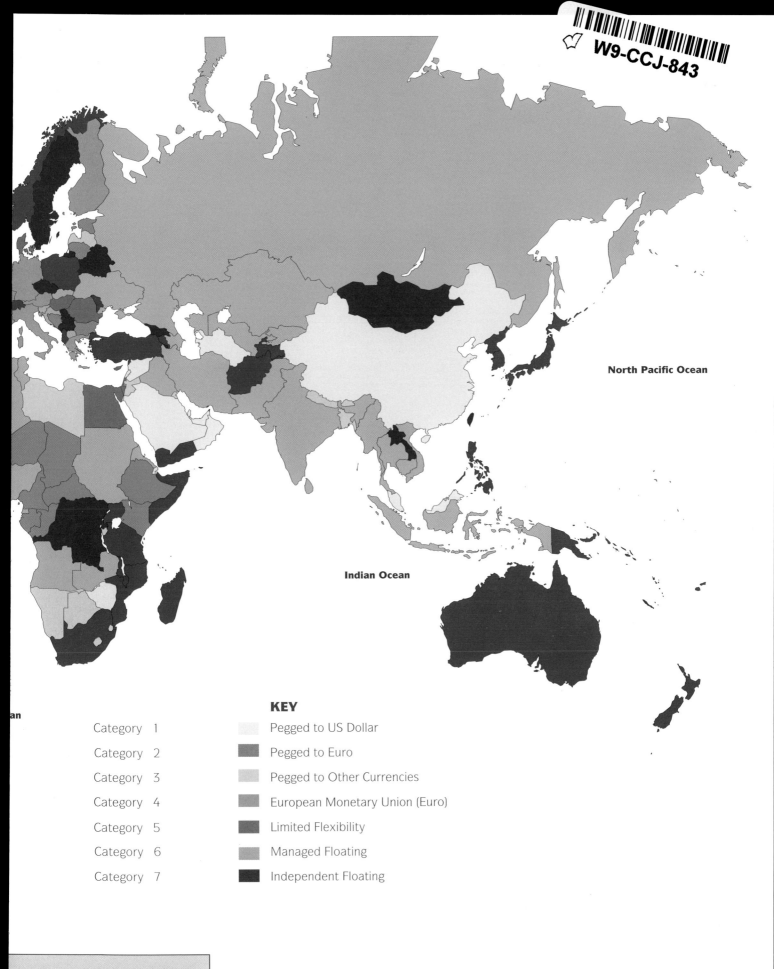

North Pacific Ocean

Indian Ocean

KEY

Category 1	Pegged to US Dollar
Category 2	Pegged to Euro
Category 3	Pegged to Other Currencies
Category 4	European Monetary Union (Euro)
Category 5	Limited Flexibility
Category 6	Managed Floating
Category 7	Independent Floating

rangements

This map is not to scale

International Financial Management
CANADIAN PERSPECTIVES

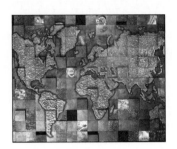

Cheol S. Eun
Georgia Institute of Technology

Bruce G. Resnick
Wake Forest University

Donald J.S. Brean
Rotman School of Management
University of Toronto

McGraw Hill

Toronto Montréal Boston Burr Ridge, IL Dubuque, IA Madison, WI New York
San Francisco St. Louis Bangkok Bogotá Caracas Kuala Lumpur Lisbon London
Madrid Mexico City Milan New Delhi Santiago Seoul Singapore Sydney Taipei

ISBN: 0-07-091228-9

2 3 4 5 6 7 8 9 10 TCP 0 9 8 7 6

Printed and bound in Canada

Care has been taken to trace ownership of copyright material contained in this text; however, the publisher will welcome any information that enables them to rectify any reference or credit for subsequent editions.

Vice President, Editorial and Media Technology: Patrick Ferrier
Executive Sponsoring Editor: Lynn Fisher
Developmental Editor: Daphne Scriabin
Sales Manager: Megan Farrell
Senior Marketing Manager: Kelly Smyth
Manager, Editorial Services: Kelly Dickson
Supervising Editor: Joanne Limebeer
Copy Editor: Rohini Herbert
Senior Production Coordinator: Jennifer Wilkie
Editorial Coordinator: Stephanie Hess
Composition: Bill Renaud
Cover Design: Dianna Little
Printer: Transcontinental Printing Group

National Library of Canada Cataloguing in Publication Data

Eun, Cheol S.
    International financial management: Canadian Perspectives / Cheol S. Eun, Bruce G. Resnick, Donald J. S. Brean.

Includes bibliographical references and index.
ISBN 0-07-091228-9

    1. International finance—Textbooks. 2. International business
enterprises—Finance—Textbooks. I. Resnick, Bruce G. II. Brean, Donald J. S., 1945- III. Title.

HG3881.E95 2004   658.15'99   C2004-904583-0

To Elizabeth
C.S.E.

To Donna
B.G.R.

To Tess
D.J.S.B.

About the Authors

Cheol S. Eun,

Georgia Institute of Technology

Cheol S. Eun is the Thomas R. Williams Professor of International Finance at the DuPree College of Management, Georgia Institute of Technology. He has held appointments at the University of Minnesota, the University of Maryland where he received the Krowe Teaching Excellence Award, the Wharton School of the University of Pennsylvania, and the Esslingen University of Technology in Germany. Professor Eun's research on international finance appears in leading research journals including the *Journal of Finance, Journal of Banking and Finance, Journal of International Money and Finance and Management Science.*

Professor Eun chairs the annual Fortis/Georgia Tech Conference on International Finance, which promotes research on international finance in a forum for academics, practitioners, and regulators. He serves as a consultant to national and international organizations, including the World Bank and the Korean Development Institute, advising on capital market liberalization, global capital, and exchange risk management.

Bruce G. Resnick,

Wake Forest University

Bruce G. Resnick is the Joseph M. Bryan Professor of Banking and Finance at the Babcock Graduate School of Management of Wake Forest University. He has also taught at Indiana University, the University of Minnesota, California State University, and the Helsinki School of Economics. Professor Resnick has served as resident director of the Centre for European Studies at the University of Limburg in The Netherlands. His research interests include efficiency of options and futures markets and empirical tests of asset pricing. A major focus is the optimal design of internationally diversified portfolios controlled for parameter uncertainty and exchange rate risk. In recent years, Professor Resnick has investigated international portfolio investment strategies applying information in the yield curve. His research has been published in major academic journals in finance. Bruce Resnick is an associate editor for the *Journal of Financial Research, Journal of Multinational Financial Management* and the *Journal of Economics and Business.*

Donald J. S. Brean,

Rotman School of Management
University of Toronto

Donald J.S. Brean is a professor of finance and economics in the Rotman School of Management at the University of Toronto and former Associate Dean. He has held academic appointments at leading universities in Europe, Asia, and Africa including Cambridge University, Ecole Superieure de Commerce Paris, University of Siena, Johannes Kepler University in Austria, University of Nairobi, Nankai University (China), and Chulalongkorn University in Bangkok. He has published extensively in taxation, international finance, risk management, industrial organization, corporate governance. and economic policy.

Professor Brean advises numerous international agencies and governments including the Canadian Federal Department of Finance, The United Nations Development Program, The World Bank, and The International Monetary Fund. He is the editor of the highly acclaimed *Taxation in Modern China*, a research volume dealing with fiscal reform and financial development in China. He is co-editor (with John Hull) of the professional series, *The Advisors Guide to Financial Research.* Recent special issues deal with international finance and risk management.

Contents in Brief

Contents

Preface

Our Reason for Writing This Textbook

International Financial Management: Canadian Perspectives builds on the structure and the success of *International Financial Management* by Eun and Resnick.

As the world becomes more economically integrated through expanded trade and cross-border investment, international finance likewise becomes ever more crucial. For Canada, in particular, our economic and financial involvement with the rest of the world represents an especially large share of our industrial activity, our growth, and our risk. Relatively more business done by Canadian firms involves foreign currencies than is the case in any other modern nation.

Our impressive volume of trade and foreign investment presents uniquely Canadian financial challenges. For one thing, Canadian business must contend with a flexible and sometimes volatile exchange rate. While exchange rate risk is not new, the structure of contracts, hedging instruments, and market settlements are oriented to the major currencies—the American dollar, the euro, and the yen—rather than minor currencies, such as the Canadian dollar. Canadian corporate decision makers are well advised to learn of the various new and increasingly sophisticated financial instruments available to manage risks that stem from the distinct position of Canadian business.

Another uniquely Canadian aspect of international financial management stems from our close proximity to—and substantial business with—the United States. Canadian corporations inevitably become involved with American bond dealers, investment banks, and securities firms that naturally have an American orientation. As Canadian firms deal with foreign markets and institutions whose interests and perspectives are generally non-Canadian, our side is challenged to be creative in addressing our concerns.

The *theory* of international finance is essentially the same for all countries and companies. The problem is in the practical matter of *application. International Financial Management: Canadian Perspectives* is the first international finance text to address the unique international concerns of Canadian businesses. The data, cases, illustrations, institutional detail, and, above all, strategic perspectives for management solidly reflect the Canadian point of view.

The material is most effectively learned when it is well grounded in the basics. Consequently, we initially devote several early chapters to the fundamental concepts of international finance, including the nature of currency markets and the determinants of the value of the exchange rate. Thereafter, applied managerial concepts emerge logically by extension of the theory into the real world. Professional readers are able to recognize immediate applicability, while students are provided with a framework for analysis that will serve them well in their future careers.

Our goal is to present well-organized, managerially relevant coverage of topics in international finance that take advantage of our many years of teaching, research, and professional consultancy.

Uniquely Canadian Perspectives and Content

Here is a sampling of uniquely Canadian perspectives and content found throughout the text:

Chapter 1: Globalization discussed from the Canadian perspective, illustrating the role of Canadian corporations

Chapter 2: The modern history of the Canadian dollar exchange rate ... and a note on Canadian-born Robert Mundell, Nobel Laureate in Economics for his work on exchange rates

Chapter 3: Detailed discussion of the Canadian Balance of Payments

Chapter 4: The market for foreign exchange with extensive examples involving the Canadian dollar

Chapter 5: The international parity conditions—with Canadian empirical content

Chapter 6: Canadian banks in global financial markets

Chapter 7: The international bond market—how Canadians borrow from and lend to foreigners

Chapter 8: An overview of international equity markets that includes a section on Canadian cross-listed shares

Chapter 9: Currency options and futures are illustrated, with a detailed example of hedging currency risk in the sale of Bombardier aircraft to Air Wisconsin

Chapter 10: Currency and interest rate swaps are illustrated through contracts involving Canadian companies and the Canadian dollar

Chapter 11: International portfolio investment with pertinent data on returns, variances and covariances expressed in Canadian dollar returns

Chapter 13: Transaction exposure addressed from a Canadian perspective, with illustrations including the LCBO and a money market hedge constructed for Bombardier to hedge the risk of a sale of aircraft to Austrian Airways denominated in euro

Chapter 14: Translation exposure discussed from a Canadian managerial perspective—applying CICA Section 1650. Corporate illustrations include Four Seasons Hotels, Shell Canada, and consolidation of the international accounts of Maple Corporation

Chapter 15: Foreign direct investment and cross-border acquisition are illustrated by Reebock's recent takeover of CCM

Chapter 17: Analysis of capital budgeting develops an extensive example based on Canada's Research-in-Motion investing in the United Kingdom

Chapter 18: Multinational cash management illustrated in the context of a multinational corporation with a Canadian affiliate

Chapter 20: Discussion of international taxation includes reference to rules, rates, and regulations that are in Canadian policy and legislation

Chapter 21: An overview of corporate governance highlights issues of pressing concern for Canadian businesses including comparison and contrast of alternative approaches to governance in various countries

Pedagogical Features

Chapter Outline: At the beginning of each chapter, a numbered chapter outline ties the chapter objectives into the numbered headings in each chapter. A statement of purpose details the objectives of the chapter.

CHAPTER OUTLINE	**10.1** Types of Swaps **10.7** Variations of Basic Currency and Interest Rate Swaps

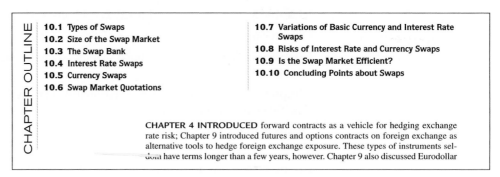

10.1 Types of Swaps
10.2 Size of the Swap Market
10.3 The Swap Bank
10.4 Interest Rate Swaps
10.5 Currency Swaps
10.6 Swap Market Quotations

10.7 Variations of Basic Currency and Interest Rate Swaps
10.8 Risks of Interest Rate and Currency Swaps
10.9 Is the Swap Market Efficient?
10.10 Concluding Points about Swaps

CHAPTER 4 INTRODUCED forward contracts as a vehicle for hedging exchange rate risk; Chapter 9 introduced futures and options contracts on foreign exchange as alternative tools to hedge foreign exchange exposure. These types of instruments seldom have terms longer than a few years, however. Chapter 9 also discussed Eurodollar

Examples: These are integrated throughout the text, providing students with immediate application of the text concepts.

> **EXAMPLE** **4.1** **Correspondent Banking Relationship** As an example of how the network of correspondent bank accounts facilitates international foreign exchange transactions, consider Ottawa Importer arranging the finance of an order of merchandise from Dutch Exporter of Amsterdam. The order is invoiced in euros at €200,000. Ottawa Importer will contact his local bank, CIBC, and inquire about the €/$ exchange rate. The quote is €1 = $1.53. If Ottawa Importer accepts this exchange rate, then CIBC will debit Ottawa Importer's demand deposit account for $306,000, which equals €200,000 times $1.53. CIBC will instruct its correspondent bank in Amsterdam, ING, to debit CIBC's correspondent bank account €200,000 and to credit that amount to Dutch Exporter. CIBC will than debit its books €200,000 as an offset to the $306,000 debit to Ottawa Importers account, to reflect the decrease in its correspondent bank account with ING. ∎

Exhibits: In each chapter, extensive graphs and tables provide visual illustration of important concepts.

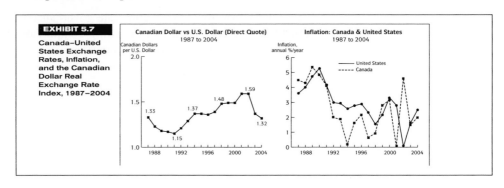

EXHIBIT 5.7

Canada–United States Exchange Rates, Inflation, and the Canadian Dollar Real Exchange Rate Index, 1987–2004

International Finance in Practice Boxes: Selected chapters contain International Finance in Practice boxes. These real-world illustrations offer students a practical look at the major concepts presented in the chapter.

INTERNATIONAL FINANCE IN PRACTICE

Contagion without Borders

The lessons taught by the "Tequila Effect" or the "Brazilian Sneeze"

Economists are developing a fascinating body of work around how international markets interact and behave during times of economic crises. The extension of this work could prove seminal to how institutional investors model their portfolios and manage risk.

The phenomenon known as financial contagion is the cross-border financial shock that propagates between countries and cannot be explained by examining standard channels of interaction, such as trade links.

Shift contagion refers to changes in the normal strength of transmission mechanisms, including the fundamental channels of trade links, financial links, monetary policy and common shocks affecting those links. Fundamental channels are the oldest and best understood of all linkages between countries. Bilateral trade relationships, for example, are most often believed responsible for transmitting financial, market and economic shocks across countries.

Annotated Web Resources: Web Resources appear in the margins within each chapter to serve as a quick reference of pertinent chapter-related websites. Each URL listed also includes a short statement on what can be found at that specific site.

Supplementary Material: Some topics are by nature more complex than others. The chapter sections that contain such material are indicated by the section heading "Supplementary Material'" and are in blue type. These sections may be skipped without loss of continuity, enabling the instructor to easily tailor the reading assignments to the students. End-of-chapter Questions and Problems relating to the Supplementary Material sections of the text are also indicated by blue type.

Supplementary Material

18.2 Reduction in Precautionary Cash Balances

Up to this point, we have handled the multilateral netting of intera (Exhibit 18.6) *and* the net receipts of the affiliates from the transact parties (Exhibit 18.8) as two separate sets of cash flows through the c itory. While it was easier to develop the concepts in that manner, it practical, or efficient to do it that way in practice. Instead, the tw flows can be bilaterally netted, with the resulting net sums going th depository. This will further reduce the number, size, and expense of transactions for the MNC. Exhibit 18.9 calculates the net amount of f affiliates to flow through the central depository.

Key Words: One of the most interesting aspects of studying international finance is learning new terminology. All key terms are presented in boldfaced type when they are first introduced, and they are defined thoroughly in the chapter. A list of key words is presented at the end of the chapter with convenient page references and a full glossary is found at the back of the text.

Summary: A short summary concludes each chapter, providing students with a handy overview of key concepts for review.

SUMMARY	This chapter introduced currency futures and options on foreign exchange. These instruments are useful for speculating and hedging foreign exchange rate movements. In later chapters, it will be shown how to use these vehicles for hedging purposes.
	1. Forward, futures, and options contracts are derivative, or contingent claim, securities. That is, their value is derived or contingent upon the value of the asset that underlies these securities.
	2. Forward and futures contracts are similar instruments, but there are differences. Both are contracts to buy or sell a certain quantity of a specific underlying asset at some specific price in the future. Futures contracts, however, are exchange traded, and there are standardized features that distinguish them from the tailor-made

End-of-Chapter Questions and Problems: A set of end-of-chapter questions and problems is provided for each chapter. This material can be used by students on their own to test their understanding of the material or as homework exercises assigned by the instructor. Questions and Problems relating to the Supplementary Material sections of the text are indicated by blue type.

QUESTIONS	1. Describe the differences between foreign bonds and Eurobonds. Also discuss why Eurobonds make up the lion's share of the international bond market.
	2. Briefly define each of the major types of international bond market instruments, noting their distinguishing characteristics.
	3. Why do most international bonds have high Moody's or Standard & Poor's credit ratings?
	4. What factors does Standard & Poor's analyze in determining the credit rating it assigns a sovereign government?

CFA Problems: Many chapters include questions from CFA exams. These CFA problems, indicated by the CFA logo, show students the relevancy of what is expected of certified professional analysts.

CFA®
PROBLEMS

10. Omni Advisors, an international pension fund manager, plans to sell equities denominated in Swiss francs (CHF) and purchase an equivalent amount of equities denominated in South African rands (ZAR).

Omni will realize net proceeds of three million CHF at the end of 30 days and wants to eliminate the risk that the ZAR will appreciate relative to the CHF during this 30-day period. The following exhibit shows current exchange rates between the ZAR, CHF, and the American dollar (USD).

Currency Exchange Rates

Maturity	ZAR/US$		CHF/US$	
	Bid	Ask	Bid	Ask
Spot	6.2681	6.2789	1.5282	1.5343
30-day	6.2538	6.2641	1.5226	1.5285
90-day	6.2104	6.2200	1.5058	1.5115

Questions with Excel Software: An icon indicates which end-of-chapter questions throughout the book are linked to the software program created by the authors. See page xxiii for more information on the software.

11. Do problem 10 again, assuming an American put option instead of a call option.

12. Use the European option-pricing models developed in the chapter to value the call of problem 10 and the put of problem 11. Assume the annualized volatility of the

Web Exercises: Internet Exercises are included at the end of each chapter to highlight specific topics and to prompt the student to search the Internet for specific data. The student is then able to analyze the data found to solve the exercise.

INTERNET EXERCISE

1. *Bond Markets Online* is an Internet magazine with articles of current interest to bond market participants. Go to the website www.bondmarkets.com/ newsletters/2002/global902.shtml to see what current events are of concern in the global bond market.

Mini Cases: Almost every chapter includes a mini case for student analysis of multiple concepts covered throughout the chapter. These Mini Case problems show students how the theory and concepts in the textbook relate to the everyday world.

Illustrated **MINI CASE** Research In Motion/Europe

Research In Motion (RIM) of Waterloo, Ontario, is a world leader in mobile communications. RIM developed and manufactures BlackBerry, the stunningly successful wireless handheld communicator with access to e-mail, Internet, and phone, along with organizer features.

Research in Motion has been exporting BlackBerries to Europe for several years. European sales are currently 9,600 units a year and have been increasing at a rate of 5 percent. The European marketing manager believes that a manufacturing facility in Europe offers real advantages in production efficiencies. A local presence in Europe is also strategically wise in view of the potential market expansion driven by European enlargement.

Reference and Suggested Readings: At the end of each chapter a list of selected references and suggested readings is presented, allowing the student to easily locate references that provide additional information on specific topics.

Technology Solutions

Online Learning Centre

More and more students are studying online. That is why we offer an Online Learning Centre (OLC) that follows *International Financial Management: Canadian Perspectives* chapter by chapter. You do not have to build or maintain anything, and it is ready to go the moment you and your students type in the URL:

www.mcgrawhill.ca/college/eun

As your students study, they can refer to the OLC website for such benefits as:

- Online Quizzes
- Globe and Mail newsfeeds
- Annotated Web Links
- Internet Questions
- Finance Around the World

- Study to Go
- Excel files
- Chapter Outlines
- Glossary and Key Terms
- Chapter Summary

Remember, the *International Financial Management: Canadian Perspectives* OLC content is flexible enough to use with any course management platform currently available. If your department or school is already using a platform, we can help. For information on our course management services, contact your *i*-Learning Sales Specialist or see "Superior Service" on page xxii.

Classroom Performance System (CPS)

Bring interactivity into the classroom or lecture hall. CPS, by eInstruction, is a student response system using wireless connectivity. It gives instructors and students immediate feedback from the entire class. The response pads are remotes that are easy to use and engage students.

- CPS helps increase student preparation, interactivity, and active learning so you can receive immediate feedback and know what students understand.

- CPS allows you to administer quizzes and tests, and provide immediate grading.

- With CPS, you can create lecture questions that can be multiple-choice, true/false, and subjective. You can even create questions on-the-fly as well as conduct group activities.

- CPS not only allows you to evaluate classroom attendance, activity, and grading for your course as a whole, but CPSOnline allows you to provide students with an immediate study guide. All results and scores can easily be imported into Excel and can be used with various classroom management systems.

CPS ready content is available for use with Eun/Resnick/Brean: *International Financial Management: Canadian Perspectives*. Please contact your *i*-Learning Sales Specialist for more information on how you can integrate CPS into your finance classroom.

Mobile Learning

STUDY TO GO   The businesses and companies of today want their new employees to be adept in all aspects of the changing business environment. They are quick to tell us they want graduates with the skills of tomorrow . . . today. From laptops to cell phones to PDAs, the new medium is mobility.

As a leader in technology and innovation, McGraw-Hill Ryerson has developed material providing students with optimum flexibility for use anytime, anywhere they need to study—whether with a laptop, PDA, or tablet. These innovations provide instructors with a number of exciting ways to integrate technology into the learning process.

With **Study To Go**, we have introduced wireless activities as a part of our Online Learning Centre. Now, whether you are waiting in line, riding on transit, or just filling some spare time, homework and practice are just a click away.

Course Management

PAGEOUT   McGraw-Hill Ryerson's course management system, PageOut, is the easiest way to create a website for your international finance course. There is no need for HTML coding, graphic design, or a thick how-to book. Just fill in a series of boxes in plain English, and click on one of our professional designs. In no time, your course is online!

For the integrated instructor, we offer *International Financial Management: Canadian Perspectives* content for complete online courses. Whatever your needs, you can customize the *International Financial Management: Canadian Perspectives* Online Learning Centre content and author your own online course materials. It is entirely up to you. You can offer online discussion and message boards that will complement your office hours, and reduce the lines outside your door. Content cartridges are also available for course management systems, such as WebCT and Blackboard. Ask your *i*-Learning Sales Specialist for details.

Superior Service

SUPERIOR SERVICE   Service takes on a whole new meaning with McGraw-Hill Ryerson and *International Financial Management: Canadian Perspectives*. More than just bringing you the textbook, we have consistently raised the bar in terms of innovation and educational research—both in finance and in education in general. These investments in learning and the education community have helped us understand the needs of students and educators across the country and allowed us to foster the growth of truly innovative, integrated learning.

INTEGRATED LEARNING   Your Integrated Learning Sales Specialist is a McGraw-Hill Ryerson representative who has the experience, product knowledge, training, and support to help you assess and integrate any of our products, technology, and services into your course for optimum teaching and learning performance. Whether it is using our test bank software, helping your students improve their grades, or putting your entire course online, your *i*Learning Sales Specialist is there to help you do it. Contact your local *i*Learning Sales Specialist today to learn how to maximize all of McGraw-Hill Ryerson's resources!

iLEARNING SERVICES PROGRAM   McGraw-Hill Ryerson offers a unique *i*Services package designed for Canadian faculty. Our mission is to equip providers of higher education with superior tools and resources required for excellence in teaching. For additional information, visit *www.mcgrawhill.ca/highereducation/iservices*.

TEACHING, TECHNOLOGY & LEARNING CONFERENCE SERIES   The educational environment has changed tremendously in recent years, and McGraw-Hill Ryerson continues to be committed to helping you acquire the skills you need to succeed in this new milieu. Our innovative Teaching, Technology & Learning Conference Series brings faculty together from across Canada with 3M Teaching Excellence award winners to share teaching and learning best practices in a collaborative and stimulating environment. Preconference workshops on general topics, such as teaching large classes and technology integration, will also be offered. We will also work with you at your own institution to customize workshops that best suit the needs of your faculty.

RESEARCH REPORTS INTO MOBILE LEARNING AND STUDENT SUCCESS
These landmark reports, undertaken in conjunction with academic and private sector advisory boards, are the result of research studies into the challenges professors face in helping students succeed and the opportunities that new technology presents to impact teaching and learning.

Comprehensive Teaching and Learning Package

For the Instructor

Instructor's Online Learning Centre The Online Learning Centre (OLC) contains a password-protected site with downloadable supplements for instructors; visit us at *www.mcgrawhill.ca/college/eun*. The site offers downloadable supplements and Page-Out, the McGraw-Hill Ryerson course website development centre. A list of matching cases is also included which provides suggested Harvard Business School Publishing Cases linked to each chapter in the text.

CaseLink *International Financial Management: Canadian Perspectives* is a **CaseLink** textbook. **CaseLink** makes it simple to connect leading case studies to chapters in this text. Instructors can create their own customized casebook for use in their course. Please contact your local *i*-Learning Sales Specialist for additional detail or follow the link from the Instructor's OLC.

Instructor's CD-ROM The CD-ROM includes the following Instructor Supplements:

> **Instructor's Manual/Test Bank**—Includes detailed suggested answers and solutions to the problems and multiple-choice test questions for each chapter.

> **PowerPoint Presentation System**—PowerPoint slides for use in classroom lecture settings, adapted by Charles Schell, University of Northern British Columbia.

For the Student

Student Online Learning Centre Prepared by Semih Yildirim, University of Saskatchewan, the OLC offers such aids as Online Quizzes, Internet Exercises, Annotated Web Links, Excel Templates, Study To Go, *Globe and Mail* newsfeeds and more. The *International Financial Management, Canadian Perspectives* Online Learning Centre is located at *www.mcgrawhill.ca/college/eun*.

The site includes Excel-based software that can be used with this book. This international finance software has three main programs:

- A currency options pricing program allows students to price put and call options on foreign exchange.
- A hedging program allows the student to compare forward, money market instruments, futures, and options for hedging exchange risk.
- A portfolio optimization program based on the Markowitz model allows for examining the benefits of international portfolio diversification.

The three programs can be used to solve certain end-of-chapter problems (marked with an Excel icon) or assignments the instructor devises. A Software Users's Guide is also provided.

Acknowledgements

We are indebted to many colleagues for insight and guidance throughout the development process. Their careful work enabled us to create a text that is current, accurate, and modern in its approach. Among all who helped in this endeavour:

Raymond Canon, University of Western Ontario
Francesca Carrieri, McGill University
Gilles Chemla, University of British Columbia
Dorethee Feils, University of Alberta
Arvind Jain, Concordia University
Keith MacInnes, York University
Basma Majerbi, McGill University
Michael McIntyre, Carleton University
Asmo Palasvirta, Memorial University
Duane Rockerbie, University of Lethbridge
John Rumsey, Dalhousie University
Charles Schell, University of Northern British Columbia
Jacques Schnabel, Wilfrid Laurier University
David Stangeland, University of Manitoba

A special word of gratitude for assistance on specific issues goes out to Professors Joel Amernic, Laurence Booth, Craig Doidge, Myron Gordon, John Hull, Tom McCurdy, Gordon Richardson, and Alan White, all of the Rotman School of Management, University of Toronto. Ambrus Kecskes provided valuable comments from an informed reader's perspective.

The wise counsel and especially the patience of the professional staff of McGraw-Hill Ryerson are sincerely appreciated. Lynn Fisher proposed the project, and Daphne Scriabin ensured that it happened. Rohini Herbert and Joanne Limebeer were remarkably skilled in their editorial tasks.

DJSB

International Financial Management
CANADIAN PERSPECTIVES

Foundations of International Financial Management

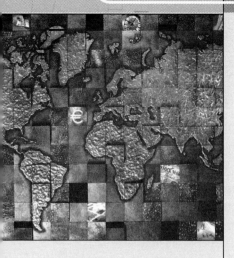

OUTLINE

PART ONE lays the macroeconomic foundation for all the topics to follow. A thorough understanding of this material is essential for understanding the advanced topics covered in the remaining sections.

CHAPTER 1 provides an introduction to International Financial Management. The chapter discusses why it is important to study international finance and distinguishes international finance from domestic finance.

CHAPTER 2 introduces the various types of international monetary systems under which the world economy can function and has functioned at various times. The chapter traces the historical development of the world's international monetary systems from the early 1800s to the present. Additionally, a detailed discussion of the European Monetary System of the European Union is presented.

CHAPTER 3 presents balance-of-payment concepts and accounting. The chapter shows that even a country must keep its "economic house in order" or else it will experience current account deficits that will undermine the value of its currency.

CHAPTER 4 provides an introduction to the organization and operation of the spot-and-forward foreign exchange market. This chapter describes institutional arrangements of the foreign exchange market and details of how foreign exchange is quoted and traded worldwide.

CHAPTER 5 presents the fundamental international parity relationships among exchange rates, interest rates, and inflation rates. An understanding of these parity relationships is essential for practising financial management in a global setting.

Globalization and the Multinational Firm

MORE THAN MOST, Canadians realize that virtually all business is *international* business and, likewise, that all finance is ultimately *international* finance.

A quick run across the country illustrates how economically integrated Canada is with the rest of the world. Electricity originating in Newfoundland keeps the lights on in New England. New Brunswick is home to a global communications nexus. Oysters and potatoes from Prince Edward Island are world famous. Nova Scotia's universities export quality education. Bombardier of Quebec ranks among the top three aircraft manufacturers in the world. Cross-border trade between Ontario and Michigan exceeds the total value of trade between the United States and Japan. Manitoba and Saskatchewan are among the world's most efficient agriculture producers, with much of the output sold abroad. Alberta is the reason that Canada is a major energy exporter. Beautiful British Columbia, Canada's gateway to Asia, is a major world supplier of wood products and minerals.

Canada exports a great deal and also imports almost as much. Canadian business is forced to be outward looking. As exporters, Canadian businesses compete directly with businesses abroad. Imports, on the other hand, expose domestic Canadian business to the cold winds of competition. We are a very open economy.

Business requires finance. International business deals with *international* finance. Exports generate receipts in foreign currencies. Imports require payments in foreign currencies. Not just goods and services but capital, too, can be exported or imported. Canadian companies and governments borrow substantial amounts of money from foreign sources. Those funds represent capital imports. On the other hand, when Canadian firms invest abroad, capital moves out of Canada. Alcan, Bombardier, CN, and Dofasco or moving further along the alphabet to Laidlaw, McCain and Nortel—these are prominent Canadian firms that operate globally from a Canadian base.

This book deals with international finance—focusing on markets, players, decisions, and strategies. We deal with international financial issues from a Canadian perspective. The Canadian point of view is crucial. Opportunities and challenges that confront Canadians in international financial matters are often distinctly Canadian. Foreign exchange risk involving the Canadian dollar, for example, is a uniquely Canadian concern. The laws and regulations that govern how Canadian financial markets connect to the world—such as our bond markets, stock markets, and even our system of taxation—have Canadian characteristics that shape transactions within these markets.

A special characteristic of Canada and Canadian business is our close commercial ties to the United States. Ninety percent of Canadians live within 100 kilometres of the American border. Canada and the United States generate the largest bilateral volume of trade in the world. Eighty-five percent of Canadian exports are shipped to the United States. Seventy percent of our imports come from the United States. The Canada–United States Free Trade Agreement, signed in 1988 and broadened to the **North American Free Trade Agreement (NAFTA)** in 1994, represents the most comprehensive trade agreement in the world, governing not just trade but also cross-border investment and legal procedures to deal with disputes. Money and capital flows freely back and forth across the Canada–United States border with the result that our bond and stock markets are highly integrated. Indeed, one of the most important influences on Canadian interest rates is American interest rates. In this respect, Canada enjoys the economic advantages—and risks—of being a close neighbour to the world's largest economy.

On international financial matters, then, Canadian concerns are naturally tilted toward the United States. Nevertheless, Canada has a significant degree of financial independence from the United States and from all other nations as well. This is where the Canadian perspective on international finance comes strongly to the fore. In Canada, we have our own currency, our own central bank—The Bank of Canada—and our own capital markets and financial institutions. Above all, Canada maintains a *flexible* exchange rate. Throughout much of this book, the flexibility of our exchange rate—which suggests exchange rate volatility as well as exchange rate uncertainty—emerges as the central factor that distinguishes international finance from its purely domestic counterpart. Canada has a specific exchange rate with each of the many currencies of the world, including the American dollar, of course, but also the new euro, the British pound, the Japanese yen, the Mexican peso, and more than one hundred others.

In a world of business in which borders are becoming less of a barrier, it is essential for managers and corporate decision makers to fully understand vital international aspects of financial management.

1.1 What Is Special about International Finance?

While we may be convinced of the importance of studying international finance, we must still ask ourselves, "What is special about international finance?" Put another way, how is international finance different from purely domestic finance (if such a thing exists)? Three major dimensions set international finance apart from domestic finance:

1. Foreign exchange risk and political risk
2. Differences in regulations, tax law, and government policies
3. The greater set of business opportunities for production and investment

As we will see, these major dimensions of international finance reflect the fact that sovereign nations have the right and power to issue their own currencies; to formulate their own economic policies; to impose taxes; and to regulate the movement of goods, services, and capital across their borders. Before moving on, it is useful to briefly illustrate each of the key dimensions of international financial management.

Foreign Exchange and Political Risk

One of Canada's most important exports to Mexico is Canola, a genetically engineered oil-seed produced in the prairie provinces. Canadian exporters of Canola, such as Advanta Seeds of Winnipeg, are vulnerable to changes in the exchange rate between the Canadian dollar and the currency of the nation to which they are exporting, in this case Mexico. If the Mexican peso were to depreciate sharply against the Canadian dollar, as it did in the famous "Tequila crisis" of 1994, the peso price of Canola would immediately rise. Advanta Seeds would see sales of their product drop as it becomes more costly for Mexicans.

Lost sales and lower profits—all due to an unexpected change in the Canadian dollar–Mexican peso exchange rate. The risk of such losses is **foreign exchange risk**.

Advanta and other Canadian exports would have faced similar difficulty in the wake of the Asian financial crises of 1997, when the value of the Thai baht, the Korean won, and the Malaysian ringgit all fell sharply against other currencies, including the Canadian dollar. When firms are involved in foreign sales, they are potentially exposed to foreign exchange risk that they would not normally encounter in purely domestic transactions.

In the modern world of flexible exchange rates, exchange rates fluctuate continuously in unpredictable ways. This has been the case since the early 1970s, when a regime of fixed exchange rates among the major currencies—including the American dollar, the British pound, the Japanese yen, and the German deutschmark—was abandoned. Canada, prior to that move, was somewhat unique among nations for allowing the Canadian dollar to "float" against the American dollar, although in very narrow range. Exhibit 1.1 illustrates that our exchange rate volatility increased dramatically after 1973. Note in particular the relatively low volatility between 1962 and 1970 followed by substantial volatility thereafter. At the far right of the graph, the deep downward spike reflects the sharp appreciation of the Canadian dollar against the American dollar in 2003. The spike is negative because Canadian dollar appreciation means a reduction in Canadian dollars required to buy an American dollar—from $1.57 to $1.30.

Another form of risk that firms may encounter in an international setting is **political risk**. Political risk ranges from unexpected changes in tax rules to outright expropriation of assets held by foreigners. Political risk arises from the fact that a sovereign nation can change the "rules of the game" and the affected parties may not have effective recourse. We can continue with the example of Canadian exports of Canola to illustrate political risk. As a genetically engineered agricultural product, Canola is viewed by some Counties as undesirable. In 2002, China banned the import of Canola, wiping out a $200-million-dollar market for Canadian producers.

EXHIBIT 1.1

Monthly Percentage Change in Canadian Dollar–American Dollar Exchange Rate

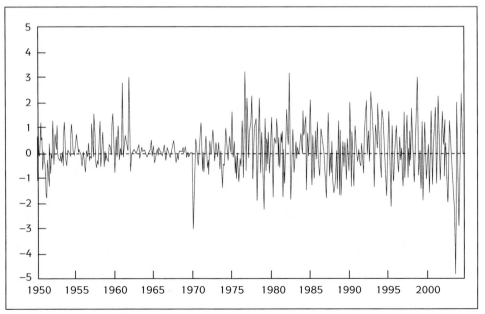

Source: International Monetary Fund, *International Financial Statistics,* various issues.

In another illustrative case of political action causing commercial loss to a multinational enterprise, Canada in 1997 passed legislation banning the use of the gasoline additive MMT from interprovincial trade and importation into Canada. In 1998, the Ethyl Corporation, an American-owned importer of MMT into Canada, initiated a claim challenging the legislation under NAFTA Chapter 11, the section that defines the limits of government action (by parties to NAFTA) that adversely affects foreign firms. The Government of Canada settled the claim out of court, paying $13 million to Ethyl, the firm's costs and lost profits in Canada. Ethyl dropped its claims against the Government of Canada. The case illustrates how international agreements, such as NAFTA, can mitigate political risk by providing a means by which foreign companies can seek recourse. However, the Ethyl case also caused alarm over whether the provisions of NAFTA could be used to limit sovereign powers of regulation in the fields of environment and public health.

Market Imperfections

Although the world economy is much more integrated today than was the case 10 or 20 years ago, a variety of barriers still hamper free movements of people, goods, services, and capital across national boundaries. These barriers include legal restrictions, excessive transaction and transportation costs, and discriminatory taxation. The world markets are thus highly imperfect. As we will discuss later, **market imperfections,** which represent various frictions and impediments preventing markets from functioning perfectly, play an important role in motivating multinational corporations (MNCs) to locate production overseas. Honda, a Japanese automobile company, for instance, established production facilities in Alliston, Ontario, mainly to circumvent a 6.1-percent tax that Canada imposes on imported finished vehicles. One might even say that MNCs are a product of market imperfections.

Imperfections in world financial markets tend to restrict the extent to which investors can diversify their portfolios. An interesting example involves the Nestlé Corporation, a well-known Swiss MNC. Nestlé used to issue two different classes of common shares—bearer shares and registered shares. Foreigners were allowed to hold only bearer shares. As Exhibit 1.2 shows, bearer shares used to trade for about twice the

EXHIBIT 1.2

Daily Prices of Nestlé's Bearer and Registered Shares

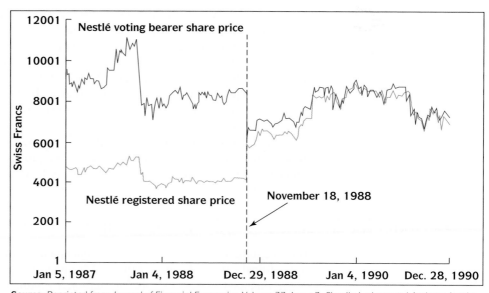

Source: Reprinted from *Journal of Financial Economics,* Volume 37, Issue 3, Claudio Loderer and Andreas Jacobs, "The Nestlé Crash," pp. 315–339, 1995, with kind permission from Elsevier Science S.A., P.O. Box 564, 1001 Lausanne, Switzerland.

price of registered shares, which were exclusively reserved for Swiss residents.[1] This kind of price disparity is a uniquely international phenomenon that is attributable to market imperfections.

On November 18, 1988, however, Nestlé lifted restrictions imposed on foreigners, allowing them to hold registered as well as bearer shares. After this announcement, the price spread between the two types of Nestlé shares narrowed drastically. As Exhibit 1.2 shows, the price of bearer shares declined sharply, whereas that of registered shares rose sharply. This implies that there was a major transfer of wealth from foreign shareholders to domestic shareholders. Foreigners holding Nestlé bearer shares were exposed to political risk in a country that is widely viewed as a haven from such risk. The Nestlé episode illustrates both the importance of considering market imperfections in international finance and the peril of political risk.

Expanded Opportunity Set

When firms engage in business beyond their own national borders, when they become transnational or multinational, they benefit from an **expanded opportunity set**. When firms locate production abroad, penetrate foreign markets, or tap the capital markets of other countries, they are operating in a global context. Firms with a global perspective scan the world for investment opportunities, for low cost resources, and for foreign markets to develop.

Four Seasons Hotels, a world leader in the high-end hospitality sector, began life in Toronto but expanded to Paris, New York, and Milan among other cities as Four Seasons grew to global prominence. Similarly, McCain Foods of New Brunswick now operates in more than 30 countries. While McCain is primarily associated with French fries—they produce one-third of all frozen French fries in the world—McCain is actually exporting its technology and managerial skill. When CN, formerly Canadian National, was developing a strategy for growth, it bought two mid-western American railway companies and restructured CN from an east-west Canadian railway to a continental logistics system. When Barrick, the Toronto-based mining company, looks for exploration and production opportunities, it looks to Australia, Peru, Chile, and Tanzania. When Barrick raises capital for these capital-intensive activities, it issues shares simultaneously in Toronto, New York, London, Paris, and Zurich.

These well-known Canadian companies illustrate the successful identification and pursuit of expanded opportunities in each of their respective industries. However, their roots are in Canada, just as the roots of Roots Canada are in Canada, but its business perspective and growth prospects are global.

Individual investors can also benefit greatly if they invest internationally, rather than domestically. Suppose you have a given amount of money to invest in shares. You may invest the entire amount in Canadian (domestic) shares. Alternatively, you may allocate the funds across domestic and foreign shares. If you diversify internationally, the resulting international portfolio may have a lower risk or a higher return (or both) than a purely domestic portfolio. This can happen mainly because shares returns tend to covary much less across countries than within a given country. Once you are aware of overseas investment opportunities and are willing to diversify internationally, you face a much expanded opportunity set and you can benefit from it. It just does not make sense to play in only one corner of the sandbox.

1.2 Goals for International Financial Management

The foregoing discussion implies that understanding and managing foreign exchange and political risks and coping with market imperfections have become important parts of the financial manager's job. *International Financial Management* is designed to

---

[1] Bearer and registered shares of Nestlé had the same claims on dividends but differential voting rights. Chapter 16 provides a detailed discussion of the Nestlé case.

provide today's financial managers with an understanding of the fundamental concepts and the tools necessary to be effective global managers. Throughout, the text emphasizes how to deal with exchange risk and market imperfections, using the various instruments and tools that are available at the same time maximizing the benefits from an expanded global opportunity set.

Effective financial management, however, is more than the application of the newest business techniques or operating more efficiently. There must be an underlying goal. The fundamental goal of sound financial management is shareholder wealth maximization. **Shareholder wealth maximization** means that the firm makes all business decisions and investments with an eye toward making the owners of the firm—the shareholders—better off financially, or more wealthy, than they were before.

Whereas shareholder wealth maximization is generally accepted as the ultimate goal of financial management in "Anglo-Saxon" countries, such as Australia, Canada, the United Kingdom, and especially the United States, it is not as widely embraced a goal in other parts of the world. In such countries as France and Germany, for example, shareholders are generally viewed as one among several "stakeholders" of the firm, others being employees, customers, suppliers, banks, and so forth. European managers tend to consider the promotion of the firm's stakeholders' overall welfare as the most important corporate goal. In Japan, on the other hand, many companies form a small number of interlocking business groups called *keiretsu,* such as Mitsubishi, Mitsui, and Sumitomo, which arose from the consolidation of family-owned business empires. Japanese managers tend to regard the prosperity and growth of their *keiretsu* as the critical goal; for instance, they tend to strive to maximize market share, rather than shareholder wealth.

It must be pointed out, however, that as capital markets become more liberalized and internationally integrated, even managers in France, Germany, Japan and other non–Anglo-Saxon countries are beginning to pay serious attention to shareholder wealth maximization. In Germany, for example, companies are now allowed to repurchase shares, if necessary, for the benefit of shareholders. In accepting an unprecedented $183 billion takeover offer by Vodafone AirTouch, a leading British wireless phone company, Klaus Esser, CEO of Mannesmann of Germany cited shareholder interests: "The shareholders clearly think that this company, Mannesmann, a great company, would be better together with Vodafone AirTouch. . . . The final decision belongs to shareholders."[2]

Obviously, the firm could pursue other goals. This does not mean, however, that the goal of shareholder wealth maximization is merely an alternative or that the firm should enter into a debate as to its appropriate fundamental goal. Quite the contrary. If the firm seeks to maximize shareholder wealth, it will most likely simultaneously be accomplishing other legitimate goals that are perceived as worthwhile. Shareholder wealth maximization is a long-run goal. A firm cannot stay in business to maximize shareholder wealth if it treats employees poorly, produces shoddy merchandise, wastes raw materials and natural resources, operates inefficiently, or fails to satisfy customers. Only a well-managed business firm that profitably produces what is demanded in an efficient manner can expect to stay in business in the long run and thereby provide employment opportunities.

While managers are hired to run the company for the interests of shareholders, there is no guarantee that they will actually do so. As shown by a series of recent corporate scandals at some companies, such as Enron and Parmalat, managers, when they are not closely monitored, may pursue their own private interests at the expense of shareholders. Extensive corporate malfeasance and accounting manipulations at these companies eventually drove them into financial distress and bankruptcy, devastating shareholders

---

[2]The source for this information is *The New York Times,* February 4, 2000, p. C9.

and employees alike. Regretably, some senior managers enriched themselves enormously in the process. Clearly, the boards of directors, the ultimate guardians of the interests of shareholders, failed to perform their duties at these companies. In the wake of these corporate calamities that have undermined the credibility of the free market system, the society has painfully learned the importance of **corporate governance,** that is, the financial and legal framework for regulating the relationship between a company's management and its shareholders. Needless to say, the corporate governance problem is not confined to advanced industrial nations. In fact, it can be a much more serious problem in many other parts of the world, especially emerging and transition economies, such as Indonesia, Korea, China, and Russia, where legal protection of shareholders is weak or virtually nonexistent.

Shareholders are the owners of the business; their capital is at risk. It is only equitable that they receive a fair return on their investment. Private capital may not be forthcoming for the business firm if it intends to accomplish any other objective. As we will discuss shortly, the massive privatization that is currently taking place in the developing and formerly socialist countries, which will eventually enhance the standard of living of these countries' citizens, depends on private investment. It is, thus, vitally important to strengthen corporate governance so that shareholders receive fair returns on their investments. In what follows, we discuss in detail: (1) the globalization of the world economy, (2) the growing role of MNCs in the world economy, and (3) the organization of the text.

1.3   Globalization of the World Economy: Recent Trends

The term "globalization" became a popular buzzword for describing business practices in the last few decades, and it appears as if it will continue to be a key word for describing business management throughout the new century. In this section, we review a few key trends of the world economy: (1) the emergence of globalized financial markets, (2) the advent of the euro, (3) the continued trade liberalization and economic integration, and (4) large-scale privatization of state-owned enterprises.

Emergence of Globalized Financial Markets

The 1980s and 1990s saw a rapid integration of international capital and financial markets. The impetus for globalized financial markets initially came from the governments of major countries that had begun to deregulate their foreign exchange and capital markets. For example, in 1980, Japan deregulated its foreign exchange market, and in 1985, the Tokyo Stock Exchange admitted as members a limited number of foreign brokerage firms. The London Stock Exchange (LSE) began admitting foreign firms as full members in February 1986.

Perhaps the most celebrated deregulation, however, occurred in London on October 27, 1986, and is known as the "Big Bang." On that date, as on "May Day" in 1975 in the United States, the London Stock Exchange eliminated fixed brokerage commissions. In Europe, financial institutions are allowed to perform both investment-banking and commercial-banking functions. Hence, the London affiliates of foreign commercial banks were eligible for membership on the LSE. These changes gave London the most open and competitive capital markets in the world. It worked. Today, the competition to be in London is especially fierce among the world's major financial firms.

Canada, too, is actively involved in financial sector deregulation. In a significant break from the past, Canadian chartered banks are now allowed to own and operate brokerage houses—such as TDCanada Trusts' TDWaterhouse. Canadian banks are also major players in corporate and investment banking with offices in the world's major financial centres.

The United States recently repealed the Glass-Steagall Act, which restricted commercial banks from investment banking activities (such as underwriting corporate securities), further promoting competition among financial institutions. Even the developing countries, such as Chile, Mexico, and Korea, began to liberalize by allowing foreigners to directly invest in their financial markets.

Deregulated financial markets and heightened competition in financial services provide a natural environment for financial innovations that result in the introduction of various financial instruments. Examples of innovation include currency futures and options, multicurrency bonds, international mutual funds, country funds, and foreign stock index futures. Corporations also play an active role in integrating the world financial markets by listing their shares across borders. Such well-known companies as Seagram, Sony, Toyota Motor, Fiat, Telefonos de Mexico, KLM, British Petroleum, Glaxo, and DaimlerChrysler are directly listed and traded on several stock exchanges throughout the world. IBM and GM are listed on the Brussels, Frankfurt, London, and Paris stock exchanges. Such cross-border listings of shares allow investors to buy and sell foreign shares as if they were domestic shares, facilitating international investments.[3]

Last but not least, advances in computer and telecommunications technologies contribute in no small measure to the emergence of global financial markets. These technological advancements, especially the Internet-based information technologies, give investors around the world immediate access to the most recent news and information affecting their investments, sharply reducing information costs. Also, computerized order-processing and settlement procedures reduce the costs of international transactions. The relative cost index of computing power declined from a level of 100 in 1960 to 15.6 in 1970, 2.9 in 1980, and only 0.5 in 1999. As a result of these technological developments and the liberalization of financial markets, cross-border financial transactions have exploded in recent years.

www.imf.org

Offers an overview of globalization and ways in which countries may gain from the process.

Advent of the Euro

The advent of the euro at the start of 1999 represents a momentous event in the history of the world financial system that has profound ramifications for the world economy. Currently, more than 300 million Europeans in 12 countries (Austria, Belgium, Finland, France, Germany, Greece, Ireland, Italy, Luxembourg, the Netherlands, Portugal, and Spain) are using the common currency on a daily basis. No single currency has circulated so widely in Europe since the days of the Roman Empire. Considering that 10 more countries, including the Czech Republic, Hungary, and Poland, joined the European Union (EU) by the year 2004, and that many of them will adopt the euro relatively soon, the **transaction domain** of the euro will become larger than that of the American dollar in the near future.

Once a country adopts the common currency, it forgoes its own monetary policy. The common monetary policy for the euro zone is now formulated by the **European Central Bank** (ECB) located in Frankfurt. The ECB is legally mandated to maintain price stability for the euro zone. Considering the sheer size of the euro zone in terms of population, economic output, and world trade share as well as the prospect of monetary stability in Europe, the euro has strong potential for becoming another global currency, rivalling the American dollar for dominance in international trade and finance. Reflecting the significance of the euro's introduction, Professor Robert Mundell, who is often referred to as the intellectual father of the euro, recently stated: "The creation of the euro area will eventually, but inevitably, lead to competition with the dollar area, both from the standpoint of excellence in monetary policy and in the enlistment of other currencies."[4] The world, thus, faces the prospects of a bipolar international monetary system.

Since its inception in 1999, the euro has already brought about revolutionary changes in European finance. For instance, by redenominating corporate and

---

[3]Various studies indicate that the liberalization of capital markets tends to lower the cost of capital. See, for example, Peter Henry, "Stock Market Liberalization, Economic Reform, and Emerging Market Equity Prices," *Journal Finance* 2000, pp. 529–64.

[4]Source: Robert Mundell, "Currency Area, Volatility and Intervention," *Journal of Policy Modeling 22* (3), 281–99.

Why We Believe in the Euro

By Jürgen Schrempp, CEO of DaimlerChrysler

In our company, we don't mean to waste even a day in putting the euro to work. On Jan. 1, 1999—day one for the new currency—our company will switch over completely to the euro as the internal and external unit of account. We expect to be one of the first German-based companies—perhaps *the* first—to make such a complete change. We'll also encourage our suppliers within Euroland to invoice us in euros from the very beginning. Our Euroland customers, of course, will have the option of paying in either euros or their domestic currency until 2001.

Nearly all major European companies are in favor of the single currency. But having recently agreed on a historic, transatlantic merger with Chrysler Corp. of the United States, we feel especially attuned to the forces of global competition that make the euro so essential. For our new company, DaimlerChrysler AG, and for Germany and Europe as a whole, economic and monetary union will bring substantial and lasting benefits as we take our place in the interdependent world of the 21st century.

Those benefits will take shape—indeed, are already occurring—in several realms at once. First and most fundamental is the political. The single currency will push the countries of Europe into cooperating more and more in seeking solutions to common economic problems. As they do so, they'll grow increasingly intertwined politically.

At the same time, the euro will unleash powerful market forces certain to transform the way Europeans live and work. The years ahead will bring increased efficiency, greater productivity, higher overall living standards and lower unemployment. For businesses, a common currency will reduce transaction costs—eliminating, among other things, the unnecessary waste of resources involved in dealing with several European currencies. At present, doing business across borders means having to buy and sell foreign currencies—and taking the risk that sudden changes in their relative value could upend an otherwise sound business strategy. The risks can be hedged, of course, but only at a cost that must ultimately be borne by customers.

The market forces unleashed by the euro will be felt not just by corporate managers but also by political leaders. Business executives are already working to rationalize their companies, enhancing productivity and improving labor flexibility. Elected officials, facing competition as they try to attract the investments that create jobs, will eventually lower corporate tax rates and streamline regulation. In so doing, governments will give corporations a boost, like the reduction in the cost of capital that came about as countries tightened their fiscal and monetary policies in preparation for EMU.

These changes are mutually reinforcing. And as they take hold, Euroland companies will grow more confident

government bonds and shares from 12 different currencies into the common currency, the euro has precipitated the emergence of continent-wide capital markets in Europe characterized by depth and liquidity. Companies all over the world benefit from this development by raising capital more easily and on favourable terms in Europe. In addition, the recent surge in European merger and acquisition (M&A) activities, cross-border alliances among financial exchanges, and lessening dependence on the banking sectors for capital raising are all manifestations of the profound effects of the euro. The International Finance in Practice box, "Why We Believe in the Euro," presents an upbeat view of the euro expressed by Jürgen Schrempp, CEO of DaimlerChrysler.

Since the end of World War I, the American dollar has played the role of the dominant global currency, displacing the British pound. As a result, foreign exchange rates of currencies are quoted against the dollar and the lion's share of currency trading involves the dollar on either the buy or the sell side. Similarly, international trade in primary commodities, such as petroleum, coffee, wheat, and gold, is conducted using the American dollar as the invoice currency. Reflecting the dominant position of the dollar in the world economy, central banks of the world hold a major portion of their external reserves in dollars. The ascendance of the dollar reflects several key factors, such as the dominant size of the American economy, mature and open capital markets, price stability, and the political and military power of the United States. The dominant global currency status of the dollar confers upon the United States many special privileges,

about committing resources to long-term projects. A look at the level of corporate mergers in recent years shows that managers have already stepped up their strategic decision making. Europe saw 237 such deals last year, worth $250 billion, of which 25 percent were European cross-border transactions. In 1995, by contrast, there were just 100 deals, worth $168 billion—and only 17 percent were European cross-border transactions.

Euroland will be a strong base for companies striving to compete globally. In 1997 its combined population numbered 290 million, compared with 268 million for the United States and 126 million for Japan. Its combined GDP was $6.3 trillion, versus $7.8 trillion for the United States and $4.2 trillion for Japan. Euroland already trades with the rest of the world as much as the United States does, and the picture will change in favor of Europe as soon as the United Kingdom, and others who have stayed out of the first wave, join the currency union. Such a development—the sooner the better—is something we would very much welcome.

Launching the new euro is one thing; successfully managing the EMU process in the years ahead is quite another. Implementation poses major challenges. Some will be technical; others will have to do with maintaining a unity of purpose among a diverse group of nations, regions, peoples and cultures. I believe, however, that Europe possesses the unshakable political will and financial expertise needed to keep this endeavor on track.

It will help that—as we at DaimlerChrysler well know—some of the payoffs are immediate and obvious.

Currently, one third of our group's revenues are earned in Deutsche marks, but nearly three quarters of our costs are incurred in that currency. That makes planning harder and running the company more complex. But with the coming of the euro, the disparity between our DM costs and DM revenues will diminish. As of January, 50 percent of our revenues will be in euros, with 80 percent of our costs incurred in the same currency.

How will the euro affect our ability to compete in the United States, our main export market outside the EU? In a word, positively. Higher productivity and a stable "home" currency will allow us to maintain a competitive pricing structure. Such long-term consistency in our business practices is something our U.S. customers have come to appreciate.

One final point. Thanks to the single market and the pending introduction of a single currency, Europe has matured both politically and economically. As a major transatlantic player, DaimlerChrysler is now in a position to communicate an important message to its business partners in that other great single-currency market, the United States. Working through the World Trade Organization and other groups, the globe has made great progress toward free and fair trade over the years. Now let us together examine opportunities for removing some of the remaining obstacles to trade between Europe and the United States. The beneficiaries will be consumers on both sides of the Atlantic.

Source: *Newsweek*, Special Issue. Winter 1998, p. 38. Reprinted with permission.

such as the ability to run trade deficits without having to hold foreign exchange reserves, that is, "deficits without tears." American firms conduct a large portion of international transactions in dollars without bearing exchange risks. However, once economic agents start to use the euro in earnest as an invoice, vehicle, and reserve currency, the dollar may have to share the aforementioned privileges with the euro.[5]

Trade Liberalization and Economic Integration

International trade, which has been the traditional link between national economies, continue to expand. As Exhibit 1.3 shows, the ratio of merchandise exports to GDP for the world has increased from 7 percent in 1950 to 21.9 percent in 2003. This implies that over the same time period, international trade increased nearly three times as fast as world GDP. For some countries, international trade grew much faster; for Germany, the ratio rose from 6.2 percent to 34.2 percent, while for Taiwan, it grew from 2.5 percent to 47.2 percent over the same time period. Latin American countries, such as Argentina and Brazil, have relatively low export-to-GDP ratios. This reflects the

---

[5]A recent study by Eun and Lai, 2002, "The Power Contest in FX Markets: The Euro vs. the Dollar," indicates that within three years since its inception, the euro has succeeded in establishing its own currency bloc in Europe, comprising the currencies of Croatia, Czech Republic, Hungary, Norway, Slovakia, Slovenia, Sweden, and Switzerland. The study, however, shows that the American dollar remains the dominant global currency. In contrast, the Japanese yen does not have its own currency bloc in Asia.

EXHIBIT 1.3

Long-Term Openness in Perspective
(Merchandise Exports/GDP at 1990 Prices, in Percent)

Country	1870	1913	1929	1950	1973	2001	2003
United States	2.5	3.7	3.6	3.0	5.0	7.2	7.9
Canada	12.0	12.2	15.8	13.0	19.9	41.1	45.2
Australia	7.4	12.8	11.2	9.1	11.2	17.6	19.1
United Kingdom	12.0	17.7	13.3	11.4	14.0	19.0	22.4
Germany	9.5	15.6	12.8	6.2	23.8	31.1	34.2
France	4.9	8.2	8.6	7.7	15.4	24.7	25.1
Spain	3.8	8.1	5.0	1.6	5.0	19.0	23.6
Japan	0.2	2.4	3.5	2.3	7.9	10.7	10.7
Korea	0.0	1.0	4.5	1.0	8.2	36.0	39.4
Taiwan	0.0	2.5	5.2	2.5	10.2	45.2	47.3
Thailand	2.1	6.7	6.6	7.0	4.5	59.4	62.6
Argentina	9.4	6.8	6.1	2.4	2.1	9.9	13.1
Brazil	11.8	9.5	7.1	4.0	2.6	10.3	11.3
Mexico	3.7	10.8	14.8	3.5	2.2	28.7	33.6
World	5.0	8.7	9.0	7.0	11.2	19.7	21.9

Source: Various issues of *World Financial Markets,* JP Morgan, and *International Financial Statistics,* IMF.

inward-looking, protectionist economic policies these countries pursued in the past. Even these once-protectionist countries are now increasingly pursuing free-market and open-economy policies because of the gains from international trade.

The principal argument for international trade is based on the **theory of comparative advantage,** advanced by David Ricardo in his seminal book, *Principles of Political Economy* (1817). According to Ricardo, it is mutually beneficial for countries to specialize in the production of those goods they can produce most efficiently and trade such goods among them. Suppose England produces textiles most efficiently, whereas France produces wine most efficiently. It then makes sense for England to specialize in the production of textiles and France in the production of wine, and for the two countries to then trade their products. By doing so, the two countries can increase their combined production of textiles and wine, which, in turn, allows both countries to consume more of both goods. This argument remains valid even if one country can produce both goods more efficiently than the other country.[6] Ricardo's theory has a clear policy implication: *Liberalization of international trade will enhance the welfare of the world's citizens.* In other words, international trade is not a "zero-sum" game in which one country benefits at the expense of another country—the view held by the "mercantilists." Rather, international trade is an "increasing-sum" game in which all players become winners.

The theory of comparative advantage provides a powerful intellectual rationale for free trade among nations. Currently, international trade is being liberalized at both the global and regional levels. At the global level, the **General Agreement on Tariffs and Trade (GATT),** which is a multilateral agreement among member countries, has played a key role in dismantling barriers to international trade. Since it was established in 1947, GATT has been successful in gradually eliminating and reducing tariffs, subsidies, quotas, and other barriers to trade. Through various rounds of talks, the GATT worked to (1) reduce import tariffs worldwide by an average of 38 percent, (2) increase the proportion of duty-free products from 20 percent to 54 percent for industrialized countries, and (3) extend the rules of world trade to cover agriculture, such services as banking and insurance, and intellectual property rights. It also created a permanent **World Trade Organization (WTO)** to replace GATT. The WTO has more power to enforce the rules of international trade. China recently joined the WTO. China's WTO membership will further legitimize the idea of free trade.

www.wto.org/

The World Trade Organization website covers news and data about international trade development.

---

[6]Readers are referred to Appendix 1A for a detailed discussion of the theory of comparative advantage.

On the regional level, formal arrangements among countries have been instituted to promote economic integration. The **European Union (EU)** is a prime example. The European Union is the direct descendent of the European Community (formerly the European Economic Community), which was established to foster economic integration among the countries of Western Europe. Today, the EU includes 25 member states that have eliminated barriers to the free flow of goods, capital, and people. The member states of the EU hope this move will strengthen its economic position relative to the United States and Japan. In 1999, 12 member countries of the EU successfully adopted a single common currency, the euro, which may rival the American dollar as a dominant currency for international trade and investment. The launch of the euro has spurred a rush by European companies to seeking pan-European and global alliances. Merger and acquisition deals in Europe totalled $1.2 trillion in 1999, exceeding the figure for American deals for the first time. The EU recently enlarged to include some formerly socialist countries, such as Poland, Hungary, and the Czech Republic.

Whereas the economic and monetary union planned by the EU is one of the most advanced forms of economic integration, a free trade area is the most basic. In 1994, Canada, the United States, and Mexico entered into the North American Free Trade Agreement (NAFTA). Canada is the United States' largest trading partner, and Mexico is the third-largest. In a free trade area, all impediments to trade, such as tariffs and import quotas, are eliminated among members. The terms of NAFTA call for phasing out tariffs over a 15-year period. Many observers believe that NAFTA will foster increased trade among its members, resulting in an increase in the number of jobs and the standard of living in all member countries. It is interesting to note from Exhibit 1.3 that for Canada, the ratio of exports to GDP increased dramatically from 19.2 percent in 1973 to 45.2 percent in 2003.

Privatization

The economic integration and globalization that began in the 1980s picked up speed in the 1990s via privatization. Through **privatization,** a country divests itself of the ownership and operation of a business venture by turning it over to the free market system. Privatization did not begin with the fall of the Berlin Wall; nevertheless, its pace accelerated since the collapse of communism in the Eastern Bloc countries. It is ironic that the very political and economic system that only a short while ago extolled the virtues of state ownership should so dramatically be shifting toward capitalism by shedding state-operated businesses.

Privatization can be viewed in many ways. In one sense, it is a denationalization process. When a national government divests itself of a state-run business, it gives up part of its national identity. Moreover, if the new owners are foreign, the country may simultaneously be importing a cultural influence that did not previously exist. Privatization is frequently viewed as a means to an end. One benefit of privatization for many less-developed countries is that the sale of state-owned businesses brings to the national treasury hard-currency foreign reserves. The sale proceeds are often used to pay down sovereign debt that has weighed heavily on the economy. Additionally, privatization is often seen as a cure for bureaucratic inefficiency and waste; some economists estimate that privatization improves efficiency and reduces operating costs by as much as 20 percent.

There is no one single way to privatize state-owned operations. The objectives of the country seem to be the prevailing guide. For the Czech Republic, speed was the overriding factor. To accomplish privatization en masse, the Czech government essentially gave away its businesses to the Czech people. For a nominal fee, vouchers were sold that allowed Czech citizens to bid on businesses as they went on the auction block. From 1991 to 1995, more than 1,700 companies were turned over to private hands. Moreover, three-quarters of the Czech citizens became shareholders in these newly privatized firms.

In Russia, there has been an "irreversible" shift to private ownership. More than 80 percent of the country's nonfarm workers are now employed in the private sector.

Eleven million apartment units have been privatized, as have half of the country's 240,000 other business firms. Via a Czech-style voucher system, 40 million Russians now own shares in over 15,000 medium- to large-size corporations that recently became privatized through mass auctions of state-owned enterprises.

1.4 Multinational Corporations

In addition to international trade, foreign direct investment by MNCs is a major force driving globalization of the world economy. There are about 62,000 MNCs in the world with over 500,000 foreign affiliates.[7] Throughout the 1990s, foreign direct investment by MNCs grew at the annual rate of about 10 percent. In comparison, international trade grew at the rate of 3.5 percent during the same period. MNCs' worldwide sales reached $16 trillion in 2002, compared with about $10 trillion of world exports in the same year. As indicated in the International Finance in Practice box on page 16, MNCs are reshaping the structure of the world economy.

A **multinational corporation (MNC)** is a business firm incorporated in one country that has production and sales operations in several other countries. The term suggests a firm obtaining raw materials from one national market and financial capital from another, producing goods with labour and capital equipment in a third country, and selling the finished product in yet other national markets. Indeed, some MNCs have operations in dozens of different countries. MNCs obtain financing from major money centres around the world in many different currencies to finance their operations. Global operations force the treasurer's office to establish international banking relationships, place short-term funds in several currency denominations, and effectively manage foreign exchange risk.

Exhibit 1.4 lists the top 40 of the largest 100 MNCs ranked by the size of foreign assets. The list was compiled by the United Nations Conference on Trade and Development (UNCTAD). Many of the firms on the list are well-known MNCs with household names because of their presence in consumer product markets. For example, General Motors, Royal/Dutch Shell, Toyota, Daimler-Benz, IBM, Philip Morris, British Petroleum, Unilever, Nestlé, Sony, and Siemens are names recognized by most people. By country of origin, American MNCs, with 28 out of the total of 100, represent the largest group. The United Kingdom ranks second with 16 in the top 100, followed by France with 13, Germany with 12, and Japan with 8. It is interesting to note that some firms from smaller countries can be extremely multinational. Philips Electronics of the Netherlands, for instance, derive about 98 percent of its sales from overseas markets.

In *The World Investment Report*s' ranking of the top 100 nonfinancial multinational corporations in 2001, Canada is represented by The Thomson Corporation (number 55), Nortel (56), which has since fallen off the list, and Bell Canada Enterprises at number 97.

MNCs gain from their global presence in a variety of ways. First of all, MNCs can benefit from economies of scale by (1) spreading research and development (R&D) expenditures and advertising costs over their global sales, (2) pooling global purchasing power over suppliers, (3) utilizing their technological and managerial know-how globally with minimum additional costs, and so forth. Furthermore, MNCs can use their global presence to take advantage of low-cost labour available in certain developing countries while gaining access to special R&D capabilities in advanced nations. MNCs can, indeed, leverage their global presence to boost their profit margins and create shareholder value.

www.unctad.org/wir/

This UNCTAD website provides a broad coverage of cross-border investment activities by multinational corporations.

---

[7]The source for this information is the United Nation's *World Investment Report 2003*.

EXHIBIT 1.4 The World's Top 40 Nonfinancial MNCs Ranked by Foreign Assets, 2001 (Millions of Dollars)

Ranking by Foreign Assets	Corporation	Home Economy	Industry	Assets Foreign	Assets Total	Sales Foreign	Sales Total
1	Vodafone	United Kingdom	Telecommunications	187,792	207,458	24,602	32,744
2	General Electric	United States	Electrical & electronic equip.	180,031	495,210	39,914	125,913
3	BP	United Kingdom	Petroleum expl./ref./distr.	111,207	141,158	141,225	175,389
4	Vivendi Universal	France	Diversified	91,120	123,156	29,652	51,423
5	Deutsche Telekom AG	Germany	Telecommunications	90,657	145,802	11,836	43,309
6	Exxonmobil Corporation	United States	Petroleum expl./ref./distr.	89,426	143,174	145,814	209,417
7	Ford Motor Company	United States	Motor vehicles	81,169	276,543	52,983	162,412
8	General Motors	United States	Motor vehicles	75,379	323,969	45,256	177,260
9	Royal Dutch/Shell Group	United Kingdom/Netherlands	Petroleum expl./ref./distr.	73,492	111,543	72,952	135,211
10	TotalFinaElf	France	Petroleum expl./ref./distr.	70 030	78 500	74 647	94 418
11	Suez	France	Electricity, gas, and water	69,345	79,280	29,919	37,975
12	Toyota Motor Corporation	Japan	Motor vehicles	68,400	144,793	59,880	108,880
13	Fia Spa	Italy	Motor vehicles	48,749	89,264	24,860	52,002
14	Telefonica SA	Spain	Telecommunications	48,122	77,011	14,303	27,775
15	Volkswagen Group	Germany	Motor vehicles	47,480	92,520	57,426	79,376
16	ChevronTexaco Corp.	United States	Petroleum expl./ref./distr.	44,943	77,572	57,673	104,409
17	Hutchison Whampoa Ltd.	Hong Kong, China	Diversified	40,9899	55,281	6,092	11,415
18	News Corporation	Australia	Media	35,650	40,007	13,880	15,087
19	Honda Motor Co. Ltd.	Japan	Motor vehicles	35,257	52,056	40,088	55,955
20	E.On	Germany	Electricity, gas, and water	33,990	87,755	22,744	71,419
21	Nestlé	Switzerland	Food & Beverages	33,065	55,821	34,704	50,717
22	RWE Group	Germany	Electricity, gas, and water	32,809	81,024	23,151	58,039
23	IBM	United States	Electrical & electronic equip.	32,800	88,313	50,651	85,866
24	ABB	Switzerland	Machinery and equipment	30,586	32,305	18,876	19,382
25	Unilever	United Kingdom/Netherlands	Diversified	30,529	46,922	28,675	46,803
26	ENI Group	Italy	Petroleum expl./ref./distr.	29,935	55,584	19,437	43,861
27	BMW AG	Germany	Motor vehicles	29,901	45,415	25,304	34,482
28	Philips Electronics	Netherlands	Electrical & electronic equip.	29,416	34,070	27,598	28,992
29	Carrefour SA	France	Retail	29,342	41,172	31,513	62,294
30	Electricité De France	France	Electricity, gas, and water	28,141	120,124	12,468	36,502
31	Repsol YPF SA	Spain	Petroleum expl./ref./distr.	27,028	45,575	13,752	39,135
32	Sony Corporation	Japan	Electrical & electronic equip.	26,930	61,393	38,605	57,595
33	Aventis SA	France	Pharmaceuticals	26,368	34,761	13,377	20,567
34	Wal-Mart Stores	United States	Retail	26,324	83,451	35,485	217,799
35	DaimlerChrysler AG	Germany/United States	Motor vehicles	25,795	183,765	43,556	137,051
36	Lafarge SA	France	Construction Materials	24,906	26,493	10,537	12,280
37	Nissan Motor Co. Ltd.	Japan	Motor vehicles	24,382	54,113	29,078	47,091
38	AES Corporation	United States	Electricity, gas, and water	23,902	36,736	5,809	9,327
39	Roche Group	Switzerland	Pharmaceuticals	22,794	25,289	17,156	17,463
40	BASF AG	Germany	Chemicals	20,872	32,671	17,108	29,136

Source: *World Investment Report 2003*, United Nations.

INTERNATIONAL FINANCE
I N   P R A C T I C E

Multinationals More Efficient

Foreign-owned manufacturing companies in the world's most highly developed countries are generally more productive and pay their workers more than comparable locally-owned businesses, according to the Organisation for Economic Co-operation and Development.

The Paris-based organisation also says that the proportion of manufacturing under foreign ownership in European Union countries rose substantially during the 1990s, a sign of increasing economic integration.

In a report on the global role of multinationals, the OECD points out that for some countries, the level of production abroad by foreign subsidiaries of national businesses was comparable to total exports from these countries.

The finding underlines the increasing importance in the world economy of large companies with bases scattered across the globe.

Gross output per employee, a measure of productivity, in most OECD nations tends to be greater in multinationals than in locally-owned companies, the report says.

This is partly a factor of the multinationals being bigger and more geared to operating according to world-class levels of efficiency. But it also reflects their ability to transfer new thinking in production technologies through an international factory network.

Reflecting the greater efficiencies, workers in foreign-owned plants tend to earn more money than those in locally-owned ones.

In Turkey, employees of multinationals earn double the wages of their counterparts. The equivalent figure in the UK is 23 per cent and in the US it is 9 per cent.

In the EU in 1998, a quarter of total manufacturing production was controlled by a foreign subsidiary of a

Foreign companies' share in manufacturing production
1998 or lastest year (%)

Source: OECD, Activities of Foreign Affiliates database

bigger company compared to 17 per cent in 1990. The figure has probably increased since then, and is expected to climb further as the impact of the euro tightens the link between member countries' economies.

Measuring Globalisation: The Role of Multinationals in OECD Economies. For details see www.oecd.org

Source: Peter Marsh, *Financial Times,* March 20, 2002, p. 6. Reprinted with permission.

1.5   Organization of the Text

International Financial Management contains 21 chapters divided into four parts. Part One, Foundations of International Financial Management, contains five chapters on the fundamentals of international finance. This section lays the macroeconomic foundation for all the topics to follow. A thorough understanding of this material is essential for understanding the advanced topics covered in the remaining sections.

Chapter 2 introduces the student to the various types of international monetary systems under which the world economy can function and has functioned at various times. Extensive treatment is given to the differences between fixed and flexible exchange rate regimes. The chapter traces the historical development of the world's international monetary systems from the early 1800s to the present. A detailed discussion of the European Monetary System of the European Union is presented. Chapter 3 presents balance-of-payment concepts and accounting. The chapter is designed to show that even a national government must keep its "economic house in order" or else it will experience current account deficits that will undermine the value of its currency. This chapter also shows how the balance of payments reveals the sources of demand and

16

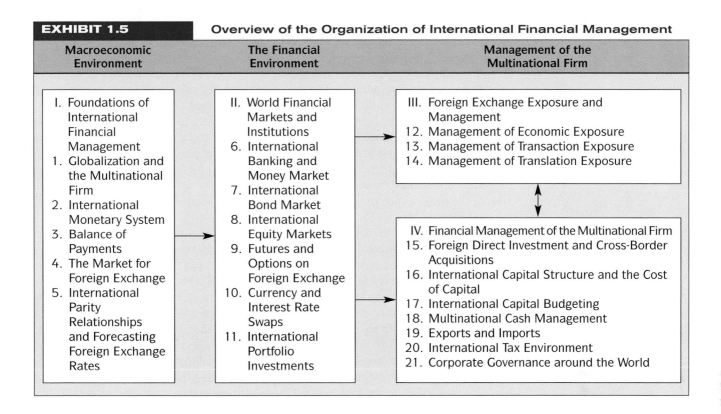

EXHIBIT 1.5 Overview of the Organization of International Financial Management

Macroeconomic Environment	The Financial Environment	Management of the Multinational Firm
I. Foundations of International Financial Management 1. Globalization and the Multinational Firm 2. International Monetary System 3. Balance of Payments 4. The Market for Foreign Exchange 5. International Parity Relationships and Forecasting Foreign Exchange Rates	II. World Financial Markets and Institutions 6. International Banking and Money Market 7. International Bond Market 8. International Equity Markets 9. Futures and Options on Foreign Exchange 10. Currency and Interest Rate Swaps 11. International Portfolio Investments	III. Foreign Exchange Exposure and Management 12. Management of Economic Exposure 13. Management of Transaction Exposure 14. Management of Translation Exposure IV. Financial Management of the Multinational Firm 15. Foreign Direct Investment and Cross-Border Acquisitions 16. International Capital Structure and the Cost of Capital 17. International Capital Budgeting 18. Multinational Cash Management 19. Exports and Imports 20. International Tax Environment 21. Corporate Governance around the World

supply of a country's currency. It concludes by surveying the balance-of-payments trends in major countries.

Chapter 4 provides an introduction to the organization and operation of the spot-and-forward foreign exchange market. It describes institutional arrangements of the foreign exchange markets and details of how foreign exchange is quoted and traded worldwide. Chapter 5, in turn, presents some of the fundamental international parity relationships among exchange rates, interest rates, and inflation rates. An understanding of these parity relationships, which are manifestations of market equilibrium, is essential for astute financial management in a global setting. Chapter 5 begins with the derivation of *interest rate parity*, showing the interrelationship between the interest rates of two countries and the spot and forward exchange rates between the same two countries. Similarly, the theory of *purchasing power parity (PPP)* is developed, showing the relationship between a change in exchange rate between two countries and the relative values of their inflation rates. The limitations of PPP are clearly detailed. The chapter concludes with a discussion of forecasting exchange rates using parity relationships and other fundamental and technical forecasting techniques.

The chapters in Part One lay the macroeconomic foundation for *International Financial Management.* Exhibit 1.5 provides a diagram that shows the text layout. The diagram shows discussion moving from a study of macroeconomic foundations to a study of the financial environment in which the firm and the financial manager must function. Financial strategy and decision making can be discussed intelligently only after one has an appreciation of the financial environment.

Part Two, World Financial Markets and Institutions, provides a thorough discussion of international financial institutions, financial assets, and marketplaces and develops the tools necessary to manage exchange rate uncertainty. Chapter 6, International Banking and the Money Market, begins the section. The chapter differentiates between international and domestic bank operations and examines the institutional differences between various types of international banking offices. International banks and their clients make up the Eurocurrency market and form the core of the international money market. The chapter includes a discussion of the features and characteristics of the major international money market instruments: forward rate agreements, Euronotes, Euro-medium-term notes, and Eurocommercial paper. The chapter concludes with an examination of the international debt crisis that severely jeopardized the economic viability of many of the world's largest banks during the past decade.

Chapter 7 distinguishes between foreign bonds and Eurobonds, which together make up the international bond market. It discusses the advantages to the issuer of sourcing funds from the international bond market as opposed to raising funds domestically. It describes both the underwriting procedure for issuing new Eurobonds and the procedure for trading existing international bonds in the secondary market. A discussion of the major types of international bonds is included in the chapter. The chapter concludes with a discussion of international bond ratings.

Chapter 8 covers international equity markets. There is not a separate international equity market that operates parallel to domestic equity markets. Instead, the equity shares of certain corporations have broad appeal to international investors, rather than just investors from the country in which the corporation is incorporated. Chapter 8 documents the size of equity markets in both the developed and the developing countries. Various methods of trading equity shares in the secondary markets are discussed. The chapter discusses the advantages to the firm of cross-listing equity shares in more than one country.

Chapter 9 provides an extensive treatment of exchange-traded currency futures and options contracts. The chapter covers the institutional details of trading these derivative securities and also develops basic valuation models for pricing them. We believe that derivative securities are best understood if one also understands what drives their value. How to use derivative securities is saved for Chapters 13 and 14, which examine the topics of transaction exposure and translation exposure.

Approximately 30 percent of the bonds issued in the world end up being involved in an interest rate or currency swap. Chapter 10 provides an extensive treatment of both types of swaps. The chapter provides detailed examples and real-life illustrations of swap arrangements that highlight the cash flows between counterparties while delineating the risks inherent in swap transactions. Swap pricing is also covered.

Chapter 11 covers international portfolio investment. The chapter begins by examining the benefits to the investor from diversifying his or her portfolio internationally, rather than just domestically. It shows that the gains from international diversification come from the lower correlations that typically exist among international assets in comparison with those existing among domestic assets. The chapter documents the potential benefits from international diversification that are available to all national investors. An appendix shows how the rewards from international diversification can be further enhanced by using derivative contracts to hedge the exchange rate risk in the portfolio.

Part Three, Foreign Exchange Exposure and Management, comprises three chapters, one each devoted to the topics of economic, transaction, and translation exposure management. Chapter 12 covers economic exposure, that is, the extent to which the value of the firm will be affected by unexpected changes in exchange rates. The chapter provides a way to measure economic exposure, discusses its determinants, and presents methods for managing and hedging economic exposure. Several real-life illustrations are provided.

Chapter 13 covers the management of transaction exposure that arises from contractual obligations denominated in a foreign currency. Several methods for hedging this exposure are compared and contrasted: the forward hedge, the futures hedge, the money market hedge, and the options hedge. The chapter also discusses why an MNC should hedge, a debatable subject in the minds of both academics and practitioners.

Chapter 14 covers translation exposure or, as it is sometimes called, accounting exposure. Translation exposure refers to the effect that an unanticipated change in exchange rates will have on the consolidated financial reports of an MNC. The chapter discusses, compares, and contrasts the various methods for translating financial statements denominated in foreign currencies. The chapter includes a discussion of managing translation exposure using funds adjustment and the pros and cons of using balance sheet and derivatives hedges.

Part Four, Financial Management of the Multinational Firm, covers topics on financial management practices for the MNC. The section begins with Chapter 15 on foreign direct investment, which discusses why MNCs make capital expenditures in productive capacity in foreign lands, rather than just produce domestically and then export to overseas markets. The chapter also deals with an increasingly popular form of foreign investment, cross-border mergers and acquisitions. The chapter includes a full treatment of the political risk associated with foreign investment.

Chapter 16 deals with the international capital structure and the cost of capital of an MNC. An analytical argument is presented showing that the firm's cost of equity capital is lower when its shares trade internationally, rather than just in the home country. Moreover, the cost of debt can be reduced if debt capital is sourced internationally. The result of international trading of equity and sourcing debt in the international bond market is a lower weighted average cost of capital, which increases the net present value of capital expenditures as well as the value of the firm.

Chapter 17 presents the adjusted present value (APV) framework, which is useful for a parent firm in analyzing a capital expenditure in foreign operations. The APV framework is a value additivity model that determines the present value of each relevant cash flow of a capital project by discounting at a rate of discount consistent with the risk inherent in the cash flow.

Chapter 18 covers issues in cash management for the MNC. The chapter begins with an illustration of a cash management system for an MNC. It is shown that if a centralized cash depository is established and if the parent firm and its foreign affiliates employ a multinational netting system, the number of foreign cash flows can be reduced, thus saving the firm money and giving the MNC better control of its cash. It is also shown that managing cash transactions through a centralized depository that administers a precautionary cash balance portfolio reduces the systemwide investment in cash. Transfer pricing strategies are explored as a means for reducing an MNC's worldwide tax liability. Further, transfer pricing strategies and other methods are considered as means for removing blocked funds from a host country.

Chapter 19 provides a brief introduction to trade financing and countertrade. Through the use of an example, a typical foreign trade transaction is traced from beginning to end. The example shows the three primary documents used in trade financing: letter of credit, time draft, and bill of lading. The example also shows how a time draft can become a negotiable money market instrument, called a banker's acceptance. The chapter concludes with a discussion of countertrade transactions, which are reciprocal promises between a buyer and a seller to purchase goods or services from one another.

Chapter 20 examines the international tax environment. The chapter opens with a discussion on the theory of taxation, exploring the issues of tax neutrality and tax equity. Different methods of taxation—income tax, withholding tax, value-added tax— are considered next. Income tax rates in select countries are compared, as are the withholding tax rates that exist through tax treaties between Canada and various countries. The chapter concludes with a treatment of the organizational structures MNCs can use for reducing tax liabilities.

The text concludes with Chapter 21, which deals with the important issue of corporate governance. Among other things, the chapter explains how separation of ownership and control in modern corporations gives rise to agency problems—conflict of interest between agents (managers) and principals (shareholders)—and how different countries deal with the problem using different corporate governance frameworks. The chapter also discusses the practical issue of how to improve corporate governance practices so that the interests of managers and shareholders can be better aligned.

SUMMARY

This chapter provided an introduction to *International Financial Management.*

1. It is essential to study "international" financial management because we now live in a highly globalized and integrated world economy. Owing to the (a) continuous liberalization of international trade and investment, and (b) rapid advances in telecommunications and transportation technologies, the world economy will become even more integrated.

2. Three major dimensions distinguish international finance from domestic finance. They are (a) foreign exchange and political risks, (b) market imperfections, and (c) an expanded opportunity set.

3. Financial managers of MNCs must learn to manage foreign exchange and political risks using proper tools and instruments, deal with (and take advantage of) market imperfections, and benefit from the expanded investment and financing opportunities. By doing so, financial managers contribute to shareholder wealth maximization, which is the ultimate goal of international financial management.

4. The theory of comparative advantage states that economic well being is enhanced if countries produce those goods for which they have comparative advantage and then trade those goods. The theory of comparative advantage provides a powerful rationale for free trade. Currently, international trade is becoming liberalized at both the global and the regional levels. At the global level, the WTO plays a key role in promoting free trade. At the regional level, the European Union and NAFTA play a vital role in dismantling trade barriers within regions.

5. A major economic trend of the present decade is the rapid pace with which former state-owned businesses are being privatized. With the fall of communism, many Eastern Bloc countries began stripping themselves of inefficient business operations formerly run by the state. Privatization has placed a new demand on international capital markets to finance the purchase of the former state enterprises, and it has also brought about a demand for new managers with international business skills.

6. In modern times, corporate capital and control of industrial technology are at the heart of one country's comparative advantage over another country. These controllers of capital and know-how are multinational corporations (MNCs). Today, it is not uncommon for an MNC to produce merchandise in one country on capital equipment financed by funds raised in a number of different currencies through issuing securities to investors in many countries and then selling the finished product to customers in yet other countries.

KEY WORDS

corporate governance, *8*
European Central Bank, *9*
European Union (EU), *13*
expanded opportunity set, *6*
foreign exchange risk, *4*
General Agreement on Tariffs and Trade (GATT), *12*

market imperfections, *5*
multinational corporation (MNC), *14*
North American Free Trade Agreement (NAFTA), *3*
political risk, *4*
privatization, *13*

shareholder wealth maximization, *7*
theory of comparative advantage, *12*
transaction domain *9*
World Trade Organization (WTO), *12*

QUESTIONS

1. Why is it important to study international financial management?
2. How is international financial management different from domestic financial management?
3. Discuss the three major trends that have prevailed in international business during the last two decades.

4. How is Canada's economic well being enhanced through free international trade in goods and services?

5. What considerations might limit the extent to which the theory of comparative advantage is realistic?

6. What are multinational corporations (MNCs), and what economic roles do they play?

7. Critics of the North American Free Trade Agreement (NAFTA) in both the United States and Canada feared the loss of American jobs to Mexico, where labour is cheaper to hire workers. What are the merits and demerits of this position on NAFTA? Considering recent economic developments in North America, how would you assess the position on NAFTA?

8. In 1995, a working group of French chief executive officers was set up by the Confederation of French Industry (CNPF) and the French Association of Private Companies (AFEP) to study the French corporate governance structure. The group reported the following, among other things: "The board of directors should not simply aim at maximizing share values as in the U.K. and the U.S. Rather, its goal should be to serve the company, whose interests should be clearly distinguished from those of its shareholders, employees, creditors, suppliers and clients but still equated with their general common interest, which is to safeguard the prosperity and continuity of the company." Evaluate the above recommendation of the working group.[8]

9. Emphasizing the importance of voluntary compliance, as opposed to enforcement, in the aftermath of such corporate scandals as those involving Enron and World-Com, American President George W. Bush stated that while tougher laws might help, "ultimately, the ethics of American business depends on the conscience of America's business leaders." Describe your view on this statement.

10. Suppose you are interested in investing in the shares of Nokia Corporation of Finland, which is a world leader in wireless communication. But before you make your investment decision, you would like to learn about the company. Visit the website of CNN Financial Network (www.cnnfn.com) and collect information about Nokia, including the recent share price history and analysts' views of the company. Discuss what you learn about the company. Also discuss how the instantaneous access to information via the Internet would affect the nature and workings of financial markets.

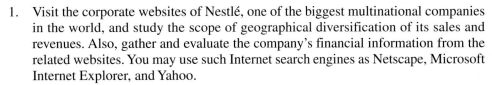

INTERNET EXERCISES

1. Visit the corporate websites of Nestlé, one of the biggest multinational companies in the world, and study the scope of geographical diversification of its sales and revenues. Also, gather and evaluate the company's financial information from the related websites. You may use such Internet search engines as Netscape, Microsoft Internet Explorer, and Yahoo.

2. Go to the website for McCain Food. Get a sense of the corporate history and its global presence. Since McCain is not a public company, you will not find publicly available financial information.

---

[8]This question draws on the article by François Degeorge, "French Boardrooms Wake Up Slowly to the Need for Reform," in the Complete MBA Companion in Global Business, *Financial Times*, 1999, pp. 156–60.

MINI CASE

Nike's Decision

Nike, an American-based company with a globally recognized brand name, manufactures athletic shoes in such Asian developing countries as China, Indonesia, and Vietnam using subcontractors and sells the products in the United States and foreign markets. The company has no production facilities in the United States. In each of those Asian countries where Nike has production facilities, the rates of unemployment and underemployment are quite high. The wage rate is very low in those countries by American standards; the hourly wage rate in the manufacturing sector is less than one dollar in each of those countries, compared with about $18 in the United States. In addition, workers in those countries often operate in poor and unhealthy environments, and their rights are not well protected. Understandably, the Asian host countries are eager to attract foreign investments, such as Nike's, to develop their economies and raise the living standards of their citizens. Recently, however, Nike came under worldwide criticism for its practice of hiring workers for such a low pay—"next to nothing" in the words of critics—and condoning the poor working conditions in the host countries.

Evaluate and discuss various ethical as well as economic ramifications of Nike's decision to invest in those Asian countries.

REFERENCES & SUGGESTED READINGS

Basic Finance References

Bodie, Zvi, Kane, J., P. Ryan, and S. Perrakis. *Investments*, 4th Canadian edition. Toronto; McGraw-Hill Ryerson, 2003.

Ross, Stephen A., W. Westerfield, F. Jaffee, and G. Roberts. Corporate Finance, 3rd Canadian edition. Toronto: McGraw-Hill Ryerson, 2002.. *Corporate Finance,* 6th ed. New York: Irwin/McGraw-Hill, 2002.

International Accounting References

Al Hashim, Dhia D., and Jeffrey S. Arpan. *International Dimensions of Accounting,* 3rd ed. Boston: PWS-Kent, 1992.

Meuller, Gerhard G., Helen Gernon, and Gary Meek. *Accounting: An International Perspective,* 5th ed. Burr Ridge, Ill.: Richard D. Irwin, 2000.

International Economics References

Baker, Stephen A. *An Introduction to International Economics.* San Diego: Harcourt Brace Jovanovich, 1990.

Husted, Steven, and Michael Melvin. *International Economics,* 5th ed. Reading, Mass.: Addison-Wesley, 2000.

Krugman, Paul R., and Maurice Obstfeld. *International Economics: Theory and Policy,* 6th ed. Reading, Mass.: Addison-Wesley, 2002.

Rivera-Batiz, Francisco L., and Luis Rivera-Batiz. *International Finance and Open Economy Macroeconomics,* 2nd ed. Upper Saddle River, N.J.: Prentice Hall, 1994.

Gains from Trade: The Theory of Comparative Advantage

The theory of comparative advantage was originally advanced by the 19th-century economist David Ricardo as an explanation for why nations trade with one another. The theory claims that economic well being is enhanced if each country's citizens produce that which they have a comparative advantage in producing relative to the citizens of other countries and then trade products. Underlying the theory are the assumptions of free trade between nations and that the factors of production (land, buildings, labour, technology, and capital) are relatively immobile. Consider the example described in Exhibit A.1 as a vehicle for explaining the theory.

Exhibit A.1 assumes two countries, A and B, which each produce only food and textiles, but they do not trade with one another. Country A and B each have 60,000,000 units of input. Each country presently allocates 40,000,000 units to the production of food and 20,000,000 units to the production of textiles. Examination of the exhibit shows that Country A can produce five kilograms of food with one unit of production or three metres of textiles. Country B has an absolute advantage over Country A in the production of both food and textiles. Country B can produce 15 kilograms of food or four metres of textiles with one unit of production. When all units of production are employed, Country A can produce 200,000,000 kilograms of food and 60,000,000 metres of textiles. Country B can produce 600,000,000 kilograms of food and 80,000,000 metres of textiles. Total output is 800,000,000 kilograms of food and 140,000,000 metres of textiles. Without trade, each nation's citizens can consume only what they produce.

While it is clear from the examination of Exhibit A.1 that Country B has an absolute advantage in the production of food and textiles, it is not so clear that Country A (B) has a relative advantage over Country B (A) in producing textiles (food). Note that in using units of production, Country A can "trade off" one unit of production needed to produce five kilograms of food for three metres of textiles. Thus, a metre of textiles has an *opportunity cost* of 5/3 = 1.67 kilograms of food, or a kilogram of food has an opportunity cost of 3/5 = 0.60 metres of textiles. Analogously, Country B has an opportunity cost of 15/4 = 3.75 kilograms of food per metre of textiles, or 4/15 = 0.27 metres of textiles per kilogram of food. When viewed in terms of opportunity costs, it is clear that Country A is relatively more efficient in producing textiles and Country B is relatively more efficient in producing food. That is, Country A's (B's) opportunity cost for producing textiles (food) is less than Country B's (A's). A *relative efficiency* that shows up via a lower opportunity cost is referred to as a comparative advantage.

Exhibit A.2 shows that when there are no restrictions or impediments to free trade, such as import quotas, import tariffs, or costly transportation, the economic well being of the citizens of both countries is enhanced through trade. Exhibit A.2 shows that Country A has shifted 20,000,000 units from the production of food to the production of textiles where it has a comparative advantage and that Country B has shifted 10,000,000 units from the production of textiles to the production of food where it has a comparative advantage. Total output is now 850,000,000 kilograms of food and 160,000,000 metres of textiles. Suppose that Country A and Country B agree on a price of 2.50 kilograms of food for one metre of textiles, and that Country A sells Country B 50,000,000 metres of textiles for 125,000,000 kilograms of food. With free trade, Exhibit A.2 makes it clear that the citizens of each country have increased their consumption of food by 25,000,000 kilograms and textiles by 10,000,000 metres.

EXHIBIT A.1

Input/Output without Trade

		Country		
		A	B	Total
I.	Units of input (000,000)			
	Food	40	40	
	Textiles	20	20	
II.	Output per unit of input (kgs or metres)			
	Food	5	15	
	Textiles	3	4	
III.	Total output (kgs or metres) (000,000)			
	Food	200	600	800
	Textiles	60	80	140
IV.	Consumption (kgs or metres) (000,000)			
	Food	200	600	800
	Textiles	60	80	140

EXHIBIT A.2

Input/Output with Free Trade

		Country		
		A	B	Total
I.	Units of input (000,000)			
	Food	20	50	
	Textiles	40	10	
II.	Output per unit of input (kgs or metres)			
	Food	5	15	
	Textiles	3	4	
III.	Total output (kgs or metres) (000,000)			
	Food	100	750	850
	Textiles	120	40	160
IV.	Consumption (kgs or metres) (000,000)			
	Food	225	625	850
	Textiles	70	90	160

PROBLEMS

1. Country C can produce seven kilograms of food or four metres of textiles per unit of input. Compute the opportunity cost of producing food instead of textiles. Similarly, compute the opportunity cost of producing textiles instead of food.

2. Consider the no-trade input/output situation presented in the following table for countries X and Y. Assuming that free trade is allowed, develop a scenario that will benefit the citizens of both countries.

Input/Output without Trade

		Country		
		X	Y	Total
I.	Units of input (000,000)			
	Food	70	60	
	Textiles	40	30	
II.	Output per unit of input (kgs or metres)			
	Food	17	5	
	Textiles	5	2	
III.	Total output (kgs or metres) (000,000)			
	Food	1,190	300	1,490
	Textiles	200	60	260
IV.	Consumption (kgs or metres) (000,000)			
	Food	1,190	300	1,490
	Textiles	200	60	260

CHAPTER 2

International Monetary System

THIS CHAPTER EXAMINES the international monetary system that defines the financial environment in which multinational corporations operate. The international monetary system includes the foreign exchange markets where values of exchange rates are determined. As mentioned in Chapter 1, exchange rates among major currencies, such as the American dollar, the euro, the British pound, and the Japanese yen, have been floating since the fixed exchange rate regime—know as the Bretton Woods Agreement—was abandoned in 1973.

Earlier, from 1950 to 1962, when most other nations in the world were on fixed rates, Canada maintained a flexible exchange rate. Canada's concern was that a fixed exchange rate would contribute to inflation in Canada as Canadian exports at the time were strong—especially to Europe, which was rebuilding following the war. Capital was also flowing into Canada. Canada intended the "managed float" to be temporary and to be kept within a small range, plus-or-minus 1 percent of US$0.91, but this proved to be much too restrictive. In fact, in 1957, the Canadian dollar touched US$1.06. In1962, Canada fixed the exchange rate at US$0.925, again with a commitment to keep it within plus-or-minus one percent of that figure. In 1970, following several episodes of sharp swings in the Current Account Balance, Canada announced that the exchange rate would float. Since then, the external value of the Canadian dollar— the exchange rate—has been determined in the markets for foreign exchange.

Floating exchange rates are a fact of modern life and a source of concern for all businesses. Exchange rate changes can present opportunities as well as pleasant or unpleasant surprises. It is crucial for firms to carefully measure and manage their exchange rate risk and exposure. The complex international monetary arrangements imply that for adroit financial decision making, it is essential for managers to appreciate the arrangements and workings of the international monetary system.

The **international monetary system** is the *institutional framework within which international payments are made, movements of capital are accommodated,* and *exchange rates among currencies are determined.* It is a complex set of institutions, rules, and policies regarding exchange rates, international payments, and the international flow of capital. The international monetary system has evolved over time and will continue to do so in the future as fundamental economic and political conditions under-lying the world economy continue to shift. In this chapter, we review the history of the international monetary system and contemplate its future prospects. In addition, we compare and contrast the alternative exchange rate systems, that is, fixed versus flexible exchange rates.

2.1 Evolution of the International Monetary System

The international monetary system went through several distinct stages of evolution. These stages are summarized as follows:

1. Bimetallism: Before 1875.
2. Classical gold standard: 1875–1914.
3. Interwar period: 1915–1944.
4. Bretton Woods system: 1945–1972.
5. Flexible exchange rate regime: Since 1973.

We now examine each of the five stages in some detail.

2.2 Bimetallism: Before 1875

Prior to the 1870s, many countries had **bimetallism,** that is, a double standard, in that free coinage was maintained for both gold and silver. In Great Britain, for example, bimetallism was maintained until 1816 (after the conclusion of the Napoleonic Wars), when Parliament passed a law maintaining free coinage of gold only, abolishing the free coinage of silver. In the United States, bimetallism was adopted by the *Coinage Act* of 1792 and remained a legal standard until 1873, when Congress dropped the silver dollar from the list of coins to be minted. France, on the other hand, introduced and maintained its bimetallism from the French Revolution to 1878. Some other countries, such as China, India, Germany, and Holland, were on the silver standard.

The international monetary system before the 1870s can be characterized as "bimet-allism" in the sense that both gold and silver were used as international means of pay-ment and that the exchange rates among currencies were determined by either their gold or silver contents.[1] Around 1870, for example, the exchange rate between the British pound, which was fully on a gold standard, and the French franc, which was officially on a bimetallic standard, was determined by the gold content of the two cur-rencies. On the other hand, the exchange rate between the franc and the German mark, which was on a silver standard, was determined by the silver content of the currencies. The exchange rate between the pound and the mark was determined by their exchange rates against the franc. It is also worth noting that due to various wars and political upheavals, some major countries, such as the United States, Russia, and Austria-Hun-gary, had irredeemable currencies at one time or another during the period 1848–1879. One might say that the international monetary system was less than fully *systematic* up until the 1870s.

Countries that were on the bimetallic standard often experienced the well-known phenomenon referred to as **Gresham's law.** Since the exchange ratio between the two metals was fixed officially, only the abundant metal was used as money, driving more scarce metal out of circulation. This is Gresham's law, according to which "bad" (abun-dant) money drives out "good" (scarce) money. For example, when gold from newly discovered mines in California and Australia poured into the market in the 1850s, the

---

[1]This does not imply that each individual country was on a bimetallic standard. In fact, many countries were on either a gold standard or a silver standard by 1870.

value of gold became depressed, causing overvaluation of gold under the French official ratio, which equated a gold franc to a silver franc $15\frac{1}{2}$ times as heavy. As a result, the franc effectively became a gold currency.

2.3 Classical Gold Standard: 1875–1914

Mankind's fondness for gold as a storage of wealth and means of exchange dates back to antiquity and was shared widely by diverse civilizations. Christopher Columbus once said, "Gold constitutes treasure, and he who possesses it has all he needs in this world." The first full-fledged **gold standard,** however, was not established until 1821 in Great Britain, when notes from the Bank of England were made fully redeemable for gold. As previously mentioned, France was effectively on the gold standard beginning in the 1850s and formally adopted the standard in 1878. The newly emergent German empire, which was to receive a sizable war indemnity from France, converted to the gold standard in 1875, discontinuing free coinage of silver. The United States adopted the gold standard in 1879 and Russia and Japan in 1897.

One can say roughly that the *international* gold standard existed as a historical reality during the period 1875–1914. The majority of countries got off gold in 1914, when World War I broke out. The classical gold standard as an international monetary system thus lasted for about 40 years. During this period, London became the centre of the international financial system, reflecting Britain's advanced economy and its preeminent position in international trade.

An *international* gold standard can be said to exist when, in most major countries, (1) gold alone is assured of unrestricted coinage, (2) there is two-way convertibility between gold and national currencies at a stable ratio, and (3) gold may be freely exported or imported. In order to support unrestricted convertibility into gold, banknotes need to be backed by a gold reserve of a minimum stated ratio. In addition, the domestic money stock should rise and fall as gold flows in and out of the country. The above conditions were roughly met between 1875 and 1914.

Under the gold standard, the exchange rate between any two currencies will be determined by their gold content. For example, suppose that the pound is pegged to gold at six pounds per ounce, whereas one ounce of gold is worth 12 francs. The exchange rate between the pound and the franc should then be two francs per pound. To the extent that the pound and the franc remain pegged to gold at given prices, the exchange rate between the two currencies will remain stable. There were, indeed, no significant changes in exchange rates among the currencies of such major countries as Great Britain, France, Germany, and the United States during the entire period. For example, the dollar–sterling exchange rate remained within a narrow range of $4.84 and $4.90 per pound. Highly stable exchange rates under the classical gold standard provided an environment that was conducive to international trade and investment.

Under the gold standard, misalignment of the exchange rate will be automatically corrected by cross-border flows of gold. In the above example, suppose that one pound is trading for 1.80 francs at the moment. Since the pound is undervalued in the exchange market, people will buy pounds with francs, but not francs with pounds. For people who need francs, it would be cheaper first to buy gold from the Bank of England and ship it to France and sell it for francs. For example, suppose that you need to buy 1,000 francs using pounds. If you buy 1,000 francs in the exchange market, it will cost you £555.56 at the exchange rate of Fr1.80/£. Alternatively, you can buy 83.33 = 1,000/12 ounces of gold from the Bank of England for £500:

$$£500 = (1,000/12) \times 6$$

Then you could ship it to France and sell it to the Bank of France for 1,000 francs. This way, you can save about £55.56.[2] Since people only want to buy, not sell, pounds at the exchange rate of Fr1.80/£, the pound will eventually appreciate to its fair value, namely, Fr2/£.

Under the gold standard, international imbalances of payment are corrected automatically. Consider a situation where Great Britain exported more to France than it imported from France. This kind of trade imbalance would not persist under the gold standard. Net exports from Great Britain to France would trigger a net flow of gold in the opposite direction. This flow of gold leads to a lower price level in France and, at the same time, a higher price level in Great Britain. (Recall that under the gold standard, the domestic money stock rises or falls as the country experiences an inflow or outflow of gold.) The resultant change in the relative price level, in turn, would slow exports from Great Britain and encourage exports from France. As a result, the initial net export from Great Britain would eventually disappear. This adjustment mechanism is referred to as the **price-specie-flow mechanism,** which is attributed to David Hume, a Scottish philosopher.[3]

Despite its demise a long time ago, the gold standard still has ardent supporters in academic, business, and political circles, who view it as an ultimate hedge against price inflation. Gold has a natural scarcity, and no one can increase its quantity at will. Therefore, if gold serves as the sole base for domestic money creation, the money supply cannot get out of control and cause inflation. In addition, if gold is used as the sole international means of payment, then countries' balance of payments is regulated automatically via the movements of gold.[4]

The gold standard, however, has a few key shortcomings. First of all, the supply of newly minted gold is so restricted that the growth of world trade and investment can be seriously hampered for the lack of sufficient monetary reserves. The world economy can face deflationary pressures. Second, whenever government finds it politically necessary to pursue national objectives that are inconsistent with maintaining the gold standard, it can abandon the gold standard. In other words, the international gold standard *per se* has no mechanism to compel each major country to abide by the rules of the game.[5] For such reasons, it is not very likely that the classical gold standard will be restored in the foreseeable future.

2.4   Interwar Period: 1915–1944

World War I ended the classical gold standard in August 1914, as major countries, such as Great Britain, France, Germany, and Russia, suspended redemption of banknotes in gold and imposed embargoes on gold exports. After the war, many countries, especially Germany, Austria, Hungary, Poland, and Russia, suffered hyperinflation. The German experience provides a classic example of hyperinflation: by the end of 1923, the wholesale price index in Germany was more than one trillion times as high as its prewar level. Freed from wartime pegging, exchange rates among currencies fluctuated in the early 1920s. During this period, countries widely used "predatory" depreciations of their currencies as a means of gaining advantages in the world export market.

---

[2]In this example, we ignored shipping costs. But as long as the shipping costs do not exceed £55.56, it is still advantageous to buy francs via "gold export" than via the foreign exchange market.

[3]The price-specie-flow mechanism will work only if governments are willing to abide by the rules of the game by letting the money stock rise and fall as gold flows in and out. Once government demonetizes (neutralizes) gold, the mechanism will break down. In addition, the effectiveness of the mechanism depends on the price elasticity of the demand for imports.

[4]The balance of payments will be discussed in detail in Chapter 3.

[5]This point need not be viewed as a weakness of the gold standard *per se*, but it casts doubt on the long-term feasibility of the gold standard.

As major countries began to recover from the war and stabilize their economies, they attempted to restore the gold standard. The United States, which replaced Great Britain as the dominant financial power, spearheaded efforts to restore the gold standard. With only mild inflation, the United States was able to lift restrictions on gold exports and return to a gold standard in 1919. In Great Britain, Winston Churchill, the Chancellor of the Exchequer, played a key role in restoring the gold standard in 1925. Besides Great Britain, such countries as Switzerland, France, and the Scandinavian countries restored the gold standard by 1928.

The international gold standard of the late 1920s, however, little more than a façade. Most major countries gave priority to the stabilization of domestic economies and systematically followed a policy of **sterilization of gold** by matching inflows and outflows of gold, respectively, with reductions and increases in domestic money and credit. The Federal Reserve of the United States, for example, kept some gold outside the credit base by circulating it as gold certificates. The Bank of England also followed the policy of keeping the amount of available domestic credit stable by neutralizing the effects of gold flows. In a word, countries lacked the political will to abide by the "rules of the game," and so the automatic adjustment mechanism of the gold standard was unable to work.

Even the façade of the restored gold standard was destroyed in the wake of the Great Depression and the accompanying financial crises. Following the stock market crash and the onset of the Great Depression in 1929, many banks, especially in Austria, Germany, and the United States, suffered sharp declines in their portfolio values, touching off runs on the banks. Against this backdrop, Britain experienced a massive outflow of gold, due to chronic balance-of-payment deficits and lack of confidence in the pound sterling. Despite coordinated international efforts to rescue the pound, British gold reserves continued to fall to the point where it was impossible to maintain the gold standard. In September 1931, the British government suspended gold payments and let the pound float. As Great Britain got off gold, Canada, Sweden, Austria, and Japan followed suit by the end of 1931. The United States got off gold in April 1933 after experiencing a spate of bank failures and outflows of gold. Lastly, France abandoned the gold standard in 1936 because of the flight from the franc, which, in turn, reflected the economic and political instability following the inception of the socialist Popular Front government led by Leon Blum. Paper standards came into being when the gold standard was abandoned.

In sum, the interwar period was characterized by economic nationalism, halfhearted attempts and failure to restore the gold standard, economic and political instabilities, bank failures, and panicky flights of capital across borders. No coherent international monetary system prevailed during this period, with profoundly detrimental effects on international trade and investment.

2.5 Bretton Woods System: 1945–1972

In July 1944, representatives of 44 nations gathered at Bretton Woods, New Hampshire, to discuss and design the postwar international monetary system. After lengthy discussions and bargaining, representatives succeeded in drafting and signing the Articles of Agreement of the International Monetary Fund (IMF), which constitutes the core of the **Bretton Woods system.** The agreement was subsequently ratified by the majority of countries to launch the IMF in 1945. The IMF embodied an explicit set of rules about the conduct of international monetary policies and was responsible for enforcing these rules. Delegates also created a sister institution, the International Bank for Reconstruction and Development (IBRD), better known as the World Bank, that was chiefly responsible for financing individual development projects.

In designing the Bretton Woods system, representatives were concerned with how to prevent the recurrence of economic nationalism with destructive "beggar-thy-neighbour" policies and how to address the lack of clear rules of the game plaguing the interwar years. The British delegates led by John Maynard Keynes proposed an international clearing union that would create an international reserve asset called "bancor." Countries would accept payments in bancor to settle international transactions, without limit. They would also be allowed to acquire bancor by using overdraft facilities with the clearing union. On the other hand, the American delegates, headed by Harry Dexter White, proposed a currency pool to which member countries would make contributions and from which they might borrow to tide themselves over during short-term balance-of-payments deficits. Both delegates desired exchange rate stability without restoring an international gold standard. The American proposal was largely incorporated into the Articles of Agreement of the IMF.

Under the Bretton Woods system, each country established a **par value** in relation to the American dollar, which was pegged to gold at $35 per ounce. This point is illustrated in Exhibit 2.1. Each country was responsible for maintaining its exchange rate within ±1 percent of the adopted par value by buying or selling foreign exchanges, as necessary. However, a member country with a "fundamental disequilibrium" may be allowed to make a change in the par value of its currency. Under the Bretton Woods system, the American dollar was the only currency that was fully convertible to gold; other currencies were not directly convertible to gold. Countries held American dollars, as well as gold, for use as an international means of payment. Because of these arrangements, the Bretton Woods system can be described as a dollar-based **gold-exchange standard.** A country on the gold-exchange standard holds most of its reserves in the form of currency of a country that is *really* on the gold standard.

Advocates of the gold-exchange system argue that the system economizes on gold because countries can use not only gold but also foreign exchanges as an international means of payment. Foreign exchange reserves offset the deflationary effects of limited addition to the world's monetary gold stock. Another advantage of the gold-exchange system is that individual countries can earn interest on their foreign exchange holdings, whereas gold holdings yield no returns. In addition, countries save on transaction costs associated with transporting gold across countries under the gold-exchange system. An ample supply of international monetary reserves coupled with stable exchange rates provided an environment highly conducive to the growth of international trade and investment throughout the 1950s and 1960s.

Professor Robert Triffin warned, however, that the gold-exchange system was programmed to collapse in the long run. To satisfy the growing need for reserves, the United States had to run balance-of-payments deficits continuously. Yet, if the United States ran perennial balance-of-payments deficits, it would eventually impair the public confidence in the dollar, triggering a run on the dollar. Under the gold-exchange

EXHIBIT 2.1

The Design of the Gold-Exchange System

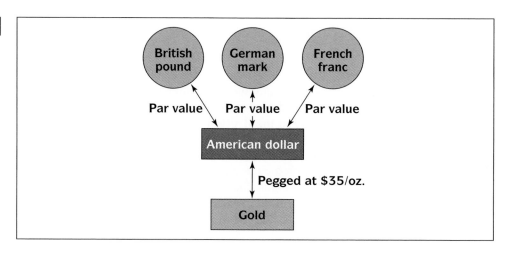

system, the reserve-currency country should run balance-of-payments deficits to supply reserves, but if such deficits are large and persistent, they can lead to a crisis of confidence in the reserve currency itself, causing the downfall of the system. This dilemma, known as the **Triffin paradox,** was indeed responsible for the eventual collapse of the dollar-based gold-exchange system in the early 1970s.

The United States began to experience trade deficits with the rest of the world in the late 1950s, and the problem persisted into the 1960s. By the early 1960s, the total value of the American gold stock, when valued at $35 per ounce, fell short of foreign dollar holdings. This naturally created concern about the viability of the dollar-based system. Against this backdrop, President Charles de Gaulle prodded the Bank of France to buy gold from the U.S. Treasury, unloading its dollar holdings. Efforts to remedy the problem centred on (1) a series of dollar defence measures taken by the American government, and (2) the creation of a new reserve asset, **special drawing rights (SDRs),** by the IMF.

In 1963, President John Kennedy imposed the Interest Equalization Tax (IET) on American purchases of foreign securities in order to stem the outflow of dollars. The IET was designed to increase the cost of foreign borrowing in the American bond market. In 1965, the Federal Reserve introduced the American voluntary Foreign Credit Restraint Program (FCRP), which regulated the amount of dollars American banks could lend to American multinational companies engaged in foreign direct investments. In 1968, these regulations became legally binding. Such measures as IET and FCRP lent a strong impetus to the rapid growth of the Eurodollar market, which is a transnational, unregulated fund market.

To partially alleviate the pressure on the dollar as the central reserve currency, the IMF created an artificial international reserve called the SDR in 1970. The SDR, which is a basket currency comprising major individual currencies, was allotted to the members of the IMF, who could then use it for transactions among themselves or with the IMF. In addition to gold and foreign exchanges, countries could use the SDR to make international payments.

Initially, the SDR was designed to be the weighted average of 16 currencies of those countries whose shares in world exports exceeded more than 1 percent. The percentage share of each currency in the SDR was about the same as the country's share in world exports. In 1981, however, the SDR was greatly simplified to comprise only five major currencies: American dollar, German mark, Japanese yen, British pound, and French franc. As Exhibit 2.2 shows, the weight for each currency is updated periodically, reflecting the relative importance of each country in the world trade of goods and services and the amount of the currencies held as reserves by the members of the IMF. Currently, the SDR comprises of four major currencies—American dollar (45 percent weight), euro (29 percent), Japanese yen (15 percent), and British pound (11 percent).

The SDR is used not only as a reserve asset but also as a denomination currency for international transactions. Since the SDR is a "portfolio" of currencies, its value tends to be more stable than the value of any individual currency included in the SDR. The portfolio nature of the SDR makes it an attractive denomination currency for international commercial and financial contracts under exchange rate uncertainty.

http://fx.sauder.ubc.ca

Provides a list of all the currencies of the world with information on each country's exchange rate regime. Also provides current and historical exchange rates.

EXHIBIT 2.2

The Composition of the Special Drawing Right (SDR)[a]

Currencies	1981–85	1986–90	1991–95	1996–2000	2001–2005
American dollar	42%	42%	40%	39%	45%
Euro	—	—	—	—	29
German mark	19	19	21	21	—
Japanese yen	13	15	17	18	15
British pound	13	12	11	11	11
French franc	13	12	11	11	—

[a]The composition of the SDR changes every five years.
Source: The International Monetary Fund.

The efforts to support the dollar-based gold-exchange standard, however, turned out to be ineffective in the face of expansionary monetary policy and rising inflation in the United States, which were related to the financing of the Vietnam War and the Great Society program. In the early 1970s, it became clear that the dollar was overvalued, especially relative to the mark and the yen. As a result, the German and Japanese central banks had to make massive interventions in the foreign exchange market to maintain their par values. Given the unwillingness of the United States to control its monetary expansion, the repeated central bank interventions could not solve the underlying disparities. In August 1971, American President Nixon suspended the convertibility of the dollar into gold and imposed a 10-percent import surcharge. The foundation of the Bretton Woods system cracked under the strain.

In an attempt to save the Bretton Woods system, 10 major countries, known as the Group of Ten, met at the Smithsonian Institution in Washington, D.C., in December 1971. They reached the **Smithsonian Agreement,** according to which (1) the price of gold was raised to $38 per ounce, (2) each of the other countries revalued its currency against the American dollar by up to 10 percent, and (3) the band within which the exchange rates were allowed to move was expanded from 1 percent to 2.25 percent in either direction.

The Smithsonian Agreement lasted for little more than a year before it came under attack again. Clearly, the devaluation of the American dollar was not sufficient to stabilize the situation. In February 1973, the dollar came under heavy selling pressure, again prompting central banks around the world to buy dollars. The price of gold was further raised from $38 to $42 per ounce. By March 1973, European and Japanese currencies were allowed to float, completing the decline and fall of the Bretton Woods system. Since then, the exchange rates among such major currencies as the dollar, the pound, and the yen have been fluctuating against each other.

2.6 The Flexible Exchange Rate Regime: 1973–Present

The flexible exchange rate regime that followed the demise of the Bretton Woods system was ratified after the fact in January 1976 when the IMF members met in Jamaica and agreed to a new set of rules for the international monetary system. The key elements of the **Jamaica Agreement** include the following:

1. Flexible exchange rates were declared acceptable to the IMF members, and central banks were allowed to intervene in the exchange markets to iron out unwarranted volatilities.

2. Gold was officially abandoned (i.e., demonetized) as an international reserve asset. Half of the IMF's gold holdings was returned to the members and the other half was sold, with the proceeds to be used to help poor nations.

3. Non–oil-exporting countries and less-developed countries were given greater access to IMF funds.

The IMF continued to provide assistance to countries facing balance-of-payments and exchange rate difficulties. The IMF, however, extended assistance and loans to the member countries on the condition that those countries follow the IMF's macroeconomic policy prescriptions. This "conditionality," which often involves deflationary macroeconomic policies and elimination of various subsidy programs, provoked resentment among the people of the developing countries receiving the IMF's balance-of-payments loans.

As can be expected, exchange rates have become substantially more volatile since March 1973 than they were under the Bretton Woods system. Exhibit 2.3 summarizes the behaviour of the dollar exchange rate since 1965. The exhibit shows the exchange rate between the American dollar and a weighted basket of 21 other major currencies. The

EXHIBIT 2.3

The Value of the American Dollar since 1965[a]

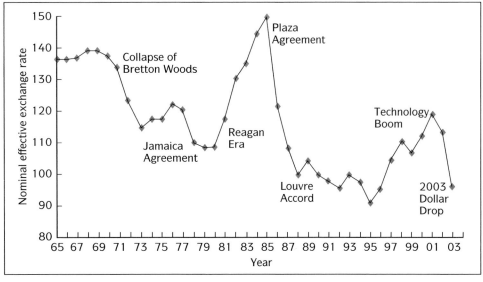

[a]The value of the American dollar represents the nominal effective exchange rate index (1990 = 100) with weights derived from trade among 22 industrialized countries.
Source: The International Monetary Fund.

http://fx.sauder.ubc.ca

Provides a list of all the currencies of the world with information on each country's exchange rate regime. Also provides current and historical exchange rates.

decline of the dollar between 1970 and 1973 represents the transition from the Bretton Woods to the flexible exchange rate system. The most conspicuous phenomena shown in Exhibit 2.3 are the dollar's spectacular rise between 1980 and 1984 and its equally spectacular decline between 1985 and 1988. These unusual episodes merit some discussion.

Following the American presidential election of 1980, the Reagan administration ushered in a period of growing American budget deficits and balance-of-payments deficits. The American dollar, however, experienced a major appreciation throughout the first half of the 1980s because of the large-scale inflows of foreign capital caused by unusually high real interest rates available in the United States. To attract foreign investment to help finance the budget deficit, the United States had to offer high real interest rates. The heavy demand for dollars by foreign investors pushed up the value of the dollar in the exchange market.

The value of the dollar reached its peak in February 1985 and then began a persistent downward drift until it stabilized in 1988. The reversal in the exchange rate trend partially reflected the effect of the record-high American trade deficit, about $160 billion in 1985, brought about by the soaring dollar. The downward trend was also reinforced by concerted government interventions. In September 1985, the so-called G-5 countries (France, Japan, Germany, the United Kingdom, and the United States) met at the Plaza Hotel in New York and reached what became known as the **Plaza Accord.** They agreed that it would be desirable for the dollar to depreciate against most major currencies to solve the American trade deficit problem and expressed their willingness to intervene in the exchange market to realize this objective. The slide of the dollar that had begun in February was further precipitated by the Plaza Accord.

As the dollar continued its decline, the governments of the major industrial countries began to worry that the dollar may fall too far. To address the problem of exchange rate volatility and other related issues, the G-7 economic summit meeting was convened in Paris in 1987.[6] The meeting produced the **Louvre Accord,** according to which:

1. The G-7 countries would cooperate to achieve greater exchange rate stability.

2. The G-7 countries agreed to more closely consult and coordinate their macroeconomic policies.

---

[6]The G-7 is composed of Canada, France, Japan, Germany, Italy, the United Kingdom, and the United States.

The Louvre Accord marked the inception of the **managed-float system,** under which the G-7 countries would jointly intervene in the exchange market to correct over- or undervaluation of currencies. Since the Louvre Accord, exchange rates became relatively more stable for a while. During the period 1996–2001, however, the American dollar generally appreciated, reflecting a robust performance of the American economy fuelled by the technology boom. During this period, foreigners invested heavily in the United States to participate in the booming American economy and stock markets. This helped the dollar to appreciate.

2.7 The Current Exchange Rate Arrangements

Although the most actively traded currencies of the world, such as the dollar, the yen, the pound, and the euro, fluctuate against each other, a significant number of the world's smaller currencies are pegged to single currencies, particularly the American dollar and the euro, or baskets of currencies, such as the SDR. The current exchange rate arrangements as classified by the IMF are provided in Exhibit 2.4.

As can be seen from the exhibit, the IMF currently classifies exchange rate arrangements into eight separate regimes:[7]

Exchange arrangements with no separate legal tender: The currency of another country circulates as the sole legal tender or the country belongs to a monetary or currency union in which the same legal tender is shared by the members of the union. Examples include Ecuador, El Salvador, and Panama using the American dollar and the 12 euro zone member countries (such as France, Germany, and Italy) sharing the common currency, the euro.

Currency board arrangements: A monetary regime based on an explicit legislative commitment to exchange domestic currency for a specified foreign currency at a fixed exchange rate, combined with restrictions on the issuing authority to ensure the fulfillment of its legal obligation. Examples include Hong Kong fixed to the American dollar and Estonia fixed to the euro.

Other conventional fixed peg arrangement: The country pegs its currency (formally or *de facto*) at a fixed rate to a major currency or a basket of currencies where the exchange rate fluctuates within a narrow margin of less than 1 percent, plus or minus, around a central rate. Examples include China, Malaysia, and Saudi Arabia.

Pegged exchange rates within horizontal bands: The value of the currency is maintained within margins of fluctuation around a formal or *de facto* fixed peg that are wider than at least 1 percent, plus or minus, around a central rate. Examples include Denmark, Egypt, and Hungary.

Crawling pegs: The currency is adjusted periodically in small amounts at a fixed, preannounced rate or in response to changes in selective quantitative indicators. Examples are Bolivia and Costa Rica.

Exchange rates within crawling bands: The currency is maintained within certain fluctuation margins around a central rate that is adjusted periodically at a fixed preannounced rate or in response to changes in selective quantitative indicators. Examples are Israel, Romania, and Venezuela.

Managed floating with no preannounced path for the exchange rate: The monetary authority influences the movements of the exchange rate through active intervention in the foreign exchange market without specifying, or precommitting to, a preannounced path for the exchange rate. Examples include Algeria, Singapore, and Thailand.

[7]We draw on IMF classifications provided in *International Financial Statistics.*

Independent floating: The exchange rate is market determined, with any foreign exchange intervention aimed at moderating the rate of change and preventing undue fluctuations in the exchange rate, rather than at establishing a level for it. Examples include Australia, Brazil, Canada, Korea, Mexico, the United Kingdom, Japan, Switzerland, and the United States.

As of December 2001, a large number of countries (41), including Australia, Canada, Japan, the United Kingdom, and the United States, allow their currencies to float independently against other currencies; the exchange rates of these countries are essentially determined by market forces. Forty-two countries, including India, Russia, and Singapore, have some forms of "managed floating" system that combines market forces and government intervention in setting the exchange rates. In contrast, 40 countries do not have their own national currencies. For example, 14 central and western African countries jointly use the CFA-franc, which is fixed to the euro through the French franc. Eight countries, including Hong Kong and Estonia, on the other hand, maintain national currencies, but they are permanently fixed to such hard currencies as the American dollar or euro. The remaining countries adopt a mixture of fixed and floating exchange rate regimes. As is well known, the European Union pursued Europe-wide monetary integration by first establishing the European Monetary System and then the European Monetary Union. These topics deserve a detailed discussion.

2.8 European Monetary System

According to the Smithsonian Agreement, which was signed in December 1971, the band of exchange rate movements was expanded from the original plus or minus 1 percent to plus or minus 2.25 percent. Members of the European Economic Community (EEC), however, decided on a narrower band of ± 1.125 percent for their currencies. This scaled-down, European version of the fixed exchange rate system that arose concurrently with the decline of the Bretton Woods system was called the **snake**. The name "snake" was derived from the way the EEC currencies moved closely together within the wider band allowed for other currencies like the dollar.

The EEC countries adopted the snake because they felt that stable exchange rates among the EEC countries were essential for promoting intra-EEC trade and deepening economic integration. The snake arrangement was replaced by the **European Monetary System (EMS)** in 1979. The EMS, which was originally proposed by German Chancellor Helmut Schmidt, was formally launched in March 1979. Among its chief objectives are:

1. To establish a "zone of monetary stability" in Europe.
2. To coordinate exchange rate policies *vis-à-vis* the non-EMS currencies.
3. To pave the way for the eventual European monetary union.

At the political level, the EMS represented a Franco-German initiative to speed up the movement toward European economic and political unification. All EEC member countries, except the United Kingdom and Greece, joined the EMS. The two main instruments of the EMS are the European Currency Unit and the Exchange Rate Mechanism.

The **European Currency Unit (ECU)** was a "basket" currency constructed as a weighted average of the currencies of member countries of the European Union (EU). The weights were based on each currency's relative GNP and shares in intra-EU trade. The ECU served as the accounting unit of the EMS and played an important role in the workings of the exchange rate mechanism.

The **Exchange Rate Mechanism (ERM)** refers to the procedure by which EMS member countries collectively manage their exchange rates. The ERM was based on a "parity grid" system, which was a system of par values among ERM currencies. The par values in the parity grid were computed by first defining the par values of EMS curren-

EXHIBIT 2.4   Exchange Rate Regimes and Anchors of Monetary Policy (As of December 31, 2001)[1]

Exchange Rate Regime (Number of Countries)	Monetary Policy Framework				
	Exchange Rate Anchor	Monetary Aggregate Target	Inflation Targeting Framework	Fund-Supported or Other Monetary Program	Other
Exchange Arrangements with No Separate Legal Tender (40)	**Another currency as legal tender** Ecuador, El Salvador[10], Kiribati, Marshall Islands, Rep. of, Micronesia, Fed. States of, Palau, Panama, San Marino — **ECCU** Antigua & Barbuda, Dominica, Grenada, St. Kitts & Nevis, St. Lucia, St. Vincent & the Grenadines — **CFA Franc Zone** — **WAEMU** Benin[†], Burkina Faso[†], Côte d'Ivoire[†], Guinea-Bissau[†], Mali[†], Niger[†], Senegal[†], Togo — **CAEMC** Cameroon[†], C. African Rep.[†], Chad[†], Congo, Rep. of[†], Equatorial Guinea, Gabon[†]				**Euro Area** Austria, Belgium, Finland, France, Germany, Greece, Ireland, Italy, Luxembourg, Netherlands, Portugal, Spain
Currency Board Arrangements (8)	Argentina[†], Bosnia and Herzegovina[†], Brunei Darussalam, Bulgaria[†], China, P.R.: Hong Kong, Djibouti[†], Estonia[†], Lithuania[†]				
Other Conventional Fixed Peg Arrangements (Including De Facto Peg Arrangements under Managed Floating) (40)	**Against a single currency (30)** Aruba, Bahamas, The[2], Bahrain, Kingdom of, Bangladesh, Barbados, Belize, Bhutan, Cape Verde, China, P. R. Mainland[*3], Comoros[5], Iran[3], Jordan[†3], Lebanon[3], Lesotho[†], Macedonia, FYR[†3], Malaysia, Maldives[3], Namibia, Nepal, Netherlands Antilles, Oman, Qatar[3,4], Saudi Arabia[3,4], Sudan[7], Suriname[2,3], Swaziland, Syrian Arab Republic[2], Turkmenistan[3], United Arab Emirates[3,4], Zimbabwe[3] — **Against a composite (10)** Botswana[2], Fiji, Kuwait, Latvia[†], Libyan A.J., Malta, Morocco, Samoa, Seychelles, Vanuatu	China, P.R.: Mainland[*3]			
Pegged Exchange Rates within Horizontal Bands (5)[10]	**Within a cooperative arrangement ERM II (1)** Denmark — **Other band arrangements (4)** Cyprus, Egypt[6], Hungary[*], Tonga		Hungary[*]		
Crawling Pegs (4)	Bolivia[†], Costa Rica[7], Nicaragua[†], Solomon Islands[7]				

Exchange Rates within Crawling Bands (6)[7]	Belarus, Honduras†, Israel*, Romania†[3], Uruguay†, Venezuela, Rep. Bolivariana		Israel*		
Managed Floating with No Preannounced Path for Exchange Rate (42)		Ghana†, Guinea†, Guyana†, Indonesia†[3], Jamaica†[3], Mauritius, São Tomé and Príncipe†, Slovenia, Sri Lanka†, Tunisia	Thailand†	Azerbaijan, Cambodia[2], Croatia, Ethiopia, Iraq, Kazakhstan, Kenya, Kyrgyz Republic, Lao PDRy[2], Mauritania, Nigeria, Pakistan, Russian Federation, Rwanda, Trinidad & Tobago, Ukraine, Vietnam, Yugoslavia, Fed. Rep. of, Zambia	Algeria, Angola, Burundi, Dominican Rep.[2], Eritrea, Guatemala, India, Myanmar[2,3], Paraguay, Singapore, Slovak Republic, Uzbekistan[2]
Independently Floating (41)		Gambia, The†, Malawi†, Mongolia†, Peru[11], Philippines†, Sierra Leone†, Turkey†, Yemen†	Australia, Brazil[9], Canada, Chile[2], Colombia†, Czech Rep., Iceland, Korea, Mexico, New Zealand, Norway, Poland, South Africa, Sweden, United Kingdom	Albania, Armenia, Congo, Dem. Rep., Georgia, Madagascar, Moldova, Mozambique, Tajikistan, Tanzania, Uganda	Afghanistan[2,8], Haiti, Japan, Liberia, Papua New Guinea, Somalia[2,8], Switzerland, United States

Source: International Financial Statistics, August 2002.

Note: "Country" in this publication does not always refer to a territorial entity that is a state as understood by international law and practice; the term also covers the euro area and some nonsovereign territorial entities for which statistical data are provided internationally on a separate basis.

[1] A country with * indicates that the country adopts more than one nominal anchor in conducting monetary policy. It should be noted, however, that it would not be possible, for practical reasons, to infer from this table which nominal anchor plays the principal role in conducting monetary policy.

[2] Member maintained exchange regimes involving more than one market. The regime shown is that maintained in the major market.

[3] The indicated country has a *de facto* regime which differs from its *de jure* regime.

[4] Exchange rates are determined on the basis of a fixed relationship to the SDR, within margins of up to ±7.25%. However, because of the maintenance of a relatively stable relationship with the American dollar, these margins are not always observed.

[5] Comoros has the same arrangement with the French Treasury as do the CFA Franc Zone countries.

[6] The band width for these countries is: Cyprus (±2.25%), Denmark (±2.25%), Egypt (±3%), Hungary (±15%), and Tonga (±5%).

[7] The band for these countries is: Belarus (±5%), Honduras (±7%), Israel (±7%), Romania (unannounced), Uruguay (±3%), and República Bolivariana de Venezuela (±7.5%).

[8] There is no relevant information available for the country.

[9] Brazil maintains a Fund-supported program.

[10] For El Salvador, the printing of new colones, the domestic currency, is prohibited, but the existing stock of colones will continue to circulate, along with the American dollar, as legal tender until all notes physically wear out.

[11] Peru's exchange rate regime has been reclassified, retroactively, as Peru has been maintaining an independently floating exchange rate.

cies in terms of the ECU. These par values are called the ECU central rates. The ECU central rates of the German mark and the French franc were DM1.949 per ECU and Fr6.538 per ECU. This implied that the parity between the two member currencies Fr6.538/DM1.949 = Fr3.353/DM. The parity grid was computed by referring to the ECU central rates set by the European Commission.

When the EMS was launched in 1979, a currency was allowed to deviate from the parities with other currencies by a maximum of plus or minus 2.25 percent, with the exception of the Italian lira, for which a maximum deviation of plus or minus 6 percent was allowed. In 1993, however, the band was widened to a maximum of plus or minus 15 percent. When a currency was at the lower or upper bound, the central banks of both countries were required to intervene in the foreign exchange markets to keep the market exchange rate within the band. To intervene in the exchange markets, the central banks could borrow from a credit fund to which member countries contributed gold and foreign reserves.

Since the EMS members were less than fully committed to coordinating their economic policies, the EMS went through a series of realignments. The Italian lira, for instance, was devalued by 6 percent in 1985 and again by 3.7 percent in 1990. In 1992, Italy and the United Kingdom pulled out of the ERM as high German interest rates were inducing massive capital flows into Germany. Following German reunification in October 1990, the German government experienced substantial budget deficits, which were not accommodated by the monetary policy. Germany would not lower its interest rates for fear of inflation, and the United Kingdom and Italy were not willing to raise their interest rates (which was necessary to maintain their exchange rates) for fear of higher unemployment. Italy, however, rejoined the ERM in 1996 in an effort to participate in the European monetary union.

Despite the recurrent turbulence in the EMS, European Union members met at Maastricht (the Netherlands) in 1991 and signed the **Maastricht Treaty.** According to the treaty, the member states of the European Union committed irrevocably to fix exchange rates by January 1, 1999, and subsequently to introduce a common European currency, replacing individual national currencies. The European Central Bank, to be located in Frankfurt, Germany, would be solely responsible for the issuance of common currency and conducting monetary policy in the European Union. National central banks of individual countries would then function as regional member banks of the European system. Exhibit 2.5 provides a chronology of the European Union.

To pave the way for the European Monetary Union (EMU), the member states of the European Union agreed to closely coordinate their fiscal, monetary, and exchange rate policies and achieve a *convergence* of their economies. Specifically, each member country shall strive to: (1) keep the ratio of government budget deficits to gross domestic product (GDP) below 3 percent, (2) keep gross public debts below 60 percent of GDP, (3) achieve a high degree of price stability, and (4) maintain its currency within the prescribed exchange rate ranges of the ERM.

2.9 The Euro and the European Monetary Union

On January 1, 1999, an epochal event took place in the arena of international finance: Eleven of 15 EU countries adopted a common currency called the **euro,** voluntarily giving up their monetary sovereignty. The euro-11 includes Austria, Belgium, Finland, France, Germany, Ireland, Italy, Luxembourg, the Netherlands, Portugal, and Spain. Four member countries of the European Union—Denmark, Greece, Sweden, and the United Kingdom—did not join the first wave. Greece, however, joined the euro club in 2001 when it could satisfy the convergence criteria.

The advent of a European single currency, which may potentially rival the American dollar as a global currency, has profound implications for various aspects of international finance. In this section, we (1) describe briefly the historical background for the euro and

EXHIBIT 2.5

Chronology of the
European Union

1951	The treaty establishing the European Coal and Steel Community (ECSC), which was inspired by French Foreign Minister Robert Schuman, was signed in Paris by six countries: France, Germany, Italy, the Netherlands, Belgium, and Luxembourg.
1957	The treaty establishing the European Economic Community (EEC) was signed in Rome.
1968	The Custom Union became fully operational; trade restrictions among the EEC member countries were abolished and a common external tariff system was established.
1973	The United Kingdom, Ireland, and Denmark became EEC members.
1978	The EEC became the European Community (EC).
1979	The European Monetary System (EMS) was established for the purpose of promoting exchange rate stability among the EC member countries.
1980	Greece became an EC member.
1986	Portugal and Spain became EC members.
1987	The *Single European Act* was adopted to provide a framework within which the common internal market could be achieved by the end of 1992.
1991	The Maastricht Treaty was signed and subsequently ratified by 12 member states. The treaty establishes a timetable for fulfilling the European Monetary Union (EMU). The treaty also commits the EC to political union.
1994	The European Community was renamed the European Union (EU).
1995	Austria, Finland, and Sweden became EU members.
1999	A common European currency, the euro, was adopted by 11 EU member countries.
2001	Greece adopted the euro on January 1.
2002	Euro notes and coins were introduced; national currencies were withdrawn from circulation.

its implementation process, (2) discuss the potential benefits and costs of the euro from the perspective of the member countries, and (3) investigate the broad impacts of the euro on international finance in general.

A Brief History of the Euro

Considering that no European currency has been in circulation since the fall of the Roman Empire, the advent of the euro in January 1999, indeed, qualifies as a historical event. The launch of the euro marks the first time that sovereign countries voluntarily have given up their monetary independence to foster economic integration. The euro, thus, represents a historically unprecedented experiment, the outcome of which will have far-reaching implications. If the experiment succeeds, for example, both the euro and the dollar will dominate the world of international finance.

The euro represents a step toward the ever deepening integration of Europe, which began in earnest with the formation of the European Economic Community in 1958. As discussed previously, the European Monetary System (EMS) was created in 1979 to establish a European zone of monetary stability; members were required to restrict fluctuations of their currencies. In 1991, the Maastricht European Council reached agreement on a draft Treaty on the European Union, which called for the introduction of a single European currency by 1999. The European Monetary System merged into the **European Monetary Union (EMU)** on January 1, 1999. The euro became the common currency. For a three-year transition period, each member of the EMU continued to keep its own currency in circulation—the German mark, the French franc, and the Dutch guilder, for example. Meanwhile, financial statements, public accounts, and contracts were expressed in both the new euro values and the old domestic currency values. The European Central Bank formally took on new authority and responsibility for monetary policy within the EMU.

www.ecb.int/

Website of the European Central Bank offers a comprehensive coverage of the euro and links to EU central banks.

As the euro was introduced, each national currency of the euro-11 countries was *irrevocably* fixed to the euro at a conversion rate as of January 1, 1999. The conversion rates are provided in Exhibit 2.6. National currencies, such as the French franc, German mark, and Italian lira, are no longer independent currencies. Rather, they are just different denominations of the same currency, the euro. On January 1, 2002, euro notes and coins were introduced in circulation, while national bills and coins were gradually withdrawn. Once the changeover was completed by July 1, 2002, the legal-tender status of national currencies was cancelled, leaving the euro as the sole legal tender in the euro-12 countries.

Monetary policy for the euro-12 countries is conducted by the European Central Bank (ECB) headquartered in Frankfurt, Germany. The primary purpose of the ECB is to maintain price stability. The independence of the ECB is legally guaranteed so that in conducting its monetary policy, it will not be unduly subjected to political pressure from any member country or institution. By and large, the ECB is modelled after the German Bundesbank, which was highly successful in achieving price stability in Germany.

The national central banks of the euro-12 countries have not disappeared. Together with the European Central Bank, they form the **European System of Central Banks (ESCB).** The responsibilities of the ESCB are threefold: (1) to define and implement the common monetary policy of the Union; (2) to conduct foreign exchange operations; and (3) to hold and manage the official foreign reserves of the euro member states. In addition, governors of national central banks sit on the Governing Council of the ECB. Although national central banks must follow the policies of the ECB, they continue to perform important functions in their jurisdiction, such as distributing credit, collecting resources, and managing payment systems.

From the perspective of those outside of Europe, bilateral exchange rates *vis-à-vis* the euro are important indicators of the strength and stability of Europe's new common currency. Exhibit 2.7 presents data since euro-inception until June 2004 for the Canadian dollar-euro exchange rate along with the American dollar-euro rate. At the launch of the euro, the Canadian dollar-euro rate was 1.79 Canadian dollars per euro, while the initial American dollar-euro rate was 1.18 American dollars per euro. Immediately thereafter, the euro started a downward slide against both North American dollars, reaching a low of 1.25 Canadian dollars in October 2000 and 0.825 American dollars in the same month. The Canadian and American dollars tend to be highly correlated in their movements *vis-à-vis* the euro.

EXHIBIT 2.6	1 Euro Is Equal to:	
Euro Conversion Rates	Austrian schilling	13.7603
	Belgian franc	40.3399
	Dutch guilder	2.20371
	Finnish markka	5.94573
	French franc	6.55957
	German mark	1.95583
	Irish punt	0.78756
	Italian lira	1936.27
	Luxembourg franc	40.3399
	Portuguese escudo	200.482
	Spanish peseta	166.386
	Canadian dollar*	1.655
	U.S. dollar*	1.214
	Japanese yen*	132.000
	Special Drawing Rights (SDR)*	0.8235

*Represents the market exchange rates of 19 June 2004.

Exchange Rates since the Euro's Inception for Canadian Dollar and American Dollar

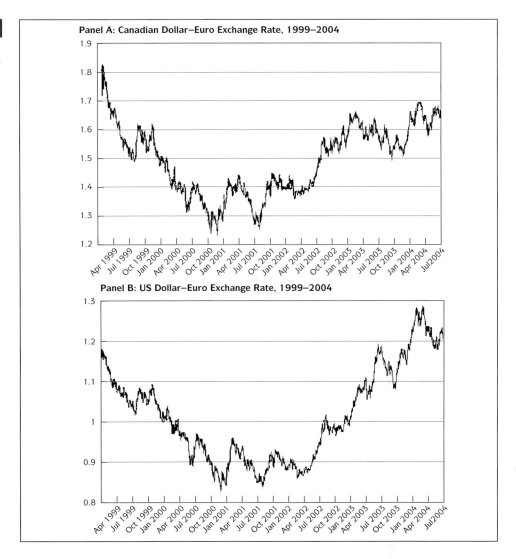

Panel A: Canadian Dollar–Euro Exchange Rate, 1999–2004

Panel B: US Dollar–Euro Exchange Rate, 1999–2004

With the early decline of the euro, it appeared that the new currency was more fragile than first anticipated. However, by April 2002, the euro began to recapture the value that it had lost against other currencies, including both the Canadian and the American dollars. By January 2004, the euro had strengthened to 1.29 American dollars per euro, substantially above its "launch" value five years earlier. Meanwhile, against the Canadian dollar—which had gained strength against the American dollar—the euro rose to 1.65 Canadian dollars per euro which compares with its "launch value" of 1.79.

What Are the Benefits of the Monetary Union?

The Euro-12 countries obviously decided to form a monetary union with a common currency because they believed the benefits from such a union would outweigh the associated costs—in contrast to those eligible countries that chose not to adopt the single currency. It is thus important to understand the potential benefits and costs of monetary union.

What are the main benefits from adopting a common currency? The most direct and immediate benefits are reduced transaction costs and the elimination of exchange rate uncertainty. There was a popular saying in Europe that if one travelled through all 15 EU countries, changing money in each country into its currency but not actually spending it, one would return home with only half the original amount. However, when countries use the same currency, such transactions costs are reduced substantially.

These savings accrue to practically all economic agents, benefiting individuals, companies, and governments. Although it is difficult to estimate accurately the magnitude of foreign exchange transaction costs, a consensus estimation is around 0.4 percent of Europe's GDP.

Economic agents also benefit from the elimination of exchange rate uncertainty. Companies no longer suffer currency loss from intra–euro zone transactions. Companies that used to hedge exchange risk now save hedging costs. As price comparison becomes easier because of the common currency, consumers can benefit from comparison shopping. Increased price transparency promotes Europe-wide competition, exerting downward pressure on prices. Reduced transaction costs and the elimination of currency risk together have the net effect of promoting cross-border investment and trade within the euro zone. By furthering economic integration of Europe, the single currency promotes corporate restructuring via mergers and acquisitions, encourages optimal business location decisions, and ultimately strengthens the international competitive position of European companies. Thus, the enhanced efficiency and competitiveness of the European economy can be regarded as the third major benefit of the monetary union.

The advent of the common European currency also helps create conditions conducive to the development of continental capital markets. In the past, national currencies and localized legal/regulatory frameworks resulted in largely illiquid, fragmented capital markets in Europe, which prevented European companies from raising capital on competitive terms. The common currency and the integration of European financial markets pave the way for a European capital market in which both European and non-European companies can raise money at favourable rates.

Last but not least, sharing a common currency promotes political cooperation and peace in Europe. The founding fathers of the European Union, including Jean Monnet, Paul-Henri Spaak, Robert Schuman, and their successors, took a series of economic measures designed to link the European countries together. They envisioned a new Europe in which economic interdependence and cooperation among regions and countries would replace nationalistic rivalries which so often led to calamitous wars in the past. In this context, Helmut Kohl, a former German chancellor, said that the European Monetary Union was a "matter of war and peace." A stable, continentally accepted euro advances the political integration of Europe.

Costs of Monetary Union

www.columbia.edu/~ram15

This homepage of Professor Robert Mundell provides a synopsis of his academic works, Nobel lecture, etc.

The main cost of monetary union is the loss of national monetary and exchange rate policy independence. Suppose Finland, a country heavily dependent on the paper and pulp industries, faces a sudden drop in world paper and pulp prices. This price drop could severely hurt the Finnish economy, causing unemployment and income decline while scarcely affecting other euro zone countries. Finland, thus, faces an "asymmetric shock." Generally speaking, a country is more prone to asymmetric shocks when its economy is less diversified and more trade-dependent.

If Finland maintained monetary independence, the country could consider lowering domestic interest rates to stimulate the weak economy as well as letting its currency depreciate to boost foreigners' demand for Finnish products. But because Finland has joined the EMU, the country no longer has these policy options at its disposal. Further, with the rest of the euro zone unaffected by Finland's particular problem, the ECB is not likely to tune its monetary policy to address a local Finnish shock. In other words, a common monetary policy dictated in Frankfurt cannot address asymmetric economic shocks that affect only a particular country or subregion; it can only deal with euro zone–wide shocks.

If, however, wage and price levels in Finland are flexible, then the country may still be able to deal with an asymmetric shock; lower wage and price levels in Finland would have economic effects similar to those of a depreciation of the Finnish currency. Furthermore, if capital flows freely across the euro zone and workers are willing to relocate to where jobs are, then again much of the asymmetric shock can be absorbed without monetary adjustments. If these conditions are not met, however, the asymmetric shock could cause a recession in the affected country. In this case, monetary union could become a costly venture. The concept of an **optimum currency area,** originally conceived by Robert Mundell in 1961, suggests that the relevant criterion for identifying and designing a common currency zone is the degree of factor (i.e., capital and labour) mobility within the zone. A high degree of factor mobility provides an adjustment mechanism as an alternative to country-specific monetary/currency adjustments.

Considering the high degree of capital and labour mobility in Canada, one might argue that Canada approximates an optimum currency area. It would be suboptimal for each province to issue its own currency. Canadian workers are highly mobile within Canada, moving to wherever job opportunities are. In contrast, unemployed workers in Helsinki, for example, are not very likely to move to Milan or Stuttgart for job opportunities because of cultural, religious, linguistic, and other barriers. The stability pact of EMU, designed to discourage irresponsible fiscal behaviour in the post-EMU era, also constrains the Finnish government to restrict its budget deficit to 3 percent of GDP at most. At the same time, Finland cannot expect to receive transfer payments from Brussels because of a rather low degree of fiscal integration among the EU countries. These considerations taken together suggest that the European Monetary Union could involve significant economic costs. An empirical study by von Hagen and Neumann (1994) identified Austria, Belgium, France, Luxembourg, the Netherlands, and Germany as nations that satisfy the conditions for an optimum currency area. However, Denmark, Italy, and the United Kingdom do not. It is interesting to note that Denmark and the United Kingdom actually chose to stay out of the EMU. Von Hagen and Neumann's study suggests that Italy joined the EMU prematurely. The International Finance in Practice box, "Mundell Wins Nobel Prize in Economics," explains Professor Mundell's view on the monetary union.

Prospects of the Euro: Some Critical Questions

Will the euro succeed? The first real test of the euro will come when the euro zone experiences major asymmetric shocks. A successful response to these shocks will require wage, price, and fiscal flexibility. A cautionary note is in order: Asymmetric shocks can occur even within a country. In Canada, for example, when oil prices jump as they did in the 1970s and, more recently, in 2004, oil-consuming regions, such as the eastern provinces, suffer adverse effects, whereas Alberta, a major oil-producing province, experiences a boom. Likewise, in Italy, the highly industrialized Genoa–Milan region and the southern Mezzogiorno, an underdeveloped region, can be in very different phases of the business cycle. But these countries have managed their economies with a common national monetary policy. Although asymmetric shocks are no doubt more serious internationally, one should be careful not to exaggerate their significance as an impediment to monetary union. In addition, since the advent of the EMS in 1979, the EMU member countries have restricted their monetary policies in order to maintain exchange rate stability in Europe. Considering that intra–euro zone trade accounts for about 60 percent of foreign trade of the euro-12 countries, benefits from the EMU are likely to exceed substantially the associated costs. Furthermore, leaders in political and business circles in Europe have invested substantial political capital in the success of the euro. It seems safe to predict that the euro will be a success.

Will the euro become a global currency to rival the American dollar? The American dollar has been the dominant global currency since the end of World War I, replacing the British pound as the currency of choice in international commercial and financial transactions. Even after the American dollar went off the gold standard in 1971, it retained its dominant position in the world economy. This dominance was possible because the dollar was backed by the sheer size of the American economy and the relatively sound monetary policy of the Federal Reserve. Now, as can be seen from

Mundell Wins Nobel Prize for Economics

Robert A. Mundell, one of the intellectual fathers of both the new European common currency and Reagan-era supply-side economics, won the Nobel Memorial Prize for Economic Science.

Mr. Mundell conducted innovative research into common currencies when the idea of the euro, Europe's new currency, was still a fantasy. The 66-year-old Columbia University professor, a native of Canada, also examined the implications of cross-border capital flows and flexible foreign-exchange rates when capital flows were still restricted and currencies still fixed to each other.

"Mundell chose his problems with uncommon—almost prophetic—accuracy in terms of predicting the future development of international monetary arrangements and capital markets," the selection committee said in announcing the prize.

An eccentric, white-haired figure who once bought an abandoned Italian castle as a hedge against inflation, Mr. Mundell later became a hero of the economic Right with his dogged defense of the gold standard and early advocacy of the controversial tax-cutting, supply-side economics that became the hallmark of the Reagan administration.

While the Nobel committee sidestepped his political impact in awarding Mr. Mundell the $975,000 prize for his work in the 1960s, his conservative fans celebrated the award as an endorsement of supply-side thinking.

"I know it will take a little longer, but history eventually will note that it was Mundell who made it possible for Ronald Reagan to be elected president," by providing the intellectual backing for the Reagan tax cuts, wrote conservative economist Jude Wanniski on his Web site.

Mr. Mundell's advocacy of supply-side economics sprang from his work in the 1960s examining what fiscal and monetary policies are appropriate if exchange rates

Mundell's View

Great currencies and great powers according to Robert Mundell:

Country	Period
Greece	7th–3rd C. B.C.
Persia	6th–4th C. B.C.
Macedonia	4th–2nd C. B.C.
Rome	2nd C. B.C.–4th C.
Byzantium	5th–13th C.
Franks	8th–11th C.
Italian city states	13th–6th C.
France	13th–18th C.
Holland	17th–18th C.
Germany (thaler)	14th–19th C.
France (franc)	1803–1870
Britain (pound)	1820–1914
U.S. (dollar)	1915–present
E.U. (euro)	1999

Source: The Euro and the Stability of the International Monetary System, Robert Mundell, Columbia University.

are either fixed—as they were prior to the collapse of the gold-based Bretton Woods system in the early 1970s—or floating, as they are in the U.S. and many other countries today.

One major finding has since become conventional wisdom: When money can move freely across borders, policy makers must choose between exchange-rate stability and an independent monetary policy. They can't have both.

Mr. Mundell's work has long had an impact on policy makers. In 1962, he wrote a paper addressing the

Exhibit 2.8, the euro zone is comparable with the United States in terms of population size, GDP, and international trade share. Exhibit 2.8 also shows that the euro is as important a denomination currency as the dollar in international bond markets. In contrast, the Japanese yen plays an insignificant role in international bond markets. As previously discussed, there is little doubt that the ECB will pursue a sound monetary policy. Considering both the size of the euro zone economy and the mandate of the ECB, the euro is likely to emerge as the second global currency in the near future, ending the dollar's sole dominance. The Japanese yen is likely to be a junior partner in the dollar–euro condominium. However, the emergence of the euro as another global currency may prompt Japan and other Asian countries to explore cooperative monetary arrangements for the region.

Kennedy administration's predicament of how to spur the economy while facing a balance-of-payments deficit. "The only correct way to do it was to have a tax cut and then protect the balance of payments by tight money," he recalled in a 1996 interview. The Kennedy administration eventually came around to the same way of thinking.

Mr. Mundell traces the supply-side movement to a 1971 meeting of distinguished economists, including Paul Volcker and Paul Samuelson, at the Treasury Department. At the time, most economists were stumped by the onset of stagflation—a combination of inflationary pressures, a troubled dollar, a worsening balance of payments and persistent unemployment. They thought any tightening of monetary or fiscal policy would bolster the dollar and improve the balance of payments, but worsen unemployment. An easing of monetary or fiscal policy might generate jobs, but weaken the dollar, lift prices and expand the balance-of-payments deficit.

Mr. Mundell suggested a heretical solution: Raise interest rates to protect the dollar, but cut taxes to spur the economy. Most others in the room were aghast at the idea, fearing tax cuts would lead to a swelling budget deficit—something many nonsupply-siders believe was exactly what happened during the Reagan years.

"I knew I was in the minority," he said in an 1988 interview. "But I thought my vote should count much more than the others because I understood the subject."

At the University of Chicago early in his career, Mr. Mundell befriended a student named Arthur Laffer, and together they were at the core of the supply-side movement. Even today, Mr. Mundell predicts similar policies will be necessary to keep the U.S. economic expansion going. "Monetary policy isn't going to be enough to stay up there and avoid a recession," he said in an interview yesterday. "We'll have to have tax reduction, too."

While in Chicago, he found himself constantly at odds with Milton Friedman, who advocated monetary rules and floating exchange rates. Mr. Mundell joined Colum-bia in 1974, two years before Mr. Friedman won the economics Nobel.

Ever the maverick, Mr. Mundell remains a fan of the gold standard and fixed exchange rates at a time when they're out of favor with most other economists. "You have fixed rates between New York and California, and it works perfectly," he said.

The Nobel committee also praised Mr. Mundell's research into common currency zones, which laid the intellectual foundation for the 11-country euro. In 1961, when European countries still clung to their national currencies, he described the circumstances in which nations could share a common currency.

"At the time, it just seemed like such a wacko thing to work on, and that's why it's so visionary," said Kenneth Rogoff, a Harvard economist.

In particular, Mr. Mundell argued that in any successful currency zone, workers must be able to move freely from areas that are slowing to areas that are booming. Some critics suggest the euro nations don't fit his description.

But Mr. Mundell believes the new currency will eventually challenge the dollar for global dominance. "The benefits will derive from transparency of pricing, stability of expectations and lower transactions costs, as well as a common monetary policy run by the best minds that Europe can muster," Mr. Mundell wrote last year. He began working on the euro project as a consultant to European monetary authorities in 1969.

Outside academia, Mr. Mundell has led a colorful life. Worried about the onset of inflation in the late 1960s, he bought and renovated a 16th century Italian castle originally built for Pandolfo Petrucci, the "Strong Man of Siena." Mr. Mundell has four children, who range in age from one to 40.

Source: Michael M. Phillips, *The Wall Street Journal,* October 14, 1999. p. A2. © 1999 Dow Jones & Company, Inc. All Rights Reserved Worldwide.

EXHIBIT 2.8

Macroeconomic Data for Major Economies[a]

Economy	Population (Million)	GDP ($ Billion)	Annual Inflation	World Trade Share	International Bonds Outstanding ($ Billion)
United States	278.1	10,209.3	2.8%	17.9%	2,283.8
Euro-12	304.8	6,804.7	2.2	17.8	2,185.4
Japan	126.8	3,775.8	−0.6	6.6	94.5
United Kingdom	59.6	1,439.8	2.1	6.1	749.0

[a]The inflation rate is the annual average from 1999 to 2001. GDP is estimated on the basis of purchasing power parity as of the end of 2001. The remaining data are the 2001 figures.
Sources: *The World Factbook* 2001, published by the CIA; *National Accounts of OECD Countries* 2002; *International Financial Statistics;* and *BIS Quarterly Review,* June 2002.

2.10 The Mexican Peso Crisis

On December 20, 1994, the Mexican government under new president Ernesto Zedillo announced its decision to devalue the peso against the dollar by 14 percent. This decision, however, touched off a stampede to sell pesos as well as Mexican shares and bonds. As Exhibit 2.9 shows, by early January 1995, the peso fell against the American dollar by as much as 40 percent, forcing the Mexican government to float the peso. As concerned international investors reduced their holdings of emerging market securities, the peso crisis rapidly spilled over to other Latin American and Asian financial markets.

Faced with an impending default by the Mexican government and the possibility of a global financial meltdown, the Clinton administration, together with the International Monetary Fund (IMF) and the Bank for International Settlement (BIS), put together a $53 billion package to bail out Mexico.[8] As the bailout plan was put together and announced on January 31, the world's, as well as Mexico's, financial markets began to stabilize.

The Mexican peso crisis is significant in that it is perhaps the first serious international financial crisis touched off by cross-border flight of portfolio capital. International mutual funds are known to have invested more than $45 billion in Mexican securities during a three-year period prior to the peso crisis. As the peso fell, fund managers quickly liquidated their holdings of Mexican securities as well as other emerging market securities. This had a highly destabilizing, contagious effect on the world financial system. The same point is discussed in the International Finance in Practice box, "The New World Order of Finance" on page 47.

As the world's financial markets are becoming more integrated, this type of contagious financial crisis is likely to occur more often. Two lessons emerge from the peso crisis. First, it is essential to have a multinational safety net in place to safeguard the world financial system from the peso-type crisis. No single country or institution can handle a potentially global crisis alone. In addition, in the face of rapidly changing market conditions, usually slow and parochial political processes cannot cope with rapidly changing market conditions. In fact, the Clinton administration faced stiff opposition in Congress and from

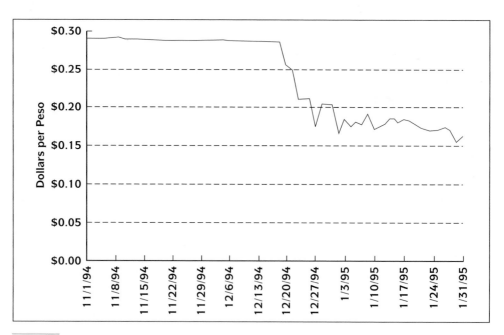

EXHIBIT 2.9

American Dollar versus Mexican Peso Exchange Rate
(November 1, 1994–January 31, 1995)

[8]The United States contributed $20 billion out of its Exchange Stabilization Fund, whereas IMF and BIS contributed, respectively, $17.8 billion and $10 billion. Canada, the Latin American countries, and commercial banks collectively contributed $5 billion.

The New World Order of Finance

Global financial panics erupt every decade or so. But even by historical standards, Mexico's currency collapse ranks among the scariest. With the crisis stretching into its seventh week, investors were stampeding. Worse yet, the panic was spreading from Buenos Aires to Budapest. Even the dollar was taking an unexpected shellacking. Some were bracing for another 1987 crash—not just in Mexico City, but in New York, London, and Tokyo.

It took forceful action to stop the runaway markets before they dragged the world economy down with them: $49.8 billion in loans and guarantees for Mexico from the U.S. and its allies. Some bankers say the total could reach $53 billion or more. Certainly, this will go down as the largest socialization of market risk in international history.

Ambitious Labor

With the U.S. spreading the gospel of democracy and free-market economics throughout the developing world, Clinton and his cohorts had little choice but to assemble the megaplan. As the club of emerging-market nations expands, the rich nations' obligation to provide a safety net for poorer trading partners is growing exponentially. America and its allies must mount a collective drive to ensure global monetary and economic stability—much like their efforts to maintain geopolitical order in the post-cold-war era.

Such ambitious labor is needed because the nature of financial markets has changed since Latin America's last financial crisis in 1982. Back then, it was gunslinger bankers who lent to Latin America. Because banks could lend for the long haul and absorb losses, they were a valuable shock absorber for the financial system. When enough Latin loans eventually went bad, it still took years to craft and conclude their restructuring.

Since then, bankers have wised up. Now, others with a

shorter time horizon make the emerging-market deals. This time, it was mutual-, hedge-, and pension-fund gunslingers who provided the capital. Mexico attracted $45 billion in mutual-fund cash in the past three years. And when the peso dived, fund managers bolted. In this global market, all it takes is a phone call to Fidelity to send money hurtling toward Monterey—or zooming back. And world leaders should be able to act with similar speed.

Clinton's $40 billion in loan guarantees for Mexico got nowhere because Congress objected to bailing out Wall Street. Legislators also did not like the U.S. shouldering most of the cost. They were right. Emerging markets will stay volatile, and countries and investors shouldn't expect a handout every time an economy hits a rough patch. And when a rescue is necessary, it should be global.

Bridge the Gap

Europe and Japan, after all, will benefit from a healthy Mexican economy and thus should bear the burden of supporting it in times of crisis. Likewise, Washington should be obliged to lend a hand to European or Asian allies if Poland or Indonesia come unglued. One way to keep the next crisis at bay: bridge the gap between short-term money and long-term investment needs.

In addition, emerging economies need to take steps to immunize themselves from the vagaries of a fund-dominated world. It would help a lot if more of them developed mandatory pension schemes to build up domestic savings. Along with that should come privatization. With capital so flighty, it may take hard decisions to make money stay put. But if the first world wants to encourage capitalism, it will have to underwrite it—even if the cost is huge.

Source: Reprinted from February 13, 1995 issue of *Business Week* by special permission, © 1995 by The McGraw-Hill Companies, Inc.

foreign allies when it was working out a bailout package for Mexico. As a result, early containment of the crisis was not possible. Fortunately, the G-7 countries endorsed a $50 billion bailout fund for countries in financial distress, which would be administered by the IMF, and a series of increased disclosure requirements to be followed by all countries. The reluctance of the outgoing Salinas administration to disclose the true state of the Mexican economy, that is, the rapid depletion of foreign exchange reserves and serious trade deficits, contributed to the sudden collapse of the peso.

Second, Mexico depended excessively on foreign portfolio capital to finance its economic development. In hindsight, the country should have saved more domestically and depended more on long-term, rather than short-term, foreign capital investments. As Professor Robert MacKinnon of Stanford University pointed out, a flood of foreign money had two undesirable effects. It led to an easy credit policy on domestic borrowings, which caused Mexicans to consume more and save less. Foreign capital influx also caused a higher domestic inflation and an overvalued peso, which hurt Mexico's trade balances.

2.11 The Asian Currency Crisis

On July 2, 1997, the Thai baht, which had been largely fixed to the American dollar, was suddenly devalued. What at first appeared to be a local financial crisis in Thailand quickly escalated into a global financial crisis, first spreading to other Asian countries—Indonesia, Korea, Malaysia, and the Philippines—then far afield to Russia and Latin America, especially Brazil. As can be seen from Exhibit 2.10, at the height of the crisis, the Korean won fell by about 50 percent in its dollar value from its precrisis level, whereas the Indonesian rupiah fell an incredible 80 percent.

The Asian crisis is the third major currency crisis of the 1990s, preceded by the crises of the European Monetary System (EMS) of 1992 and the Mexican peso in 1994–1995. The Asian crisis, however, turned out to be far more serious than its two predecessors in terms of the extent of contagion and the severity of resultant economic and social costs. Following the massive depreciations of local currencies, financial institutions and corporations with foreign-currency debts in the afflicted countries were driven to financial distress and many were forced to default. Worse, the currency crisis led to a deep, widespread, and long-lasting recession in East Asia, a region that, for more than a decade, had enjoyed the most rapidly growing economy in the world. At the same time, many lenders and investors from the developed countries also suffered large capital losses from their investments in emerging-market securities. For example, Long-Term Capital Management (LTCM), one of the largest and, until then, profitable hedge funds, experienced a near bankruptcy due to its exposure to Russian bonds. In mid-August 1998, the Russian ruble fell sharply from 6.3 rubles per dollar to about 20 rubbles per dollar. The prices of Russian shares and bonds also fell sharply. The Federal Reserve System, which feared a domino-like systematic financial failure in the United States, orchestrated a $3.5-billion bailout of LTCM in September 1998.

Given the global effects of the Asian currency crisis and the challenges it poses for the world financial system, it would be useful to understand its origins and causes and discuss how similar crises might be prevented in the future.

EXHIBIT 2.10   **Asian Currency Crisis**

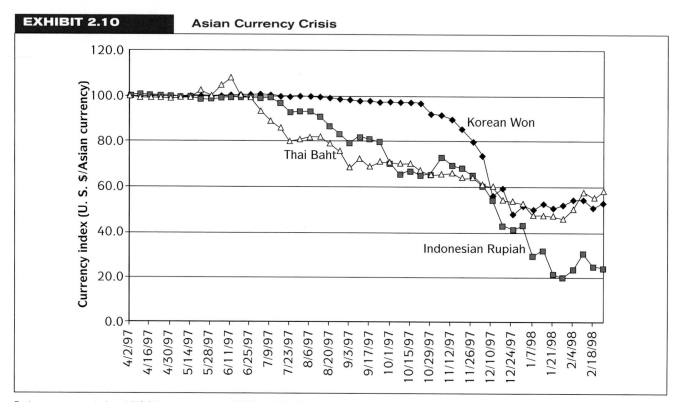

Exchange rates are indexed (US $/Asian currency on 4/2/97 = 100). Exchange rates on 4/2/97: 0.00112 US $/Korean won, 0.03856 US $/Thai baht, and 0.00041 US $/Indonesian rupiah.

Origins of the Asian Currency Crisis

Several factors are responsible for the onset of Asian currency crisis: a weak domestic financial system, free international capital flows, the contagion effects of changing market sentiment, and inconsistent economic policies. In recent years, both the developing and the developed countries were encouraged to liberalize their financial markets and allow free flows of capital across countries. As capital markets liberalized, both firms and financial institutions in the Asian developing countries eagerly borrowed foreign currencies from American, Japanese, and European investors who were attracted to these fast-growing emerging markets for extra returns for their portfolios. In 1996 alone, for example, five Asian countries—Indonesia, Korea, Malaysia, the Philippines, and Thailand—enjoyed a new inflow of private capital worth $93 billion. In contrast, there was a net outflow of $12 billion flowed out of these five countries in 1997.

Large inflows of private capital resulted in a credit boom in the Asian countries in the early and mid-1990s. The credit boom was often directed to speculations in real estate and stock markets as well as to investments in marginal industrial projects. Fixed or stable exchange rates also encouraged unhedged financial transactions and excessive risk taking by both lenders and borrowers, who were not much concerned with exchange risk. As asset prices declined (as happened in Thailand prior to the currency crisis), in part due to the government's effort to control the overheated economy, the quality of banks' loan portfolios also declined as the same assets were held as collateral for the loans. Clearly, banks and other financial institutions in the afflicted countries practised poor risk management and were poorly supervised. In addition, their lending decisions were often influenced by political considerations, likely leading to suboptimal allocation of resources. However, the so-called crony capitalism was not a new condition, and the East Asian economies achieved an economic miracle under the same system.

Meanwhile, the booming economy with a fixed or stable nominal exchange rate inevitably brought about appreciation of the real exchange rate. This, in turn, resulted in a marked slowdown in export growth in such Asian countries as Thailand and Korea. In addition, a long-lasting recession in Japan and the yen's depreciation against the dollar hurt Japan's neighbours, further worsening the trade balances of the Asian developing countries. If the Asian currencies had been allowed to depreciate in real terms, which was not possible because of the fixed nominal exchange rates, such catastrophic, discrete changes of the exchange rates as observed in 1997 might have been avoided.

In Thailand, as the run on the baht started, the Thai central bank initially injected liquidity to the domestic financial system and tried to defend the exchange rate by drawing on its foreign exchange reserves. With its foreign reserves declining rapidly, the central bank eventually decided to devalue the baht. The sudden collapse of the baht touched off a panicky flight of capital from other Asian countries with a high degree of financial vulnerability. From Exhibit 2.11, we see that the three Asian countries hardest hit by the crisis are among the most financially vulnerable as measured by (1) the ratio of short-term foreign debts to international reserve, and (2) the ratio of broad money, M2 (which represents the banking sector's liabilities) to international reserve. Contagion of the currency crisis was caused, at least in part, by the panicky, indiscriminate flight of capital from the Asian countries for fear of a spreading crisis. Fear, thus, became self-fulfilling. As lenders withdrew their capital and refused to renew short-term loans, the former credit boom turned into a credit crunch, hurting creditworthy as well as marginal borrowers.

As the crisis unfolded, the International Monetary Fund (IMF) came to rescue the three hardest-hit Asian countries—Indonesia, Korea, and Thailand—with bailout plans. As a condition for the bailing out, however, the IMF imposed a set of austerity measures—such as raising domestic interest rates and curtailing government expenditures—that were designed to support the exchange rate. Since these austerity measures, contractionary in nature, were implemented when the economies had already been contracting because of a severe credit crunch, the Asian economies consequently suffered a deep, long-lasting recession. According to a World Bank report (1999), one-year declines in industrial production of 20 percent or more in Thailand and Indonesia are comparable with those in the United States and Germany during the Great Depression.

EXHIBIT 2.11   **Financial Vulnerability Indicators**

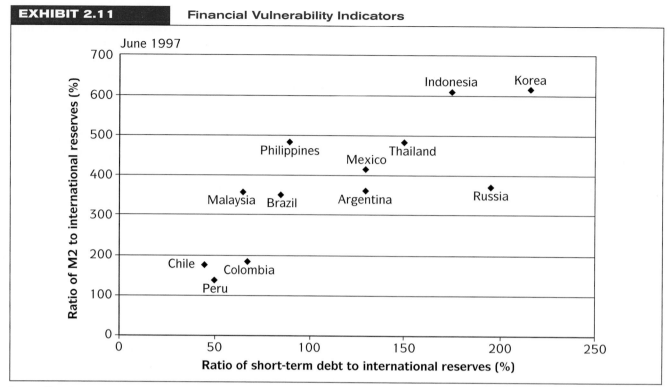

Source: The World Bank, International Monetary Fund.

One can thus argue that the IMF initially prescribed the wrong medicine for the afflicted Asian economies. The IMF bailout plans were also criticized on another ground: moral hazard. IMF bailouts may breed dependency in the developing countries and encourage risk taking on the part of international lenders.

Lessons from the Asian Currency Crisis

Generally speaking, liberalization of financial markets when combined with a weak, underdeveloped domestic financial system tends to create an environment susceptible to currency and financial crises. Interestingly, both Mexico and Korea experienced a major currency crisis within a few years after joining the Organization for Economic Cooperation and Development (OECD), which required a significant liberalization of financial markets. It seems safe to recommend that countries first strengthen their domestic financial system and then liberalize their financial markets.

www.adb.org

Provides a broad coverage of Asian financial developments.

A number of measures can and should be undertaken to strengthen a nation's domestic financial system. Among other things, the government should strengthen its system of financial-sector regulation and supervision. One way of doing so is to sign on to the "Core Principle of Effective Banking Supervision" drafted by the Basle Committee on Banking Supervision and to monitor its compliance with the principle. In addition, banks should be encouraged to base their lending decisions solely on economic merits, rather than political considerations. Furthermore, firms, financial institutions, and the government should be required to provide the public with reliable financial data in a timely fashion. A higher level of disclosure of financial information and the resultant transparency about the state of the economy will make it easier for all the concerned parties to monitor the situation better and mitigate the destabilizing cycles of investor euphoria and panic accentuated by the lack of reliable information.

Even if a country decides to liberalize its financial markets by allowing cross-border capital flows, it should encourage foreign direct investments and equity and long-term bond investments; it should not encourage short-term investments that can be reversed overnight, causing financial turmoil. As Chile has successfully implemented, some form of **"Tobin tax"** on the international flow of hot money can be useful. Throwing some sand in the wheels of international finance can have a stabilizing effect on the world's financial markets.

A fixed but adjustable exchange rate is problematic in the face of integrated international financial markets. Such a rate arrangement often invites speculative attack at the time of financial vulnerability. Countries should not try to restore the same fixed exchange rate system unless they are willing to impose capital controls. According to the so-called "trilemma" that economists are fond of talking about, a country can attain only two of the following three conditions: (1) a fixed exchange rate, (2) free international flows of capital, and (3) an independent monetary policy. If a country would like to maintain monetary policy independence to pursue its own domestic economic goals and still would like to keep a fixed exchange rate between its currency and other currencies, then the country should restrict free flows of capital. China and India were not noticeably affected by the Asian currency crisis because both countries maintain capital controls, segmenting their capital markets from the rest of the world. Hong Kong was less affected by the crisis for a different reason. Hong Kong has fixed its exchange rate permanently to the American dollar via a currency board and allowed free flows of capital; in consequence, Hong Kong gave up its monetary independence. A **currency board** is an extreme form of the fixed exchange rate regime under which local currency is "fully" backed by the dollar (or another chosen standard currency). Hong Kong has essentially dollarized its economy. To avoid currency crises, a country can have a really fixed exchange rate or flexible exchange rate, but not a fixed yet adjustable exchange rate, when international capital markets are integrated.

A recent episode with the Argentine peso, however, shows that even a currency board arrangement cannot be completely safe from a possible collapse. Exhibit 2.12 shows how the peso–dollar exchange rate, fixed at parity throughout much of the 1990s, collapsed in January 2002. Short of a complete dollarization (as is the case with Panama, for example), a currency board arrangement can collapse, unless the arrangement is backed by the political will and economic discipline to defend it. When the peso was first linked to the American dollar at parity in February 1991, initial economic effects were quite positive: Argentina's chronic inflation fell dramatically and foreign investment began to pour in, leading to an economic boom. Over time, however, the peso has appreciated against the majority of currencies as the American dollar became increasingly stronger in the second half of the 1990s. A strong peso hurt exports from Argentina and caused a protracted economic downturn that eventually led to the abandonment of the peso–dollar parity in January 2002. This change, in turn, caused severe economic and political distress in the country. In contrast, Hong Kong was able to successfully defend its currency board arrangement during the Asian financial crisis, a major stress test for the arrangement.

EXHIBIT 2.12

Collapse of the Currency Board Arrangement in Argentina

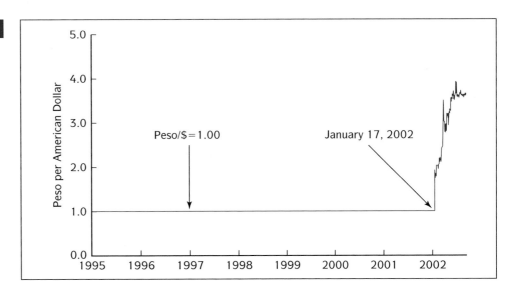

2.12   Fixed versus Flexible Exchange Rate Regimes

Since some countries, including Canada, prefer flexible exchange rates, while others, notably the members of the EMU and many developing countries, prefer to maintain fixed exchange rates, it is worthwhile to examine some of the arguments advanced in favour of fixed versus flexible exchange rates.

The key arguments for flexible exchange rates rest on (1) easier external adjustments, and (2) national policy autonomy. Suppose a country is experiencing a balance-of-payments deficit at the moment. This means that there is an excess supply of the country's currency at the prevailing exchange rate in the foreign exchange market. Under a flexible exchange rate regime, the external value of the country's currency will simply depreciate to the level at which there is no excess supply of the country's currency. At the new exchange rate level, the balance-of-payments disequilibrium will disappear.

As long as the exchange rate is allowed to be determined according to market forces, external balance will be achieved automatically. Consequently, the government does not have to take policy actions to correct the balance-of-payments disequilibrium. With flexible exchange rates, therefore, the government can use its monetary and fiscal policies to pursue whatever economic goals it chooses. Under a fixed rate regime, however, the government may have to take contractionary (expansionary) monetary and fiscal policies to correct the balance-of-payments deficit (surplus) at the existing exchange rate. Since policy tools need to be committed to maintaining the exchange rate, the government cannot use the same policy tools to pursue other economic objectives. As a result, the government loses its policy autonomy under a fixed exchange rate regime.

Using the British pound as the representative foreign exchange, Exhibit 2.13 illustrates the preceding discussion on how the balance-of-payment disequilibrium is corrected under alternative exchange rate regimes. As is the case with most other commodities, the demand for British pounds would be downward sloping, whereas the supply of British pounds would be upward sloping. Suppose that the exchange rate for American dollars is initially $1.40/£. As can be seen from the exhibit, the demand for British pounds far exceeds the supply (i.e., the supply of dollars far exceeds the demand) at this exchange rate. The United States experiences trade (or balance of payment) deficits. Under the flexible exchange rate regime, the dollar will simply depreciate to a new level of exchange rate, $1.60/£, at which the excess demand for British pounds (and, thus, the trade deficit) will disappear. Now, suppose that the exchange rate is "fixed" at $1.40/£ and, thus, the excess demand for British pounds cannot be eliminated by the exchange rate adjustment. Facing this situation, the U.S. Federal Reserve Bank may initially draw on its foreign exchange reserve holdings to satisfy the

---

EXHIBIT 2.13

External Adjustment Mechanism: Fixed versus Flexible Exchange Rates

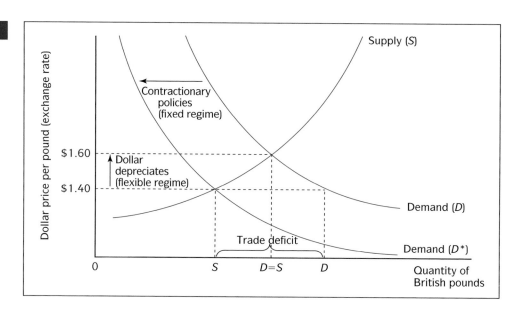

excess demand for British pounds. If the excess demand persists, however, the American government may have to resort to contractionary monetary and fiscal policies so that the demand curve can shift to the left (from D to D^* in the exhibit) until the excess demand for British pounds can be eliminated at the fixed exchange rate, $1.40/£. In other words, it is necessary for the government to take policy actions to maintain the fixed exchange rate.

A possible drawback of the flexible exchange rate regime is that exchange rate uncertainty may hamper international trade and investment. Proponents of the fixed exchange rate regime argue that when future exchange rates are uncertain, businesses tend to shun foreign trade. Since countries cannot fully benefit from international trade under exchange rate uncertainty, resources will be allocated suboptimally on a global basis. Proponents of the fixed exchange rate regime argue that fixed exchange rates eliminate such uncertainty and, thus, promote international trade. However, to the extent that firms can hedge exchange risk by means of currency forward or options contracts, uncertain exchange rates do not necessarily hamper international trade.

As the above discussion suggests, the choice between the alternative exchange rate regimes is likely to involve a trade-off between national policy independence and international economic integration. If countries would like to pursue their respective domestic economic goals, they are likely to pursue divergent macroeconomic policies, rendering fixed exchange rates infeasible. On the other hand, if countries are committed to promoting international economic integration (as is the case with the core members of the European Union like France and Germany), the benefits of fixed exchange rates are likely to outweigh the associated costs.

A "good" (or ideal) international monetary system should provide (1) liquidity, (2) adjustment, and (3) confidence. In other words, a good IMS should be able to provide the world economy with sufficient monetary reserves to support the growth of international trade and investment. It should also provide an effective mechanism that restores the balance-of-payments equilibrium whenever it is disturbed. Lastly, it should offer a safeguard to prevent crises of confidence in the system that result in panicked flights from one reserve asset to another. Politicians and economists should keep these three criteria in mind when they design and evaluate the international monetary system.

SUMMARY

This chapter provides an overview of the international monetary system, which defines an environment in which multinational corporations operate.

1. The international monetary system can be defined as the institutional framework within which international payments are made, the movements of capital are accommodated, and exchange rates among currencies are determined.

2. The international monetary system went through five stages of evolution: (a) bimetallism, (b) classical gold standard, (c) interwar period, (d) Bretton Woods system, and (e) flexible exchange rate regime.

3. The classical gold standard spanned 1875 to 1914. Under the gold standard, the exchange rate between two currencies is determined by the gold contents of the currencies. Balance-of-payments disequilibrium is automatically corrected through the price-specie-flow mechanism. The gold standard still has ardent supporters who believe that it provides an effective hedge against price inflation. Under the gold standard, however, the world economy can be subject to deflationary pressure due to the limited supply of monetary gold.

4. To prevent the recurrence of economic nationalism with no clear "rules of the game" witnessed during the interwar period, representatives of 44 nations met at Bretton Woods, New Hampshire, in 1944 and adopted a new international monetary system. Under the Bretton Woods system, each country established a par value in relation to the American dollar, which was fully convertible to gold. Countries used foreign exchanges, especially the American dollar, as well as gold

as international means of payments. The Bretton Woods system was designed to maintain stable exchange rates and economize on gold. The Bretton Woods system eventually collapsed in 1973 mainly because of American domestic inflation and the persistent balance-of-payments deficits.

5. The flexible exchange rate regime that replaced the Bretton Woods system was ratified by the Jamaica Agreement. Following a spectacular rise and fall of the American dollar in the 1980s, major industrial countries agreed to cooperate to achieve greater exchange rate stability. The Louvre Accord of 1987 marked the inception of the managed-float system under which the G-7 countries would jointly intervene in the foreign exchange market to correct over- or undervaluation of currencies.

6. In 1979, the EEC countries launched the European Monetary System (EMS) to establish a "zone of monetary stability" in Europe. The two main instruments of the EMS are the European Currency Unit (ECU) and the Exchange Rate Mechanism (ERM). The ECU is a basket currency comprising the currencies of the EMS members and serves as the accounting unit of the EMS. The ERM refers to the procedure by which EMS members collectively manage their exchange rates. The ERM is based on a parity grid that the member countries are required to maintain.

7. On January 1, 1999, eleven European countries including France and Germany adopted a common currency called the euro. Greece adopted the euro in 2001. The advent of a single European currency, which may eventually rival the American dollar as a global vehicle currency, will have major implications for the European as well as world economy. The euro-12 countries will benefit from reduced transaction costs and the elimination of exchange rate uncertainty. The advent of the euro will also help develop continentwide capital markets where companies can raise capital at favourable rates.

8. Under the European Monetary Union (EMU), the common monetary policy for the euro-12 countries is formulated by the European Central Bank (ECB) located in Frankfurt. The ECB is legally mandated to maintain price stability in Europe. Together with the ECB, the national central banks of the euro-12 countries form the European System of Central Banks (ESBC), which is responsible for defining and implementing the common monetary policy for the EMU.

9. While the core EMU members, including France and Germany, apparently prefer the fixed exchange rate regime, other major countries, such as the United States and Japan, are willing to live with flexible exchange rates. Under the flexible exchange rate regime, governments can retain policy independence because the external balance will be achieved by the exchange rate adjustments, rather than by policy intervention. Exchange rate uncertainty, however, can potentially hamper international trade and investment. The choice between the alternative exchange rate regimes is likely to involve a trade-off between national policy autonomy and international economic integration.

KEY WORDS

bimetallism, *26*
Bretton Woods system, *29*
currency board, *51*
euro, *38*
European Currency Unit (ECU), *35*
European Monetary System (EMS), *35*
European Monetary Union (EMU), *39*
Exchange Rate Mechanism (ERM), *35*

European System of Central Banks (ESCB), *40*
gold-exchange standard, *30*
gold standard, *27*
Gresham's law, *26*
international monetary system, *25*
Jamaica Agreement, *32*
Louvre Accord, *33*
Maastricht Treaty, *38*

managed-float system, *34*
optimum currency area, *43*
par value, *30*
Plaza Accord, *33*
price-specie-flow mechanism, *28*
Smithsonian Agreement, *32*
snake, *35*

special drawing rights   sterilization of gold, *29*   Triffin paradox, *31*
   (SDRs), *31*   "Tobin tax," *50*

QUESTIONS

1. Explain Gresham's law.

2. Explain the mechanism that restores the balance-of-payments equilibrium when it is disturbed under the gold standard.

3. Suppose that the pound is pegged to gold at six pounds per ounce, whereas the franc is pegged to gold at 12 francs per ounce. This, of course, implies that the equilibrium exchange rate should be two francs per pound. If the current market exchange rate is 2.2 francs per pound, how would you take advantage of this situation? What would be the effect of shipping costs?

4. Discuss the advantages and disadvantages of the gold standard.

5. What were the main objectives of the Bretton Woods system?

6. Comment on the proposition that the Bretton Woods system was programmed to an eventual demise.

7. Explain how special drawing rights (SDR) are constructed. Also, discuss the circumstances under which the SDR was created.

8. Explain the arrangements and workings of the European Monetary System (EMS).

9. There are arguments for and against the alternative exchange rate regimes.

   a. List the advantages of the flexible exchange rate regime.

   b. Criticize the flexible exchange rate regime from the viewpoint of the proponents of the fixed exchange rate regime.

   c. Rebut the above criticism from the viewpoint of the proponents of the flexible exchange rate regime.

10. In an integrated world financial market, a financial crisis in a country can be quickly transmitted to other countries, causing a global crisis. What kind of measures would you propose to prevent the recurrence of an Asia-type crisis?

11. Discuss the criteria for a "good" international monetary system.

12. Once capital markets are integrated, it is difficult for a country to maintain a fixed exchange rate. Explain why this may be so.

13. Assess the possibility for the euro to become another global currency rivalling the American dollar. If the euro really becomes a global currency, what impact will it have on the American dollar and the world economy?

INTERNET EXERCISES

1. Using the data from http://fx.sauder.ubc.ca, first plot the daily exchange rate between the euro and the American dollar since January 1, 2002, and try to explain why the exchange rate behaved the way it did.

2. Repeat the exercise with the Canadian dollar and the euro.

MINI CASE

Will the United Kingdom Join the Euro Club?

When the euro was introduced in January 1999, the United Kingdom was conspicuously absent from the list of European countries adopting the common currency. Although the current Labour government led by Prime Minister Tony Blair appears to be in favour of joining the euro club, it is not clear at the moment if that will actually happen. The opposition Tory party is not in favour of adopting the euro and thus giving up monetary sovereignty of the country. Public opinion is also divided on the issue.

Whether the United Kingdom will eventually join the euro club is a matter of considerable importance for the future of the European Union as well as that of the United Kingdom. If the United Kingdom, with its sophisticated finance industry, joins, it will most certainly propel the euro into a global currency status rivalling the American dollar. The United Kingdom, for its part, will firmly join the process of economic and political unionization of Europe, abandoning its traditional balancing role.

Investigate the political, economic, and historical situations surrounding British participation in the European economic and monetary integration, and write your own assessment of the prospect of the United Kingdom joining the euro club. In doing so, assess from the British perspective, among other things, (1) potential benefits and costs of adopting the euro, (2) economic and political constraints facing the country, and (3) the potential impact of British adoption of the euro on the international financial system, including the role of the American dollar.

REFERENCES & SUGGESTED READINGS

Brean, Donald J.S. "Financial Liberalization in Canada: Historical, Institutional and Economic Perspectives," in *International Financial Reform,* Albert Berry and Gustavo Indart, eds., London: Transaction Publishers, 2003.

Cooper, Richard N. *The International Monetary System: Essays in World Economics.* Cambridge, Mass.: MIT Press, 1987.

Courchene, Thomas J. and Richard G. Harris. "North American Monetary Union: Analytical Principles and Operational Guidelines: *The North American Journal of Economics and Finance* Volume 11, Issue 1 (August 2000), pp. 3–18.

Eichengreen, Barry. *The Gold Standard in Theory and History.* Mathuen: London, 1985, pp. 39–48.

Friedman, Milton. *Essays in Positive Economics.* Chicago: University of Chicago Press, 1953.

Grubel, Herbert G. "The Merit of a Canada–US Monetary Union," *The North American Journal of Economics and Finance* Volume 11, Issue 1 (August 2000), pp. 19–40.

Jorion, Philippe. "Properties of the ECU as a Currency Basket," *Journal of Multinational Financial Management* 1 (1991), pp. 1–24.

Machlup, Fritz. *Remaking the International Monetary System: The Rio Agreement and Beyond.* Baltimore: Johns Hopkins Press, 1968.

Mundell, Robert. "A Theory of Optimum Currency Areas." *American Economic Review* 51 (1961), pp. 657–65.

———. "Currency Areas, Volatility and Intervention," *Journal of Policy Modeling* 22 (2000), pp. 281–99.

Murray, John. "Why Canada Needs a Flexible Exchange Rate," *The North American Journal of Economics and Finance* Volume 11, Issue 1 (August 2000), pp. 41–60.

Nurkse, Ragnar. *International Currency Experience: Lessons of the Interwar Period.* Geneva: League of Nations, 1944.

Powell, James. *A History of The Canadian Dollar.* Ottawa: The Bank of Canada (1999). Available in pdf from *www.bankofcanada.ca/en/dollar_book/full_text_e.htm*

Robson, William B.P. and David Laidler. *The Awkward Economics and Politics of North American Monetary Integration.* Toronto: C.D. Howe Institute, July 2002.

Solomon, Robert. *The International Monetary System, 1945–1981.* New York: Harper & Row, 1982.

Stiglitz, Joseph. "Reforming the Global Economic Architecture: Lessons from Recent Crisis," *Journal of Finance* 54 (1999), pp. 1508–21.

TD Economics. *Loonie Tunes: Understanding the Rally in the Canadian Dollar and Its Consequences;* A Special Report on the Canadian Dollar by the Economics Department of TDCanadaTrust (2004). Available in pdf from *www.td.com/economics.*

Tobin, James. "Financial Globalization," unpublished manuscript presented at American Philosophical Society, 1998.

Triffin, Robert. *Gold and the Dollar Crisis.* New Haven, Conn.: Yale University Press, 1960.

CHAPTER 3

Balance of Payments

CHAPTER OUTLINE

3.1 Canada's Balance of Payments

Canada is one of the most economically "open" nations in the world. Canada's trade—its exports and imports—amounts to a whopping 83 percent of national income. Much of that trade, close to 85 percent, is with the United States. Canada's financial markets are highly integrated with world financial markets, again predominantly with markets in the United States. Vast volumes of finance flow back and forth across the border. Over the past 15 years, spurred by the Canada–United States Free Trade Agreement of 1989 and NAFTA of 1994, the external side of Canada's economy has grown at impressive rates.

Exhibit 3.1 uses a conventional measure of "openness" to illustrate the ever-expanding share of trade in Canada's gross domestic product (GDP). Exhibit 3.2 shows the dramatic growth of international financial flows to and from Canada.

Canada's commerce with other nations is recorded in the accounts that make up the **Balance of Payments**. In this chapter, we look at these accounts in some detail. The numbers highlight the importance of international trade and foreign investment. Moreover, since Canada's trade and cross-border investment involve some form of exchange of Canadian dollars for foreign currency, we will see how developments in the Balance of Payments influence the exchange rate—the "external value" of the Canadian dollar.

The word "payments" in the Balance of Payments refers to payments to foreigners for things that Canadians buy from abroad—imported cars or clothing, trips to Europe, or an American government bond—as well as payments to Canadians for Canadian products and services that foreigners want—for example, oil or natural gas, insurance services from ManuLife, or shares in Bombardier. All such payments involving international transactions, whether they are inbound or outbound from Canada, are recorded in Canadian dollars.

When Canadians want to buy foreign goods, services, or financial assets, Canadian dollars must be sold in order to buy foreign currency for those transactions. Likewise, Canadian dollars must be purchased by foreigners in order to buy the Canadian currency to buy Canadian goods, services, or financial assets.

As we shall soon see, the Balance of Payments must "balance." However, within that balance, there are pressures that can cause the Canadian exchange rate to strengthen or weaken. In view of our keen focus on the Canadian exchange rate—what determines its value and, above all, what causes it to change—a solid grasp of the Balance of Payments is the appropriate first step toward understanding the forces that determine the exchange rate.

EXHIBIT 3.1

Canada's Increasing "Openness": 1980–2002

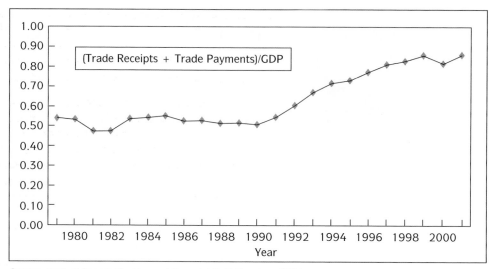

Source: Bank of Canada Banking and Financial Statistics, June 2004.

3.2 Balance of Payments Accounts

Canada's international transactions are grouped into three accounts that make up the Balance of Payments:

1. The Current Account
2. The Capital Account
3. The Reserve Account

The **Current Account** records—on a quarterly or annual basis—flows of exports, imports, investment income and international financial transfers. Transactions that involve foreign purchases of Canadian dollars (to buy Canadian goods or services or to travel in Canada) are recorded as "credits." Transactions that involve Canadian purchases of foreign currencies (when Canadians import goods or services, when Canadi-

EXHIBIT 3.2

Canada's International Financial Flows: 1980–2002

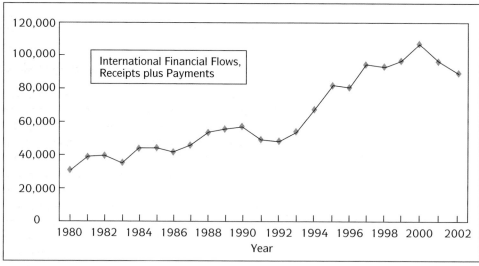

Source: Bank of Canada Banking and Financial Statistics, June 2004.
Figures are drawn from the "Investment Income" section of the Current Account—Interest, Dividends and Reinvested Earnings.

ans travel abroad, or when Canada pays interest or dividends to foreigners) are recorded as "debits."

The **Capital Account** records—on a quarterly or annual basis—flows of capital that move into or out of Canada within the period. For example, if an American buys a bond issued by a Canadian government or corporation, this represents an inflow of capital to Canada. Such transactions are recorded in the Capital Account as "credits." On the other hand, if a Canadian buys a bond issued by a foreign government or corporation, this represents an outflow of Canadian capital. Such transactions enter the Capital Account as "debits."

The **Reserve Account** of the Balance of Payments records changes in the amount of "official" foreign exchange reserves held by the Bank of Canada. In Canada and most industrial nations, such changes tend to be small relative to the total foreign exchange for commercial and international investment purposes.

Exhibit 3.3 provides a variety of specific examples of transactions that enter the Current Account and the Capital Account of the Canadian Balance of Payments. Exhibit 3.4 shows selected entries in the Current Account and the Capital Account of the Canadian Balance of Payments for the year 2002.

The **Balance of Payments** *Identity* is an accounting relationship that in principle (that is, aside from statistical errors) must hold. The Balance of Payments Identity is:

$$BCA + BKA + BRA = 0$$

where:

BCA = Balance on Current Account
BKA = Balance on Capital Account
BRA = Balance on Reserves Account

EXHIBIT 3.3		
Examples of Entries in Canada's Balance of Payments Accounts	**Credits**	**Debits**
	Current Account	*Current Account*
	a. The Alberta Natural Gas Company exports natural gas to California.	a. Ford (Canada) buys automobile transmissions from a supplier in Michigan.
	b. Bombardier of Montreal sells aircraft to Australia.	b. The LCBO buys wine from Italy.
	c. Corel of Ottawa sells a licence to a Mexican software producer.	c. The CN Tower pays an insurance premium to Lloyds of London.
	d. The Barenaked Ladies give a concert in New York and deposit their receipts in a Toronto Bank.	d. Tom McNeil of Charlottetown goes to the London School of Economics and takes $20,000 to pay tuition and expenses.
	e. Canada hosts the G8 Summit in Halifax, and 1,000 foreign press visit the city for five days.	e. Canada Drugs pays a patent royalty to Novo of Sweden.
	f. The Ontario Teachers Pension Fund receives $100,000 in dividends on its holdings of Microsoft (USA) shares.	f. Hydro Quebec pays interest on its bonds to bondholders in Switzerland.
	Capital Account	*Capital Account*
	g. Fidelity Mutual Fund of New York buys 10,000 shares of Nortel Networks (Bramalea)	g. Altamira Investments (Toronto) buys shares in Xerox (USA).
	h. Societe General of Paris buys Province of Nova Scotia bonds.	h. Saskatchewan Teachers Superannuation Commission buys State of Montana bonds.
	i. Professor Jones moves from Harvard to McGill and transfers his personal assets from Boston to Montreal.	i. Barrick buys a gold mine in Peru.
		j. Irving Oil of New Brunswick buys gas stations in Maine.

EXHIBIT 3.4

Canada's Balance of Payments: Selected Items (2002) in billions of C$

	Credits	Debits
Current Account		
1. Exports & Income Receipts		
1.0 Total	498.4	
1.1 Merchandise	410.3	
1.2 Services	58.2	
1.3 Investment Income Receipts	29.9	
Interest	2.3	
Dividends	27.6	
2. Imports & Income Payments		
2.0 Total		482.7
2.1 Merchandise		356.2
2.2 Services		66.2
2.3 Investment Income Payments		60.3
Interest		29.3
Dividends		31.0
3. Transfers (net)	1.4	
Capital Account		
4. Direct Investment		
4.1 Canadian Direct Investment Abroad		43.7
4.2 Direct Investment in Canada	33.6	
5. Portfolio Investment		
5.1 Outward, from Canada (net)		31.7
5.2 Inward, to Canada (net)	30.5	
Balance of Current Account (1.0 − 2.0 + 3)	17.1	
Balance on Capital Account (4.2 + 5.2 − 4.1 − 5.1)	−11.3	
Increase in Official Reserves	5.0	
Statistical Discrepency	−0.8	

Source: Bank of Canada: Banking and Financial Statistics, April 2003; Table J1 and J2.

The Balance on Reserves Account serves as a foreign exchange buffer managed by the government or the central bank—The Bank of Canada, for example. In countries with governments or central banks that actively intervene in the foreign market to "fix" their exchange rate against one of the world's major currencies, such as the American dollar or the euro, the Reserves Account is drawn down to buy one's own currency in order to raise its "external" value or to resist a fall in value. Most industrial nations tend to do very little exchange rate fixing. Consequently, changes in the Balance on Reserves Account tend to be small and random, and hence for all practical purposes, the key Balance of Payments relationship is that the Balance on Current Account equals the Balance on Capital Account.

The Current Account

Exhibit 3.4 highlights a number of points that characterize Canada as a trading nation. On the Current Account, the value of our exports and investment income receipts from abroad exceeds the value of its imports and investment income payments paid to foreigners. For business-minded people who think in terms of cash flow, this suggests that Canada enjoys a positive operating cash flow in its business dealings with the rest of the world. It is interesting to look a little closer at the composition of these cash flows.

Canada enjoys a highly favourable balance of merchandise trade (line items 1.1 and 2.1). In practical terms, the total value of Canadian exports of such items as forest products, minerals, energy, agricultural products, airplanes, and automobiles exceeds the value of the imported merchandise—such as electronics, clothing, and food products from warmer climates. A graphical summary of Canada's merchandise trade over the past 22 years is presented in Exhibit 3.5.

In respect of services, the so-called "**invisible trade**," Canada generally runs a small deficit (line items 1.2 and 2.2). Patent royalties, fees for movies, travel, insurance, consultants and engineering are the sorts of "invisible" import items in this category.

The largest gap between debits and credits on Current Account involves Line items 1.3 and 2.3, Investment Income Receipts and Investment Income Payments. The Canadian outflow of these financial payments far exceeds the inflow of receipts from abroad. This imbalance reflects Canada's heritage as a small country that over the years has imported vast amounts of capital for nation building and industry. Canadian industry ranks among the most capital intensive in the world. Capital is used intensively in mining, energy, forestry, fishing, and manufacturing. Governments have also imported capital to build the national infrastructure—including roads, bridges, and telecommunication networks. The foreign capital that has been drawn to Canada is paid for through interest and dividends.

The Balance on Current Account was positive in 2002. That is to say, in 2002, Canada generated more receipts through exports and income on foreign investments than it paid out for imports and the payments to foreign investors. Without judging the economic merits of a positive balance, one should note that a positive Balance on Current Account is a relatively new phenomenon for Canada. Through virtually all of the 1980s and 1990s, Canada had a negative Balance on Current Account due, in large measure, to the high interest burden of foreign debt—for the most part, corporations and provinces that sold bonds to foreign investors.

Before turning to the Capital Account, which we will do in a moment, it is useful to draw a crucial link between the Current Account and the Capital Account. The positive Balance on Current Account in 2002 can be interpreted as Canada and Canadians earning more foreign exchange—American dollars, euros, Mexican pesos and so on—than needed to purchase things with those currencies. The "excess foreign exchange" on the Current Account must be spent somehow and so it is used to purchase foreign financial assets. As a result, the overall Balance of Payments balances, which means that the surplus (or deficit) on the Current Account corresponds to the deficit (or surplus) on the Capital Account.

The Current Account balance, especially the trade balance, tends to be sensitive to changes in the exchange rate. When the Canadian dollar appreciates relative to the American dollar, for example, as it did sharply in the first half of 2003, then Canadian-

EXHIBIT 3.5

Canada's Trade in
Goods and Services:
1980–2002

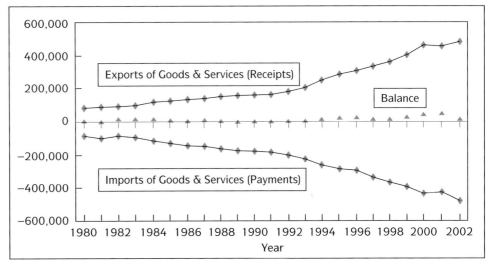

Source: Bank of Canada Banking and Financial Statistics, June 2004.

produced goods become more expensive in the export market. Meanwhile, the stronger Canadian dollar makes imports cheaper. As Canadian exports fall and imports rise, the trade balance deteriorates.

One would predict that the **trade balance**, exports minus imports, would improve if a country's currency depreciated against the currency of its major trading partners. Indeed so, but adjustments generally require time to work themselves through. The length of time required to adjust production plans and contracts with foreign customers results in lags that result in a predictable pattern in the trade balance following a change in the exchange rate.

The classic reaction pattern of the trade balance to a currency depreciation is referred to as the **J-curve effect**. This is illustrated in Exhibit 3.6. The J-curve depicts an initial deterioration and eventual improvement of the trade balance following the currency depreciation. The explanation is due to the difficulty and costliness of adjustment in production and marketing in international trade. One observes short-term inelasticity or lack of price-responsiveness of exports and imports to the change in the exchange rate. Following a currency depreciation, some importers continue to import at the higher import price before they find alternative domestic sources. Likewise, exporters require time before they fully exploit the new opportunities in their markets abroad. In the transition immediately following a currency depreciation, the country's import bill tends to rise, while export receipts tend not to respond immediately. The net effect is deterioration of the trade balance. In the longer run, adjustments take place, imports fall, exports rise, and the trade balance improves.

The Capital Account

The Capital Account records sales to foreigners of Canadian financial assets and Canadian purchases of foreign financial assets. The Balance on Capital Account is simply the difference between the value of foreign purchases of Canadian financial assets and Canadian purchases of foreign financial assets.

There are two main categories of financial assets recorded in the Capital Account—direct investment and portfolio investment. The economic and industrial characters of these two categories of cross-border investment are significantly different, and that difference is especially pertinent to the types of issues that arise in international financial management.

EXHIBIT 3.6

A Currency Depreciation and the Time-Path of the Trade Balance: The J-Curve Effect

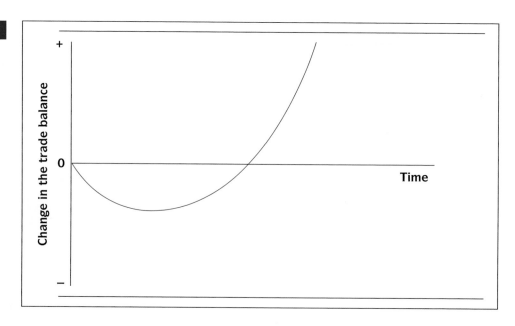

Foreign direct investment (FDI) is what multinational enterprises do. When McCain Foods of New Brunswick sets up a food processing plant in France, when the Bank of Montreal expands operations of its wholly owned Harris Bank of Chicago, or when media giant Quebecor doubles its printing facilities in New Delhi, these corporate investments represent Canadian outbound foreign direct investment. The distinguishing features of foreign direct investment are ownership and control in a corporate context. McCain, the Bank of Montreal, and Quebecor are directly involved in the ownership, control, and management of their operations abroad. These Canadian-based multinational companies assign their corporate names, and they transfer technology, trade-marks, marketing, and strategy to their subsidiaries abroad. In the Capital Account of the Balance of Payments for a particular year, McCain's contribution to outbound foreign direct investment would consist of the new direct investment—in the form of corporate equity—made in that year. So, when McCain sets up the food processing plant in France with equity injections of $10 million per year in 2004 and 2005, $10 million is recorded as a debit in the Capital Account in each of those years. Reinvested earnings and non–arm's-length (intrafirm) debt are also recorded in the Capital Account.

While foreign direct investment is recorded in the Capital Account, the subsequent flow of earnings on that capital is recorded as investment income in the Current Account. Since the difference between the Current Account and the Capital Account hinges on the difference between foreign-source income and foreign investment, if McCain earns $1 million on its operations in France and then immediately reinvests those earnings in the French subsidiary, the Current Account would record $1 million of foreign investment income (a credit) while the Capital Account would record $1 million of foreign direct investment (a debit).

Portfolio investment refers to (1) changes in Canadian holdings of noncontrolling equity in foreign companies, (2) foreign holdings of noncontrolling equity in Canadian companies, (3) Canadian holdings of debt issued by foreigners, and (4) foreign holdings of debt issued by Canadians. Canadian purchases of shares of foreign companies, foreign purchases of shares in Canadian companies, Canadian purchases of foreign bonds, and foreign purchases of Canadian bonds are the main transaction categories for portfolio investment. The Capital Account records net changes under each of these categories. The principal purpose is to report the totals and the composition of Canadian lending to foreigners and foreign lending to Canada. Illustrative examples are presented in Exhibit 3.3.

To put the foregoing points into specific numbers, in 2002, Canada sent $44 billion of foreign direct investment abroad, while foreigners directly invested $34 billion in Canada. Outbound portfolio investment—Canada lending to foreigners—amounted to $32 billion, while inbound portfolio investment amounted approximately the same value, $31 billion. Canada added $5 billion to foreign reserves.

The motives for foreign direct investment are the conventional motives of business in an international setting. Firms "go abroad" to expand their markets or to take advantage of more profitable sites of production. For example, Molson's finds the Latin American market tantalizing and a good strategic move. In 2000, Molson entered this market by acquiring Bavaria, a leading beer brand in Brazil. On the other hand, foreign firms find Canada an attractive destination for investment, either for market access or for resources. For instance, Stora Enso of Finland or Weyerhaeuser of the State of Washington have been aggressive investors in the Canadian forest industry by buying Canadian companies. We will look into such decisions in greater detail in Chapters 15 to 17.

The $1.2 billion in net cross-border portfolio investment is driven by somewhat different concerns. Portfolio capital seeks out attractive bond interest, noncontrolling equity returns, diversification, and tax advantages. As we shall see in Chapter 8 (on international equity markets) and Chapter 11 (on bond portfolio investment), the

EXHIBIT 3.7	Balances on the Current (BCA) and Capital (BKA) Accounts of Five Major Countries: 1982–2002 (US$ billion)[a]								
	China		Japan		Germany		United Kingdom		United States	
Year	BCA	BKA	BCA	BKA	BCA	BKA	BCA	BKA	BCA	BKA
1982	5.7	0.6	6.9	−11.6	4.9	−2.0	8.0	−10.6	−11.6	16.6
1983	4.2	−0.1	20.8	−19.3	4.6	−6.6	5.3	−7.1	−44.2	45.4
1984	2.0	−1.9	35.0	−32.9	9.6	−9.9	1.8	−2.8	−99.0	102.1
1985	−11.4	9.0	51.1	−51.6	17.6	−15.4	3.3	−0.7	−124.5	128.3
1986	−7.0	5.0	85.9	−70.7	40.9	−35.5	−1.3	5.0	−150.5	150.2
1987	0.3	4.5	84.4	−46.3	46.4	−24.9	−8.1	28.2	−166.5	157.3
1988	−3.8	6.2	79.2	−61.7	50.4	−66.0	−29.3	33.9	−127.7	131.6
1989	−4.3	3.8	63.2	−76.3	57.0	−54.1	−36.7	28.6	−104.3	129.5
1990	12.0	0.1	44.1	−53.2	48.3	−41.1	−32.5	32.5	−94.3	96.5
1991	13.3	1.3	68.2	−76.6	−17.7	11.5	−14.3	19.0	−9.3	3.5
1992	6.4	−8.5	112.6	−112.0	−19.1	56.3	−18.4	11.7	−61.4	57.4
1993	−11.6	13.4	131.6	−104.2	−13.9	−0.3	−15.5	21.0	−90.6	91.9
1994	6.9	23.5	130.3	−105.0	−20.9	18.9	−2.3	3.8	−132.9	127.6
1995	1.6	20.9	111.0	−52.4	−22.6	29.8	−5.9	5.0	−129.2	138.9
1996	7.2	24.5	65.9	−30.7	−13.8	12.6	−3.7	3.2	−148.7	142.1
1997	29.7	6.1	94.4	−87.8	−1.2	−2.6	6.8	−11.0	−166.8	167.8
1998	31.5	−6.3	120.7	−116.8	−6.4	17.63	−8.0	0.2	−217.4	151.6
1999	21.1	5.2	106.9	−31.1	−18.0	−40.5	−31.9	31.0	−324.4	367.9
2000	20.5	2.0	116.9	−75.5	−18.7	13.2	−28.8	26.2	−444.7	443.6
2001	17.4	4.3	87.8	−98.1	1.7	8.5	−33.7	28.0	−393.7	461.1
2002	35.4	6.4	112.5	−102.0	43.4	−16.2	−26.7	24.7	−480.9	498.6

[a]The balance on the capital account (BKA) includes statistical discrepancies.
Source: IMF, *International Financial Statistics Yearbook,* various issues.

world's capital markets offer the advantage of a wide array of financial investment in risk categories, industries, and currencies that are otherwise unavailable if money is kept exclusively at home.

External Balance and the Exchange Rate

In principle, the Current Account and the Capital Account should balance each other out. If Canada buys more goods, services, and the like than it sells (i.e., if Canada runs a current account deficit), it must finance that deficit. A current account deficit is financed by means of a capital account surplus. In theory, therefore, since the balance of payments is the sum of the current account and the capital account, the balance of payments is always zero.

To a rough approximation, a Current Account deficit indicates that a nation has spent more than it has earned. In that case, other nations lend money to the nation in Current Account deficit to finance the difference between its income and spending. The nation-as-a-whole borrows money from the rest of the world by means of the net sale of financial assets. Of course, the net sale of financial assets to the rest of the world is that nation's Capital Account surplus. Again, we see that a deficit on current account is mirrored by a surplus on capital account such that the balance of payments "balances."

Current Account surpluses or deficits may or may not be a matter of economic or policy concern, depending on specific circumstances. Surpluses or deficits in either account are not necessarily problematic. For example, as a relatively new and rapidly growing country in the 20th century, Canada often experienced strong inflows of both direct investment and portfolio investment. These inflows helped Canada grow and prosper. In contrast, and more recently, there have been occasions when Canadians have substantially increased their investment abroad. Such circumstances have led to a Capital Account deficit balanced by a Current Account surplus.

In view of our focus on international financial management at the corporate level, impatient managers may find the macroeconomics perspective on external balance—the relation between the Current Account and the Capital Account—to be somewhat distant from their immediate concerns about exchange rates and exchange rate risk. As we shall see in later chapters that deal directly with the management of foreign exchange risk—Chapters 12, 13 and 14—foreign exchange *risk* and exchange rate *volatility* are, for all practical purposes, the same thing. Exchange rate volatility is a macroeconomic phenomenon with microeconomic (corporate level) implications.

Short-term volatility in the exchange rate is often perplexing for international corporate financial management. If the Current Account deficit or surplus is always offset by the Capital Account surplus or deficit, what sort of "imbalance" causes the exchange rate to change, especially in the short-run, say, day to day, week to week, or within six months? To answer this question in a way that managers and business students have a unique advantage in understanding, it helps to view the surplus on the Capital Account as essentially "loans" from financiers in the rest of the world to the country in Current Account deficit. Such loans are attracted to capital importing nations by interest rates. The interest rate is an important mechanism for "balancing" the Capital Account and the Current Account. The points can be illustrated by the case of the United States over the past 20 years.

Exhibit 3.8a shows that since 1982, the United States has experienced continuous deficits on Current Account and continuous surpluses on its Capital Account. The size of the American Current Account deficits is far greater than that of any other country experienced over this period (see Canada's in Exhibit 3.8b). Looking at the more recent years—through the 1990s—the American Current Account deficit has grown steadily, owing, in large part, to the investment boom driven by the impressive increases in American industrial productivity, especially in high-end manufacturing, such as electronics and information technology. The fact that these Current Account deficits were financed through Capital Account surpluses reflects on the enormous capacity of the United States to borrow from the rest of the world, that is, the capacity of the United States to sell financial assets to foreigners.

By 2002, the American Current Account deficit had swollen to more than $500 billion. Meanwhile the investment boom had subsided, the United States teetered on the verge of recession and interest rates had fallen to historic lows. The question for American "external balance" was whether the rest of the world would continue to buy and hold the American financial assets that had underwritten past Current Account deficits and that were also necessary for further deficits.

If the rest of the world becomes uncomfortable with mounting loans to the United States, and if they reduce the flow of capital to the United States, that is, reduce the Capital Account surpluses, then one of two things (or a combination of the two) will occur. Either American interest rates must rise to attract new capital inflows or the American dollar will fall against other currencies as foreign financiers' willingness to buy American dollars (to buy American financial assets) subsides. In either case, the American Current Account will shrink to match the reduced capital inflows. For example, if the American dollar falls, imports become more costly for Americans and American exports become cheaper on world markets, and hence the American trade balance improves. On the other hand, if American interest rates rise, the American economy is negatively affected and imports fall, likewise improving the American trade balance and reducing the overall need for capital imports. The International Finance in Practice Box, "The Dollar and the Deficit" (page 68) addresses issues associated with the American Current Account deficit.

Exhibit 3.7 also reveals that Japan has had an unbroken string of Current Account surpluses since 1982 despite the fact that the value of the yen rose steadily until the mid-1990s. As the Balance of Payments dictates, during this period, Japan exported capital (Capital Account deficits). Japan invested heavily in foreign shares and bonds,

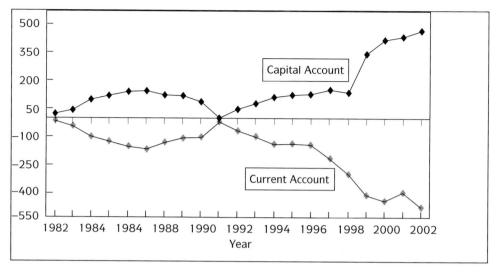

Source: IMF, *International Financial Statistics*, various issues.

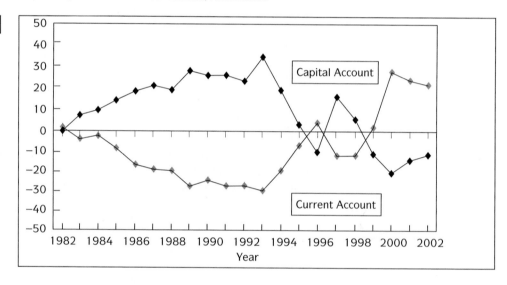

businesses and real estate to recycle its huge and persistent Current Account surpluses. Consequently, Japan emerged as the world's largest creditor nation—largely to the United States—as the United States became overwhelmingly the world's largest debtor nation.

The Current Account imbalances in the United States and Japan evolved over a protracted period of 20 years or so. They are macroeconomic phenomena. To move directly to the issue of what causes much shorter-term movements in the exchange rate, we begin by assuming that at any point in time, the exchange rate between two countries is in equilibrium, a concept to be explored in more detail in Chapter 5.

Any news of an *unexpected* boost to a macroeconomic factor—news that points to greater economic strength or higher interest rates, for example—is likely to trigger a strengthening of that county's currency. For instance, the Canadian dollar is likely to rise relative to the American dollar on news of the following sort:

Statistics Canada Reports Surprise Jump in Canadian Output

The Bank of Canada Announces Higher-than-Expected Interest Rate Hike

Industrial Unemployment Well Below Forecast Values

Exports Up Sharply Above Trend

Oil and Energy Prices Jump 10 Percent

These headlines all suggest an element of surprise in terms of one or another of macroeconomic forces that play on the exchange rate. News that the economy is stronger or more vibrant than was previously thought will generally strengthen the exchange rate, whereas unexpected negative news—concerning economic growth, investment, employment, or exports—will generally cause a nation's currency to weaken. In terms of exchange rate volatility, "news" is, by definition, new and equally likely to be good or bad. Therefore, in the very short-term at least, the movement of the exchange rate is random. Consequently, the best estimate of tomorrow's exchange rate is today's exchange rate.

3.3 Balance-of-Payments Trends in Major Countries

Considering the significant attention that balance-of-payments data receive in the news media, it is useful to closely examine balance-of-payments trends in some of the major countries. Exhibit 3.7 provides the balance on the current account (BCA) as well as the balance on the capital account (BKA) for each of six key countries—the United States, Canada, Germany, the United Kingdom, Japan, and China during the period 1982–2000.

Exhibit 3.8 shows first that the United States has experienced continuous deficits on the current account since 1982 and continuous surpluses on the capital account. Clearly, the magnitude of American current account deficits is far greater than any that other countries ever experienced during the 19-year sample period. In 2003, the American current account deficit reached $500 billion. The American balance-of-payments trend is illustrated in Exhibit 3.8. This situation has led some politicians and commentators to lament that Americans are living far beyond their means. As a matter of fact, the net international investment position of the United States turned negative in 1987 for the first time in decades and continued to deteriorate. The overseas debt burden of the United States—the difference between the value of foreign-owned assets in the United States and the value of American-owned assets abroad—reached about $2,500 billion at the end of 2003, when valued by the replacement cost of the investments made abroad and at home. As recently as 1986, the United States was a net creditor nation, with about $35 billion more in assets overseas than foreigners owned in the United States. The International Finance in Practice box "The Dollar and the Deficit" addresses the issues associated with the American trade deficit.

Second, Exhibit 3.7 reveals that Japan has had an unbroken string of current account surpluses since 1982 despite the fact that the value of the yen rose steadily until the mid-1990s. As can be expected, during this period Japan realized continuous capital account deficits; Japan invested heavily in foreign shares and bonds, businesses, real estate, art objects, and the like to recycle its huge, persistent current account surpluses. Consequently, Japan emerged as the world's largest creditor nation, whereas the United States became the largest debtor nation. The persistent current account disequilibrium has been a major source of friction between Japan and its key trading partners, especially the United States. In fact, Japan has often been criticized for pursuing **mercantilism** to ensure continuous trade surpluses.[7]

Third, like the United States, the United Kingdom recently experienced continuous current account deficits, coupled with capital account surpluses. The magnitude, however, is far less than that of the United States. Germany, on the other hand, traditionally had current account surpluses. Since 1991, however, Germany has been experiencing

---

[7]Mercantilism, which originated in Europe during the period of absolute monarchies, holds that precious metals like gold and silver are the key components of national wealth and that a continuing trade surplus should be a major policy goal as it ensures a continuing inflow of precious metals and, thus, continuous increases in national wealth. Mercantilists, therefore, abhor trade deficits and argue for imposing various restrictions on imports. Mercantilist ideas were criticized by such British thinkers as David Hume and Adam Smith. Both argued that the main source of wealth of a country is its productive capacity, not precious metals.

The Dollar and the Deficit

The dollar is looking vulnerable. It is propped up not by the strength of America's exports but by vast imports of capital. America, a country already rich in capital, has to borrow from abroad almost $2 billion net every working day to cover a current-account deficit forecast to reach almost $500 billion this year.

To most economists, this deficit represents an unsustainable drain on world savings. If the capital inflows were to dry up, some reckon that the dollar could lose a quarter of its value. Only Paul O'Neill, America's treasury secretary, appears unruffled. The current-account deficit, he declares, is a "meaningless concept", which he talks about only because others insist on doing so.

The dollar is not just a matter for America, because the dollar is not just America's currency. Over half of all dollar bills in circulation are held outside American's borders, and almost half of America's Treasury bonds are held as reserves by foreign central banks. The euro cannot yet rival this global reach. International financiers borrow and lend in dollars, and international traders use dollars, even if Americans are at neither end of the deal. No asset since gold has enjoyed such widespread acceptance as a medium of exchange and store of value. In fact, some economists, such as Paul Davidson of the University of Tennessee and Ronald McKinnon of Stanford University, take the argument a step further (see references at end). They argue that the world is on a de facto dollar standard, akin to the 19th-century gold standard.

For roughly a century up to 1914, the world's main currencies were pegged to gold. You could buy an ounce for about four pounds or twenty dollars. The contemporary "dollar standard" is a looser affair. In principle, the world's currencies float in value against each other, but in reality few float freely. Countries fear losing competitiveness on world markets if their currency rises too much against the greenback; they fear inflation if it falls too far. As long as American prices remain stable, the dollar therefore provides an anchor for world currencies and prices, ensuring that they do not become completely unmoored.

In the days of the gold standard, the volume of money and credit in circulation was tied to the amount of gold in a country's vaults. Economies laboured under the "tyranny" of the gold regime, booming when gold was abundant, deflating when it was scarce. The dollar standard is a more liberal system. Central banks retain the right to expand the volume of domestic credit to keep pace with the growth of the home economy.

Eventually, however, growth in the world's economies translates into a growing demand for dollar assets. The more money central banks print, the more dollars they like to hold in reserve to underpin their currency. The more business is done across borders, the more dollars traders need to cover their transactions. If the greenback is the new gold, Alan Greenspan, the Federal Reserve chairman, is the world's alchemist, responsible for concocting enough liquidity to keep world trade bubbling along nicely.

But America can play this role only if it is happy to allow foreigners to build up a huge mass of claims on its assets—and if foreigners are happy to go along. Some economists watch with consternation as the rest of the world's claims on America outstrip America's claims on the rest of the world. As they point out, even a dollar bill is an American liability, a promise of ultimate payment by the US Treasury. Can America keep making these promises to foreigners, without eventually emptying them of value?

According to Mr Davidson, the world cannot risk America stopping. America's external deficit means an extra $500 billion is going into circulation in the world economy each year. If America reined in its current account, international commerce would suffer a liquidity crunch, as it did periodically under the gold standard. Hence America's deficit is neither a "meaningless concept" nor a lamentable drain on world savings. It is an indispensable fount of liquidity for world trade.

Spigot by Nature

But is the deficit sustainable? Many of America's creditors, Mr McKinnon argues, have a stake in preserving the dollar standard, whatever the euro's potential charms. In particular, a large share of America's more liquid assets are held by foreign central banks, particularly in Asia, which dare not offload them for fear of undermining the competitiveness of their own currencies. "Willy nilly," Mr McKinnon says, "foreign governments cannot avoid being important creditors of the United States." China, for one, added $60 billion to its reserves in the year to June by ploughing most of its trade surplus with America back into American assets.

This is not the first time America's external deficits have raised alarm. In 1966, as America's post-war trade surpluses began to dwindle, *The Economist* ran an article entitled "The dollar and world liquidity: a minority view." According to this view, the build-up of dollar claims by foreigners was not a "deficit" in need of "correction". Rather, the American capital market was acting like a global financial intermediary, providing essential liquidity to foreign governments and enterprises. In their own ways, Mr Davidson and Mr McKinnon echo this minority view today. A "correction" of America's current deficit, they say, would create more problems than it would solve. Whether the world's holders of dollars will always agree remains to be seen.

"Financial Markets, Money and the Real World" by Paul Davidson. Edward Elgar 2002.

"The International Dollar Standard and Sustainability of the U.S. Current Account Deficit" by Ronald McKinnon 2001. Available on www.stanford.edu/~mckinnon/papers.htm

Source: *The Economist,* September 14, 2002, p. 74. Reprinted with permission.

current account deficits. This is largely due to German reunification and the resultant need to absorb more output domestically to rebuild the East German region. This has left less output available for exports.

Fourth, like Japan, China tends to have a surplus on current account. Unlike Japan, however, China tends to realize a surplus on capital account as well. In 2002, for instance, China had a $35.4 billion surplus on current account and, at the same time, a $6.4 billion surplus on the capital account. This implies that China's official reserve holdings must have gone up for the year. In fact, China's official reserves have increased sharply in recent years, reaching about $400 billion in 2003.

While perennial balance-of-payments deficits or surpluses can be a problem, each country need not achieve balance-of-payments equilibrium every year. Suppose a country is currently experiencing a trade deficit because of the import demand for capital goods that are necessary for economic development projects. In this case, the trade deficit can be self-correcting in the long run because once the projects are completed, the country may be able to export more or import less by substituting domestic products for foreign imports. In contrast, if the trade deficit is the result of importing consumption goods, the situation will not correct by itself. Thus, what matters is the nature and causes of the disequilibrium.

SUMMARY

1. The balance of payments can be defined as the statistical record of a country's international transactions over a certain period of time presented in the form of double-entry bookkeeping.

2. In the balance of payments, any transaction resulting in a receipt from foreigners is recorded as a credit, with a positive sign, whereas any transaction resulting in a payment to foreigners is recorded as a debit, with a minus sign.

3. A country's international transactions can be grouped into three main categories: the current account, the capital account, and the official reserve account. The current account includes exports and imports of goods and services, whereas the capital account includes all purchases and sales of assets such as shares, bonds, bank accounts, real estate, and businesses. The official reserve account covers all purchases and sales of international reserve assets, such as dollars, foreign exchanges, gold, and SDRs.

4. The current account is divided into four subcategories: merchandise trade, services, factor income, and unilateral transfers. Merchandise trade represents exports and imports of tangible goods, whereas trade in services includes payments and receipts for legal, engineering, consulting, and other performed services and tourist expenditures. Factor income consists of payments and receipts of interest, dividends, and other income on previously made foreign investments. Lastly, unilateral transfer involves unrequited payments, such as gifts, foreign aid, and reparations.

5. The capital account is divided into three subcategories: direct investment, portfolio investment, and other investment. Direct investment involves acquisitions of controlling interests in foreign businesses. Portfolio investment represents investments in foreign shares and bonds that do not involve acquisitions of control. Other investment includes bank deposits, currency investment, trade credit, and the like.

6. When we compute the cumulative balance of payments including the current account, capital account, and the statistical discrepancies, we obtain the overall balance or official settlement balance. The overall balance is indicative of a country's balance-of-payments gap that must be accommodated by official reserve

transactions. If a country must make a net payment to foreigners because of a balance-of-payments deficit, the country should either run down its official reserve assets, such as gold, foreign exchanges, and SDRs, or borrow anew from foreigners.

7. A country can run a balance-of-payments surplus or deficit by increasing or decreasing its official reserves. Under the fixed exchange rate regime, the combined balance on the current and capital accounts will be equal in size, but opposite in sign, to the change in the official reserves. Under the pure flexible exchange rate regime where the central bank does not maintain any official reserves, a current account surplus or deficit must be matched by a capital account deficit or surplus.

KEY WORDS

balance of payments, *57*
balance-of-payments identity (BOPI), *59*
capital account, *59*
current account, *58*

foreign direct investment (FDI), *63*
invisible trade, *61*
J-curve effect, *62*

mercantilism, *67*
portfolio investment, *63*
reserve account, *59*
trade balance, *62*

QUESTIONS

1. Define *balance of payments.*
2. Why would it be useful to examine a country's balance-of-payments data?
3. The United States has run current account deficits continuously since the early 1980s. What do you think are the main causes for the deficits? What are the global consequences of continuous American current account deficits?
4. In contrast to the United States, Japan has realized continuous current account surpluses. What could be the main causes for these surpluses? Is it desirable to have continuous current account surpluses?
5. Comment on the following statement: "When Canada imports more than it exports, it is necessary for Canada to import capital from foreign countries to finance its current account deficits."
6. Explain how a country can run an overall balance-of-payments deficit or surplus.
7. Explain *official reserve assets* and its major components.
8. Explain how to compute the overall balance, and discuss its significance.
9. Since the early 1980s, foreign portfolio investors have purchased a significant portion of U.S. Treasury bond issues. Discuss the short-term and long-term effects of foreigners' portfolio investment on the American balance of payments.
10. Describe the *balance-of-payments identity,* and discuss its implications under the fixed and flexible exchange rate regimes.
11. Occasionally, a country will have a current account deficit and at the same time have a capital account deficit. Explain how this can happen.
12. Explain how each of the following transactions will be classified and recorded in the debit and credit of the Canadian balance of payments:
    a. A Japanese insurance company purchases Government of Ontario bonds and pays out of its bank account kept in Toronto.
    b. A Canadian citizen has a meal at a restaurant in Paris and pays with her Royal Bank VISA card.
    c. An Indian immigrant living in Halifax sends a cheque drawn on his Halifax bank account as a gift to his parents living in New Delhi.

d. A Canadian computer programmer is hired by a British company for consulting and gets paid from a Canadian bank account maintained by the British company.

13. Construct the balance-of-payment table for Japan for the year of 1998 which is comparable in format to Exhibit 3.4, and interpret the numerical data. You may consult *International Financial Statistics* published by the IMF or search for useful websites for the data yourself.

INTERNET EXERCISE

Study the website of the International Monetary Fund (IMF), www.imf.org/external, and discuss the role of the IMF in dealing with balance-of-payment and currency crises.

MINI CASE

Mexico's Balance-of-Payments Problem

Recently, Mexico experienced large-scale trade deficits, depletion of foreign reserve holdings, and a major currency devaluation in December 1994, followed by the decision to freely float the peso. These events also brought about a severe recession and higher unemployment in Mexico. Since the devaluation, however, the trade balance has improved.

Investigate the Mexican experiences in detail, and write a report on the subject. In the report, you may:

1. Document the trend in Mexico's key economic indicators, such as the balance of payments, the exchange rate, and foreign reserve holdings, during the period 1994.1 through 1995.12.

2. Investigate the causes of Mexico's balance-of-payments difficulties prior to the peso devaluation.

3. Discuss what policy actions might have prevented or mitigated the balance-of-payments problem and the subsequent collapse of the peso.

4. Derive lessons from the Mexican experience that may be useful for other developing countries.

In your report, you may identify and address any other relevant issues concerning Mexico's balance-of-payments problem. *International Financial Statistics* published by the IMF provides basic macroeconomic data on Mexico.

REFERENCES & SUGGESTED READINGS

Edwards, Sebastian. *Real Exchange Rates, Devaluation and Adjustment: Exchange Rate Policy in Developing Countries.* Cambridge, Mass.: MIT Press, 1989.

Grabbe, Orlin. *International Financial Markets.* New York: Elsevier, 1991.

Kemp, Donald. "Balance of Payments Concepts—What Do They Really Mean?," *Federal Reserve Bank of St. Louis Review,* (July 1975), pp. 14–23.

Ohmae, Kenichi. "Lies, Damned Lies and Statistics: Why the Trade Deficit Doesn't Matter in a Borderless World," *Journal of Applied Corporate World,* (Winter, 1991), pp. 98–106.

Salop, Joan, and Erich Spitaller. "Why Does the Current Account Matter?" International Monetary Fund, *Staff Papers,* (March 1980), pp. 101–34.

U.S. Department of Commerce. "Report of the Advisory Committee on the Presentation of the Balance of Payments Statistics," *Survey of Current Business,* (June, 1991), pp. 18–25.

Yeager, Leland. *International Monetary Relations.* New York: Harper & Row, 1965.

The Relationship between Balance of Payments and National Income Accounting

This section is designed to explore the mathematical relationship between balance-of-payments accounting and national income accounting and to discuss the implications of this relationship. National income (Y), or gross national product (GNP), is identically equal to the sum of nominal consumption (C) of goods and services, private investment expenditures (I), government expenditures (G), and the difference between exports (X) and imports (M) of goods and services:

$$\text{GNP} \equiv Y \equiv C + I + G + X - M. \tag{3A.1}$$

Private savings (S) is defined as the amount left from national income after consumption and taxes (T) are paid:

$$S \equiv Y - C - T, \text{ or} \tag{3A.2}$$

$$S \equiv C + I + G + X - M - C - T. \tag{3A.3}$$

Noting that the BCA ≡ X − M, equation (3A.3) can be rearranged as:

$$(S - I) + (T - G) \equiv X - M \equiv \text{BCA}. \tag{3A.4}$$

Equation (3A.4) shows that there is an intimate relationship between a country's BCA and how the country finances its domestic investment and pays for government expenditures. In equation (3A.4), (S − I) is the difference between a country's savings and investment. If (S − I) is negative, it implies that a country's domestic savings is insufficient to finance domestic investment. Similarly, (T − G) is the difference between tax revenue and government expenditures. If (T − G) is negative, it implies that tax revenue is insufficient to cover government spending and a government budget deficit exists. This deficit must be financed by the government issuing debt securities.

Equation (3A.4) also shows that when a country imports more than it exports, its BCA will be negative because through trade foreigners obtain a larger claim to domestic assets than the claim the country's citizens obtain to foreign assets. Consequently, when BCA is negative, it implies that government budget deficits and/or part of domestic investment are being financed with foreign-controlled capital. In order for a country to reduce a BCA deficit, one of the following must occur:

1. For a given level of S and I, the government budget deficit (T − G) must be reduced.
2. For a given level of I and (T − G), S must be increased.
3. For a given level S and (T − G), I must fall.

The Market for Foreign Exchange

CALPERS, THE CALIFORNIA pension fund, purchases one million Canadian dollars in order to buy shares in Research in Motion of Waterloo. DeutscheBank of Frankfurt arranges to buy 10 million Canadian dollars for a German customer who is purchasing real estate in Nova Scotia. WisconsinAir of Milwaukee needs 200 million Canadian dollars to acquire a fleet of commuter airplanes from Bombardier of Montreal. A construction firm in Tokyo buys 15 million Canadian dollars to pay for a shipment of softwood lumber from British Columbia.

These sorts of transactions—industrial firms and financial institutions buying Canadian dollars with foreign currency—take place every day in the world of international trade and cross-border investment. The purchase of Canadian dollars with foreign currency is a crucial step taken by foreigners to pay for Canadian exports or to invest in Canadian financial assets.

Likewise, Canadians and non-Canadians alike use their Canadian dollars to buy foreign currencies—for example, American dollars, euros, yen, or Swedish krona. The Alberta Treasury might buy 10 million American dollars to retire a bond denominated in American dollars that the province had issued five years ago. Or Magna, the giant auto parts manufacturer in Ontario, goes to its bank to buy 15 million euros to pay for machinery imported from Germany. Perhaps Volvo (Canada) of Halifax buys five million Swedish krona to pay management fees to the Volvo head office in Sweden. Calpers of California, mentioned above, would be selling Canadian dollars if it decided to unwind its position in Research in Motion.

Firms, governments, financial institutions, and ordinary citizens are frequently involved—indeed they are constantly involved, if we look at it at a reasonable level of aggregation—in purchases of foreign currencies to buy foreign things (imports) from foreign suppliers. Foreign currencies are also required by those who want to make financial investments in foreign assets or to retire outstanding foreign debt.

The purchase of Canadian dollars with foreign currencies and the purchase of foreign currencies with Canadian dollars are typical transactions in the global market for foreign exchange. The purpose of this chapter is to describe this fascinating market in some detail, outlining its functions and operations as well as its institutional make-up. Our concerns are Canadian, but our perspective is global.

The market for foreign exchange is the largest financial market in the world by virtually any standard. It is open somewhere in the world every day, 24 hours a day. The market is involved in products—currencies and contracts related to currencies—that are liquid, costless to store and transportable at the speed of light. In 2002, The Bank of International Settlements (BIS) estimated the worldwide daily volume of trading in the spot and forward foreign exchange at US$1.2 trillion. This is equivalent to US$300 per day for every person on earth. Exhibit 4.1 presents a pie chart showing the shares of global foreign exchange turnover.

Broadly defined, the **foreign exchange (FX or FOREX)** market encompasses the conversion of purchasing power from one country into another—as when American purchasing power comes to Canada to buy Bombardier aircraft—but in addition the FX market involves bank deposits of foreign currency, credit denominated in foreign currency, foreign trade financing, trading in foreign currency options and futures contracts, and currency swaps. One chapter cannot adequately cover all these topics. In this chapter, we confine our discussion to the spot and forward markets for foreign exchange. Later, in Chapter 9, we examine currency futures and options contract, and in Chapter 10, we look at swaps.

This chapter begins with an overview of the function and structure of the foreign exchange market and the major market participants that trade currencies in this market. Following is a discussion of the spot market for foreign exchange. This section explains how to read spot market quotations, derives cross-rate quotations, and develops the concept of triangular arbitrage as a means of ensuring market efficiency. The chapter concludes with a discussion of the forward market for foreign exchange. Forward market quotations are presented, the purpose of the market is discussed, and the purpose of swap rate quotations is explained.

This chapter lays the foundation for much of the discussion throughout the remainder of the text. Without a solid understanding of how the foreign exchange market works, international finance cannot be studied in an intelligent manner. As authors, we urge you to read this chapter carefully and thoughtfully.

www.ny.frb.org.

This is the website of the Federal Reserve Bank of New York. The online article titled "The Basics of Foreign Trade and Exchange" can be downloaded for study. The report titled *The Foreign Exchange and Interest Rate Derivatives Markets Survey: Turnover in the United States* can also be downloaded.

4.1   Function and Structure of the FOREX Market

The structure of the foreign exchange market is an outgrowth of one of the primary functions of a commercial banker: to assist clients in the conduct of international commerce. For example, a corporate client desiring to import merchandise from abroad would need a source for foreign exchange if the import was invoiced in the exporter's home currency. Alternatively, the exporter might need a way to dispose of foreign

EXHIBIT 4.1

Shares of Reported Global Foreign Exchange Turnover, 2001

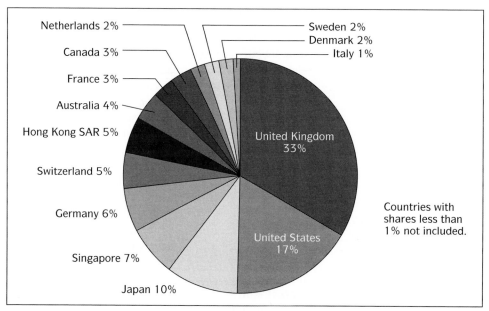

Note: Percent of total reporting foreign exchange turnover, adjusted for intracountry double-counting.
Source: *Foreign Currency Exchange,* Federal Reserve Bank of New York, www.ny.frb.org.

exchange if payment for the export was invoiced and received in the importer's home currency. Assisting in foreign exchange transactions of this type is one of the services that commercial banks provide for their clients and one that bank customers expect from their bank.

The spot and forward foreign exchange market is an **over-the-counter (OTC) market**; that is, trading does not take place in a central marketplace where buyers and sellers congregate. Rather, the foreign exchange market is a worldwide linkage of bank currency traders, nonbank dealers, and FX brokers who assist in trades connected to one another via a network of telephones, telex machines, computer terminals, and automated dealing systems. Reuters and EBS are the largest vendors of quote screen monitors used in trading currencies. The communications system of the foreign exchange market is second to none, including industry, governments, the military, and national security and intelligence operations.

Twenty-four-hour-a-day currency trading follows the sun around the globe. Three major market segments can be identified: Australasia, Europe, and North America. Australasia includes the trading centres of Sydney, Tokyo, Hong Kong, Singapore, and Bahrain; Europe includes Zurich, Frankfurt, Paris, Brussels, Amsterdam, and London; and North America includes New York, Montreal, Toronto, Chicago, San Francisco, and Los Angeles. Most trading rooms operate over a nine- to 12-hour working day, although some banks have experimented with operating three eight-hour shifts in order to trade around the clock. Especially active trading takes place when the trading hours of the Australasia centres and the European centres overlap and when the European and North American centres overlap. More than half of the trading in North America occurs between 8:00 A.M. and noon eastern standard time (1:00 P.M. and 5:00 P.M. Greenwich Mean Time [London]), when the European markets were still open. Certain trading centres have a more dominant effect on the market than others. For example, trading diminishes dramatically in the Australasian market segment when the Tokyo traders are taking their lunch break! Exhibit 4.2 provides a general indication of the participation level in the global FX market by showing electronic trades per hour.

FX Market Participants

The market for foreign exchange can be viewed as a two-tier market. One tier is the **wholesale** or **interbank market** and the other tier is the **retail** or **client market**. FX market participants can be categorized into five groups: international banks, bank customers, nonbank dealers, FX brokers, and central banks.

International banks provide the core of the FX market. Approximately 100 to 200 banks worldwide actively "make a market" in foreign exchange, that is, they stand will-

EXHIBIT 4.2

The Circadian Rhythms of the FX Market

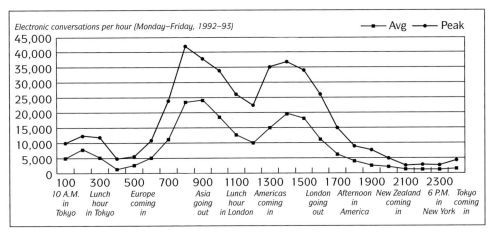

Electronic conversations per hour (Monday–Friday, 1992–93) —■— Avg —●— Peak

Note: Time (0100–2400 hours, Greenwich Mean Time).
Source: Sam Y. Cross, *All About the Foreign Exchange Market in the United States,* Federal Reserve Bank of New York, www.ny.frb.org.

ing to buy or sell foreign currency for their own account. These international banks serve their retail clients, the *bank customers,* in conducting foreign commerce or making international investment in financial assets that require foreign exchange. Bank customers broadly include multinational corporations (MNCs), money managers, and private speculators. According to 2002 BIS statistics, retail or bank client transactions account for approximately 13 percent of FX trading volume. The other 87 percent of trading volume is from interbank trades between international banks or nonbank dealers. *Nonbank dealers* are large nonbank financial institutions, such as investment banks, whose size and frequency of trades make it cost-effective to establish their own dealing rooms to trade directly in the interbank market for their foreign exchange needs. Nonbank dealers account for approximately 30 percent of interbank trading volume.

Part of the interbank trading among international banks involves adjusting the inventory positions they hold in various foreign currencies. However, most interbank trades are *speculative* or *arbitrage* transactions, where market participants attempt to correctly judge the future direction of price movements in one currency versus another or attempt to profit from temporary price discrepancies in currencies between competing dealers. Market psychology is a key ingredient in currency trading, and a dealer can often infer another's trading intention from the currency position being accumulated.

FX brokers match dealer orders to buy and sell currencies for a fee but do not take a position themselves. Brokers have knowledge of the quotes offered by many dealers in the market. Consequently, interbank traders will use a broker primarily to disseminate as quickly as possible a currency quote to many other dealers. In recent years, since the introduction and increased usage of electronic dealing systems, the use of brokers has declined because the computerized systems duplicate many of the same services at much lower fees. The BIS reports that among major currency pairs, about 50 to 70 percent of turnover is conducted through electronic dealing systems.

Since the exchange *rate* is determined in the market for foreign exchange and since the exchange rate is of crucial concern to government and policy makers, there is a question of the extent to which governments—through their central banks—should intervene in the foreign exchange market in order to push the exchange rate up or down. A lower exchange rate, for example, encourages exports and discourages imports. Such matters are of particular concern in Canada where 45 percent of our GDP is touched by trade and more than 85 percent of our trade involves just one country, the United States. On the specific issue of *exchange rate intervention* by the Bank of Canada, the key point is that the Bank does not do much of it. First of all, large as it is, the Bank of Canada is still a very small player in the foreign exchange market, even for the Canadian dollar. The main policy instrument that the Bank uses to influence the exchange rate (and also inflation) is the interest rate. The Bank is in a position to influence Canadian short-term interest rates. A bump-up in Canadian short-term interest rates attracts foreign capital to Canada and, in the process, this raises demand for Canadian dollars, which, in turn, puts upward pressure on the exchange rate. Lowering Canadian short-term interest rates has the opposite effect.

In fact, the central banks of most industrial countries remain largely neutral in the international markets for foreign exchange. They are involved to the extent that they deal in foreign exchange for operational purposes, for example, as they manage their nations' foreign exchange reserves. However, central banks of industrialized nations seldom intervene actively to achieve a specific value for their exchange rate. They, at most, serve a stabilizing function, dampening some of the volatility in the exchange in times of particular stress, such as during the political uncertainty that gripped Canada during the 1995 Quebec Referendum on Separation or amidst the global chaos of the Asian Financial Crisis of 1997. Other, less dramatic episodes call for a regular steadying influence of the central bank.

There is little evidence that industrialized countries can effectively intervene in the foreign exchange market to influence the value of their exchange rate for any length of time. Perhaps the best known recent cases that illustrate the limits to central banks' power to resist the relentless forces of foreign exchange markets occurred in the early 1990s when both the United Kingdom and Italy lost huge volumes of foreign exchange reserves as well as the battle to maintain the value of their currencies—the pound and the lira—at exchange rates to which they made commitments to the European Monetary System.

Japan is somewhat of an exception to the passivity of central banks. Japan has been more willing than most industrialized nations to intervene in the foreign exchange market for extended periods. It has proven to be a costly exercise. The International Finance in Practice box on page 78 provides an interesting insight into a day in the life of a central bank trader for the Bank of Japan.

Correspondent Banking Relationships

The interbank market is a network of **correspondent banking relationships**, with large commercial banks maintaining demand deposit accounts with one another, called correspondent banking accounts. The correspondent bank account network allows for the efficient functioning of the foreign exchange market.

> **EXAMPLE 4.1** **Correspondent Banking Relationship** As an example of how the network of correspondent bank accounts facilitates international foreign exchange transactions, consider Ottawa Importer arranging the finance of an order of merchandise from Dutch Exporter of Amsterdam. The order is invoiced in euros at €200,000. Ottawa Importer will contact his local bank, CIBC, and inquire about the €/$ exchange rate. The quote is €1 = $1.53. If Ottawa Importer accepts this exchange rate, then CIBC will debit Ottawa Importer's demand deposit account for $306,000, which equals €200,000 times $1.53. CIBC will instruct its correspondent bank in Amsterdam, ING, to debit CIBC's correspondent bank account €200,000 and to credit that amount to Dutch Exporter. CIBC will then debit its books €200,000 as an offset to the $306,000 debit to Ottawa Importer's account, to reflect the decrease in its correspondent bank account with ING. ∎

This rather contrived example assumes that CIBC and Dutch Exporter both have bank accounts with ING. A more realistic interpretation is to recognize that within Europe, the sophistication of the banking system is such that Ottawa Importer can directly contact its correspondent bank in Holland, say ING, confident that ING will have relationships with Dutch Importer's bank and will hold funds and release funds for Ottawa Importer appropriate to the shipment.

The *Society for Worldwide Interbank Financial Telecommunications (SWIFT)* allows international commercial banks to communicate instructions of the type in this example to one another. SWIFT is a private nonprofit message transfer system with headquarters in Brussels with intercontinental switching centres in the Netherlands and in the United States (which serves Canada). The *Clearing House Interbank Payments System (CHIPS)* provides a clearinghouse for the interbank settlements (primarily in American dollars) between intenational banks. Returning to our example, suppose CIBC first needed to purchase euros in order to have them for transfer to Dutch Exporter. CIBC can use CHIPS for settling the purchase of euros from American dollars from, say, Barclays, with instructions via SWIFT to Barclays to deposit the euros in its account with ING and to ING to transfer ownership to Dutch Exporter. The transfer between Barclays and ING would, in turn, be executed through correspondent bank accounts or through the European clearinghouse.

In August 1995, *Exchange Clearing House Limited (ECHO)*, the first global clearinghouse for settling interbank FOREX transactions, began operation. ECHO was a multilateral netting system that on each settlement date netted a client's payments and receipts in each currency, regardless of whether they are due to or from multiple

INTERNATIONAL FINANCE
IN PRACTICE

Fearless Dealers

Central-Bank Traders Have an Advantage: Their Employers Don't Demand Profits

Tokyo—Tetsuya Nishida says his wife will be relieved when he gets his next assignment at the Bank of Japan.

Right now, the 32-year-old Mr. Nishida is a front-line soldier in the central bank's struggle to rein in the currency markets. He's one of nine currency traders at the Bank of Japan's cluttered, second-floor trading desk in downtown Tokyo. It's a grueling job; Mr. Nishida starts watching the markets when he wakes at 6 A.M. and often doesn't finish work until 11 P.M.

The past year, Mr. Nishida's trades often haven't been the least bit profitable. But that's part of his mission.

Of all central banks, the Bank of Japan has battled currency speculators the hardest. By some estimates, it bought more than $50 billion of dollars in the two years ended March 31, 1988, even though the dollar kept falling in value. With only limited success, Mr. Nishida and his colleagues were selling valuable yen in hopes of braking the dollar's fall.

A shy, conservatively dressed man, Mr. Nishida never set out to be a big-time currency trader. He was an English major at Sophia University in Japan, unlike most Bank of Japan employees, who studied law or economics at prestigious Tokyo University. When Mr. Nishida joined the central bank, he headed into the more tranquil research department. That job let him hone his English for a year at Johns Hopkins University in Baltimore.

But the Bank of Japan's tradition is to rotate employees through a wide range of departments. That's a big contrast with, say, the U.S. or West German central banks, which prefer to have lifetime currency dealers. So in June 1987, Mr. Nishida's turn came up.

Trading currencies "is just one step in one's overall career at the bank," says Zenta Nakajima, head of the foreign-exchange division at the Bank of Japan. "We don't train [dealers]. They've got to pick up expertise while they're here."

Mr. Nishida took quickly to his new setting. "This is the only place in the bank where you can get a real sense of market activities," he says. Upon awakening on a typical day, Mr. Nishida scans the newspapers and television for news of overnight markets and heads for the office. Before an 8 A.M. meeting, he reads the overnight messages from central banks around the world and phones dealers at Japanese and foreign banks in Tokyo.

Mr. Nishida won't talk about his trades, but central-bank dealers often trade in $10 million or bigger chunks. On a busy day, they can pound the market with as much as $500 million or $1 billion of total buying or selling. An advantage of working for a central bank, as opposed to a private bank, is that dealers don't have to worry about turning a profit.

"The important thing for central bankers is to be able to part with dollars or yen and not look back," says Richard Koo, senior economist at the Nomura Research Institute. "Their strength in the market comes from the fact that they can toss dollars and yen and not suffer losses." Other traders "fear those who have nothing to lose," Mr. Koo adds.

Recent market conditions suggest that the Bank of Japan's dollar-buying binge has earned some vindication. Exchange-rate stability of a sort has been achieved, and the Japanese economy is growing briskly with little threat of inflation.

As for Mr. Nishida, he says he faces plenty of stress but survives by always trying to look ahead. "I don't continue to be sorry for things already done," he says. "We may make some mistakes. But my motto is to forget about what isn't necessary."

Source: Kathryn Graven, *The Wall Street Journal*, September 23, 1988, p. R31. Reprinted by permission of *The Wall Street Journal*, ©1988 Dow Jones & Company, Inc. All Rights Reserved Worldwide.

counterparties. Multilateral netting eliminates the risk and inefficiency of individual settlement. In 1997, CLS Services Limited merged with ECHO. Currently, operation of the system has been suspended.

4.2 The Spot Market

The **spot market** involves almost the immediate purchase or sale of foreign exchange. Typically, cash settlement is made two business days (excluding holidays of either the buyer or the seller) after the transaction for trades between the American dollar and a non–North American currency. For regular spot trades between the American dollar

EXHIBIT 4.3

Average Daily Foreign Exchange Turnover by Instrument and Counterparty, 2004

Instrument/Counterparty	Turnover in US$ (millions)		Percent
Spot		$621	35
With reporting dealers	301		20
With other financial institutions	213		10
With nonfinancial customers	108		5
Outright Forwards		208	12
With reporting dealers	73		4
With other financial institutions	80		4
With nonfinancial customers	56		4
Foreign Exchange Swaps		944	53
With reporting dealers	562		35
With other financial institutions	293		14
With nonfinancial customers	89		4
Total		$1,880	100

Note: Turnover is net of local and cross-border interdealer double-counting.
Source: Table E.1.1 in the *Triennial Central Bank Survey*, Bank for International Settlements, Basle, September 2004.

and the Mexican peso or the Canadian dollar, settlement takes only one business day.[1] According to BIS statistics, spot foreign exchange trading accounted for 33 percent of FX trades in 2001. Exhibit 4.3 provides a detailed analysis of foreign exchange turnover by instrument and counterparty.

Spot Rate Quotations

Spot rate currency quotations can be stated in direct or indirect terms. To understand the difference, let us refer to Exhibit 4.4. The exhibit shows currency quotations for November 3, 2003. The first two columns provide **direct quotations** from the American perspective, that is, the price of one unit of the foreign currency priced in American dollars. For example, the spot quote for one British pound is $1.6944. (Forward quotations for one-, three-, and six-month contracts, which will be discussed in a following section, appear directly under the spot quotations for four currencies.) The second two columns provide **indirect quotations** from the American perspective, that is, the price of one American dollar in the foreign currency. For example, in the third column, we see that the Monday spot quote for one dollar in British pound sterling is £0.5902. Obviously, the direct quotation from the American perspective is an indirect quote from the British viewpoint, and the indirect quote from the American perspective is a direct quote from the British viewpoint.

It is common practice among currency traders worldwide to both price and trade currencies against the American dollar. For example, BIS statistics indicate that in 2004, 89 percent of currency trading in the world involved the American dollar on one side of the transaction. In recent years, however, the use of other currencies has been increasing, especially in dealing done by smaller regional banks. For example, in Europe many European currencies were traded against the deutschemark. Overall, in 2004, 37 percent of all currency trading worldwide involved the euro on one side of the transaction. With respect to other major currencies, 20 percent involved the Japanese yen, 17 percent the British pound, 6 percent the Swiss franc, and 4 percent the Canadian dollar. Exhibit 4.5 provides a detailed analysis of foreign exchange turnover by currency.

---

[1]The banknote market for converting small amounts of foreign exchange, which travellers are familiar with, is different from the spot market.

EXHIBIT 4.4

Exchange Rates

	US$ Equivalent	Local Currency per US$	Canadian $ Equivalent	Local Currency per Canadian $
The foreign exchange mid-range rates below apply to trading among banks in amounts of US$1 million or more as quoted at 4 p.m Eastern time by Reuters and other sources. Retail transactions provide fewer units of foreign currency per dollar.				
Argentina (Peso)	0.3490	2.8653	0.4602	2.1728
Australia (Dollar)	0.7078	1.4128	0.9334	1.0714
Bahrain (Dinar)	2.6525	0.3770	3.4979	0.2859
Brazil (Real)	0.3489	2.8662	0.4601	2.1735
Canada (Dollar)	0.7583	1.3187	1.0000	1.0000
1-month forward	0.7572	1.3207	—	—
3-months forward	0.7552	1.3242	—	—
6-months forward	0.7525	1.3289	—	—
Chile (Peso)	0.001596	627	0.002105	475
China (Renminbi)	0.1208	8.2781	0.1593	6.2775
Colombia (Peso)	0.0003477	2876	0.0005	2181
Czech Republic (Koruna)	0.03618	27.6396	0.0477	20.9597
Denmark (Krone)	0.1558	6.4185	0.2055	4.8673
Ecuador (US Dollar)	1.0000	1.0000	1.3187	0.7583
Egypt (Pound)	0.1634	6.1200	0.2155	4.6409
Hong Kong (Dollar)	0.1288	7.7640	0.1698	5.8876
Hungary (Forint)	0.004447	224.87	0.005864	170.5245
India (Rupee)	0.022070	45.3104	0.029104	34.3599
Indonesia (Rupiah)	0.000118	8496	0.000155	6443
Israel (Shekel)	0.2226	4.4924	0.2935	3.4067
Japan (Yen)	0.009096	109.94	0.011995	83.3688
1-month forward	0.009104	109.84	0.012005	83.2955
3-months forward	0.009124	109.60	0.012032	83.1130
6-months forward	0.009152	109.27	0.012069	82.8587
Jordan (Dinar)	1.4104	0.7090	1.8599	0.5377
Kuwait (Dinar)	3.3972	0.2944	4.4799	0.2232
Lebanon (Pound)	0.000661	1514	0.000871	1148
Malaysia (Ringgit)	0.2632	3.7994	0.3471	2.8812
Malta (Lira)	2.7185	0.3678	3.5849	0.2789
Mexico (Peso)	0.0908	11.0132	0.1197	8.3516
New Zealand (Dollar)	0.6137	1.6295	0.8093	1.2357
Norway (Krone)	0.1407	7.1073	0.1855	5.3896
Pakistan (Rupee)	0.017430	57.3723	0.022985	43.5067
Peru (new Sol)	0.2879	3.4734	0.3797	2.6340
Philippines (Peso)	0.018050	55.4017	0.023803	42.0123
Poland (Zloty)	0.2477	4.0371	0.3266	3.0615
Russia (Ruble)	0.033380	29.9581	0.044018	22.7179
Saudi Arabia (Riyal)	0.2666	3.7509	0.3516	2.8444
Singapore (Dollar)	0.5749	1.7394	0.7581	1.3191
Slovak Republic (Koruna)	0.027950	35.7782	0.036858	27.1314
South Africa (Rand)	0.1452	6.8871	0.1915	5.2226
South Korea (Won)	0.000845	1183	0.001114	897
Sweden (Krona)	0.1277	7.8309	0.1684	5.9383
Switzerland (Franc)	0.7459	1.3407	0.9836	1.0167
1-month forward	0.7464	1.3398	0.9843	1.0160
3-months forward	0.7476	1.3376	0.9859	1.0143
6-months forward	0.7492	1.3348	0.9880	1.0122
Taiwan (Dollar)	0.02947	33.9328	0.0389	25.7320
Thailand (Baht)	0.02503	39.9521	0.0330	30.2965
Turkey (Lira)	0.00000067	1492537	0.00000088	1131825
United Kingdom (Pound)	1.6944	0.5902	2.2344	0.4475
1-month forward	1.6907	0.5915	2.2295	0.4485
3-months forward	1.6826	0.5943	2.2188	0.4507
6-months forward	1.6705	0.5986	2.2029	0.4539
United Arab (Dirham)	0.2723	3.6724	0.3591	2.7849
Uruguay (Peso)	0.0351	28.4900	0.0463	21.6046
Venezuela (Bolivar)	0.000626	1597.44	0.000826	1211.38
SDR (IMF)	1.4318	0.6984	1.8881	0.5296
Euro	1.1584	0.8633	1.5276	0.6546

Special Drawing Rights (SDR) are based on a weighted sum of exchange rates for the American dollar, Euro, British pound, and Japanese yen.

Source: *The Wall Street Journal*, 3 November, 2003. Reprinted by permission of *The Wall Street Journal*, 2002 Dow Jones & Company, Inc. All Rights Reserved Worldwide. Canadian dollar figures are authors' calculations from the American dollar data.

EXHIBIT 4.5

Average Daily Foreign Exchange Turnover by Currency against All Other Currencies, 2004

Currency	Turnover Stated in US$ (000)	Percent
American dollar	$1,667,560	89
Euro	689,360	37
Japanese yen	381,640	20
Pound sterling	317,720	17
Swiss franc	114,680	6
Canadian dollar	78,960	4
Australian dollar	103,400	6
Other currencies	198,340	11
Total—double-counted	$3,760,000	200
Total—not double-counted	$1,880,000	100

Note: Since there are two sides to each transaction, each currency is reported twice. Turnover is net of local and cross-border interdealer double-counting. Estimated gaps in reporting of $27,000,000 brings the total to approximately $1,880,000,000, the estimated daily average turnover figure.
Source: Tabulated from data in Table E.1.1 in the *Triennial Central Bank Survey*, Bank for International Settlements, Basle, September 2004.

Most currencies in the interbank market are quoted in **European terms**, that is, the American dollar is priced in terms of the foreign currency (an indirect quote from the American perspective). By convention, however, it is standard practice to price certain currencies in terms of the American dollar, or in what is referred to as **American terms** (a direct quote from the American perspective). Prior to 1971, the British pound was a nondecimal currency; that is, a pound was not naturally divisible into 10 subcurrency units. Thus, it was cumbersome to price decimal currencies in terms of the pound. By necessity, the practice developed of pricing the British pound, as well as the Australian dollar, New Zealand dollar, and Irish punt in terms of decimal currencies, and this convention continues today. When the common euro currency was introduced, it was decided that it also would be quoted in American terms. To the uninitiated, this can be confusing, and it is something to bear in mind when examining currency quotations.

In this textbook, we will use the following notation for spot rate quotations. In general, $S(j/k)$ will refer to the price of one unit of currency k in terms of currency j. Thus, the American term quote for an American dollar in exchange for British pounds on Monday, November 1, is $S(\$/£) = 1.6944$. The corresponding European quote is $S(£/\$) = £0.5902$. When the context is clear as to what terms the quotation is in, the less cumbersome S will be used to denote the spot rate.

It should be intuitive that the American and European term quotes are reciprocals of one another. That is,

$$S(\$/£) = \frac{1}{S(£/\$)}$$

$$1.6944 = \frac{1}{0.5902} \tag{4.1}$$

and

$$S(£/\$) = \frac{1}{S(\$/£)}$$

$$0.5902 = \frac{1}{1.6944} \tag{4.2}$$

The Bid-Ask Spread

Up to this point in our discussion, we have ignored the bid-ask spread in FX transactions. Interbank FX traders buy currency for inventory at the **bid price** and sell from inventory at the higher **offer** or **ask price**. Consider the Reuters quotations from Exhibit 4.4. What are they, bid or ask? In a manner of speaking, the answer is both, depending on whether one is referring to the American or European term quotes. Note the wording directly under the *Exchange Rates* title. The key to our inquiry is the sentence that reads: "Retail transactions provide fewer units of foreign currency per dollar." The word "provide" implies that the quotes in the third and fourth columns under the "Currency per U.S. $" heading are buying, or bid quotes. Thus the European term quotations are interbank bid prices.

To be more specific about the £/$ quote we have been using as an example, we can specify that it is a bid quote by writing $S(£/\$_b) = 0.5902$, meaning the bank dealer will bid, or pay, £0.5902 for one dollar. However, if the bank dealer is buying dollars for British pound sterling, it must be selling British pounds for American dollars. This implies that the $/£ quote we have been using as an example is an ask quote, which we can designate as $S(\$/£_a) = 1.6944$. That is, the bank dealer will sell one British pound for $ 1.6944.

Returning to the reciprocal relationship between European and American term quotations, the recognition of the bid-ask spread implies:

$$S(\$/£_a) = \frac{1}{S(£/\$_b)} \qquad\qquad (4.3)$$

In American terms, the bank dealer is asking $1.6944 for one British pound; that means the bank dealer is willing to pay, or bid, less. Interbank bid-ask spreads are quite small. Let us assume the bid price is $0.0005 less than the ask; thus, $S(\$/£_b) = 1.6939$. Similarly, the bank dealer will want an ask price in European terms greater than its bid price. The reciprocal relationship between European and American term quotes implies:

$$S(£/\$_a) = \frac{1}{S(\$/£_b)} \qquad\qquad (4.4)$$

$$= \frac{1}{1.6939}$$

$$= 0.5904$$

Thus, the bank dealer's ask price of £0.5904 per dollar is, indeed, greater than its bid price of £0.5902.

Spot FX Trading

Exhibit 4.4 indicates that for most currencies, quotations are carried out to four decimal places in both American and European terms. However, for some currencies (e.g., the Japanese yen, Slovakian koruna, South Korean won) quotations in European terms are carried out only to two or three decimal places, but in American terms, the quotations may be carried out to as many as eight decimal places (see, for example, the Turkish lira).

In the interbank market, the standard-size trade among large banks in the major currencies is for the American-dollar equivalent of $10,000,000, or "ten dollars" in trader jargon. Dealers quote both the bid and the ask, willing to either buy or sell up to $10,000,000 at the quoted prices. Spot quotations are good for only a few seconds. If a trader cannot immediately make up his mind whether to buy or sell at the proffered prices, the quotes are likely to be withdrawn.

In conversation, interbank FX traders use a shorthand abbreviation in expressing spot currency quotations. Consider the $/£ bid-ask quotes from above, $1.6939–$1.6944. The "1.69" is known as the *big figure,* and it is assumed to be known by all traders. The second two digits to the right of the decimal place are referred to as the *small figure.*

Since spot bid-ask spreads are typically around 5 "points," it is unambiguous for a trader to respond with "39–44" when asked what is his quote for British pound sterling. Similarly, "97 to 02" is a sufficient response for a quote of $1.6997–$1.7002, where the big figures are 1.69 and 1.70, respectively, for the bid and ask quotes.

The establishment of the bid-ask spread will facilitate acquiring or disposing of inventory. Suppose most $/£ dealers are trading at $1.6939–$1.6944. A trader believing the pound will soon appreciate substantially against the dollar will desire to acquire a larger inventory of British pounds. A quote of "40–45" will encourage some traders to sell at the higher than market bid price but also dissuade other traders from purchasing at the higher offer price. Analogously, a quote of "38–43" will allow a dealer to lower his pound inventory if he thinks the pound is ready to depreciate.

The retail bid-ask spread is wider than the interbank spread; that is, lower bid and higher ask prices apply to the smaller sums traded at the retail level. This is necessary to cover the fixed costs of a transaction that exist regardless of which tier the trade is made in.

Interbank trading rooms are typically organized with individual traders dealing in a particular currency. The dealing rooms of large banks are set up with traders dealing against the American dollar in all the major currencies: the Japanese yen, euro, Canadian dollar, Swiss franc, and British pound, plus the local currency if it is not one of the majors. Individual banks may also specialize by making a market in regional currencies or in the currencies of less-developed countries, again all versus the American dollar. Additionally, banks will usually have a cross-rate desk where trades between two currencies not involving the American dollar are handled. It is not uncommon for a trader of an active currency pair to make as many as 1,500 quotes and 400 trades in a day. In smaller European banks accustomed to more regional trading, dealers will frequently quote and trade versus the euro.

A bank trading room is a noisy, busy place. Currency traders are typically young, high-energy people, who are capable of interpreting new information quickly and making high-stakes decisions. The International Finance in Practice box on pages 84–85, titled "Young Traders Run Currency Markets," depicts the sense of excitement and the electric atmosphere one finds in a bank dealing room.

Cross-Exchange Rate Quotations

Let us ignore the transaction costs of trading temporarily while we develop the concept of a cross-rate. A **cross-exchange rate** is an exchange rate between a currency pair where neither currency is the American dollar. It is useful to bear in mind that in 90 percent of foreign currency transactions, regardless of where they occur, the American dollar is on one side of the transaction. The cross-exchange rate can be calculated from the American dollar exchange rates for the two currencies, using either European or American term quotations. For example, the €/£ cross-rate can be calculated from American term quotations as follows:

$$S(\text{€/£}) = \frac{S(\$/\text{£})}{S(\$/\text{€})} \qquad (4.5)$$

where from Exhibit 4.4,

$$S(\text{€/£}) = \frac{1.6944}{1.1584} = 1.4627$$

That is, if £1 cost $1.6944 and €1 cost $1.1584, the cost of £1 in euros is €1.4627. In European terms, the calculation is

$$S(\text{€/£}) = \frac{S(\text{€/\$})}{S(\text{£/\$})} \qquad (4.6)$$

$$= \frac{0.8633}{0.5902}$$

$$= 1.4627.$$

Young Traders Run Currency Markets

NEW YORK—Surrounded by flashing currency prices, ringing phones and screaming traders, Fred Scala offers his view of people who use economic analysis to forecast currency rates. "They may be right," he says, "but they don't know how to pull the trigger."

Mr. Scala knows how.

At age 27, he is Manufacturers Hanover Trust Co.'s top dealer in German marks. Yesterday morning alone, he traded about $500 million in marks, darting in and out of the market 100 times. As the dollar inched up, he bought. As it retreated, he sold. "We're mercenaries, soldiers of fortune," he says. "We have no alliances. We work for the bank."

Currency traders like Mr. Scala are riding high these days. As politicians dicker about what to do about the dollar after last month's stock-market crash, young traders at the world's top 30 to 50 banks hold day-to-day control of the currency markets. And unlike their shell-shocked counterparts at stock-trading desks, currency dealers are making nearly all the right bets.

Bravo for Lira Trader

A look at Manufacturers Hanover's trading desk shows this trading mentality in firm command. As traders arrive yesterday at 7 A.M., the lira trader, Scott Levy, gets a hero's welcome. He had bought $55 million of lira the night before, switched some of it into German marks, and benefited from a rising mark in overnight Asian trading.

"I did quite well," he tells colleagues, as he takes his seat. A Hong Kong trader woke him up at home with a 4 A.M. phone call—but helped Mr. Levy unwind his position at a profit of more than $165,000. Other traders greet him with "high five" handslaps, like a football player who has just scored a touchdown.

The next 90 minutes are consumed by a blizzard of trades with European banks. Computerized dealing systems let traders do business with London, Frankfurt or Zurich by the push of a button, without even a phone call. Typically, Manufacturers Hanover will buy "five dollars"— trader jargon for $5 million—then resell it at a razor-thin profit margin seconds later.

At 9:03 A.M., the first of the day's big news headlines hits the screen. "U.S. Commerce Under Secretary Says Dollar Is Now Competitive," a new monitor reports.

"That's good for the dollar," says Mr. Remigio. He and Mr. Scala buy $10 million at a rate of 1.7080 marks.

Moments later, a senior bank trader walks by and asks why the dollar is rising. Mr. Remigio starts to explain the new views expressed by the Commerce under secretary.

"What the hell does he know?" another trader snaps.

The issue is settled. In a flurry of four transactions, Manufacturers Hanover dumps the $10 million it just bought, and sells another $8 million as well. It gets rates ranging from 1.7088 to 1.7107 marks. The slight gain from its purchase price is infinitesimal to anyone but a currency trader. To Messrs. Scala and Remigio, it is $500 quick profit for the bank.

Difficult Stretch

About 1 P.M., the mark traders encounter their one difficult stretch of the day. They have sold dollars, expecting further drops. But the dollar is inching up. Mr. Scala twirls his phone cord around his finger and taps his feet. Mr. Remigio slams his phone down, snarling: "It's up, it's up, it's going up."

Rather than fight the momentary trend, the traders begin buying dollars. "The dollar is going uptown," Mr. Remigio declares. He holds his new positive position on the dollar for only a brief spell, but profits from it as well.

All morning, calls from incoming banks and customers light up dealers' phone boards, which hold 120 direct phone lines. Only around 11 A.M. does the most important phone line—the one in the bottom left-hand corner, begin blinking at Manufacturers Hanover's mark desk. It is the Federal Reserve Bank of New York, agent for the U.S. government. And for a moment, Mr. Scala doesn't see the line light up.

"When that line comes in, you've got to pick it up quick," Mr. Remigio chides his partner. "They could be wanting to deal."

The New York Fed in fact deals with any of a dozen big New York banks when it enters the market to buy or sell

---

Analogously,

$$S(£/€) = \frac{S(\$/€)}{S(\$/£)}$$

$$= \frac{1.1584}{1.6944}$$

$$= 0.6837$$

(4.7)

currencies, and it often doesn't let one bank know about its dealings with another. This time the Fed just wants information about the dollar. "It goes up. It goes down. It goes all around," the Fed's trader asks over the phone. "What's going on?"

Reading Fed Signals

Mr. Scala tries to offer a quick summary of market activity. Then he asks the Fed: "Is there any level you want me to call you back at?"

With his low-key question, Mr. Scala is trying to get at perhaps the most important piece of information in the foreign-exchange market. Traders' one big worry currently is that if the dollar falls too fast, the Fed and foreign central banks may barge in with big buy orders to prop up the dollar. If a trader knows what dollar rate worries the Fed, he can better prepare for any possible intervention.

"Yeah," says the Fed trader. "Call me if it gets to 1.7075."

A little later, the dollar does slip to that level. Mr. Scala calls the Fed. But instead of placing a big buy order, the Fed trader just says: "Call me back if it goes much lower."

Around this time, Manufacturers Hanover's mark traders back off from some bearish market positions they have taken against the dollar. But that is straightforward profit-taking, the traders say, unrelated to the Fed's call.

The trading frenzy continues until about noon New York time, when the European trading day ends. Only then can Manufacturers' New York traders relax. "It's like a ball and chain," complains James Young, senior sterling trader. "I can't go out to lunch."

For their efforts, the mark traders break even after making about 200 trades involving nearly $1 billion. The bank's entire currency-trading operation did better however, bringing in a profit of about $300,000 for the day.

While young traders are in the front lines, big banks like Manufacturers Hanover have top managers looking over their shoulders, setting position limits and trying to make sure the bank doesn't get stuck with unexpected losses. But the foreign-exchange market has grown so fast, and takes such a toll on traders, that there are few veterans.

Mr. Remigio, the 27-year-old No. 2 mark trader, received an M.B.A. from Hofstra University before coming to Manufacturers Hanover a couple of years ago. His colleague, Mr. Scala, has only a high-school diploma. Mr. Scala has something more valuable to the bank, though: nearly a decade of experience. He started as a broker's clerk, then advanced to trading when he was all of 20. Individual traders, many still in their 20s, earn more than $100,000 a year in salary and bonus.

The Role of Luck

But there are no illusions about succeeding on skill alone around the trading room. Within reach of nearly every trader is a good-luck charm. At the desk where Japanese yen are traded, dealers can rub the tummy of a cherubic statuette or slap a bobbing-head doll representing Japan's rising sun. It then cries out, in Japanese: "Try, you can do it!" The Japanese writing on a headband wrapped around a speaker phone reads: "We're definitely going to win!"

Traders joke that for them, 10 minutes is a long-term outlook. One of Manufacturers Hanover's economists, Marc M. Goloven, says he can sense the difference when he visits trading floors to get a feel for market trends. "When I sit down there, I can feel the tension rising," he says. "That's tough duty. I sympathize with them." His one quibble, he says, is that many traders "aren't attuned to looking at [economic] fundamentals as much as we think they should."

Down in the trading room, the traders generally agree. "I like to see what the economist thinks, but he's thinking long-term," says James Young, Manufacturer's top sterling trader. "And there are 13 floors between here and long-term."

Bank officials doubt that the dollar's decline is over. "It isn't un-American" to sell dollars and profit from the currency's decline, Mr. Young says. "It's how the game is played."

The dollar's chronic slump is worrying for the U.S. economy, adds Mr. Remigio. But there's no room at the trading desk for sentimentality. "I don't like seeing the dollar down here," he says. "My money doesn't buy as much when I travel overseas. But in trading, if the thing's going down, I'm going to sell it."

Source: Charles W. Stevens, *The Wall Street Journal,* November 5, 1987, p. 26. Excerpted from *The Wall Street Journal,* ©1987 Dow Jones & Company, Inc. All Rights Reserved Worldwide.

and

$$S(£/€) = S(£/\$)/S(€/\$)$$
$$= 0.5902/0.8633$$
$$= 0.6837$$

(4.8)

Equations 4.5 to 4.8 imply that given N currencies, one can calculate a triangular matrix of the $(N \times (N - 1))/2$ cross-exchange rates. Daily in the *Financial Times* appear the 36 cross-exchange rates for all pair combinations of nine currencies and stated as

S(j/k) and S(k/j). Exhibit 4.6 presents an example of the table for Monday, November 3, 2003. Reading across a row for a country, say, Canada, each cell in the row indicates the number of units of each foreign currency designated in the column-headings, say, the Danish kroner, that can be purchased with one Canadian dollar. Reading down a column indicates the number of units of the column-currency, again, say, the Canadian dollar, that are required to purchase a unit of the respective foreign currency. Looking at the extreme upper-right and lower-left cells in the table, in the first instance, we see that one Canadian dollar will buy 0.751 American dollars and then, correspondingly, that 1.33 Canadian dollars are required to purchase one American dollar.

Alternative Expressions for the Cross-Exchange Rate

For some purposes, it is easier to think of cross-exchange rates calculated as the product of an American term and a European exchange rate, rather than as the quotient of two American term or two European term exchange rates. For example, substituting $S(€/\$)$ for $1/S(\$/€)$ allows Equation 4.5 to be rewritten as:

$$S(€/£) = S(\$/£) \times S(€/\$) \qquad (4.9)$$
$$= 1.6944 \times 0.8633$$
$$= 1.4627$$

In general terms,

$$S(j/k) = S(\$/k) \times S(j/\$) \qquad (4.10)$$

and taking reciprocals of both sides of Equation 4.10 yields

$$S(k/j) = S(k/\$) \times S(\$/j) \qquad (4.11)$$

The Cross-Rate Trading Desk

Most interbank trading goes through the American dollar. Suppose a bank customer wants to trade out of British pound sterling into Swiss francs. In dealer jargon, a nondollar trade such as this is referred to as a **currency against currency** trade. The bank will frequently (or effectively) handle this trade for its customer by selling British pounds for American dollars and then selling American dollars for Swiss francs. At first blush, this might seem ridiculous. Why not just sell the British pounds directly for Swiss francs? To answer this question, let us return to Exhibit 4.6 of the cross-exchange rates. Suppose a bank's home currency was one of the nine currencies in the exhibit and that it made markets in the other eight currencies. The bank's trading room would typically be organized with eight trading desks, each for trading one of the non-dollar currencies against the American dollar. A dealer needs only to be concerned with making a market in his nondollar currency against the dollar. However, if each of the nine currencies was traded directly with the others, the dealing room would need to accommodate 36 trading desks. Or worse, individual traders would be responsible for making a market in several currency pairs, say, the €/\$, €/£, and €/SF, instead of just the

EXHIBIT 4.6		Exchange Cross Rates								
		C$	DKr	€	Y*	NKr	SKr	SFr	£	US$
Canada	C$	1.000	4.873	0.656	83.452	5.397	5.941	1.022	0.448	0.751
Denmark	DKr	0.205	1.000	0.135	17.132	1.080	1.220	0.210	0.092	0.154
Euro	€	1.530	7.436	1.000	127.330	8.235	9.061	1.560	0.684	1.145
Japan	Y	1.200	5.842	0.786	1.000	5.842	7.122	1.225	0.537	0.900
Norway	NKr	0.186	0.903	0.122	15.469	1.000	1.101	0.189	0.083	0.139
Sweden	SKr	0.169	0.821	0.110	14.057	0.821	1.000	0.172	0.075	0.126
Switzerland	SFr	0.979	4.770	0.642	81.680	5.283	5.815	1.000	0.438	0.735
United Kingdom	£	2.237	10.884	1.464	186.380	12.054	13.269	2.283	1.000	1.676
United States	US$	1.333	6.494	0.874	111.200	7.192	7.916	1.362	0.597	1.000

*Yen per 100
Source: *Financial Times*, November 3, 2003.

€/$. This would entail an informational complexity that would be virtually impossible to handle.

Banks handle currency against currency trades, such as for the bank customer who wants to trade out of British pounds into Swiss francs, at the cross-rate desk. Recall from Equation 4.10 that a $S(SF/£)$ quote can be obtained from the product of $S($/£)$ and $S(SF/$)$. Recognizing transaction costs implies the following restatement of Equation 4.10:

$$S(SF/£_b) = S($/£_b) \times S(SF/$_b) \tag{4.12}$$

The bank will quote its customer a selling (bid) price for the British pounds in terms of Swiss francs determined by multiplying its American term bid price for British pounds and its European term bid price (for American dollars) stated in Swiss francs.

Taking reciprocals of Equation 4.12 yields

$$S(£/SF_a) = S(£/$_a) \times S($/SF_a) \tag{4.13}$$

which is analogous to Equation 4.11. In terms of our example, Equation 4.13 says the bank could alternatively quote its customer an offer (ask) price for Swiss francs in terms of British pounds determined by multiplying its European term ask price (for American dollars) stated in British pounds by its American term ask price for Swiss francs.

Triangular Arbitrage

Certain banks specialize in making a direct market between nondollar currencies, pricing at a narrower bid-ask spread than the cross-rate spread. Nevertheless, the implied cross-rate bid-ask quotations imposes a discipline on the nondollar market makers. If their direct quotes are not consistent with cross-exchange rates, a triangular arbitrage profit is possible. **Triangular arbitrage** is the process of trading out of the American dollar into a second currency, then trading it for a third currency, which is, in turn, traded for American dollars. The purpose is to earn an arbitrage profit via trading from the second to the third currency when the direct exchange rate between the two is not in alignment with the cross-exchange rate.

EXAMPLE 4.2 **Calculating the Cross-Exchange Rate Bid-Ask Spread** Let us assume (as we did earlier) that the $/£ bid-ask prices are $1.6939 – $1.6944 and the £/$ bid-ask prices are £0.5902 – £0.5904.

Let us also assume the $/€ bid-ask prices are $1.1581 – $1.1586 and the €/$ bid-ask prices are €0.8630 – €0.8636. These bid and ask prices and Equation 4.12 imply that $S(€/£_b) = $1.6939 \times 0.8630 = 1.4620$. The reciprocal of $S(€/£_b)$, or Equation 4.13, implies that $S(£/€_a) = 0.5904 \times 1.1586 = 0.6840$.

Analogously, equation 4.13 suggests that $S(€/£_a) = 1.6944 \times 0.8636 = 1.4633$, and its reciprocal implies that $S(£/€_b) = 0.6834$.

That is, the €/£ bid-ask prices are €1.4620 – €1.4633 and the £/€ bid-ask prices are 0.6834 – 0.6840.

Note that the cross-rate bid-ask spreads are much larger than the American or European bid-ask spreads. For example, the €/£ bid-ask spread is 0.0013 versus the €/$ spread of $0.0005. The £/€ bid-ask spread is 0.0006 versus the $/€ spread of $0.0005, which is a sizable difference, since a British pound is priced in excess of one American dollar. The implication is that cross-exchange rates *implicitly* incorporate the bid-ask spreads of the two transactions that are necessary for trading out of one nondollar currency and into another. Hence, even when a bank makes a direct market in one nondollar currency versus another, the trade is effectively going through the dollar because the "currency against currency" exchange rate is consistent with a cross-exchange rate calculated from the dollar exchange rates of the two currencies. Exhibit 4.7 provides a more detailed presentation of cross-rate foreign exchange translations.

■

| **EXAMPLE** | **4.3** | **Taking Advantage of Triangular Arbitrage Opportunities** |

To illustrate triangular arbitrage, assume the cross-rate trader at Deutsche Bank notices that Credit Lyonnais is buying dollars at $S(€/\$_b) = 0.8631$, the same as Deutsche Bank's bid price. Similarly, he notices that Barclays Bank is offering dollars for pounds at $S(\$/£_b) = 1.6939$, also the same as Deutsche Bank. Next, he finds that BNP Paribas is making a direct market between the euro and the pound with a current ask price of $S(€/£_a) = 1.4600$.

The cross-rate formula and the American and European quotes, as we saw above, imply that the €/£ *bid* price should be no lower than $S(€/£)_b = 1.6939 * 0.8631 = 1.4620$. Yet, BNP Paribas is offering to sell British pounds at a rate of only 1.4600!

A triangular arbitrage profit is available if Deutsche Bank traders are quick enough.

A sale of $5,000,000 to Credit Lyonnais for euros will yield $5,000,000 × 0.8631 which equals €4,315,500. The €4,315,500 will be immediately resold to BNP Paribas for British pounds, that is, €4,315,500/1.4600 which amounts to £2,955,822. Then, to complete the triangle, the British pounds are sold for dollars at £2,955,822 × 1.6939 or $5,006,867.

The result is an arbitrage profit of $6,867.

BNP Paribas obviously must raise its asking price above €1.4600 / £1. The cross-exchange rates (from Exhibit 4.7) indicate €/£ bid-ask prices of €1.4620 – €1.4633. These prices imply that BNP Paribas can deal inside the spread and sell for less than €1.4633 but not less than €1.4620. An ask price of €1.4625 would eliminate the arbitrage profit. At that price, the €4,315,500 would be resold into pounds for £2,905,769, which, in turn, would yield only £2,905,769 × 1.6939 or $4,998,398. An attempt at the triangular trip would result in a loss of $1,692.

In today's technology-intensive FX market, many FX trading rooms around the world have developed in-house software that receives a digital feed of real-time FX prices from the EBS Spot electronic brokering system to continuously scan for triangular arbitrage opportunities. Opportunities are exploited almost instantaneously through programmed trades in the relevant configuration. Exhibit 4.8 presents a diagram and a summary of our triangular arbitrage example.

Spot Foreign Exchange Market Microstructure

Market microstructure refers to the basic mechanics of how a marketplace operates. Five recent empirical studies on FX market microstructure shed light on the operation of the spot FX marketplace. Huang and Masulis (1999) study spot FX rates on DM/$ trades over the period October 1992 to September 1993. They find that bid-ask spreads in the spot FX market increase with FX exchange rate volatility and decrease with dealer competition. These results are consistent with models of market microstructure. They also find that the bid-ask spread decreases when the percentage of large dealers in the marketplace increases. They conclude that dealer competition is a fundamental determinant of the spot FX bid-ask spread.

Lyons (1998) tracks the trading activity of a DM/$ trader at a large New York bank over a period of five trading days. The dealer was extremely profitable over the study period, averaging profits of $100,000 per day on volume of $1 billion. Lyons is able to disentangle total trades into those that are speculative and those that are nonspeculative, or where the dealer acts as a financial intermediary for a retail client. He determines that the dealer's profits come primarily from the dealer's role as an intermediary. This makes sense, since speculative trading is a zero-sum game among all speculators, and in the long-run, it is unlikely that any one trader has a unique advantage. Interestingly, Lyons finds that the half-life of the dealer's position in nonspeculative trades is

Bank Quotations	American Terms		European Terms	
	Bid	Ask	Bid	Ask
British pounds	1.6939	1.6944	0.5902	0.5904
Euros	1.1581	1.1586	0.8631	0.8636

a. Bank Customer wants to sell £1,000,000 for Euros. The Bank will sell American dollars (buy British pounds) for $1.6939. The sale yields Bank Customer:

£1,000,000 × $1.6939 = $1,693,900

The Bank will buy dollars (sell Euros) for €0.8631. The sale of dollars yields Bank Customer:

$1,693,900 x €0.8630 = €1,462,005

Bank Customer has effectively sold British pounds at a €/£ bid price of

€1,462,005/£1,000,000 = €1.4620/£1.00.

b. Bank Customer wants to sell €1,000,000 for British pounds. The Bank will sell American dollars (buy Euros) for €0.8636. The sale yields Bank Customer:

€1,000,000/0.8636 = $1,157,943

The Bank will buy dollars (sell British pounds) for $1.6944. The sale of dollars yields Bank Customer:

$1,157,943/1.6944 = €683,394

Bank customer has effectively bought British pounds at a €/£ ask price of

€1,000,000/£ 683,394 = €1.4633/£ 1.00.

From parts (a) and (b), we see the currency against currency bid-ask spread for British pounds is €1.4620 − €1.4633.

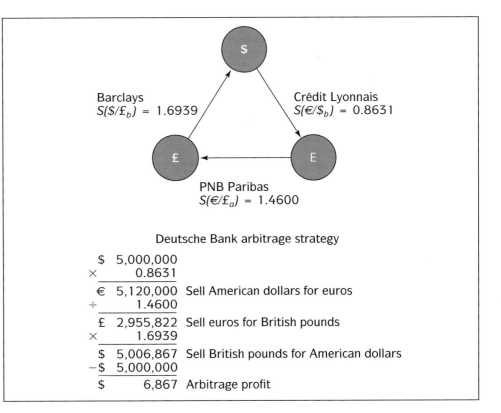

Barclays
$S(\$/£_b) = 1.6939$

Crédit Lyonnais
$S(€/\$_b) = 0.8631$

PNB Paribas
$S(€/£_a) = 1.4600$

Deutsche Bank arbitrage strategy

$	5,000,000	
×	0.8631	
€	5,120,000	Sell American dollars for euros
÷	1.4600	
£	2,955,822	Sell euros for British pounds
×	1.6939	
$	5,006,867	Sell British pounds for American dollars
−$	5,000,000	
$	6,867	Arbitrage profit

only 10 minutes! That is, the dealer typically trades or swaps out of a nonspeculative position within 20 minutes.

Ito, Lyons, and Melvin (1998) study the role of private information in the spot FX market. They examine ¥/$ and DM/$ between September 1994 and March 1995. Their study provides evidence against the common view that private information is irrelevant, since all market participants are assumed to possess the same set of public information. Their evidence comes from the Tokyo foreign exchange market, which prior to December 1994, closed for lunch between noon and 1:30 P.M. After December 21, 1994, the variance in spot exchange rates increased during the lunch period relative to the period of closed trading. This was true for both ¥/$ and DM/$ trades, but more so for the ¥/$ data, which is to be expected since ¥/$ trading is more intensive in the Tokyo FX market. Ito, Lyons, and Melvin attribute these results to a greater revelation of private information in trades being allocated to the lunch hour. This suggests that private information is, indeed, an important determinant of spot exchange rates.

Cheung and Chinn (2001) conducted a survey of foreign exchange traders in order to explore several aspects of exchange rate dynamics not typically observable in trading data. In particular, they are interested in traders' perceptions about news events—innovations in macroeconomic variables—that cause movements in exchange rates. The traders they survey respond that the bulk of the adjustment to economic announcements regarding unemployment, trade deficits, inflation, GDP, and the Federal funds rate takes place within one minute. In fact, "about one-third of the respondents claim that full price adjustment takes place in less than 10 seconds"! They also find that central bank intervention does not appear to have a substantial impact on exchange rates, but intervention does increase market volatility. Dominguez (1998) confirms this latter finding.

4.3 The Forward Market

In conjunction with spot trading, there is also a forward foreign exchange market. The **forward market** involves contracting today for the future purchase or sale of foreign exchange. The forward price may be the same as the spot price, but usually it is higher (at a premium) or lower (at a discount) than the spot price. Forward exchange rates are quoted on most major currencies for a variety of maturities. Bank quotes for maturities of 1, 3, 6, 9, and 12 months are readily available. Quotations on nonstandard, or broken-term, maturities are also available. Maturities extending beyond one year are becoming more frequent, and for good bank customers, a maturity extending out to five, and even as long as 10 years, is possible.

Forward Rate Quotations

To learn how to read forward exchange rate quotations, let us go back to Exhibit 4.4. Note that **forward rate** quotations appear directly under the spot rate quotations for four major currencies—British pound, Canadian dollar, Japanese yen, and Swiss franc—in one-, three- and six-month maturities. The settlement date of, for example, a three-month forward transaction is three calendar months from the spot settlement date for the currency. That is, if today is November 1, 2004 and spot settlement is November 3, then the forward settlement date would be February 3, 2005, a period of 94 days from November 1.

In this textbook, we use the following notation for forward rate quotations. In general F_N (j/k) refers to the price of one unit of currency k in terms of currency j for delivery in N months. N equalling 1 denotes a one-month maturity based on a 360-day banker's year. Thus, N equaling 3 denotes three-month maturity. When the context is clear, the simpler notation F is used to denote a forward exchange rate. Forward quotes are either direct or indirect, one being the reciprocal of the other. From the American perspective, reflecting the quotes in Exhibit 4.4. taken from *The Wall Street Journal*, a direct forward quote is in American dollar terms.

From the Canadian point of view, a *direct* quote for an American dollar—spot or forward—is expressed in Canadian dollar terms, such as "1.3187," indicating 1.3187 Canadian dollars for one American dollar. On the other hand, an *indirect* quote, from the Canadian perspective, of the exchange rate would be "0.7583", indicating 75.83 American cents per Canadian dollar.

As an example, let us consider the *direct* quotes (from the Canadian perspective) of forward rates involving the Canadian dollar and the American dollar. For convenience and clarity, the spot rate is defined as $S(C/US)$ and similarly as $F_N(C/US)$ forward rates. We see that:

$$S(C/US) = 1.3187$$
$$F_1(C/US) = 1.3207$$
$$F_3(C/US) = 1.3242$$
$$F_6(C/US) = 1.3289$$

From these quotations, we can see that from the Canadian perspective, the American dollar is trading at a forward *premium* to the Canadian dollar and that the premium increases out to six months. In other words, the forward premium is greater the further the forward contract settlement date is from November 3. The forward market is "pricing in" a weakening of the Canadian dollar *vis-à-vis* the American dollar. The forward market demands more and more Canadian dollars per one American dollar the further out in time we go. A significant element of implicit forecasting or "market thinking" about currency depreciation or appreciation is built into the structure of forward foreign exchange rates.

Indirect quotations are the reciprocal of direct quotations. In indirect terms from the Canadian perspective, the spot and forward quotes, S(US/C) and FN (US/C), involving the Canadian dollar and the American dollar are:

$$S(US/C) = 0.7583$$
$$F_1(US/C) = 0.7572$$
$$F_3(US/C) = 0.7552$$
$$F_6(US/C) = 0.7525$$

From these quotations, we see that in *indirect* terms the Canadian dollar is trading at a forward discount to the American dollar and that the discount increases out to six months. This is exactly what we should expect, since *indirect* quotations are reciprocals of *direct* quotations. The "pricing in" of a weakening of the Canadian dollar *vis-à-vis* the American dollar is reflected in the smaller number of American dollars per Canadian dollar that is offered in the forward market the further out in time one goes.

One can buy (take a *long* position) or sell (take a *short* position) in a foreign exchange forward contract. Bank customers can contact the foreign exchange desk of their bank to buy or sell a specific sum of FX for delivery on a certain date. Likewise interbank traders, who do the vast bulk of forward foreign exchange trading, can establish long or short positions with traders from other banks.

Exhibit 4.9 graphs both the long and short positions for a three-month forward contract to buy American dollars with Canadian dollars. The contract is expressed in *direct* Canadian dollar terms, $F_3(C/US)$. $F_3(C/US)$ is priced at 1.3242 Canadian dollars per American dollar.

The *long* position in this contract commits the party to buy the contract amount of American dollars at a rate of C$1.3242 on the contract maturity date of February 3, 2004, with settlement two days later. The short position in the contract commits the party to deliver the contract amount of American dollars at a rate of C$1.3242 on the settlement date.

The graph in Exhibit 4.9 measures profits or losses (per unit of the contract currency) on the vertical axis. The horizontal axis shows the spot price of foreign exchange on the maturity date of February 3, 2004. Since neither the long position nor the short position has a pay-off if the spot rate on February 3 is identical to the

EXHIBIT 4.9

Graph of Long and
Short Position in
Three-month Forward
Contract to Deliver
U.S. Dollars

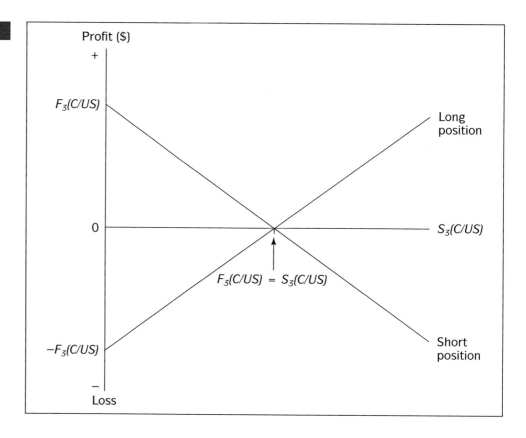

$F_3(C/US)$ of 1.3242, the line of pay-off for the long position and the line of pay-off for the short position intersect at $F_3(C/US)$ at zero pay-off.

The line of pay-off for the long position is upward sloping indicating that if the spot rate is above 1.3242 on February 3, the holder of the long position makes a profit. If the spot rate on February 3 is above 1.3242, then the holder of the long position pays C$1.3242 for American dollars that are worth somewhat more than C$1.3242. In other words, the long position on a American dollar forward contract pays off in Canadian dollar terms if the Canadian dollar weakens.

On the other hand, the line of pay-off for the short position is downward sloping indicating that if the spot rate is above 1.3242 on February 3, the holder of the short position incurs a loss. If the spot rate on February 3 is above 1.3242, then the holder of the short position must deliver American dollars for C$1.3242 per American dollar at a time when American funds cost somewhat more than that in Canadian dollar terms. In other words, a short position on an American dollar forward contract is a losing position if the Canadian dollar weakens.

EXAMPLE 4.4 A Speculative Forward Position It is November 3, 2003. The American dollar/Swiss franc trader at Citibank in New York has just heard from the bank's economic forecasting unit that the Swiss franc is likely to fall in value against the American dollar to a level less than the forward rate that several other banks are currently offering. If the trader decides to act on this information, he will take a short position in a three-month $/SF forward contract. Let us say that he does act. He phones the S/SF trader at Chemical Bank. He sells SF5,000,000 against dollars at $0.7476 with delivery on February 3, 2004.

continued

EXAMPLE 4.4 **Continued**

Suppose the forecast proves to be correct and on February 3, the spot $/SF is $0.7400. The trader can buy the Swiss francs spot at $0.7400 and deliver it under the forward contract where he receives $0.7476 per Swiss franc. The trade has made a speculative profit of ($0.7476 − $0.7400) = $0.0076 per unit. This is illustrated in Exhibit 4.10. The total profit from the trade is $38,000 = (5,000,000 × $0.0076). If, on the other hand, the American dollar depreciates against the Swiss franc and the spot rate turns out to be 0.7500 on February 3, 2004, then the speculator would have lost ($0.7500 − $0.7476) = $0.0024 per unit, for a total loss of $12,000.

■

EXHIBIT 4.10

Graph of Long and Short Position in the Three-Month Swiss Franc Contract

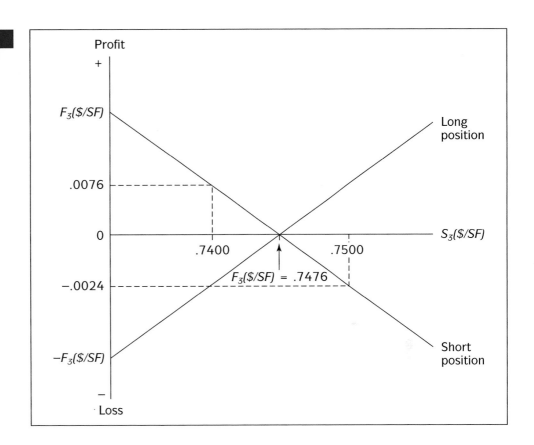

Forward Cross-Exchange Rates

Forward cross-exchange rate quotations are calculated in an analogous manner to spot cross-rates, and so it is not necessary to provide detailed examples. In generic terms,

$$F_N(j/k) = \frac{F_N(\$/k)}{F_N(\$/j)} \qquad (4.14)$$

or

$$F_N(j/k) = \frac{F_N(j/\$)}{F_N(k/\$)} \qquad (4.15)$$

and

$$F_N(k/j) = \frac{F_N(\$/j)}{F_N(\$/k)} \qquad (4.16)$$

or

$$F_N(k/j) = \frac{F_N(k/\$)}{F_N(j/\$)}$$

(4.17)

Swap Transactions

Forward trades can be classified as outright or swap transactions. In conducting their trading, bank dealers do take speculative positions in the currencies they trade, but more often, traders offset the currency exposure inherent in a trade. From the bank's standpoint, an **outright forward transaction** is an uncovered speculative position in a currency, even though it might be part of a currency hedge to the bank customer on the other side of the transaction. Swap transactions provide a means for the bank to mitigate the currency exposure in a forward trade. A **swap transaction** is the simultaneous sale (or purchase) of spot foreign exchange against a forward purchase (or sale) of approximately an equal amount of the foreign currency.

Swap transactions account for approximately 56 percent of interbank FX trading, whereas outright trades are 11 percent. (See Exhibit 4.3.) Because interbank forward transactions are most frequently made as part of a swap transaction, bank dealers in conversation among themselves use a shorthand notation to quote bid and ask forward prices in terms of *forward points* that are either added to or subtracted from the spot bid and ask quotations.

EXAMPLE 4.5 **Forward Point Quotations** Recall the $/£ spot bid-ask rates of $1.6939 – $1.6944 developed previously. With reference to these rates, forward prices might be displayed as:

Spot	1.6939–1.6944
One-Month	39–37
Three-Month	57–53
Six-Month	145–138

When the second number in a forward point pair is smaller than the first, the dealer understands that the forward points are subtracted from the spot bid and ask prices to obtain the outright forward rates. For example, the spot bid price of $1.6939 minus 0.0039 (or 39 points) equals $1.6900, the one-month bid price. The spot ask price of $1.6944 minus 0.0037 (or 37 points) equals $1.6907, the one-month ask price. Analogously, the three-month outright forward bid-ask rates are $1.6882 – $1.6891 and the six-month outright forward bid-ask rates are $1.6794 – $1.6806. The following table summarizes the calculations:

Spot		1.6939 – 1.6944
	Forward Point Quotations	**Outright Forward Quotations**
One-Month	39–37	1.6900–1.6907
Three-Month	57–54	1.6882–1.6891
Six-Month	145–138	1.6794–1.6806

Three things are notable about the outright forward prices. First, the British pound is trading at a forward discount to the (American) dollar. Second, all bid prices are less than the corresponding ask prices, as they must be for a trader to be willing to make a market. Third, the bid-ask spread increases in time to maturity, as is typical. These three conditions prevail only *because* the forward points are subtracted from the spot prices. As a check, note that in points the spot bid-ask spread is 5 points, the one-month forward spread is 7 points, the three-month spread is 9 points, and the six-month spread is 12 points.

continued

EXAMPLE **4.5** **Continued**

If the British pound was trading at a forward premium to the dollar, the second number in each forward pair would be larger than the first number in the pair. The trader would know to *add* the points to the spot bid and ask prices to obtain the outright forward bid and ask rates. For example, if the three-month and six-month point-pairs were 54–57 and 138–145, the corresponding three-month and six-month bid-ask spreads would be $1.6993 – $1.7001 and $1.7077 – $1.7089, that is, increasing in term to maturity.

■

Quoting forward rates in terms of forward points is convenient for two reasons. First, forward points may remain constant for long periods of time, even if the spot rate fluctuates frequently. Second, in swap transactions where the trader is attempting to minimize currency exposure, the actual spot and outright forward rates are often of no consequence. What is important is the premium or discount differential measured in forward points. To illustrate, suppose a bank customer wants to sell dollars three months forward against British sterling. The bank can handle this trade for its customer and simultaneously neutralize the exchange rate risk in the trade by selling (borrowed) dollars spot against British pounds. The bank will lend sterling for three months until pounds are needed to deliver against the dollars it has purchased forward. The dollars received will be used to liquidate the dollar loan. Implicit in this transaction is the interest rate differential between the dollar borrowing rate and the pound sterling lending rate. The interest rate differential is captured by the forward premium or discount measured in forward points. As a rule, when the interest rate of the foreign currency is greater than the interest rate of the quoting currency, the outright forward rate is less than the spot exchange rate, and *vice versa*. This will become clear in the following chapter on international parity relationships.

Forward Premium

It is common to express the premium or discount of a forward rate as an annualized percentage deviation from the spot rate. The forward premium (or discount) is useful for comparing against the interest rate differential between two countries, as we will see more clearly in Chapter 5 on international parity relationships. The **forward premium** or **discount** can be expressed in *direct* terms. Obviously, if a currency is trading at a premium (discount) in direct terms, it will be at a discount (premium) in indirect terms.

EXAMPLE **4.6** **Calculating the Forward Position** The formula for calculating the forward premium or discount in direct terms for currency *j* against currency *k* is :

$$f_{N,j/k} = \frac{F_N(k/j) - S(k/j)}{S(k/j)} \times 360/\text{days}$$

When the context is clear, the forward premium will be simply stated as *f*. The premium is expressed as an annualized percent.

As an example of the calculation of the forward premium, let us use the November 3, 2003, quotes from Exhibit 4.4 for the three-month forward for the Canadian dollar (C$) versus the American dollar (US$). We see that in direct-Canadian terms, the Canadian dollar is selling at a forward premium to the American dollar. The calculation is:

continued

EXAMPLE 4.6   Continued

$$f_{94,(C\$/US\$)} = \frac{(C\$/US\$) - S(C\$/US\$)}{S(C\$/US\$)} \times 360/94$$

$$= \frac{1.3242 - 1.3187}{1.3187} \times 360/94 = 0.0160$$

We see that the three-month forward premium is 0.0160 or 1.60 percent. In words, we say that the Canadian dollar is trading at a 1.60 percent premium versus the American dollar for delivery in 94 days. In *direct* terms of Canadian dollars per the American dollar, the forward premium indicates that the market is pricing in a weakening of the Canadian dollar.

Turning to the *indirect* quote,

$$f_{94,(US\$/C\$)} = \frac{(US\$/C\$) - S(US\$/CS\$)}{S(US\$/CS\$)} \times 360/94$$

$$= \frac{0.7552 - 0.7583}{0.7583} \times 360/94 = 0.0157$$

We see that the three-month forward premium is −0.0157 or −1.57 percent. In words, we say that the Canadian dollar is trading at a 1.57 percent discount versus the American dollar for delivery in 94 days. In *indirect* terms of American dollars per Canadian dollar, the forward discount again indicates that the market is pricing in a weakening of the Canadian dollar in the forward rate structure that calls for fewer American dollars per the Canadian dollar for delivery in three months from now versus today.

SUMMARY

This chapter presents an introduction to the market for foreign exchange. Broadly defined, the foreign exchange market encompasses the conversion of purchasing power from one currency into another, bank deposits of foreign currency, the extension of credit denominated in a foreign currency, foreign trade financing, and trading in foreign currency options and futures contracts. This chapter limits the discussion to the spot and forward markets for foreign exchange. The other topics are covered in later chapters.

1. The FX market is the largest and most active financial market in the world. It is open somewhere in the world 24 hours a day, 365 days a year.

2. The FX market is divided into two tiers: the retail or client market and the wholesale or interbank market. The retail market is where international banks service their customers who need foreign exchange to conduct international commerce or trade in international financial assets. The great majority of FX trading takes place in the interbank market among international banks that are adjusting inventory positions or conducting speculative and arbitrage trades.

3. The FX market participants include international banks, bank customers, nonbank FX dealers, FX brokers, and central banks.

4. In the spot market for FX, nearly immediate purchase and sale of currencies take place. In the chapter, notation for defining a spot rate quotation was developed. Additionally, the concept of a cross-exchange rate was developed. It was determined that nondollar currency transactions must satisfy the bid-ask spread determined from the cross-rate formula or a triangular arbitrage opportunity exists.

5. In the forward market, buyers and sellers can transact today at the forward price for the future purchase and sale of foreign exchange. Notation for forward exchange rate quotations was developed. The use of forward points as a shorthand method for expressing forward quotes from spot rate quotations was presented. Additionally, the concept of a forward premium was developed.

KEY WORDS

American terms, *81*
ask price, *82*
bid price, *81*
client market, *75*
correspondent banking relationships, *77*
cross-exchange rate, *83*
currency against currency, *86*
direct quotation, *79*

European terms, *81*
foreign exchange (FX or FOREX) market, *74*
forward market, *90*
forward premium/discount, *95*
forward rate, *90*
indirect quotation, *79*
interbank market, *75*
offer price, *82*

outright forward transaction, *94*
over-the-counter (OTC) market, *75*
retail market, *75*
spot market, *78*
spot rate, *79*
swap transaction, *94*
triangular arbitrage, *87*
wholesale market, *75*

QUESTIONS

1. Give a full definition of the market for foreign exchange.
2. What is the difference between the retail or client market and the wholesale or interbank market for foreign exchange?
3. Who are the market participants in the foreign exchange market?
4. How are foreign exchange transactions between international banks settled?
5. What is meant by a currency trading at a discount or at a premium in the forward market?
6. Why does most interbank currency trading worldwide involve the American dollar?
7. Banks find it necessary to accommodate their clients' needs to buy or sell FX forward, in many instances for hedging purposes. How can the bank eliminate the currency exposure it has created for itself by accommodating a client's forward transaction?
8. A $/€ bank trader is currently quoting a *small figure* bid-ask of 35–40, when the rest of the market is trading at C$1.3436–C$1.3441. What is implied about the trader's beliefs by his prices?
9. What is triangular arbitrage? What is a condition that will give rise to a triangular arbitrage opportunity?

PROBLEMS

1. Using Exhibit 4.4, calculate a cross-rate matrix for the euro, Swiss franc, Japanese yen, and British pound. Use the most current American term quotes to calculate the cross-rates so that the triangular matrix resulting is similar to the portion above the diagonal in Exhibit 4.6.
2. Using Exhibit 4.4, calculate the one-, three-, and six-month forward cross-exchange rates between the Canadian dollar and the Swiss franc using the most current quotations. State the forward cross-rates in "Canadian" terms.
3. Restate the following one-, three-, and six-month outright forward European term bid-ask quotes in forward points.

Spot	1.3431–1.3436
One-Month	1.3432–1.3442
Three-Month	1.3448–1.3463
Six-Month	1.3488–1.3508

4. Using the spot and outright forward quotes in problem 3, determine the corresponding bid-ask spreads in points.

5. Using Exhibit 4.4, calculate the one-, three-, and six-month forward premium or discount for the Canadian dollar in European terms. For simplicity, assume each month has 30 days.

6. Using Exhibit 4.4, calculate the one-, three-, and six-month forward premium or discount for the British pound in American terms using the most current quotations. For simplicity, assume each month has 30 days.

7. Given the following information, what are the NZD/SGD currency against currency bid-ask quotations?

| Bank Quotations | American Terms | | European Terms | |
	Bid	Ask	Bid	Ask
New Zealand dollar (NZ$)	.4660	.4667	2.1427	2.1459
Singapore dollar (SG$)	.5705	.5710	1.7513	1.7528

8. Assume you are a trader with Deutsche Bank. From the quote screen on your computer terminal, you notice that Dresdner Bank is quoting €1.0242/$1 and Credit Suisse is offering SF1.5030/$1. You learn that UBS is making a direct market between the Swiss franc and the euro, with a current €/SF quote of 0.6750. Show how you can make a triangular arbitrage profit by trading at these prices. (Ignore bid-ask spreads for this problem.) Assume you have $5,000,000 with which to conduct the arbitrage. What happens if you initially sell dollars for Swiss francs? What €/SF price will eliminate triangular arbitrage?

9. The current spot exchange rate is $1.55/£ and the three-month forward rate is $1.50/£. On the basis of your analysis of the exchange rate, you are pretty confident that the spot exchange rate will be $1.52/£ in three months. Assume that you would like to buy or sell £1,000,000.

   a. What actions do you need to take to speculate in the forward market? What is the expected dollar profit from speculation?

   b. What would be your speculative profit in dollar terms if the spot exchange rate actually turns out to be $1.46/£?

10. Omni Advisors, an international pension fund manager, plans to sell equities denominated in Swiss francs (CHF) and purchase an equivalent amount of equities denominated in South African rands (ZAR).

    Omni will realize net proceeds of three million CHF at the end of 30 days and wants to eliminate the risk that the ZAR will appreciate relative to the CHF during this 30-day period. The following exhibit shows current exchange rates between the ZAR, CHF, and the American dollar (USD).

Currency Exchange Rates

| Maturity | ZAR/US$ | | CHF/US$ | |
	Bid	Ask	Bid	Ask
Spot	6.2681	6.2789	1.5282	1.5343
30-day	6.2538	6.2641	1.5226	1.5285
90-day	6.2104	6.2200	1.5058	1.5115

    a. Describe the currency transaction that Omni should undertake to eliminate currency risk over the 30-day period.

    b. Calculate the following:

- The CHF/ZAR cross currency rate Omni would use in valuing the Swiss equity portfolio.
- The current value of Omni's Swiss equity portfolio in ZAR.
- The annualized forward premium or discount at which the ZAR is trading versus the CHF.

INTERNET EXERCISES

1. A currency trader makes a market in a currency and attempts to generate speculative profits from dealing against other currency traders. Today, electronic dealing systems are frequently used by currency traders. The most widely used spot trading system is EBS Spot. Go to their website, www.ebsp.com/products/MarketDataEBS_rates.jsp, which presents a sample view of the monitor screen seen by traders. What is meant by the terms "touch high/low" and "market high/low" that you see on the screen?

2. In addition to the historic currency symbols, such as, $, ¥, £, and €, there is an official three-letter symbol for each currency that is recognized worldwide. These symbols can be found at the Bloomberg website: www.bloomberg.com/markets/wcvl.html. Go to this site. What is the currency symbol for the Congo franc? The Guyana dollar?

MINI CASE

Shrewsbury Herbal Products, Ltd.

Shrewsbury Herbal Products, located in central England close to the Welsh border, is an old-line producer of herbal teas, seasonings, and medicines. Their products are marketed all over the United Kingdom and in many parts of continental Europe as well.

Shrewsbury Herbal generally invoices in British pound sterling when it sells to foreign customers in order to guard against adverse exchange rate changes. Nevertheless, it has just received an order from a large wholesaler in central France for £320,000 of its products, conditional upon delivery being made in three months' time and the order invoiced in euros.

Shrewsbury's controller, Elton Peters, is concerned with whether the pound will appreciate versus the euro over the next three months, thus eliminating all or most of the profit when the euro receivable is paid. He thinks this an unlikely possibility, but he decides to contact the firm's banker for suggestions about hedging the exchange rate exposure.

Mr. Peters learns from the banker that the current spot exchange rate in €/£ is €1.5641; thus, the invoice amount should be €500,512. Mr. Peters also learns that the three-month forward rates for the pound and the euro versus the American dollar are $1.5188/£1 and $0.9727/€1, respectively. The banker offers to set up a forward hedge for selling the franc receivable for pound sterling based on the €/£ cross-forward exchange rate implicit in the forward rates against the American dollar.

What would you do if you were Mr. Peters?

REFERENCES & SUGGESTED READINGS

Bank for International Settlements. *Triennial Central Bank Survey.* Basle, Switzerland: Bank for International Settlements, March 2002.

Cheung, Yin-Wong, and Menzie David Chinn. "Currency Traders and Exchange Rate Dynamics: A Survey of the US Market." *Journal of International Money and Finance* 20 (2001), pp. 439–71.

Coninx, Raymond G. F. *Foreign Exchange Dealer's Handbook,* 2nd ed. Burr Ridge, Ill.: Dow Jones-Irwin, 1986.

Copeland, Laurence S. *Exchange Rates and International Finance,* 2nd ed. Wokingham, England: Addison-Wesley, 1994.

Dominguez, Kathryn M. "Central Bank Intervention and Exchange Rate Volatility." *Journal of International Money and Finance* 17 (1998), pp. 161–90.

D'Souza, Chris. *A Market Microstructure Analysis of Foreign Exchange Intervention in Canada.* Bank of Canada Working Paper 2002–16 (Financial Markets Department). Ottawa: Bank of Canada, 2002.

Federal Reserve Bank of New York. *The Foreign Exchange and Interest Rate Derivatives Markets Survey: Turnover in the United States.* New York: Federal Reserve Bank of New York, 2001.

"The Foreign-Exchange Market: Big." *The Economist,* (September 23, 1995).

Grabbe, J. Orlin. *International Financial Markets,* 3rd ed. Upper Saddle River, N.J.: Prentice Hall, 1996.

Graven, Kathryn. "Fearless Dealers: Central-Bank Traders Have an Advantage: Their Employers Don't Demand Profits." *The Wall Street Journal,* (September 23, 1988), p. R31.

Huang, Roger D., and Ronald W. Masulis. "FX Spreads and Dealer Competition across the 24-Hour Trading Day." *Review of Financial Studies* 12 (1999), pp. 61–93.

International Monetary Fund. *International Capital Markets: Part I. Exchange Rate Management and International Capital Flows.* Washington, D.C.: International Monetary Fund, 1993.

Ito, Takatoshi, Richard K. Lyons, and Michael T. Melvin. "Is There Private Information in the FX Market? The Tokyo Experiment." *Journal of Finance* 53 (1998), pp. 1111–30.

Lyons, Richard K. "Profits and Position Control: A Week of FX Dealing." *Journal of International Money and Finance* 17 (1998), pp. 97–115.

McCallum, John. "Seven Issues in the Choice of an Exchange Rate Regime for Canada," *Current Analysis,* Economics Department, Royal Bank of Canada (1999).

Murray, John, Lawrence Schembri, and Pierre St-Amant. "Revisiting the Case for Flexible Exchange Rates in North America," *The North American Journal of Economics and Finance,* Vol. 14, Issue 2 (2000), pp. 207–400.

Swiss Bank Corporation. *Foreign Exchange and Money Market Operations.* Basle, Switzerland: Swiss Bank Corporation, 1987.

UBS Wartung. *Foreign Exchange and Money Market Transactions.* This book can be found and downloaded at www.ubswarburg.com/fx_swiss/.

CHAPTER 5

International Parity Relationships and Forecasting Foreign Exchange Rates

This chapter examines the international *parity conditions* that govern the exchange rate between pairs of currencies. The parity conditions offer the economic explanation for the value of the exchange rate and also for the rate of change of the exchange rate. The parity conditions are the foundation of most models of forecasting exchange rates.

The parity conditions reflect the international Law of One Price, the fundamental idea that two things that are identical ought to sell for the same price. Whereas the Law of One Price, sometimes called Purchasing Power Parity, is crucial in international trade—essentially the idea that traded goods tend to have the same price everywhere—we will focus on the financial aspect of the Law of One Price and deal with financial assets, capital flows, and interest rates.

Since *arbitrage* plays a crucial role in the following discussion, we will define it at the outset. **Arbitrage** is *the simultaneous purchase and sale of equivalent assets for the purpose of generating a certain and riskless profit.* An arbitrager sells an over-priced asset and buys an identical underpriced asset.

As long as profitable arbitrage opportunities exist, the market cannot be in equilibrium. Conversely and usefully, a market is said to be in equilibrium when no profitable arbitrage opportunities exist. In international finance, *interest rate parity* is an important zero-arbitrage relationship.

5.1 Interest Rate Parity

Interest rate parity (IRP) is a zero-arbitrage condition that must hold when international financial markets are in equilibrium. Interest rate parity, in effect, means that financial assets of similar risk in two countries yield the same rate of return, regardless of the currency in which the assets are denominated.

Consider two alternative ways of investing 100 dollars. You could invest the $100 in Canada in a one-year Government of Canada bond. The Canadian bond pays the Canadian interest rate, $i_\$$. Alternatively, you could invest in a one-year British government bond that pays the British interest rate, $i_£$.

Note that the example is constructed with Canadian and British bonds that are both considered riskless and have one-year maturity. In other words, they are in the same (zero) risk class, and they have the same maturity.

The investment in Canada will result in cash at maturity of $100(1 + i_\$)$. This is a certain amount of Canadian dollars.

To invest in the United Kingdom, on the other hand, you must carry out the following three-step procedure:

1. Pay $100 to buy British pounds at the prevailing spot exchange rate (S). This will provide you with £100 (1/S).

2. Invest the pounds at the British interest rate. This will result in cash at maturity of £100 (1/S) $(1 + i_£)$. This is a certain amount of British pounds.

3. Sell the maturity value of the British investment *forward* at the forward exchange rate (F). This will result in cash at maturity of £100 (1/S) $(1 + i_£)$ F. This is a certain amount of Canadian dollars.

The investment in the United Kingdom begins with Canadian dollars and ends with Canadian dollars. Canadian dollars are sold (spot) for pounds at the beginning, and pounds were sold (forward) to result in Canadian dollars at the end. From your point of view as a Canadian investor, your investment in British bonds is *hedged*. At the outset, you know the British interest rate, the spot exchange rate, and the forward exchange rate, and hence you know for certain the number of Canadian dollars that you will end up with at the maturity of the British investment.

The "effective" dollar interest rate from the British investment is $(F/S) (1 + i_£) - 1$.

Zero-arbitrage equilibrium dictates that the future dollar proceeds (or, equivalently, the dollar interest rates) from investing in Canada or in the United Kingdom is the same, that is:

$$\$100 (1 + i_\$) = \$100 (F/S) (1 + i_£)$$

or

$$(1 + i_\$) = (F/S) (1 + i_£) \tag{5.1}$$

This is a formal statement of interest rate parity. It represents the Law of One Price applied to international money market instruments.

If IRP, in fact, holds, the immediate implication is that it makes no difference where the Canadian investor invests. The dollar return will be the same whether the investment is in Canadian bonds or British bonds. In other words, arbitrage opportunities do not exist. The *net cashflow* from investing in British bonds versus Canadian bonds is zero. This is illustrated in Exhibit 5.1.

Exhibit 5.1 traces the transactions of a Canadian investor's purchase of British bonds in the situation in which IRP holds. The slight difference from the previous example is that the Canadian investor borrows in Canada to finance the investment. The Canadian investor borrows $1, converts that dollar to British pounds at the spot rate (S), and sells the pound-proceeds forward at the forward rate (F). The net cashflow is zero, indicative of the absence of an arbitrage opportunity.

Zero-arbitrage profits mean that

$$(1 + i_£) F - (1 + i_\$) S = 0 \tag{5.2}$$

This, upon simple rearrangement, is the same result as equation 5.1.

EXHIBIT 5.1	Transactions	CF_0	CF_1
Dollar Cash Flows to an Arbitrage Portfolio	1. Borrow in Canada	S_0	$-S_1 (1 + i_\$)$
	2. Lend in Britain	$-\$S_0$	$S_1 (1 + i_£)$
	3. Sell the £ receivable forward*	0	$(1 + i_£)(F - S_1)$
	Net cash flow	0	$(1 + i_£) F - (1 + i_\$) S_0$

*Selling the £ receivable forward will not result in any cash flow at the present time, that is $CF_0 = 0$.
At maturity, the seller of "forward pounds-for-dollars" will receive $(F - S_1)$ for each pound sold forward.
S_1 denotes the spot exchange rate at maturity.

Interest rate parity is often approximated as[1]

$$(i_\$ - i_£) = (F - S)/S \qquad (5.3)$$

Equation 5.3 indicates that interest rate parity implies an explicit linkage between the interest rates in two countries. The "linkage" is explicit in the relationship between the spot rate of exchange and the forward rate. Specifically, the interest rate will be higher in Canada than in the United Kingdom when the Canadian dollar is at a forward discount, that is $F > S$.

Recall that the exchange rates, S and F, represent the dollar prices of one unit of foreign currency. When the dollar is at a forward discount, the implication is that the dollar is expected to depreciate against the British pound. If so, the Canadian interest rate (in equilibrium) must be higher than the British interest rate to compensate for the expected depreciation of the dollar. Otherwise, investors would shy away from dollar-denominated securities. On the other hand, the Canadian interest rate will be lower than the British interest rate when the dollar is at a forward premium, that is when $F < S$. In general, equation 5.3 indicates that under interest rate parity the forward exchange rate will deviate from the spot exchange rate whenever the interest rates in the two countries are not the same.

When IRP holds, you will be indifferent to investing your money in Canada or Britain with forward hedging. However, if IRP does not hold, you will prefer one country to the other. You will be better off investing in Canada if $(1 + i_\$)$ is greater than $(F/S)(1 + i_£)$. You will be better off investing in the United Kingdom if $(1 + i_\$)$ is less than $(F/S)(1 + i_£)$.

When you need to borrow, you will choose to borrow where the dollar interest is lower. It is better to borrow in Canada when $(1 + i_\$)$ is less than $(F/S)(1 + i_£)$.

When IRP does not hold, the situation gives rise to **covered interest arbitrage (CIA)** opportunities. To explain the covered interest arbitrage process, it is convenient to work with a numerical example.

EXAMPLE 5.1 **The Adjustment Process** Suppose that the annual interest rate is 5 percent in Canada and 7 percent in the United Kingdom. The spot exchange rate is $2.20/£. The forward exchange rate is $2.18/£.

In terms of our notation, $i_\$ = 5\%$, $i_£ = 7\%$, $S = \$2.20$ and $F = \$2.18$.

Assume that an arbitrager can borrow up to $1,000,000 or £454,545. The latter figure (in pounds) is equivalent to $1,000,000 at the spot exchange rate.

Let us check to see if IRP is holding under current market conditions. Substituting the given data, we find,

$$(F/S)(1 + i_£) = (2.18/2.20)(1.07) = 1.0603$$

which is not equal to $(1 + i\$) = 1.05$. Specifically, we find that the current market conditions are characterized by:

$$(1 + i_\$) < (F/S)(1 + i_£) \qquad (5.4)$$

Interest rate parity is not holding, implying that a profitable arbitrage opportunity exists. Since the interest rate in Canada is lower than the effective dollar interest rate on a British investment, arbitrage transactions involve borrowing in Canada and lending in the United Kingdom.

continued

---

[1] Equation 5.3 is an approximate version. The exact version is $(i_\$ - i_£) = [(F-S)/S](1 + i_£)$. To determine if an arbitage opportunity exists, one should use the exact version of IRP.

EXAMPLE 5.1 **Continued**

The arbitrager can carry out the following transactions:

1. In Canada, borrow $1,000,000. Repayment in one year will be $1,050,000 = $1,000,000 × 1.05.
2. Buy £454,545 spot using the $1,000,000
3. Invest £454,545 in British securities. The maturity value will be £486,364 = £454,545 × 1.07 .
4. Sell £486,364 forward in exchange for $1,060,273 = £486,364 ($2.18/£).

In one year, when everything matures, the arbitrager will receive the full maturity value of the British investment, that is £486,364. The arbitrage will deliver the pound amount to the counterparty of the forward contract and will receive $1,060,273 in return. Out of this dollar amount, the initial loan plus interest, $1,050,000 will be repaid. The arbitrager still has $10,273 (= $1,060,273 − $1,050,000) left in his account. This is the arbitrage profit. In making this certain profit, the arbitrager neither invested any money out of his own pocket nor bore any risk. He, indeed, carried out "covered interest arbitrage," which means that he borrowed at one interest rate and simultaneously loaned the funds at another interest rate, all the while with the exchange risk fully covered via forward hedging. Exhibit 5.2 provides a summary of the covered interest arbitrage transactions.

How long will this arbitrage opportunity last? A simple answer is: only for a short while. As soon as deviations from IRP are detected, informed traders will immediately carry out CIA transactions. As a result of these arbitrage activities, IRP will be restored quite quickly. To see this, let us get back to our numerical example, which induced covered interest arbitrage activities. Since every trader will (1) borrow in Canada as much as possible, (2) lend in the United Kingdom, (3) buy the pound spot, and, at the same time, (4) sell the pound forward, the following adjustments will occur to the initial market condition described in equation 5.4:

1. The interest rate will rise in Canada ($i_\$\uparrow$).
2. The interest rate will fall in the United Kingdom ($i_\pounds\downarrow$).
3. The pound will appreciate in the spot market ($S\uparrow$).
4. The pound will depreciate in the forward market ($F\downarrow$).

These adjustments will raise the left hand side of equation 5.4 and, at the same time, lower the right hand side until both sides are equalized, restoring IRP.

The adjustment process is depicted in Exhibit 5.3. The initial market condition described by equation 5.4 is represented by point A in the exhibit, substantially off the IRP line. CIA activities will increase the interest rate differential (as indicated by the

EXHIBIT 5.2	Transactions	CF$_0$	CF$_1$
Covered Interest Arbitrage: Cash Flow Analysis	1. Borrow $1,000,000	$1,000,000	−$1,050,000
	2. Buy £ spot	−$1,000,000 £454.545	
	3. Lend £454.545	−£454.545	£486,364
	4. Sell £486,364 forward		−£486,364 $1,060,273
	Net cash flow	0	$10,273

horizontal arrow) and, at the same time, lower the forward premium/discount (as indicated by the vertical arrow). Since the foreign exchange and money markets share the burden of adjustments, the actual path of adjustment to IRP can be depicted by the dotted arrow. When the initial market condition is located at point *B*, IRP will be restored partly by an increase in the forward premium, $(F - S)/S$, and partly by a decrease in the interest rate differential, $i_\$ - i_£$.

Interest Rate Parity and Exchange Rate Determination

As a zero-arbitrage equilibrium condition involving the (spot) exchange rate, IRP has an immediate implication for exchange rate determination. To see why, let us reformulate the IRP relationship in terms of the spot exchange rate:

$$S = \left[\frac{1 + i_£}{1 + i_\$}\right]F \tag{5.5}$$

Equation 5.5 indicates that given the forward exchange rate, the spot exchange rate depends on relative interest rates. All else equal, an increase in the Canadian interest rate will lead to a higher foreign exchange value of the dollar.[2] This is so because a higher Canadian interest rate will attract capital to the Canada, increasing the demand for dollars. In contrast, a decrease in the Canadian interest rate will lower the foreign exchange value of the dollar.

In addition to relative interest rates, the forward exchange rate is an important factor in spot exchange rate determination. Under certain conditions the forward exchange rate can be viewed as the expected future spot exchange rate conditional on all relevant information being available now, that is,

$$F = E(S_{t+1}|I_t) \tag{5.6}$$

where S_{t+1} is the future spot rate when the forward contract matures, and I_t denotes the set of information currently available.[3] When equations 5.5 and 5.6 are combined,

EXHIBIT 5.3

The Interest Rate Parity Diagram

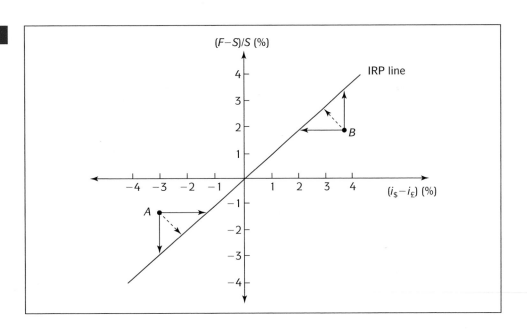

---

[2]A higher Canadian interest rate $(i_\$\uparrow)$ will lead to a lower spot exchange rate $(S\downarrow)$, which means a stronger dollar. *S* represents the number of Canadian dollars per pound.

[3]The set of relevant information includes money supplies, interest rates, trade balances, and so on that influences exchange rates.

we obtain,

$$S = \left[\frac{1 + i_£}{1 + i_\$}\right] E(S_{t+1}|I_t) \tag{5.7}$$

Two things are noteworthy from equation 5.7. First, "expectation" plays a key role in exchange rate determination. Specifically, the expected future exchange rate is shown to be a major determinant of the current exchange rate; when people "expect" the exchange rate to go up in the future, it goes up now. People's expectations thus become self-fulfilling. Second, exchange rate behaviour is driven by news events. People form expectations based on the information (I_t) they possess. As they receive news continuously, they update their expectations continuously. As a result, the exchange rate tends to exhibit *dynamic* and *volatile* short-term behaviour, responding to various news events. By definition, news events are unpredictable, making forecasting future exchange rates an arduous task.

When the forward exchange rate F is replaced by the expected future spot exchange rate, $E(S_{t+1})$ in equation 5.3, we obtain:

$$(i_\$ - i_£) = E(e) \tag{5.8}$$

where $E(e)$ is the expected rate of change in the exchange rate, that is, $[E(S_{t+1}) - S_t]/S_t$. Equation 5.8 states that the interest rate differential between a pair of countries is (approximately) equal to the expected rate of change in the exchange rate. This relationship is known as the **uncovered interest rate parity.** If, for instance, the annual interest rate is 5 percent in Canada and 7 percent in the United Kingdom, as assumed in our numerical example, uncovered IRP suggests that the pound will depreciate against the dollar by about 2 percent, that is, $E(e) = -2\%$.

Reasons for Deviations from Interest Rate Parity

Although IRP tends to hold quite well, it may not hold precisely all the time for at least two reasons: transaction costs and capital controls.

In our previous examples of CIA transactions, we implicitly assumed, among other things, that no transaction costs. In that case, for each dollar borrowed at the Canadian interest rate ($i_\$$), the arbitrager could realize the following amount of positive profit:

$$(F/S)(1 + i_£) - (1 + i_\$) > 0 \tag{5.9}$$

In reality, transaction costs do exist. The interest rate at which the arbitrager borrows, i^a, tends to be higher than the rate at which he lends, i^b, reflecting the bid-ask spread. Likewise, there are bid-ask spreads in the foreign exchange market as well. The arbitrager has to buy foreign exchange at the higher ask price and sell it at the lower bid price. Each of the four variables in equation 5.9 can be regarded as representing the midpoint of the spread.

Because of spreads, arbitrage profit from each dollar borrowed may become non-positive:

$$(F^b/S^a)(1 + i_£^b) - (1 + i_\$^a) \le 0 \tag{5.10}$$

where the superscripts a and b to the exchange rates and interest rates denote the ask and bid prices, respectively. This is so because

$$(F^b/S^a) < (F/S)$$
$$(1 + i_£^b) < (1 + i_£)$$
$$(1 + i_\$^a) > (1 + i_\$)$$

If the arbitrage profit turns negative because of transaction costs, the current deviation from IRP does not represent a profitable arbitrage opportunity. Thus, the IRP line in Exhibit 5.4 can be viewed within a band around it. Only IRP deviations outside the band, such as point *C,* represent profitable arbitrage opportunities. IRP deviations

EXHIBIT 5.4

Interest Rate Parity with Transaction Costs

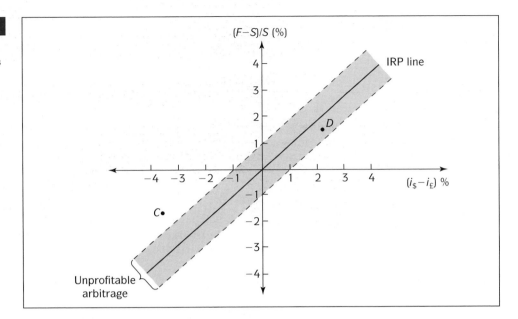

within the band, such as point *D,* would not represent profitable arbitrage opportunities. The width of this band will depend on the size of transaction costs.

Another major reason for deviations from IRP is capital controls imposed by governments. For various macroeconomic reasons, governments sometimes restrict capital flows, inbound and/or outbound. Instruments to restrict capital inflow or outflow include taxes or explicit controls. Capital controls were often imposed by governments in an effort to improve the balance-of-payments situations and to keep the exchange rate at a desirable level.

An interesting historical example is provided by Japan, where capital controls were imposed on and off until December 1980, when the Japanese government liberalized international capital flows. Otani and Tiwari (1981) investigated the effect of capital controls on IRP deviations during the period 1978–81. They computed deviations from interest rate parity (DIRP) as follows:[4]

$$\text{DIRP} = [(1 + i_{¥})S/(1 + i_{\$})F] - 1 \tag{5.11}$$

where:

$i_{¥}$ = interest rate on three-month Gensaki bonds.[5]

$i_{\$}$ = interest rate on three-month euro-dollar deposits.

S = yen/dollar spot exchange rate in Tokyo.

F = yen/dollar three-month forward exchange rate in Tokyo.

Deviations from IRP computed as above are plotted in Exhibit 5.5. If IRP holds strictly, deviations from it would be randomly distributed, with the expected value of zero.

Exhibit 5.5, however, shows that deviations from IRP hardly hover around zero. The deviations were quite significant at times until near the end of 1980. They were the greatest during 1978. This can be attributed to various measures the Japanese government took to discourage capital inflows, which was done to keep the yen from appreciating. As these measures were removed in 1979, the deviations were reduced. They increased again considerably in 1980, however, reflecting an introduction of capital

---

[4]Readers can convince themselves that DIRP in equation 5.11 will be zero if IRP holds exactly.

[5]Gensaki bonds, issued in the Tokyo money market, are sold with a repurchase agreement. While interest rates on Gensaki bonds are determined by market forces, they can still be affected by various market imperfections.

EXHIBIT 5.5

Deviations from Interest Rate Parity: Japan, 1978–1981 (in percent)

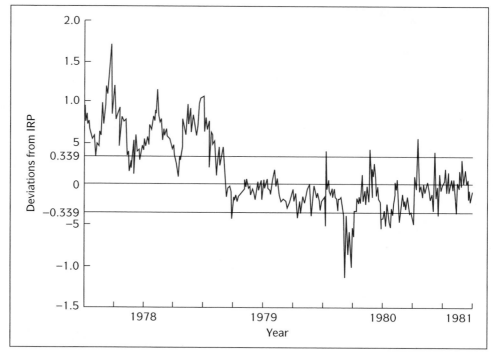

Note: Daily data were used in computing the deviations. The zone bounded by +0.339 and −0.339 represents the average width of the band around the IRP for the sample period.
Source: I. Otani and S. Tiwari, "Capital Controls and Interest Rate Parity: The Japanese Experience, 1978–81," *IMF Staff Papers* 28 (1981), pp. 793–815.

control; Japanese financial institutions were asked to discourage foreign currency deposits.

In December 1980, Japan adopted the new *Foreign Exchange and Foreign Trade Control Law,* which generally liberalized foreign exchange transactions. Not surprisingly, the deviations hover around zero in the first quarter of 1981. The empirical evidence presented in Exhibit 5.5 closely reflects changes in capital controls during the study period. This implies that deviations from IRP, especially in 1978 and 1980, do not represent unexploited profit opportunities; rather, they reflect the existence of significant barriers to cross-border arbitrage.

5.2 Purchasing Power Parity

When the law of one price is applied internationally to a *standard commodity basket,* we have the concept of **purchasing power parity** (PPP): the exchange rate between currencies of two countries should be equal to the ratio of the countries' price levels.

Let $P_\$$ be the dollar price of the standard commodity basket in Canada and $P_£$ the pound price of the same basket in the United Kingdom. Formally, PPP states that the exchange rate between the dollar and the pound should be

$$S = P_\$/P_£ \tag{5.12}$$

where S is the dollar price of one pound. PPP implies that if the standard commodity basket costs $200 in Canada and £100 in the United Kingdom, then the exchange rate should be $2.00 per pound:

$$\$2/£ = \$200/£100$$

If the price of the commodity basket is higher in Canada, say, $300, then PPP dictates that the exchange rate should be higher, that is, $3/£.

To give an alternative interpretation to PPP, let us rewrite equation 5.12 as follows:

$$P_\$ = S \times P_£$$

This equation states that the dollar price of the commodity basket in Canada, $P_\$$, must be the same as the dollar price of the basket in the United Kingdom, that is, $P_£$ multiplied by S. In other words, PPP requires that the price of the standard commodity basket be the same across countries when measured in a common currency. Clearly, PPP is the manifestation of the law of one price applied to the standard consumption basket. As discussed in the International Finance in Practice box "Big MacCurrencies," PPP is a way of defining the equilibrium exchange rate.

As a light-hearted guide to the "correct" level of exchange rate, *The Economist* each year compiles local prices of Big Macs around the world and computes the so-called "Big Mac PPP," the exchange rate that would equalize the hamburger prices between America and elsewhere. To compare this PPP and the actual exchange rate, a currency may be judged to be either undervalued or overvalued. In April 2002, a Big Mac cost (on average) $2.49 in America and 2.50 pesos in Argentina. Thus, the Big Mac PPP would be about one peso per dollar. The actual exchange rate, however, is 3.13 pesos per dollar, implying that the peso is vastly undervalued. In contrast, the Big Mac PPP for Switzerland is 2.53 Swiss francs per dollar, compared with the actual exchange rate of 1.66 francs per dollar. This implies that the Swiss franc is overvalued.

The PPP relationship of equation 5.12 is called the *absolute* version of PPP. When the PPP relationship is presented in the "rate of change" form, we obtain the *relative* version:

$$e = (\pi_\$ - \pi_£)/(1 + \pi_£) \approx \pi_\$ - \pi_£ \tag{5.13}$$

where e is the rate of change in the exchange rate and $\pi_\$$ and $\pi_£$ are the inflation rates in Canada and United Kingdom, respectively. For example, if the inflation rate is 6 percent per year in Canada and 4 percent in the United Kingdom, then the pound should appreciate against the dollar by about 2 percent, that is, $e = 2$ percent, per year. It is noted that even if absolute PPP does not hold, relative PPP may hold.[6]

PPP Deviations and the Real Exchange Rate

Whether PPP holds or not has important implications for international trade. If PPP holds and thus the differential inflation rates between countries are exactly offset by exchange rate changes, countries' competitive positions in world export markets will not be systematically affected by exchange rate changes. However, if there are deviations from PPP, changes in nominal exchange rates cause changes in the **real exchange rates,** affecting the international competitive positions of countries. This, in turn, would affect countries' trade balances.

The real exchange rate, q, which measures deviations from PPP, can be defined as follows:[7]

$$q = \frac{1 + \pi_\$}{(1 + e)(1 + \pi_£)} \tag{5.14}$$

First, note that if PPP holds, that is, $(1 + e) = (1 + \pi_\$)/(1 + \pi_£)$, the real exchange rate will be unity, $q = 1$. When PPP is violated, however, the real exchange rate will deviate from unity. Suppose, for example, the annual inflation rate is 5 percent in Canada and 3.5 percent in the United Kingdom, and the dollar depreciated against the pound by 4.5 percent. Then, the real exchange rate is 0.97:

$$q = (1.05)/(1.045)(1.035) = 0.97$$

www.economist.com/
markets/Bigmac/Index.cfm

Offers a discussion of
exchange rate theory using
Big Mac Index.

---

[6]From equation 5.13, we obtain $(1 + e) = (1 + \pi_\$)/(1 + \pi_£)$. Rearranging the above expression we obtain $e = (\pi_\$ - \pi_£)/(1 + \pi_£)$, which is approximated by $e = \pi_\$ - \pi_£$ as in equation 5.12.

[7]The real exchange rate measures the degree of deviations from PPP over a certain period of time, assuming that PPP held roughly at a starting point. If PPP holds continuously, the real exchange rate will remain unity.

In the above example, the dollar depreciated by more than is warranted by PPP, strengthening the competitiveness of Canadian industries in the world market. If the dollar depreciates by less than the inflation rate differential, the real exchange rate will be greater than unity, weakening the competitiveness of Canadian industries. To summarize,

$q = 1$: Competitiveness of the domestic country unaltered.

$q < 1$: Competitiveness of the domestic country improves.

$q > 1$: Competitiveness of the domestic country deteriorates.

Exhibit 5.6 plots the real "effective" exchange rates for the American dollar, euro (Germany), Japanese yen, and Mexican peso since 1970. The rates plotted in Exhibit 5.6 are, however, the real effective exchange rate "indices" computed using 1995 rates as the base, that is, 1995 = 100. The real effective exchange rate is a weighted average of bilateral real exchange rates, with the weight for each foreign currency determined by the country's share in the domestic country's international trade. The real effective exchange rate rises if domestic inflation exceeds inflation abroad and the nominal exchange rate fails to depreciate to compensate for the higher domestic inflation rate. Thus, if the real effective exchange rate rises (falls), the domestic country's competitiveness declines (improves). It is noted that the real effective exchange rate of the Mexican peso falls sharply periodically, reflecting devaluations of the peso.

Real versus Nominal Exchange Rates—A Closer Look

If Purchasing Power Parity—the "international law of one price"—held at all times, which it certainly does not, the exchange rate between two currencies would continuously adjust to reflect the difference in inflation between the two countries. On the other hand, if the exchange rate does not adjust to fully reflect the difference between the two countries' inflation rates, the *real* exchange rate is altered. This result underlies the distinction between the *nominal* exchange rate (the exchange rate that you "see") and the *real* exchange rate. The latter takes explicit account of purchasing power parity or deviations from it.

EXHIBIT 5.6

Real Effective Exchange Rates for Selected Currencies

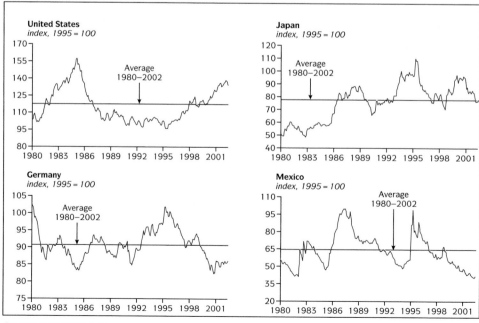

Source: Datastream.com.

The *nominal–real* distinction is important for understanding the influence of exchange rates on a nation's competitiveness. We will briefly examine the *nominal–real* distinction in two specific contexts:

1. the nominal exchange rate changes despite no inflation differential between two countries, and
2. the nominal exchange rate is steady despite an inflation differential between two countries.

Let us make the first context even more specific. Say, we have zero inflation in both Canada and the United States. Now, let us also say that the Canadian dollar appreciates against the American dollar, from C$1.50/US$1 to C$1.40/US$1. With Canadian dollar appreciation, Canadian goods become more expensive for Americans while American goods become cheaper for Canadians. The *real* value of the Canadian dollar has risen. Canada experiences a rise in the *real* exchange rate.

> *In general, if an exchange rate appreciates more than the difference between the rates of inflation in the two countries, then the country that experiences the nominal exchange rate appreciation also experiences a rise in its real exchange rate. The other country experiences a fall in its real exchange rate.*

Now, to deal with the second context, where the nominal exchange rate is steady despite an inflation differential between two countries, let us be specific and say that the Canada–United States exchange rate is slow to adjust to a Canada–United States inflation differential. Let us also say that American inflation exceeds Canadian inflation. In other words, the nominal price of goods in the United States rises faster than the price of goods in Canada. Since the exchange rate does not fully adjust for the inflation differential, American consumers will soon discover that goods imported from Canada are cheaper than American goods. Canadians will discover that American goods have become more expensive. Canada experiences a fall in the *real* exchange rate.

> *In general, if an international inflation differential is not reflected in depreciation of the currency of the country with higher inflation, then the country with higher inflation experiences a rise in its real exchange rate while the country with lower inflation experiences a reduction in the real value of its exchange rate.[8]*

Exhibit 5.7 illustrates the recent 18-year history of the nominal and real values of the Canadian exchange rate *vis-à-vis* the American dollar. The top chart presents the values of the exchange rate with a *direct* quote—the number of Canadian dollars required to purchase one American dollar. The second chart graphs the values of the exchange rate using the *indirect* quote—the value of the Canadian dollar expressed in terms of American dollars.

The third chart in Exhibit 5.7 presents rates of inflation in Canada and in the United States in each year of the 18-year period. In most years since 1990 (with 2002 being a striking exception), Canadian inflation has been below inflation in the United States.

---

[8]This type of effect led to the 1971–1973 collapse of the Bretton Woods fixed exchange rate regime that had been in place since 1944. The main strain was between the United States and Germany. By 1971, the United States had experienced several years of substantial inflation. Germany had relatively low inflation. The inevitable rise in the real exchange rate (from the American perspective) resulted in a large and widening American trade deficit. Germany, on the other hand, had a substantial trade surplus that put "demand pressure" on the German economy, largely from the United States. The fixed exchange regime in effect meant that the United States was "exporting" its inflation to Germany and, to a lesser extent, Japan. Meanwhile, the United States was bleeding foreign exchange reserves via capital outflows. When the stable exchange rate regime finally collapsed, the American dollar depreciated sharply against all other major currencies, first by 9 percent in 1971 and then by 11 percent in 1973.

EXHIBIT 5.7

Canada–United States Exchange Rates, Inflation, and the Canadian Dollar Real Exchange Rate Index, 1987–2004

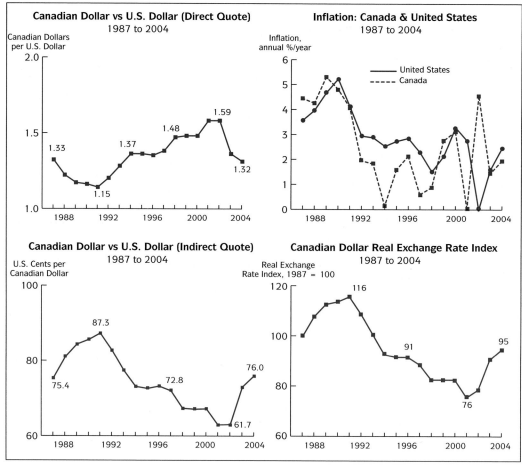

Source: *Bank of Canada Review* (Banking and Financial Statistics, June 2004, Table 11 (Exchange Rates) and Table 48 (Prices Indices). Figure "Inflation: Canada & US" adapted from Statistics Canada CANSIM database http://cansim2.statscan.ca, Series V121701, D139105, B3400.

Finally, the bottom chart in Exhibit 5.7 integrates data on the nominal exchange rate and inflation differentials into a Real Exchange Rate Index for the period 1987 to 2004.[9] A year-over-year rise in the index indicates a rise in the Canadian real exchange rate. A year-over-year fall in the index indicates a fall in the Canadian real exchange rate. We see that the index rose sharply from 1987 to 1991, a period in which the Bank of Canada committed to austere monetary policy and high interest rates in an effort to rid the country of inflation. In 1991, Canada's merchandise trade balance touched its lowest level in the entire 1980–2004 period, in large part due to the exceptionally high real value of the Canadian exchange rate (but also in part due to the 1991–1992 recession in the United States). From 1992 to 2001, the real exchange rate index fell 35 percent, from 116 to 76, puzzling most economists who deal with these issues. Since then the index has bounced back 25 percent (July 2004).

Evidence on Purchasing Power Parity

As is clear from the above discussions, whether PPP holds in reality is a question of considerable importance. In view of the fact that PPP is the manifestation of the law of one price applied to a standard commodity basket, it will hold only if the prices of con-

---

[9]The Real Exchange Rate Index equals the nominal exchange rate (indirect quote) in year *t* divided by the ratio of the American Price Index to the Canadian Price Index in the same year *t*. The two price indexes are normalized to the same base value in the year t_0. The Real Exchange Rate Index is normalized to a value of 100 for the year 1987. This computational approach is consistent with equation 5.14.

EXHIBIT 5.8

A Guide to World
Prices: March 1999[a]

Location	Fast Food (1 unit)	Aspirin (100.units)	Man's Haircut (1 unit)	Camera Film (24 exposures)
Athens	$4.43	$2.87	$17.76	$4.52
Copenhagen	$7.98	$5.71	$27.46	$7.81
Hong Kong	$2.65	$10.33	$36.16	$2.70
London	$5.76	$15.26	$21.28	$6.55
Los Angeles	$4.37	$7.91	$13.17	$3.49
Madrid	$4.91	$15.36	$12.56	$3.50
Mexico City	$4.50	$13.39	$6.70	$4.20
Munich	$5.52	$13.15	$23.20	$3.79
Paris	$4.76	$12.62	$20.46	$5.25
Rio de Janeiro	$2.15	$20.67	$13.95	$3.60
Rome	$4.98	$25.40	$25.79	$4.24
Sydney	$3.92	$8.54	$14.75	$4.19
Tokyo	$5.56	$17.78	$46.37	$4.03
Toronto	$4.20	$5.17	$11.43	$3.31
Vienna	$5.25	$7.55	$22.90	$3.36
Average	$4.73	$12.11	$20.93	$4.30
Standard Deviation	$1.35	$6.18	$10.26	$1.33
Coefficient of Variation[b]	0.29	0.51	0.49	0.31

[a]Prices include sales tax and value-added tax except in the United States location.
[b]The coefficient of variation is obtained from dividing the standard deviation by the average. It thus provides a
measure of dispersion adjusted for the magnitude of the variable.
Source: Runzheimer International.

stituent commodities are equalized across countries in a given currency and if the composition of the consumption basket is the same across countries.

The PPP has been the subject of a series of tests, yielding generally negative results. For example, in his study of disaggregated commodity arbitrage between Canada and the United States, Richardson (1978) was unable to detect commodity arbitrage for a majority of commodity classes. Richardson reported: "The presence of commodity arbitrage could be rejected with 95 percent confidence for at least 13 out of the 22 commodity groups" (p. 346). Although Richardson did not directly test PPP, his findings can be viewed as highly negative news for PPP. If commodity arbitrage is imperfect between neighbouring countries, such as the United States and Canada, that have relatively few trade restrictions, PPP is not likely to hold much better for other pairs of countries.

Exhibit 5.8, "A Guide to World Prices," also provides evidence against commodity price parity. The price of aspirin (100 units) ranges from $2.87 in Athens to $25.40 in Rome. Likewise, a cost of a man's haircut ranges from $6.70 in Mexico City to $46.37 in Tokyo. It cost seven times more to have a haircut in Tokyo than in Mexico City. The price differential, however, is likely to persist because haircuts are simply not tradable. In comparison, the price disparity for camera film is substantially less. This can be attributable to the fact that camera film is a highly standardized commodity that is actively traded across national borders.

Generally unfavourable evidence about PPP suggests substantial barriers to international commodity arbitrage. Obviously, commodity prices can diverge between countries up to the transportation costs without triggering arbitrage. If it costs $50 to ship a tonne of rice from Thailand to Korea, the price of rice can diverge by up to $50 in either direction between the two countries without violating PPP. Likewise, deviations from PPP can result from tariffs and quotas imposed on international trade.

As is well recognized, some commodities never enter into international trade. Examples of such **nontradables** include haircuts, medical services, housing, and the like. These items are either immovable or inseparable from the providers of these services. Suppose a quality haircut costs $20 in Toronto but the comparable haircut costs

Big MacCurrencies

Currency forecasters have had it hard in recent years. Most expected the euro to rise after its launch in 1999, yet it fell. When America went into recession last year, the dollar was tipped to decline; it rose. So to help forecasters really get their teeth into exchange rates, *The Economist* has updated its Big Mac index.

Devised 16 years ago as a light-hearted guide to whether currencies are at their "correct" level, the index is based on the theory of purchasing-power parity (PPP). In the long run, countries' exchange rates should move towards rates that would equalise the prices of an identical basket of goods and services. Our basket is a McDonald's Big Mac, produced in 120 countries. The Big Mac PPP is the exchange rate that would leave hamburgers costing the same in America as elsewhere. Comparing these with actual rates signals if a currency is under- or overvalued.

The first column of the table shows the local-currency prices of a Big Mac. The second converts these into dollars. The average American price has fallen slightly over the past year, to $2.49. The cheapest Big Mac is in Argentina (78 cents), after its massive devaluation; the most expensive ($3.81) is in Switzerland. (More countries are listed on our website.) By this measure, the Argentina peso is the most undervalued currency and the Swiss franc the most overvalued.

The third column calculates Big Mac PPPs. Dividing the Japanese price by the American price, for instance, gives a dollar PPP of ¥105, against an actual exchange rate of ¥130. This implies that the yen is 19% undervalued. The euro is only 5% undervalued relative to its Big Mac PPP, far less than many economists claim. The euro area may have a single currency, but the price of a Big Mac varies widely, from €2.15 in Greece to €2.95 in France. However, that range has narrowed from a year ago. And prices vary just as much within America, which is why we use the average price in four cities.

The Australian dollar is the most undervalued rich-world currency, 35% below McParity. No wonder the Australian economy was so strong last year. Sterling, by contrast, is one of the few currencies that is overvalued against the dollar, by 16%; it is 21% too strong against the euro.

Overall, the dollar now looks more overvalued against the average of the other big currencies than at any time in the life of the Big Mac index. Most emerging-market currencies also look cheap against the dollar. Over half the emerging-market currencies are more than 30% undervalued. That implies that any currency close to McParity (e.g., the Argentine peso last year, or the Mexican peso today) will be overvalued against other emerging-market rivals.

Adjustment back towards PPP does not always come through a shift in exchange rates. It can also come about partly through price changes. In 1995 the yen was 100% overvalued. It has since fallen by 35%; but the price of a Japanese burger has also dropped by one-third.

Every time we update our Big Mac index, readers complain that burgernomics does not cut the mustard. The Big Mac is an imperfect basket. Hamburgers cannot be traded across borders; prices may be distorted by taxes, different profit margins or differences in the cost of non-tradable goods and services, such as rents. Yet it seems to pay to follow burgernomics.

In 1999, for instance, the Big Mac index suggested that the euro was already overvalued at its launch, when nearly every economist predicted it would rise. Several studies confirm that, over the long run, purchasing-power parity—including the Big Mac PPP—is a fairly good guide to exchange-rate movements.

Still, currencies can deviate from PPP for long periods. In the early 1990s the Big Mac index repeatedly signaled that the dollar was undervalued, yet it continued to slide for several years until it flipped around. Our latest figures suggest that, sooner or later, the mighty dollar will tumble; relish for fans of burgernomics.

Source: "Economics Focus Big MacCurrencies," *The Economist*, April 27, 2002, p. 76.

only $7 in Mexico City. Obviously, you cannot import haircuts from Mexico. Either you have to travel to Mexico or a Mexican barber must travel to Toronto, both of which, of course, are impractical in view of travel costs and immigration laws. Consequently, the Canadian–Mexican price differential for haircuts will persist. As long as there are nontradables, PPP will not hold in its absolute version. If PPP holds for tradables and the relative prices between tradables and nontradables are maintained, then PPP can hold in its relative version. These conditions, however, are not likely to hold.

Even if PPP may not hold in reality, it can still play a useful role in economic analysis. First, one can use the PPP-determined exchange rate as a benchmark in deciding if a country's currency is undervalued or overvalued against other currencies. Second,

The hamburger standard

	Big Mac prices		Implied PPP* of the dollar	Actual dollar exchange rate 23/04/02	Under (−)/over (+) valuation against the dollar, %
	in local currency	in dollars			
United States†	$2.49	2.49	-	-	-
Argentina	Peso 2.50	0.78	1.00	3.13	−68
Australia	A$3.00	1.62	1.20	1.86	−35
Brazil	Real 3.60	1.55	1.45	2.34	−38
Britain	£1.99	2.88	1.25‡	1.45‡	+16
Canada	C$3.33	2.12	1.34	1.57	−15
Chile	Peso 1,400	2.16	562	655	−14
China	Yuan 10.50	1.27	4.22	8.28	−49
Czech Rep	Koruna 56.28	1.66	22.6	34.0	−33
Denmark	DKr24.75	2.96	9.94	8.38	+19
Euro area	€2.67	2.37	0.93§	0.89§	−5
Hong Kong	HK$11.20	1.40	4.50	7.80	−42
Hungary	Forint459	1.69	184	272	−32
Indonesia	Rupiah 16,000	1.71	6,426	9,430	−32
Israel	Shekel 12.00	2.51	4.82	4.79	+1
Japan	¥262	2.01	105	130	−19
Malaysia	M$5.04	1.33	2.02	3.8	−47
Mexico	Peso 21.90	2.37	8.80	9.28	−5
New Zealand	NZ$3.95	1.77	1.59	2.24	−29
Peru	New Sol 8.50	2.48	3.41	3.43	−1
Philippines	Peso 65.00	1.28	26.1	51.0	−49
Poland	Zloty 5.90	1.46	2.37	4.04	−41
Russia	Rouble 39.00	1.25	15.7	31.2	−50
Singapore	S$3.30	1.81	1.33	1.82	−27
South Africa	Rand 9.70	0.87	3.90	10.9	−64
South Korea	Won 3,100	2.36	1,245	1,304	−5
Sweden	SKr26.00	2.52	10.4	10.3	+1
Switzerland	SFr6.30	3.81	2.53	1.66	+53
Taiwan	NT$70.00	2.01	28.1	34.8	−19
Thailand	Baht 55.00	1.27	22.1	43.3	−49
Turkey	Lira 4,000,000	3.06	1,606,426	1,324,500	+21
Venezuela	Bolivar 2,500	2.92	1,004	857	+17

*Purchasing-power-parity: local price divided by price in United States
†Average of New York, Chicago, San Francisco, and Atlanta
‡Dollars per pound
§Dollars per euro
Source: McDonald's; *The Economist.*

one can often make more meaningful international comparisons of economic data using PPP-determined, rather than market-determined, exchange rates. This point is highlighted in Exhibit 5.9, "How Large Is India's Economy?"

Suppose you want to rank countries in terms of gross national product (GNP). If you use market exchange rates, you can either underestimate or overestimate the true GNP values. Exhibit 5.9 provides the GNP values of the major countries in 2001 computed using both PPP and market exchange rates. A country's ranking in terms of GNP value is quite sensitive to which exchange rate is used. India provides a striking example. When the market exchange rate is used, India ranks 12th, lagging behind such countries as Canada, Spain, and Brazil. However, when the PPP exchange rate is

EXHIBIT 5.9

How Large Is India's Economy?

PPP exchange rate		Rank	Market exchange rate	
$10.17 trillion	U.S.	1	U.S.	$10.17 trillion
$5.51	China	2	Japan	$4.25
$3.36	Japan	3	Germany	$1.87
$2.55	India	4	U.K.	$1.41
$2.19	Germany	5	France	$1.30
$1.54	France	6	China	$1.16
$1.53	U.K.	7	Italy	$1.09
$1.51	Italy	8	Canada	$0.68
$1.34	Brazil	9	Mexico	$0.62
$1.30	Russia	10	Spain	$0.58
$0.89	Mexico	11	Brazil	$0.50
$0.89	Canada	12	India	$0.48
$0.86	Korea	13	Korea	$0.42
$0.80	Spain	14	Netherlands	$0.37
$0.65	Indonesia	15	Australia	$0.37

Sources: Organization for Economic Cooperation and Development and the World Bank. All figures are for 2001.

used, India moves up to fourth after Japan, but ahead of Germany, France, and the United Kingdom. China also moves up from sixth to second, ahead of Japan, when the PPP exchange rate is used. In contrast, such countries as Canada and Spain move down in the GNP ranking when PPP exchange rates are used.

5.3 Fisher Effects

Another parity condition we often encounter in the literature is the **Fisher effect.** The Fisher effect holds that *an increase (decrease) in expected inflation rate will cause a proportionate increase (decrease) in the nominal interest rate.* Formally, the Fisher effect can be written as follows:

$$i_\$ = \rho_\$ + E(\pi_\$) + \rho_\$ E(\pi_\$) \approx \rho_\$ + E(\pi_\$) \tag{5.15}$$

where $\rho_\$$ denotes the equilibrium expected "real" interest rate in Canada.[10]

For example, suppose the expected real interest rate is 2 percent per year in Canada. Given this, the Canadian (nominal) interest rate will be entirely determined by expected inflation. If, for instance, the expected inflation rate is 4 percent per year, the nominal interest rate will then be about 6 percent. With a 6-percent interest rate, the lender will be compensated for the expected erosion of the purchasing power of money while still expecting to realize a 2-percent real return. The Fisher effect should hold in each country. The expected inflation rate is the difference between the nominal and real interest rates in each country, that is,

$$E(\pi_\$) = (i_\$ - \rho_\$)/(1 + \rho_\$) \approx i_\$ - \rho_\$$$
$$E(\pi_£) = (i_£ - \rho_£)/(1 + \rho_£) \approx i_£ - \rho_£$$

Now, let us assume that the real interest rate is the same between countries, that is, $\rho_\$ = \rho_£$, because of unrestricted capital flows. When we substitute the above results into the relative PPP in its expectational form in equation (5.13), we obtain

$$E(e) = (i_\$ - i_£)/(1 + i_£) \approx i_\$ - i_£ \tag{5.16}$$

---

[10]It is noted that equation 5.15 obtains from the relationship: $(1 + i_\$) = (1 + \rho_\$)(1 + E(\pi_\$))$.

which is known as the **international Fisher effect (IFE).**[11] IFE suggests that the nominal interest rate differential reflects the expected change in exchange rate. For instance, if the interest rate is 5 percent per year in Canada and 7 percent in the United Kingdom, the Canadian dollar is expected to appreciate against the British pound by about 2 percent per year.

Lastly, when the international Fisher effect is combined with IRP, that is, $(F - S)/S = (i_\$ - i_£)/(1 + i_£)$, we obtain

$$(F - S)/S = E(e) \tag{5.17}$$

which is referred to as **forward expectations parity (FEP).** Forward parity states that any forward premium or discount is equal to the expected change in the exchange rate. When investors are risk-neutral, forward parity will hold as long as the foreign exchange market is informationally efficient. Otherwise, it need not hold even if the market is efficient. Exhibit 5.10 summarizes the parity relationships discussed so far.[12]

5.4 Forecasting Exchange Rates

http://fx.sauder.ubc.ca

Provides historical time series of exchange rates.

In our world of flexible exchange rates, many business decisions must take account of forecasts of exchange rates. Understandably, forecasting exchange rates as accurately as possible is a matter of vital importance for currency traders who are actively engaged in speculating, hedging, and arbitrage in the foreign exchange markets. It is also a vital concern for multinational corporations that are formulating international sourcing, production, financing, and marketing strategies. The quality of these corporate decisions depend on the accuracy of exchange rate forecasts.

Some corporations generate their own forecasts, while others subscribe to outside services for a fee. While forecasters use a wide variety of forecasting techniques, most can be classified into three distinct approaches:

- Efficient market approach
- Fundamental approach
- Technical approach

Let us briefly examine each of these approaches.

Efficient Market Approach

Financial markets are said to be efficient if the current asset prices fully reflect all the available and relevant information. The **efficient market hypothesis** (EMH) has strong implications for forecasting.

If foreign exchange markets are efficient, the current exchange rate reflects all relevant information pertinent to the value of the exchange rate, such as money supplies, inflation rates, trade balances, and output growth. The exchange rate will then change only when the market receives new information. Since news, by definition, is unpredictable, the exchange rate will change randomly over time. In other words, incremental changes in the exchange rate are independent of the past history of the

---

[11]The international Fisher effect is the same as the uncovered IRP previously discussed. While the Fisher effect should hold in an efficient market, the international Fisher effect need not hold even in an efficient market unless investors are risk-neutral. Generally speaking, the interest rate differential may reflect not only the expected change in the exchange rate but also a risk premium.

[12]Suppose that the Fisher effect holds both in Canada and in the United Kingdom and that the real interest rate is the same in both the countries. As shown in Exhibit 5.10, the Fisher effect (FE) then implies that the interest rate differential should be equal to the expected inflation differential. Furthermore, when forward parity and PPP are combined, we obtain what might be called "forward-PPP" (FPPP), that is, the forward premium/discount is equal to the expected inflation differential.

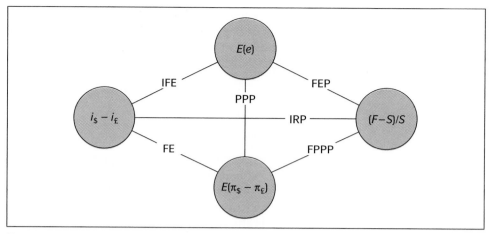

Notes:
1. With the assumption of the same real interest rate, the Fisher effect (FE) implies that the interest rate differential is equal to the expected inflation rate differential.
2. If both purchasing power parity (PPP) and forward expectations parity (FEP) hold, then the forward exchange premium or discount will be equal to the expected inflation rate differential. The latter relationship is denoted by the forward-PPP, that is, FPPP in the exhibit.
3. IFE stands for the international Fisher effect.

exchange rate. If the exchange rate, indeed, follows a random walk, the future exchange rate is expected to be the same as the current exchange rate, that is,

$$S_t = E(S_{t+1})$$

In a sense, the **random walk hypothesis** suggests that today's exchange rate is the best predictor of tomorrow's exchange rate.

While researchers found it difficult to reject the random walk hypothesis for exchange rates on empirical grounds, there is no theoretical reason why exchange rates should follow a pure random walk. The parity relationships we discussed previously indicate that the current forward exchange rate can be viewed as the market's consensus forecast of the future exchange rate based on the available information (I_t) if the foreign exchange markets are efficient, that is,

$$F_t = E(S_{t+1}|I_t)$$

To the extent that interest rates are different between two countries, the forward exchange rate will be different from the current spot exchange rate. This means that the future exchange rate should be expected to be different from the current spot exchange rate.

Those who subscribe to the efficient market hypothesis may predict the future exchange rate using either the current spot exchange rate or the current forward exchange rate. But which one is better? Agmon and Amihud (1981) compared the performance of the forward exchange rate with that of the random walk model as a predictor of the future spot exchange rate. The forward exchange rate failed to outperform the random walk model in predicting the future exchange rate. The two prediction models based on the efficient market hypothesis registered largely comparable performances.

Predicting exchange rates using the efficient market approach has two advantages. First, since the efficient market approach is based on market-determined prices, it is costless to generate forecasts. Both the current spot and forward exchange rates are public information. As such, everyone has free access to it. Second, given the efficiency of foreign exchange markets, it is difficult to outperform the market-based forecasts unless the forecaster has access to private information that is not yet reflected in the current exchange rate.

Fundamental Approach

www.oecd.org

Provides macroeconomic data useful for fundamental analysis.

The "fundamental approach" to exchange rate forecasting is a much more complex and data-intensive exercise. Analysis of this type is typically done by large financial institutions, such as the Bank of Canada, or the research divisions of the commercial banks.

While there are many models of exchange rate behaviour, we will briefly outline one typical structure that reflects captures the idea that exchange rates are driven by monetary conditions and expectations of economic growth, as we outlined in Chapter 3.

The "model" takes the following form:

$$s = \alpha + \beta_1(m - m^*) + \beta_2(y - y^*) + u \tag{5.18}$$

where:

s = the rate of change of the spot exchange rate
m = the expected rate of growth of domestic money
m^* = the expected rate of growth of money in the foreign country
y = the expected rate of real economic growth in the domestic economy
y^* = the expected rate of real economic growth in the foreign economy
u = an error term

The theory underlying this model is twofold. First, the country that expands its money supply relatively faster will incur relatively more inflation and can expect to see its exchange rate fall. Second, the country that experiences relatively greater economic growth can expect its exchange rate to rise on that account. This latter effect indirectly works through a higher real interest in the more rapidly growing country, which attracts capital inflows and boosts the exchange rate.

The exchange rate is defined as units of domestic currency required to purchase one unit of the foreign currency. For example, if it takes C$1.40 to purchase one American dollar, the exchange rate is 1.40. With this "direct" quote, a higher exchange rate is simply a lower numerical value of the quote, say, from $1.40 to $1.36 per American dollar. As a result, we would expect β_1 to be positive and β_2 to be negative. The model parameters, β_1 and β_2 are estimated from the past history of the relationship between the rate of change of the exchange rate exchange rate (s) and the explanatory variables, $(m - m^*)$ and $(y - y^*)$.

The application of the exchange rate forecasting model is a three step process:

Step 1: Estimation of the structural model (equation 5.18) to determine empirical values for the parameters, α, β_1 and β_2.

Step 2: Estimation of future values of the independent explanatory variables m, m^*, y, and y^*.

Step 3: Substituting the estimated (forecast) values of the independent variables into the estimated structural model to generate the exchange rate forecast.

If, for example, the forecaster wants to predict the rate of change of the exchange rate over the next year, he would estimate the values of the independent variables over the next year and substitute these explanatory variables into the structural model.

The fundamental approach to exchange rate forecasting has three main difficulties. First, one must forecast a set of independent variables to forecast the exchange rates. Forecasting the former will certainly be subject to errors and may not be necessarily easier than forecasting the latter. Second, the parameter values, that is, α and β's, that are estimated using historical data may change over time because of changes in government policies and/or the underlying structure of the economy. Either difficulty can diminish the accuracy of forecasts even if the model is correct. Third, the model itself can be wrong. For example, the model described by equation 5.18 may be wrong. The forecast generated by a wrong model cannot be reliably accurate.

Not surprisingly, researchers found that the fundamental models failed to more accurately forecast exchange rates than either the forward rate model or the random walk model. Meese and Rogoff (1983), for example, found that the fundamental models developed on the basis of the monetary approach did worse than the random walk model even if realized (true) values were used for the independent variables. They also confirmed that the forward rate did not do better than the random walk model. In the words of Meese and Rogoff:

> Ignoring for the present the fact that the spot rate does no worse than the forward rate, the striking feature…is that none of the models achieves lower, much less significantly lower, RMSE than the random walk model at any horizon.…The structural models in particular fail to improve on the random walk model in spite of the fact that their forecasts are based on realized values of the explanatory variables.[13] (p. 12)

Technical Approach

www.forexe.com

Provides information about technical analysis and currency charts.

The technical approach to exchange rate forecasting first analyzes the past behaviour of exchange rates for the purpose of identifying "patterns" and then projects these patterns into the future to generate forecasts. Clearly, the technical approach is based on the premise that *history repeats itself*. The technical approach, thus, is at odds with the efficient market approach. At the same time, it differs from the fundamental approach in that it does not use the key economic variables, such as money supplies or trade balances, for the purpose of forecasting. However, technical analysts sometimes consider various transaction data, such as trading volume, outstanding interests, and bid-ask spreads, to aid their analyses.

An example of technical analysis is provided by the moving average cross-over rule illustrated in Exhibit 5.11. Many technical analysts or chartists compute moving averages as a way of separating short- and long-term trends from the vicissitudes of daily exchange rates. Exhibit 5.11 illustrates how exchange rates may be forecast on the basis of the movements of short- and long-term moving averages. Since the short-term moving average (SMA) weighs recent exchange rate changes more heavily than the long-term moving average (LMA), the SMA will lie below (above) the LMA when the British pound is falling (rising) against the dollar. This implies that one can forecast exchange rate movements on the basis of the cross-over of the moving averages. According to this rule, a cross-over of the SMA above the LMA at point A signals that the British pound is appreciating. On the other hand, a cross-over of the SMA below the LMA at point D signals that the British pound is depreciating.

While academic studies tend to discredit the validity of **technical analysis,** many traders depend on technical analyses for their trading strategies. If a trader knows that other traders use technical analysis, it can be rational for the trader to use technical analysis, too. If enough traders use technical analysis, the predictions based on it can become self-fulfilling to some extent, at least in the short run.

Performance of the Forecasters

Because predicting exchange rates is difficult, many firms and investors subscribe to professional forecasting services for a fee. Since an alternative to subscribing to professional forecasting services is to use a market-determined price, such as the forward exchange rate, it is relevant to ask: *Can professional forecasters outperform the market?*

An answer to the above question was provided by Richard Levich, who evaluated the performances of 13 forecasting services using the forward exchange rate as a benchmark. Under certain conditions, the forward exchange rate can be viewed as the market's consensus forecast of the future exchange rate.[14] These services use different

---

[13]RMSE, which stands for root mean squared error, is the criterion that Meese and Rogoff used in evaluating the accuracy of forecasts.

[14]These conditions are: (a) the foreign exchange markets are efficient, and (b) the forward exchange rate does not contain a significant risk premium.

EXHIBIT 5.11

Moving Average Cross-over Rule: A Technical Analysis

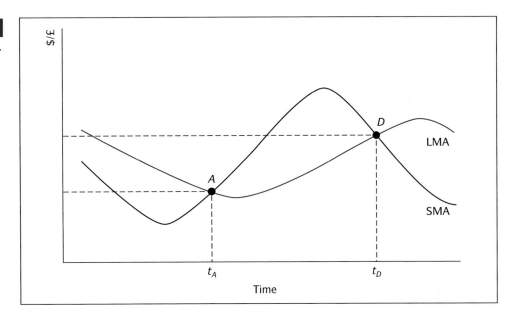

methods of forecasting, such as econometric, technical, and judgmental. In evaluating the performance of forecasters, Levich computed the following ratio:

$$R = \text{MAE(S)}/\text{MAE(F)} \tag{5.19}$$

where:

MAE(S) = mean absolute forecast error of a forecasting service.

MAE(F) = mean absolute forecast error of the forward exchange rate as a predictor.[15]

If a professional forecasting service provides more accurate forecasts than the forward exchange rate, that is, MAE(S) < MAE(F), then the ratio R will be less than unity for the service. If the service fails to outperform the forward exchange rate, the ratio R will be greater than unity.

Exhibit 5.12 provides the R ratios for each service for the American dollar exchange rates of nine major foreign currencies for a three-month forecasting horizon. The most striking finding presented in the exhibit is that only 24 percent of the entries, 25 out of 104, are less than unity. This, of course, means that the professional services as a whole clearly failed to outperform the forward exchange rate.[16] In other words, they failed to beat the market.

However, there are substantial variations in the performance records across individual services. In the cases of services 4 and 11, for instance, every entry is greater than unity. In contrast, for service 13, which is Wharton Econometric Forecasting Associates, the majority of entries, seven out of nine, are less than unity. It is also clear from the exhibit that the performance record of each service varies substantially across

---

[15]The mean absolute forecast error (MAE) is computed as follows:

$$\text{MAE} = \Sigma_i |P_i - A_i|/n$$

where P is the predicted exchange rate, A is the actual (realized) exchange rate, and n is the number of forecasts made. The MAE criterion penalizes the over- and underestimation equally. If a forecaster has perfect foresight so that $P = A$ always, then MAE will be zero.

[16]Levich found that the same qualitative result holds for different horizons like one month, six months, and 12 months.

EXHIBIT 5.12   **Performance of Exchange Rate Forecasting Services**

Currency	Forecasting Services												
	1	2	3	4	5	6	7	8	9	10	11	12	13
Canadian dollar	1.29	1.13	1.00	1.59	0.99	1.08	n.a.	1.47	1.17	1.03	1.47	1.74	0.80
British pound	1.11	1.24	0.91	1.44	1.09	0.98	1.05	1.09	1.27	1.69	1.03	1.22	1.01
Belgian franc	0.95	1.07	n.a.	1.33	1.17	n.a.	n.a.	0.99	1.21	n.a.	1.06	1.01	0.77
French franc	0.91	0.98	1.02	1.43	1.27	n.a.	0.98	0.92	1.00	0.96	1.03	1.16	0.70
German mark	1.08	1.13	1.07	1.28	1.19	1.35	1.06	0.83	1.19	1.07	1.13	1.04	0.76
Italian lira	1.07	0.91	1.09	1.45	1.14	n.a.	1.12	1.12	1.00	1.17	1.64	1.54	0.93
Dutch guilder	0.80	1.10	n.a.	1.41	1.06	n.a.	n.a.	0.91	1.26	1.26	1.10	1.01	0.81
Swiss franc	1.01	n.a.	1.08	1.21	1.32	n.a.	n.a.	0.86	1.06	1.04	1.04	0.94	0.63
Japanese yen	1.42	1.05	1.02	1.23	1.08	1.45	1.09	1.24	0.94	0.47	1.31	1.30	1.79

Note: Each entry represents the R ratio defined in equation 5.19. If a forecasting service outperforms (underperforms) the forward exchange rate, the R ratio will be less (greater) than unity.
Source: Richard Levich, "Evaluating the Performance of the Forecasters," in Richard Ensor, ed., *The Management of Foreign Exchange Risk,* 2nd ed. (Euromoney Publications, 1982).

currencies. The R ratio for Wharton, for example, ranges from 0.63 for the Swiss franc to 1.79 for the Japanese yen. Wharton Associates clearly has difficulty in forecasting the dollar/yen exchange rate. Service 10, on the other hand, convincingly beat the market in forecasting the yen exchange rate, with an R ratio of 0.47! This suggests that consumers need to discriminate among forecasting services depending on what currencies they are interested in. Lastly, note that service 12, which is known to use technical analysis, outperformed neither the forward rate nor other services. This result certainly does not add credence to the technical approach to exchange rate forecasting.

In a more recent study, Eun and Sabherwal (2002) evaluated the forecasting performances of 10 major commercial banks from around the world. They used the data from *Risk,* a London-based monthly publication dealing with practical issues related to derivative securities and risk management. During the period April 1989 to February 1993, *Risk* published forecasts provided by the banks for exchange rates 3, 6, 9, and 12 months ahead. These forecasts were made for the American dollar exchange rates of the British pound, German mark, Swiss franc, and Japanese yen on the same day of the month by all the banks. This is a rare case where banks' exchange rate forecasts were made available to the public. Since commercial banks are the market makers as well as key players in foreign exchange markets, they should be in a position to observe the order flows and the market sentiments closely. It is, thus, interesting to check how these banks perform.

In evaluating the performance of the banks, Eun and Sabherwal used the spot exchange rate as the benchmark. Recall that if you believe the exchange rate follows a random walk, today's spot exchange rate can be taken as the prediction of the future spot exchange rate. They, thus, computed the forecasting accuracy of each bank and compared it with that of the current spot exchange rate, that is, the rate prevailing on the day when forecast is made. In evaluating the performance of banks, they computed the following ratio:

$$R = MSE(B) / MSE(S)$$

where:

MSE(B) = mean squared forecast error of a bank.

MSE(S) = mean squared forecast error of the spot exchange rate.

If a bank provides more accurate forecasts than the spot exchange rate, that is, MSE(B) < MSE(S), then the ratio R will be less than unity, that is, $R<1$.

Exhibit 5.13 provides the computed R ratios for each of the 10 sample banks as well as the forward exchange rate. Overall, the majority of entries in the exhibit exceed

EXHIBIT 5.13   Forecasting Exchange Rates: Do Banks Know Better?

Currency	Forecast Lead (months)	ANZ Bank (Australia)	Banque-Paribas (France)	Barclays Bank (United Kingdom)	Chemical Bank (U.S.)	Commerz Bank (Germany)	Generale Bank (France)	Harris Bank (U.S.)	Ind. Bank of Japan (Japan)	Midland-Montagu (United Kingdom)	Union Bank (Switzerland)	Forward Rate
British pound	3	2.09	1.31	1.08	1.33	1.31	1.41	1.95	1.10	1.10	0.98	1.02
	6	1.60	1.12	0.92	0.96	1.01	1.17	1.97	0.94	1.11	0.96	1.04
	9	1.42	1.04	0.81	0.88	0.78	0.97	1.65	0.81	0.99	1.09	0.83
	12	1.06	0.84	0.60	1.07	0.72	0.77	1.69	0.68	0.95	1.16	1.02
German mark	3	1.98	1.39	1.09	1.19	1.59	1.39	1.95	1.14	1.26	1.00	1.01
	6	1.15	1.53	1.16	1.03	1.21	1.21	1.97	1.07	1.27	1.05	1.00
	9	0.92	1.45	1.33	0.99	0.85	0.96	1.71	1.00	1.09	0.93	1.06
	12	0.80	1.19	1.14	1.16	0.62	0.97	1.51	1.00	0.87	1.16	0.96
Swiss franc	3	2.15	1.47	1.13	1.26	1.66	1.32	1.98	1.05	1.19	1.03	1.02
	6	1.18	1.58	1.30	0.98	1.29	1.35	1.88	1.04	1.24	1.05	1.00
	9	0.88	1.46	1.38	0.84	0.96	1.10	1.66	0.96	1.13	0.87	0.99
	12	0.67	1.16	1.15	0.88	0.74	1.01	1.40	0.91	0.98	1.01	0.94
Japanese yen	3	3.52	2.31	1.46	1.44	1.73	2.19	2.51	1.52	2.16	1.80	1.08
	6	2.32	2.43	1.55	1.39	1.59	1.62	2.31	1.62	1.68	1.70	1.06
	9	2.54	2.73	1.80	1.57	1.60	1.85	2.22	1.90	1.74	1.97	0.99
	12	2.70	2.61	1.83	1.79	1.44	1.97	1.89	1.93	1.68	2.00	1.10

Source: Cheol Eun and Sanjiv Sabherwal, "Forecasting Exchange Rates: Do Banks Know Better?", *Global Finance Journal*, (2002), pp. 195–215.

unity, implying that these banks as a whole could not outperform the random walk model. However, some banks significantly outperformed the random walk model, especially in the longer run. For example, in forecasting the British pound exchange rate 12 months into the future, Barclays Bank ($R = 0.60$), Commerz Bank ($R = 0.72$), and Industrial Bank of Japan ($R = 0.68$) provided more accurate forecasts, on average, than the random walk model. Likewise, Commerz Bank outperformed the random walk model in forecasting the German mark and Swiss franc rates 12 months into the future. But these are more exceptional cases. It is noted that no bank, including the Japanese bank, could beat the random walk model in forecasting the Japanese yen rate at any lead. The last column of Exhibit 5.13 shows that the R-ratio for the forward exchange rate is about unity, implying that the performance of the forward rate is comparable with that of the spot rate.

SUMMARY

This chapter provides a systematic discussion of the key international parity relationships and two related issues, exchange rate determination and prediction. A thorough understanding of parity relationships is essential for astute financial management.

1. Interest rate parity (IRP) holds that the forward premium or discount should be equal to the interest rate differential between two countries. IRP represents a zero-arbitrage equilibrium condition that should hold in the absence of barriers to international capital flows.

2. If IRP is violated, one can lock in guaranteed profit by borrowing in one currency and lending in another, with exchange risk hedged via forward contract. As a result of this covered interest arbitrage, IRP will be restored.

3. IRP implies that in the short run, the exchange rate depends on (a) the relative interest rates between two countries, and (b) the expected future exchange rate. Other things being equal, a higher (lower) domestic interest rate will lead to appreciation (depreciation) of the domestic currency. People's expectations concerning future exchange rates are self-fulfilling.

4. Purchasing power parity (PPP) states that the exchange rate between two countries' currencies should be equal to the ratio of their price levels. PPP is a manifestation of the law of one price applied internationally to a standard commodity basket. The relative version of PPP states that the rate of change in the exchange rate should be equal to the inflation rate differential between countries. The existing empirical evidence, however, is generally negative on PPP. This implies that substantial barriers to international commodity arbitrage exist.

5. There are three distinct approaches to exchange rate forecasting: (a) the efficient market approach, (b) the fundamental approach, and (c) the technical approach. The efficient market approach uses such market-determined prices as the current exchange rate or the forward exchange rate to forecast the future exchange rate. The fundamental approach uses various formal models of exchange rate determination for forecasting purposes. The technical approach, on the other hand, identifies patterns from the past history of the exchange rate and projects it into the future. Empirical evidence indicates that neither the fundamental nor the technical approach outperforms the efficient market approach.

KEY WORDS

arbitrage, *101*
covered interest arbitrage, *103*
efficient market hypothesis, *117*

Fisher effect, *116*
forward expectations parity, *117*
interest rate parity, *101*

international Fisher effect, *117*
monetary approach, *129*
nontradables, *113*

QUESTIONS

1. Give a full definition of *arbitrage.*

2. Discuss the implications of interest rate parity for exchange rate determination.

3. Explain the conditions under which the forward exchange rate will be an unbiased predictor of the future spot exchange rate.

4. Explain purchasing power parity, both the absolute and relative versions. What causes deviations from purchasing power parity?

5. Discuss the implications of the deviations from purchasing power parity for countries' competitive positions in the world market.

6. Explain and derive the international Fisher effect.

7. Researchers found that it is very difficult to forecast future exchange rates more accurately than the forward exchange rate or the current spot exchange rate. How would you interpret this finding?

8. Explain the random walk model for exchange rate forecasting. Can it be consistent with technical analysis?

9. Derive and explain the monetary approach to exchange rate determination.

10. Explain the following three concepts of purchasing power parity (PPP):

    a. The law of one price.

    b. Absolute PPP.

    c. Relative PPP.

11. Evaluate the usefulness of relative PPP in predicting movements in foreign exchange rates on:

    a. Short-term basis (for example, three months).

    b. Long-term basis (for example, six years).

PROBLEMS

1. Suppose that the treasurer of Weston's has an extra cash reserve of $10 million to invest for six months. The six-month interest rate is 4 percent per annum in the Canada and 5 percent per annum in Germany. Currently, the spot exchange rate is €0.65 per dollar and the six-month forward exchange rate is €0.66 per dollar. The treasurer of Weston's does not wish to bear any exchange risk. Where should he invest?

2. While you were visiting Paris, you purchased a Renault for €10,000, payable in three months. You have enough cash at your bank in Vancouver, which pays 0.35 percent interest per month, compounding monthly, to pay for the car. Currently, the spot exchange rate is $1.45/€ and the three-month forward exchange rate is $1.40/€. In Paris, the money market interest rate is 2 percent for a three-month investment. There are two alternative ways of paying for your Renault.

   a. Keep the funds at your bank in Canada and buy €10,000 forward.

   b. Buy a certain Euro amount spot today and invest the amount in Europe for three months so that the maturity value becomes equal to €10,000. Evaluate each payment method. Which method would you prefer? Why?

3. Currently, the spot exchange rate is $1.50/€ and the three-month forward exchange rate is $1.49/€. The three-month interest rate is 4 percent per annum in Canada and 5 percent per annum in Europe. Assume that you can borrow as much as $1,500,000 or €1,000,000.

   a. Determine whether interest rate parity is currently holding.

   b. If IRP is not holding, how would you carry out covered interest arbitrage? Show all the steps and determine the arbitrage profit.

   c. Explain how IRP will be restored as a result of covered arbitrage activities.

4. Suppose that the current spot exchange rate is €0.65/$ and the three-month forward exchange rate is €0.64/$. The three-month interest rate is 5.6 percent per annum in Canada and 5.40 percent per annum in France. Assume that you can borrow up to $1,000,000 or €1,060,000.

   a. Show how to realize a certain profit via covered interest arbitrage, assuming that you want to realize profit in terms of dollars. Also determine the size of your arbitrage profit.

   b. Assume that you want to realize profit in terms of euros. Show the covered arbitrage process and determine the arbitrage profit in euros.

5. *The Economist* reports that the interest rate per annum is 5 percent in Canada and 50 percent in Turkey. Why do you think the interest rate is so high in Turkey? On the basis of the reported interest rates, how would you predict the change of the exchange rate between the Canadian dollar and the Turkish lira?

6. As of November 1, 1999, the exchange rate between the Brazilian real and the American dollar was R$1.95/$. The consensus forecast for the American and Brazil inflation rates for the next one-year period is 2.6 percent and 20 percent, respectively. What would you forecast the exchange rate to be at around November 1, 2000?

7. Omni Advisors, an international pension fund manager, uses the concepts of purchasing power parity (PPP) and the International Fisher Effect (IFE) to forecast spot exchange rates. Omni gathers the financial information as follows:

Base price level	100
Current Canadian price level	105
Current South African price level	111
Base rand spot exchange rate	$0.175
Current rand spot exchange rate	$0.158
Expected annual Canadian inflation	7%
Expected annual South African inflation	5%
Expected Canadian one-year interest rate	10%
Expected South African one-year interest rate	8%

Calculate the following exchange rates (ZAR refers to the South African rand):

   a. The current ZAR spot rate in dollars that would have been forecast by PPP.

   b. Using the IFE, the expected ZAR spot rate in dollars one year from now.

   c. Using PPP, the expected ZAR spot rate in dollars four years from now.

8. Suppose that the current spot exchange rate is €1.50/£ and the one-year forward exchange rate is €1.60/£. The one-year interest rate is 5.4 percent in euros and 5.2 percent in pounds. You can borrow at most €1,000,000 or the equivalent pound amount, that is, £666,667, at the current spot exchange rate.

   a. Show how you can realize a guaranteed profit from covered interest arbitrage. Assume that you are a euro-based investor. Also determine the size of the arbitrage profit.

   b. Discuss how interest rate parity may be restored as a result of the above transactions.

   c. Suppose you are a pound-based investor. Show the covered arbitrage process and determine the pound profit amount.

9. Due to the integrated nature of their capital markets, investors in both Canada and the United Kingdom require the same real interest rate, 2.5 percent, on their lending. There is a consensus in capital markets that the annual inflation rate is likely to be 3.5 percent in Canada and 1.5 percent in the United Kingdom for the next three years. The spot exchange rate is currently $1.50/£.

   a. Compute the nominal interest rate per annum in both Canada and the United Kingdom, assuming that the Fisher effect holds.

   b. What is your expected future spot dollar–pound exchange rate in three years from now?

   c. Can you infer the forward dollar–pound exchange rate for one-year maturity?

INTERNET EXERCISE

You provide foreign exchange consulting services based on technical (chartist) analysis. Your client would like to have a good idea about the Canadian dollar and Mexican peso exchange rate six months into the future. First plot the past exchange rates and try to identify patterns that can be projected into the future. What forecast exchange rate would you offer to your client? You may download exchange rate data from www.pacific.commerce.ubc.ca/xr/data.html.

MINI CASE

Turkish Lira and Purchasing Power Parity

Veritas Emerging Market Fund specializes in investing in the emerging stock markets of the world. Mr. Henry Mobaus, an experienced hand in international investment and your boss, is currently interested in Turkish stock markets. He thinks that Turkey will eventually be invited to negotiate its membership in the European Union. If this happens, it will boost stock prices in Turkey. But, at the same time, he is quite concerned with the volatile exchange rates of the Turkish currency. He would like to understand what drives Turkish exchange rates. Since the inflation rate is much higher in Turkey than in the United States, he thinks that purchasing power parity may be holding at least to some extent. As a research assistant for him, you are assigned to check this out. In other words, you have to study and prepare a report on the following question: Does purchasing power parity hold for the Turkish lira–American dollar exchange rate? Among other things, Mr. Mobaus would like you to do the following:

1. Plot past exchange rate changes against the differential inflation rates between Turkey and the United States for the last four years.

2. Regress the rate of exchange rate changes on the inflation rate differential to estimate the intercept and the slope coefficient, and interpret the regression results.

Data sources: You may download consumer price index data for the United States and Turkey from the following website: www.oecd.org/EN/statistics/0,,EN-statistics-0-nodirectorate-no-no-no-0,00.html "hot file" (Excel format). You may download exchange rate data from the website: www.pacific.commerce.ubc.ca/xr/data.html.

**REFERENCES &
SUGGESTED
READINGS**

Abuaf, N. and P. Jorion. "Purchasing Power Parity in the Long Run." *Journal of Finance* 45 (1990), pp. 157–74.

Alexius, A., and J. Nilsson. "Real Exchange Rate Fundamentals: Evidence from 15 OECD Countries," *Open Economies Review*, 11 (2000), pp. 383–97.

Aliber, R. "The Interest Rate Parity: A Reinterpretation." *Journal of Political Economy* (1973), pp. 1451–59.

Adler, Michael, and Bruce Lehman. "Deviations from Purchasing Power Parity in the Long Run." *Journal of Finance* 38 (1983), pp. 1471–87.

Baillie, Richard T., and Tim Bollerslev. "The Forward Premium Anomaly Is Not as Bad as You Think," *Journal of International Money and Finance* (August 2000), pp. 471–88.

Baxter, M. "Real Exchange Rates and Real Interest Differentials: Have We Missed the Business Cycle Relationship?" *Journal of Monetary Economics*, 33 (1994), pp. 5–37.

Brean, D.J.S. "International Portfolio Capital: The Wedge of the Withholding Tax," *National Tax Journal* (June 1984), pp. 239–47.

Chadha, B., and E. Prasad. "Real Exchange Rate Fluctuations and the Business Cycle," *IMF Staff Papers* 44 (1997), pp. 328–55.

Frenkel, Jacob. "Flexible Exchange Rates, Prices and the Role of News: Lessons from the 1970s." *Journal of Political Economy* 89 (1981), pp. 665–705.

Frenkel, Jacob, and Richard Levich. "Covered Interest Arbitrage: Unexploited Profits?" *Journal of Political Economy* 83 (1975), pp. 325–38.

Frankel, Jeffrey. "Flexible Exchange Rate: Experience versus Theory," *Journal of Portfolio Management* (Winter 1989), pp. 45–54.

Froot, Kenneth A., and Richard H. Thaler. "Anomalies: Foreign Exchange," *Journal of Economic Perspectives* (Summer 1990), pp.179–92.

Gauthier, Céline, and David Tessier. "Supply Shocks and Real Exchange Dynamics: Canadian Evidence," Bank of Canada Working Paper (Monetary and Financial Analysis Department) 2002–31, November 2002.

Keynes, John M. *Monetary Reform.* New York: Harcourt Brace, 1924.

Kravis, I., and R. Lipsey. "Price Behavior in the Light of Balance of Payment Theories." *Journal of International Economics* (1978), pp. 193–246.

Lafrance, Robert, and Pierre St-Amant. "Real Exchange Rate Indexes for the Canadian Dollar," *Bank of Canada Review* (Autumn 1999), pp.19–28.

Lafrance, Robert, and Pierre St-Amant. "Exchange Rate Fundamentals and the Canadian Dollar," *Bank of Canada Review* (Autumn 1995), pp.17–33.

Larsen, Glen, and Bruce Resnick. "International Parity Relationships and Tests for Risk Premia in Forward Foreign Exchange Rates." *Journal of International Financial Markets, Institutions and Money* 3 (1993), pp. 33–56.

Levich, Richard. "Evaluating the Performance of the Forecasters," in Richard Ensor (ed.), *The Management of Foreign Exchange Risk,* 2nd ed. Euromoney Publication, 1982, pp. 121–34.

Lothian, James R., and Mark P. Taylor. "Real Exchange Rate Behavior: The Recent Float from the Perspective of the Past Two Centuries," *Journal of Political Economy* (June 1996).

Meese, Richard, and Kenneth Rogoff. "Empirical Exchange Rate Models of the Seventies: Do They Fit Out of Sample?" *Journal of International Economics* 14 (1983), pp. 3–24.

Mishkin, Frederick S. "Are Real Interest Rates Equal Across Countries? An International Investigation of Parity Conditions," *Journal of Finance* (December 1984), pp. 1345–57.

Richardson, J. "Some Empirical Evidence on Commodity Arbitrage and the Law of One Price." *Journal of International Economics* 8 (1978), pp. 341–52.

Purchasing Power Parity and Exchange Rate Determination

Although PPP itself can be viewed as a theory of exchange rate determination, it also serves as a foundation for a more complete theory, namely, the **monetary approach.** The monetary approach is based on two basic tenets: purchasing power parity and the quantity theory of money.

From the **quantity theory of money,** we obtain the following identity that must hold in each country:

$$P_\$ = M_\$ V_\$ / y_\$ \tag{5A.1A}$$

$$P_£ = M_£ V_£ / y_£ \tag{5A.1B}$$

where M denotes the money supply, V the velocity of money, measuring the speed at which money is being circulated in the economy, y the national aggregate output, and P the general price level; the subscripts denote countries. When the above equations are substituted for the price levels in the PPP equation 5.12, we obtain the following expression for the exchange rate:

$$S = (M_\$/M_£)(V_\$/V_£)(y_£/y_\$) \tag{5A.2}$$

According to the monetary approach, what matters in the exchange rate determination are:

1. The relative money supplies.
2. The relative velocities of money.
3. The relative national outputs.

All else being equal, an increase in the Canadian money supply will result in a proportionate depreciation of the dollar against the pound. So will an increase in the velocity of the dollar, which has the same effect as an increased supply of dollars. But an increase in Canadian output will result in a proportionate appreciation of the dollar.

The monetary approach, which is based on PPP, can be viewed as a long-run theory of exchange rate determination, since the monetary approach does not allow for price rigidities. It assumes that prices adjust fully and completely, which is unrealistic in the short run. Prices of many commodities and services are often fixed over a certain period of time. A good example of short-term price rigidity is the wage rate set by a labour contract. Despite this apparent shortcoming, the monetary approach remains an influential theory and serves as a benchmark in modern exchange rate economics.

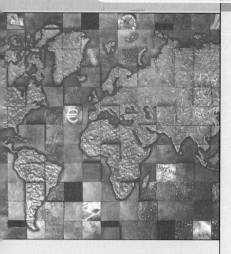

PART TWO

World Financial Markets and Institutions

PART TWO provides a thorough discussion of international financial institutions, assets, and marketplaces and develops the tools necessary to manage exchange rate uncertainty.

CHAPTER 6 differentiates between international bank and domestic bank operations and examines the institutional differences of various types of international banking offices. International banks and their clients constitute the Eurocurrency market and form the core of the international money market.

CHAPTER 7 distinguishes between foreign bonds and Eurobonds, which together make up the international bond market. The advantages of sourcing funds from the international bond market as opposed to raising funds domestically are discussed. A discussion of the major types of international bonds is included in the chapter.

CHAPTER 8 covers international equity markets. The chapter begins with a statistical documentation of the size of equity markets in both the developed and the developing countries. Various methods of trading equity shares in the secondary markets are discussed. Additionally, the chapter provides a discussion of the advantages to the firm of cross-listing equity shares in more than one country.

CHAPTER 9 provides an extensive treatment of exchange-traded currency futures and options contracts. Basic valuation models are developed.

CHAPTER 10 covers currency and interest rate swaps.

CHAPTER 11 covers international portfolio investment. It documents that the potential benefits from international diversification are available to all national investors.

International Banking and Money Market

"WORLD" FINANCIAL MARKETS involve a global network of financial institutions that facilitate the financing of international trade and foreign investment. Banks are the major players. Whenever business crosses borders or whenever one currency is exchanged for another, a bank or a combination of banks is there to facilitate the international financial transactions.

To begin discussion of world financial markets and institutions, we take up two fundamental topics—international banking and international money market operations.

We open this chapter with an outline of the services provided by international banks for their corporate clients. While any bank could be termed "international" if it offers such services as currency exchange or foreign currency deposits, a more substantial determination of being "international" is whether the bank has a network of branches or subsidiaries abroad. The major Canadian banks, we shall see, easily meet this test. Likewise, many foreign banks maintain permanent operations in Canada.

The second part of the chapter focuses on the Eurocurrency market, the creation of Eurocurrency deposits by international banks and the nature of Eurocurrency loans. We explain Euronotes, Eurocommercial paper, and forward rate agreements. The prefix "Euro" in these expressions is no longer literal. It is a carryover from a time when international finance sought out the relatively unregulated financial environment of Europe to avoid domestic banking regulations, especially on the part of American-based international business. "Euro" is now understood to refer to financial instruments that are subject to the financial regulations of no specific country.

Eurofinancial instruments are denominated in major currencies. The distinguishing characteristic is that the financial instrument is issued in a country other than the country from which the currency is derived. For example, if Siemens of Germany issues commercial paper denominated in American dollars and the paper is bought by the Standard Chartered Bank of England, these are American-dollar Eurotransactions. It would still be an American-dollar Euro issue, even if American-owned CitiBank bought some of the Siemens paper.

6.1 International Banking Services

Multinational business is multicurrency business. When Toronto-based Four Seasons receives foreign hotel earnings in American dollars, euros, or yen, the "banking" of those foreign funds is done by Canadian banks chosen by Four Seasons. In the evolution of international business—such as Four Seasons but also Barrick's offshore gold mining, McCain Foods operations around the world, or CN's major expansion into the United States—domestic banks tend to travel hand-in-hand internationally with the industrial companies that they serve. Whereas the industrial companies know how to establish hotels or how to operate mines, food processing plants, or transportation systems, they turn to banks to provide deposit accounts in various local currencies and to facilitate such transactions as converting foreign earnings into Canadian dollars. Domestic banks that have been involved with nonfinancial companies for many years generally continue to provide banking services when these companies venture abroad. This, of course, requires the domestic banks to establish their own operating facilities abroad.

The major features that distinguish international banks from strictly domestic banks are the types of deposits that they accept and the currency-denomination of the investments they make. International banks borrow (by accepting deposits), lend, and intermediate in a variety of currencies. International banks facilitate their clients' export and import operations by arranging trade finance. When, for example, Inniskillen Wines of Niagara exports a million dollar shipment of ice wine to France, an international bank—perhaps the Bank of Nova Scotia through its branch in Paris—will receive the French importer's payment in euros and convert these funds into Canadian dollars, all the while attending to important legal and contractual matters to secure the wine delivery through its various steps.

In the finance of international trade, banks often assist clients in hedging exchange rate risk in foreign currency receivables and payables through forward and options contracts. The advisory services of international banks to their corporate clients extend to cash management, project financing, and a range of risk management services.

With their skills and systems to deal in foreign exchange for clients, international banks also trade currencies and foreign exchange products for their own account. Virtually all international trade finance and payments on international investments ultimately flow through international banks. The global network of banks involved in foreign currency operations, giving rise to an enormous volume of interbank foreign currency transactions, "make the market" in foreign currencies. Spot rates, forward rates and the various intercurrency products that are priced off exchange rates and their risks, such as options and futures, are determined in markets in which international banks carry out essentially all the transactions.

International banks frequently form loan syndicates wherein several banks team up to lend large sums to multinational corporations (MNCs) for investment and project financing or to sovereign governments that go to the global markets to issue bonds.

The World's Largest Banks

Exhibit 6.1 lists the world's 50 largest banks ranked by assets as of fiscal year-end 2001. The exhibit shows each bank's shareholder equity, total assets, and net income stated in millions of American dollars. We see that 9 of the world's 50 largest banks are from the United States; 6 each from Japan and the United Kingdom; 5 each from Germany and France; 4 from China; 3 from the Netherlands; and 2 each from Australia, Belgium, Italy, Spain, and Switzerland. Canada and Sweden each have one bank that ranks among the world's 50 largest.

From Exhibit 6.1, one might correctly surmise that the world's major international finance centres are New York, Tokyo, London, Paris, Frankfurt, Zurich, and perhaps even Beijing. However, by far the most important international financial centres are the great trio of London, New York, and Tokyo, which have developed in these settings of liberal yet solid banking regulations. These three financial centres are frequently referred to as *full service centres* because the major banks that operate in them typically provide a full range of services.

EXHIBIT 6.1	The World's 50 Largest Banks (in Millions of American dollars, as of fiscal year-end 2001)				
Rank	Bank	Country	Shareholder Equity	Total Assets	Net Income
1	Citigroup	U.S.	81,247	1,051,450	14,126
2	Mizuho Bank/Mizuho Corp Bank	Japan	56,622	1,286,529	1,794
3	HSBC Holdings	U.K.	52,469	695,877	5,406
4	Bank of America	U.S.	48,521	621,764	6,792
5	JPMorgan Chase	U.S.	41,099	693,575	1,694
6	Deutsche Bank	Germany	41,050	813,361	148
7	Royal Bank of Scotland Group	U.K.	40,940	535,287	3,844
8	Sumitomo Mitsui Banking Corp.	Japan	40,186	957,695	1,063
9	HypoVereinsbank	Germany	31,790	645,013	831
10	UFJ Bank Ltd	Japan	30,313	720,984	−1,685
11	Groupe Crédit Agricole	France	29,384	498,961	1,105
12	UBS	Switzerland	28,474	749,045	2,972
13	Wachovia Corporation	U.S.	28,455	330,452	1,619
14	Wells Fargo & Company	U.S.	27,214	307,569	3,423
15	Santander Central Hispano	Spain	26,954	317,239	2,202
16	Bank of China	China	26,387	406,118	955
17	BNP Paribas	France	25,441	731,047	3,559
18	Bank of Tokyo-Mitsubishi	Japan	24,706	721,577	−1,116
19	Barclays	U.K.	23,970	517,676	3,578
20	Credit Suisse Group	Switzerland	23,262	611,115	948
21	Industrial & Commercial Bank of China (CBC)	China	23,105	524,194	740
22	Banco Bilbao Vizcaya Argentaria	Spain	21,736	273,935	2,093
23	Bank One Corporation	U.S.	20,226	268,954	2,638
24	HBOS	U.K.	20,132	453,267	2,433
25	Norinchukin Bank	Japan	17,827	483,309	944
26	Société Générale	France	17,661	453,972	1,908
27	FleetBoston Financial	U.S.	17,608	203,638	931
28	Lloyds TSB Group	U.K.	17,065	343,336	3,629
29	Rabobank Nederland	Netherlands	16,688	322,094	1,144
30	US Bancorp	U.S.	16,461	171,390	1,707
31	Agricultural Bank of China	China	16,279	263,971	36
32	ABN Amro Group	Netherlands	15,700	529,144	2,861
33	ING Bank	Netherlands	15,672	392,725	1,207
34	Washington Mutual Inc	U.S.	14,063	242,506	3,114
35	China Construction Bank	China	13,876	305,871	911
36	IntesaBCI	Italy	13,270	278,936	822
37	Dresdner Bank	Germany	13,141	448,820	159
38	Abbey National	U.K.	12,674	311,936	1,852
39	Commerzbank	Germany	11,608	444,062	90
40	National Australia Bank	Australia	11,604	184,591	1,026
41	**Royal Bank of Canada**	**Canada**	**11,509**	**227,618**	**1,528**
42	Groupe Crédit Mutuel CIC	France	11,484	274,092	825
43	DZ-Bank	Germany	11,427	322,963	101
44	UniCredito Italiano	Italy	10,988	184,590	1,288
45	Asahi Bank	Japan	10,981	250,483	−63
46	Groupe Caisses d'Epargne	France	10,764	305,651	776
47	Fortis Bank	Belgium	10,561	334,827	3,901
48	Nordea Group	Sweden	10,473	213,964	1,389
49	Commonwealth Bank of Australia	Australia	10,075	117,074	1,217
50	Dexia Group	Belgium	9,806	311,230	1,263

Source: Excerpted from *Euromoney*, June 2002, p. 114.

One tier below London, New York, and Tokyo, we have a larger number of important regional financial centres, including Frankfurt, Paris, and Zurich as well as Singapore, Hong Kong, Johannesburg, Beirut, and Buenos Aires. Toronto fits nicely in this second tier given its importance as the financial centre of Canada with strong ties to world markets.

6.2 Types of International Banking Offices

The services and operations of international banks are a function of the regulatory environment in which the bank operates and the type of banking facility established. Following is a discussion of the major types of international banking offices, detailing the purpose of each and the regulatory rationale for its existence. The discussion moves from correspondent bank relationships, through which minimal service can be provided to a bank's customers, to a description of offices providing a fuller array of services, to those that have been established by regulatory change aimed at minimizing domestic restrictions on international finance.

Correspondent Bank

The large banks in the world generally have a correspondent relationship with other banks in all the major financial centres in which they do not have their own banking operation. A **correspondent bank relationship** is established when two banks maintain a correspondent bank account with one another. For example, a large Toronto bank will have a correspondent bank account in a Vienna bank, and the Vienna bank will maintain one with the Toronto bank.

The correspondent banking system enables a bank's MNC clients to conduct business worldwide through the firm's local bank or its contacts. Correspondent banking services centre around foreign exchange conversions that arise through the international transactions the MNC makes. However, correspondent bank services also include assistance with trade financing, such as honouring letters of credit and accepting drafts drawn on the correspondent bank. An MNC needing foreign local financing for one of its subsidiaries may rely on its local bank to provide it with a letter of introduction to the correspondent bank in the foreign country.

The correspondent bank relationship is beneficial because a bank can service its MNC clients at low cost and without the need of bank personnel physically located in many countries. A disadvantage is that the bank's clients may not receive the level of service through the correspondent bank that they would if the bank had its own foreign facilities to service its clients.

Representative Offices

A **representative office** is a small service facility staffed by parent bank personnel that is designed to assist MNC clients of the parent bank in dealings with the bank's correspondents. It is a way for the parent bank to provide its MNC clients with a level of service greater than that provided through merely a correspondent relationship. The parent bank may open a representative office in a country in which it has many MNC clients or at least an important client. Representative offices also assist MNC clients with information about local business practices, economic information, and credit evaluation of the MNC's foreign customers.

Foreign Branches

A **foreign branch bank** operates much like a local bank, but legally it is a part of the parent bank. As such, a branch bank is subject to the banking regulations of both its home country and the country in which it operates. Canadian branch banks in foreign countries are regulated from Canada under the *Bank Act* and similar legislation that peretains to Canadian banks operating in foreign countries.

There are several reasons why a parent bank might establish a branch bank abroad. The primary one is that the bank organization can provide a much fuller range of services for its MNC customers through a foreign branch office than it can through a representative office. For example, branch bank loan limits are based on the capital of the parent bank, not the branch bank. Consequently, a branch bank will likely be able to extend a larger loan to a customer than a locally chartered subsidiary bank of the parent. The books of a foreign branch are part of the parent bank's books. Thus, a branch bank system allows customers much faster cheque clearing than does a correspondent bank network because the debit and credit procedure is handled internally within one organization.

Another reason a Canadian parent bank may establish a foreign branch bank is to compete on a local level with the banks of the host country. Foreign branches are not subject to Canadian reserve requirements on deposits and are not required to have Canadian Deposit Insurance (CDI) insurance on deposits. Consequently, branch banks are on the same competitive level as local banks in terms of their cost structure in making loans.

Branch banking is the most popular way for Canadian banks to expand operations overseas. The networks of Canadian branch banks are extensive in the United States and Europe. Many branch banks are operated as "shell" branches in offshore banking centres, a topic covered later in this section.

Subsidiary and Affiliate Banks

A **subsidiary bank** is a locally incorporated bank that is either wholly owned or owned in major part by a foreign parent. An **affiliate bank** is one that is only partially owned but not controlled by its foreign parent. Both subsidiary and affiliate banks operate under the banking laws of the country in which they are incorporated. Canadian parent banks find subsidiary and affiliate banking structures desirable because they are allowed to underwrite securities.

Foreign-owned subsidiary banks in Canada tend to locate in major centres of financial and commercial activity, such as Vancouver, Toronto, and Montreal.

Edge Act Banks

In the United States, international banking by American domestic banks has a unique federal regulation that has a bearing on how Canadian banks operate in the United States. **Edge Act banks** are federally chartered subsidiaries of American banks that are physically located in the United States and are allowed to engage in a full range of international banking activities. Senator Walter E. Edge sponsored the 1919 amendment to the *Federal Reserve Act* to allow American banks to be competitive with the services foreign banks could supply their customers. Edge Act banks can accept foreign deposits, extend trade credit, finance foreign projects abroad, trade foreign currencies, and engage in investment banking activities with American citizens involving foreign securities. As such, Edge Act banks do not compete directly with the services provided by American commercial banks.

Foreign banks operating in the United States may establish Edge Act banks. Thus, both American and foreign Edge Act banks operate on an equal competitive basis.

Edge Act banks are not prohibited from owning equity in business corporations, as are domestic commercial banks. Thus, it is *through* the Edge Act that American parent banks own foreign banking subsidiaries and have ownership positions in foreign banking affiliates.

Offshore Banking Centres

A significant portion of the external banking activity takes place through offshore banking centres. An **offshore banking centre** is a country whose banking system is organized to permit external accounts beyond the normal economic activity of the country. The International Monetary Fund recognizes the Bahamas, Bahrain, the Cayman Islands, Hong Kong, the Netherlands Antilles, Panama, and Singapore as major offshore banking centres.

Offshore banks operate as branches or subsidiaries of the parent bank. The principal features that make a country attractive for establishing an offshore banking operation are virtually total freedom from host-country governmental banking regulations—for example, low reserve requirements and no deposit insurance, low taxes, a favourable time zone that facilitates international banking transactions, and, to a minor extent, strict banking secrecy laws. It should not be inferred that offshore host governments tolerate or encourage poor banking practices, as entry is usually confined to the largest and most reputable international banks.

The primary activities of offshore banks are to seek deposits and grant loans in currencies other than the currency of the host government. Offshore banking was spawned in the late 1960s when the U.S. Federal Reserve authorized American banks to establish "shell" branches, which need be nothing more than a post office box in the host country. The actual banking transactions were conducted by the parent bank. The purpose was to allow smaller American banks the opportunity to participate in the growing Eurodollar market without having to bear the expense of setting up operations in a major European money centre. Most offshore banking centres continue to serve as locations for shell branches, but Hong Kong and Singapore have developed into full service banking centres that now rival London, New York, and Tokyo.

6.3 Capital Adequacy Standards

www.bis.org.

This is the official website of the Bank for International Settlements. It is quite extensive. One can download many papers on international bank policies and reports containing statistics on international banks, capital markets, and derivative securities markets. There is also a web page that provides a link to the websites of most central banks in the world.

A concern of bank regulators worldwide and of bank depositors is the safety of bank deposits. **Bank capital adequacy** refers to the amount of equity capital and other securities a bank holds as reserves against risky assets to reduce the probability of a bank failure. In a 1988 agreement known as the **Basle Accord**, after the Swiss city in which it is headquartered, the Bank for International Settlements (BIS) established a framework for measuring bank capital adequacy for banks in the Group of Ten countries and Luxembourg. The BIS is the central bank for clearing international transactions between national central banks and also serves as a facilitator in reaching international banking agreements among its members.

The Basle Accord called for a minimum bank capital adequacy ratio of 8 percent of risk-weighted assets for banks that engage in cross-border transactions. The accord divides bank capital into two categories: Tier I Core capital, which consists of shareholder equity and retained earnings, and Tier II Supplemental capital, which consists of internationally recognized nonequity items, such as preferred shares and subordinated bonds. Supplemental capital is allowed to count for no more than 50 percent of total bank capital, or no more than 4 percent of risk-weighted assets. In determining risk-weighted assets, four categories of risky assets are each weighted differently. More risky assets receive a higher weight. Government obligations are weighted at zero percent, short-term interbank assets are weighted at 20 percent, residential mortgages at 50 percent, and other assets at 100 percent. Thus, a bank with $100 million in each of the four asset categories would have the equivalent of $170 million in risk-weighted assets. It would need to maintain $13.6 million in capital against these investments, of which no more than one-half of this amount, or $6.8 million, could be Tier II capital.

The 1988 Basle Capital Accord has been widely adopted throughout the world by national bank regulators. Nevertheless, it is not without problems. National banking supervisors have criticised the arbitrary nature of the *"rules-based"* Basle Capital Accord, especially the constant 8 percent minimum capital assigned to risk-weighted assets. The argument is that risk is not constant throughout the business cycle. Thus, it may be preferable to require banks to keep more than the 8 percent minimum in the expansionary phase of a business cycle to guard against the more risky operating environment usually associated with an economic downturn. Furthermore, the 8 percent minimum was set with the banks of industrial countries in mind. The Basle Capital Accord has been adopted by many developing countries that experience longer and more severe business cycles than do the developed countries, in which case 8 percent capital on risk-weighted assets is probably not adequate.

An additional problem with the "rules-based" 1988 Basle Capital Accord has to do with the type of business in which banks engage. Bank trading in equity, interest rate, and exchange rate derivative products has escalated in recent years. Many of these products did not exist when the Basle Accord was drafted. Notwithstanding the criticisms with respect to traditional credit risk, the capital adequacy standards of the 1988 Basle Accord are not sufficient to safeguard against the market risk from derivatives trading. Barings Bank, for example, which collapsed in 1995 due, in part, to the activities of a rogue derivatives trader, was considered to be a safe bank by the Basle capital adequacy standards.

A 1996 amendment to the 1988 accord requires commercial banks engaging in significant trading activity to set aside additional capital to cover the market risks inherent in their trading accounts. The amendment allows banks to use internally developed portfolio models to assess adequate capital requirements. Instead of using a "rules-based" approach to determining adequate bank capital, they may apply a *risk-focused* approach that relies on modern portfolio theory.

The bank's portfolio is the monetary value of its on- and off-balance sheet trading account positions. Estimating the portfolio standard deviation of return allows the bank's value-at-risk to be calculated. **Value-at-risk (VAR)** is the loss that will be exceeded with a specified probability over a specified time horizon. The amendment requires VAR to be calculated daily according to the criterion that there be only 1 percent chance that the maximum loss over a 10-day time period will exceed the bank's capital. VAR is calculated as VAR = Portfolio Value × Daily Standard Deviation of Return × Confidence Interval Factor × $\sqrt{\text{Horizon}}$. The confidence interval factor is the appropriate z-value from the standard normal density function associated with the maximum level of loss that is tolerable. For example, the 1 percent VAR for a portfolio of \$400 million with a daily portfolio standard deviation of 0.75 percent for a 10-day planning horizon is \$22.07 million = \$400 million × .0075 × 2.326 × $\sqrt{10}$, where 2.326 is the z-value associated with a one-tail 99 percent confidence interval. That is, there is only a 1 percent chance that the loss during a 10-day period will exceed \$22.07 million. Assuming accurate inputs into the VAR formula, the bank would be required to maintain an equivalent amount of capital as an explicit cushion against its price risk exposure.

As an estimate of capital adequacy, VAR is only as good as the accuracy of its inputs. The true portfolio standard deviation is never known and must be estimated. Thus, implementing VAR analysis is subject to the problem of *estimation risk,* or *parameter uncertainty,* which modern portfolio theory, in general, is subject to. The Basle Committee on Banking Supervision is aware of this and other implementation problems. To address them, the capital charge for a bank that uses its own internal proprietary model to estimate VAR is the larger of the previous day's VAR, or three times the average of the daily VAR of the proceeding 60 business days.

Recognizing the deficiencies of the 1988 accord, the Basle Committee has drafted the New Basel Capital Accord, known as Basel II. The New Capital Accord was finalized in late 2003, with implementation in 2006. The proposed new capital adequacy framework will incorporate three mutually reinforcing pillars that allow banks and supervisors to evaluate the risks that banks face. The three pillars are: minimum capital requirements, a supervisory review process, and the effective use of market discipline. With respect to the first pillar, a bank's minimum 8 percent capital ratio will be calculated on the sum of the bank's credit, market, and operational risks. Operational risks include such threats as computer failure and fraud. In determining the bank's risk-weighted assets, weights for high-quality corporate credits will be reduced. Weights in excess of 100 percent will be assigned for certain low-quality exposures. In determining adequate capital, banks will be allowed to calculate their own market risks, such as VAR analysis. The second pillar is designed to ensure that each bank

www.riskmetrics.com

This is a website of Risk Metrics Group, one of the pioneers in applying value-at-risk techniques. It has a subsite devoted to educational matters. For example, interested students can take an on-line course on market and credit risk management called "Managing Risk."

has a sound internal process in place to properly assess the adequacy of its capital based on a systematic and continuous evaluation of its risks. Implementation of this pillar encourages supervisory intervention at the national level with the authority to require capital in excess of the minimum. The third pillar seeks to enhance bank disclosure standards to bolster the role that market participants have in encouraging banks to hold adequate capital.

6.4 International Money Market

Eurocurrency Market

The core of the international money market is the Eurocurrency market. A **Eurocurrency** is a *time* deposit of money in an international bank located in a country different from the country that issued the currency. For example, Eurodollars are deposits of American dollars in banks located outside of the United States, Eurosterling are deposits of British pound sterling in banks outside of the United Kingdom, and Euroyen are deposits of Japanese yen in banks outside of Japan. The prefix *Euro* is something of a misnomer, since the bank in which the deposit is made does not have to be located in Europe. The depository bank could be located in Europe, the Caribbean, or Asia. Indeed, Eurodollar deposits can be made in offshore shell branches or **International Banking Facilities (IBFs)**, where the physical dollar deposits are actually with the American parent bank. An "Asian dollar" market exists, with headquarters in Singapore, but it can be viewed as a major division of the Eurocurrency market.

The origin of the Eurocurrency market can be traced back to the 1950s and early 1960s, when the former Soviet Union and Soviet-bloc countries sold gold and commodities to raise hard currency. Because of anti-Soviet sentiment, these Communist countries were afraid of depositing their American dollars in American banks for fear that the deposits could be frozen or taken. Instead, they deposited their American dollars in a French bank whose telex address was EURO-BANK. Since that time, dollar deposits outside the United States have been called Eurodollars and banks accepting Eurocurrency deposits have been called **Eurobanks**.[1]

The Eurocurrency market is an *external* banking system that runs parallel to the *domestic* banking system of the country that issued the currency. Both banking systems seek deposits and make loans to customers from the deposited funds. Euro-deposits are not subject to reserve requirements or deposit insurance; hence, the cost of operations is less. Because of the reduced cost and regulatory structure, the Eurocurrency market has grown spectacularly since its inception.

The Eurocurrency market operates at the *interbank* and/or *wholesale* level. The majority of Eurocurrency transactions are interbank transactions, involving sums of $1,000,000 or more. Eurobanks with surplus funds lend to Eurobanks that need loanable funds. The rate charged by banks with excess funds is referred to as the *interbank offered rate*; they accept interbank deposits at the *interbank bid rate*. The spread is generally one-eighth of 1 percent for major Eurocurrencies.

London has historically been, and remains, the major Eurocurrency financial centre. The name of the city gives rise to the **London Interbank Offered Rate (LIBOR)**, the reference rate in London for Eurocurrency deposits. To be clear, there is a LIBOR for Eurodollars, Euro–Canadian dollars, Euroyen, and even euros. In other financial centres, other reference rates are used. For example, *SIBOR* is the Singapore Interbank Offered Rate, *PIBOR* is the Paris Interbank Offered Rate, and *BRIBOR* is the Brussels Interbank Offered Rate. Competition forces the various interbank rates for a particular Eurocurrency to be close to one another.

The 1999 launch of the common euro currency of 11 countries that make up the European Economic and Monetary Union created a need for a new interbank offer rate. To dispel the confusion as to whether one is referring to the common euro currency or

---

[1]See Rivera-Batiz and Rivera-Batiz (1994) for an account of the historical origin of the Eurocurrency market.

www.euribor.org

This website provides a brief history of the Euro common currency and a discussion of EURIBOR.

another Eurocurrency, such as Eurodollars, *international* currencies is replacing "Eurocurrencies" and *prime* banks replace Eurobanks. **EURIBOR** is the rate at which interbank deposits of the euro are offered by one prime bank to another in the euro zone.

In the wholesale money market, Eurobanks accept Eurocurrency fixed time deposits and issue **negotiable certificates of deposit (NCDs)**. In fact, these are the preferable ways for Eurobanks to raise loanable funds, as the deposits tend to be for a lengthier period and the acquiring rate is often slightly less than the interbank rate. Denominations are at least $500,000, but sizes of $1,000,000 or larger are more typical. Rates on Eurocurrency deposits are quoted for maturities ranging from one day to several years; however, more standard maturities are for 1, 2, 3, 6, 9, and 12 months. Exhibit 6.2 shows sample Eurocurrency interest rates. Appendix 6A illustrates the creation of the Eurocurrency.

Exhibit 6.3 shows the year-end values in billions of American dollars of international bank credit for the years 1997 through 2003. The 2003 column shows that the gross value of international bank credits was $13,528.7 billion and that interbank credits accounted for $6,327.6 billion, or about half the total. The major currencies denominating these were the American dollar, the euro, and the Japanese yen. Since the source of international bank credits are international deposits, these amounts indicate the size of the Eurocurrency market.

Approximately 95 percent of wholesale Eurobank deposits come from fixed time deposits, the remainder from NCDs. There is an interest penalty for the early withdrawal of funds from a fixed time deposit. NCDs, on the other hand, being negotiable, can be sold in the secondary market if the depositor suddenly needs funds prior to scheduled maturity. The NCD market began in 1967 in London for Eurodollars. EuroCDs for currencies other than the American dollar are offered by banks in London and in other financial centres, but the secondary market for nondollar NCDs is not very liquid.

Eurocredits

Eurocredits are short- to medium-term loans of Eurocurrency extended by Eurobanks to corporations, sovereign governments, nonprime banks, or international organizations. The loans are denominated in currencies other than the home currency of the Eurobank. Because these loans are frequently too large for a single bank to handle, Eurobanks will band together to form a bank lending **syndicate** to share the risk.

The credit risk on these loans is greater than on loans to other banks in the interbank market. Thus, the interest rate on Eurocredits must compensate the bank, or banking syndicate, for the added credit risk. On Eurocredits originating in London, the base lending rate is LIBOR. The lending rate on these credits is stated as LIBOR $+X$ percent, where X is the lending margin charged depending upon the creditworthiness of the borrower. Rollover pricing was created on Eurocredits so that Eurobanks do not end up paying more on Eurocurrency time deposits than they earn from the loans. Thus, a Eurocredit may be viewed as a series of shorter-term loans, where at the end of each time

EXHIBIT 6.2	Eurocurrency Interest Rate Quotations: August 19, 2002					
Jul 6	**Short Term**	**7 Days' Notice**	**One Month**	**Three Months**	**Six Months**	**One Year**
Euro	$3\,5/16$–$3\,1/4$	$3\,5/16$–$3\,7/32$	$3\,11/32$–$3\,1/4$	$3\,3/8$–$3\,9/32$	$3\,13/32$–$3\,3/8$	$3\,17/32$–$3\,7/16$
Danish Krone	$3\,7/16$–$3\,11/32$	$3\,9/16$–$3\,7/16$	$3\,9/16$–$3\,13/32$	$3\,9/16$–$3\,13/32$	$3\,11/16$–$3\,9/16$	$3\,23/32$–$3\,19/32$
Sterling	$4\,1/2$–$4\,3/8$	4–$3\,29/32$	$3\,31/32$–$3\,7/8$	$3\,31/32$–$3\,7/8$	$4\,1/32$–$3\,31/32$	$4\,7/32$–$4\,1/8$
Swiss Franc	$1\,3/32$–$19/32$	$3/4$–$19/32$	$3/4$–$21/32$	$27/32$–$23/32$	$7/8$–$25/32$	$1\,1/8$–$1\,1/32$
Canadian Dollar	$2\,13/16$–$2\,11/16$	$2\,25/32$–$2\,11/16$	$2\,27/32$–$2\,11/16$	$2\,15/16$–$2\,13/16$	$3\,1/16$–$2\,29/32$	$3\,3/16$–$3\,1/16$
American Dollar	$1\,27/32$–$1\,23/32$	$1\,13/16$–$1\,11/16$	$1\,13/16$–$1\,11/16$	$1\,13/16$–$1\,23/32$	$1\,25/32$–$1\,21/32$	$1\,31/32$–$1\,7/8$
Japanese Yen	$1/32$–$1/16$	$1/32$–$1/16$	$1/16$–$1/32$	$1/16$–$1/32$	$3/32$–$1/32$	$1/8$–$1/32$
Singapore $	$3/4$–$3/4$	$1\,1/16$–$9/16$	$15/16$–$9/16$	$15/16$–$9/16$	$7/8$–$5/8$	1–$3/4$

Source: Reuters.

EXHIBIT 6.3	International Bank Credit (at Year-End in Billions of American Dollars)						
	1997	**1998**	**1999**	**2000**	**2001**	**2002**	**2003**
Type Credit							
Gross international bank credit	10,382.7	11,048.2	11,194.4	12,270.0	13,047.4	12,849.7	13,528.7
Interbank credit	5,097.7	5,563.2	5,812.7	6,242.1	6,470.6	6,690.2	7,201.1
Net international bank credit	5,285.0	5,485.0	5,381.7	6,027.9	6,576.8	6,159.5	6,327.6

Source: *International Banking and Financial Market Developments,* Bank for International Settlements, p. 6, May 1998; p. 6, June 1999; p. A7, June 2002.

period (generally three or six months), the loan is rolled over and the base lending rate is repriced to current LIBOR over the next time interval of the loan.

Exhibit 6.4 shows the relationship among the various interest rates discussed in this section. On August 19, 2002, American domestic banks paid 1.70 percent for six-month NCDs. The prime lending rate, the base rate charged the bank's most credit-worthy corporate clients, was 4.75 percent. This represents a spread of 3.05 percent for the bank to cover operating costs and earn a profit. By comparison, Eurobanks also accept six-month Eurodollar time deposits, say, Eurodollar NCDs, at a rate of 1.70 percent. The rate charged for Eurodollar credits is LIBOR + X percent, where any lending margin less than 3.01 percent appears to make the Eurodollar loan more attractive than the prime rate loan. Since lending margins typically fall in the range of $1/4$ percent to 3 percent, with the median rate being $1/2$ percent to $1\frac{1}{2}$ percent, the exhibit shows the narrow borrowing-lending spreads of Eurobankers in the Eurodollar credit market. This seems to suggest that borrowers can obtain funds more cheaply in the Eurodollar market. However, international competition in recent years has forced American commercial banks to lend domestically at subprime rates.

EXAMPLE | 6.1 | Rollover Pricing of a Eurocredit   Teltrex International can borrow $3,000,000 at LIBOR plus a lending margin of 0.75 percent per annum on a three-month rollover basis from Barclays in London. Suppose that three-month LIBOR is currently $5^{17}\!/_{32}$ percent. Further suppose that over the second three-month interval, LIBOR falls to $5\frac{1}{8}$ percent. How much will Teltrex pay in interest to Barclays over the six-month period for the Eurodollar loan?

Solution: $3,000,000 × (0.0553125 + 0.0075)/4 + $3,000,000 ×
(0.05125 + 0.0075)/4 = $47,109.38 + $44,062.50
= $91,171.88

EXHIBIT 6.4

Comparison of American Lending and Borrowing Rates with Eurodollar Rates on August 19, 2002[a]

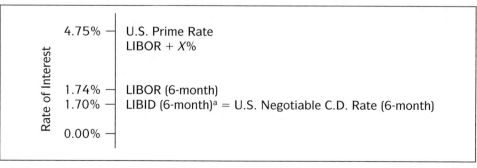

[a]LIBID denotes the London Interbank Bid rate.

A major risk Eurobanks face in accepting Eurodeposits and in extending Eurocredits is interest rate risk resulting from a mismatch in the maturities of the deposits and credits. For example, if deposit maturities are longer than credit maturities and interest rates fall, the credit rates will be adjusted downward while the bank is still paying a higher rate on deposits. Conversely, if deposit maturities are shorter than credit maturities and interest rates rise, deposit rates will adjust upward while the bank is still receiving a lower rate on credits. Only when deposit and credit maturities are perfectly matched will the rollover feature of Eurocredits allow the bank to earn the desired deposit-loan rate spread.

A **forward rate agreement (FRA)** is an interbank contract that allows the Eurobank to hedge the interest rate risk in mismatched deposits and credits. The size of the market is enormous. At year-end 2001, the notional value of FRAs outstanding was $7.737 billion. An FRA involves two parties, a buyer and a seller, where:

1. the buyer agrees to pay the seller the increased interest cost on a notional amount if interest rates fall below an agreement rate, or

2. the seller agrees to pay the buyer the increased interest cost if interest rates increase above the agreement rate.

FRAs are structured to capture the maturity mismatch in standard-length Eurodeposits and credits. For example, the FRA might be on a six-month interest rate for a six-month period beginning three months from today and ending nine months from today; this would be a "three against nine" FRA. The following time line depicts this FRA example.

| Start | Agreement Period (3 Months) | Cash Settlement | FRA Period (6 Months) | End |

The payment amount under an FRA is calculated as the absolute value of:

$$\frac{\text{Notional Amount} \times (SR - AR) \times days/360}{1 + (SR \times days/360)}$$

where SR denotes the settlement rate, AR denotes the agreement rate, and $days$ denotes the length of the FRA period.

EXAMPLE 6.2 **Three against Six Forward Rate Agreement**

As an example, consider a bank that has made a three-month Eurodollar loan of US$3,000,000 against an offsetting six-month Eurodollar deposit. The bank's concern is that three-month LIBOR will fall below expectations and the Eurocredit is rolled over at the new lower base rate, making the six-month deposit unprofitable.[2] To protect itself, the bank could sell a $3,000,000 "three against six" FRA. The FRA will be priced such that the agreement rate is the expected three-month dollar LIBOR in three months.

continued

---

[2]Consistent with the Unbiased Expectations Hypothesis (UEH), the agreement rate AR is the expected rate at the beginning of the FRA period. For example, in a "three against six" FRA, the AR can be calculated from the forward rate that ties together current three-month LIBOR and six-month LIBOR:

$$([1 + (6 \text{ mth LIBOR})(T_2/360)]/[1 + (3 \text{ mth LIBOR})(T_1/360)] - 1) \times 360/(T_2 - T_1)$$
$$= f \times 360/(T_2 - T_1) = AR,$$

where T_2 and T_1 are, respectively, the actual number of days to maturity of the six-month and three-month Eurocurrency periods and f is the forward rate.

EXAMPLE 6.2 | Continued

Assume *AR* is 6 percent and the actual number of days in the three-month FRA period is 91. Thus, the bank expects to receive $45,500 (= $3,000,000 × 0.06 × 91/360) as the base amount of interest when the Eurodollar loan is rolled over for a second three-month period. If *SR* (i.e., three-month market LIBOR) is 5⅛ percent, the bank will receive only $38,864.58 in base interest, or a shortfall of $6,635.42. Since *SR* is less than *AR*, the bank will profit from the FRA it sold. It will receive from the buyer in three months a cash settlement at the beginning of the 91-day FRA period equaling the present value of the *absolute* value of [$3,000,000 × (0.05125 − 0.06) × 91/360] = $6,635.42. This *absolute* present value is:

$$\frac{\$3,000,000 \times (0.05125 - 0.06) \times 91/360}{1 + (0.05125 \times 91/360)}$$

$$= \frac{\$6,635.42}{1.01295}$$

$$= \$6,550.59$$

The sum, $6,550.59, equals the present value as of the *beginning* of the 91-day FRA period of the shortfall of $6,635.42 from the expected Eurodollar loan proceeds that are needed to meet the interest on the Eurodollar deposit. Had *SR* been greater than *AR*, the bank would have paid the buyer the present value of the excess amount of interest above what was expected from rolling over the Eurodollar credit. In this event, the bank would have effectively received the agreement rate on its three-month Eurodollar loan, which would have made the loan a profitable transaction.

FRAs can be used for speculative purposes also. If one believes rates will be less than the *AR,* the sale of an FRA is the suitable position. In contrast, the purchase of an FRA is the suitable position if one believes rates will be greater than the *AR.*

Euronotes

Euronotes are short-term notes underwritten by a group of international investment or commercial banks called a "facility." A client-borrower makes an agreement with a facility to issue Euronotes in its own name for a period of time, generally three to 10 years. Euronotes are sold at a discount from face value and pay back the full face value at maturity. Euronotes typically have maturities of from three to six months. Borrowers find Euronotes attractive because the interest expense is usually slightly less—typically LIBOR plus ⅛ percent—in comparison with syndicated Eurobank loans. The banks find them attractive to issue because they earn a small fee from the underwriting or supply the funds and earn the interest return.

Eurocommercial Paper

Eurocommercial paper, like domestic commercial paper, is an unsecured short-term promissory note issued by a corporation or a bank and placed directly with the investment public through a dealer. Like Euronotes, Eurocommercial paper is sold at a discount from face value. Maturities typically range from one to six months.

The vast majority of Eurocommercial paper is American dollar–denominated. There are, however, a number of differences between the American and Eurocommercial paper markets. The maturity of Eurocommercial paper tends to be about twice as long as American commercial paper. For this reason, the secondary market is more active than for American paper. Additionally, Eurocommercial paper issuers tend to be of much lower quality than their American counterparts; consequently, yields tend to be higher.[3]

Exhibit 6.5 shows the year-end value of the Euronote and Eurocommercial paper market in billions of American dollars for the years 1997 through 2001.

---

[3]See Dufey and Giddy (1994) for a list of the differences between the American and Eurocommercial paper markets.

EXHIBIT 6.5

Size of the Euronote Market at Year-End
(in Billions of American dollars)

Instrument	1997	1998	1999	2000	2001
Euronotes	73.5	61.6	84.8	270.5	154.6
Eurocommercial Paper	110.4	132.7	175.2	223.3	243.1
Total	183.8	194.3	260.0	493.8	397.7

Source: *International Banking and Financial Market Developments,* Bank for International Settlements, Table 13A, p. 70, June 1999; Table 13A, p. 70, June 2000; Table 13A, p. A86, June 2002.

6.5 International Debt Crises

Certain principles define sound banking behaviour. At least five of these principles—namely, avoid an undue concentration of loans to single activities, individuals, or groups; expand cautiously into unfamiliar activities; know your counterparty; control mismatches between assets; and beware that your collateral is not vulnerable to the same shocks that weaken the borrower—are especially relevant in international banking. Nevertheless, violation of the first two of these principles by some of the largest international banks in the world have been responsible for **international debt crises** caused by lending to the sovereign governments of some **less-developed countries (LDCs).**

History

On August 20, 1982, Mexico asked more than 100 American and foreign banks to forgive its $68 billion in loans. Soon Brazil, Argentina, and more than 20 other developing countries announced similar problems in making the debt service on their bank loans. At the height of the crisis, Third World countries owed $1.2 *trillion*!

It appeared as if the crisis might bring down some of the world's largest banks. The World Bank estimated that 19 LDCs had debt outstanding equivalent to 53.6 percent of GNP in 1989. Interest payments alone amounted to 22.3 percent of export income. The international banking community was obviously shaken.

The origin of the Latin American debt crisis was oil. In the early 1970s, the Organization of Petroleum Exporting Countries (OPEC) became the dominant supplier of oil worldwide. Throughout this time period, OPEC raised oil prices dramatically. As a result of these price rises, OPEC amassed a tremendous amount of American dollars, the currency generally demanded as payment from the oil-importing countries.

OPEC deposited billions in Eurodollar deposits; by 1976, the deposits amounted to nearly $100 billion. Eurobanks were faced with a huge problem of lending these funds in order to generate interest income to pay the interest on the deposits. Third World countries were only too eager to assist the eager Eurobankers in accepting Eurodollar loans that could be used for economic development *and* for payment of oil imports. The lending process became circular and known as *petrodollar recycling*: Eurodollar loan proceeds were used to pay for new oil imports; some of the oil revenues from the developed countries and the LDCs were redeposited, and the deposits were re-lent to Third World borrowers.

OPEC raised oil prices again in the late 1970s. The high oil prices were accompanied by high inflation and high unemployment in the industrialized countries. Tight monetary policies instituted in a number of the major industrialized countries led to a global recession and a decline in the demand for commodities, such as oil, and in commodity prices. The same economic policies led to higher real interest rates, which increased the borrowing costs of the LDCs, since most of the bank borrowing was denominated in American dollars and had been made on a floating-rate basis. The collapse of commodity prices and the resultant loss of income made it impossible for the LDCs to meet their debt service obligations. As an indication of the magnitude of the involvement of some of the banks in LDC loans at the height of the crisis, Exhibit 6.6 lists the 10 largest American bank lenders *just* to Mexico.

Ten Biggest American Bank Lenders to Mexico (in Billions of American dollars as of September 30, 1987)

Bank	Outstanding to Mexico	Loan Loss Reserves for Developing Country Loans
Citicorp	$2.900	$3.432
BankAmerica Corp.	2.407	1.808
Manufacturers Hanover Corp.	1.883	1.833*
Chemical New York Corp.	1.733	1.505*
Chase Manhattan Corp.	1.660	1.970
Bankers Trust New York Corp.	1.277	1.000
J. P. Morgan & Co.	1.137	1.317
First Chicago Corp.	0.898	0.930
First Interstate Bancorp.	0.689	0.500
Wells Fargo & Co.	0.587	0.760

*As of June 30, 1987.

Source: *The Wall Street Journal*, December 30, 1987. Reprinted by permission of *The Wall Street Journal*, © 1987 Dow Jones & Company, Inc. All Rights Reserved Worldwide.

Why would the international banks make such risky loans to LDC sovereign governments in the first place? One reason obviously was that they held vast sums of money in Eurodollar deposits that needed to be quickly placed to start producing interest income. Banks were simply too eager and not careful enough in analyzing the risks they were undertaking in lending to unfamiliar borrowers. Many American banks claim that there was official *arm-twisting* from Washington to assist the economic development of the Third World countries. Nevertheless, had the bankers and Washington policy makers been better versed in economic history, perhaps the LDC debt crisis might have been avoided, or at least mitigated. The International Finance in Practice box on page 146 presents an article documenting a clear warning by David Hume, the 18th-century Scottish economist, about the dangers of sovereign lending.

Debt-for-Equity Swaps

In the midst of the LDC debt crisis, a secondary market developed for LDC debt at prices discounted significantly from face value. The secondary market consisted of approximately 50 creditor banks, investment banks, and boutique market makers. The LDC debt was purchased for use in **debt-for-equity swaps**. As part of debt rescheduling agreements among the bank lending syndicates and the debtor nations, creditor banks would sell their loans for American dollars at discounts from face value to MNCs desiring to make equity investment in subsidiaries or local firms in the LDCs. An LDC central bank would buy the bank debt from an MNC at a smaller discount than the MNC paid, but in local currency. The MNC would use the local currency to make preapproved new investment in the LDC that was economically or socially beneficial to the LDC and its populace.

Exhibit 6.7 diagrams a hypothetical debt-for-equity swap. The exhibit shows a MNC purchasing $100 million of Mexican debt (either directly or through a market maker) from a creditor bank for $60 million, that is, at a 40 percent discount from face value. The MNC then redeems the $100 million note from the Mexican central bank for the equivalent of $80 million in Mexican pesos at the current exchange rate. The Mexican pesos are invested in a Mexican subsidiary of the MNC or in an equity position in an LDC firm. The MNC has paid $60 million for $80 million in Mexican pesos.

During the midst of the LDC debt crisis, Latin American debt was going at an average discount of approximately 70 percent. The September 10, 1990, issue of *Barron's* quotes Brazilian sovereign debt at 21.75 cents per dollar, Mexican debt at 43.12 cents, and Argentinean debt at only 14.25 cents.

Real-life examples of debt-for-equity swaps abound. Chrysler invested $100 million in pesos in Chrysler de Mexico from money obtained from buying Mexican debt at a 56 percent discount. Volkswagen paid $170 million for $283 million in Mexican debt,

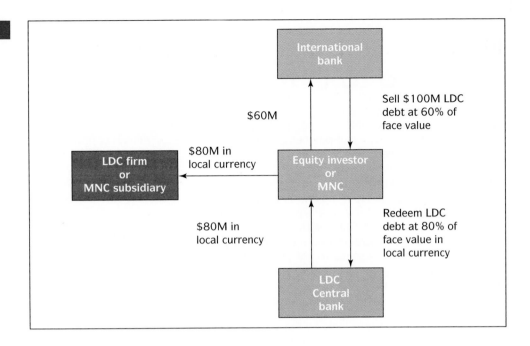

which it swapped for the equivalent of $260 million of pesos. In a more complicated deal, CitiBank, acting as a market maker, paid $40 million to another bank for $60 million of Mexican debt, which was swapped with Banco de Mexico, the Mexican central bank, for $54 million worth of pesos later used by Nissan to expand a truck plant outside of Mexico City.

Who benefits from a debt-for-equity swap? All parties are presumed to, or else the swap would not have taken place. The creditor bank benefits from getting an unproductive loan off its books and at least a portion of the principal repaid. The market maker obviously benefits from earning the bid-ask spread on the discounted loan amount. The LDC benefits in two ways. The first benefit comes from being able to pay off a "hard" currency loan (generally at a discount from face value) on which it cannot meet the debt service with its own local currency. The second benefit comes from the new productive investment made in the country, which was designed to foster economic growth. The equity investor benefits from the purchase of LDC local currency needed to make the investment at a discount from the current exchange rate.

Third World countries have only been open to allowing debt-for-equity swaps for certain types of investment. The LDC obtains the local currency to redeem the hard currency loan by printing it. This obviously increases the country's money supply and is inflationary. Thus, LDCs have only allowed swaps where the benefits of the new equity investment were expected to be greater than the harm caused to the economy by increased inflation. Acceptable types of investments have been in:

1. Export-oriented industries, such as automobiles, that will bring in hard currency.

2. High-technology industries that will lead to larger exports, improve the technological base of the country, and develop the skills of its people.

3. Tourist industry, such as resort hotels, that will increase tourism and visitors bringing hard currency.

4. Low-income housing developments that will improve the standard of living of some of the populace.

MLDC Lenders Should Have Listened to David Hume

David Hume, the 18th-century Scottish philosopher-economist, is known for formulating (1) the price-specie flow mechanism of balance-of-payments adjustment, (2) the doctrine of the neutrality of money, and (3) the classical theory of interest. Not so well known are his remarks on the external debt of sovereign nations. More's the pity. For those remarks, as contained in his 1752 essay "Of Public Credit," are particularly apropos to the current problem of Third World debt. Had modern policy makers and bankers heeded his words, they might have avoided the sorry sequence of overlending, over-borrowing, debt mismanagement, waste and potential default that he foresaw.

Hume thought no good could result from borrowing:

If the abuses of treasures [held by the state] be dangerous by engaging the state in rash enterprizes in confidence of its riches; the abuses of mortgaging are more certain and inevitable; poverty, impotence, and subjection to foreign powers.

Nations, presuming they can find the necessary lenders, are tempted to borrow without limit and to squander the funds on unproductive projects:

It is very tempting to a minister to employ such an expedient as enables him to make a great figure during his administration without overburthening the people with taxes or exciting any immediate clamorous against himself. The practice, therefore, of contracting debt will almost infallibly be abused in every government. It would scarcely be more imprudent to give a prodigal son a credit in every banker's shop in London than to empower a statesman to draw bills in this manner upon posterity.

Eventually, however, interest must be paid and the burden of debt service charges will fall heavily on the poor:

The taxes which are levied to pay the interest of these debts are . . . an oppression on the poorer sort.

Those same taxes "hurt commerce and discourage industry" and thus inhibit economic development and condemn the borrowing nation to continuing poverty. The debt burden will also pauperize the prosperous merchant and landowning classes that constitute the main bulwark of political freedom and stability. With the pauperization of the middle class:

No expedient at all remains for resisting tyranny: Elections are swayed by bribery and corruption alone: And the middle power between king and people being totally removed, a grievous despotism must infallibly prevail. The landowners [and merchants] despised for their oppressions, will be utterly unable to make any opposition to it.

The Solution: Brady Bonds

Today, most debtor nations and creditor banks would agree that the international debt crisis is effectively over. U.S. Treasury Secretary Nicholas F. Brady of the first Bush administration is largely credited with designing a strategy in the spring of 1989 to resolve the problem. Brady's solution was to offer creditor banks one of three alternatives: (1) convert their loans to marketable bonds with a face value equal to 65 percent of the original loan amount; (2) convert the loans into collateralized bonds with a reduced interest rate of 6.5 percent; or (3) lend additional funds to allow the debtor nations to get on their feet. As one can imagine, few banks chose the third alternative. The second alternative called for extending the debt maturities by 25 to 30 years and the purchase by the debtor nation of zero-coupon U.S. Treasury bonds with a corresponding maturity to guarantee the bonds and make them marketable. These bonds have come to be called **Brady bonds**.

By 1992, Brady bond agreements had been negotiated in many countries, including Argentina, Brazil, Mexico, Uruguay, Venezuela, Nigeria, and the Philippines. By August of 1992, 12 of 16 major debtor nations had reached refinancing agreements accounting for 92 percent of their outstanding private bank debt. In total, over $100 billion in bank debt has been converted to Brady bonds.

Can one imagine a more accurate assessment of the political situation in many Third World debtor nations?

Hume even foresaw the emigration of capital and labour to escape the burden of servicing debt held by foreign banks. Referring to England, then an underdeveloped nation, he said:

> As foreigners possess a great share of our national funds, they render the public, in a manner tributary to them, and may in time occasion by transport of our people and our industry.

As a country's debt expands, it eventually exceeds the taxable capacity to service it. Once this constraint is reached, Hume foresaw attempts to repudiate the debt. Contrary to Walter Wriston's dictum that sovereign nations never default, Hume argued that they would act on the belief that "either the nation must destroy public credit, or public credit will destroy the nation."

Such default, he thought, would hurt a nation's credit only temporarily. So forgetful and gullible are foreign banks that they would soon offer loans on the same generous terms and debt would flourish as before:

> So great dupes are the generality of mankind that notwithstanding such a violent shock to public credit as a voluntary bankruptcy in England would occasion, it would not probably be long ere credit would again revive in as flourishing a condition as before.

Forget rational expectations, said Hume; nobody behaves rationally all the time. People are destined to be fooled over and over again:

> Mankind are in all ages caught by the same baits: The same tricks played over and over again still trepan them. The heights of popularity and patriotism are still the beaten road to power and tyranny; flattery to treachery; standing armies to arbitrary governments; and the glory of God to the temporal interest of the clergy.

Because of the gullibility of lenders, "the fear of an everlasting destruction of credit . . . is a needless bugbear." In fact, a nation that has just defaulted may be a better credit risk than one that has not yet done so:

> A opulent knave . . . is a preferable debtor to an honest bankrupt: For the former, in order to carry on business, may find it his interest to discharge his debts where they are not exorbitant: The latter has it not in his power.

Hume's advice to would-be creditors: Lend sparingly. For once a country has borrowed beyond its taxable capacity, it will be tempted to default. From the debtor's viewpoint, debt repudiation may seem less costly than bleeding the nation dry in a vain effort to service the debt.

Hume, although prescient, was hardly infallible. He predicted that England would default on its large and rising debt within 50 years. His prediction was never realized. England's debt-service capacity exceeded his estimate.

Source: *The Wall Street Journal*, February 21, 1989, p. A20. Reprinted by permission of *The Wall Street Journal*, © 1989 Dow Jones & Company, Inc. All Rights Reserved Worldwide.

Japanese Banking Crisis

The Japanese banking system ended fiscal year 2001 with its fifth deficit in seven years. Cumulative losses over the seven-year period total ¥15 trillion (US$115 billion), an amount equivalent to almost 60 percent of shareholders' capital at the beginning of the period. Superficially, the Japanese banking system looks healthy, with a capital ratio of $10\frac{1}{2}$ percent. This figure, however, disguises the fact that over 40 percent of bank capital comes from an equal combination of public funds and deferred tax credits that can only be realized as offsets against profit within a five-year time period. The profit potential for Japanese banks is also questionable. A fundamental problem is the low margin charged on loans, resulting from strong competition from government-sponsored loans, government pressure to provide loans to small businesses on favourable terms, and the hesitation of bankers to charge an adequate rate to borrowers with whom they have close relationships.

The history of the Japanese banking crisis is a result of a complex combination of events and the structure of the Japanese financial system. In Japan, commercial banks have historically served as the financing arm and the centre of a collaborative group of business firms known as *keiretsu*. Keiretsu members have cross-holdings of one another's equity and ties of trade and credit. Typically, these equity shares are not traded. Additionally, Japanese banks frequently hold large equity positions in *keiretsu* members, which, in turn, tend to be highly levered in comparison to American business firms. The robust Japanese economy of the late 1980s, fuelled by large trade surpluses, created an economic environment of rapidly accelerating financial and real asset prices. Japanese banks, flush with cash and a desire to gain worldwide market share, engaged in tremendous lending both at home and abroad. A significant amount of this was in the form of real estate loans. During this time, Japanese firms had little trouble in servicing their bank loans.

The collapse of the Japanese stock market set in motion a downward spiral for the entire Japanese economy, and, in particular, Japanese banks. The Japanese stock market bubble burst at year-end 1989. As of September 2002, it stood at less than a third of its value at the peak. The downturn in the Japanese economy and the drop in Japanese real estate values put in jeopardy massive amounts of bank loans to corporations. Meanwhile, the concurrent downturn in the American economy resulted in a drop in value of real estate investments there.

The state of the Japanese banking system is, indeed, dire. Currently, nonperforming loans total ¥32 trillion (US$245 billion). At current low interest rates it is not too difficult for bank customers to meet periodic interest payments. Moreover, today's low rates have reduced the cost for banks to continue carrying nonperforming loans on their books. However, it is questionable whether these same customers will be able to make debt service obligations when interest rates turn up or whether they have the incentive or means to eventually pay off the loans. It is unlikely that the Japanese banking crisis will be rectified anytime soon. At least two important factors make this true. First, the Japanese financial system does not have a legal infrastructure that allows for an expedient method to restructure bad bank loans. Secondly, Japanese bank managers have little incentive to change outdated business practices because of the interrelations that exist between bank shareholders and bank customers.

The Asian Crisis

As noted in Chapter 2, the Asian crisis began in mid-1997 when Thailand devalued the baht. Subsequently, other Asian countries devalued their currencies by letting them float—ending their pegged value with the American dollar. Not since the LDC debt crisis have international financial markets experienced such widespread turbulence. The troubles, which began in Thailand, soon affected other countries in the region and also emerging markets in other regions.[4]

Interestingly, the Asian crisis followed a period of economic expansion in the region financed by record private capital inflows. Bankers from the G-10 countries actively sought to finance the growth opportunities in Asia by providing businesses in the region with a full assortment of products and services. Domestic price bubbles in East Asia, particularly in real estate, were fostered by these capital inflows. The simultaneous liberalization of financial markets contributed to bubbles in financial asset prices as well. The close interrelationships common among commercial firms and financial institutions in Asia resulted in poor investment decision making.

The risk exposure of the lending banks in East Asia was primarily to local banks and commercial firms, and not to sovereignties, as in the LDC debt crisis. It may have been implicitly assumed, however, that the governments would come to the rescue of their private banks should financial problems develop. The history of managed growth in the

---

[4]The discussion in this section closely follows the discussion on the Asian crisis found in *International Capital Markets: Developments, Prospects, and Key Policy Issues* (International Monetary Fund, Washington, D.C.), September 1998, pp. 1–6; and the Bank for International Settlements working paper titled "Supervisory Lessons to Be Drawn from the Asian Crisis," June 1999.

INTERNATIONAL FINANCE
IN PRACTICE

Contagion without Borders

The lessons taught by the "Tequila Effect" or the "Brazilian Sneeze"

Economists are developing a fascinating body of work around how international markets interact and behave during times of economic crises. The extension of this work could prove seminal to how institutional investors model their portfolios and manage risk.

The phenomenon known as financial contagion is the cross-border financial shock that propagates between countries and cannot be explained by examining standard channels of interaction, such as trade links.

The Contagions

Evidence of contagion and subsequent study is based on the following prominent examples:

- Tequila Effect (1994)—Mexican devaluation of the peso. Economics noticed the shock unduly influenced several Latin American markets, while the rest of the world came away relatively unscathed.
- Asian Flu (1997)—Speculative attacks in Indonesian, Korean, Malaysian and Thai markets. Almost all emerging markets—and even some developed markets—were affected. With the exception of Chile, these countries in Latin America had almost no direct trading relationships with the southeast Asian region.
- Russian Cold (1997)—Russia defaulted on its sovereign bonds and followed with a devaluation of the ruble, leading to a dramatic drop in the Russian stock market. The Russian Cold had a surprisingly large impact on international markets, given its small size relative to global market capitalization.
- Brazilian Sneeze (1999)—Speculative attack on the Brazilian real, which eventually caused the central bank to devalue the currency. The impact was smaller than the Russian or Asian crises, and did not have a consistent effect on other emerging markets.
- The NASDAQ Rash (2000)—Drop in the NASDAQ index and rise in its volatility. The losses sustained from this shock in the majority of the emerging markets were greater than in the U.S. market. As well, the impact was widespread in all developed markets.

Shift Contagion

There are two schools of thought identifying when contagion is taking place: shift contagion and pure contagion.

Shift contagion refers to changes in the normal strength of transmission mechanisms, including the fundamental channels of trade links, financial links, monetary policy and common shocks affecting those links. Fundamental channels are the oldest and best understood of all linkages between countries. Bilateral trade relationships, for example, are most often believed responsible for transmitting financial, market and economic shocks across countries.

Pure Contagion

Pure contagion refers to non-fundamental links. The transmission channels relate to investors' expectations and behaviour. The "herding" theory of investor behaviour, for example, focuses on the notion that individuals copy others in their group, acting on the perception that others have better information. They key points here are that imitation may be rewarded and individuals have an intrinsic preference for conformity.

Every country has contagious links both directly and indirectly to other nations. These links are present all the time, not just during the crises. With the integration of global markets, this means that contagion can spread quickly and affect developed and emerging markets, regardless of whether or not there is an apparent disconnect. What's more, many of the linkages cannot be controlled through macroeconomic policy decisions.

Advancements in the study of financial contagion and subsequent application of this learning to the institutional investment arena will result in:

- A better understanding of the stability relationship between international markets and how they move together;
- An improved forecasting ability for these markets;
- More robust Value-at-Risk (VaR) and asset allocation modelling; and,
- Improved buy/sell decisions during times of market distress.

Author: Robert F. Boston, CFA, MFC Global Investment Management. **Source:** *Canadian Investment Review*, Summer 2003.

region at least suggested that the economic and financial system, as an integral unit, could be managed in an economic downturn. This did not turn out to be the case. The Asian crisis is the most recent, but yet another, example of banks making a multitude of poor loans.

It is doubtful if the international debt crisis or the Asian crisis has taught banks a lasting lesson about the risks of lending to sovereign governments or large amounts of funds targeted to specific regions of the world. For some reason, bankers always seem willing to lend huge amounts to borrowers with a limited potential to repay. Regardless, there is no excuse for not properly evaluating the potential risks of an investment or loan. In lending to a sovereign government or making loans to private parties in distant parts of the world, the risks are unique, and a proper analysis of the economic, political, and social factors that constitute **political risk** is warranted. (See International Finance in Practice Box "Contagion without Borders.") While this subject might fit nicely with the current discussion, we leave it instead for the next chapter on the international bond market and Chapter 15 on direct foreign investment.

SUMMARY

In this chapter, the topics of international banking, the international money market, and the Third World debt crisis were discussed. This chapter begins the textbook's six-chapter sequence on world financial markets and institutions.

1. International banks can be characterized by the types of services they provide. International banks facilitate the imports and exports of their clients by arranging trade financing. They also arrange foreign currency exchange, assist in hedging exchange rate exposure, trade foreign exchange for their own account, and make a market in currency derivative products. Some international banks seek deposits of foreign currencies and make foreign currency loans to nondomestic bank customers. Additionally, some international banks may participate in the underwriting of international bonds if banking regulations allow.

2. Various types of international banking offices include correspondent bank relationships, representative offices, foreign branches, subsidiaries and affiliates, Edge Act banks, offshore banking centres, and International Banking Facilities. The reasons for the various types of international banking offices and the services they provide vary considerably.

3. The core of the international money market is the Eurocurrency market. A Eurocurrency is a time deposit of money in an international bank located in a country different from the country that issued the currency. For example, Eurodollars, which make up the largest part of the market, are deposits of American dollars in banks outside of the United States. The Eurocurrency market is headquartered in London. Eurobanks are international banks that seek Eurocurrency deposits and make Eurocurrency loans. The chapter illustrated the creation of Eurocurrency and discussed the nature of Eurocredits, or Eurocurrency loans.

4. Other main international money market instruments include forward rate agreements, Euronotes, and Eurocommercial paper.

5. Capital adequacy refers to the amount of equity capital and other securities a bank holds as reserves against risky assets to reduce the probability of a bank failure. The BIS 1988 Basle Capital Accord establishes a "rules-based" framework establishing the capital charge to safeguard depositors. This framework has been widely adopted throughout the world by national bank regulators. A 1996 amendment to the accord develops a "risk-focused" approach to capital adequacy for protection against the price risk exposure of its trading accounts. The amendment requires banks to determine their value-at-risk (VAR) according to the criterion that there be only a 1-percent chance that the maximum loss over a 10-day time period will exceed the bank's capital. A New Basel Capital Accord, designed to correct several deficiencies in the 1988 accord, is expected to be implemented by year-end 2006.

6. The international debt crisis was caused by international banks lending more to Third World sovereign governments than they should have. The crisis began during the 1970s when OPEC countries flooded banks with huge sums of Eurodollars that needed to be lent to cover the interest being paid on the deposits. Because of a subsequent collapse in oil prices, high unemployment, and high inflation, many less-developed countries could not afford to meet the debt service on their loans. The huge sums involved jeopardized some of the world's largest banks, in particular, American banks that had lent most of the money. Debt-for-equity swaps were one means by which some banks shed themselves of problem Third World debt. But the main solution was collateralized Brady bonds, which allowed the less-developed countries to reduce the debt service on their loans and extend the maturities far into the future.

7. The Asian crisis began in mid-1997. The troubles, which began in Thailand, soon affected other countries in the region and also emerging markets in other regions. Not since the LDC debt crisis have international financial markets experienced such widespread turbulence. The crisis followed a period of economic expansion in the region financed by record private capital inflows. Bankers from industrialized countries actively sought to finance the growth opportunities. The risk exposure of the lending banks in East Asia was primarily to local banks and commercial firms, and not to sovereignties, as in the LDC debt crisis. Nevertheless, the political and economic risks were not correctly assessed. The Asian crisis is the most recent example of commercial banks making a multitude of poor loans.

KEY WORDS

affiliate bank, *135*
bank capital
   adequacy, *136*
Basle Accord, *136*
Brady bonds, *146*
correspondent bank
   relationship, *134*
debt-for-equity swap, *144*
Edge Act bank, *135*
Eurobank, *138*
Eurocommercial
   paper, *142*
Eurocredit, *139*

Eurocurrency, *138*
Euronote, *142*
Euro Interbank
   Offered Rate
   (EURIBOR), *139*
foreign branch bank, *134*
forward rate agreement
   (FRA), *141*
International Banking
   Facility (IBF), *138*
international debt
   crisis, *143*

less-developed countries
   (LDCs), *143*
London Interbank Offered
   Rate (LIBOR), *138*
negotiable certificate of
   deposit (NCD), *139*
offshore banking
   centre, *135*
political risk, *150*
representative office, *134*
subsidiary bank, *135*
syndicate, *139*
value-at-risk (VAR), *137*

QUESTIONS

1. Briefly discuss some of the services that international banks provide their customers and the marketplace.

2. Briefly discuss the various types of international banking offices.

3. How does the deposit-loan rate spread in the Eurodollar market compare with the deposit-loan rate spread in the domestic American banking system? Why?

4. What is the difference between the Euronote market and the Eurocommercial paper market?

5. Briefly discuss the cause and the solution(s) to the international bank crisis involving less-developed countries.

6. What warning did David Hume, the 18th-century Scottish philosopher-economist, give about lending to sovereign governments?

PROBLEMS

1. Grecian Tile Manufacturing of Athens, Georgia, borrows $1,500,000 at LIBOR plus a lending margin of 1.25 percent per annum on a six-month rollover basis from a London bank. If six-month LIBOR is $4\frac{1}{2}$ percent over the first six-month interval and $5\frac{3}{8}$ percent over the second six-month interval, how much will Grecian Tile pay in interest over the first year of its Eurodollar loan?

2. A bank sells a "three against six" $3,000,000 FRA for a three-month period beginning three months from today and ending six months from today. The purpose of the FRA is to cover the interest rate risk caused by the maturity mismatch from having made a three-month Eurodollar loan and having accepted a six-month Eurodollar deposit. The agreement rate with the buyer is 5.5 percent. There are actually 92 days in the three-month FRA period. Assume that three months from today the settlement rate is $4\frac{7}{8}$ percent. Determine how much the FRA is worth and who pays who—the buyer pays the seller or the seller pays the buyer.

3. Assume the settlement rate in problem 2 is $6\frac{1}{8}$ percent. What is the solution now?

4. A three-against-nine FRA has an agreement rate of 4.75 percent. You believe six-month LIBOR in three months will be 5.125 percent. You decide to take a speculative position in a FRA with a $1,000,000 notional value. There are 183 days in the FRA period. Determine whether you should buy or sell the FRA and what your expected profit will be if your forecast is correct about the six-month LIBOR rate.

5. The Fisher effect (Chapter 5) suggests that nominal interest rates differ between countries because of differences in the respective rates of inflation. According to the Fisher effect and your examination of the one-year Eurocurrency interest rates presented in Exhibit 6.2, order the currencies from the eight countries from highest to lowest in terms of the size of the inflation premium embedded in the nominal interest rates for August 19, 2002.

6. A bank has a $500 million portfolio of investments and bank credits. The daily standard deviation of return on this portfolio is 0.666 percent. Capital adequacy standards require the bank to maintain capital equal to its VAR calculated over a 10-day holding period at a maximum 1-percent loss level. What is the capital charge for the bank?

INTERNET EXERCISES

1. Exhibit 6.4 compares the spread between the prime borrowing rate and dollar LIBOR. Go to the Bloomberg website www.bloomberg.com/markets/rates.html to see the current spread for terms to maturity between one month and one year.

2. In this chapter, we noted that universal banks provide a host of services to corporate clients. Bank of America, one of the world's largest banks, is an example of a universal bank. Go to its website www.corp.bankofamerica.com/portal/portal/controller/controller.jsp?path=iegr/global_rch/content.xml to view the global services they provide.

MINI CASE

Detroit Motors' Latin American Expansion

It is September 1990, and Detroit Motors of Detroit, Michigan, is considering establishing an assembly plant in Latin America for a new utility vehicle it has just designed. The cost of the capital expenditures has been estimated at $65,000,000. There is not much of a sales market in Latin America, and virtually all output would be exported to the United States for sale. Nevertheless, an assembly plant in Latin America is attractive for at least two reasons. First, labour costs are expected to be half what Detroit Motors would have to pay in the United States to union workers. Since the assembly plant will be a new facility for a newly designed vehicle, Detroit Motors does not expect any hassle from its American union in establishing the plant in Latin America. Secondly, the chief financial officer (CFO) of Detroit Motors believes that a debt-for-equity swap can be arranged with a least one of the Latin American countries that has not been able to meet its debt service on its sovereign debt with some of the major American banks.

The September 10, 1990, issue of *Barron's* indicated the following prices (cents on the dollar) on Latin American bank debt:

Brazil	21.75
Mexico	43.12
Argentina	14.25
Venezuela	46.25
Chile	70.25

The CFO is not comfortable with the level of political risk in Brazil and Argentina and has decided to eliminate them from consideration. After some preliminary discussions with the central banks of Mexico, Venezuela, and Chile, the CFO has learned that all three countries would be interested in hearing a detailed presentation about the type of facility Detroit Motors would construct, how long it would take, the number of locals that would be employed, and the number of units that would be manufactured per year. Since it is time-consuming to prepare and make these presentations, the CFO would like to approach the most attractive candidate first. He has learned that the central bank of Mexico will redeem its debt at 80 percent of face value in a debt-for-equity swap, Venezuela at 75 percent, and Chile 100 percent. As a first step, the CFO decides an analysis based purely on financial considerations is necessary to determine which country looks like the most viable candidate. You are asked to assist in the analysis. What do you advise?

REFERENCES & SUGGESTED READINGS

Bank for International Settlements. "Overview of the Amendment to the Capital Accord to Incorporate Market Risks." Basle: Bank for International Settlements, January 1996.

Bank for International Settlements. "A New Capital Adequacy Framework." Basle: Bank for International Settlements, June 1999.

Bank for International Settlements. "Supervisory Lessons to Be Drawn from the Asian Crisis." Basle: Bank for International Settlements, June 1999.

Bank for International Settlements. "The New Basel Capital Accord: An Explanatory Note." Basle: Bank for International Settlements, January 2001.

Bank for International Settlements. *72nd Annual Report.* Basle: Bank for International Settlements, July 2002.

Baughn, William H., and Donald R. Mandich. *The International Banking Handbook.* Burr Ridge, Ill.: Dow-Jones Irwin, 1983.

Barry, Andrew. "The Lust for Latin Debt: Yield-Seeking Funds Downplay Perils in Brady Bonds." *Barron's* (August 16, 1993).

Beder, Tanya Styblo. "VAR: Seductive but Dangerous." *Financial Analysts Journal* (September/ October 1995), pp. 12–24.

Bodie, Zvi, Alex Kane, and Alan J. Marcus. *Investments,* 5th ed. New York: McGraw Hill/Irwin, 2002.

Chung, Sam Y. "Portfolio Risk Measurement: A Review of Value at Risk." *Journal of Alternative Investments* (Summer 1999), pp. 34–42.

Deak, Nicholas L., and JoAnne Celusak. *International Banking.* New York: New York Institute of Finance, 1984.

Dufey, Gunter, and Ian Giddy. *The International Money Market,* 2nd ed. Upper Saddle River, N.J.: Prentice Hall, 1994.

Eng, Maximo V., Francis A. Lees, and Laurence J. Maurer. *Global Finance,* 2nd ed. Reading, Mass.: Addison-Wesley, 1998.

Feldstein, Martin. "A Wrong Turn in LDC Debt Management." *The Wall Street Journal* (March 5, 1989).

Goldberg, Lawrence G., and Robert Grosse. "Location Choice of Foreign Banks in the United States." *Journal of Economics and Business* 46 (1994), pp. 367–79.

Hartman, Philipp, Michele Manna, and Andrés Manyanares. "The Microstructure of the Euro Money Market." *Journal of International Money and Finance* 20 (2001), pp. 895–948.

Hultman, Charles W. *The Environment of International Banking.* Englewood Cliffs, N.J.: Prentice Hall, 1990.

International Monetary Fund. *International Capital Markets: Part I. Exchange Rate Management and International Capital Flows.* Washington, D.C.: International Monetary Fund, April 1993.

International Monetary Fund. *International Capital Markets: Part II. Systemic Issues in International Finance.* Washington, D.C.: International Monetary Fund, August 1993.

International Monetary Fund. *International Capital Markets: Developments, Prospects, and Policy Issues.* Washington, D.C.: International Monetary Fund, September 1994.

International Monetary Fund. *International Capital Markets: Developments, Prospects, and Policy Issues.* Washington, D.C.: International Monetary Fund, August 1995.

International Monetary Fund. *International Capital Markets: Developments, Prospects, and Key Policy Issues.* Washington, D.C.: International Monetary Fund, September 1998.

Johansson, Frederik, Michael J. Seiler, and Mikael Tjarnberg. "Measuring Downside Portfolio Risk." *Journal of Portfolio Management* (Fall 1999), pp. 96–107.

Jorion, Phillipe. "Risk^2: Measuring the Risk in Value at Risk." *Financial Analysts Journal* (November/December 1996), pp. 47–56.

Ju, Xiongwei and Neil Pearson. "Using Value-at-Risk to Control Risk Taking: How Wrong Can You Be?" *Journal of Risk* 1 (1999), pp. 5–36.

Lopez, Jose. "Regulatory Evaluation of Value-at-Risk." *Journal of Risk* 1 (1999), pp. 37–63.

Marton, Andrew. "The Debate over Debt-for-Equity Swaps." *Institutional Investor* (February 1987), pp. 177–80.

"A Mexican Standoff on the Debt Crisis, 1982." *The Wall Street Journal* (November 30, 1989).

Mulford, David C. "Moving beyond the Latin Debt Crisis," *The Wall Street Journal* (August 21, 1992).

Pool, John C., and Stephen C. Stamos, Jr. *International Economic Policy.* Lexington, Mass.: Lexington Books, 1989.

Reimer, Bianca. "A Way to Turn Debt from a Burden to a Boon." *Business Week* (December 22, 25, and 28, 1986).

Rivera-Batiz, Francisco L., and Luis Rivera-Batiz. *International Finance and Open Economy Macroeconomics.* 2nd ed. Upper Saddle River, N.J.: Prentice Hall, 1994.

Rugman, Alan M., and Shyan J. Kamath. "International Diversification and Multinational Banking." In Sarkis J. Khoury and Alo Ghosh, eds., *Recent Developments in International Banking and Finance.* Lexington, Mass.: Lexington Books, 1987.

Saunders, Anthony. *Financial Institutions Management,* 3rd ed. New York: Irwin/McGraw-Hill, 2000.

Shirreff, David. "Danger—Kids at Play." *Euromoney* (March 1995), pp. 43–46.

Shirreff, David. "Risk Scientists Look beyond Their Silos." *Euromoney* (May 1999), pp. 32–33.

Smith, Roy C., and Ingo Walter. *Global Banking.* New York: Oxford University Press, 1997.

"Swap Shop: The Whys and Ways of the Market in LDC." *Barron's* (September 4, 1989).

Torres, Craig. " 'Bridge' Loans to Latin America Rise, but Some Wonder If the Toll Is Too High." *The Wall Street Journal* (August 25, 1993).

Eurocurrency Creation

As an illustration, consider the following simplified example of the creation of Eurodollars. Assume an American Importer purchases $100 of merchandise from a German Exporter and pays for the purchase by drawing a $100 cheque on his American chequing account (demand deposit). Further assume the German Exporter deposits the $100 cheque received as payment in a demand deposit in the American bank (which in actuality represents the entire American commercial banking system). This transaction can be represented by T accounts, where changes in assets are on the left and changes in liabilities are on the right side of the T, as follows:

American Commercial Bank	
	Demand Deposits
	American Importer −$100
	German Exporter +$100

At this point, all that has changed in the American banking system is that ownership of $100 of demand deposits has been transferred from domestic to foreign control.

The German Exporter is not likely to leave his deposit in the form of a demand deposit for long, as no interest is being earned on this type account. If the funds are not needed for the operation of the business, the Germany Exporter can deposit the $100 in a time deposit in a bank outside the United States and receive a greater rate of interest than if the funds were put in a American time deposit. Assume the German Exporter closes out his demand deposit in the American Bank and redeposits the funds in a London Eurobank. The London Eurobank credits the German Exporter with a $100 time deposit and deposits the $100 into its correspondent bank account (demand deposit) with the American Bank (banking system). These transactions are represented as follows by T accounts:

American Commercial Bank	
	Demand Deposits
	German Exporter −$100
	London Eurobank +$100

London Eurobank			
Demand Deposits		*Time Deposits*	
Amercian Bank	+$100	German Exporter	+$100

Two points are noteworthy from these transactions. First, ownership of $100 of demand deposits has again been transferred (from the German Exporter to the London Eurobank), but the entire $100 still remains on deposit in the American Bank. Second, the $100 time deposit of the German Exporter in the London Eurobank represents the creation of Eurodollars. This deposit exists *in addition* to the dollars deposited in the United States. Hence, no dollars have flowed out of the American banking system in the creation of Eurodollars.

The London Eurobank will soon lend out the dollars, as it cannot afford to pay interest on a time deposit on which it is not earning a return. To whom will the London Eurobank lend the dollars? Most obviously, to a party needing dollars for a dollar-denominated business transaction or to an investor desiring to invest in the United

States. Let us assume that a Dutch Importer borrows $100 from the London Eurobank for the purpose of purchasing from an American Exporter merchandise for resale in the Netherlands. The T accounts representing these transactions are as follows:

London Eurobank

Demand Deposits			
American Bank	−$100		
Loans			
Dutch Importer	+$100		

American Commercial Bank

	Demand Deposits	
	London Eurobank	−$100
	Dutch Importer	+$100

Dutch Importer

Demand Deposits		Loan from	
in American Bank	+$100	London Eurobank	+$100

Note from these transactions that the London Eurobank transfers ownership of $100 of its demand deposits held in the American Commercial Bank to the Dutch Importer in exchange for the $100 loan.

The Dutch Importer will draw a cheque on its demand deposit in the American Bank to pay the American Exporter for the merchandise shipment. The American Exporter will deposit the cheque in his American Bank demand deposit. These transactions are represented as follows:

Dutch Importer

Demand Deposit	
in American Bank	−$100
Inventory	+$100

American Exporter

Inventory	−$100
Demand Deposit	
in American Bank	+$100

American Commercial Bank

	Demand Deposit	
	Dutch Importer	−$100
	American Exporter	+$100

The T accounts show that $100 of demand deposits in the American Bank have changed ownership, going from the control of the Dutch Exmporter to the American Exporter—or from foreign to American ownership. The original $100, however, never left the American banking system.

International Bond Market

THIS CHAPTER CONTINUES the discussion of international capital markets and institutions, focusing on the international bond market. The chapter should be especially useful for the financial officer of an MNC interested in sourcing new debt capital in the international bond market, as well as for the international investor interested in international fixed-income securities.

The chapter opens with statistics on the size of the world's bond markets and the major currencies in which bonds are denominated. The next section presents some useful definitions that describe exactly what is meant by the international bond market. The accompanying discussion distinguishes market segments and the various types of bond instruments traded in them. An examination of the currency distribution of the international bond market and the nationality and the type of borrower follows. Trading practices in the Eurobond market are discussed next. The chapter concludes with a discussion of international bond credit ratings and bond market indexes that are useful for performance analysis.

7.1 The World's Bond Markets: A Statistical Perspective

Exhibit 7.1 presents an overview of the world's bond markets. It shows the amounts of domestic and international bonds outstanding denominated in the major currencies. As of June 2003, the face value of bonds outstanding in the world was US$45,400. Domestic bonds account for the largest share of outstanding bonds, equalling $35,655 billion, or 79 percent, of the total.

The American dollar, the euro, and the yen are the currencies in which the majority of domestic and international bonds are denominated. Proportionately more domestic bonds are denominated in yen (19 percent) than are international bonds (4 percent), while more international bonds than domestic bonds are denominated in the euro (41 percent versus 17.1 percent) and pound sterling (7 percent versus 3 percent).

7.2 Foreign Bonds and Eurobonds

The international bond market encompasses two basic market segments: foreign bonds and Eurobonds. A **foreign bond** issue is one offered by a foreign borrower to the

EXHIBIT 7.1	Amounts of Domestic and International Bonds Outstanding As of June 2003, Billions of American Dollars					
Currency	Domestic	Percent	International	Percent	Total	Percent
American dollar	16,764	47	4,211	43	20,976	46
Euro	6,269	18	4,009	41	10,278	23
Pound sterling	1,093	3	668	7	1,760	4
Yen	6,910	19	427	4	7,337	16
Canadian dollar	619	2	68	1	686	2
Other	4,000	11	365	4	4,365	10
Total	35,655	100	9,748	100	45,402	100

Source: *International Banking and Financial Market Developments*, Bank for International Settlements, Tables 13 B and 16 A, September 2003.

investors in a national capital market and denominated in that nation's currency. An example is a German multinational corporation (MNC) issuing dollar-denominated bonds to American investors. A **Eurobond** issue is one denominated in a particular currency but sold to investors in national capital markets other than the country that issued the denominating currency. An example is a Dutch borrower issuing dollar-denominated bonds to investors in the United Kingdom, Switzerland, and the Netherlands. The markets for foreign bonds and Eurobonds operate in parallel with the domestic national bond markets, and all three market groups compete with one another.

Exhibit 7.2 presents the amounts of international bonds outstanding for 1997 through 2002 classified by the amounts by type of issue. The amounts of international bonds have increased steadily each year. At year-end 1997, $3,323 billion in bonds were outstanding; in 2002, the amount was $8,758 billion, a 165-percent increase.

In any given year, roughly 80 percent of new international bonds are likely to be Eurobonds, rather than foreign bonds. Eurobonds are known by the currency in which they are denominated, for example, American dollar Eurobonds, yen Eurobonds, and Swiss franc Eurobonds, or, correspondingly, Eurodollar bonds, Euroyen bonds, and EuroSF bonds. Foreign bonds, on the other hand, frequently have colourful names that designate the country in which they are issued. For example, *Yankee* bonds are dollar-denominated foreign bonds originally sold to American investors, *Samurai* bonds are yen-denominated foreign bonds sold in Japan, and *Bulldogs* are pound sterling–denominated foreign bonds sold in the United Kingdom.

Bearer Bonds and Registered Bonds

Eurobonds are usually bearer bonds. With a **bearer bond,** possession is evidence of ownership. The issuer does not keep records indicating the current owner of a bond. With **registered bonds,** the owner's name is on the bond and it is recorded by the issuer, or the owner's name is assigned to a bond serial number recorded by the issuer. When a registered bond is sold, a new bond certificate is issued with the new owner's name, or the new owner's name is assigned to the bond serial number.

American security regulations require Yankee bonds and American corporate bonds sold to American citizens to be registered. Bearer bonds are very attractive to investors

EXHIBIT 7.2		1997	1998	1999	2000	2001	2002
International Bond Amounts Outstanding Classified by Major Instruments Year-End, 1997-2002, Billions American Dollars	*Instrument*						
	Straight-fixed rate	2,390	2,968	3,634	4,158	4,832	6,257
	Floating-rate notes	736	925	1,236	1,479	1,736	2,193
	Convertible issues	152	188	218	231	261	299
	With equity warrants	45	23	18	11	10	11
	Total	3,323	4,103	5,106	5,880	6,839	8,758

Source: *International Banking and Financial Market Developments*, Bank for International Settlements, Table 13 B, September 2003.

desiring privacy and anonymity—attractive features for tax planning. Consequently, investors will generally accept a lower yield on bearer bonds than on registered bonds of comparable terms, making them a less costly source of funds for the issuer to service.

National Security Regulations

Foreign bonds must meet the security regulations of the country in which they are issued. This means that publicly traded Yankee bonds must meet the same regulations as American domestic bonds. Securities sold in the United States to public investors must be registered with the Securities and Exchange Commission (SEC), and a prospectus disclosing detailed financial information about the issuer must be provided and made available to prospective investors. The expense of the registration process, the time delay it creates in bringing a new issue to market (four additional weeks), and the disclosure of information that many foreign borrowers consider private historically have made it desirable for foreign borrowers to raise American dollars in the Eurobond market. The shorter length of time in bringing a Eurodollar bond issue to market, and the lower rate of interest that borrowers pay for Eurodollar bond financing in comparison with Yankee bond financing are two major reasons why the Eurobond segment of the international bond market is roughly four times the size of the foreign bond segment. Since Eurobonds do not have to meet national security regulations, name recognition of the issuer is an extremely important factor in being able to source funds in the international capital market.

Eurobonds sold in the United States may not be sold to American citizens. To prevent this, the initial purchaser receives the bearer bond only after a 90-day waiting period and presentation of identification that one is not an American citizen. Of course, nothing prevents an American investor from repurchasing bearer bonds in the secondary market after 90 days.

Withholding Taxes

Prior to 1984, the United States required a 30-percent withholding tax on interest paid to nonresidents who held American government or corporate bonds. Moreover, American firms issuing Eurodollar bonds from the United States were required to withhold the tax on interest paid to foreigners. In 1984, the withholding tax law was repealed. American corporations were allowed to issue domestic bearer bonds to nonresidents, but Congress would not grant this privilege to the Treasury.

The repeal of the withholding tax law caused a substantial shift in the relative yields on American government and Eurodollar bonds. Prior to 1984, top-quality Eurodollar bonds sold overseas traded at lower yields than American Treasury bonds of similar maturities that were subject to the withholding tax. Afterwards, the situation was reversed; foreign investors found the safety of registered U.S. Treasury bonds without the withholding tax more attractive than higher yields on corporate Eurodollar bond issues.

When it was in effect, the American withholding tax on interest paid to foreigners resulted in a substantial amount of American corporate borrowings from Europe—more than 90 percent—being channelled through the tiny tax haven of the Netherlands Antilles. The Netherlands Antilles had a tax treaty with the United States that stipulated a zero withholding tax rate on American-source interest paid on bonds issued from the Netherlands Antilles. As a result, interest payments from the United States could flow through to European recipients (who, of course, registered their bonds in the Netherlands Antilles) without the burden of the American withholding tax as long as the interest flowed through the Netherlands Antilles. When the withholding tax was repealed, the so-called "Dutch Treat" was no longer sought out by American corporate borrowers.

Canadian corporate borrowers are also familiar with withholding taxes and their potential effect of the after-tax cost of borrowing abroad. For many years, Canada imposed a withholding tax on interest paid to foreigners, in particular, interest paid by a Canadian corporation to a bondholder in, say, the United States. The rate of withholding tax was punitive, ranging from 15 to 25 percent of the interest payment. When it was in effect, the withholding tax forced Canadian corporate borrowers to rely heavily on the relatively small Canadian bond market. It drove a wedge between Canadian borrowing rates and the "world" interest rate, and it discouraged capital from flowing into Canada. When the tax was scrapped in 1975, these adverse effects promptly disappeared.

Today, most industrial nations cooperate through tax treaties to maintain low or zero rates of withholding taxes on interest paid on arm's-length (that is, *not* intracorporate) borrowing. This enlightened tax policy on international capital is analogous to the elimination of tariffs on traded goods.

Other Regulatory Changes

Two other features of American security regulations have a significant effect on the international bond market. SEC *Rule 415*, instituted in 1982, provides for "shelf registration." **Shelf registration** allows an issuer to preregister a securities issue and then shelve the securities for later sale when financing is actually needed. Shelf registration has, thus, eliminated the time delay in bringing a foreign bond issue to market in the United States, but it has not eliminated the information disclosure that many foreign borrowers find too expensive and/or objectionable. SEC *Rule 144A* allows qualified institutional investors in the United States to trade in private placement issues that do not have to meet the strict information disclosure requirements of publicly traded issues. SEC rule 144A was designed to make the American capital markets more competitive with the Eurobond market. A large portion of the 144A market is composed of Yankee bonds.

Global Bonds

Global bond issues were first offered in 1989. A **global bond** issue is a large international bond offering by a single borrower that is simultaneously sold in North America, Europe, and Asia. Global bonds follow the registration requirements of domestic bonds but have the fee structure of Eurobonds. Global bond offerings enlarge the borrower's opportunities for financing at reduced costs. Purchasers, mainly institutional investors, like the increased liquidity of the issues and have been willing to accept lower yields. The largest corporate global bond issue, to date, is the $14.6 billion Deutsche Telekom multicurrency offering. The issue includes three American dollar tranches with five-, 10-, and 30-year maturities totalling $9.5 billion, two euro tranches with five - and 10-year maturities totalling €3 billion, two British pound sterling tranches with five- and 30-year maturities totalling £950 million, and one five-year Japanese yen tranche of ¥90 billion. Another large global bond issue is the AT&T package of $2 billion of 5.625 percent notes due 2004, $3 billion of 6.000 percent notes due 2009, and $3 billion of 6.500 percent notes due 2029 issued in March 1999. The Republic of Italy issued one of the largest sovereign global bond issues in September 1993, a package of $2 billion of 6.000 percent notes due 2003 and $3.5 billion of 6.875 percent debentures due 2023. One of the largest emerging markets global bond issues, to date, is the Republic of Korea package issued April 1998 of $1 billion of 8.750 percent notes due 2003 and $3 billion of 8.875 percent bonds due 2008. SEC Rule 415 and Rule 144A have likely facilitated global bond offerings, and more offerings in the future can be expected.

7.3 Types of Instruments

The international bond market has been much more innovative than the domestic bond market in the types of instruments offered to investors. In this section, we examine the major types of international bonds. We begin with a discussion of the more standard types of instruments and conclude with the more exotic innovations that have appeared in recent years.

Straight Fixed-Rate Issues

Straight fixed-rate bond issues have a designated maturity date at which the principal of the bond issue is promised to be repaid. During the life of the bond, fixed coupon payments, which are a percentage of the face value, are paid as interest to the bond-holders. In contrast to many domestic bonds, which make semiannual coupon payments, coupon interest on Eurobonds is typically paid annually. The reason is that Eurobonds are usually bearer bonds, and annual coupon redemption is more convenient for bondholders and less costly for the bond issuer as bondholders are scattered geographically. Exhibit 7.2 shows that the majority of new international bond offerings in any year are straight fixed-rate issues. The American dollar, euro, British pound sterling, and Japanese yen have been the most common currencies denominating straight fixed-rate bonds in recent years.

Euro-Medium-Term Notes

Euro-Medium-Term Notes (Euro MTNs) are typically fixed-rate notes issued by a corporation with maturities ranging from less than a year to about 10 years. Like fixed-rate bonds, Euro-MTNs have a fixed maturity and pay coupon interest on periodic dates. Unlike a bond issue, in which the entire issue is brought to market at once, a Euro-MTN issue is partially sold on a continuous basis through an issuance facility that allows the borrower to obtain funds only as needed on a flexible basis. This feature is very attractive to issuers. Euro-MTNs have become a very popular means of raising medium-term funds since they were first introduced in 1986. All the statistical exhibits in this chapter include the amounts outstanding of MTNs.

An example of straight-fixed rate bonds is the EUR 2,000,000 of 5-percent notes due in 2008, issued in March 1998 by the European Investment Bank.

Floating-Rate Notes

Floating-rate notes (FRNs) are typically medium-term bonds with coupon payments indexed to some reference rate. Common reference rates are either three-month or six-month American dollar LIBOR. Coupon payments on FRNs are usually quarterly or semiannual and in accord with the reference rate.

For example, consider a five-year FRN with coupons referenced to six-month dollar LIBOR paying coupon interest semiannually. At the beginning of every six-month period, the next semiannual coupon payment is *reset* to be $0.5 \times (\text{LIBOR} + X \text{ percent})$ of face value, where X represents the default risk premium above LIBOR the issuer must pay based on its creditworthiness. The premium is typically no larger than 1/8 percent for top-quality issuers. As an example, if X equals 1/8 percent and the current six-month LIBOR is 6.6 percent, the next period's coupon rate on a $1,000 face value FRN will be $0.5 \times (0.066 + 0.00125) \times \$1,000 = \$33.625$. If on the next reset date six-month LIBOR is 5.7 percent, the following semiannual coupon will be set at $29.125.

FRNs have interest rate risk different from that of straight fixed-rate bonds. All bonds experience an inverse price change when the market rate of interest changes. FRNs experience only mild price changes between reset dates which are relatively frequent. On the reset date, the market price will gravitate back close to par value when the next period's coupon payment is reset to the new market value of the reference rate, and subsequent coupon payments are repriced to market expectations of future values of the reference rate. That is to say that FRNs have "short duration" and, therefore, relatively small interest rate risk.

FRNs make attractive investments for investors with a strong need to preserve the principal value of the investment should they need to liquidate the investment prior to the maturity of the bonds. Exhibit 7.2 shows that FRNs are the second most common type of international bond issue. The American dollar and the euro are the two currencies denominating most outstanding FRNs.

In February 2002, the National Bank of Kuwait issued FRNs at par $450,000,000 of FRNs due 2005 indexed to three-month LIBOR plus 25 basis points.

Equity-Related Bonds

There are two types of **equity-related bonds:** convertible bonds and bonds with equity warrants. A **convertible bond** issue allows the investor to exchange the bond for a predetermined number of equity shares of the issuer. The *floor-value* of a convertible bond is its straight fixed-rate bond value. Convertibles usually sell at a premium above the larger of their straight debt value and their conversion value. Investors are usually willing to accept a lower coupon rate of interest than the comparable straight fixed coupon bond rate because they find the conversion feature attractive. **Bonds with equity warrants** can be viewed as straight fixed-rate bonds with the addition of a call option (or warrant) feature. The warrant entitles the bondholder to purchase a certain number of equity shares in the issuer at a prestated price over a predetermined period of time.

Zero-Coupon Bonds

Zero-coupon bonds are sold at a discount from face value and do not pay any coupon interest over their life. At maturity, the investor receives the full face value. Alternatively, some zero-coupon bonds originally sell for face value and at maturity the investor receives an amount in excess of face value to compensate the investor for the use of the money, but this is really nothing more than a semantic difference as to what constitutes "face value." Zero-coupon bonds have been denominated primarily in the American dollar and the Swiss franc. Japanese investors are particularly attracted to zero-coupon bonds because their tax law treats the difference between face value and the discounted purchase price of the bond as a tax-free capital gain, whereas coupon interest is taxable. More generally, zero-coupon bonds are attractive to investors who desire to avoid the reinvestment risk of coupon receipts at possibly lower interest rates.

Another form of zero-coupon bonds are stripped bonds. A **stripped bond** is a zero-coupon bond that results from stripping the coupons and principal from a coupon bond. The result is a series of zero-coupon bonds represented by the individual coupon and principal payments. This practice began in the early 1980s when several investment banks created stripped bonds to satisfy the demand for zero-coupon American Treasury securities with various maturity dates. For example, Salomon Brothers offered CATS, which is an acronym for Certificates of Accrual for Treasury Securities. The stripped bonds are actually *receipts* representing a portion of the Treasury security held in trust. In 1985, the U.S. Treasury introduced its own product called STRIPS, for Separate Trading of Registered Interest and Principal of Securities. Investment firms are allowed under Treasury regulations to sell the stripped bonds in bearer form to non-American citizens, but, as previously mentioned, the Treasury does not have this privilege. Nevertheless, the Treasury's STRIPS dominate the stripped-bond market.

Dual-Currency Bonds

Dual-currency bonds became popular in the mid-1980s. A **dual-currency bond** is a straight fixed-rate bond issued in one currency, say, Swiss francs, that pays coupon interest in that same currency. At maturity, the principal is repaid in another currency, say, American dollars. Coupon interest is frequently at a higher rate than comparable straight fixed-rate bonds. The amount of the dollar principal repayment at maturity is set at inception; frequently, the amount allows for some appreciation in the exchange rate of the stronger currency.

From the investor's perspective, a dual-currency bond includes a long-term forward contract. If the dollar appreciates over the life of the bond, the principal repayment will be worth more than a return of principal in Swiss francs. The market value of a dual-currency bond in Swiss francs should equal the sum of the present value of the Swiss franc coupon stream discounted at the Swiss market rate of interest plus the dollar principal repayment, converted to Swiss francs at the expected future exchange rate, and discounted at the Swiss market rate of interest.

Japanese firms have been large issuers of dual currency bonds. These bonds were issued and pay coupon interest in yen with the principal reimbursement in American dollars. Yen/dollar dual currency bonds are an attractive financing method for Japanese MNCs desiring to establish or expand American subsidiaries. The yen proceeds can be converted to dollars to finance the capital investment in the United States, and during the early years, the coupon payments can be made by the parent firm in yens. At

EXHIBIT 7.3

Typical Characteristics of International Bond Market Instruments

Instrument	Frequency of Interest Payment	Size of Coupon Payment	Payoff at Maturity
Straight fixed-rate	Annual	Fixed	Currency of issue
Floating-rate note	Quarterly or semiannual	Variable	Currency of issue
Convertible bond	Annual	Fixed	Currency of issue or conversion to equity shares
Straight fixed-rate with equity warrants	Annual	Fixed	Currency of issue plus equity shares from exercised warrants
Zero-coupon bond	None	Zero	Currency of issue
Dual-currency bond	Annual	Fixed	Dual currency

maturity, the dollar principal repayment can be made from dollar profits earned by the subsidiary.

Exhibit 7.3 summarizes the typical characteristics of the international bond market instruments discussed in this section.

7.4 International Bonds and Notes: Currency, Nationality, and Type of Issuer

Exhibit 7.4 presents the distribution of the amounts of international bonds and notes outstanding for the period 1997 to 2003 in each of the major currencies—the American dollar, Euro, Japanese yen, British pound sterling, Swiss franc, and Canadian dollar.

A number of salient points emerge from this table of the currency distribution of international bonds and notes. First, within this recent time period, despite the fact that the world economy was slowing, the growth of international borrowing is striking. Total issues outstanding grew at an average annual rate of 20 percent per year. Much of the growth is observed in euro-denominated issues, to such an extent that euro issues now equal American dollar issues. Euro issues grew at an average rate of 30 percent per year.

Yen-denominated international issues rose sharply from 1997 to 1999 and declined significantly thereafter. This pattern is explained, in large part, by the fact that the figures in Exhibit 7.4 are expressed in American dollars. The yen strengthened against the American dollar between 1997 and 2000 and then rose against the dollar between 2001 and 2003.

EXHIBIT 7.4

Currency Distribution of International Bond Amounts Outstanding
(At Year-End in US$Billions)

	1997	1998	1999	2000	2001	2002	2003
Currency							
American dollar	1,455	1,855	2,399	2,912	3,467	4,040	4,211
Euro	849	1,133	1,475	1,771	2,170	3,283	4,009
Pound sterling	268	324	394	453	505	619	668
Yen	453	480	531	455	409	433	427
Swiss franc	143	154	137	132	124	159	168
Canadian dollar	67	55	56	52	48	52	68
Other	88	103	114	106	118	163	197
Total	3,323	4,103	5,106	5,879	6,839	8,758	9,748

Source: *International Banking and Financial Market Developments,* Bank for International Settlements, Table 13B, September 2003 (2003 figure as of June of that year). Euro zone currencies prior to 1999.

EXHIBIT 7.5

International Bonds and Notes: Nationality and Type of Issuer
1997-2003, Billions of American Dollars

	1997	1998	1999	2000	2001	2002	2003
Nationality							
Australia	74	74	76	91	100	127	148
Canada	181	20	217	203	208	242	261
France	205	249	298	295	367	511	614
Germany	365	473	624	768	889	877	1,046
Italy	90	109	148	197	259	257	312
Japan	304	312	332	278	246	104	106
Netherlands	127	167	196	260	294	678	785
United Kingdom	289	340	437	505	572	846	953
United States	533	816	1,287	1,682	2,170	2,750	2,861
Other developed countries	501	577	658	714	788	831	1,016
Offshore centres	37	45	57	68	87	619	658
Developing countries	318	369	401	447	481	484	613
International institutions	300	371	375	374	377	432	474
Total	**3,324**	**4,106**	**5,106**	**5,882**	**6,838**	**8,758**	**9,747**
Type							
Financial institutions	1,475	1,886	2,397	3,470	4,030	6,234	6,953
Governments	710	863	1,032	1,173	1,417	868	1,013
International institutions	300	371	375	374	378	432	474
Corporate issuers	838	983	1,301	862	1,015	1,224	1,307
Total	**3,324**	**4,106**	**5,106**	**5,882**	**6,838**	**8,758**	**9,747**

Source: *International Banking and Financial Market Developments,* Bank for International Settlements, Table 13B, September 2003 (2003 figures as of June of that year).

International bonds issued in Canadian dollars represent less than one percent of the world total and less than 2 percent of the value of international issues denominated in American dollars. Since this ratio is not at all reflective of the relative size of the Canadian economy to the American economy, approximately 1:10, the relatively large role of the American dollar–denominated issues reflects the much more accepted and substantial international role of the American dollar in international finance.

The fact that the value of Canadian dollar issues did not grow over this period reflects, in part, the effects of the aggressive reduction of Canadian government debt at both the federal and provincial levels throughout this period.

Exhibit 7.5 is divided into two panels that show the nationality and the type of issuer of international bonds and notes. The top panel indicates that the United States, Germany, the United Kingdom, France, and Italy are the major issuers of international debt securities. Since the top panel of Exhibit 7.5 presents the *nationality* of the issuer without reference to the *currency* of the issue, we now see a relation between the size of the national economy and the amount of international issues outstanding. Canada, for example, has approximately one-tenth the amount of international issues of the United States.

The bottom panel of Exhibit 7.5 reveals that financial institutions—banks, in particular—issue, by far, the largest share of international bonds and notes. This reflects the prominent operational role and, indeed, the comparative advantage of banks in international finance. Banks have the global perspective and credit capacity to borrow in a variety of currencies and then to convert those borrowings into currencies according to the specific needs of their industrial and commercial clients.

7.5 International Bond Market Credit Ratings

Fitch IBCA, Moody's Investors Service, and Standard & Poor's (S&P) have for years provided credit ratings on domestic and international bonds. These three credit-rating

Sara Lee Corp. Offers 3-Year Eurobonds at 6%

Sara Lee Corp. is serving up a brand name and a shorter maturity than other recent corporate borrowers to entice buyers to its first-ever dollar Eurobonds.

The U.S. maker of consumer products, from Sara Lee cheesecake to Hanes pantyhose and Hillshire Farm meats, is selling $100 million in bonds with a 6 percent coupon.

These are three-year bonds; other corporate bond sellers including Coca-Cola Co., Unilever NV, and Wal-Mart Stores Inc., have concentrated on its five-year maturities.

"It is a well-known name and it is bringing paper to a part of the maturity curve where there is not much there," said Noel Dunn of Goldman Sachs International.

Goldman Sachs expects to find most buyers in the Swiss retail market, where "high-quality American corporate paper is their favorite buy," Dunn said.

These are the first bonds out of a $500 million Eurobond program that Sara Lee announced in August, and the proceeds will be used for general corporate purposes, said Jeffrey Smith, a spokesman for the company.

The bond is fairly priced, according to Bloomberg Fair Value analysis, which compared a bond with similar issues available in the market.

The bond offers investors a yield of 5.881 percent annually or 5.797 percent semiannually. That is 22 basis points more than they can get on the benchmark five-year U.S. Treasury note.

BFV analysis calculates that the bond is worth $100,145 on a $100,000 bond, compared with the re-offer price of $100,320. Anything within a $500 range on a $100,000 bond more or less than its BFV price is deemed fairly priced.

Sara Lee is rated "AA−" by Standard & Poor's Corp. and "A1," one notch lower, by Moody's Investors Service.

In July 1994, Sara Lee's Netherlands division sold 200 million Dutch guilders ($127 million) of three-year bonds at 35 basis points over comparable Netherlands government bonds. In January, its Australian division sold 51 million British pounds ($78 million) of bonds maturing in 2004, to yield 9.43 percent.

Source: Excerpted from Bloomberg News.

---

www.fitchibca.com

This is the website of Fitch IBCA, an international bond rating service. Information about Fitch and its philosophy can be found here.

www.moodys.com

This is the website of Moody's Investor Service. Information about the investment services that Moody's provides and their bond ratings can be found here.

www.standardandpoors.com

This is the website of Standard & Poor's, a provider of investment information, such as bond ratings. Information about S&P can be found here.

organizations classify bond issues into categories based upon the creditworthiness of the borrower. The ratings are based on an analysis of current information regarding the likelihood of default and the specifics of the debt obligation. The ratings only reflect creditworthiness and not exchange rate uncertainty.

Moody's rates bonds into nine categories, from Aaa, Aa, A, Baa, and Ba down to C. Ratings of Aaa to Baa are known as *investment grade* ratings. These issues are judged not to have any speculative elements; interest payments and principal safety appear adequate at present. The future prospects of lower-rated issues cannot be considered as well assured. Within each of the nine categories, Moody's has three numeric modifiers, 1, 2, or 3, to place an issue, respectively, at the upper, middle, or lower end of the category.

Standard & Poor's rates bond issues into 11 categories, from AAA, AA, A, BBB, and BB down to D and CI. Categories AAA to BBB are investment grade ratings. Category D is reserved for bond issues that are presently in default, and the payment of interest and/or the repayment of principal is in arrears. Category CI is reserved for income bonds on which no income is being paid. Ratings for categories AA to CCC may be modified with a plus (+) or minus (−) to reflect the relative standing of an issue to others in the category. Fitch uses ratings symbols and definitions similar to S&P's.

Eurobonds tend to have high credit ratings in comparison to domestic and foreign bonds. For example, Claes, DeCeuster, and Polfliet (2002) report that approximately 40 percent of Eurobond issues are rated AAA and 30 percent are AA. One reason may be that issuers with low credit ratings invoke their publication rights and have had them withdrawn prior to dissemination. Kim and Stulz (1988) point out that the Eurobond market is accessible only to firms that have good credit ratings and name recognition; hence, they are rated highly to begin with.

Exhibit 7.6 presents a guide to S&P's International Ratings for sovereigns, municipalities, corporations, utilities, and supranationals. As noted in Exhibit 7.5, sovereigns issue a sizable portion of all international bonds. In rating a sovereign government,

165

| **EXHIBIT 7.6** | **S&P Debt Rating Definitions** |

A Standard & Poor's corporate or municipal debt rating is a current assessment of the creditworthiness of an obligor with respect to a specific obligation. This assessment may take into consideration obligors such as guarantors, insurers, or lessees.

The debt rating is not a recommendation to purchase, sell, or hold a security, inasmuch as it does not comment as to market price or suitability for a particular investor.

The ratings are based, in varying degrees, on the following considerations:

1. Likelihood of default-capacity and willingness of the obligor as to the timely payment of interest and repayment of principal in accordance with the terms of the obligation;
2. Nature of and provisions of the obligation;
3. Protection afforded by, and relative position of, the obligation in the event of bankruptcy, reorganization, or other arrangement under the laws of bankruptcy and other laws affecting creditors rights.

Investment Grade
AAA Debt rated 'AAA' has the highest rating assigned by S&P. Capacity to pay interest and repay principal is extremely strong.

AA Debt rated 'AA' has a very strong capacity to pay interest and repay principal and differs from the highest rated issues only in small degree.

A Debt rated 'A' has a strong capacity to pay interest and repay principal although it is somewhat more susceptible to the adverse effects of changes in circumstances and economic conditions than debt in higher rated categories.

BBB Debt rated 'BBB' is regarded as having an adequate capacity to pay interest and repay principal. Whereas it normally exhibits adequate protection parameters, adverse economic conditions or changing circumstances are more likely to lead to a weakened capacity to pay interest and repay principal for debt in this category than in higher rated categories.

Speculative Grade
Debt rated 'BB,' 'B,' 'CCC,' 'CC,' and 'C' is regarded as having predominantly speculative characteristics with respect to capacity to pay interest and repay principal. 'BB' indicates the least degree of speculation and 'CCC' the highest. While such debt will likely have some quality and protective characteristics, these are outweighed by large uncertainties or exposures to adverse conditions.

BB Debt rated 'BB' has less near-term vulnerability to default than other speculative issues. However, it faces major ongoing uncertainties or exposure to adverse business, financial, or economic conditions which could lead to inadequate capacity to meet timely interest and principal payments. The 'BB' rating category is also used for debt subordinated to senior debt that is assigned an actual or implied 'BBB−' rating.

B Debt rated 'B' has a greater vulnerability to default but currently has the capacity to meet interest payments and principal repayments. Adverse business, financial, or economic conditions will likely impair capacity or willingness to pay interest and repay principal. The 'B' rating category is also used for debt subordinated to senior debt that is assigned an actual or implied 'BB' or 'BB−' rating.

CCC Debt rated 'CCC' has a currently identifiable vulnerability to default, and is dependent upon favorable business, financial, and economic conditions to meet timely payment of interest and repayment of principal. In the event of adverse business, financial, or economic conditions, it is not likely to have the capacity to pay interest and repay principal. The 'CCC' rating category is also used for debt subordinated to senior debt that is assigned an actual or implied 'B' or 'B−' rating.

CC The rating 'CC' typically is applied to debt subordinated to senior debt that is assigned an actual or implied 'CCC' rating.

C The rating 'C' typically is applied to debt subordinated to senior debt that is assigned an actual or implied 'CCC−' debt rating. The 'C' rating may be used to cover a situation where a bankruptcy petition has been filed, but debt service payments are continued.

CI The rating 'CI' is reserved for income bonds on which no interest is being paid.

D Debt rated 'D' is in payment default. The 'D' rating category is used when interest payments or principal payments are not made on the date due even if the applicable grace period has not expired, unless S&P believes that such payments will be made during such grace period. The 'D' rating also will be used upon the filing of a bankruptcy petition if debt service payments are jeopardized.

Plus (+) or minus (−): The ratings from 'AA' to 'CCC' may be modified by the addition of a plus or minus sign to show relative standing within the major rating categories.

N.R. Not rated.

Debt Obligations of Issuers outside the U.S. and its territories are rated on the same basis as domestic corporate and municipal issues. The ratings measure the creditworthiness of the obligor but do not take into account currency exchange and related uncertainties.

Source: Standard & Poor's *Credit Week*, February 5, 1996, p. 64.

EXHIBIT 7.7

Standard & Poor's Sovereign Debt Rating Methodology

Political Risk
Political system
- Form of government
- Orderliness of leadership succession
- Adaptability of political institutions

Social environment
- Living standards and income distribution
- Labour market conditions
- Cultural and demographic characteristics of population

International relations
- Integration within international economic system
- Security risk

Economic Risk
External financial position
- Size and structure of gross and net external debt
- Debt service burden
- Adequacy of international reserves

Balance-of-payments flexibility
- Structure, performance, and responsiveness of the current account
- Adequacy and composition of capital flows
- Ability of policy makers to manage external payments

Economic structure and growth
- Resource endowment, level of development, and economic diversification
- Size and composition of savings and investment
- Rate and pattern of economic growth

Economic management
- Willingness and ability to ensure economic balance
- Effectiveness of fiscal, monetary, and income policies
- Structural economic reforms

Economic prospects
- Long-term economic projections, including reasonable worst-case scenario
- Cost of policy trade-offs

Source: Standard & Poor's *Sovereign Rating Criteria*, August 1992.

S&P's analysis centres around an examination of the degree of *political risk* and *economic risk*. In assessing political risk, S&P examines the stability of the political system, the social environment, and international relations with other countries. Factors in assessing economic risk include the sovereign's external financial position, balance-of-payments flexibility, economic structure and growth, management of the economy, and economic prospects. The rating assigned a sovereign is particularly important because it usually represents the ceiling for ratings S&P will assign an obligation of an entity domiciled within that country. Exhibit 7.7 details the ratings methodology that S&P uses in rating a sovereign government.

7.6 Eurobond Market Structure and Practices

Since the Eurobond segment of the international bond market accounts for approximately 80 percent of new offerings, it is wise to know something about the Eurobond market structure and practices.

A corporate borrower looking to raise funds in the European market first contacts an investment banker to serve as **lead manager** of an underwriting syndicate that will bring the bonds to market. The **underwriting syndicate** is a group of investment banks, merchant banks, and the merchant banking arms of commercial banks that specialize in various phases of a public issuance. The lead manager will sometimes invite co-managers to form a **managing group** to help negotiate terms with the borrower, ascertain market conditions, and manage the issuance. Exhibit 7.8 ranks the top 50 debt arrangers (underwriters) of global loans, international bonds, and medium-term notes.

The managing group, along with other banks, will serve as **underwriters** for the issue, that is, they will commit their own capital to buy the issue from the borrower at a discount from the issue price. The discount, or **underwriting spread** on a Eurobond issue, is typically in the range of 2 to 2.5 percent. By comparison, the spread averages about 1 percent for domestic issues. Most of the underwriters, along with other banks, will be part of a **selling group** that sells the bonds to the investing public. The various members of the underwriting syndicate receive a portion of the spread, depending on the number and type of functions they perform. The lead manager will obviously receive the full spread, but a bank serving as only a member of the selling group will receive a smaller portion. The total elapsed time from the decision date of the borrower to issue Eurobonds until the net proceeds from the sale are received is typically five to six weeks. Exhibit 7.9 presents a tombstone (announcement) for a dollar-denominated Euro-medium-term note issue and the underwriting syndicate that brought the issue to market.

Secondary Market

Eurobonds initially purchased in the **primary market** from a member of the selling group may be resold prior to their maturities to other investors in the secondary market. The **secondary market** for Eurobonds is an over-the-counter market with principal trading in London. However, important trading is also done in other major European money centres, such as Zurich, Luxembourg, Frankfurt, and Amsterdam.

The secondary market comprises market makers and brokers connected by an array of telecommunications equipment. **Market makers** stand ready to buy or sell for their own account by quoting two-way **bid** and **ask prices**. Market makers trade directly with one another, through a broker, or with retail customers. The bid-ask spread represents their only profit; no other commission is charged.

Eurobond market makers and dealers are members of the International Securities Market Association (ISMA), a self-regulatory body based in Zurich. Market makers tend to be the same investment banks, merchant banks, and commercial banks that serve as lead managers in an underwriting. **Brokers**, on the other hand, accept buy or sell orders from market makers and then attempt to find a matching party for the other side of the trade; they may also trade for their own account. Brokers charge a small commission for their services to the market maker that engaged them. They do not deal directly with retail clients.

Clearing Procedures

www.euroclear.com

www.clearstream.com

Eurobond transactions in the secondary market require a system for transferring ownership and payment from one party to another. Two major clearing systems, Euroclear and Clearstream International, have been established to handle most Eurobond trades. Euroclear Clearance System is based in Brussels and is operated by Euroclear Bank. Clearstream, located in Luxembourg, was established in 2000 through a merger of Deutsche Börse Clearing and Cedel International, two other clearing firms.

Both clearing systems operate in a similar manner. Each clearing system has a group of depository banks that physically store bond certificates. Members of either system hold cash and bond accounts. When a transaction is conducted, electronic book entries are made that transfer book ownership of the bond certificates from the seller to the buyer and transfer funds from the purchaser's cash account to the seller's. Physical transfer of the bonds seldom takes place.

EXHIBIT 7.8

Ranking of Top Debt Managers of Global Loans, International Bonds and MTNs
(Year-ended March 31, 2001, in Millions of U.S. Dollars)

Rank	Group	Amount	Number of Issues
1	JP Morgan	461,859	1,329
2	Citigroup/Salomon Smith Barney	399,757	2,315
3	Bank of America	280,845	1,242
4	Deutsche Bank	243,483	1,573
5	Morgan Stanley	193,156	726
6	Merrill Lynch	176,167	881
7	Credit Suisse First Boston	170,951	698
8	Barclays Capital	149,907	726
9	ABN AMRO	140,819	703
10	UBS Warburg	137,624	767
11	Goldman Sachs	129,866	635
12	HSBC	100,604	1,820
13	Lehman Brothers	93,898	846
14	BNP Paribas	83,919	1,109
15	Bank One	77,949	425
16	Dresdner Kleinwort Wasserstein	75,372	407
17	Société Générale	68,467	331
18	Commerzbank	58,598	373
19	Mizuho Group	55,871	531
20	FleetBoston Financial	46,533	428
21	Bank of Tokyo-Mitsubishi	39,824	230
22	Royal Bank of Scotland	39,131	191
23	First Union	38,756	310
24	WestLB	38,505	239
25	**Bank of Nova Scotia**	**30,024**	**172**
26	Bayerische Hypo-und Vereinsbank	25,942	266
27	**Toronto-Dominion Bank**	**24,827**	**159**
28	Nomura	23,059	600
29	**RBC Dominion Securities**	**22,707**	**175**
30	Bank of New York	22,261	102
31	Credit Lyonnais	21,815	185
32	Credit Agricole Indosuez	21,735	166
33	ING Barings/BBL	19,439	121
34	**CIBC World Markets**	**15,933**	**91**
35	CDC IXIS Capital Markets	15,814	109
36	DG Bank	15,769	136
37	Bear Stearns	15,126	69
38	Sumitomo Bank	13,996	73
39	Mediobanca	12,805	21
40	Bayerische Landesbank Girozentrale	12,528	85
41	**Bank of Montreal**	**10,563**	**64**
42	Wells Fargo Bank	10,477	113
43	Wachovia Corp	10,168	69
44	Daiwa Securities	9,335	423
45	SunTrust Banks	9,003	74
46	Lloyds TSB Capital Markets	8,908	22
47	Fortis Group	8,864	90
48	Banco Bilbao Vizcaya Argentaria	8,431	107
49	PNC Bank	7,868	90
50	Banca IMI	7,410	34

Source: *Euromoney*, June 2001, p. 122.

Euroclear and Clearstream perform other functions associated with the efficient operation of the Eurobond market. (1) The clearing systems finance up to 90 percent of the inventory that a Eurobond market maker has deposited within the system. (2) The

This announcement appears as a matter of record only

Hamburgische Landesbank

Hamburgische Landesbank – Girozentrale –
(incorporated as a credit institution under public law in the Federal Republic of Germany)

Hamburgische Landesbank London Branch
Hamburgische LB Finance (Guernsey) Limited
(incorporated in Guernsey)

U.S.$2,000,000,000

Euro Medium Term Note Programme
Guaranteed in respect of Notes issued by
Hamburgische LB Finance (Guernsey) Limited by
Hamburgische Landesbank – Girozentrale –

The Programme is rated Aa1 by Moody's and AAA by Fitch IBCA

NOW RATED Aa1 BY MOODY'S

Arrangers

Merrill Lynch International

Merrill Lynch Capital Markets Bank Limited,
Frankfurt/Main Branch

Merrill Lynch Finance SA

Dealers

Credit Suisse First Boston
Hamburgische Landesbank – Girozentrale –
Merrill Lynch International
Morgan Stanley Dean Witter
Salomon Smith Barney

Deutsche Morgan Grenfell
Merrill Lynch Finance SA
J.P. Morgan Securities Ltd.
Nomura International
Warburg Dillon Read

Source: *Euromoney*, January 1999, p. 11.

clearing systems will assist in the distribution of a new bond issue. The clearing systems will take physical possession of the newly printed bond certificates in the depository, collect subscription payments from the purchasers, and record ownership of the bonds. (3) The clearing systems also distribute coupon payments. The borrower pays to the clearing system the coupon interest due on the portion of the issue held in the depository, which, in turn, credits the appropriate amounts to the bond owners' cash accounts.

7.7 International Bond Market Indexes

There are several international bond market indexes. Some of the best known are the J.P. Morgan and Company Domestic Government Bond Indices and their Global Government Bond Index. J.P. Morgan publishes a government bond index for 18 individual countries: Australia, Canada, Belgium, Denmark, France, Germany, Italy, Japan, the Netherlands, Spain, Sweden, the United Kingdom, the United States, New Zealand, Ireland, Finland, Portugal, and South Africa. Each bond index includes only

www.jpmorgan.com

This is the website of J.P. Morgan and Company, an international investment banking firm. This is an extensive website detailing products and services of the firm.

government bonds in five maturity categories: 1–3 years, 3–5 years, 5–7 years, 7–10 years, and 10-plus years. The Global Government Bond Index is a value-weighted representation of the 18 government bond indexes.

The J.P. Morgan Domestic and Global Government Bond Indices are widely referenced and used frequently as benchmarks of international bond market performance. The index values for six of the Domestic Government Indices, European Monetary Union Government Bond Index (EMU), the 18-country Global Government Bond Index, and an Emerging Market Government Bond Index (EMBI) appear daily in *The Wall Street Journal*. Exhibit 7.10 provides an example of these indexes. Note that the index values are provided in local currency terms and in American dollar terms. One-day, one-month and three-month total rates of return are provided for each index in local and American dollar terms.

Exhibit 7.10 shows that *The Wall Street Journal* also publishes daily values of yields to maturity for Japanese, German, British, and Canadian Government Bonds of various terms to maturity. These data allow for one to compare the term structures of interest rates from these major industrialized countries with one another. Another source of international bond data is the coupon rates, prices, and yields to maturity found in the daily "Benchmark Government Bonds" table in the *Financial Times*. Exhibit 7.11 provides an example.

EXHIBIT 7.10 International Bond Market Data Provided Daily in The Wall Street Journal

International Government Bonds

Coupon	Maturity Mo/Yr	Price	Change	Yield*	Coupon	Maturity Mo/Yr	Price	Change	Yield*
Japan (3 p.m. Tokyo)					Germany (5 p.m. London)				
4.60%	09/04	109.47	—	0.04%	4.25%	02/05	101.41	+0.13	3.639%
3.20	09/06	112.02	+0.02	0.23	5.00	02/06	103.53	+0.24	3.903
1.30	06/12	100.35	—	1.26	5.00	07/12	103.43	+0.30	4.559
1.90	06/22	99.43	+0.22	1.94	5.50	01/31	107.63	+0.45	4.989
United Kingdom (5 p.m. London)					Canada (3 p.m. Eastern Time)				
8.00%	06/03	103.29	+0.03	3.791%	5.00%	12/03	102.34	+0.11	3.136%
7.50	12/06	111.43	+0.15	4.538	6.00	09/05	106.08	n.a.	3.876
5.00	03/12	102.72	+0.33	4.644	5.50	06/09	104.13	+0.82	4.804
4.25	06/32	96.57	+0.50	4.449	8.00	06/27	130.24	−0.18	5.589

*Equivalent to semi-annual compounded yields to maturity.

Total Rates of Return on International Bonds
In percent, based on J.P. Morgan Government Bond Index, Dec. 31, 1987 = 100

	Local Currency Terms					American Dollar Terms				
	Index Value	1 Day	1 Mo	3 Mos	Since 12/31	Index Value	1 Day	1 Mo	3 Mos	Since 12/31
Japan	216.49	0.00	+0.20	+1.12	+1.73	220.08	−0.35	−2.46	+6.71	+11.97
Britain	404.06	+0.30	+2.46	+6.15	+6.03	326.87	+0.11	−0.91	+11.02	+11.15
Germany	262.99	+0.29	+1.74	+5.10	+5.20	205.79	+0.21	−2.17	+11.30	+15.27
France	350.02	+0.29	+1.73	+5.02	+5.21	276.81	+0.21	−2.17	+11.21	+15.28
Canada	381.83	+0.60	+1.60	+5.17	+4.81	315.26	+0.14	−0.75	+3.03	+6.29
Netherlands	280.90	+0.28	+1.75	+5.19	+5.39	219.47	+0.20	−2.16	+11.39	+15.48
EMU-d	185.13	+0.29	+1.75	+4.97	+5.30	147.27	+0.22	−2.16	+11.16	+15.38
Global-a	315.08	+0.31	+1.58	+4.48	+5.16	270.73	+0.17	−0.96	+8.54	+12.22
EMBI + -b	200.70	+0.51	−2.10	−6.45	+0.18	200.70	+0.51	−2.10	−6.45	+0.18

a-18 intl. gov. markets b-external-currency emerging mkt. debt, Dec. 31, 1993 = 100.   d-Jan. 2, 1995 = 100.
Source: *The Wall Street Journal*, August 21, 2002, p. C10. Reprinted by permission of *The Wall Street Journal*, © 1996 Dow Jones & Company, Inc. All Rights Reserved Worldwide.

EXHIBIT 7.11

International
Government Bond
Market Data
Provided Daily in
the Financial Times

World Bond Prices
BENCHMARK GOVERNMENT BONDS

Aug 19	Redemption Date	Coupon	Bid Price	Bid Yield	Year Chg Yld
Australia	09/04	9.000	107.4934	5.13	+0.04
	06/11	5.750	100.2306	5.71	−0.06
Austria	10/04	3.400	99.3600	3.71	−0.32
	07/12	5.000	101.7000	4.78	−0.23
Belgium	04/04	7.250	105.7700	3.64	−0.39
	09/12	5.000	101.4000	4.82	−0.26
Canada	06/04	3.500	100.1000	3.44	−0.98
	06/11	6.000	105.8000	5.17	−0.28
Denmark	11/03	5.000	101.3100	3.88	−0.58
	11/11	6.000	107.8800	4.91	−0.12
Finland	11/03	3.750	100.2000	3.57	−0.49
	02/11	5.750	106.9500	4.73	−0.24
France	01/04	4.000	100.5800	3.55	−0.45
	01/07	3.750	98.3900	4.15	−0.20
	04/12	5.000	102.2900	4.70	−0.15
	10/32	5.750	110.5800	5.06	−0.40
Germany	03/04	4.250	100.9700	3.58	−0.38
	02/07	4.000	99.4300	4.14	−0.12
	01/12	5.000	102.9300	4.60	−0.15
	01/31	5.500	107.0000	5.03	−0.34
Greece	01/04	6.600	104.0000	3.59	−0.52
	05/12	5.250	102.1100	4.97	−0.29
Ireland	10/05	3.500	98.6300	3.97	−0.11
	04/13	5.000	101.1300	4.86	−0.07
Italy	03/04	4.500	101.4000	3.57	−0.47
	03/07	4.500	101.0900	4.23	−0.24
	02/12	5.000	101.6100	4.79	−0.28
	02/33	5.750	108.0800	5.22	−0.46
Japan	03/04	3.400	105.3372	0.03	−0.03
	03/07	0.700	101.7717	0.31	−0.06
	12/11	1.400	101.9374	1.18	−0.13
	12/21	2.200	104.5847	1.92	−0.10
Netherlands	01/04	5.750	102.8900	3.58	−0.45
	07/12	5.000	101.9800	4.74	−0.17
New Zealand	04/04	8.000	103.4380	5.78	−0.36
	11/11	6.000	96.9940	6.44	−0.20
Norway	11/04	5.750	98.1400	6.64	−0.27
	05/11	6.000	97.4600	6.38	+0.06
Portugal	08/04	3.625	98.1000	4.53	+0.05
	09/13	5.450	104.3300	4.93	−0.20
Spain	10/04	4.650	101.8900	3.73	−0.32
	10/11	5.350	104.3000	4.76	−0.34
Sweden	01/04	5.000	100.4500	4.64	+0.28
	03/11	5.250	100.8200	5.12	+0.10

EXHIBIT 7.11

Continued

Aug 19	Redemption Date	Coupon	Bid Price	Bid Yield	Year Chg Yld
Switzerland	04/04	6.500	108.2500	1.35	−1.53
	06/12	2.750	97.8700	3.00	−0.23
UK	12/03	6.500	103.1200	4.00	−0.99
	12/06	7.500	111.2800	4.58	−0.49
	03/12	5.000	102.3900	4.69	−0.20
	06/32	4.250	96.0800	4.49	—
US	02/04	3.000	101.4686	2.02	−1.62
	11/06	3.500	100.9074	3.27	−1.15
	02/12	4.875	104.3766	4.31	−0.53
	02/31	5.375	104.3836	5.08	−0.35

London close. New York mid-day. Source: FT Interactive Data.
Yields: Local market standard/Annualized yield basis. Yields shown for Italy exclude withholding tax at 12.5 per cent payable by nonresidents.
Source: *Financial Times*, August 20, 2002, p. 20. Reprinted with permission.

SUMMARY

This chapter introduces and discusses the international bond market. The chapter presents a statistical perspective of the market, noting its size, an analysis of the market segments, the types of instruments issued, the major currencies used to denominate international bonds, and the major borrowers by nationality and type. Trading practices of the Eurobond market are examined, as are credit ratings for international bonds and international bond market indexes.

1. At year-end 2002, there were over $45 trillion in domestic bonds outstanding and over $6.8 trillion in international bonds. The three major currencies that are used to denominate bonds are the American dollar, euro, and yen.

2. A foreign bond issue is one offered by a foreign borrower to investors in a national capital market and denominated in that nation's currency. A Eurobond issue is one denominated in a particular currency but sold to investors in national capital markets other than the country that issues the denominating currency.

3. The Eurobond segment of the international bond market is roughly four times the size of the foreign bond segment. The two major reasons for this stem from the fact that the American dollar is the currency most frequently sought in international bond financing. First, Eurodollar bonds can be brought to market more quickly than Yankee bonds because they are not offered to American investors and, thus, do not have to meet the strict SEC registration requirements. Second, Eurobonds are typically bearer bonds that provide anonymity to the owner and, thus, allow a means for avoiding taxes on the interest received. Because of this feature, investors are generally willing to accept a lower yield on Eurodollar bonds in comparison with registered Yankee bonds of comparable terms, where ownership is recorded. For borrowers the lower yield means a lower cost of debt service.

4. Straight fixed-rate bonds are the most frequent type of international bond issue, and floating-rate notes are the second. Other types of issues found in the international bond market are convertible bonds, bonds with equity warrants, zero-coupon bonds, stripped bonds, and dual-currency bonds.

5. Fitch IBCA, Moody's Investors Service, and Standard & Poor's provide credit ratings on most international bond issues. A disproportionate share of Eurobonds have high credit ratings. The evidence suggests this is because the Eurobond market is accessible only to firms that have good credit ratings to begin with. An

entity's credit rating is usually never higher than the rating assigned the sovereign government of the country in which it resides. S&P's analysis of a sovereign includes an examination of political risk and economic risk.

6. New Eurobond issues are offered in the primary market through an underwriting syndicate hired by the borrower to bring the bonds to market. The secondary market for Eurobonds is an over-the-counter arrangement with principal trading done in London.

7. The investment banking firm of J.P. Morgan and Company provides some of the best international bond market indexes that are frequently used for performance evaluations. J.P. Morgan publishes a Domestic Government Bond Index for 18 individual countries, a euro zone Government Index, a Global Government Bond Index, and an Emerging Market Bond Index.

KEY WORDS

ask price, *168*
bearer bond, *158*
bid price, *168*
bond with equity
    warrants, *162*
broker, *168*
convertible bond, *161*
dual-currency bond, *162*
equity-related bond, *161*
Eurobond, *158*

Euro-medium-term note
    (Euro-MTN), *161*
floating-rate note
    (FRN), *161*
foreign bond, *157*
global bond, *160*
lead manager, *168*
managing group, *168*
market makers, *168*
primary market, *168*
registered bond, *158*

secondary market, *168*
selling group, *168*
shelf registration, *160*
straight fixed-rate
    bond, *160*
stripped bond, *162*
underwriters, *168*
underwriting spread, *168*
underwriting
    syndicate, *168*
zero-coupon bond, *162*

QUESTIONS

1. Describe the differences between foreign bonds and Eurobonds. Also discuss why Eurobonds make up the lion's share of the international bond market.

2. Briefly define each of the major types of international bond market instruments, noting their distinguishing characteristics.

3. Why do most international bonds have high Moody's or Standard & Poor's credit ratings?

4. What factors does Standard & Poor's analyze in determining the credit rating it assigns a sovereign government?

5. Discuss the process of bringing a new international bond issue to market.

6. You are an investment banker advising a Eurobank about a new international bond offering it is considering. The proceeds are to be used to fund Eurodollar loans to bank clients. What type of bond instrument would you recommend that the bank consider issuing? Why?

7. What should a borrower consider before issuing dual-currency bonds? What should an investor consider before investing in dual-currency bonds?

PROBLEMS

1. Your firm has just issued five-year floating-rate notes indexed to six-month American dollar LIBOR plus $\frac{1}{4}$ percent. What is the amount of the first coupon payment your firm will pay per US$1,000 of face value, if six-month LIBOR is currently 7.2 percent?

2. The discussion of zero-coupon bonds in the text gave an example of two zero-coupon bonds issued by Commerzbank. The DM300,000,000 issue due in 1995 sold at 50 percent of face value, and the DM300,000,000 due in 2000 sold at $33\frac{1}{3}$

percent of face value; both were issued in 1985. Calculate the implied yield to maturity of each of these two zero-coupon bond issues.

3. Consider 8.5 percent Swiss franc/American dollar dual-currency bonds that pay $666.67 at maturity per SF1,000 of par value. What is the implicit SF/$ exchange rate at maturity? Will the investor be better off or worse off at maturity if the actual SF/$ exchange rate is SF1.35/$1?

INTERNET EXERCISE

Bond Markets Online is an Internet magazine with articles of current interest to bond market participants. Go to the website www.bondmarkets.com/newsletters/2002/global902.shtml to see what current events are of concern in the global bond market.

MINI CASE

Sara Lee Corporation's Eurobonds

The *International Finance in Practice* boxed reading (see p. 165) in the chapter discussed a three-year $100-million Eurobond issue by Sara Lee Corporation. The article also mentions other bond issues recently placed by various foreign divisions of Sara Lee. What thoughts do you have about Sara Lee's debt-financing strategy?

REFERENCES & SUGGESTED READINGS

Anderson, Torben Juul. *Euromarket Instruments*. New York: New York Institute of Finance, 1990.

Bank for International Settlements. *73rd Annual Report*. Basle: BIS, 2003.

Claes, A., Marc J. K. DeCeuster, and R. Polfliet. "Anatomy of the Eurobond Market." *European Financial Management* 8, no. 3 (2002).

Dosoo, George. *The Eurobond Market*, 2nd ed. New York: Woodhead, Faulkner, 1992.

Gallant, Peter. *The Eurobond Market*. New York: Woodhead, Faulkner, 1988.

Gowland, D. H., ed. *International Bond Markets*. London: Routledge, 1991.

Grabbe, J. Orlin. *International Financial Markets*, 3rd ed. Upper Saddle River, N.J.: Prentice Hall, 1996.

International Monetary Fund. *International Capital Markets: Developments and Prospects*. Washington, D.C.: International Monetary Fund, 2003.

Jones, Frank J., and Frank J. Fabozzi. *International Government Bond Markets*. Chicago: Probus, 1992.

Kim, Yong Cheol, and Rene M. Stultz. "The Eurobond Market and Corporate Financial Policy: A Test of the Clientele Hypothesis." *Journal of Financial Economics* 22 (1988), pp. 189–205.

Lederman, Jess, and Keith K. H. Park, eds. *The Global Bond Markets*. Chicago: Probus, 1991.

Van Horne, James C. *Financial Market Rates and Flows*, 6th ed. Upper Saddle River, N.J.: Prentice Hall, 2001.

CHAPTER 8

International Equity Markets

CHAPTER OUTLINE

8.1 A Statistical Perspective
8.2 International Equity Market Benchmarks
8.3 World Equity Benchmark Shares

8.4 Trading in International Equities
8.5 Factors Affecting International Equity Returns

THIS CHAPTER FOCUSES on equity markets, or how ownership in publicly owned corporations is traded throughout the world. It discusses both the *primary* sale of new common shares by corporations to initial investors and how previously issued common shares are traded between investors in the *secondary* markets. This chapter is useful for understanding how companies source new equity capital and provides useful institutional information for investors interested in diversifying their portfolio internationally.

The chapter begins with an overview of the world's equity markets. Statistics are provided to show the comparative sizes and trading opportunities in various secondary equity marketplaces in both the developed and the developing countries. Differences in market structures are also explored, and comparative transaction costs of equity trading are presented. Following this, the discussion moves to the benefits of multiple listing of a corporation's shares on more than one national stock exchange. The related issue of sourcing new equity capital from primary investors in more than the home national market is also examined. The chapter concludes with a discussion of the factors that affect equity valuation.

8.1 A Statistical Perspective

Before we can intelligently discuss international equity markets, it is helpful to understand where the major national equity markets are located, some information about their relative sizes, and the opportunities for trading and ownership.

Market Capitalization of Developed Countries

At year-end 2003, total market capitalization of the world's equity markets stood at $31,500 billion. Of this amount, 90 percent is accounted for by the market capitalization of the major equity markets from 23 countries. Exhibit 8.1 shows the market capitalizations for these 23 developed countries for 1996 through 2003. Over the eight-year period, their total market capitalization increased 76 percent, from $17,911 billion to $31,500 billion.

The growth in market capitalization was not evenly spread among the developed countries. For example, North America registered an increase of 84 percent over the eight-year period, whereas the increase in the European markets was over 100 percent. The Far East, however, registered only a 21-percent increase.

Measures of Liquidity

A liquid stock market is one in which investors can buy and sell shares quickly at close to the current quoted prices. A measure of **liquidity** for a stock market is the turnover

176

EXHIBIT 8.1

Market Capitalization of Equity Markets in Developed Countries (1997-2003, Billions of American Dollars)

Region or Country	1996	1997	1998	1999	2000	2003
Europe	4,947	5,939	7,697	9,607	9,124	10,106
Austria	34	36	34	33	30	33
Belgium	120	137	246	185	182	202
Denmark	72	94	99	105	108	120
Finland	63	73	155	349	294	326
France	591	674	991	1,475	1,447	1,603
Germany	671	825	1,094	1,432	1,270	1,407
Ireland	12	49	67	69	82	91
Italy	258	345	570	728	768	851
Luxembourg	33	34	35	36	34	38
Netherlands	379	469	603	695	640	709
Norway	57	67	47	64	65	72
Portugal	24	39	63	66	61	68
Spain	243	290	402	432	504	558
Sweden	247	273	279	373	328	363
Switzerland	402	575	689	693	792	877
United Kingdom	1,740	1,996	2,374	2,933	2,576	2,853
Far East	4,039	3,063	3,287	5,810	4,325	4,900
Australia	312	296	329	428	373	393
Hong Kong	449	413	343	609	623	663
Japan	3,089	2,217	2,496	4,547	3,157	3,620
New Zealand	39	31	25	28	19	21
Singapore	150	106	94	198	153	203
North America	8,970	11,877	13,994	17,436	15,945	16,500
Canada	486	568	543	801	841	900
United States	8,484	11,309	13,451	16,635	15,104	15,600
Total Developed Markets	17,911	20,886	24,968	32,844	29,119	31,500

Source: Derived from various issues of *Emerging Stock Markets Factbook,* International Finance Corporation and Standard & Poor's.

ratio; that is, the ratio of stock market transactions over a period of time divided by the size, or market capitalization, of the stock market. Generally, the higher the turnover ratio, the more liquid the secondary stock market is, indicating ease in trading.

Exhibit 8.2 presents turnover ratio percentages for 23 equity markets of the developed countries for the five years beginning with 1996. The turnover ratio varies considerably over time for most national equity markets. The table also indicates that most national equity markets had very high turnover ratios, with the great majority in excess of 50 percent turnover per year.

Primary and Secondary Markets

The expression "equity market" has two distinct—but interrelated—meanings. First, the equity market is the formal market to which business goes when it wants to "raise equity." A firm raises equity by selling shares. When a firm first "goes public" by selling shares or when it sells additional shares into the market, it is involved in the so-called ***primary* market** which simply means that the shares are, indeed, new to the market. An initial sale of shares or the sale of additional shares means that money flows directly to the firm that issues those shares. That money is then available to the firm to invest in machinery, equipment, buildings, and working capital or perhaps to buy another firm. The very first time that a firm sells shares is referred to as an initial public offering or IPO.

A smoothly functioning, efficient, properly regulated equities market—"stock market," if you prefer—is crucially important for industry and economic development, since it serves as a key source of fresh finance for industry.

EXHIBIT 8.2

Turnover Ratio of Equity Markets in the Developed Countries (Transactions in US$/Year-End Market Capitalization in US$)

Region or Country	1996	1997	1998	1999	2000
Europe					
Austria	60	69	109	38	30
Belgium	22	22	22	28	21
Denmark	48	50	NA	60	86
Finland	36	50	39	44	64
France	47	60	58	62	74
Germany	115	125	127	108	79
Iceland	8	NA	NA	4	51
Italy	40	58	84	83	104
Luxembourg	2	2	3	3	3
Netherlands	90	61	63	145	101
Norway	62	70	77	90	93
Portugal	29	54	76	63	86
Spain	103	156	174	179	211
Sweden	55	65	73	73	111
Switzerland	98	86	92	78	82
United Kingdom	33	42	49	52	67
Far East					
Australia	48	45	47	28	57
Hong Kong	37	118	60	51	61
Japan	41	56	38	53	70
New Zealand	23	27	57	45	46
Singapore	28	60	54	67	52
North America					
Canada	55	63	69	54	77
United States	84	90	98	124	201

Source: Calculated from data from various issues of *Emerging Stock Markets Factbook,* International Financial Corporation, and Standard & Poor's.

Once issued by companies and purchased by investors, the shares are then available to be traded among investors. Once they have been issued, shares traded among investors do not supply fresh funds to the firms whose shares are traded in the equities markets. Such trading gives rise to the second meaning of "equities market"—the *secondary* **market**.

The volume of transactions in the secondary market is vastly greater than the volume of new issues in the primary market. You might think of the ratio as 99 to 1.

The primary and secondary markets are related in significant ways. The secondary market provides liquidity for investors. The large variety of shares available in relatively small denominations allows the investor to build a diversified portfolio and, thus, to manage risk. Equally importantly, the secondary market continuously determines prices for all traded equities. Since the prevailing share price is important for the firm that wants to sell additional shares (a firm naturally wants to sell new shares at the highest possible price per share) the secondary market provides price "signals" for firms when they consider raising equity capital—which, of course, takes us back to the primary market.

When the equities markets function well—free of distortion, manipulation, and inefficiencies—then industrial finance is more readily available and more likely to be channelled to its most productive use. On the other hand, if the equities markets are poorly developed, industry is forced to rely on internal funds or debt that is intermediated by banks. Such capital is generally less flexible and is less inclined to finance riskier investments that are often the impetus for growth, and so-called *intermediated debt* (or bank loans) tends to be allocated to industry on a somewhat arbitrary and *ad hoc* basis.

These are unfortunate characteristics of financial markets, including equities markets, that are not well developed.

Equities markets are complex systems that involve not just the stock market itself but also the supporting participation of brokerages, investment banks, and regulatory agencies. The efficiency and strength of a nation's equities market depend directly on the integrity of the commercial legal system, regulation, and the supporting functions of accounting and communications. In Canada and in other advanced nations, such as those listed in Exhibit 8.1, financial institutional development tends to be taken for granted by corporations looking to raise equity capital relatively smoothly and at reasonable cost. A striking feature of international finance, as we shall discuss shortly, is the *integration* of various national equities markets throughout the world as companies *cross-list* their shares on several stock exchanges—in both Toronto and New York, for example—which results in a number of advantages for both firms and investors.

In recent years, most national stock markets have become automated for at least some of the issues traded on them. The first was the Toronto Stock Exchange, which introduced the Computer Assisted Trading System (CATS) in 1977. An automated trading system electronically stores and displays public orders on a continuous basis, and allows public traders to cross orders with one another to execute trades without the assistance of exchange personnel. Automated systems are successful largely because orders can be filled faster and more efficiently, since fewer exchange personnel are needed. Indeed, in some countries, the exchange trading floor has been completely eliminated. The old trading floor at the Toronto Stock Exchange has been turned into a showplace of modern art and design!

Automated, computer-facilitated trading naturally lends itself to **continuous** **trading**. Continuous trading is desirable for actively traded issues. On the other hand, **call markets** and **crowd trading** as it is called—involving traders and **specialists** crying out bids and offers in the noisy "pit" while recording trades on bits of paper—has advantages for thinly traded issues. Person-to-person trading and the buffering role of the specialists smooth the trading process and mitigate the effects of short-term imbalances between bids and offers.

Exhibit 8.3 provides a summary of the locations and market trading systems of various major stock markets throughout the world. The exhibit also shows the typical taxes applicable to equity trades and the number of business days required to settle a trade.

8.2 International Equity Market Benchmarks

As a benchmark of activity or performance of a given national equity market, an index of the shares traded on the secondary exchange (or exchanges) of a country is used. Several national equity indexes are available for use by investors.

To this point, the exhibits of this chapter have presented data from stock market indexes prepared by Standard & Poor's. Each year S&P publishes its *Emerging Stock Markets Factbook,* which provides a variety of statistical data on stock markets of both emerging and developed countries. The *Factbook* is an excellent source that is carried by many university libraries and provides annual comparative statistics in an easy-to-read format.

The indexes prepared and published by Morgan Stanley Capital International (MSCI) are an excellent source of national stock market performance. Through its monthly publication, *Morgan Stanley Capital International Perspective,* MSCI presents return and market capitalization data for 24 national stock market indexes from the developed countries. In constructing each of these indexes, an attempt is made to include equity issues representing at least 60 percent of the market capitalization of each industry within the country. The shares in each country index are market-value weighted, that is, the proportion of the index a share represents is determined by its

EXHIBIT 8.3			Trading Practices and Costs of Major Equity Markets	
Country	**Primary Market**	**System**	**Taxes**	**Settlement**
Argentina	Buenos Aires	Auction market; automated; OTC	.0951% + 20% of commission	Trade date + 3 days
Australia	National market	Automated	Off shore: none; domestic: 10% of commission	Trade date + 3 days
Austria	Vienna	Automated quote and market-making	.02–.1% turnover tax	Trade date + 3 days
Belgium	Brussels	Euronext	None for nonresidents	Trade date + 3 days
Brazil	Sao Paulo	Crowd trading; automated	Fee: .035%	Trade date + 3 days
Canada	Toronto	Automated	None	Trade date + 3 days
Czech Republic	Prague	Automated and OTC	.080–.125%; OTC: 0%	Trade date + 5 days; OTC: Negotiable
Chile	Santiago	Major Shares: automated; Others: crowd trading	Cumulative schedule from .50%–0%	Trade date + 2 days
China	Shenzhen and Shanghai	Automated	Shenzhen: .2841% Shanghai: .28%	Trade date + 3 days
Colombia	Bogotá	Automated	None	Trade date + 3 days
Denmark	Copenhagen	Automated	None	Trade date + 3 days
Egypt	Cairo, Alexandria	Automated	.025%	Trade date + 2 days (sell); Trade date + 3 days (buy)
Finland	Helsinki	Automated	None	Trade date + 3 days
France	Paris	Euronext	VAT on commission; None for foreigners	Trade date + 3 days
Germany	Frankfurt	Automated and floor trading	.04–.08%	Trade date + 3 days (Foreign) Trade date + 2 days (Domestic)
Greece	Athens	Automated	Fees: .30% on sales	Trade date + 3 days
Hong Kong	Hong Kong	Automated	.012%	Trade date + 2 days
Hungary	Budapest	Automated	None	Trade date + 5 days
India	National Stock Exchange; Bombay Stock Exchange	Automated	.50% on buys	Trade date + 5 days
Indonesia	Jakarta	Automated	.153%	Trade date + 4 days
Ireland	Dublin	Automated	1.00% on purchases	Trade date + 3 days
Israel	Tel Aviv	Automated	None	Trade date + 2 days
Italy	Milan	Automated	None for nonresidents	Trade date + 3 days
Japan	Tokyo, Osaka	Automated	None	Trade date + 3 days
Malaysia	Kuala Lumpur	Automated	.04%	Trade date + 3 days
Mexico	Mexico City	Automated	.05%	Trade date + 2 days
Netherlands	Amsterdam	Automated with liquidity of provider	None	Trade date + 3 days
New Zealand	National Integrated Market	Automated	None	Trade date + 3 days
Norway	Oslo	Automated	None	Trade date + 3 days
Peru	Lima	Automated and crowd trading	.2272%	Trade date + 3 days
Philippines	Manila	Automated	Buying: .76% Selling: .50%	Trade date + 3 days
Poland	Warsaw	Automated	.04%	Trade date + 3 days
Portugal	Lisbon	Euronext	Listed .015%; OTC .04–.05%	Trade date + 3 days

(continued)

EXHIBIT 8.3		Continued		
Country	**Primary Market**	**System**	**Taxes**	**Settlement**
Russia	Moscow	OTC automated quotation and dealer quotation	.3% sellers and domestic buyers	Trade date + 7 to 15 days
Singapore	Singapore	Automated	.05% (Max SGD200)	Trade date + 3 days
South Africa	Johannesburg	Automated	.25% on buys	Tuesday following trade week
South Korea	Seoul	Automated	.30%–.50% on sales	Trade date + 2 days
Spain	Madrid	Automated and crowd trading(<3%)	None	Trade date + 3 days
Sweden	Stockholm	Automated and call market	None	Trade date + 3 days
Switzerland	Zurich	Automated	.085%	Trade date + 3 days
Taiwan	Taipei	Automated	.3% on sells	Trade date + 1 day
Thailand	Bangkok	Automated	VAT .0175%	Trade date + 3 days
Turkey	Istanbul	Automated	None	Trade date + 2 days
United Kingdom	London	Automated and automated dealer quotation system	.50% on purchases	Trade date + 3 days
United States	New York and OTC	Specialist: NYSE and AMEX; Automated quotation: NASDAQ OTC	USD 15 per USD 1 million sale value	Trade date + 3 days
Venezuela	Caracas	Automated	1% on sales	Trade date + 3 days

Source: Excerpted from *Guide to Global Equity Markets,* 11th ed., UBS Warburg, April 2002.

proportion of the total market capitalization of all shares in the index. MSCI publishes a market-value-weighted World Index comprising 23 of its country indexes. The World Index includes approximately 2,600 share issues of major corporations in the world. MSCI also publishes several regional indexes: the European, Australasia, Far East (EAFE) Index comprising approximately 1,000 shares from 21 countries; the North American Index composed of the United States and Canada; the Far East Index (three countries); several Europe Indexes (depending upon whether individual constituent countries are included); the Nordic Countries Index (four countries); and the Pacific Index (five countries). The EAFE Index is widely followed, and it is representative of World Index excluding North American stock market performance. Daily values of several of the MSCI country indexes and the World Index can be found in *The Wall Street Journal.* MSCI also publishes dozens of industry indexes, each of which includes equity issues from the respective industry from the countries it follows.

MSCI also publishes 26 national emerging stock market indexes for the developing countries, covering approximately 1,700 securities. Additionally, MSCI publishes several regional emerging markets indexes. The Emerging Markets Free version of these indexes recognizes that some countries impose ownership restrictions on shares by foreigners. In this case, the constituent national indexes are excluded or underweighted to recognize the particular restriction in order to provide an index representative of investments that can be freely made.

The Dow Jones Company (DJ) provides stock market index values for a number of countries. The values and percentage changes of these indexes can be found daily in *The Wall Street Journal.* The data are presented in local currency terms and for comparative purposes in American dollars. Exhibit 8.4 presents an example of the daily report of these indexes as found in *The Wall Street Journal.*

EXHIBIT 8.4

Example of Dow Jones
Country Stock Market
Indexes

Best and Worst Performing DJ Country Indexes
Ranked by % change, on an American dollar basis

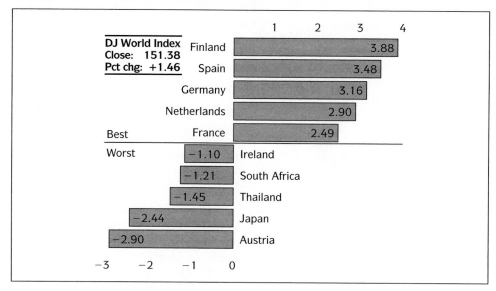

Dow Jones Country Indexes
August 19, 2002 5:15 p.m. ET

In American dollar terms

Country	Index	Chg	% Chg	YTD %Chg	Country	Index	Chg	% Chg	YTD %Chg
Australia	150.47	−0.40	−0.27	−2.38	Mexico	142.57	+1.38	+0.98	−9.44
Austria	95.59	−2.85	−2.90	+10.95	Netherlands	219.50	+6.18	+2.90	−14.66
Belgium	163.84	+2.92	+1.81	−3.91	New Zealand	109.74	+0.22	+0.20	+6.80
Brazil	154.12	−0.54	−0.35	−38.97	Norway	117.11	−1.25	−1.06	−6.31
Canada	158.47	+0.78	+0.49	−12.03	Philippines	50.38	−0.43	−0.85	−5.70
Chile	121.04	+0.22	+0.18	−12.00	Portugal	112.09	+0.35	+0.31	−19.46
Denmark	167.90	+2.65	+1.60	−10.35	Singapore	111.81	+0.75	+0.68	+3.16
Finland	604.87	+22.57	+3.88	−36.66	South Africa	78.06	−0.96	−1.21	+10.56
France	162.39	+3.95	+2.49	−16.02	South Korea	91.17	−0.19	−0.21	+18.08
Germany	136.83	+4.19	+3.16	−17.45	Spain	144.41	+4.86	+3.48	−13.69
Greece	101.18	−0.34	−0.33	−13.02	Sweden	162.00	+2.05	+1.28	−31.38
Hong Kong	170.37	−0.29	−0.17	−12.71	Switzerland	282.80	+3.90	+1.40	−3.79
Indonesia	35.73	−0.05	−0.14	+40.43	Taiwan	94.41	−0.91	−0.95	−11.70
Ireland	252.90	−2.81	−1.10	−15.99	Thailand	34.08	−0.50	−1.45	+19.79
Italy	128.39	+2.60	+2.07	−6.82	U.K.	147.29	+2.00	+1.38	−11.64
Japan	63.09	−1.58	−2.44	+1.30	U.S.	220.52	+4.83	+2.24	−17.32
Malaysia	99.92	+0.04	+0.04	+9.06	Venezuela	20.42	—	—	−40.83

Source: *The Wall Street Journal,* August 20, 2002, p. C14. Reprinted by permission of *The Wall Street Journal,* © 2002 Dow Jones & Company, Inc. All Rights Reserved Worldwide.

In addition to their own Dow Jones country stock market indexes, *The Wall Street Journal* also reports values and percentage changes in local currency values of the major stock market indexes of the national exchanges or markets from various countries in the world. Many of these indexes are prepared by the stock markets themselves or well-known investment advisory firms. Exhibit 8.5 presents a list of the indexes that appear daily in *The Wall Street Journal.*

EXHIBIT 8.5	
Major National Stock Market Indexes	

Country	Index
Argentina	**Merval**
Australia	**All Ordinaries**
Belgium	**Bel-20**
Brazil	**Sao Paulo Bovespa**
Canada	**S&P/TSX Composite: TSX Venture Composite**
Chile	**Santiago IPSA**
China	**Dow Jones China 88**
China	**Dow Jones Shanghai**
China	**Dow Jones Shenzhen**
Europe	**DJ STOXX (Euro)**
Europe	**DJ STOXX 50**
Euro Zone	**DJ Euro STOXX**
Euro Zone	**DJ Euro STOXX 50**
France	**Paris CAC 40**
Germany	**Frankfurt Xetra DAX**
Hong Kong	**Hang Seng**
India	**Bombay Sensex**
Israel	**Tel Aviv 25**
Italy	**Milan MIBtel**
Japan	**Tokyo Nikkei 225**
Japan	**Tokyo Nikkei 300**
Japan	**Tokyo Topix Index**
Mexico	**I.P.C. All-Share**
Netherlands	**Amsterdam AEX**
Singapore	**Straits Times**
South Africa	**Johannesburg All Share**
South Korea	**KOSPI**
Spain	**IBEX 35**
Sweden	**SW All Share**
Switzerland	**Zurich Swiss Market**
Taiwan	**Weighted**
U.K.	**London FTSE 100-share**
U.K.	**London FTSE 250-share**
United States	
American Stock Exchange Composite	
Dow Jones Industrial Average	
National Association of Security Dealers	
Automated Quotation Composite	
New York Stock Exchange Composite	
Russell 2000	
Standard & Poor's 500	
Wilshire 5000	
Value-Line	

Source: *The Wall Street Journal,* August 20, 2002, p. C14. Reprinted by permission of *The Wall Street Journal,* © 2002 Dow Jones & Company, Inc. All Rights Reserved Worldwide.

8.3 World Equity Benchmark Shares

Recently, Barclays Global Investors introduced World Equity Benchmark Shares (WEBS) as vehicles to facilitate investment in country funds. WEBS are country-specific baskets of shares designed to replicate the MSCI country indexes of 20 countries and three regions. They trade as shares on the American Stock Exchange.

WEBS are subject to U.S. Securities and Exchange Commission (SEC) and Internal Revenue Service (IRS) diversification requirements. These requirements prohibit the

http://www.iunits.com/english
/index.cfm

This website describes the
WEBS, created by Barclays
Global Investors.

investment of more than 50 percent of the fund in five or fewer securities, or 25 percent of the fund in a single security. Thus, for some countries, the WEB does not perfectly replicate the MSCI country fund. Nevertheless, WEBS are a low-cost, convenient way for investors to hold diversified investments in several different countries. Eleven new country WEBS are expected to start trading soon.

8.4   Trading in International Equities

During the 1980s, world capital markets began a trend toward greater global integration. Several factors account for this movement. First, investors began to realize the benefits of international portfolio diversification. Second, major capital markets became more liberalized through the elimination of fixed trading commissions, the reduction in governmental regulation, and measures taken by the European Union to integrate their capital markets. Third, new computer and communications technology facilitated efficient and fair securities trading through order routing and execution, information dissemination, and clearance and settlement. Fourth, multinational corporations (MNCs) realized the benefits of sourcing new capital internationally. In this section, we explore some of the major effects that greater global integration has had on the world's equity markets. We begin by examining the cross-listing of shares.

Cross-Listing of Shares

Cross-listing refers to a firm having its equity shares listed on one or more foreign exchanges, in addition to the home country stock exchange. Cross-listing is not a new concept; however, with the increased globalization of world equity markets, the amount of cross-listing has exploded in recent years. In particular, MNCs often cross-list their shares, but non-MNCs also cross-list.

Exhibit 8.6 presents the total number of companies listed on various national stock exchanges in the world and the breakdown of the listings between domestic and foreign for 2001. The exhibit also shows the number of new listings and the domestic-foreign split for 2001. Some foreign companies are listed on virtually all national stock exchanges of the developed countries. Several exchanges have a large proportion of foreign listings. In fact, the Luxembourg Stock Exchange has more foreign than domestic listings, while on the Swiss bourse, the foreign listings are over 50 percent.

A firm may decide to cross-list its shares for many reasons:

1. Cross-listing provides a means to expand the investor base for a firm's shares, thus potentially increasing the demand for the shares. Increased demand for a company's shares may increase the market price. Greater market demand and a broader investor base may also improve the liquidity of the security.

2. Cross-listing establishes name recognition of the company in a new capital market, thus paving the way for the firm to source new equity or debt capital from local investors as demands dictate.

3. Cross-listing brings the firm's name before more investor and consumer groups. Local consumers (investors) may more likely become investors in (consumers of) the company's shares (products) if the company's shares (products) are locally available. International portfolio diversification is facilitated for investors if they can trade the security on their own stock exchanges.

4. Cross-listing may mitigate the possibility of a hostile takeover of the firm through the broader investor base created for the firm's shares.

Cross-listing of a firm's shares obligates the firm to adhere to the securities regulations of its home country as well as the regulations of the countries in which it is cross-listed. Cross-listing in the United States means the firm must meet the accounting and disclosure requirements of the SEC. Reconciliation of a company's financial statements to American standards can be a laborious process, and some foreign firms are reluctant to disclose hidden reserves. For foreign firms desiring to have their shares

EXHIBIT 8.6		Total, Domestic, and Foreign Company Listings on Major National Stock Exchanges for 2001					
		Total Listings			**New Listings**		
Region	Exchange	Total	Domestic	Foreign	Total	Domestic	Foreign
North America	AMEX	606	558	48	44	39	5
	Bermuda	50	22	28	7	1	6
	Canadian Venture Exchange	2,688	2,688	0	277	277	0
	Chicago	5	5	0	0	0	0
	Mexico	172	167	5	4	3	1
	Nasdaq	4,063	3,618	445	144	123	21
	NYSE	2,400	1,939	461	144	93	51
	Toronto	1,299	1,261	38	84	81	3
South America	Buenos Aires	119	116	3	3	3	0
	Lima	227	204	23	12	6	6
	Santiago	249	248	1	3	3	0
	Sao Paulo	441	438	3	10	10	0
Europe, Africa, Middle East	Athens	314	313	1	21	21	0
	Barcelona	689	684	5	115	115	0
	Bilbao	347	344	3	49	49	0
	Budapest	56	55	1	1	1	0
	Copenhagen	217	208	9	5	4	1
	Deutsche Börse	983	748	235	21	21	0
	Euronext	1,132	1,132	NA	46	34	12
	Helsinki	155	152	3	9	9	0
	Irish	87	68	19	2	1	1
	Istanbul	311	310	1	1	1	0
	Italy	294	288	6	18	18	0
	Johannesburg	532	510	22	11	11	0
	Lisbon	99	97	2	2	1	1
	Ljubljana	151	151	0	15	15	0
	London	2,332	1,923	409	245	236	9
	Luxembourg	257	48	209	9	1	8
	Madrid	1,480	1,458	22	458	452	6
	Malta	12	12	0	2	2	0
	Oslo	212	186	26	17	12	5
	Stockholm	305	285	20	24	19	5
	Swiss Exchange	412	263	149	21	14	7
	Tehran	297	297	0	12	12	0
	Tel-Aviv	649	648	1	16	15	1
	Valencia	508	505	3	61	61	0
	Vienna	113	99	14	8	6	2
	Warsaw	230	230	0	9	9	0
Asia, Pacific	Australian	1,410	1,334	76	80	72	8
	Colombo	238	238	0	2	2	0
	Hong Kong	867	857	10	88	88	0
	Jakarta	315	315	0	31	31	0
	Korea	688	688	0	16	16	0
	Kuala Lumpur	807	804	3	20	20	0
	New Zealand	195	145	50	15	14	1
	Osaka	1,335	1,335	0	55	55	0
	Philippines	232	230	2	3	3	0
	Singapore	492	424	68	37	29	8
	Taiwan	586	584	2	70	69	1
	Thailand	385	385	0	10	10	0
	Tokyo	2,141	2,103	38	93	92	1

Source: Table I.1, p. 86 and Table I.2., p. 87 from *FIBV Annual Report and Statistics 2001.*

traded only among large institutional investors, rather than listed on an exchange, less rigorous accounting and disclosure requirements apply under SEC Rule 144A. Rule 144A share sales are often acceptable to family-owned companies, which for privacy or tax reasons operate their business with generally unacceptable accounting standards.

Canadian Cross-Listed Shares

Many of Canada's largest corporations list their shares in New York and other foreign stock exchanges as well as on Canadian exchanges. As of November 2003, there were 181 Canadian firms listed on exchanges in the United States. Most of the Canadian companies (80 of the 181) are listed on The New York Stock Exchange, while 78 were listed on the NASDAQ. The remaining 23 are listed on regional exchanges or on the American Stock Exchange (AMEX). A small number of Canadian firms (23) are listed on the London Stock Exchange.

The NYSE list includes the major Canadian banks and financials—the Bank of Montreal (BMO), the Royal Bank of Canada (RBC) Financial, Toronto-Dominion (TD), Scotiabank, and Manulife—as well as industrials, such as BCE, CN, Domtar, EnCana, Ipsco, Intrawest, Rogers Media, Shaw Communications, and Suncor. Canadian (TSX) companies listed on the NYSE and the NASDAQ simultaneously account for more than two-thirds of the current market capitalization of TSX-listed firms. Waterloo-based Research in Motion (RIM) reports that two-thirds of the trading in its shares takes place in New York on the NASDAQ.

Only the largest Canadian firms have sufficient size to meet the minimum capitalization requirement of, for instance, the NYSE. When they do, however, international cross-listing offers distinct advantages to both the firm and its investors. The firm has enhanced visibility and access to a substantially larger potential pool of equity for new issues. From the investors' point of view, cross-listed shares are followed up—or monitored—by a larger number of professional analysts which means that investors are generally better informed. Furthermore, the expanded diversification effects as Canadian shares are held together with American shares in American portfolios can lower the risk and the cost of capital of cross-listed firms, which means higher equity value.

A leading Canadian expert on international cross-listing, Usha Mittoo of the University of Manitoba, has carefully examined the performance of Canadian firms that have listed their shares on stock exchanges in the United States. Mittoo finds that before listing in the United States, a typical Canadian firm has enjoyed a dramatic run-up in its value with above-average rate return on equity on a risk-adjusted basis. In other words, Canadian firms that list in the United States show strong performance at home beforehand. That strong stock performance continues for some time after listing in the United States, reflecting a fall in the Canadian companies' cost of equity. The value of trading of Canadian shares, a measure of liquidity, also increases following American listing—by approximately 40 percent in terms of trading value per month.

Now the bad news. A number of empirical studies, including the work by Mittoo, demonstrate that despite the pre- and early post-American-listing rise in equity value (or fall in cost of equity), the long-run performance of American listings of Canadian firms is significantly different from that in the short-term. Whereas, on average, the firms that list on American exchanges have outperformed the market index by 30 to 40 percent in the year prior to listing, after the listing they underperform their at-home Canadian peers on average for three years.

Why Canadian firms underperform after listing in the United States is puzzling, but there are various explanations. First, it could reflect "selection bias." Firms that enjoy an impressive rise in value in Canada and then opt to list abroad may have misread a one-off boost that is not sustainable. The underperformance following American listing may represent performance and values reverting to more normal levels. Alternatively, Canadian firms and their enthusiastic advisors may overlook certain important costs in an international equity issue—such as the "road show"—as well as the risk of being subject to very close scrutiny from a larger number of analysts.

Regardless of the explanation, one implication is clear. Listing in the United States is no guarantee of a lower cost of equity capital in the long run. Each firm must carefully evaluate its foreign-listing decision in light of all factors—earnings growth, risk, liquidity, and transactions costs—that bear on this significant step in the firm's international corporate strategy.

Yankee Stock Offerings

Since the beginning of the 1990s, many foreign companies, Latin American in particular, have listed their shares on American exchanges to prime the American equity market for future **Yankee stock** offerings, that is, the direct sale of new equity capital to American public investors. This was a break from the past for the Latin American companies, which typically sold restricted 144A shares to large investors. Three factors appear to be fuelling the sale of Yankee stocks. One is the push for privatization by many Latin American and Eastern European government-owned companies. A second factor is the rapid growth in the economies of the developing countries. The third reason is the expected large demand for new capital by Mexican companies now within the North American Free Trade Agreement (NAFTA).

The European Stock Market

Western and Eastern Europe have more than 20 national equity markets, where at least 15 different languages are spoken. Several combinations and trading arrangements have been formed among these national stock exchanges in recent years, but as yet, there is not a single European stock market that comprises all national markets, and it does not appear as if one will exist in the near future.

The closest thing to a "European stock market" is Euronext, which was created in September 2000, as a result of a merger of the Amsterdam Exchange, Brussels Exchange, and the Paris Bourse. The three markets are wholly owned subsidiaries of Euronext N.V., doing business as Euronext Amsterdam, Euronext Brussels, and Euronext Paris. Euronext creates a single trading platform serving all members at each of the three subsidiary exchanges. A single order book exists for each share, allowing for transparency and liquidity. A single clearinghouse and payment and delivery system facilitates trading.

In June 2001, the Portuguese stock exchange merged with Euronext. In 2001, a cross-access and cross-trading agreement was signed between Euronext and the Luxembourg, Helsinki, and Warsaw stock exchanges. Thus, it appears that a European stock exchange is in the process of developing.

Another noteworthy European trading arrangement is NASDAQ Europe. NASDAQ Europe is a result of NASDAQ Stock Market, Inc. acquiring the European Association of Securities Dealers Automated Quotation System (EASDAQ) as a subsidiary. NASDAQ desires to create the world's first truly global securities market. NASDAQ Europe is a pan-European stock market that operates independently of any national European exchanges. It offers low-cost cross-border trading similar to trading on NASDAQ in the United States. It expects to offer trading in both European and American shares.

www.euronext.com

This is the official website of Euronext.

www.nasdaqeurope.com

This is the official website of NASDAQ Europe.

American Depository Receipts

Foreign shares can be traded directly on a national stock market, but most often they are traded in the form of a *depository receipt*. For example, Yankee stock issues often trade on American exchanges as **American Depository Receipts (ADRs).** An ADR is a receipt representing a number of foreign shares that remain on deposit with the American depository's custodian in the issuer's home market. The bank serves as the transfer agent for the ADRs, which are traded on the listed exchanges in the United States or in the over-the-counter (OTC) market. The first ADRs began trading in 1927 as a means of eliminating some of the risks, delays, inconveniences, and expenses of trading the actual shares of foreign companies. The ADR market has grown significantly over the years; in 2002, there were approximately 2,200 ADR programs, representing issuers from more than 80 countries. Approximately 600 ADRs trade on American exchanges. Similarly, *Global Depository Receipts* allow foreign firms to

www.adr.com

This website sponsored by J.P. Morgan tells you everything there is to know about ADRs. See in particular the online book titled *The ADR Reference Guide.*

trade principally on the London and Luxembourg stock exchanges, and *Singapore Depository Receipts* trade on the Singapore Stock Exchange. Exhibit 8.7 shows a tombstone for a Global Depository Receipt.

ADRs offer the American investor many advantages over trading directly in the underlying shares on the foreign exchange. Non-American investors can also invest in ADRs, and frequently do so, rather than invest in the underlying shares because of the investment advantages. These advantages include:

1. ADRs are denominated in dollars, trade on an American stock exchange, and can be purchased through the investor's regular broker. By contrast, trading in the underlying shares would likely require the investor to set up an account with a broker from the country where the company issuing the shares was located, make a currency exchange and arrange for the shipment of the share certificates or the establishment of a custodial account.

2. Dividends received on the underlying shares are collected and converted to dollars by the custodian and paid to the ADR investor, whereas investment in the underlying shares requires the investor to collect the foreign dividends and make a currency conversion. Moreover, tax treaties between the United States and some countries lower the dividend tax rate paid by nonresident investors. Consequently, American investors in the underlying shares need to file a form to get a refund on the tax difference withheld. ADR investors, however, receive the full dollar equivalent dividend, less only the applicable taxes.

3. ADR trades clear in three business days as do American equities, whereas settlement practices for the underlying shares vary in foreign countries.

4. ADR price quotes are in American dollars.

EXHIBIT 8.7

Global Depository Receipt Tombstone

CIB

COMMERCIAL INTERNATIONAL BANK (EGYPT) S.A.E.

International Offering of
9,999,000 Global Depository Receipts

corresponding to
999,900 Shares (nominal Value of E£100 per Share)

at an
Offer price of US$11.875 per Global Depository Receipt

Seller
National Bank of Egypt

Global Co-ordinator
Co Lead Managers
Robert Fleming & Co. Limited Salomon Brothers International Limited
UBS Limited

Domestic Advisor
Commercial International Investment Company S.A.E.

ING ☙ BARINGS

July 1996

Source: *Euromoney*, October 1998, p. 127.

5. ADRs (except Rule 144A issues) are registered securities that provide for the protection of ownership rights, whereas most underlying shares are bearer securities.

6. An ADR investment can be sold by trading the depository receipt to another investor in the American stock market, or the underlying shares can be sold in the local stock market. In this case, the ADR is delivered for cancellation to the bank depository, which delivers the underlying shares to the buyer.

7. ADRs frequently represent a multiple of the underlying shares, rather than a one-for-one correspondence, to allow the ADR to trade in a price range customary for American investors. A single ADR may represent more or less than one underlying share, depending on the per-share value.

There are two types of ADRs: sponsored and unsponsored. *Sponsored* ADRs are created by a bank at the request of the foreign company that issued the underlying security. The sponsoring bank often offers ADR holders an assortment of services, including investment information and portions of the annual report translated into English. Sponsored ADRs are the only ones that can be listed on the American stock markets. All new ADR programs must be sponsored. *Unsponsored* ADRs—some dating back prior to 1980 still exist—were usually created at the request of an American investment banking firm without direct involvement by the foreign issuing firm. Consequently, the foreign company may not provide investment information or financial reports to the depository on a regular basis or in a timely manner. The depository fees of sponsored ADRs are paid by the foreign company. ADR investors pay the depository fees on unsponsored ADRs. Unsponsored ADRs may have several issuing banks, with the terms of the offering varying from bank to bank.

Five empirical studies document some important findings about the ADR market. Rosenthal (1983), using a time series of weekly, biweekly, and monthly rates of return over the time period of 1974 through 1978 for 54 ADRs, find that the ADR market was weak-form efficient. That is, abnormal trading profits are not likely from studying historical price data.

Park (1990) finds that a substantial portion of the variability in (i.e., change in) ADR returns is accounted for by variation in the share price of the underlying security in the home market; however, information observed in the American market is also an important factor in the ADR return-generating process.

Officer and Hoffmeister (1987) and Kao, Wei, and Vu (1991) examine ADRs as vehicles for constructing diversified equity portfolios. Officer and Hoffmeister use a sample of 45 ADRs and 45 domestic shares. For each, they calculate monthly rates of return for the period 1973 through 1983. They find that as few as four ADRs combined with four domestic shares allow the investor to reduce portfolio risk by as much as 25 percent without any reduction in expected return.

Kao, Wei, and Vu use 10 years of monthly return data covering the time period 1979 through 1989 for ADRs with underlying shares from the United Kingdom, Australia, Japan, the Netherlands, and Sweden. They find that an internationally diversified portfolio of ADRs outperforms both an American stock market and a world stock market benchmark on a risk-adjusted basis. Country ADR portfolio from all countries, except Australia, also outperforms the American and world benchmarks, but only country ADR portfolio from the United Kingdom, Japan, and the Netherlands outperforms their home country stock market benchmark.

Jayaraman, Shastri, and Tandon (1993) examine the effect of the listing of ADRs on the risk and return of the underlying shares. They find positive abnormal performance (i.e., return in excess of the expected equilibrium return) of the underlying security on the initial listing date. They interpret this result as evidence that an ADR listing provides the issuing firm with another market from which to source new equity capital. Additionally, they find an increase in the volatility of (change in) returns of the underlying shares. They interpret this result as consistent with the theory that traders with proprietary information will attempt to profit from their knowledge by taking advantage of price discrepancies caused by information differentials between the ADR and underlying security markets.

The International Finance in Practice box on page 192 discusses buying foreign shares directly and through ADRs and mutual funds.

Global Registered Shares

The merger of Daimler Benz AG and Chrysler Corporation in 1998 created Daimler-Chrysler AG, a German firm. The merger was hailed as a landmark event for global equity markets because it simultaneously created a new type of equity share called Global Registered Shares (GRS). GRS are one share traded globally, unlike ADRs, which are receipts for bank deposits of home-market shares and traded on foreign markets. The primary exchanges for DaimlerChrysler GRS are the Frankfurt Stock Exchange and the NYSE; however, they are traded on a total of 20 exchanges worldwide. The shares are fully fungible—a GRS purchased on one exchange can be sold on another. They trade in both American dollars and euros. A new global share registrar that links the American and German transfer agents and registrars needed to be created to facilitate clearing. The main advantages of GRS over ADRs appear to be that all shareholders have equal status and direct voting rights. The main disadvantage of GRS appears to be the greater expense in establishing the global registrar and clearing facility. GRS have met with limited success; many companies that considered them opted instead for ADRs.[1]

EXAMPLE | 8.1 | DaimlerChrysler AG Shares in DaimlerChrysler AG—the result of the merger of Daimler Benz AG, the famous German automobile manufacturer, and Chrysler Corporation—trade on both the Frankfurt Stock Exchange in Germany and on the New York Stock Exchange. On the Frankfurt bourse, Daimler-Chrysler closed at a price of €47.50 on Tuesday, August 19, 2002. On the same day, DaimlerChrysler closed in New York at $46.91 per share. To prevent arbitrage between trading on the two exchanges, the shares have to trade at the same price when adjusted for the exchange rate. We see that this is true. The $/€ exchange rate on August 19 was $0.9764/€1. Thus, €47.50 × $0.9764 = $46.38, an amount very close to the closing price in New York of $46.91. The difference is easily explainable by the fact that the New York market closes several hours after the Frankfurt exchange, and thus market prices had changed slightly.

8.5 | Factors Affecting International Equity Returns

Before closing this chapter, it is beneficial to explore some of the empirical evidence about which factors influence equity returns. After all, to construct an efficiently diversified international portfolio of shares, one must estimate the expected return and the variance of returns for each security in the investment set plus the pairwise correlation structure. It may be easier to accurately estimate these parameters if a common set of factors affect equity returns. Some likely candidates are macroeconomic variables that influence the overall economic environment in which the firm issuing the security conducts its business; exchange rate changes between the currency of the country issuing the shares and the currency of other countries where suppliers, customers, and investors of the firm reside; and the industrial structure of the country in which the firm operates.

---

[1]Much of the information in this section is from the 1999 clinical study by G. Andrew Karolyi.

Macroeconomic Factors

Two recent studies test the influence of various macroeconomic variables on share returns. Solnik (1984) examines the effect of exchange rate changes, interest rate differentials, the level of the domestic interest rate, and changes in domestic inflation expectations. He finds that international monetary variables have only weak influence on equity returns in comparison with domestic variables. In another study, Asprem (1989) finds that changes in industrial production, employment, and imports, the level of interest rates, and an inflation measure explain only a small portion of the variability of equity returns for 10 European countries but that substantially more of the variation is explained by an international market index.

Exchange Rates

Adler and Simon (1986) examine the exposure of a sample of foreign equity and bond index returns to exchange rate changes. They find that changes in exchange rates generally explain a larger portion of the variability of foreign bond indexes than foreign equity indexes but that some foreign equity markets are more exposed to exchange rate changes than are the respective foreign bond markets. Their results suggest that it would likely be beneficial to hedge (i.e., protect) foreign stock investment against exchange rate uncertainty.

In another study, Eun and Resnick (1988) find that the cross-correlations among major stock markets and exchange markets are relatively low but positive. This result implies that the exchange rate changes in a given country reinforce the stock market movements in that country as well as in the other countries examined.

Industrial Structure

Studies examining the influence of industrial structure on foreign equity returns are inconclusive. In a study examining the correlation structure of national equity markets, Roll (1992) concludes that the industrial structure of a country is important in explaining a significant part of the correlation structure of international equity index returns. He also finds that industry factors explained a larger portion of stock market variability than did exchange rate changes.

In contrast, Eun and Resnick (1984) find for a sample of 160 shares from eight countries and 12 industries that the pairwise correlation structure of international security returns can be better estimated from models that recognize country factors, rather than industry factors. Similarly, using individual share return data for 829 firms, from 12 countries, and representing seven broad industry groups, Heston and Rouwenhorst (1994) conclude "that industrial structure explains very little of the cross-sectional difference in country return volatility, and that the low correlation between country indices is almost completely due to country specific sources of variation."

Both Rouwenhorst (1999) and Beckers (1999) examine the effect of the EMU on European equity markets and come up with opposite conclusions. Rouwenhorst concludes that country effects in share returns have been larger than industry effects in Western Europe since 1982 and that this situation continued throughout the 1993–1998 period when interest rates were converging and fiscal and monetary policies were being harmonized in the countries entering the European Monetary Union (EMU). On the other hand, Beckers finds an increase in correlations between markets and between the same sector in different markets arising from the European integration of fiscal, monetary, and economic policies. He concludes that the increase in pairwise correlations in these countries represents a reduction in the diversification benefits from investing in the euro zone.

Griffin and Karolyi (1998) examine the effect of industrial structure on covariances by studying whether a difference exists in the effect between traded-goods industries and non–traded-goods industries. They find that the cross-country covariances are larger for firms within a given industry than the cross-country covariances across firms in different industries in traded-goods industries. In contrast, for non–traded-goods industries, there is little difference in cross-country covariances between firms in the same industry and those in different industries.

Buying Foreign Stocks from U.S. Brokers Gets Easier

Maybe you have a hunch about Mazda's stock. Or maybe you just *know* that Peru's telephone company is going to be the next hot play from Latin America.

Until recently, it would have been difficult to make more of your idea than cocktail chatter. Neither stock is listed in any form in the U.S. and most brokers wouldn't buy shares overseas in an amount small enough for an individual investor's portfolio.

But now U.S. brokerage houses are handling more foreign stocks for small investors. Merrill Lynch & Co. now trades about 4,000 foreign stocks that aren't listed in the U.S., for retail clients—up from only around 600 two years ago, thanks to its recent acquisition of Smith New Court Securities Ltd., a British brokerage firm. Travelers Group's Smith Barney Inc. trades about 1,000 foreign issues for its retail clients, and a nest of discount brokers across the U.S. now specializes in selling foreign stocks cheap to small investors.

U.S. institutions are unwittingly helping small investors pick among foreign stocks, too. Retail brokers can trade more foreign stocks during the U.S. working day, largely because U.S. pension funds and other big investors in this country have more foreign shares to buy and sell. As a result, "more and more people are realizing that they have the access to buy foreign shares" in the U.S., says James Heitzer, an investment adviser at Renaissance Financial Securities Inc. in Atlanta, a brokerage firm that trades foreign stocks.

Be warned. Buying foreign stocks carries risks beyond those normally associated with buying domestic stocks. Financial reports, if they come at all, may not be in English. Foreign markets aren't as strictly regulated as the U.S. market. And many foreign stocks carry the risk that the currency in which they are denominated could fall against the U.S. dollar, either eroding an otherwise big gain or exacerbating a loss.

If that daunts you, consider investing overseas through other vehicles. Mutual funds hold enough different securities to keep you from holding too many of your eggs in one basket. And American depository receipts—the restricted number of certificates that represent foreign shares but are listed on U.S. markets—are subject to the same Securities and Exchange Commission rules as U.S. stocks.

But "the advantage of buying individual [foreign] stocks is that you are making your own decisions" over a broader range of securities than are included among ADRs, says Vivian Lewis, the New York–based publisher of Global Investing, a newsletter for individuals who like to do their stock-picking overseas.

When looking for a brokerage firm to trade foreign stocks, insist on dealing only with staff that "know how to trade pink sheet stocks," Ms. Lewis says. (A U.S. investor can also open an account with a foreign brokerage house, she notes. But most foreign brokers with offices in the U.S. cater to institutional investors.)

A full-service firm has one distinct advantage over discount brokerages when it comes to picking foreign stocks: research. Merrill Lynch, for instance, offers its small clients the same foreign research that it gives U.S. institutional investors. That research comes from analysts who specialize in watching Asia, Europe, Latin America, Canada and South Africa.

To understand the value of that, consider the hassles Ms. Lewis faced when she wanted to assess Peru's telecommunications company on her own. The only English-speaker she found by phone at the company's headquarters was in the procurement department, and knew little about the company's general health. Eventually, Ms. Lewis had to call Spain and question an official of a Spanish concern that held some of the Peruvian company's shares. For such reasons, Marquette de Bary does much of its business with U.S. investors who are living abroad and know about foreign markets first hand.

Once you own a foreign stock, you will face other hurdles. The most difficult may be keeping a tab on a foreign company through financial reports that are far more lax than those in the U.S. If a foreign company with $10 million in assets has at least 500 U.S. shareholders, it must furnish the SEC with the financial statements it files in its home market. But the SEC won't do anything if those statements are false, and it won't insist that the foreign company use U.S. accounting standards.

Foreign filings usually don't provide all the information that U.S. filings must. That means you might know nothing about how a company pays its executives or how its individual units are performing. Many foreign companies don't even file statements quarterly, as U.S. companies must, but only once or twice a year.

The result can be "very messy," says Paul Broderick, operations manager at Barry Murphy. In 1993, he discovered that a Malaysian company whose shares many of his clients held was offering rights for new shares—only two days before the offering was due to expire.

Source: Excerpted from Robert Steiner, *The Wall Street Journal*, June 7, 1996, p. C1. Reprinted with permission of *The Wall Street Journal,* © 1996 Dow Jones & Company, Inc. All Rights Reserved Worldwide.

SUMMARY

This chapter provides an overview of international equity markets. The material is designed to provide an understanding of how MNCs source new equity capital outside of their own domestic primary market and to provide useful institutional information to investors interested in diversifying their portfolio internationally.

1. The chapter began with a statistical perspective of the major equity markets in the developed countries.

2. A variety of international equity benchmarks were also presented. Knowledge of where to find comparative equity market performance data is useful. Specifically, Standard & Poor's, Morgan Stanley Capital International, and the Dow Jones Country Stock Market indexes were discussed. Also, a list of the major national stock market indexes prepared by the national exchanges or major investment advisory services was presented.

3. A considerable amount of discussion was devoted to differences in secondary equity market structures. Secondary markets have historically been structured as dealer or agency markets. Both of these types of market structure can provide for continuous market trading, but noncontinuous markets tended to be agency markets. Over-the-counter trading, specialist markets, and automated markets allow for continuous market trading. Call markets and crowd trading are each types of noncontinuous trading market systems. Trading costs—commissions and taxes—on various national equity markets were summarized in a table comparing market characteristics. It was noted that most national stock markets are now automated for at least some of the issues traded on them.

4. Cross-listing of a company's shares on foreign exchanges was extensively discussed. A firm may cross-list its shares to establish a broader investor base for its shares; establish name recognition in foreign capital markets; and pave the way for sourcing new equity and debt capital from investors in these markets. Yankee stock offerings, or sale of foreign shares to American investors, were also discussed. Yankee stocks trade on American markets as American depository receipts (ADRs), which are bank receipts representing a multiple of foreign shares deposited in an American bank. ADRs eliminate some of the risks, delays, inconveniences, and expenses of trading actual shares.

5. Several empirical studies that tested for factors that might influence equity returns indicate that domestic factors, such as the level of domestic interest rates and expected changes in domestic inflation, as opposed to international monetary variables, have the greatest effect on national equity returns. Industrial structure does not appear to be of primary importance. Equity returns are also found to be sensitive to own-currency exchange rate changes.

KEY WORDS

American depository
   receipt (ADR), *187*
call market, *179*
continuous trading, *179*

cross-listing, *184*
crowd trading, *179*
liquidity, *176*
primary market, *177*

secondary market, *178*
specialist, *179*
Yankee stock, *187*

QUESTIONS

1. Get a current copy of *The Wall Street Journal* and find the *Dow Jones Country Indexes* listing in Section C of the newspaper. Examine the 12-month changes in American dollars for the various national indexes. How do the changes from your table compare with the 12-month changes from the sample provided in the text-book as Exhibit 8.4? Are they all of similar size? Are the same national indexes positive and negative in both listings? Discuss your findings.

2. As an investor, what factors would you consider before investing in the emerging stock market of a developing country?

3. Compare and contrast the various types of secondary market trading structures.

4. Discuss any benefits you can think of for a company to (a) cross-list its equity shares on more than one national exchange, and (b) to source new equity capital from foreign investors as well as domestic investors.

5. Why might it be easier for an investor desiring to diversify his portfolio internationally to buy depository receipts, rather than the actual shares of the company?

6. Why do you think the empirical studies about factors affecting equity returns basically showed that domestic factors were more important than international factors, and, secondly, that industrial membership of a firm was of little importance in forecasting the international correlation structure of a set of international shares?

PROBLEMS

1. On the Milan bourse, Fiat shares closed at €11.17 per share on Tuesday, August 19, 2002. Fiat trades as an ADR on the NYSE. One underlying Fiat share equals one ADR. On August 19, the $/€ spot exchange rate was $0.9764/€1. At this exchange rate, what is the no-arbitrage American dollar price of one ADR?

2. If Fiat ADRs were trading at $15 when the underlying shares were trading in Milan at €11.17, what could you do to earn a trading profit? Use the information in problem 1, above, to help you and assume that transaction costs are negligible.

INTERNET EXERCISES

1. The Bloomberg website provides current values of many of the international stock indexes presented in Exhibit 8.5 at the website www.quote.bloomberg.com/cgi-bin/regionalind.cgi?config=wei. Go to this website and determine what country's stock markets are trading higher and lower today. Is there any current news event that might influence the way different national markets are trading today?

2. The J.P. Morgan website www.adr.com/ provides online data on trading in ADRs. Go to this website to view today's total trading volume in ADRs and the year-to-date trading volume. What are the top 10 individual ADRs by trading volume? By dollar value? Does there seem to be a similarity in industry (such as telecom) represented by the top ADRs, or are they from a variety of different industries? Recall from the chapter that the effect of industrial structure on international share returns is an unresolved issue.

MINI CASE

San Pico's New Stock Exchange

San Pico is a rapidly growing Latin American developing country. The country is blessed with miles of scenic beaches that have attracted tourists by the thousands in recent years to new resort hotels financed by joint ventures of San Pico businessmen and moneymen from the Middle East, Japan, and the United States. Additionally, San Pico has good natural harbours that are conducive for receiving imported merchandise from abroad and exporting merchandise produced in San

Pico and other surrounding countries that lack access to the sea. Because of these advantages, many new businesses are being started in San Pico.

Presently, shares are traded in a cramped building in La Cobijio, the nation's capital. Admittedly, the San Pico Stock Exchange system is rather archaic. Twice a day an official of the exchange will call out the name of each of the 43 companies whose shares trade on the exchange. Brokers wanting to buy or sell shares for their clients then attempt to make a trade with one another. This crowd trading system has worked well for over one hundred years, but the government desires to replace it with a new modern system that will allow greater and more frequent opportunities for trading in each company and will allow for trading the shares of the many new startup companies that are expected to trade in the secondary market. Additionally, the government administration is rapidly privatizing many state-owned businesses in an attempt to foster their efficiency, obtain foreign exchange from the sale, and convert the country to a more capitalist economy. The government believes that it could conduct this privatization faster and perhaps at more attractive prices if it had a modern stock exchange facility where the shares of the newly privatized companies will eventually trade.

You are an expert in the operation of secondary stock markets and have been retained as a consultant to the San Pico Stock Exchange to offer your expertise in modernizing the stock market. What would you advise?

REFERENCES & SUGGESTED READINGS

Adler, Michael, and David Simon. "Exchange Rate Surprises in International Portfolios." *The Journal of Portfolio Management* 12 (1986), pp. 44–53.

Asprem, Mads. "Stock Prices, Assets Portfolios and Macroeconomic Variables in Ten European Countries." *Journal of Banking and Finance* 13 (1989), pp. 589–612.

Batista, Venilia, Teresa Palmiero, and Jacqueline Grosch Lobo. *The Euromoney Guide to World Equity Markets 2002*. London: Euromoney Books, 2002.

Becker, Stan. "Investment Implications of a Single European Capital Market." *Journal of Portfolio Management* (Spring 1999), pp. 9–17.

Eun, Cheol S., and S. Sabherwal, "Cross-Border Listings and Price Discovery: Evidence from U.S.-Listed Canadian Stocks." *Journal of Finance* Vol. 58, No. 2 (2003), pp. 549–75.

Eun, Cheol S., and Bruce G. Resnick. "Exchange Rate Uncertainty, Forward Contracts, and International Portfolio Selection." *Journal of Finance* 43 (1988), pp. 197–215.

Foerster, Stephen R., and G. Andrew Karolyi. "The Effects of Market Segmentation and Investor Recognition on Asset Prices: Evidence from Foreign Stocks Listings in the United States." *Journal of Finance* 54 (1999), pp. 981–1013.

Griffin, John M., and G. Andrew Karolyi. "Another Look at the Role of the Industrial Structure of Markets for International Diversification Strategies." *Journal of Financial Economics* 50 (1998), pp. 351–73.

Herman, Tom, and Michael R. Sesit. "ADRs: Foreign Issues with U.S. Accents." *The Wall Street Journal* (February 8, 1990).

Heston, Steven L., and K. Geert Rouwenhorst. "Does Industrial Structure Explain the Benefits of International Diversification?" *Journal of Financial Economics* 36 (1994), pp. 3–27.

Jayaraman, Narayanan, Kuldeep Shastri, and Kishore Tandon. "The Impact of International Cross Listings on Risk and Return: The Evidence from American Depository Receipts." *Journal of Banking and Finance* 17 (1993), pp. 91–103.

Kao, G., K. C. Wenchi, John Wei, and Joseph Vu. "Risk-Return Characteristics of the American Depository Receipts." Unpublished working paper, 1991.

Karmin, Craig. "More-Efficient WEBS Provide Alternative to Closed-End Funds." *The Wall Street Journal* (July 6, 1999), p. R12.

Karolyi, G. Andrew. "DaimlerChrysler AG, The First Truly Global Share." Ohio State University working paper (September 1999).

Karolyi, G. Andrew, "Why Do Firm's List Abroad? A Survey of the Evidence and Its Managerial Implications," New York University Salomon Bros. Centre Monograph, Vol. 7, No. 1 (1998).

Lederman, Jess, and Keith K. H. Parks, eds. *The Global Equity Markets*. Chicago: Probus, 1991.

Merjos, Anna. "Lure of Faraway Places: ADRs Grow in Numbers and Popularity." *Barron's* (April 16, 1990).

Miller, Darius P. "The Market Reaction to International Cross-Listings: Evidence from Depository Receipts." *Journal of Financial Economics* 51 (1999), pp. 103–23.

Mittoo, Usha R., "The Value of U.S. Listing." *Canadian Investment Review,* Vol. 16, No. 3 (Fall 2003), pp. 31–37.

Muscarella, Chris J., and Michael R. Vetsuypens. "Stock Splits: Signaling or Liquidity? The Case of ADR 'solo-splits'." *Journal of Financial Economics* 42 (1996), pp. 2–26.

Officer, Dennis T., and J. Ronald Hoffmeister. "ADRs: A Substitute for the Real Thing?" *Journal of Portfolio Management* (Winter 1987), pp. 61–65.

Park, Jinwoo. *The Impact of Information on ADR Returns and Variances: Some Implications,* unpublished Ph.D. dissertation from The University of Iowa, 1990.

Parks, Keith K. H., and Antoine W. Van Agtmael, eds. *The World's Emerging Stock Markets.* Chicago: Probus, 1993.

Roll, Richard. "Industrial Structure and the Comparative Behavior of International Stock Market Indexes." *Journal of Finance* 47 (1992), pp. 3–42.

Rosenthal, Leonard. "An Empirical Test of the Efficiency of the ADR Market." *Journal of Banking and Finance* 7 (1983) pp. 17–29.

Rouwenhorst, K. Geert. "European Equity Markets and the EMU." *Financial Analysts Journal,* (May/June 1999), pp. 57–64.

Schwartz, Robert A. *Equity Markets.* New York: Harper and Row, 1988.

Siconolfi, Michael. "Foreign Firms Step Up Offerings in U.S." *The Wall Street Journal* (June 1, 1992).

Solnik, Bruno. "Capital Markets and International Monetary Variables." *Financial Analysts Journal* 40 (1984), pp. 69–73.

Stulz, René, "Globalization, Corporate Finance and the Cost of Capital." *Journal of Applied Corporate Finance,* Vol. 12, No. 3. (1999), pp. 8–25.

Torres, Craig. "Latin American Firms Break with Past, Scramble to Be Listed on U.S. Exchanges." *The Wall Street Journal* (September 28, 1993).

Werner, Ingrid M., and Allan W. Kleidon. "U.K. and U.S. Trading of British Cross-Listed Stocks: An Intraday Analysis of Market Integration." *The Review of Financial Studies* 9 (1996), pp. 619–64.

Wu, Congsheng, and Chuck C.Y. Kwok. "Why Do U.S. Firms Choose Global Equity Offerings?" *Financial Management* 31 (2002), pp. 47–65.

Futures and Options on Foreign Exchange

ON FEBRUARY 27, 1995, Barings PLC, the oldest merchant bank in the United Kingdom, was placed in "administration" by the Bank of England because of losses that exceeded the bank's entire $860 million in equity capital. The cause of these losses was a breakdown in Barings' risk-management system that allowed a single rogue trader to accumulate and conceal an unhedged $27 billion position in various exchange-traded futures and options contracts, primarily the Nikkei 225 stock index futures contract traded on the Singapore International Monetary Exchange. The losses occurred when the market moved unfavourably against the trader's speculative positions. The trader recently completed a prison term in Singapore for fraudulent trading. Barings was taken over by the ING Group, the Dutch banking and insurance conglomerate.

As this story implies, futures and options contracts can be very risky investments, indeed, when used for speculative purposes. Nevertheless, they are also important risk-management tools. In this chapter, we introduce exchange-traded currency futures contracts, options contracts, and options on currency futures that are useful for both speculating on foreign exchange price movements and hedging exchange rate uncertainty. These contracts make up part of the foreign exchange market that was introduced in Chapter 4, where we discussed spot and forward exchange rates.

The discussion begins by comparing forward and futures contracts and noting the similarities and differences between the two. We discuss the markets where futures are traded, the currencies on which contracts are written, contract specifications for the various currency contracts, and Eurodollar interest rate futures contracts. These are useful for hedging short-term dollar interest rate risk in much the same way as forward rate agreements, introduced in Chapter 6.

Next, options contracts on foreign exchange are introduced, comparing and contrasting the options and the futures markets. The exchanges where options are traded are identified and contract terms are specified. We discuss the over-the-counter options market. Basic option-pricing boundary relationships are illustrated using actual market prices. We outline how a speculator might use currency options. The chapter closes with the development of a currency option-pricing model.

This chapter and the knowledge gained about forward contracts in Chapters 4 and 5 set the stage for Chapters 12, 13, and 14, which explain how these vehicles are used for hedging foreign exchange risk.

9.1 Futures Contracts: Some Preliminaries

In Chapter 4, a *forward contract* was defined as a vehicle for buying or selling a stated amount of foreign exchange at a stated price per unit at a specified time in the future. Both forward and futures contracts are classified as **derivative** or **contingent claim securities** because their values are derived from or contingent upon the value of the underlying security. A **futures** contract is similar to a forward contract but with a crucial distinction. A forward exchange contract is tailor-made for a client by his international bank; in contrast, a futures contract has **standardized** features and is **exchange traded,** that is, traded on organized exchanges, rather than over the counter.

The main standardized features of future contracts are the **contract size** specifying the amount of the underlying foreign currency for future purchase or sale and the **maturity date** of the contract. A futures contract is written for a specific amount of foreign currency, rather than for a tailor-made sum. Hence, a position in multiple contracts may be necessary to establish a sizable hedge or speculative position. Futures contracts have specific **delivery months** during the year in which contracts mature on a specified day of the month.

To establish a futures position, an **initial margin** must be deposited into a collateral account. The initial margin is generally equal to about 2 percent of the contract value. Either cash or Treasury bills may be used to meet the margin requirement. The account balance will fluctuate through daily settlement, as following discussion will make clear. The margin put up by the contract holder can be viewed as "good-faith" money that he will fulfill his side of the financial obligation.

The major difference between a forward contract and a futures contract is the way the underlying asset is priced for future purchase or sale. A forward contract states a price for the future transaction. By contrast, a futures contract is settled-up, or **marked-to-market,** daily at the settlement price at the close of daily trading on the exchange.

A buyer of a futures contract (one who holds a **long** position) in which the settlement price is higher (lower) than the previous day's settlement price has a positive (negative) settlement for the day. Since a long position entitles the owner to purchase the underlying asset, a higher (lower) settlement price means the futures price of the underlying asset has increased (decreased). Consequently, a long position in the contract is worth more (less). The change in settlement prices from one day to the next determines the settlement amount. That is, the change in settlement prices per unit of the underlying asset, multiplied times the size of the contract, equals the size of the daily settlement to be added to (or subtracted from) the long's margin account.

Analogously, the seller of the futures contract (**short** position) will have his margin account increased (or decreased) by the amount the long's margin account is decreased (or increased). Thus, futures trading between the long and the short is a **zero-sum game;** that is, the sum of the long and short's daily settlement is zero.

If the investor's margin account falls below a **maintenance margin** level (roughly equal to 75 percent of the initial margin), **variation margin** must be added to the account to bring it back to the initial margin level in order to keep the position open. An investor who suffers a liquidity crunch and cannot deposit additional margin money will have his position liquidated by his broker.

The marking-to-market feature of futures markets means that market participants realize their profits or suffer their losses on a day-to-day basis, rather than all at once at maturity as with a forward contract. At the end of daily trading, a futures contract is analogous to a new forward contract on the underlying asset at the new settlement price with a one-day-shorter maturity. Because of daily marking-to-market, the futures price will converge through time to the spot price on the last day of trading in the contract. That is, the final settlement price at which any transaction in the underlying asset will transpire is the spot price on the last day of trading. The effective price is, nevertheless, the original futures contract price, once the profit or loss in the margin account is included. Exhibit 9.1 summarizes the differences between forward and futures contracts.

Two types of market participants are necessary for a derivatives market to operate: **speculators** and **hedgers.** A speculator attempts to profit from a change in the futures price. To do this, the speculator will take a long or short position in a futures contract, depending upon his expectations of future price movement. A hedger, on the other hand, wants to avoid price variation by locking in a purchase price of the underlying asset through a long position in the futures contract or a sales price through a short position. In effect, the hedger passes off the risk of price variation to the speculator, who is better able, or at least more willing, to bear this risk.

Both forward and futures markets for foreign exchange are very liquid. A **reversing trade** can be made in either market that will close out, or neutralize, a position.[1] In forward markets, approximately 90 percent of all contracts result in the short making delivery of the underlying asset to the long. This is natural given the tailor-made terms of forward contracts. By contrast, only about 1 percent of currency futures contracts result in delivery. While futures contracts are useful for speculation and hedging, their standardized delivery dates are unlikely to correspond to the actual future dates when foreign exchange transactions will transpire. Thus, they are generally closed out in a reversing trade. The **commission** that buyers and sellers pay to transact in the futures market is a single amount paid upfront that covers the *round-trip* transactions of initiating and closing out the position. These days, through a discount broker, the commission charge can be as little as $15 per currency futures contract.

EXHIBIT 9.1	
Differences between Futures and Forward Contracts	*Trading Location* Futures: Traded competitively on an organized exchange. Forward: Traded by bank dealers via a network of telephones, telex machines, and computerized dealing systems. *Contractual Size* Futures: Standardized amount of the underlying asset. Forward: Tailor-made to the needs of the participant. *Settlement* Futures: Daily settlement, or marking-to-market, by the futures clearinghouse through the participant's margin account. Forward: Participant buys or sells the contractual amount of the underlying asset from the bank at maturity at the forward (contractual) price. *Expiration Date* Futures: Standardized delivery dates. Forward: Tailor-made delivery date that meets the need of the investor. *Delivery* Futures: Delivery of the underlying asset is seldom made. Usually, a reversing trade is transacted to exit the market. Forward: Delivery of the underlying asset is commonly made. *Trading Costs* Futures: Bid-ask spread plus broker's commission. Forward: Bid-ask spread plus indirect bank charges via compensating balance requirements.

---

[1]In the forward market, the investor holds offsetting positions after a reversing trade; in the futures market, the investor actually exits the marketplace.

In futures markets, a **clearinghouse** serves as the third party to all transactions. That is, the buyer of a futures contract effectively buys from the clearinghouse, and the seller sells to the clearinghouse. This feature of futures markets facilitates active secondary market trading because the buyer and the seller do not have to evaluate one another's creditworthiness. The clearinghouse is made up of *clearing members.* Individual brokers who are not clearing members must deal through a clearing member to clear a customer's trade. In the event of default of one side of a futures trade, the clearing member stands in for the defaulting party and then seeks restitution from that party. The clearinghouse's liability is limited because a contractholder's position is marked-to-market daily. Given this organizational structure, the clearinghouse responsibly maintains the futures margin accounts for the clearing members.

Frequently, a futures exchange may have a **daily price limit** on the futures price, that is, a limit as to how much the settlement price can increase or decrease from the previous day's settlement price. Forward markets do not have this. Obviously, when the price limit is hit, trading will halt as a new market-clearing equilibrium price cannot be obtained. Exchange rules exist for expanding the daily price limit in an orderly fashion until a market-clearing price can be established.

9.2 Currency Futures Markets

www.cme.com

This is the website of the Chicago Mercantile Exchange. It provides detailed information about the futures contracts and futures options contracts traded on it.

www.phlx.com

This is the website of the Philadelphia Stock Exchange and the Philadelphia Board of Trade. It provides detailed information about the shares and derivative products that trade on the exchanges.

www.numa.com/ref/exchange.htm

This is the website of Numa Directory. It provides the website address of most of the shares and derivative exchanges in the world.

On May 16, 1972, trading first began at the Chicago Mercantile Exchange (CME) in currency futures contracts. Trading activity in currency futures has expanded rapidly at the CME. In 1978, only two million contracts were traded; this figure stood at over 20 million contracts in 2001. Most CME currency futures trade in a March, June, September, and December expiration cycle, with the delivery date being the third Wednesday of the expiration month. The last day of trading is the second business day prior to the delivery date. Regular trading in CME currency futures contracts takes place each business day from 7:20 A.M. to 2:00 P.M. Chicago time. Additional CME currency futures trading takes place Monday through Thursday on the GLOBEX$_2$ trading system from 4:30 P.M. to 4:00 P.M. Chicago time. On Sundays trading begins at 5:30 P.M. GLOBEX$_2$ is a worldwide automated order-entry and matching system for futures and options that facilitates trading after the close of regular exchange trading. Exhibit 9.2 summarizes the basic CME currency contract specifications.

The Philadelphia Board of Trade (PBOT), a subsidiary of the Philadelphia Stock Exchange, introduced currency futures trading in July 1986. The PBOT contracts trade in the same expiration cycle as the CME currency futures, plus two additional near-term months. The delivery date is also the third Wednesday of the expiration month, with the last day of trading being the preceding Friday. The trading hours of the PBOT contracts are 2:30 A.M. to 2:30 P.M. ET, except for the Canadian dollar, which trades between 7:00 A.M. and 2:30 P.M. ET. Exhibit 9.2 shows the currencies and the size of the contracts traded on the PBOT.

In addition to the CME and the PBOT, currency futures trading takes place on the New York Board of Trade, the Mer Der Exchange in Mexico, the BM&F Exchange in Brazil, the Budapest Commodity Exchange, and the Korea Futures Exchange.

9.3 Basic Currency Futures Relationships

Exhibit 9.3 shows quotations for CME futures contracts. For each delivery month for each currency, we see the opening price quotation, the high and low quotes for the trading day—in this case Thursday, January 8, 2004—and the settlement price. Each quotation is presented in American terms, that is $F(US\$/i)$. (We use the same symbol F for futures prices as well as for forward prices and we shall explain why shortly.) For each contract, the **open interest** is also reported. This is the total number of long or short contracts outstanding for the particular delivery month. Note that the open interest is

EXHIBIT 9.2

**Currency Futures
Contract
Specifications***

Currency	Contract Size	Exchange
Price Quoted in American Dollars		
Australian dollar	AD100,000	CME, PBOT
Brazilian real	BR100,000	CME
British pound	£62,500	CME, PBOT
Canadian dollar	CD100,000	CME, PBOT
Euro FX	EUR125,000	CME
Japanese yen	¥12,500,000	CME, PBOT
Mexican peso	MP500,000	CME
New Zealand dollar	NE100,00	CME
Russian ruble	RU2,500,000	CME
South African rand	RA500,000	CME
Swiss franc	SF125,000	CME, PBOT
Cross-Rate Futures		
(Underlying Currency/Price Currency)		
Euro FX/British pound	EUR125,000	CME
Euro FX/Japanese yen	EUR125,000	CME
Euro FX/Swiss franc	EUR125,000	CME

*CME denotes Chicago Mercantile Exchange; PBOT denotes Philadelphia Board of Trade.
Sources: Chicago Mercantile Exchange website, www.cme.com and Philadelphia PBOT Board of Trade website, www.phlx.com.

greatest for the **nearby** contract, in this case the March 2004 contract. Since few of these contracts will actually result in delivery, if we were to follow the open interest in the contracts through time, we would see the number of contracts for each different currency decrease as the last day of trading, March 15, 2004, approaches. This reflects increasing activity in *reversing trades*. We would also notice increased open interest in the June 2004 contract as trading interest in the soon-to-be nearby contract picks up. In general, open interest (loosely an indicator of demand) typically decreases with the term to maturity of most futures contracts.

EXAMPLE 9.1 **Reading Futures Quotations** As an example of reading futures quotations, let us use the June 2004 Canadian dollar contract. From Exhibit 9.3, we see that on Thursday, January 8, 2004, the contract opened for trading at a price of $0.7737/C$. All prices are in American dollars per Canadian dollar, which, for clarity, we will refer to as C$. The pricing and quotes in American dollars are both conventional and reasonable, as the pricing is being done through a market based in Chicago.

Throughout the day, the June 2004 Canadian dollar futures contract traded in a range of $0.7695/C$ (low) to $0.7800 (high). Throughout its lifetime, the June 2004 contract has traded in the range of $0.6201/C$ (low) to $0.7800 (high). The settlement ("closing") price was $0.7761/C$. The open interest, or number, of the June 2004 contract outstanding was 2,685.

At the settlement price of $0.7761/C$, the holder of a long position in one contract is committing himself to paying US$77,610 for C$100,000 on the delivery day, June 14, 2004, if he actually takes delivery. Note that the settlement price increased $0.0052 from the previous day. That is, it increased from $0.7709/C$ to $0.7761/C$. Both the buyer and the seller of the contract would have had their accounts marked-to-market by the change in the settlement price. That is, one holding a long position from the previous day would have US$520 (= $.0052 × CD$100,000) added to his margin account and the short would have US$520 subtracted from his account. ∎

| EXHIBIT 9.3 | | Chicago Mercantile Exchange Currency Futures Contract Quotations | | | | | | |

	Open	High	Low	Settle	Change	Lifetime High	Lifetime Low	Open Interest
Canadian Dollar (CME) 100,000 Canadian dollars; US$ per C$								
March	.7730	.7819	.7699	.7783	.0052	.7819	.6150	69,665
June	.7737	.7800	.7695	.7761	.0052	.7800	.6201	2,685
September	.7670	.7765	.7670	.7742	.0052	.7765	.6505	1,410
December	.7710	.7738	.7710	.7723	.0052	.7740	.6940	683
Est vol 21,113; vol Wed 12,125; open interest 74,152, +1,077								
Japan Yen (CME) ¥12.5 million; US$ per ¥ (.00)								
March	.9435	.9459	.9426	.9436	-.0003	.9464	.8240	151,192
June	.9464	.9477	.9460	.9465	-.0003	.9500	.8496	7,450
Est vol 7,639; vol Wed 12,036; open interest 158,697, +2,442								
British Pound (CME) £62,500; US$ per £								
March	1.8085	1.8267	1.8015	1.8222	.0125	1.8267	1.5654	60,923
Est vol 19,478; vol Wed 13,233; open interest 61,338, +1,192								
Swiss Franc (CME) 125,000 francs; US$ per SF								
March	.8079	.8183	.8022	.8164	.0086	.8183	.7060	48,218
June	.8156	.8194	.8049	.8180	.0086	.8194	.7117	190
Est vol 19,478; vol Wed 13,233; open interest 61,338, +1,192								
Australian Dollar (CME) A$100,000; US per A$								
March	.7610	.7700	.7589	.7686	.0065	.7700	.5193	61,297
June	.7539	.7611	.7528	.7603	.0065	.7611	.5645	582
Est vol 7,616; vol Wed 7,748; open interest 62,018, +966								
Mexican Peso (CME) 500,00 Mexican Pesos, US$ per MP								
March	.09122	.09170	.09090	.09127	.00020	.09330	.08600	29,620
June	.09020	.09030	.09000	.09022	.00020	.09030	.08495	413
Est vol 8,304; vol Wed 11,368; open interest 30,400, +1,692								
EURO FX (CME) €125,000; US$ per €								
March	1.2606	1.2758	1.2537	1.2739	.0117	1.2788	1.0425	122,092
June	1.2569	1.2728	1.2510	1.2710	.0117	1.2757	1.0570	888
December	1.2543	1.2660	1.2543	1.2663	.0117	1.2670	1.0735	177
Est vol 83,003; vol Wed 69,655; open interest 123,255, −3,187								

Source: *The Wall Street Journal*, Friday 9 January 2004, p.C12. Reprinted by permission of *The Wall Street Journal*.

Even though marking-to-market is an important operational difference between the futures market and the forward market, it has little effect on the pricing of futures contracts as opposed to the way that forward contracts are priced. To see this, note the pattern of the spot and forward exchange rates for American dollar versus the Canadian dollar on January 8, 2004. As before, these are expressed in terms of American dollars per one Canadian dollar.

SPOT	0.7803		
1 month forward	0.7792		
2 months forward	0.7782	March Futures Price	0.7783
3 months forward	0.7773		
6 months forward	0.7759	June Futures Price	0.7761
12 months forward	0.7718	December Futures Price	0.7723

To the extent that the forward rates are "predicting" future spot exchange rates, the futures rates are doing so as well. In both series—forward rates and futures rate—we see the respective markets "predicting" a slight weakening of the Canadian dollar *vis-à-vis* the American dollar—hence a slight strengthening of the American dollar. Both the forward rate structure and the futures price structure display a similar chronological depreciating pattern. Thus, both the forward market and the futures market are useful for **price discovery** or obtaining the market's forecast of the spot exchange rate at different future dates.

Example 9.1 implies that futures are priced very similarly to forward contracts. In Chapter 5, we developed the Interest Rate Parity (IRP) model, which states that the forward price for delivery at time *T* is

$$F_T(\$/i) = S_0(\$/i)\frac{(1 + r_\$)^T}{(1 + r_i)^T} \tag{9.1}$$

We will use the same equation to define the futures price. This should work well since the similarities between the forward and the futures markets allow arbitrage opportunities if the prices between the markets are not roughly in accord.[2] (See Example 9.2.)

EXAMPLE 9.2 **Speculating and Hedging with Currency Futures** Suppose a trader takes a position on January 9, 2004, in one June Canadian dollar futures contract at US$0.7761. The trader holds the position until the last day of trading when the spot rate is, say, 0.7570/C$. This will also be the final settlement price because of **price convergence**. The trader's profit or loss depends upon whether he had a long or a short position in the June Canadian dollar contract. If he had a long position and if he was a speculator with no underlying position in Canadian dollars, he would have suffered a cumulative loss in his margin account of –$1,910 [= ($0.7570 – $0.7761) × C$100,000] from January 9 through June 14. This amount would have been subtracted from his margin account through daily marking-to-market. If he takes delivery, he will pay out-of-pocket US$75,700 for the Canadian $100,000, that is, the spot value. The effective cost, however, is US$77,610 (= US$75,700 + US$1,910) recognizing the amount subtracted from his margin money. Alternatively, as a hedger wanting to buy C$100,000 on June 14 for US$0.7761/C$, our trader effectively locked in a purchase price of US$77,610 from a long position in the June Canadian dollar futures contract.

If the trader had taken a short position and he was a speculator with no underlying position in Canadian dollars, he would capture a cumulative gain of US$1,910 [= (US$0.7761 – US$0.7570) × C$100,000] from January 9 through June 14 that would have been added to his margin account as a result of daily marking-to-market. If he makes delivery of the Canadian dollars, he will receive US$75,700 for the C$100,000, that is, the spot value. The effective amount that he receives, however, is US$77,610 (= US$75,700 + US$1,910) recognizing the amount that has accumulated in his margin account. Alternatively, as a hedger seeking to sell C$100,000 on June 14 for US$0.7761/C$, our traded effectively locked in a sales price of US$77,610 from a short position in the June Canadian dollar future contract. Exhibit 9.4 graphs these long and short future positions. ∎

Speculating and Hedging with Currency Futures: Managerial Perspectives

To put our discussion of Canadian dollar futures contract in a *managerial* context, it is useful to consider the sort of Canadian company or organization that might be interested in hedging with Canadian dollar futures. Let us say that Bombardier, the Montreal-based aircraft manufacturer, has sold aircraft to Wisconsin Air and that in the schedule of payments,

---

[2]As a theoretical proposition, Cox, Ingersoll, and Ross (1981) show that forward and futures prices should not be equal unless interest rates are constant or can be predicted with certainty. For practical purposes, it is not necessary to be theoretically specific.

EXHIBIT 9.4

Graph of Long and Short Positions in the June 2004 Canadian Dollar Futures Contract

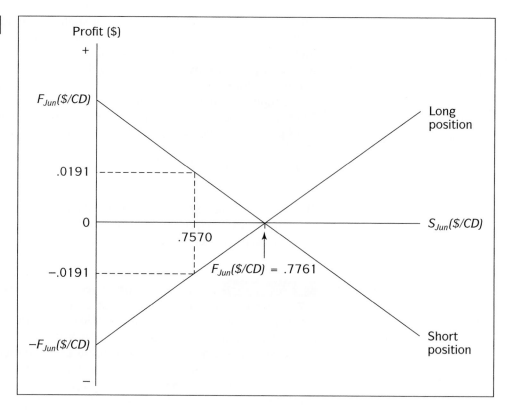

Bombardier will receive US$1,000,000 on June 14, 2004. (It is now January 2004.) As Bombardier wants certainty in its *Canadian* cashflows, Bombardier would want to hedge its exposure to the foreign exchange risk created by its American dollar receivable. Bombardier would need to take a *long* position in the June Canadian dollar futures contract.

There are two practical concerns to keep in mind as we set up a futures hedge for Bombardier. First, Bombardier's receivable is in American dollars but the Canadian dollar futures contract is specified in terms of C$100,000. Second, these contracts are created and traded in the United States and they are settled in American dollars. The following illustration continues as if Bombardier uses the services of an American-based broker who deals in foreign currency futures contracts on the Chicago Mercantile Exchange.

How many June contracts should Bombardier buy? As a starting point, it is useful to think of the *expected* number of Canadian dollars Bombardier will receive in June if the receivable is not hedged. The price of the June futures contract, at US$0.7761/C$ is a reasonable indicator, indicating that the Bombardier can expect to receive 1,000,000*(1/0.7761) or C$1,288,494 in June. But, of course, this (unhedged) expected figure is subject to substantial risk. Bombardier can address this risk by buying 13 June futures contracts at US$0.7761/C$.

Bombardier would be required to put US$1,350 per contract in a margin account.[3] This initial margin is (US$1,350 × 13) or US$17,550. The direct cost to Bombardier

---

[3]The required margin on a foreign currency futures contract is specified by the market on which the contract is traded, for example, the Chicago Mercantile Exchange. The required margin is subject to change. The margin requirement is typically increased as the volatility of the "underlying" increases which in our discussion refers to the volatility of the Canadian dollar : American dollar exchange rate. In January 2004, the required margin on one Canadian dollar futures contract (with a contract amount of C$100,000) is US$1,350 or approximately C$1,750 at the prevailing January 2004 spot rate. This is a bit less than the 2 percent margin requirement that earlier we suggested is typical. The CME's margin requirement for the Canadian dollar futures contract has *not* been changed through the rather steep run-up of the Canadian dollar from April 2003 to January 2004. At the April 2003 exchange rate of 0.6750 the margin requirement of US$1,350 was exactly C$2,000 or 2 percent of the contract value.

of this margin commitment is the cost of borrowing US$17,550 for five months. Expressed in Canadian dollars, that direct cost is ((US$17,550 / 0.7803) × 0.07 × (5/12)) assuming a Canadian interest rate of 7 percent. The second cost of the hedge is the broker's commission when buying the futures contracts and again when taking delivery of the Canadian dollars in June and closing out the margin account. The commission is US$25 per contract both in and out of the contract, or US$50 per contract on the entire arrangement, which amounts to US$650. Converting this to Canadian dollars at the January spot rate (0.7803), the commission is C$833.

Bombardier's cost of constructing a hedge with13 June Canadian dollar futures contracts is then:

Commission	$ 833
Interest on margin	656
Total[4]	$1,489

This cash expense of $1,489 can be viewed as the cost of Bombardier's insurance against a fall in the value of the American dollar *vis-à-vis* the Canadian dollar over the next five months. Of course, since the hedge mechanism is Canadian dollar futures contracts, Bombardier forgoes the "upside," that is a stronger American dollar *vis-à-vis* the Canadian dollar, while being protected on the "downside."

Our second illustration of the use of Canadian dollar futures looks at risky situation faced by the treasurer of the Province of Nova Scotia. The treasurer must make a payment of US$1,000,000 on June 14, 2004, to retire Province of Nova Scotia bonds denominated in American dollars. As before, we look at the situation as if it is January 2004.

To hedge the foreign exchange risk with Canadian dollar futures contracts, the Nova Scotia treasurer needs to be *short* an appropriate number of contracts. This problem is simply the reverse of Bombardier's situation that we have just outlined. The Nova Scotia treasurer can address the foreign exchange risk by selling 13 June futures contracts at US$0.7761/C$. The initial margin, the broker's commissions, and the interest on margin are all exactly the same as for Bombardier. For $1,489, the treasurer of Novas Scotia can hedge the foreign exchange risk involved in his bond retirement problem.

9.4 Eurodollar Interest Rate Futures Contracts

www.simex.com.sg

This is the website of the Singapore International Monetary Exchange. It provides detailed information about the derivative products traded on it.

To this point, we have considered only futures contracts written on foreign exchange. Nevertheless, future contracts are traded on many different underlying assets. One particularly important contract is the Eurodollar interest rate futures traded on the Chicago Mercantile Exchange and the Singapore International Monetary Exchange (SIMEX). The Eurodollar contract has become the most widely used futures contract for hedging short-term American dollar interest rate risk. It can be used by Eurobanks as an alternative (see problem 7 at the end of this chapter) to the forward rate agreement (FRA) we considered in Chapter 6 for hedging interest rate risk due to a maturity mismatch between Eurodollar deposits and rollover Eurocredits. Other Eurocurrency futures contracts that trade are the Euroyen, the EuroSwiss, and the EURIBOR, which began trading after the introduction of the euro.

The CME Eurodollar futures contract is written on a hypothetical $1,000,000 90-day deposit of Eurodollars. The contract trades in the March, June, September, and

[4]There are two small adjustments to this total cost figure that one might add. First, for simplicity in our illustration we assumed that the full broker's commissions—in and out—was both paid in January (in American dollars) and hence were converted to Canadian dollars at the January spot rate. In fact, the commission at the close would likely be paid in June and hence perhaps ought to be converted to Canadian dollars at the June futures rate. Second, the margin account is maintained in American dollars. This American dollar exposure has not been hedged. If the American dollar rises (falls) against the Canadian dollar from January to June, the Canadian dollar value of the change in the margin account is a foreign exchange loss (gain).

December cycle. The hypothetical delivery date is the third Wednesday of the delivery month. The last day of trading is two business days prior to the delivery date. The contract is a cash settlement contract. That is, the delivery of a $1,000,000 Eurodollar deposit is not actually made or received. Instead, final settlement is made through realizing profits or losses on the margin account on the delivery date on the basis of the final settlement price on the last day of trading. Exhibit 9.5 presents an example of CME Eurodollar futures quotations. Note that contracts trade out many years into the future.

EXAMPLE 9.3 Reading Eurodollar Futures Quotations

Eurodollar futures prices are stated as an index number of three-month LIBOR, calculated as: $F = 100 - \text{LIBOR}$. For example, from Exhibit 9.5 we see that the June 2003 contract (with hypothetical delivery on June 18, 2003) had a settlement price of 97.64 on Monday, August 19, 2002. The implied three-month LIBOR yield is, thus, 2.36 percent. The minimum price change is one basis point (bp). On $1,000,000 of face value, a one-basis-point change represents $100 on an annual basis. Since the contract is for a 90-day deposit, one basis point corresponds to a $25 price change.

EXAMPLE 9.4 Eurodollar Futures Hedge   As an example of how this contract can be used to hedge interest rate risk, consider the treasurer of a multinational corporation (MNC), who on August 19, 2002, learns that his firm expects to receive $20,000,000 in cash from a large sale of merchandise on June 21, 2003. The money will not be needed for a period of 90 days. Thus, the treasurer should invest the excess funds for this period in a money market instrument, such as a Eurodollar deposit.

The treasurer also notes that three-month LIBOR is currently 1.77 percent. The implied three-month LIBOR rate in the June 2003 contract is considerably higher at 2.36 percent. Additionally, the treasurer notes that the pattern of future expected three-month LIBOR rates implied by the pattern of Eurodollar futures prices suggests that it is expected to increase through time. Nevertheless, the treasurer believes that a 90-day rate of return of 2.36 percent is a decent rate to "lock in," and so he decides to hedge against lower three-month LIBOR in June 2003. By hedging, the treasurer is locking in a certain return of $118,000 (= $20,000,000 × 0.0236 × 90/360) for the 90-day period the MNC has $20,000,000 in excess funds.

To construct the hedge, the treasurer will need to buy, or take a long position, in Eurodollar futures contracts. At first, it may seem counterintuitive that a long position is needed, but remember, a decrease in the implied three-month LIBOR yield causes the Eurodollar futures price to increase. To hedge the interest rate risk in a $20,000,000 deposit, the treasurer will need to buy 20 June 2003 contracts.

Assume that on the last day of trading in the June 2003 contract, three-month LIBOR is 2.10 percent. The treasurer is, indeed, fortunate that he chose to hedge. At 2.10 percent, a 90-day Eurodollar deposit of $20,000,000 will generate only $105,000 of interest income, or $13,000 less than at a rate of 2.36 percent. In fact, the treasurer will have to deposit the excess funds at a rate of 2.10 percent. But the shortfall will be made up by profits from the long futures position. At a rate of 2.10 percent, the final settlement price on the June 2003 contract is 97.90 (= 100 − 2.10). The profit earned on the futures position is calculated as: [97.90 − 97.64] × 100 bp × $25 × 20 contracts = $13,000. This is precisely the amount of the shortfall.

EXHIBIT 9.5

Chicago Mercantile Exchange Eurodollar Futures Contract Quotations

	Open	High	Low	Settle	Chg	Yield Settle	Yield Chg	Open Interest
Eurodollar (CME)-$1,000,000; pts of 100%								
Aug	. . .	. . .	. . .	98.23	. . .	1.77	. . .	44,107
Sept	98.22	98.23	98.21	98.22	. . .	1.78	. . .	687,749
Oct	98.25	98.25	98.23	98.24	−.01	1.76	.01	33,143
Nov	98.26	98.26	98.24	98.26	−.01	1.74	.01	5,266
Dec	98.23	98.25	98.22	98.25	. . .	1.75	. . .	739,584
Ja03	98.20	98.20	98.19	98.20	. . .	1.80	. . .	1,933
Mar	98.00	98.04	97.98	98.04	.04	1.96	−.04	617,780
June	97.58	97.65	97.59	97.64	.03	2.36	−.03	425,705
Sept	97.21	97.20	97.13	97.19	.02	2.81	−.02	347,981
Dec	96.73	96.77	96.70	96.76	.02	3.24	−.02	292,963
Mr04	96.37	96.40	96.34	96.39	.02	3.61	−.02	183,164
June	96.11	96.14	96.08	96.12	.02	3.88	−.02	168,578
Sept	95.88	95.90	95.84	95.88	.01	4.12	−.01	127,875
Dec	95.64	95.67	95.60	95.64	.01	4.36	−.01	123,963
Mr05	95.46	95.49	95.41	95.45	. . .	4.55	. . .	106,163
June	95.27	95.31	95.20	95.26	. . .	4.74	. . .	93,989
Sept	95.13	95.14	95.04	95.09	−.01	4.91	.01	77,020
Dec	94.97	94.97	94.88	94.93	−.01	5.07	.01	55,962
Mr06	94.83	94.84	94.74	94.79	−.01	5.21	.01	56,292
June	94.67	94.69	94.59	94.64	−.01	5.36	.01	66,168
Sept	94.56	94.57	94.47	94.53	−.01	5.47	.01	48,234
Dec	94.42	94.43	94.33	94.39	−.01	5.61	.01	40,678
Mr07	94.33	94.34	94.24	94.31	. . .	5.69	. . .	30,299
June	94.23	94.24	94.14	94.21	. . .	5.79	. . .	18,623
Sp08	93.85	93.93	93.84	93.90	. . .	6.10	. . .	10,944
Dec	93.76	93.84	93.75	93.80	−.01	6.20	.01	7,807
Mr09	93.74	93.81	93.73	93.78	. . .	6.22	. . .	6,222
June	93.68	93.76	93.67	93.73	. . .	6.27	. . .	6,484
Sept	93.63	93.70	93.60	93.67	. . .	6.33	. . .	3,065
Dec	93.56	93.62	93.53	93.60	. . .	6.40	. . .	2,454
Mr10	93.56	93.62	93.53	93.59	. . .	6.41	. . .	2,807
June	93.51	93.57	93.48	93.54	. . .	6.46	. . .	2,560
Est vol 498,846; vol Fri 817,763; open int 4,486,882, −98,119.								

Source: *The Wall Street Journal,* August 20, 2002, p. C12. Reprinted by permission of *The Wall Street Journal,* © 2002 Dow Jones & Company, Inc. All Rights Reserved Worldwide.

9.5 Options Contracts: Some Preliminaries

An **option** is a contract giving the owner the right, but not the obligation, to buy or sell a given quantity of an asset at a specified price at some time in the future. Like a futures or forward contract, an option is a derivative, or contingent claim, security. Its value is derived from its definable relationship with the underlying asset—in this chapter, foreign currency, or some claim on it. An option to buy the underlying asset is a **call,** and an option to sell the underlying asset is a **put.** Buying or selling the underlying asset via the option is known as exercising the option. The stated price paid (or received) is known as the **exercise** or **striking price.** In options terminology, the buyer of an option is frequently referred to as the long, and the seller of an option is referred to as the **writer** of the option, or the short.

Because the option owner does not have to exercise the option if it is to his disadvantage, the option has a price, or **premium.** There are two types of options: American and European. The names do not refer to the continents where they are traded but, rather, to their exercise characteristics. A **European option** can be exercised only at the maturity or expiration date of the contract, whereas an **American option** can be exercised at any time during the contract. Thus, the American option allows the owner to do everything he can do with a European option, and more.

9.6 Currency Options Markets

Prior to 1982, all currency option contracts were over-the-counter options written by international banks, investment banks, and brokerage houses. Over-the-counter (OTC) options are tailor made according to the specifications of the buyer in terms of maturity length, exercise price, and the amount of the underlying currency. Generally, these contracts are written for large amounts, at least $1,000,000 of the currency serving as the underlying asset. Frequently, they are written for American dollars, with the euro, British pound, Japanese yen, Canadian dollar, and Swiss franc serving as the underlying currencies, though options are also available on less actively traded currencies. Over-the-counter options are typically European style.

In December 1982, the Philadelphia Stock Exchange (PHLX) began trading options on foreign currency. Currently, trading is in seven major currencies and the euro against the American dollar. Most trading is in *mid-month* options. These options trade in a March, June, September, and December expiration cycle with original maturities of 3, 6, 9, and 12 months, plus two near-term months so that there are always options with one-, two-, and three-month expirations. These options mature on the Friday before the third Wednesday of the expiration month.

Exhibit 9.6 shows the currencies on which options are traded at the PHLX and the amount, or size, of underlying currency per contract. Note that the size of PHLX option contracts are half the corresponding futures contract size, as noted in Exhibit 9.2. The trading hours of these contracts are 2:30 A.M. to 2:30 P.M. Philadelphia time, except for the Canadian dollar, which trades between 7:00 A.M. and 2:30 P.M.

The volume of OTC currency options trading is much larger than that of organized-exchange option trading. According to the Bank for International Settlements, in 2001 the OTC volume was approximately $60 billion per day. By comparison, exchange-traded currency option volume was approximately $1.2 billion per day, or about 10 million contracts per year. Nevertheless, the market for exchange-traded options is very important, even to the OTC market. International banks and brokerage houses frequently buy or sell standardized exchange-traded options, which they then repackage in creating the tailor-made options desired by their clients. However, at times, OTC options and forward contracts provide trading advantages over their exchange-traded counterparts, as the International Finance in Practice box on page 210 makes clear.

<table>
<tr><td rowspan="2">**EXHIBIT 9.6**

Philadelphia Stock Exchange Option Contract Specifications*</td><td>**Currency**</td><td>**Contract Size**</td><td>**Mid-Month**</td><td>**Month-End**</td><td>**Long-Term**</td></tr>
<tr><td colspan="5">*Premium Quoted in American Dollars*</td></tr>
<tr><td></td><td>Australian dollar</td><td>AD50,000</td><td>E,A</td><td>E,A</td><td>Not Traded</td></tr>
<tr><td></td><td>British pound</td><td>£31,250</td><td>E,A</td><td>E,A</td><td>E</td></tr>
<tr><td></td><td>Canadian dollar</td><td>CD50,000</td><td>E,A</td><td>E,A</td><td>Not Traded</td></tr>
<tr><td></td><td>Euro</td><td>EUR62,500</td><td>E,A</td><td>E,A</td><td>Not Traded</td></tr>
<tr><td></td><td>Japanese yen</td><td>¥6,250, 000</td><td>E,A</td><td>E,A</td><td>E</td></tr>
<tr><td></td><td>Swiss franc</td><td>SF62,500</td><td>E,A</td><td>E,A</td><td>Not Traded</td></tr>
</table>

*E denotes European-style option, A denotes American style.
Source: Philadelphia Stock Exchange, *Standardized Currency Options*, www.phlx.com

The PHLX trades a variety of options contracts in order to provide a more complete market. In addition to the *mid-month* contracts, *long-term* European-style contracts with original maturities of 18 to 24 months are traded in a June and December cycle on the British pound and the Japanese yen. The size of these contracts and the expiration procedure date are the same as the *mid-month* contracts. *Month-end* European and American-style options with original maturities of one, two, and three months began trading in 1992. All other contract terms remain the same as for the *mid-month* contracts.

The PHLX also trades currency options with custom-made contractual terms. Customized options allow users to customize the exercise price, expiration date up to two years, and the premium quotation in either units of currency or percent of underlying value for 56 currency pairs.

9.7 Currency Futures Options

The Chicago Mercantile Exchange trades American options on the currency futures contracts it offers. With these options, the underlying asset is a futures contract on the foreign currency instead of the physical currency. Options trade on each of the currency futures contracts offered by the CME (refer to Exhibit 9.2). One futures contract underlies one options contract.

Most CME futures options trade with expirations based on the most current month of the March, June, September, December expiration cycle of the underlying futures contract and two noncycle months plus four weekly expirations. For example, in January options with expirations in January, February, and March would trade on futures with a March expiration. These options expire on the second Friday prior to the third Wednesday of the options contract month. Regular trading takes place each business day from 7:20 A.M. to 2:00 P.M. Chicago time. For most contracts, extended-hour trading on the GLOBEX$_2$ system begins at 2:30 P.M. and continues until 7:05 A.M. Chicago time. On Sundays, GLOBEX$_2$ trading begins at 5:30 P.M.

Options on currency futures behave similarly to options on the physical currency, since the futures price converges to the spot price as the futures contract nears maturity. Exercise of a futures option results in a long futures position for the call buyer or the put writer and a short futures position for the put buyer or call writer. If the futures position is not offset prior to the futures expiration date, receipt or delivery of the underlying currency will, respectively, result or be required. In addition to the PHLX and the CME, there is some limited exchange-traded currency options trading at the BM&F Exchange in Brazil, on Euronext, and at the Tel-Aviv Stock Exchange.

9.8 Basic Option-Pricing Relationships at Expiration

To illustrate how currency options are priced, lets use quotations for PHLX options contracts presented in Exhibit 9.7. The exhibit shows that both European- and American-style options trade on the exchange. The American-style option quotations are the ones *without* a style designation specifically stated.

At expiration, a European option and an American option (which has not been previously exercised), both with the same exercise price, will have the same terminal value. For call options the time T expiration value can be stated per unit of foreign currency as:

$$C_{aT} = C_{eT} = Max[S_T - E, 0], \tag{9.2}$$

where C_{aT} denotes the value of the American call at expiration, C_{eT} is the value of the European call at expiration, E is the exercise price per unit of foreign currency, S_T is the expiration date spot price, and *Max* is an abbreviation for denoting the maximum of the arguments within the brackets. A call option with $S_T > E$ expires **in the money,** and

INTERNATIONAL FINANCE
I N   P R A C T I C E

Commodities: Why Isn't Currency Turmoil Sparking Future Boom?

Market turmoil usually triggers a boom in futures and options trading as hedgers scurry to cover their risks and speculators rush in search of quick profits.

But that hasn't been true of the currency pits lately.

Despite the dollar's historic slide and currency tumult in Europe this year, listed foreign-exchange derivatives have been languishing. On the Chicago Mercantile Exchange and the Philadelphia Stock Exchange, the nation's largest forums for trading currency futures and options, business fell substantially from early 1994, measured in both trading volume and the number of contracts outstanding.

Why? Exchange-traded products simply don't seem to meet the needs of most large currency traders, such as dealers, investment funds and corporations. On the immense interbank market, where $1 trillion of currency routinely changes hands a day, trading typically takes place in multimillion dollar chunks.

On the CME, by contrast, the typical contract has an underlying value of just $125,000 or less, and even the biggest amount to no more than $250,000. On a given day, only about $12 billion in CME currency contracts change hands. That's far too small for most big players, especially in major currencies like the mark or yen. The Philadelphia currency-options market is even tinier, with the average contract commanding just $45,000 of underlying value, and the daily volume running at just $1.5 billion.

Activity on the listed foreign-exchange markets is "nothing, insignificant," says David DeRosa, a director of foreign exchange trading at Swiss Bank Corp. in New York. "If you're a real player, you have to deal in the interbank market."

Even investors who would favor using listed currency derivatives find themselves driven to private, "over-the-counter" derivatives, instead. For one thing, the OTC market's well-established bank-to-bank trading network makes executing transactions there cheaper and more efficient.

"With all the trades we'd have to do to build up a position, there's a big risk of moving the market," says Mark Fitzsimmons, senior vice president of Millburn Corp., a New York-based commodity trading advisory firm, which manages about $500 million in financial futures. "We'd rather deal on the interbank market, where we can trade 24 hours and in bulk, and get a trade done very, very quickly without distorting prices."

The OTC market also frees traders from position limits and other cumbersome exchange requirements. To complete a $100 million trade on an exchange, one large institutional investor says, "we'd have to really pay up to get it done" in fees and other costs.

What's more, the Philadelphia exchange forbids speculators and hedgers from holding more than 100,000 contracts—limiting their total positions to an average $4.5 billion. And although the CME eliminated position limits on currencies a few years ago, it still requires its customers to justify their trading strategies and imposes tough reporting requirements.

Costs and hassles aren't the only things keeping big traders out of the exchanges' currency pits. Many players also see those markets as riskier than OTC markets—particularly in turbulent times.

A big reason is the listed market's relatively small size, which makes trading thinner and more volatile. The underlying value, or open interest, of OTC currency derivatives worldwide totals $14.5 trillion, according to Swaps Monitor, a newsletter that tracks the derivatives market. By contrast, total open interest of exchange-traded currency derivatives worldwide amounts to only about $450 billion—3% of that sum. And the currency pits at the CME and Philadelphia command just $70 billion and $20 billion of open interest, respectively.

While a certain measure of volatility is desirable and even necessary for a market to remain healthy, too much turmoil tends to hurt exchange-listed products by making trading even thinner and riskier. "There is a huge liquidity concern," says Swiss Bank's Mr. DeRosa.

And since the exchanges, unlike the OTC derivatives markets, don't trade actively 24 hours a day, traders risk being left in the lurch if a big market move occurs during Asian or European trading. "People are kind of scared," says Dan O'Connell, vice president of institutional foreign-exchange at First National Bank of Chicago, a unit of First Chicago Corp. "If you put on a position, and go home overnight, prices can swing dramatically and blow you out of the water."

Source: Excerpted from Suzanne McGee, "Commodities: Why Isn't Currency Turmoil Sparking Future Boom?" *The Wall Street Journal,* April 10, 1995, p. C1. Reprinted by permission of *The Wall Street Journal,* © 1995 Dow Jones & Company, Inc. All Rights Reserved Worldwide.

it will be exercised. If $S_T = E$, the option expires **at the money**. If $S_T < E$, the call option expires **out of the money,** and it will not be exercised.

A put option expires in the montey if $S_T < E$, whereas a put expires out of the money if $S_T > E$.

EXHIBIT 9.7						

Philadelphia Stock Exchange Currency Options Quotations

Options Philadelphia Exchange

			Calls		Puts	
			Vol.	Last	Vol.	Last
British Pound						156.13
31,250 Brit. Pounds-European Style						
158	Jul	16		0.23	. . .	. . .
31,250 Brit. Pounds-cents per unit.						
163	Jul	4		0.01	. . .	0.01
Euro						102.46
62,500 Euro-cents per unit.						
98	Sep		. . .	0.01	89	0.35
100	Sep		. . .	. . .	22	0.67
102	Sep		. . .	0.01	4	1.38
104	Sep		. . .	. . .	24	2.47
106	Sep	2		0.53	. . .	0.01
110	Sep	3		0.10	. . .	0.01
Japanese Yen						82.64
6,250,000 J.Yen-100ths of a cent per unit.						
80½	Sep		. . .	0.01	25	0.60
6,250,000 J.Yen-EuropeanStyle.						
80½	Sep		. . .	0.01	20	0.53
Swiss Franc						63.80
62,500 Swiss Francs-cents per unit						
67	Sep	10		0.30	. . .	. . .
68	Sep	2		0.15	. . .	. . .
Call Vol 986				Open Int 39,510		
Put Vol 3,569				Open Int 30,445		

Source: *The Wall Street Journal*, July 7, 1999, p. C14. Reprinted by permission of *The Wall Street Journal*, © 1999 Dow Jones & Company, Inc. All Rights Reserved Worldwide.

EXAMPLE 9.5 **Expiration Value of an American Call Option**

As an illustration of pricing Equation 9.2, consider the PHLX 67 Sep SF American call option from Exhibit 9.7. This option has a current premium, C_a, of 0.30 cents per SF. The exercise price is 67 cents per SF and it expires on September 10, 1999. Suppose that at expiration the spot rate is $0.7025/SF. In this event, the call option has an exercise value of 70.25 − 67 = 3.25 cents per each of the SF62,500 of the contract, or $2,031.25. That is, the call owner can buy SF62,500, worth $43,906.25 (= SF62,500 × $0.7025) in the spot market, for $41,875 (= SF62,500 × $0.67). On the other hand, if the spot rate is $0.6607/SF at expiration, the call option has a negative exercise value, 66.07 − 67 = −0.93 cents per SF. The call buyer is under no obligation to exercise the option if it is to his disadvantage, and so he should not. He should let it expire worthless, or with zero value.

Exhibit 9.8a graphs the 67 Sep SF call option from the buyer's perspective, and Exhibit 9.8b graphs it from the call writer's perspective at expiration. Note that the two graphs are mirror-images of one another. The call buyer can lose no more than the call premium but theoretically has an unlimited profit potential. The call writer can profit by no more than the call premium but theoretically can lose an unlimited amount. At an expiration spot price of $S_T = E + C_a = 67 + 0.30 = 67.30$ cents per SF, both the call buyer and writer break even, that is, neither earns nor loses anything.

The speculative possibilities of a long position in a call are clearly evident from Exhibits 9.8a and b. Anytime the speculator believes that S_T will be in excess of the breakeven point, he will establish a long position in the call. The speculator who is correct realizes a profit. If the speculator is incorrect in his forecast, the loss will be

continued

EXAMPLE   9.5   Continued

limited to the premium paid. Alternatively, if the speculator believes that S_T will be less than the breakeven point, a short position in the call will yield a profit, the largest amount being the call premium received from the buyer. If the speculator is incorrect, losses result to the extent that S_T is above the breakeven point.

Analogously, at expiration a European put and an American put will have the same value. Algebraically, the expiration value can be stated as:

$$P_{aT} = P_{eT} = Max[E - S_T, 0] \tag{9.3}$$

where P denotes the value of the put at expiration.

EXAMPLE   9.6   Expiration Value of an American Put Option

As an example of pricing Equation 9.3, consider the 104 Sep EUR American put, which has a current premium, P_a, of 2.47 cents per EUR. If S_T is $1.0307/EUR, the put contract has an exercise value of $104 - 103.07 = 0.93$ cents per EUR for each of the EUR62,500 of the contract, or $581.25. That is, the put owner can sell EUR62,500, worth $64,418.75 (= EUR62,500 × $1.0307) in the spot market, for $65,000 (= EUR62,500 × $1.04). If S_T = $1.0425/EUR, the exercise value is $104 - 104.25 = -0.25$ cents per EUR. The put buyer would not exercise the put; he should let it expire worthless with zero value.

Exhibit 9.9a graphs the 104 Sep EUR put from the buyer's perspective, and Exhibit 9.9b graphs it from the put writer's perspective at expiration. The two graphs are mirror-images of one another. The put buyer can lose no more than the put premium, and the put writer can profit by no more than the premium. The put buyer can earn a maximum profit of $E - P_a = 104 - 2.47 = 101.53$ cents per EUR if the terminal spot exchange rate is an unrealistic $0/EUR. The put writer's maximum loss is 101.53 cents per EUR. Additionally, at $S_T = E - P_a = 101.53$ cents per EUR, the put buyer and writer both break even; neither loses nor earns anything.

The speculative possibilities of a long position in a put are clearly evident from Exhibits 9.9a and b. Anytime the speculator believes that S_T will be less than the breakeven point, he will establish a long position in the put. If the speculator is correct, he will realize a profit. If the speculator is incorrect in his forecast, the loss will be limited to the premium paid. Alternatively, if the speculator believes that S_T will be in excess of the breakeven point, a short position in the put will yield a profit, the largest amount being the put premium received from the buyer. If the speculator is incorrect, very large losses can result if S_T is much smaller than the breakeven point.

9.9 American Option-Pricing Relationships

An American call or put option can be exercised at any time prior to expiration. Consequently, in a rational marketplace, American options will satisfy the following basic pricing relationships at time t prior to expiration:

$$C_a \geq Max[S_t - E, 0] \tag{9.4}$$

and

$$P_a \geq Max[E - S_t, 0] \tag{9.5}$$

These equations state that the American call and put premiums at time t will be at least as large as the immediate exercise value, or **intrinsic value,** of the call or put option. (The t subscripts are deleted from the call and put premiums to simplify the notation.) The owner of a long-maturity American option can exercise it on any date that he could exercise a shorter maturity option he held on a currency, or at some later date after the shorter maturity option expires. Therefore, it follows that all else remaining the same, the longer-term American option will have a market price at least as large as the shorter term option.

A call option with $S_t > E$ is referred to as trading in the money. If $S_t = E$ the option is trading at the money. If $S_t < E$ the call option is trading out of the money. The difference between the option premium and the option's intrinsic value is non-negative and sometimes referred to as the option's **time value.** For example, the time value for an American call is $C_a - Max[S_t - E, 0]$. The time value exists, meaning investors are willing to pay more than the immediate exercise value because the option may move more in the money, and thus become more valuable as time elapses. Exhibit 9.10 graphs the intrinsic value and time value for an American call option.

EXAMPLE 9.7 | **American Option Pricing Valuation** Let us see if Equations 9.4 and 9.5 actually hold for the 67 Sep SF American call and the 104 Sep EUR American put options we considered. For the 67 Sep SF Call,

$$0.30 \geq Max[63.80 - 67, 0] = Max[-3.20, 0] = 0.$$

Thus, the lower boundary relationship on the American call premium holds. (The spot price of 63.80 cents per SF is obtained from the beginning of the SF PHLX quotation section.) For the 104 Sep EUR put,

$$2.47 \geq Max[104 - 102.46, 0] = Max[1.54, 0] = 1.54.$$

Thus, the lower boundary relationship on the American put premium holds as well.

9.10 European Option-Pricing Relationships

The pricing boundaries for European put and call premiums are more complex because they can only be exercised at expiration. Hence, there is a time value element to the boundary expressions. Exhibit 9.11 develops the lower boundary expression for a European call.

Exhibit 9.11 compares the cost and payoffs of two portfolios an American dollar investor could make. Portfolio A involves purchasing a European call option and lending (or investing) an amount equal to the present value of the exercise price, E, at the American interest rate $r_\$$, which we assume corresponds to the length of the investment period. The cost of this investment is $C_e + E/(1 + r_\$)$. If at expiration, S_T is less than or equal to E, the call option will not have a positive exercise value, and the call owner will let it expire worthless. If at expiration, S_T is greater than E, it will be to the call owner's advantage to exercise the call; the exercise value will be $S_T - E > 0$. The risk-free loan will pay off the amount E, regardless of which state occurs at time T.

By comparison, the American dollar investor could invest in portfolio B, which consists of lending the present value of one unit of foreign currency i at the foreign interest rate r_i, which we assume corresponds to the length of the investment period. In American dollar terms, the cost of this investment is $S_t/(1 + r_i)$. Regardless of which state exists at time T, this investment will pay off one unit of foreign currency, which in American dollar terms will have value S_T.

It is easily seen from Exhibit 9.11 that if $S_T > E$, portfolios A and B pay off the same amount, S_T. However, if $S_T \leq E$, portfolio A has a larger payoff than portfolio B. It fol-

EXHIBIT 9.8A

Graph of 67 September SF Call Option: Buyer's Perspective

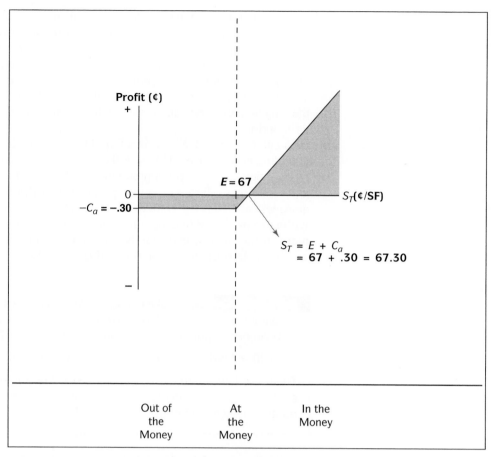

EXHIBIT 9.8B

Graph of 67 September SF Call Option: Writer's Perspective

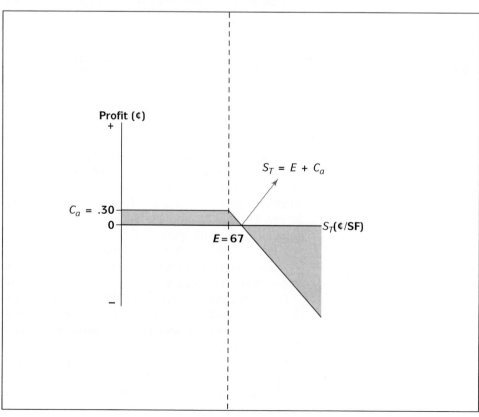

EXHIBIT 9.9A

Graph of 104 September EUR Put Option: Buyer's Perspective

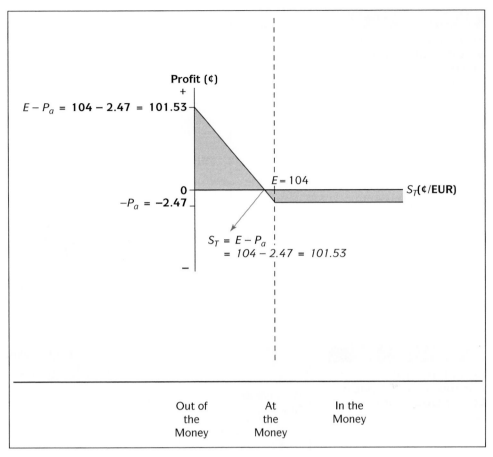

Profit (¢)

$E - P_a = 104 - 2.47 = 101.53$

$-P_a = -2.47$

$E = 104$

S_T (¢/EUR)

$S_T = E - P_a$
$= 104 - 2.47 = 101.53$

Out of the Money

At the Money

In the Money

EXHIBIT 9.9B

Graph of 104 September EUR Put Option: Writer's Perspective

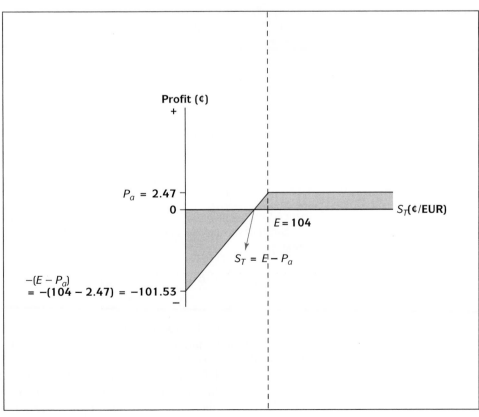

Profit (¢)

$P_a = 2.47$

$E = 104$

S_T (¢/EUR)

$S_T = E - P_a$

$-(E - P_a)$
$= -(104 - 2.47) = -101.53$

EXHIBIT 9.10

Market Value, Time Value, and Intrinsic Value of an American Call Option

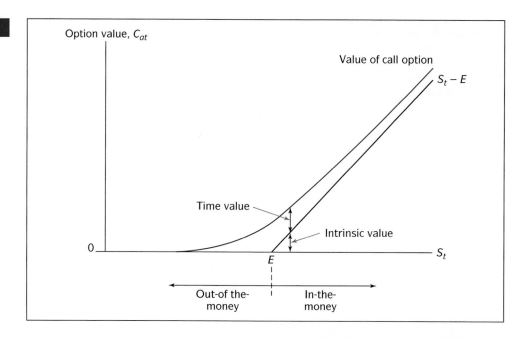

EXHIBIT 9.11

Equation for a European Call Option Lower Boundary

	Current Time	Expiration	
		$S_T \leq E$	$S_T > E$
Portfolio A:			
Buy Call	$-C_e$	0	$S_T - E$
Lend PV of E in U.S.	$\dfrac{-E/(1+r_\$)}{-C_e - E/(1+r_\$)}$	$\dfrac{E}{E}$	$\dfrac{E}{S_T}$
Portfolio B:			
Lend PV of one unit of currency i at rate r_i	$-S_t/(1+r_i)$	S_T	S_T

lows that in a rational marketplace, portfolio A will be priced to sell for at least as much as portfolio B, that is, $C_e + E/(1 + r_\$) \geq S_t /(1 + r_i)$. This implies that

$$C_e \leq Max\left[\frac{S_t}{(1 + r_i)} - \frac{E}{(1 + r_\$)}, 0\right] \qquad (9.6)$$

since the European call can never sell for a negative amount.

Similarly, it can be shown that the lower boundary pricing relationship for a European put is:

$$P_e \geq Max\left[\frac{E}{(1 + r_\$)} - \frac{S_t}{(1 + r_i)}, 0\right] \qquad (9.7)$$

The derivation of this formula is left as an exercise for the reader. (Hint: Portfolio A involves buying a put and lending spot, and portfolio B involves lending the present value of the exercise price.)

Note that both C_e and P_e are functions of only five variables: S_t, E, r_i, $r_\$$, and implicitly the term to maturity. From Equations 9.6 and 9.7, it can be determined that when all else remains the same, the call premium C_e (put premium P_e) will increase:

1. The larger (smaller) is S_t,
2. The smaller (larger) is E,
3. The smaller (larger) is r_i,
4. The larger (smaller) is $r_\$$, and
5. The larger (smaller) $r_\$$ is relative to r_i.

Implicitly, both $r_\$$ and r_i will be larger the longer the length of the option period. When $r_\$$ and r_i are not too much different in size, a European FX call and put will increase in price when the option term to maturity increases. However, when $r_\$$ is very much larger than r_i, a European FX call will increase in price, but the put premium will decrease, when the option term to maturity increases. The opposite is true when r_i is very much greater than $r_\$$.

Now, recall that IRP implies $F_T = S_t[(1 + r_\$)/(1 + r_i)]$, which, in turn, implies that $F_t/(1 + r_\$) = S_t/(1 + r_i)$. Hence, European call and put prices on spot foreign exchange, Equations 9.6 and 9.7 can be, respectively, restated as:[5]

$$C_e \geq Max\left[\frac{(F_T - E)}{(1 + r_\$)}, 0\right]$$ (9.8)

and

$$P_e \geq Max\left[\frac{(E - F_T)}{(1 + r_\$)}, 0\right]$$ (9.9)

9.11 Binomial Option-Pricing Model

The option pricing relationships we have discussed to this point have been lower boundaries on the call and put premiums, instead of exact equality expressions for the premiums. The binomial option-pricing model provides an exact pricing formula for an American call or put.[6] We will examine only a simple one-step case of the binomial model to better understand the nature of option pricing.

We want to use the binomial model to value the PHLX 67 September SF American call from Exhibit 9.7. We see from the exhibit that the option is quoted at a premium of 0.30 cents. The current spot price of the SF in American terms is $S_0 = 63.86$ cents. We will further assume that the option's volatility (annualized standard deviation of the change in the spot rate) is $\sigma = 14$ percent. The volatility on SF options has varied from less than 10 percent to over 14 percent over the past three years. This call option expires in 66 days on September 10, or in $T = 66/365 = 0.1808$ years. The one-step binomial model assumes that at the end of the option period the SF will have appreciated to $S_{uT} = S_0 \cdot u$ or depreciated to $S_{dT} = S_0 \cdot d$, where $u = e^{\sigma \cdot \sqrt{T}}$ and $d = 1/u$. The spot rate at T will be either $67.78 = 63.86 (1.06134)$ or $60.17 = 63.86 (0.94221)$, where $u = e^{0.14 \cdot \sqrt{0.1808}} = 1.06134$ and $d = 1/u = 0.94221$. At the exercise price of $E = 67$, the option will only be exercised at time T if the SF appreciates; its exercise

---

[5]An American option can be exercised at any time during its life. If it is not advantageous for the option owner to exercise it prior to maturity, the owner can let it behave as a European option, which can only be exercised at maturity. It follows from Equations 9.4 and 9.8 (for calls) and 9.5 and 9.9 (for puts) that a more restrictive lower boundary relationship for American call and put options are, respectively:

$C_a \geq Max[S_t - E, (F - E)/(1 + r_\$), 0]$ and $P_a \geq Max[E - S_t, (E - F)/(1 + r_\$), 0]$

[6]The binomial option-pricing model was independently derived by Sharpe (1978), Rendleman and Bartter (1979), and Cox, Ross, and Rubinstein (1979).

value would be $C_{uT} = 0.78 = 67.78 - 67$. If the SF depreciates it would not be rational to exercise the option; its value would be $C_{dT} = 0$.

The binominal option-pricing model only requires that $u > 1 + r_\$ > d$. The two-month Eurodollar bid rate is 5⅛ percent. Thus, $1 + r_\$ = (1.05125)^T = 1.00908$. We see that $1.06134 > 1.00908 > 0.94221$.

The binomial option-pricing model relies on the risk-neutral probabilities of the underlying asset increasing and decreasing in value. For our purposes, the risk-neutral probability of the SF appreciating is calculated as:

$$q = (F_T - S_0 \cdot d) / S_0(u - d),$$

where F_T is the forward (or futures) price that spans the option period. We will use the September SF futures price on July 6, as our estimate of $F_T(\$/SF) = \$0.6433$. Therefore,

$$q = (64.33 - 60.17)/(67.78 - 60.17) = 0.5466.$$

It follows that the risk-neutral probability of the SF depreciating is $1 - q = 1 - 0.5466 = 0.4534$.

Because the American call option can be exercised at any time, including time 0, the binomial call option premium is determined by:

$$C_0 = Max[qC_{uT} + (1 - q)C_{dT}]/(1 + r_\$), S_0 - E] \tag{9.10}$$
$$= Max[0.5466(0.78) + 0.4534(0)]/(1.00908), 63.86 - 67]$$
$$= Max[0.42, -3.14] = 0.42 \text{ cents per SF.}$$

Alternatively, (if C_{uT} is positive) the binomial call price can be expressed as:

$$C_0 = Max\{[F_T \cdot h - E((S_0 \cdot u/E)(h - 1) + 1)]/(1 + r_\$), S_0 - E\}, \tag{9.11}$$

where $h = (C_{uT} - C_{dT})/S_0(u - d)$ is the risk-free hedge ratio. The *hedge ratio* is the size of the long (short) position the investor must have in the underlying asset per option the investor must write (buy) to have a risk-free offsetting investment that will result in the investor receiving the same terminal value at time T, regardless of whether the underlying asset increases or decreases in value. For our example numbers, we see that

$$h = (0.78 - 0)/(67.78 - 60.17) = 0.1025.$$

Thus, the call premium is:

$$C_0 = Max \{[64.33(.1025) - 67((67.78/67)(0.1025 - 1) + 1)]/(1.00908), 63.86 - 67\}$$
$$= Max[0.42, -3.14] = 0.42 \text{ cents per SF.}$$

Equation 9.11 is more intuitive than Equation 9.10 because it is in the same general form as Equation 9.8. In an analogous manner, a binomial put option-pricing model can be developed. Nevertheless, for our example, the binomial call option-pricing model yielded a price that was too large compared with the actual market price of 0.30 cents. This is what we might expect with such a simple model, and when using such an arbitrary value for the option's volatility. In the next section, we consider a more refined option-pricing model.

9.12 European Option-Pricing Model

In the last section, we examined a simple one-step version of binomial option-pricing model. Instead, we could have assumed the stock price followed a multiplicative binomial process by subdividing the option period into many subperiods. In this case, S_T and C_T could be many different values. When the number of subperiods into which the option period is subdivided goes to infinity, the European call and put pricing formulas presented in this section obtain. Exact European call and put pricing formulas are:[7]

$$C_e = S_t e^{-r_i T} N(d_1) - E e^{-r_\$ T} N(d_2) \tag{9.12}$$

and

$$P_e = E e^{-r_\$ T} N(-d_2) - S_t e^{-r_i T} N(-d_1) \tag{9.13}$$

The interest rates r_i and $r_\$$ are assumed to be annualized and constant over the term to maturity T of the option contract, which is expressed as a fraction of a year.

Invoking IRP, where with continuous compounding $F_T = S_t e^{(r_\$ - r_i)T}$, C_e and P_e, Equations 9.12 and 9.13 can be, respectively, restated as:

$$C_e = [F_T N(d_1) - E N(d_2)] e^{-r_\$ T} \tag{9.14}$$

and

$$P_e = [E N(-d_2) - F_T N(-d_1)] e^{-r_\$ T} \tag{9.15}$$

where

$$d_1 = \frac{ln(F_T/E) + .5\sigma^2 T}{\sigma/\sqrt{T}}$$

and

$$d_2 = d_1 - \sigma/\sqrt{T}.$$

$N(d)$ denotes the cumulative area under the standard normal density function from $-\infty$ to d_1 (or d_2). The variable σ is the annualized volatility of the exchange rate change $ln(S_{t+1}/S_t)$. Equations 9.14 and 9.15 indicate that C_e and P_e are functions of only five variables: F_T, E, $r_\$$, T, and σ. It can be shown that both C_e and P_e increase when σ becomes larger.

The value $N(d)$ can be calculated using the NORMSDIST function of Microsoft Excel.

Equations 9.14 and 9.15 are widely used in practice, especially by international banks in trading OTC options.

EXAMPLE 9.8 **The European Option Price Model** As an example of using the European options pricing model, consider the PHLX 67 Sep SF American call option from Exhibit 9.7. We will use the European model even though the call is an American option. This is frequently done in practice, and the prices between the two option styles vary very little.[8]

The option has a premium of 0.30 American cents per SF. The option will expire on September 10—66 days from the quotation date, or $T = 66/365 = 0.1808$. We will use the September futures price on July 6, as our estimate of $F_T(\$/SF) = \$0.6433$. The rate $r_\$$ is estimated as the annualized two-month Eurodollar bid rate of 5⅛ percent. The estimated volatility is 10.7 percent.

continued

[7]The European option pricing model was developed by Biger and Hull (1983), Garman and Kohlhagen (1983), and Grabbe (1983). The evolution of the model can be traced back to European option-pricing models developed by Merton (1973) and Black (1976).

[8]Barone-Adesi and Whaley (1987) have developed an approximate American call option-pricing model that has proved quite accurate in valuing American currency call options.

EXAMPLE 9.8 | Continued

The values d_1 and d_2 are:

$$d_1 = \frac{ln(64.33/67) + 0.5(0.107)^2(0.1808)}{(0.107)\sqrt{0.1808}} = -0.8713$$

and

$$d_2 = -0.8713 - (0.107)\sqrt{0.1808} = -\sqrt{0.9168}.$$

Consequently, it can be determined that $N(-0.8713) = 0.1918$ and $N(-0.9168) = 0.1796$.

We now have everything we need to compute the model price:

$$C_e = [64.33(0.1918) - 67(0.1796)]e^{-(0.05125)(0.1808)}$$
$$= [12.3385 - 12.0332](0.9908)$$
$$= 0.30 \text{ cents per SF.}$$

As we see, the model has done a good job of valuing the SF call. The price would obviously have been higher, however, had we used a larger volatility estimate. ∎

9.13   Empirical Tests of Currency Options

Shastri and Tandon (1985) empirically test the American boundary relationships we developed in this chapter (Equations 9.4, 9.5, 9.6, 9.7, 9.8, and 9.9) using PHLX put and call data. They discover many violations of the boundary relationships but conclude that nonsimultaneous data could account for most of the violations. Bodurtha and Courtadon (1986) test the immediate exercise boundary relationships (Equations 9.4 and 9.5) for PHLX American put and call options. They also found many violations when using last daily trade data. However, when they used simultaneous price data and incorporate transaction costs, they conclude that the PHLX American currency options are efficiently priced.

Shastri and Tandon (1986) also test the European option-pricing model using PHLX American put and call data. They determine that a nonmember of the PHLX could not earn abnormal profits from the hedging strategies they examine. This implies that the European option-pricing model works well in pricing American currency options. Barone-Adesi and Whaley (1987) also find that the European option-pricing model works well for pricing American currency options that are *at* or *out of the money* but does not do well in pricing *in-the-money* calls and puts. For *in-the-money* options, their approximate American option-pricing model yields superior results.

SUMMARY

This chapter introduced currency futures and options on foreign exchange. These instruments are useful for speculating and hedging foreign exchange rate movements. In later chapters, it will be shown how to use these vehicles for hedging purposes.

1. Forward, futures, and options contracts are derivative, or contingent claim, securities. That is, their value is derived or contingent upon the value of the asset that underlies these securities.

2. Forward and futures contracts are similar instruments, but there are differences. Both are contracts to buy or sell a certain quantity of a specific underlying asset at some specific price in the future. Futures contracts, however, are exchange traded, and there are standardized features that distinguish them from the tailor-made

terms of forward contracts. The two main standardized features are contract size and maturity date.

3. Additionally, futures contracts are marked-to-market on a daily basis at the new settlement price. Hence, the margin account of an individual with a futures position is increased or decreased, reflecting daily realized profits or losses resulting from the change in the futures settlement price from the previous day's settlement price.

4. A futures market requires speculators and hedgers to effectively operate. Hedgers attempt to avoid the risk of price change of the underlying asset, and speculators attempt to profit from anticipating the direction of future price changes.

5. The Chicago Mercantile Exchange and the Philadelphia Board of Trade are the two largest currency futures exchanges.

6. The pricing equation typically used to price currency futures is the CIRP relationship, which is used also to price currency forward contracts.

7. Eurodollar interest rate futures contracts were introduced as a vehicle for hedging short-term dollar interest rate risk, in much the same way as forward rate agreements, introduced in Chapter 6.

8. An option is the right, but not the obligation, to buy or sell the underlying asset for a stated price over a stated time period. Call options give the owner the right to buy, put options the right to sell. American options can be exercised at any time during their life, European options can only be exercised at maturity.

9. Exchange-traded options with standardized features are traded on two exchanges. Options on spot foreign exchange are traded at the Philadelphia Stock Exchange, and options on currency futures are traded at the Chicago Mercantile Exchange.

10. Basic boundary expressions for put and call option prices were developed and examined using actual options-pricing data.

11. A European option-pricing model for put and call options was also presented and explained using actual market data.

KEY WORDS

American option, *208*
at-the-money, *210*
call, *207*
clearinghouse, *200*
commission, *199*
contingent claim security, *198*
contract size, *198*
daily price limit, *200*
delivery month, *198*
derivative security, *198*
European option, *208*
exchange-traded, *198*

exercise price, *207*
futures, *198*
hedger, *199*
in-the-money, *209*
initial margin, *198*
intrinsic value, *215*
long, *198*
maintenance margin, *198*
marked-to-market *198*
maturity date, *198*
nearby, *201*
open interest, *200*
option, *207*

out-of-the-money, *210*
premium, *208*
price discovery, *203*
put, *207*
reversing trade, *199*
short, *198*
speculator, *199*
standardized, *198*
striking price, *207*
time value, *215*
variation margin, *198*
writer, *207*
zero-sum game, *198*

QUESTIONS

1. Explain the basic differences between the operation of a currency forward market and a futures market.

2. In order for a derivatives market to function, two types of economic agents are needed: hedgers and speculators. Explain.

3. Why are most futures positions closed out through a reversing trade, rather than held to delivery?

4. How can the FX futures market be used for price discovery?

5. What is the major difference in the obligation of one with a long position in a futures (or forward) contract in comparison with an options contract?

6. What is meant by the terminology that an option is in, at, or out of the money?

7. List the arguments (variables) of which an FX call or put option model price is a function. How does the call and put premium change with respect to a change in the arguments?

PROBLEMS

1. Assume today's settlement price on a CME EUR futures contract is \$0.9716/EUR. You have a short position in one contract. Your margin account currently has a balance of \$1,700. The next three days' settlement prices are \$0.9702, \$0.9709, and \$0.9625. Calculate the changes in the margin account from daily marking-to-market and the balance of the margin account after the third day.

2. Do problem 1 again assuming you have a long position in the futures contract.

3. Using the quotations in Exhibit 9.3, calculate the face value of the open interest in the June 2004 Swiss franc futures contract.

4. Using the quotations in Exhibit 9.3, note that the June 2004 Mexican peso futures contract has a price of \$0.09022. You believe the spot price in June 2004 will be \$0.10000. What speculative position would you enter into to attempt to profit from your beliefs? Calculate your anticipated profits, assuming you take a position in three contracts. What is the size of your profit (loss) if the futures price is, indeed, an unbiased predictor of the future spot price and this price materializes?

5. Do problem 4 again assuming you believe the June 2004 spot price will be \$0.08000.

6. Recall the forward rate agreement (FRA) example in Chapter 6. Show how the bank can alternatively use a position in Eurodollar futures contracts to hedge the interest rate risk created by the maturity mismatch it has with the \$3,000,000 six-month Eurodollar deposit and rollover Eurocredit position indexed to three-month LIBOR. Assume the bank can take a position in Eurodollar futures contracts maturing in three months' time that have a futures price of 94.00.

7. George Johnson is considering a possible six-month, \$100-million, LIBOR-based, floating-rate bank loan to fund a project at terms shown in the table below. Johnson fears a possible rise in the LIBOR rate by December and wants to use the December Eurodollar futures contract to hedge this risk. The contract expires on December 20, 2004, has a US\$1 million contract size, and a discount yield of 7.3 percent.

Johnson will ignore the cash flow implications of marking to market, initial margin requirements, and any timing mismatch between exchange-traded futures contract cash flows and the interest payments due in March.

Loan Terms

September 20, 1999	December 20, 2004	March 20, 2005
• Borrow \$100 million at September 20 LIBOR + 200 basis points (bps)	• Pay interest for first three months	• Pay back principal plus interest
• September 20 LIBOR = 7%	• Roll loan over at December 20 LIBOR + 200 bps	

Loan initiated — First loan payment (9%) and futures contract expires — Second payment and principal

9/20/04 — 12/20/04 — 3/20/05

a. Formulate Johnson's September 20 floating-to-fixed-rate strategy using the Eurodollar future contracts discussed in the text above. Show that this strategy would result in a fixed-rate loan, assuming an increase in the LIBOR rate to 7.8 percent by December 20, which remains at 7.8 percent through March 20. Show all calculations.

Johnson is considering a 12-month loan as an alternative. This approach will result in two additional uncertain cash flows, as follows:

Loan initiated — First payment (9%) — Second payment — Third payment — Fourth payment and principal

9/20/04 — 12/20/04 — 3/20/05 — 6/20/05 — 9/20/05

b. Describe the strip hedge that Johnson could use, and explain how it hedges the 12-month loan (specify number of contracts.) No calculations are needed.

8. Jacob Bower has a liability that:
   - has a principal balance of $100 million on June 30, 2004,
   - accrues interest quarterly starting on June 30, 2004,
   - pays interest quarterly,
   - has a one-year term to maturity, and
   - calculates interest due on the basis of 90-day LIBOR (the London Interbank Offered Rate).

Bower wishes to hedge his remaining interest payments against changes in interest rates. Bower has correctly calculated that he needs to sell (short) 300 Eurodollar futures contracts to accomplish the hedge. He is considering the alternative hedging strategies outlined in the following table:

Initial Position (6/30/04) in 90-Day LIBOR Eurodollar Contracts

Contract Month	Strategy A (contracts)	Strategy B (contracts)
September 2004	300	100
December 2004	0	100
March 2005	0	100

a. Explain why strategy B is a more effective hedge than strategy A when the yield curve undergoes an instantaneous nonparallel shift.

b. Discuss an interest rate scenario in which strategy A would be superior to strategy B.

9. Use the quotations in Exhibit 9.7 to calculate the intrinsic value and the time value of the 80½ September Japanese yen American put options.

10. Assume the spot Swiss franc is $0.7000 and the six-month forward rate is $0.6950. What is the minimum price that a six-month American call option with a striking price of $0.6800 should sell for in a rational market? Assume the annualized six-month Eurodollar rate is $3\frac{1}{2}$ percent.

11. Do problem 10 again, assuming an American put option instead of a call option.

12. Use the European option-pricing models developed in the chapter to value the call of problem 10 and the put of problem 11. Assume the annualized volatility of the

Swiss franc is 14.2 percent. This problem can be solved using the FXOPM.xls spreadsheet.

13. Use the binomial option-pricing model developed in the chapter to value the call of problem 10. The volatility of the Swiss franc is 14.2 percent.

INTERNET EXERCISE

Online currency futures quotations can be found at www.castletrading.com/historiccharts.htm. Go to this website and determine in which currency there is the most trading volume today. Click on the currency name to determine in which contract expiration there is the most trading volume. Is it the near-term contract or a deferred delivery contract?

MINI CASE

The Options Speculator

A speculator is considering the purchase of five three-month Japanese yen call options with a striking price of 96 cents per 100 yen. The premium is 1.35 cents per 100 yen. The spot price is 95.28 cents per 100 yen and the 90-day forward rate is 95.71 cents. The speculator believes the yen will appreciate to $1 per 100 yen over the next three months. As the speculator's assistant, you have been asked to prepare the following:

1. Diagram the call option.
2. Determine the speculator's profit if the yen appreciates to $1/100 yen.
3. Determine the speculator's profit if the yen appreciates only to the forward rate.
4. Determine the future spot price at which the speculator will only break even.

REFERENCES & SUGGESTED READINGS

Barone-Adesi, Giovanni, and Robert Whaley. "Efficient Analytic Approximation of American Option Values." *Journal of Finance* 42 (1987), pp. 301–20.

Biger, Nahum, and John Hull. "The Valuation of Currency Options." *Financial Management* 12 (1983), pp. 24–28.

Black, Fischer. "The Pricing of Commodity Contracts." *Journal of Financial Economics* 3 (1976), pp. 167–79.

———— and Myron Scholes. "The Pricing of Options and Corporate Liabilities." *Journal of Political Economy* 81 (1973), pp. 637–54.

Bodurtha, James, Jr., and George Courtadon. "Efficiency Tests of the Foreign Currency Options Market." *Journal of Finance* 41 (1986), pp. 151–62.

Chicago Mercantile Exchange. *Using Currency Futures and Options.* Chicago: Chicago Mercantile Exchange, 1992.

Cox, John C., Jonathan E. Ingersoll, and Stephen A. Ross. "The Relation between Forward Prices and Futures Prices." *Journal of Financial Economics* 9 (1981), pp. 321–46.

Cox, John C., Stephen A. Ross, and Mark Rubinstein. "Option Pricing: A Simplified Approach." *Journal of Financial Economics* 7 (1979), pp. 229–63.

Garman, Mark, and Steven Kohlhagen. "Foreign Currency Option Values." *Journal of International Money and Finance* 2 (1983), pp. 231–38.

Grabbe, J. Orlin. "The Pricing of Call and Put Options on Foreign Exchange." *Journal of International Money and Finance* 2 (1983), pp. 239–54.

———— *International Financial Markets,* 3rd ed. Upper Saddle River, N.J.: Prentice Hall, 1996.

Merton, Robert. "Theory of Rational Option Pricing." *The Bell Journal of Economics and Management Science* 4 (1973), pp. 141–83.

Philadelphia Stock Exchange. *Understanding Foreign Currency Options* and other PHLX information brochures. Philadelphia: Philadelphia Stock Exchange, 1990.

Rendleman, Richard J., Jr., and Brit J. Bartter. "Two-State Option Pricing." *Journal of Finance* 34 (1979), pp. 1093–110.

Sharpe, William F. "Chapter 14." *Investments*. Englewood Cliffs, N.J.: Prentice Hall, 1978.

Shastri, Kuldeep, and Kishore Tandon. "Arbitrage Tests of the Efficiency of the Foreign Currency Options Market." *Journal of International Money and Finance* 4 (1985), pp. 455–68.

——— "Valuation of Foreign Currency Options: Some Empirical Tests." *Journal of Financial and Quantitative Analysis* 21 (1986), pp. 145–60.

Siegel, Daniel, and Diane Siegel. *Futures Markets*. Chicago: Dryden, 1990.

Currency and Interest Rate Swaps

CHAPTER 4 INTRODUCED forward contracts as a vehicle for hedging exchange rate risk; Chapter 9 introduced futures and options contracts on foreign exchange as alternative tools to hedge foreign exchange exposure. These types of instruments seldom have terms longer than a few years, however. Chapter 9 also discussed Eurodollar futures contracts for hedging short-term dollar-denominated interest rate risk. In this chapter, we examine interest rate swaps, both single-currency and cross-currency, which are relatively new techniques for hedging long-term interest rate risk and foreign exchange risk.

The chapter begins with some useful definitions that define and distinguish between interest rate and currency swaps. Data on the size of the interest rate and currency swap markets are presented. The next section illustrates the usefulness of interest rate swaps. The following section traces the conceptual development of currency swaps from parallel and back-to-back loans and also examines the intricacies of currency swaps. The chapter also details the risks confronting a swap dealer in maintaining a portfolio of interest rate and currency swaps and shows how swaps are priced.

10.1 Types of Swaps

In interest rate swap financing, two parties, called **counterparties,** make a contractual agreement to exchange cash flows at periodic intervals. There are two types of interest rate swaps. One is a **single-currency interest rate swap.** The name of this type is typically shortened to *interest rate swap.* The other type can be called a **cross-currency interest rate swap.** This type is usually just called a *currency swap.*

In the basic ("plain vanilla") *fixed-for-floating rate* interest rate swap, one counterparty exchanges the interest payments of a floating-rate debt obligation for the fixed-rate interest payments of the other counterparty. Both debt obligations are denominated in the same currency. Some reasons for using an interest rate swap are to better match cash inflows and outflows and/or to obtain a cost savings. There are many variants of the basic interest rate swap, some of which are discussed below.

In a **currency swap,** one counterparty exchanges the debt service obligations of a bond denominated in one currency for the debt service obligations of the other counterparty denominated in another currency. The basic currency swap involves the

Size of Interest Rate and Currency Swap Markets: Total Notional Principal Outstanding Amounts in billions of American Dollars*

Year	Interest Rate Swaps	Currency Swaps
1991	3,065	807
1992	3,851	860
1993	6,177	900
1994	8,816	915
1995	12,811	1,197
1996	19,171	1,560
1997	22,291	1,824
1998	36,262	2,253
1999	43,936	2,444
2000	48,768	3,194
2001	58,897	3,942
2002	79,161	4,509

*Notional principal is used only as a reference measure to which interest rates are applied for determining interest payments. In an interest rate swap, principal does not actually change hands. At the inception date of a swap, the market value of both sides of the swap are of equivalent value. As interest rates change, the value of the cash flows will change, and both sides may no longer be equal. This is interest rate risk. The deviation can amount to 2 to 4 percent of notional principal. Only this small fraction is subject to credit (or default) risk.
Sources: International Swaps and Derivatives Association, Inc., various year-end surveys; *International Banking and Financial Market Developments,* Bank for International Settlements, Table 18, p. 81, June 2000 and Table 19, p. A99, September 2003.

exchange of *fixed-for-fixed rate* debt service. Some reasons for using currency swaps are to obtain debt financing in the swapped denomination at a cost savings and/or to hedge long-term foreign exchange rate risk. The International Finance in Practice box on page 228 discusses the first currency swap.

10.2 Size of the Swap Market

As the International Finance in Practice box suggests, the market for currency swaps developed first. Today, however, the interest rate swap market is larger. Exhibit 10.1 provides statistics on the size and growth in the interest rate and currency swap markets. Size is measured by **notional principal,** a reference amount of principal for determining interest payments. Both markets have grown significantly since 1991, but the growth in interest rate swaps has been by far the more dramatic. The total amount of interest rate swaps outstanding increased from $3,065 billion at year-end 1991 to $79.2 trillion by the end of 2002, an increase of over 2,000 percent. Total outstanding currency swaps increased 400 percent, from $807 billion at year-end 1991 to over $4.5 trillion by year-end 2002.

While not shown in Exhibit 10.1, the five most common currencies used to denominate interest rate and currency swaps were the American dollar, euro, Japanese yen, British pound sterling, and the Swiss franc.

10.3 The Swap Bank

A **swap bank** is a generic term to describe a financial institution that facilitates swaps between counterparties. A swap bank can be an international commercial bank, an investment bank, a merchant bank, or an independent operator. The swap bank serves as either a **swap broker** or **swap dealer.** As a broker, the swap bank matches counterparties but does not assume any risk of the swap. The swap broker receives a commission for this service. Today, most swap banks serve as dealers or market makers. As a market maker, the swap bank stands willing to accept either side of a currency swap, and then later lay it off or match it with a counterparty. In this capacity, the swap bank assumes a position in the swap and therefore assumes certain risks. The dealer capacity is obviously the more risky, and the swap bank would receive a portion of the cash flows passed through it to compensate it for bearing this risk.

INTERNATIONAL FINANCE
IN PRACTICE

The World Bank's First Currency Swap

The World Bank frequently borrows in the national capital markets around the world and in the Eurobond market. It prefers to borrow currencies with low nominal interest rates, such as the deutsche mark and the Swiss franc. In 1981, the World Bank was near the official borrowing limits in these currencies but desired to borrow more. By coincidence, IBM had a large amount of deutsche mark and Swiss franc debt that it had incurred a few years earlier. The proceeds of these borrowings had been converted to dollars for corporate use. Salomon Brothers convinced the World Bank to issue Eurodollar debt with maturities matching the IBM debt in order to

enter into a currency swap with IBM. IBM agreed to pay the debt service (interest and principal) on the World Bank's Eurodollar bonds, and in turn, the World Bank agreed to pay the debt service on IBM's deutsche mark and Swiss franc debt. While the details of the swap were not made public, both counterparties benefited through a lower all-in cost (interest expense, transaction costs, and service charges) than they otherwise would have had. Additionally, the World Bank benefited by developing an indirect way to obtain desired currencies without going directly to the German and Swiss capital markets.

10.4 | Interest Rate Swaps

Basic Interest Rate Swap

EXAMPLE 10.1 A Plain Vanilla Interest Rate Swap As an example of a basic interest rate swap, consider the following example of a fixed-for-floating rate swap. Bank A is an AAA-rated international bank located in the United Kingdom. The bank needs $10,000,000 to finance floating-rate Eurodollar term loans to its clients. It is considering issuing five-year floating-rate notes indexed to LIBOR. Alternatively, the bank could issue five-year fixed-rate Eurodollar bonds at 10 percent. The FRNs make the most sense for Bank A, since it would be using a floating-rate liability to finance a floating-rate asset. In this manner, the bank avoids the interest rate risk associated with a fixed-rate issue. Bank A could end up paying a higher rate than it is receiving on its loans should LIBOR fall substantially.

Company B is a BBB-rated industrial company. It needs $10,000,000 to finance a capital expenditure with a five-year economic life. It can issue five-year fixed-rate bonds at a rate of 11.75 percent in the American dollar bond market. Alternatively, it can issue five-year FRNs at LIBOR plus 0.50 percent. The fixed-rate debt makes the most sense for Company B because it locks in a financing cost. The FRN alternative could prove very unwise should LIBOR increase substantially over the life of the note and could possibly result in the project being unprofitable.

A swap bank familiar with the financing needs of Bank A and Company B has the opportunity to set up a fixed-for-floating interest rate swap that will benefit each counterparty and the swap bank. The key, or necessary condition, giving rise to the swap is that a **quality spread differential (QSD)** exists. A QSD is the difference between the default-risk premium differential on the fixed-rate debt and the default-risk premium differential on the floating-rate debt. In general, the former is greater than the latter. The reason for this is that the yield curve for lower-quality debt tends to be steeper than the yield curve for higher-rated debt because lenders have the option not to renew, or roll over, short-term debt. Thus, they do not need to be concerned with "locking in" a high default-risk premium. Exhibit 10.2 shows the calculation of the QSD.

Given that a QSD exists, it is possible for each counterparty to issue the debt alternative that is least advantageous for it (given its financing needs), then swap interest payments, such that each counterparty ends up with the type of interest payment desired, but at a lower all-in cost than it could arrange on its own. Exhibit 10.3 diagrams a possible scenario the swap bank could arrange for the two

continued

	Company B	Bank A	Differential
EXHIBIT 10.2 **Calculation of Quality Spread Differential**			
Fixed-rate	11.75%	10.00%	1.75%
Floating-rate	LIBOR + 0.50%	LIBOR	0.50%
			QSD = 1.25%

EXHIBIT 10.3

Fixed-For-Floating Interest Rate Swap*

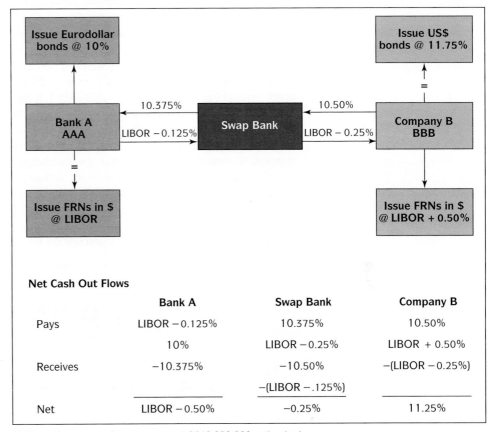

Net Cash Out Flows

	Bank A	Swap Bank	Company B
Pays	LIBOR − 0.125%	10.375%	10.50%
	10%	LIBOR − 0.25%	LIBOR + 0.50%
Receives	−10.375%	−10.50%	−(LIBOR − 0.25%)
		−(LIBOR − .125%)	
Net	LIBOR − 0.50%	−0.25%	11.25%

*Debt service expressed as a percentage of $10,000,000 notional value.

EXAMPLE 10.1 **Continued**

counterparties. The interest rates used in Exhibit 10.3 refer to the percentage rate paid per annum on the notional principal of $10,000,000.

From Exhibit 10.3, we see that the swap bank has instructed Company B to issue FRNs at LIBOR plus 0.50 percent, rather than the more suitable fixed-rate debt at 11.75 percent. Company B passes through to the swap bank 10.50 percent (on the notional principal of $10,000,000) and receives LIBOR minus 0.25 percent in return. In total, Company B pays 10.50 percent (to the swap bank) plus LIBOR + 0.50 percent (to the floating-rate bondholders) and receives LIBOR − 0.25 percent (from the swap bank) for an **all-in cost** (interest expense, transaction costs, and service charges) of 11.25 percent. Thus, through the swap, Company B has converted floating-rate debt into fixed-rate debt at an all-in cost 0.50 percent lower than the 11.75 percent fixed rate it could arrange on its own.

Similarly, Bank A was instructed to issue fixed-rate debt at 10 percent, rather than the more suitable FRNs. Bank A passes through to the swap bank LIBOR − 0.125 percent and receives 10.375 percent in return. In total, Bank A pays 10 percent (to the fixed-rate Eurodollar bondholders) plus LIBOR − 0.125 percent (to the

continued

EXAMPLE 10.1 Continued

swap bank) and receives 10.375 percent (from the swap bank) for an all-in cost of LIBOR − 0.50 percent. Through the swap, Bank A has converted fixed-rate debt into floating-rate debt at an all-in cost 0.50 percent lower than the floating rate of LIBOR it could arrange on its own.

The swap bank also benefits because it pays out less than it receives from each counterparty to the other counterparty. Note from Exhibit 10.3 that it receives 10.50 percent (from Company B) plus LIBOR − 0.125 percent (from Bank A) and pays 10.375 percent (to Bank A) and LIBOR − 0.25 percent (to Company B). The net inflow to the swap bank is 0.25 percent per annum on the notional principal of $10,000,000. In sum, Bank A has saved 0.50 percent, Company B has saved 0.50 percent, and the swap bank has earned 0.25 percent. This totals 1.25 percent, which equals the QSD. Thus, if a QSD exists, it can be split in some fashion among the swap parties resulting in lower all-in costs for the counterparties.

In an interest rate swap, the principal sums the two counterparties raise are not exchanged, since both counterparties have borrowed in the same currency. The amount of interest payments that are exchanged are based on a notional sum, which may not equal the exact amount actually borrowed by each counterparty. Moreover, while Exhibit 10.3 portrays a gross exchange of interest payments based on the notional principal, in practice, only the net difference is actually exchanged. For example, Company B would pay to the swap bank the net difference between 10.50 percent and LIBOR − 0.25 percent on the notional value of $10,000,000.

Supplementary Material

EXAMPLE 10.2 **Pricing** After the inception of an interest rate swap, it may become desirable for one and/or the other counterparty to get out of, or sell, the swap. The value of an interest rate swap to a counterparty should be the difference in the present values of the payment streams the counterparty will receive and pay on the notional principal. As an example, consider Company B from Example 10.1. Company B pays 10.50 percent to the swap bank and receives LIBOR − 0.25 percent from the swap bank on a notional value of $10,000,000. It has an all-in cost of 11.25 percent because it has issued FRNs at LIBOR + 0.50 percent.

Suppose that one year later, fixed rates have fallen from 10.50 percent to 9 percent for BBB-rated issuers. Assuming a perfectly matched swap, this will also be a reset date for the FRNs. On any reset date, the present value of the future floating-rate payments Company B will receive from the swap bank based on the notional value will always be $10,000,000. The present value of a hypothetical bond issue of $10,000,000 with four remaining 10.50 percent coupon payments at the new fixed rate of 9 percent is $10,485,960 = $1,050,000 × $PVIFA_{9\%,4}$ + $10,000,000 × $PVIF_{9\%,4}$. The value of the swap is $10,000,000 − $10,485,960 = −$485,960. Thus, Company B should be willing to pay up to $485,960 to get out of, or "sell," the swap.

10.5 Currency Swaps

Currency swaps evolved from parallel and back-to-back loans. Following the collapse of the Bretton Woods fixed exchange rate agreement, exchange rate volatility created the need among the multinational corporations (MNCs) for vehicles to hedge long-term foreign exchange exposure. While parallel and back-to-back loans are useful as tools for currency risk management and cost reduction, they were created for a different purpose.

Parallel Loans

Parallel loans were originally created as a way to circumvent exchange controls the United Kingdom imposed in the early 1970s. To encourage domestic investment, the British government imposed taxes on foreign exchange transactions involving its currency to make foreign investment more expensive and, thus, less attractive. Through a parallel loan, these taxes could be avoided.

EXAMPLE 10.3 A Parallel Loan An example will help explain the mechanics of a parallel loan. To begin with, a parallel loan involves four parties. Consider a British parent firm with a wholly owned subsidiary in Canada. The British parent could fund a capital expenditure of its subsidiary by borrowing British pound sterling in the British capital market at a fixed annual rate of 10 percent, then converting the proceeds to Canadian dollars. However, the exchange of British pounds sterling at the outset followed by periodic purchases of British pounds sterling with Canadian dollars involves substantial and costly foreign transactions. An alternative is for the Canadian subsidiary of the British parent to raise Canadian dollars directly in the Canadian capital market. Assume, however, that because the subsidiary is not well known in the Canadian capital market, it would have to borrow at a premium of 2 percent over the normal borrowing fixed rate of 11 percent.

Suppose that an analogous situation exists for a Canadian parent and its British subsidiary. The Canadian parent can borrow in Canada at a fixed rate of 11 percent, and the subsidiary would be charged 13 percent to borrow pound sterling in the British capital market.

A way around the foreign exchange transactions would be for the two parent firms to each borrow in its capital markets and to relend to the other's subsidiary. The British parent would agree to lend the British subsidiary of the Canadian parent the pounds sterling it borrowed in the British capital market at 10 percent, saving the British subsidiary 3 percent. The Canadian parent would borrow Canadian dollars at 11 percent and relend to the Canadian subsidiary of the British parent, saving it 2 percent. Moreover, since no currency exchanges are made, the parallel loan does not violate foreign exchange restrictions of either country.

Exhibit 10.4 outlines the example. Note that there is a transfer of the Canadian dollar principal between the Canadian parent and the British parent's Canadian subsidiary at inception and a transfer back at the maturity date of the loan so that the Canadian parent can repay the loan. Similarly, there is a transfer of the pound sterling principal from the British parent to the Canadian parent's subsidiary in the United Kingdom and a transfer back at the maturity date so that the British parent can retire its loan. During the term of the loans, the Canadian subsidiary of the British parent earns revenues in Canadian dollars so that it can pay the Canadian dollar debt service to the Canadian parent to pay to the Canadian lender. Similarly, the British subsidiary of the Canadian parent earns revenues in pounds sterling so that it can pay the pound sterling debt service to the British parent to pay the British lender.

■

EXHIBIT 10.4

Parallel Loan

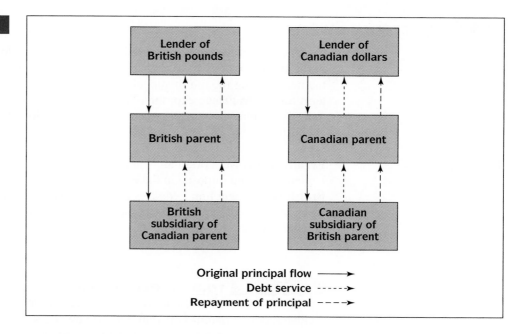

Original principal flow ⟶

Debt service - - - - -▸

Repayment of principal – – –▸

Back-to-Back Loans

EXAMPLE 10.4 A Back-to-Back Loan The **back-to-back loan** involves two parties instead of four. To continue with Example 10.3, the British and Canadian parent firms would lend directly to one another in a back-to-back loan. As Exhibit 10.5 shows, the British parent would borrow pounds sterling in the British capital market and relend the principal sum to the Canadian parent. The Canadian parent would borrow Canadian dollars in the Canadian capital market and relend the principal sum to the British parent. It is assumed that the relending is at cost. That is, the British parent relends at its borrowing cost of 10 percent and the Canadian parent relends at its cost of 11 percent. At the maturity date of the debt, the principal sums would be re-exchanged in order for the two parent firms to retire their debts in their national capital markets. Annually, each parent firm would pay to the other the annual debt service in the currency needed by the recipient to make the payment in its national capital market. In this example, the Canadian parent would pay pounds sterling to the British parent and receive Canadian dollars from the British parent.

The parent firms can obviously relend the foreign currency proceeds to a foreign subsidiary. Thus, the Canadian parent may relend the pounds sterling to its British subsidiary, and the British parent may relend the Canadian dollar proceeds to its Canadian subsidiary. The major difference between a parallel loan and a back-to-back loan is the party to whom the parent firm lends. ∎

Institutional Difficulties of Parallel and Back-to-Back Loans

There are two problems with parallel and back-to-back loans. First, both are time consuming and expensive to establish. Time must be spent searching for a party with financial needs that mirror the other party's. This search is expensive and may perhaps be fruitless. Moreover, each loan agreement is separate from the other. For example, the parallel loan agreement between the British parent and the Canadian subsidiary in the United Kingdom is independent of the loan agreement between the Canadian parent firm and the British subsidiary in Canada. Consequently, if one party defaults, say, the Canadian subsidiary, the British subsidiary is still liable to the Canadian parent. A separate registered agreement called a *rights of set-off* must be in effect to help eliminate this problem. A currency swap is a natural extension of parallel and back-to-back loans that addresses the rights of set-off as part of its basic structure.

EXHIBIT 10.5

Back-to-Back Loan

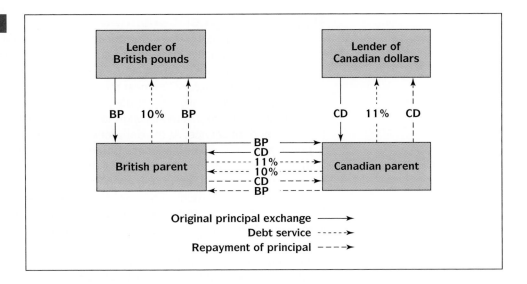

Basic Currency Swap

EXAMPLE **10.5** **A Basic Currency Swap** As an example of a basic currency swap, consider the following example. An American MNC wants to finance a capital expenditure of its German subsidiary. The project has an economic life of five years. The cost of the project is €40,000,000. At the current exchange rate of $0.90/€1, the parent firm could raise $36,000,000 in the American capital market by issuing five-year bonds at 8 percent. The parent would then convert the dollars to euros to pay the project cost. The German subsidiary would be expected to earn enough on the project to meet the annual dollar debt service and to repay the principal in five years. The only problem with this situation is that a long-term transaction exposure is created. If the dollar appreciates substantially against the euro over the loan period, it may be difficult for the German subsidiary to earn enough in euros to service the dollar loan.

An alternative is for the American parent to raise €40,000,000 in the international bond market by issuing euro-denominated Eurobonds. (The American parent might instead issue euro-denominated foreign bonds in the German capital market.) However, if the American MNC is not well known, it will have difficulty borrowing at a favourable rate of interest. Suppose the American parent can borrow €40,000,000 for a term of five years at a fixed rate of 7 percent. The current normal borrowing rate for a well-known firm of equivalent creditworthiness is 6 percent.

Assume a German MNC of equivalent creditworthiness has a mirror-image financing need. It has an American subsidiary in need of $36,000,000 to finance a capital expenditure with an economic life of five years. The German parent could raise €40,000,000 in the German bond market at a fixed rate of 6 percent and convert the funds to dollars to finance the expenditure. Transaction exposure is created, however, if the euro appreciates substantially against the dollar. In this event, the American subsidiary might have difficulty earning enough in dollars to meet the debt service. The German parent could issue Eurodollar bonds (or alternatively, Yankee bonds in the American capital market), but since it is not well known, its borrowing cost would be, say, a fixed rate of 9 percent.

A swap bank familiar with the financing needs of the two MNCs could arrange a currency swap that would solve the double problem of each MNC, that is, be confronted with long-term transaction exposure or borrow at a disadvantageous rate. The swap bank would instruct each parent firm to raise funds in its national capital market where it is well known and has a **comparative advantage** because of name

continued

EXAMPLE │ **10.5** │ **Continued**

or brand recognition. Then, the principal sums would be exchanged through the swap bank. Annually, the German subsidiary would remit to its American parent €2,400,000 in interest (6 percent of €40,000,000) to be passed through the swap bank to the German MNC to meet the euro debt service. The American subsidiary of the German MNC would annually remit $2,880,000 in interest (8 percent of $36,000,000) to be passed through to the swap bank to the American MNC to meet the dollar debt service. At the debt retirement date, the subsidiaries would remit the principal sums to their respective parents to be exchanged through the swap bank in order to pay off the bond issues in the national capital markets. The structure of this currency swap is diagrammed in Exhibit 10.6.

Exhibit 10.6 demonstrates that there is a cost savings for each counterparty because of their relative comparative advantage in their respective national capital markets. The currency swap also serves to contractually lock in a series of future foreign exchange rates for the debt service obligations of each counterparty. At inception, the principal sums are exchanged at the current exchange rate of $0.90/€1 = $36,000,000/€40,000,000. Each year, prior to debt retirement, the swap agreement calls for the counterparties to exchange $2,880,000 of interest on the dollar debt for €2,400,000 of interest on the euro debt; this is a contractual rate of $1.20/€1. At the maturity date, a final exchange, including the last interest payments and the re-exchange of the principal sums, would take place: $38,880,000 for €42,400,000. The contractual exchange rate at year 5 is, thus, $0.9170/€1. Clearly, the swap locks in foreign exchange rates for each counterparty to meet its debt service obligations over the term of the swap.

■

EXHIBIT 10.6   **$/€ Currency Swap**

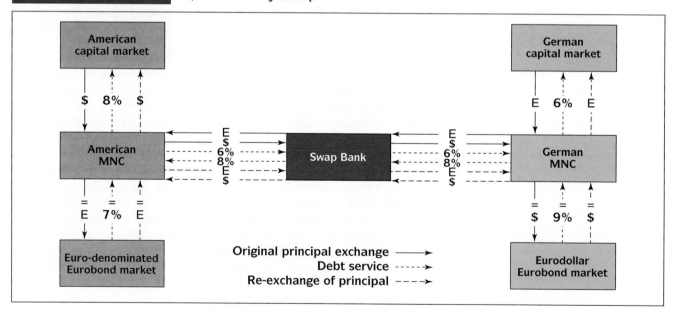

EXAMPLE 10.6 **Equivalency of Currency Swap Debt Service**

To continue with Example 10.5, it superficially appears that the German counterparty is not getting as good a deal from the currency swap as the American counterparty. The reasoning is that the German counterparty is borrowing at a rate of 6 percent (€2,400,000 per year) but paying 8 percent ($2,880,000). The American counterparty receives the $2,880,000 and pays €2,400,000. This reasoning is fraught with an ill-appreciation for international parity relationships, as Exhibit 10.7 is designed to show. In short, the exhibit shows that borrowing euros at 6 percent is equivalent to borrowing dollars at 8 percent.

Line 1 of Exhibit 10.7 shows the cash flows of the euro debt in millions. Line 2 shows the cash flows of the dollar debt in millions. The all-in-cost (AIC) for each cash flow stream is also shown for each currency. Line 3 shows the contractual foreign exchange rates between the two counterparties that are locked in by the swap agreement. Line 4 shows the foreign exchange rate that each counterparty and the market should expect on the basis of covered interest rate parity (IRP) and the forward rate being an unbiased predictor of the expected spot rate, if we can assume that IRP holds between the 6 percent euro rate and the 8 percent dollar rate. This appears reasonable, since these rates are, respectively, the best rates available for each counterparty who is well known in its national market. According to this parity relationship: $\bar{S}_t(\$/€) = S_0[1.08/1.06]^t$. For example, from the exhibit $0.934/€1 = $0.90[1.08/1.06]^2$.

Line 5 shows the equivalent cash flows in euros that have a present value of €40,000,000 at a rate of 6 percent. Without the currency swap, the German MNC would have to convert dollars into euros to meet the euro debt service. The expected rate at which the conversion would take place in each year is given by the implicit foreign exchange rates in line 4. Line 5 can be viewed as a conversion of the cash flows of line 2 via the implicit exchange rates of line 4. That is, for year 1, $2,880,000 has an expected value of €3,140,000 at the expected exchange rate of $0.917/€1. For year 2, $2,880,000 has an expected value of €3,080,000 at an exchange rate of $0.934/€1. Note that the conversion at the implicit exchange rates converts *8 percent cash flows* into *6 percent cash flows*.

The lender of €40,000,000 should be indifferent between receiving the cash flows of line 1 or the cash flows of line 5 from the borrower. From the borrower's standpoint, however, the cash flows of line 1 are free of foreign exchange risk because of the currency swap, whereas the cash flows of line 5 are not. Thus, the borrower prefers the certainty of the swap, regardless of the equivalency.

Line 6 shows in dollar terms the cash flows based on the implicit foreign exchange rates of line 4 that have a present value of $36,000,000. Line 6 can be viewed as a conversion of the 6 percent cash flows of line 1 into the 8 percent cash flows of line 6 via these expected exchange rates. A lender should be indifferent between these and the cash flow stream of line 2. The borrower will prefer to pay the cash flows of line 2, however, because they are free of foreign exchange risk. ∎

EXHIBIT 10.7	Equivalency of Currency Swap Cash Flows						
	Time of Cash Flow						
	0	1	2	3	4	5	AIC
1. Euro debt cash flow	40	−2.40	−2.40	−2.40	−2.40	−42.40	6%
2. $ Debt cash flow	36	−2.88	−2.88	−2.88	−2.88	−38.88	8%
3. Contractual FX rate	0.900	0.833	0.833	0.833	0.833	0.917	NA
4. Implicit FX rate	0.900	0.917	0.934	0.952	0.970	0.988	NA
5. Indifference euro cash flow	40	−3.14	−3.08	−3.03	−2.97	−39.35	6%
6. Indifference $ cash flow	36	−2.20	−2.24	−2.28	2.33	−41.89	8%

Note: Lines 1 and 5 present alternative cash flows in euros that have present values of €40,000,000 at a 6 percent discount rate. The cash flows in line 1 are free of exchange risk if the swap is undertaken, whereas the implicit cash flows of line 5 are not if the swap is forgone. The certain cash flows are preferable. The uncertain euro cash flows of line 5 are obtained by dividing the dollar cash flows of line 2 by the corresponding implicit FX rate of line 4. Analogously, lines 2 and 6 present alternative cash flows in American dollars that have present values of $36,000,000 at an 8 percent discount rate. The cash flows in line 2 are free of exchange risk if the swap is undertaken, whereas the implicit cash flows of line 6 are not if the swap is forgone. The certain cash flows are preferable. The uncertain dollar cash flows of line 6 are obtained by multiplying the euro cash flows of Line 1 by the corresponding implicit FX rate of Line 4.

EXAMPLE 10.7 │ Pricing the Basic Currency Swap

Suppose that a year after the American dollar–euro swap was arranged, interest rates have decreased in the United States from 8 percent to 6.75 percent and in the euro zone from 6 to 5 percent. Further assume that because the American rate decreased proportionately more than the euro zone rate, the dollar appreciated versus the euro. Instead of being $0.917/€1 as expected, it is $0.915/€1. One or both counterparties might be induced to sell their position in the swap to a swap dealer in order to refinance at the new lower rate.

The market value of the American dollar debt is $37,532,887; this is the present value of the four remaining coupon payments of $2,880,000 and the principal of $36,000,000 discounted at 6.75 percent. Similarly, the market value of the euro debt at the new rate of 5 percent is €41,418,380. The American counterparty should be willing to buy its interest in the currency swap for $37,532,887 − €41,418,380 × 0.915 = −$364,931. That is, the American counterparty should be willing to pay $364,931 to give up the stream of dollars it would receive under the swap agreement in return for not having to pay the euro stream. The American MNC is then free to refinance the $36,000,000 8 percent debt at 6.75 percent, and perhaps enter into a new currency swap.

From the German counterparty's perspective, the swap has a value of €41,418,380 − $37,532,887/0.915 = €398,831. The German counterparty should be willing to accept €398,831 to sell the swap, that is, give up the stream of euros in return for not having to pay the dollar stream. The German MNC is then in a position to refinance the €40,000,000 six percent debt at the new rate of 5 percent. The German firm might also enter into a new currency swap. ■

10.6 Swap Market Quotations

Swap banks will tailor the terms of interest rate and currency swaps to customers' needs. They also make a market in generic "plain vanilla" swaps and provide current market quotations applicable to counterparties with Aa or Aaa credit ratings. Consider a basic American dollar fixed-for-floating interest rate swap indexed to dollar LIBOR. A swap bank will typically quote a fixed-rate bid-ask spread (either semiannual or annual) versus six-month dollar LIBOR flat, that is, no credit premium. Suppose the quote for a five-year swap with semiannual payments is 8.50–8.60 percent. This means the swap bank will pay semiannual fixed-rate dollar payments of 8.50 percent against receiving six-month dollar LIBOR, or it will receive semiannual fixed-rate dollar payments at 8.60 percent against paying six-month dollar LIBOR.

It is conventional for swap banks to quote interest rate swap rates for a currency against a local standard reference in the same currency and currency swap rates against dollar LIBOR. For example, for Swiss francs suppose the bid-ask swap quotation is 6.60–6.70 percent. This means the swap bank will pay semiannual fixed-rate SF payments at 6.60 percent against receiving six-month SF (dollar) LIBOR in an interest rate (a currency) swap, or it will receive semiannual fixed-rate SF payments at 6.70 percent against paying six-month SF (dollar) LIBOR in an interest rate (a currency) swap.

It follows that if the swap bank is quoting 8.50–8.60 percent in dollars and 6.60–6.70 percent in SF against six-month dollar LIBOR, it will enter into a currency swap in which it would pay semiannual fixed-rate dollar payments of 8.50 percent in return for receiving semiannual fixed-rate SF payments at 6.70 percent, or it will receive semiannual fixed-rate dollar payments at 8.60 percent against paying semiannual fixed-rate SF payments at 6.60 percent.

As an illustration of interest rate swap quotations, on Wednesday, October 2, 2002, the following composite semiannual American dollar swap rates against six-month dollar LIBOR were listed on Bloomberg.

Term	Bid	Ask
2 Year	2.15	2.17
3 Year	2.63	2.65
4 Year	3.00	3.02
5 Year	3.31	3.34
10 Year	4.29	4.42
15 Year	4.79	4.83
20 Year	5.03	5.05

Swap banks typically build swap yield curves such as this from the 90-day LIBOR rates implied in the Eurodollar interest rate futures contracts we discussed in the previous chapter.

10.7 Variations of Basic Currency and Interest Rate Swaps

There are several variants of the basic currency and interest rate swaps we have discussed. Currency swaps, for example, need not involve the swap of fixed-rate debt. *Fixed-for-floating* and *floating-for-floating* currency rate swaps are also frequently arranged. Additionally, *amortizing* currency swaps incorporate an amortization feature in which periodically the amortized portions of the notional principals are re-exchanged. A fixed-for-floating interest rate swap does not require a fixed-rate coupon bond. A variant is a *zero-coupon-for-floating* rate swap, where the floating-rate payer makes the standard periodic floating-rate payments over the life of the swap, but the fixed-rate payer makes a single payment at the end of the swap. Another variation is the *floating-for-floating* interest rate swap. In this swap, each side is tied to a different floating rate index (e.g., LIBOR and Treasury bills) for a different frequency of the same index (such as three-month and six-month LIBOR). For a swap to be possible, a QSD must still exist. Additionally, interest rate swaps can be established on an amortizing basis, where the debt service exchanges decrease periodically through time as the hypothetical notional principal is amortized. See the International Finance in Practice box on page 239 for an interesting example of a currency swap.

10.8 Risks of Interest Rate and Currency Swaps

A swap dealer confronts a variety of risks. Some of the major ones are discussed here.
Interest-rate risk refers to the risk of interest rates changing unfavourably before the swap bank can lay off to an opposing counterparty the other side of an interest rate

swap entered into with a counterparty. As an illustration, reconsider the interest rate swap example, Example 10.1. In that example, the swap bank earns a spread of 0.25 percent. Company B passes through to the swap bank 10.50 percent per annum (on the notional principal of $10,000,000) and receives LIBOR minus 0.25 percent in return. Bank A passes through to the swap bank LIBOR 0.125 percent and receives 10.375 percent in return. Suppose the swap bank entered into the position with Company B first. If fixed rates increase substantially, say, by 0.50 percent, Bank A will not be willing to enter into the opposite side of the swap unless it receives, say, 10.875 percent. This would make the swap unprofitable for the swap bank.

Basis risk refers to a situation in which the floating-rates of the two counterparties are not pegged to the same index. Any difference in the indexes is known as the basis. For example, one counterparty could have its FRNs pegged to LIBOR, while the other counterparty has its FRNs pegged to the American Treasury bill rate. In this event, the indexes are not perfectly positively correlated, and the swap may periodically be unprofitable for the swap bank. In our example, this would occur if the Treasury bill rate was substantially larger than LIBOR.

Exchange-rate risk refers to the risk the swap bank faces from fluctuating exchange rates during the time it takes for the bank to lay off a swap it undertakes with one counterparty with an opposing counterparty.

Credit risk is the major risk faced by a swap dealer. It refers to the probability that a counterparty will default. The swap bank that stands between the two counterparties is not obligated to the defaulting counterparty, only to the nondefaulting counterparty. There is a single agreement between the swap bank and each counterparty. Thus, a swap agreement avoids the rights of set-off problem of a back-to-back or parallel loan.

Mismatch risk refers to the difficulty of finding an exact opposite match for a swap the bank has agreed to take. The mismatch may be with respect to the size of the principal sums the counterparties need, the maturity dates of the individual debt issues, or the debt service dates. Textbook illustrations typically ignore these real-life problems.

Sovereign risk refers to the probability that a country will impose exchange restrictions on a currency involved in a swap. This may make it very costly, or perhaps impossible, for a counterparty to fulfill its obligation to the dealer. In this event, provisions exist for terminating the swap, which results in a loss of revenue for the swap bank.

To facilitate the operation of the swap market, the International Swaps and Derivatives Association (ISDA) has standardized two swap agreements. One is the "Interest Rate and Currency Exchange Agreement" that covers currency swaps, and the other is the "Interest Rate Swap Agreement" that lays out standard terms for American-dollar-denominated interest rate swaps. The standardized agreements have reduced the time necessary to establish swaps and also provided terms under which swaps can be terminated early by a counterparty.

10.9   Is the Swap Market Efficient?

The two primary reasons for a counterparty to use a currency swap are to obtain debt financing in the swapped currency at an interest cost reduction brought about through comparative advantages each counterparty has in its national capital market, and/or the benefit of hedging long-run exchange rate exposure. These reasons seem straightforward and difficult to argue with, especially to the extent that name recognition is truly important in raising funds in the international bond market.

The two primary reasons for swapping interest rates are to better match maturities of assets and liabilities and/or to obtain a cost savings via the quality spread differential (QSD). In an efficient market without barriers to capital flows, the cost-savings argument through a QSD is difficult to accept. It implies that an arbitrage opportunity exists because of some mispricing of the default risk premiums on different types of debt instruments. If the QSD is one of the primary reasons for the existence of interest

Eli Lilly and Company:
The Case of the Appreciating Yen

Eli Lilly and Company (Lilly) is an international pharmaceutical company with corporate headquarters in Indianapolis, Indiana. Lilly markets its products worldwide. Being the second-largest pharmaceutical market in the world, Japan represents a particularly significant market for Lilly's products. As sales to Japan grew throughout the 1980s, Lilly became increasingly concerned about the volatility effect on overall sales and earnings performance stemming from fluctuations in the yen exchange rate.

In 1987, the company decided to investigate the possibility of developing a hedging strategy to, in effect, fix in American dollars that portion of its sales to Japan. At the time of consideration, the yen was trading in the mid ¥140/$1 range. Not too many years earlier, the yen was trading in the ¥240–¥270/$1 range. If the yen were to retreat back to those levels, obviously, Lilly's sales in terms of dollars would be significantly diminished. It was Lilly's desire, therefore, to fix future sales at current exchange rates, and the way to do that, of course, was to borrow yen, sell the yen for dollars at the current exchange rates, and service the yen debt with the future yen sales revenues. The dollars would then be used to meet current corporate requirements, and thus, the hedge would be completed.

The initial thought was for Lilly to incur yen-denominated borrowings and convert the principal into dollars. The future yen sales could then service the newly created yen liability. This idea, however, was not favoured because it would have meant adding new debt to the company's balance sheet. The alternative would be to use the yen liability to replace existing debt. The most targetable long-term debt item in Lilly's capital structure was a $150,000,000, 10.25 percent fixed-rate Eurodollar bond issue with a 1992 maturity date. These bonds were issued primarily to allow Lilly to establish name recognition and access to the European bond markets.

Unfortunately, this debt was noncallable. Had it had a call feature, the decision most likely would have been to allow for the creation of a yen liability in order to retire this higher-cost long-term source of funds.

To accomplish the same result, the financial division at Lilly conceived the idea of a currency swap, which involves no exchange of borrowings. At the current exchange rate of ¥144.1, the $150 million Eurodollar issue had a yen value of ¥21.615 billion. Lilly entertained bids from a select group of investment banks to put together a uniquely structured currency swap arrangement. One of the bids was ultimately selected, and the uniqueness of the arrangement centred around the fact that Lilly would contribute to the investment bank five annual level payments in the amount of ¥4.864 billion each during the remaining five years of the life of the Eurodollar bond issue. In return, Lilly would receive dollars each year equal to the $15,375,000 coupon payments on the bond issue plus the $150,000,000 principal repayment at the end of year 5. The level-contribution and variable-receipt arrangement was unique to the swap market, but essential to Lilly, in that it enabled the hedging of a level stream of future yen receipts. While the swap did not provide a complete hedge of all rate-affected sales revenue, it did eliminate the volatility associated with a significant percentage of those revenues. The other unique aspect of the arrangement was the adjustment for interest rate changes since the inception of the Eurodollar bond offering. Eurodollar rates had fallen from the 10.25 percent range to the 7.8 percent range, and yen rates had fallen similarly. To compensate the investment bank and the opposite party for servicing Lilly's debt at 10.25 percent, Lilly's cost of yen contribution was grossed up to 6.2 percent from the then current yen rate of less than 4 percent. Exhibit 10.8 diagrams this interesting example of a currency swap.

rate swaps, one would expect arbitrage to eliminate it over time and that the growth of the swap market would decrease. Quite the contrary has happened as Exhibit 10.1 shows; growth in interest rate swaps has been extremely large since the early 1980s. Thus, the arbitrage argument does not seem to have much merit. Indeed, Turnbull (1987) analytically shows that a QSD can exist in an efficient market. Consequently, one must rely on an argument of **market completeness** for the existence and growth of interest rate swaps. That is, all types of debt instruments are not regularly available for all borrowers. Thus, the interest rate swap market assists in tailoring financing to the type desired by a particular borrower. Both counterparties can benefit (as well as the swap dealer) through financing that is more suitable for their asset maturity structures.

EXHIBIT 10.8

Eli Lilly's Eurodollar
Bond/Yen Swap

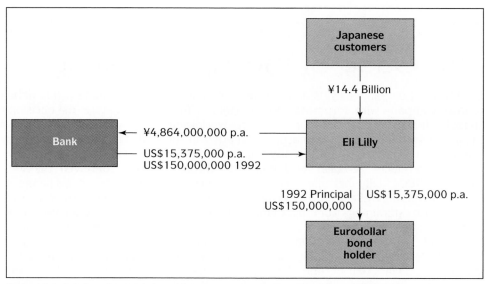

Source: Dale R. Follmer, Manager of Accounting Operations, Eli Lilly and Company.

10.10 Concluding Points about Swaps

The growth in financial swaps has been tremendous. They offer counterparties benefits and opportunities that were not previously available. Another feature of swaps is that they are off-book transactions for both the counterparties and the swap bank; that is, they do not appear as assets or liabilities on the balance sheet. The only indication that they exist is through an examination of the footnotes of the financial reports.

Swaps have become an important source of revenue for commercial banks. As swap activity increased, bank regulators became concerned that the potential liability posed by swaps might create capital adequacy problems for banks. The Federal Reserve Bank and central bankers from the Group of Ten countries and Luxembourg agree to a set of principles, called the Basle Accord, which standardizes bank capital requirements across nations. As discussed in Chapter 6, the accord established guidelines for risk-adjusted capital requirements for off-balance-sheet activities that increase a bank's risk exposure, including swaps.

SUMMARY

This chapter provides a presentation of currency and interest rate swaps. The discussion details how swaps might be used and the risks associated with each.

1. The chapter opened with definitions of an interest rate swap and a currency swap. The basic interest rate swap is a fixed-for-floating rate swap in which one counterparty exchanges the interest payments of a fixed-rate debt obligation for the floating-interest payments of the other counterparty. Both debt obligations are denominated in the same currency. In a currency swap, one counterparty exchanges the debt service obligations of a bond denominated in one currency for the debt service obligations of the other counterparty which are denominated in another currency.

2. The function of a swap bank was discussed. A swap bank is a generic term to describe a financial institution that facilitates the swap between counterparties.

The swap bank serves as either a broker or a dealer. When serving as a broker, the swap bank matches counterparties but does not assume any risk of the swap. When serving as a dealer, the swap bank stands willing to accept either side of a currency swap.

3. An example of a basic interest rate swap was presented. It was noted that a necessary condition for a swap to be feasible was the existence of a quality spread differential between the default-risk premiums on the fixed-rate and floating-rate interest rates of the two counterparties. Additionally, it was noted that there was not an exchange of principal sums between the counterparties of an interest rate swap because both debt issues were denominated in the same currency. Interest rate exchanges were based on a notional principal.

4. Pricing an interest rate swap after inception was illustrated. It was shown that after inception, the value of an interest rate swap to a counterparty should be the difference in the present values of the payment streams the counterparty will receive and pay on the notional principal.

5. The development of the currency swap market was traced to parallel and back-to-back loans. A parallel loan involves four parties. In it, one MNC borrows and relends to another's subsidiary and *vice versa*. A back-to-back loan involves only two parties. One MNC borrows and relends directly to another.

6. A detailed example of a basic currency swap was presented. It was shown that the debt service obligations of the counterparties in a currency swap are effectively equivalent to one another in cost. Nominal differences can be explained by the set of international parity relationships.

7. Pricing a currency swap after inception was illustrated. It was shown that after inception, the value of a currency swap to a counterparty should be the difference in the present values of the payment stream the counterparty will receive in one currency and pay in the other currency, converted to one or the other currency denominations.

8. In addition to the basic fixed-for-fixed currency swap and fixed-for-floating interest rate swap, many other variants exist. One variant is the amortizing swap which incorporates an amortization of the notional principals. Another variant is a zero-coupon-for-floating rate swap, in which the floating-rate payer makes the standard periodic floating-rate payments over the life of the swap, but the fixed-rate payer makes a single payment at the end of the swap. Another is the floating-for-floating rate swap. In this type of swap, each side is tied to a different floating rate index or a different frequency of the same index.

9. The reasons for the development and growth of the swap market were critically examined. It was argued that one must rely on an argument of market completeness for the existence and growth of interest rate swaps. That is, the interest rate swap market assists in tailoring financing to the type desired by a particular borrower when all types of debt instruments are not regularly available to all borrowers.

KEY WORDS

all-in cost, *229*
back-to-back loan, *232*
comparative advantage, *233*
counterparty, *226*
cross-currency interest rate swap, *226*

currency swap, *226*
market completeness, *239*
notional principal, *227*
parallel loan, *231*
quality spread differential (QSD), *228*

single-currency interest rate swap, *226*
swap bank, *227*
swap broker, *227*
swap dealer, *227*

QUESTIONS

1. Describe the difference between a swap broker and a swap dealer.
2. What is the necessary condition for a fixed-for-floating interest rate swap to be possible?
3. Describe the difference between a parallel loan and a back-to-back loan.
4. Discuss the basic motivations for a counterparty to enter into a currency swap.
5. How does the theory of comparative advantage relate to the currency swap market?
6. Discuss the risks confronting interest rate and currency swap dealers.
7. Briefly discuss some variants of the basic interest rate and currency swaps diagrammed in the chapter.
8. If the cost advantage of interest rate swaps would likely be arbitraged away in competitive markets, what other explanations exist to explain the rapid development of the interest rate swap market?
9. Assume you are the swap bank in the Eli Lilly swap discussed in the chapter. Develop an example of how you might lay off the swap to an opposing counterparty.
10. Discuss the motivational difference in the currency swap presented as Example 10.5 and the Eli Lilly and Company swap discussed in the chapter.
11. Assume a currency swap between two counterparties of comparable credit risk; each borrows at the best rate available, and yet the nominal rate of one counterparty is higher than the other. After the initial principal exchange, is the counterparty that is required to make interest payments at the higher nominal rate at a financial disadvantage to the other in the swap agreement? Explain your thinking.

PROBLEMS

1. Develop a different arrangement of interest payments among the counterparties and the swap bank in Example 10.1 that still leaves each counterparty with an all-in cost 0.50 percent below their best rate and the swap bank with a 0.25 percent inflow.
2. Alpha and Beta Companies can borrow at the following rates:

	Alpha	Beta
Moody's credit rating	Aa	Baa
Fixed-rate borrowing cost	10.5%	12.0%
Floating-rate borrowing cost	LIBOR	LIBOR + 1%

   a. Calculate the quality spread differential (QSD).
   b. Develop an interest rate swap in which both Alpha and Beta have an equal cost savings in their borrowing costs. Assume Alpha desires floating-rate debt and Beta desires fixed-rate debt.
3. Company A is an AAA-rated firm desiring to issue five-year FRNs. It finds that it can issue FRNs at six-month LIBOR + 0.125 percent or at three-month LIBOR + 0.125 percent. Given its asset structure, three-month LIBOR is the preferred index. Company B is an A-rated firm that also desires to issue five-year FRNs. It finds it can issue at six-month LIBOR + 1 percent or at three-month LIBOR + 0.625 percent. Given its asset structure, six-month LIBOR is the preferred index. Assume a notional principal of $15,000,000. Determine the QSD and set up a floating-for-floating rate swap where the swap bank receives 0.125 percent and the two counterparties share the remaining savings equally.

4. Suppose Morgan Guaranty, Ltd. is quoting swap rates as follows: 7.75–8.10 percent annually against six-month dollar LIBOR for dollars and 11.25–11.65 percent annually against six-month dollar LIBOR for British pound sterling. At what rates will Morgan Guaranty enter into a $/£ currency swap?

5. A corporation enters into a five-year interest rate swap with a swap bank in which it agrees to pay the swap bank a fixed rate of 9.75 percent annually on a notional amount of €15,000,000 and receive LIBOR. As of the second reset date, determine the price of the swap from the corporation's viewpoint assuming that the fixed-rate side of the swap has increased to 10.25 percent.

6. Karla Ferris, a fixed income manager at Mangus Capital Management, expects the current positively sloped American Treasury yield curve to shift parallel upward.

Ferris owns two $1,000,000 corporate bonds maturing on June 15, 2005, one with a variable rate based on six-month dollar LIBOR and one with a fixed rate. Both yield 50 basis points over comparable Treasury market rates, have very similar credit quality, and pay interest semiannually.

Ferris wished to execute a swap to take advantage of her expectation of a yield curve shift and believes that any difference in credit spread between LIBOR and Treasury market rates will remain constant.

a. Describe a six-month dollar LIBOR-based swap that would allow Ferris to take advantage of her expectation. Discuss, assuming Ferris's expectation is correct, the change in the swap's value and how that change would affect the value of her portfolio. [No calculations required to answer part a.]

Instead of the swap described in part a, Ferris would use the following alternative derivative strategy to achieve the same result.

b. Explain, assuming Ferris's expectation is correct, how the following *strategy* achieves the same result in response to the yield curve shift. [No calculations required to answer part b.]

Settlement Date	Nominal Eurodollar Futures Contract Value
12-15-03	$1,000,000
03-15-04	$1,000,000
06-15-04	$1,000,000
09-15-04	$1,000,000
12-15-04	$1,000,000
03-15-05	$1,000,000

c. Discuss *one* reason why these two derivative strategies provide the same result.

7. Dustin Financial owns a $10-million, 30-year maturity, noncallable corporate bond with a 6.5-percent coupon paid annually. Dustin pays annual LIBOR minus 1 percent on its three-year term time deposits.

Vega Corporation owns an annual-pay LIBOR floater and wants to swap for three years. One-year LIBOR is now 5 percent.

a. Diagram the cash flows between Dustin, Vega, Dustin's depositors, and Dustin's corporate bond. Label the following items:

• Dustin, Vega, Dustin's depositors, and Dustin's corporate bond.

• Applicable interest rate at each line and specify whether it is floating or fixed.

• Direction of each of the cash flows.

Answer problem a in the template provided.

Template for problem a:

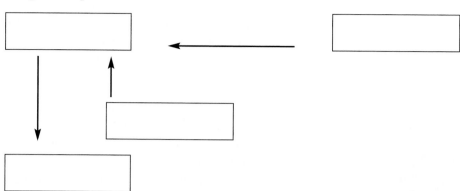

b. i. Calculate the first new swap payment between Dustin and Vega and indicate the direction of the net payment amount.

ii. Identify the net interest rate spread that Dustin expects to earn.

8. Ashton Bishop is the debt manager for World Telephone, which needs €3.33 billion Euro financing for its operations. Bishop is considering the choice between issuance of debt denominated in:

- Euros (€), or
- American dollars, accompanied by a combined interest rate and currency swap.

a. Explain *one* risk World would assume by entering into the combined interest rate and currency swap.

Bishop believes that issuing the American-dollar debt and entering into the swap can lower World's cost of debt by 45 basis points. Immediately after selling the debt issue, World would swap the American dollar payments for Euro payments throughout the maturity of the debt. She assumes a constant currency exchange rate throughout the tenor of the swap.

Exhibit 1 gives details for the two alternative debt issues. Exhibit 2 provides current information about spot currency exchange rates and the three-year life Euro/American Dollar currency and interest rate swap.

EXHIBIT 1

World Telephone
Debt Details

Characteristic	Euro Currency Debt	Dollar Currency Debt
Par value	€3.33 billion	$3 billion
Term to maturity	3 years	3 years
Fixed interest rate	6.25%	7.75%
Interest payment	Annual	Annual

EXHIBIT 2

Currency Exchange
Rate and Swap
Information

Spot currency exchange rate	$0.90 per Euro ($0.90/€1)
3-year life Euro/Dollar fixed interest rates	5.80% Euro/7.30% Dollar

b. Show the notional principal and interest payment cash flows of the combined interest rate and currency swap.

Note: Your response should show both the correct currency ($ or €) and amount for *each* cash flow.

Answer problem b in the template provided.

Template for problem b:

Cash Flows of the Swap	Year 0	Year 1	Year 2	Year 3
World pays				
Notional principal				
Interest payment				
World receives				
Notional principal				
Interest payment				

    c. State whether or not World would reduce its borrowing cost by issuing the debt denominated in American dollars, accompanied by the combined interest rate and currency swap. Justify your response with *one* reason.

INTERNET EXERCISE

The website www.finpipe.com/intrateswaps.htm provides a brief description of interest rate swaps. Links at the bottom of the screen lead to other descriptions of derivative products, including currency swaps and other types of swaps that you will find interesting. It is a good idea to bookmark this site for future reference. Use it now to see how well you understand interest rate and currency swaps. If you cannot follow the discussions, go back and reread this chapter.

MINI CASE

The Centralia Corporation's Currency Swap

The Centralia Corporation is a Canadian manufacturer of small kitchen electrical appliances. It has decided to construct a wholly owned manufacturing facility in Zaragoza, Spain, to manufacture microwave ovens for sale to the European Union market. The plant is expected to cost €4,920,000 and to take about one year to complete. The plant is to be financed over its economic life of eight years. The borrowing capacity created by this capital expenditure is $1,700,000; the remainder of the plant will be equity financed. Centralia is not well known in the Spanish or international bond market; consequently, it would have to pay 9 percent per annum to borrow euros, whereas the normal borrowing rate in the euro zone for well-known firms of equivalent risk is 7 percent. Centralia could borrow dollars in Canada at a rate of 8 percent.

Study Questions

    1. Suppose a Spanish MNC has a mirror-image situation and needs $1,700,000 to finance a capital expenditure in Canada. It finds that it must pay a 9-percent fixed rate for dollars, whereas it can borrow euros at 7 percent. The exchange rate has been forecast to be $0.80/€1 in one year. Set up a currency swap that will benefit each counterparty.

    2. Suppose that one year after the inception of the currency swap between Centralia and the Spanish MNC, the American dollar fixed rate has fallen from 8 to 6 percent and the euro zone fixed rate for euros has fallen from 7 to 5.5 percent. In both dollars and euros, determine the market value of the swap if the exchange rate is $0.8043/€1.

**REFERENCES &
SUGGESTED
READINGS**

Beidleman, Carl R., ed. *Cross Currency Swaps.* Burr Ridge, Ill.: Business One Irwin, 1992.

Campbell, Tim S., and William A. Kracaw. *Financial Risk Management.* New York: HarperCollins College Publishers, 1993.

Marshall, John F., and Kenneth R. Kapner. *The Swap Market.* 2nd ed. Miami, Fla.: Kolb, 1993.

Price, John A. M., Jules Keller, and Max Neilson. "The Delicate Art of Swaps." *Euromoney* (April 1983), pp. 118–25.

Solnik, Bruno. *International Investments,* 4th ed. Reading, Mass.: Addison-Wesley, 2000.

Smith, Clifford W., Charles W. Smithson, and Lee Macdonald Wakeman. "The Evolving Market for Swaps." *Midland Corporate Finance Journal* (Winter 1986), pp. 20–32.

———. "The Market for Interest Rate Swaps." *Financial Management* (Winter 1988), pp. 34–44.

Smithson, Charles W., Clifford W. Smith, Jr., and D. Sykes Wilford. *Managing Financial Risk.* Burr Ridge, Ill.: Irwin Professional Publishing, 1995.

Turnbull, Stuart M. "Swaps: A Zero Sum Game?" *Financial Management* (Spring 1987), pp. 15–21.

Wall, Larry D., and John J. Pringle. "Alternative Explanations of Interest Rate Swaps: A Theoretical and Empirical Analysis." *Financial Management* (Summer 1989), pp. 59–73.

International Portfolio Investment

INTERNATIONAL PORTFOLIO investment refers to the purchase of financial assets—corporate shares—that have been issued in another country and that typically are denominated in a foreign currency. For instance, when a dentist in Winnipeg buys 100 shares of Disney listed on the New York Stock Exchange, he has made an international portfolio investment. Likewise, when The Ontario Teachers Fund buys 100,000 shares of France Telecom listed on the Paris Bourse, that, too, is international portfolio investment.

A distinguishing characteristic of international portfolio investment is that investors are interested primarily in the financial return on the (foreign) investment as opposed to, say, management or control of the foreign firms whose shares they buy. The individual's investment is a very small fraction of the total public ownership of the firms whose shares are purchased. Even Ontario Teachers' Fund's 100,000 shares of France Telecom would amount to less than one-tenth of 1 percent of the total capitalization of France Telecom. Beyond their rights as shareholders, portfolio investors have no direct control or influence on the foreign firms whose shares they hold—nor do they typically want such influence or control.

International portfolio investment has grown substantially over the past three decades, much of it through large financial institutions, such as mutual funds, pension funds and trust companies. Both institutional and individual investors look more and more to diversify their personal portfolios with foreign shares.

The rapid growth in international portfolio investment reflects the globalization of financial markets. The impetus for globalized financial markets—or the "international integration" of markets—came from governments of major industrialized nations as they moved to deregulate foreign exchange and capital markets in the 1970s. For instance, in 1979, the United Kingdom dismantled its "investment dollar premium" system which imposed a heavy charge on cross-currency investments. Japan liberalized its foreign exchange markets in 1980, thus allowing its residents, for the first time, to freely invest in foreign securities. The United States and Canada reduced or eliminated taxes that had previously discouraged financial integration. Even some developing countries, for example, Brazil, India, Korea, and Mexico, took measures to allow foreigners to invest in their capital markets by offering country funds or by directly listing shares on international stock exchanges. In addition, modern advances in telecommunication and computer technologies have contributed to the globalization of investments by facilitating cross-border transactions and rapid dissemination of information around the world.

In this chapter, we look closely at the opportunities and risks involved in international portfolio investment. We note, in particular, that a prime motive for investing in foreign securities is to reduce risk below what it would otherwise be with a purely domestic portfolio. Canadian corporate equities represent only about 2.5 percent of the publicly traded equities around the world. The other 97.5 percent of shares present substantial and, for the most part, easily accessible opportunities for portfolio diversification. It is somewhat curious, then, to note that Canadians maintain close to 80 percent of their equity holdings in shares of Canadian firms, which suggests that perhaps they may be missing out on offshore opportunities. We will examine this issue of "home bias" in equity investment.

11.1   Portfolio Arithmetic—International Perspectives

Adding foreign securities to a portfolio introduces two important considerations to portfolio management. First, the world beyond one's own borders offers substantial opportunities for portfolio diversification. Second, since foreign securities are denominated in foreign currencies, the portfolio manager must contend with foreign exchange risk.

The main points concerning foreign assets can be illustrated with a simple example. Say, a Canadian portfolio manager wants to buy some British equities. He decides to buy 10 Marks & Spencer shares at a price of £10 per share. In order to buy the British shares, he must first purchase £100. Let us say that the exchange rate—dollars per pound—is C$2.30. In that case £100 costs C$230. When the foreign exchange transaction and the equities purchase are complete, the Canadian portfolio is "long" in both British equity and the British pound. The Canadian dollar value of this foreign investment is positively related to changes in the price of the security and/or the exchange rate.

Let us predict outcomes. By the end of the period, the security has risen to £110. Meanwhile, the pound has fallen against the Canadian dollar; by the end of the period, £1 is worth C$2.10. The end-of-period Canadian dollar value of the shares is C$2.10 times £110, or C$231. This figure can be compared with the original outlay of $230. From the point of view of the Canadian portfolio manager, the 10-percent gain in the pound value of the shares is almost erased by the 8.7 percent fall in the value of the pound.

The transactions and the values are summarized in Exhibit 11.1.

The key relationships in holding a foreign-denominated security can be expressed as three rates of return: (1) the return on the security itself (as earned in the foreign currency), (2) the return that results from the change in the domestic value of the foreign

EXHIBIT 11.1				
The Transactions	Time	(1) Exchange Rate ($/£)	(2) £ Value of Shares	(3) $ Value of Shares (1 × 2)
	0	2.30	100	230
	1	2.10	110	231

currency used to finance the investment, and (3) the total return which is a composite of the other two. With respect to our example, we have:

Security return in pounds:
$$r_\pounds = (110/100) - 1 = 1.10 - 1$$
$$r_\pounds = 0.10$$

Exchange rate return:
$$r_x = (2.10/2.30) - 1 = 0.913 - 1$$
$$r_x = -0.087$$

Total dollar return:
$$1 + r_{C\$} = (1 + r_\pounds)(1 + r_x)$$
$$= 1 + r_\pounds + r_x + r_\pounds r_x$$
$$r_{C\$} = r_\pounds + r_x + r_\pounds r_x$$
$$= 0.10 + (-0.087) + (0.10)(-0.087)$$
$$= 0.0043$$

The fully converted-to-dollar return on an equity investment in a foreign-denominated security depends jointly on the gain or loss on the security, together with the gain or loss on the foreign exchange transaction. A more extensive illustration with more conditional outcomes is useful for understanding how the two return-generating factors—the share price in pounds and the exchange rate—interact to create a distribution of condition returns for the Canadian investor.

In Exhibit 11.2 below, the first column presents a range of end-of-period values of 10 Marks & Spencer shares expressed in pounds. The initial £100 investment is in the middle of the column. The other cells in the column are plus-or-minus 5, 10, 15, and 20 percent of £100.

Similarly, the top row presents a range of end-of-period exchange rates between the Canadian dollar and the British pound. The values are centred on the initial $2.30 (per £1) with specific values plus-or-minus 5, 10, 15, and 20 percent of C$2.30. Values of the exchange rate greater than C$2.30 imply that the British pound has become more expensive in terms of the Canadian dollars—the pound has appreciated or the Canadian dollar has depreciated. Conversely, values less than C$2.30 imply that the British pound has become less expensive in terms of the Canadian dollars—the pound has depreciated or the Canadian dollar has appreciated.

The cells of the matrix correspond to the 81 possible discrete end-of-period pairs of the Marks & Spencer shares and the exchange rate. Each cell reports the (total) return on the investment expressed in Canadian dollars.

EXHIBIT 11.2	1.840	1.955	2.070	2.185	**2.300**	2.415	2.530	2.645	2.760
Canadian Dollar Gain 80	−36.0	−32.0	−28.0	−24.0	**−20.0**	−16.0	−12.0	−8.0	−4.0
or Loss on a British 85	−32.0	−27.8	−23.5	−19.3	**−15.0**	−10.8	−6.5	−2.3	2.0
Investment: End of 90	−28.0	−23.5	−19.0	−14.5	**−10.0**	−5.5	−1.0	3.5	8.0
Period 95	−24.0	−19.3	−14.5	−9.8	**−5.0**	−0.3	4.5	9.2	14.0
100	−20.0	**−15.0**	−10.0	**−5.0**	**0.0**	**5.0**	10.0	**15.0**	20.0
105	−16.0	−10.8	−5.5	−0.3	**5.0**	10.3	15.5	20.8	26.0
110	−12.0	−6.5	−1.0	4.5	**10.0**	15.5	21.0	26.5	32.0
115	−8.0	−2.3	3.5	9.2	**15.0**	20.8	26.5	32.3	38.0
120	−4.0	2.0	8.0	14.0	**20.0**	26.0	32.0	38.0	44.0

Each cell of the matrix presents a possible—or "joint conditional"—return to the Canadian investor that is determined by a change in the share price together with a change in the exchange rate. When we turn our attention to the risk of a foreign investment, we will see that it is necessary to break up each joint conditional return into its component parts.

The end-of-period price (in pounds) of Marks & Spencer shares determines the return on holding the British security. This return is computed before a currency conversion back into Canadian dollars. Of the nine possible—or "conditional"— end-of-period share prices, only one will occur. Each conditional end-of-period share price and hence each conditional return can be assigned a probability of happening. The probability distribution—the conditional values together with their respective probabilities—is a quantitative depiction of the fortunes of the risky shares.

Likewise the end-of-period exchange rate—and hence the return resulting from foreign exchange gain or loss—also has a probability distribution made up of nine conditional values and associated probabilities.

Holding a security denominated in a foreign currency is like holding a "portfolio" consisting of the security itself and the foreign currency. Viewed this way, the risk of a foreign security is determined in light of the variance of the return to the security (in its own currency), the variance of the exchange rate, and the covariance between the two sources of return. As with any jointly probable outcome, we compute the risk of the dollar-denominated as its standard deviation:

$$SD(r,\$) = [\text{Var }(r_i) + \text{Var }(r_x) + 2\text{ Cov}(r_i, r_x)]^{1/2}$$

As a practical matter, the covariance between the return on the shares and the exchange rate, $\text{Cov}(r_i, r_x)$, may generally be assumed to be small, close to zero. In that case, the total risk of the foreign security in our example is:

$$SD(r,\$) = [\text{Var }(r_i) + \text{Var }(r_x)]^{1/2}$$

International Portfolio Diversification

As long as movements in exchange rates are less than perfectly correlated with the return to a security denominated in the foreign currency, a foreign security may be *less* risky to an offshore investor than to a domestic investor. However, this diversification advantage from holding foreign securities is, in fact, a result of the foreign investor being "exposed" to foreign exchange risk, which essentially means that the portfolio manager is speculating on one or more foreign currencies.

Foreign exchange gains (or losses) aside, international portfolio diversification is the pursuit of an expanded set of investment opportunities—involving assets in different industries, markets, and business cycles. In other words, foreign assets are likely to have different return-generating processes, and therefore, they offer valuable opportunities for portfolio diversification. Foreign assets expand the efficient set of risky assets; they provide the opportunity for a higher Sharpe Ratio. Exhibit 11.3 illustrates the idea.

Perhaps the most direct and observable evidence of the potential for effective international portfolio diversification is in the less-than-perfect correlations of equities returns between different countries. Exhibit 11.4 presents the correlations between Canadian equities returns, as measured by the monthly return on the S&P TSX Composite, and similar indexes in each of a number of industrialized nations. We see, for example, between Canada and the United States—to cite the most obvious international investment opportunity for Canadian investors—that while the correlation between the two nations' equities returns is consistently higher than in virtually any other case, the United States–Canada correlation has weakened in recent years. This likely reflects substantial differences in American and Canadian business cycles. This incorporates such influences as the decline in resource prices that tends to hurt Canada more than the United States, the strength of American technology shares for which there

EXHIBIT 11.3

Expanding the Efficient Frontier through International Investment

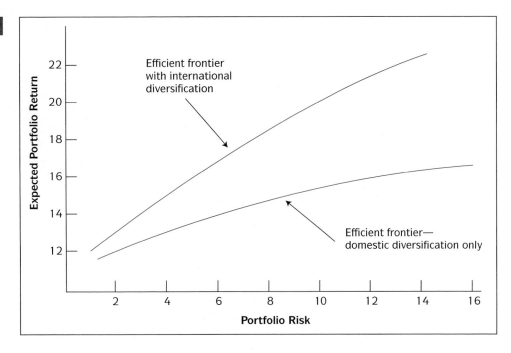

are no major Canadian counterparts, and the dramatically different performance of the American and Canadian financial sectors of late.

A cautionary note is in order here. A few studies, for example, Roll (1988) and Longin and Solnik (1995), found that international stock markets tend to move more closely together when the market volatility is higher. As was observed during the October 1987 market crash, most developed markets declined together. Considering that investors need risk diversification most precisely when markets are turbulent, this finding casts some doubt on the benefits of international diversification. However, one may say that unless investors liquidate their portfolio holdings during the turbulent period, they can still benefit from international risk diversification.

11.2 Optimal International Portfolio Selection

www.msci.com/equity/
index.html

Provides an extensive coverage of world stock markets, including historical time series of major stock market indexes around the world.

Rational investors select portfolios by considering returns as well as risk. Investors are willing to assume additional risk if they are sufficiently compensated by a higher expected return. So, we now expand our analysis to cover both risk and return. We first examine the risk-return characteristics of major world stock markets and then evaluate the potential gains from holding **optimal international portfolios.**

Exhibit 11.5 provides summary statistics of the annual returns, in Canadian dollars, for 12 major stock markets during the period 1980–2001. Let us first examine the correlation coefficients among these markets. The correlation of the Canadian equities returns with foreign markets varies from 0.49 with Australia to 0.86 with France. Norway and Germany also have relatively high correlations, 0.81 and 0.85, respectively, with the Canadian market. The German market, in fact, has relatively high correlations with many markets: for example, 0.92 with the France and 0.77 with the United States. This is likely due to a high degree of internationalization of the German economy. In contrast, the Italian and Japanese markets tend to have relatively low correlations with other markets. Generally speaking, neighbouring countries, such as Canada and the United States, and Germany and Switzerland, tend to exhibit the highest pairwise correlations, most likely due to a high degree of economic interdependence.

EXHIBIT 11.4   Canadian Dollar-Based Equity Market Returns

	1990	1991	1992	1993	1994	1995	1996	1997	1998	1999	2000	2001	2002	2003	Average Annual Return	Standard Deviation	Sharpe Ratio
Canada	−0.14	0.13	0.05	0.29	0.09	0.13	0.27	0.28	0.05	0.39	0.13	−0.10	−0.18	0.22	0.103	0.170	0.32
USA (S&P 500)	−0.05	0.32	0.16	0.15	0.07	0.34	0.21	0.44	0.33	0.16	−0.06	−0.07	−0.25	0.03	0.110	0.195	0.32
MSCI EAFE	−0.25	0.13	−0.05	0.39	0.14	0.08	0.04	0.10	0.24	0.21	−0.11	−0.16	−0.19	−0.16	0.014	0.190	−0.18
AUSTRALIA	−0.17	0.39	0.07	0.45	−0.02	0.14	0.08	0.19	0.18	0.06	0.11	0.18	−0.14	0.06	0.102	0.170	0.32
FINLAND	−0.40	−0.05	0.19	1.12	0.32	−0.06	0.40	0.50	1.15	1.84	−0.05	−0.31	−0.43	0.20	0.182	0.656	0.20
FRANCE	−0.25	0.22	0.18	0.36	−0.09	0.03	0.27	0.40	0.37	0.45	0.06	−0.13	−0.36	0.22	0.093	0.255	0.18
GERMANY	−0.21	0.11	0.03	0.53	−0.01	0.05	0.20	0.57	0.25	0.35	−0.06	−0.13	−0.46	0.13	0.062	0.279	0.05
HONG KONG	0.07	0.51	0.42	1.27	−0.25	0.20	0.31	−0.17	0.01	0.53	−0.11	−0.14	−0.21	0.13	0.126	0.409	0.19
ITALY	−0.29	0.02	0.09	0.57	0.12	−0.03	0.07	0.71	0.48	0.12	0.10	−0.18	−0.25	0.32	0.097	0.296	0.17
JAPAN	−0.41	0.01	−0.15	0.18	0.15	0.02	−0.07	−0.08	−0.05	0.40	−0.17	−0.14	−0.22	0.10	0.050	0.199	−0.49
NORWAY	−0.12	−0.13	−0.03	0.62	0.18	−0.03	0.28	0.33	−0.25	0.34	0.13	−0.05	−0.31	0.15	0.052	0.257	0.02
SPAIN	−0.25	0.20	0.01	0.71	−0.06	0.18	0.49	0.59	0.45	0.18	−0.07	−0.01	−0.31	0.09	0.119	0.309	0.23
SWITZERLAND	−0.23	0.26	0.37	0.56	−0.03	0.24	0.18	0.70	0.21	0.04	0.12	−0.15	−0.28	0.26	0.127	0.279	0.28
UK	−0.10	0.21	0.28	0.33	−0.02	0.19	0.13	0.37	0.21	0.11	−0.01	−0.07	−0.27	0.23	0.100	0.183	0.29

EXHIBIT 11.5 Canadian Dollar-Based Equity Market Return Correlations

	Canada	USA	MSCI EAFE	Australia	Finland	France	Germany	Hong Kong	Italy	Japan	Norway	Spain	Switzerland
CANADA	1.00												
USA (S&P 500)	0.58	1.00											
MSCI EAFE	0.66	0.67	1.00										
AUSTRALIA	0.49	0.58	0.68	1.00									
FINLAND	0.74	0.46	0.79	0.35	1.00								
FRANCE	0.86	0.74	0.71	0.63	0.81	1.00							
GERMANY	0.85	0.77	0.77	0.66	0.76	0.92	1.00						
HONG KONG	0.51	0.28	0.59	0.62	0.50	0.53	0.53	1.00					
ITALY	0.62	0.66	0.56	0.63	0.80	0.87	0.29	0.46	1.00				
JAPAN	0.77	0.35	0.71	0.41	0.76	0.62	0.60	0.46	0.44	1.00			
NORWAY	0.81	0.26	0.52	0.41	0.56	0.58	0.74	0.54	0.58	0.59	1.00		
SPAIN	0.72	0.75	0.77	0.74	0.63	0.83	0.92	0.53	0.82	0.44	0.62	1.00	
SWITZERLAND	0.68	0.76	0.58	0.69	0.42	0.78	0.85	0.46	0.85	0.33	0.57	0.81	1.00
UK	0.70	0.83	0.61	0.68	0.51	0.85	0.87	0.54	0.80	0.42	0.51	0.81	0.95

Exhibit 11.6 also provides summary statistics of monthly returns for 12 major stock markets expressed in American dollar returns, including the mean and standard deviation (SD) of monthly returns and the world beta measure for each market. The **world beta** measures the sensitivity of a national market to world market movements.[1] National stock markets have highly individualized risk-return characteristics. The mean return per month ranges from 0.88 percent (10.56 percent per year) for Canada to 1.71 percent (20.52 percent per year) for Sweden, whereas the standard deviation ranges from 4.43 percent for the United States to 9.58 percent for Hong Kong. Japan has the highest world beta measure, 1.20, while Switzerland has the lowest, 0.85. This means that the Japanese stock market is the most sensitive to world market movements and the American market the least sensitive.

Lastly, Exhibit 11.6 presents the historical performance measures for national stock markets, that is,

$$\text{SHP} = (\bar{R}_i - R_f)/\sigma_i \tag{11.1}$$

where $\bar{R}_i$ and σ_i are, respectively, the mean and standard deviation of returns, and R_f is the risk-free interest rate. The above expression, known as the **Sharpe performance measure (SHP),** provides a "risk-adjusted" performance measure. It represents the excess return (above and beyond the risk-free interest rate) per standard deviation risk. In Exhibit 11.6, the Sharpe performance measure is computed by using the monthly U.S. Treasury bill rate as a proxy for the risk-free interest rate.

The Sharpe performance measure computed over our sample period, 1980–2001, ranges from 0.052 for Japan and 0.057 for Canada to 0.160 for the United States and 0.161 for the Netherlands. The Dutch market performed the best, closely followed by the American and Swedish markets. The strong performance of the American market is mainly due to its low risk. The lacklustre performance of the Canadian market can be attributed to its low return, driven primarily by the depreciation of the Canadian dollar *vis-à-vis* the American dollar from 1980 to 2001. Japan's poor performance reflects the long-term stagnation of the Japanese economy since the early 1990s. The German market also registered a lacklustre performance, ranking ninth in terms of the Sharpe measure. In contrast, the British market performed reasonably well, ranking fourth, owing to a respectable mean return combined with a relatively low risk. Hong Kong has the second-highest mean return (1.53 percent per month) after Sweden but ranks sixth in terms of Sharpe performance measure, tying with France, due to its very high risk.

Using the historical performance data represented in Exhibit 11.6, we can solve for the composition of the optimal international portfolio from the perspective of American (or American dollar-based) investors.[2] Exhibit 11.8 illustrates the choice of the optimal international portfolio (OIP). The result is presented in Exhibit 11.9. As can be seen from the next-to-last column of the table, investors' optimal international portfolio comprises:

Hong Kong market	=	1.61%
Italian market	=	1.14%
Dutch market	=	29.96%
Swedish market	=	26.45%
American market	=	40.84%
Total	=	100.00%

[1]Formally, the world beta is defined as $\beta_i = \sigma_{iW}/\sigma_W^2$, where σ_{iW} is the covariance between returns to the ith market and the world market index, and σ_W^2 is the variance of the world market return. If, for example, the world beta of a market is 1.2, it means that as the world market moves up and down by 1 percent, the market goes up and down by 1.2 percent.

In their optimal international portfolio, American investors allocate the largest share, 40.84 percent, of funds to their home market, followed by the Dutch and Swedish markets. The Hong Kong and Italian markets receive relatively small weights. Seven markets—Australia, Canada, France, Germany, Japan, Switzerland, and United Kingdom—are not included in American investors' optimal international portfolio.

Similarly, we can solve for the composition of the optimal international portfolio from the perspective of each of the national investors. Since the risk-return characteristics of international stock markets vary depending on the numeraire currency used to measure returns, the composition of the optimal international portfolio will also vary across national investors using different numeraire currencies. Exhibit 11.9 presents the composition of the optimal international portfolio from the currency perspective of each national investor.

For instance, the British (or British pound–based) investors' optimal international portfolio comprises the Netherlands (43 percent), Sweden (33 percent), the United States (2.35 percent), and the United Kingdom (21 percent). Like American investors, British investors invest substantially in their domestic market, partly because the domestic market is not subject to exchange rate fluctuations and, thus, has a low risk. It is clear from the table that the three best performing markets, the Netherlands, Sweden, and the United States, are most heavily represented in the optimal international portfolios. In fact, the Dutch, Swedish, and American markets are included in every national investor's optimal international portfolio and receive the largest weights. In contrast, the Canadian, French, and German markets are not included in any optimal portfolio, while the Hong Kong and Italian markets are included in some portfolios with relatively small weights.

The last column of Exhibit 11.9 provides the composition of the optimal international portfolio in terms of the local currency (LC), constructed ignoring exchange rate changes. It is the optimal international portfolio that would have been obtained if exchange rates had not changed. As such, it can tell us the effect of currency movements on the compositions of international portfolios.

The LC optimal international portfolio comprises Australia (1.22 percent), Hong Kong (4 percent), Italy (11 percent), the Netherlands (20 percent), Sweden (40 percent), the United Kingdom (9 percent), and the United States (16 percent). It is interesting to note that the United Kingdom is included in the LC optimal portfolio but not

[2]The optimal international portfolio can be solved by maximizing the Sharpe ratio, i.e., SHP $= [E(R_p) - R_f]/\sigma_p$, with respect to the portfolio weights. Refer to Appendix 11B for a detailed discussion. The illustration of the theory and techniques of optimal international portfolio selection in this section makes convenient use of data from Morgan Stanley Capital International. The data are in American-dollar terms, and hence, the perspective is that of an American-dollar investor. For the purpose of understanding optimal international portfolio selection, the American dollar basis of the illustration is as useful for a Canadian as it is for an American resident.

Optimal portfolio selection is something of a "backward-looking" exercise. We use historical data to determine actual returns and variances of those returns in individual countries as well as covariances between countries. The historical data are relevant for the future to the extent that the relationships that they represent are stable, that is, to the extent the past is a reliable and consistent indicator of the future.

We have commented earlier on the steady decline of the value of the Canadian dollar, especially *vis-à-vis* the American dollar, from 1980 to 2000. This virtually one-way downward movement of the Canadian dollar—if investors knew that it would occur—would have signalled the investors, even Canadian investors, to stay away from Canadian equities and instead to hold shares denominated in currencies that would appreciate against the Canadian dollar. But, of course, investors could not know the fate of the Canadian dollar *ex ante*.

In regard to our illustration of the techniques of optimal international portfolio selection, the point is that in the recent history of returns, variances, and covariances of returns on national markets around the world, the Canadian data are likely an aberration and hence are unlikely to be reflective of reasonable *ex ante* Canadian-dollar–based returns, variances, and covariances.

Professionals are acutely aware of the time-varying nature of securities returns, variances, and covariances. While the techniques illustrated in this section are sound, the calibration of the mix in an optimally diversified portfolio using Canadian dollar data would give a distorted picture. A Canadian investor or portfolio manager would arrange for data to be expressed from this point forward, in Canadian-dollar terms that incorporate informed *expectations* of returns, variances, and covariances, which obviously are not captured in recent historical data.

EXHIBIT 11.6 **Summary Statistics of the Monthly Returns for 12 Major Stock Markets: 1980.1–2001.12**
(All Statistics in American Dollars)

Stock Market	Correlation Coefficients											Mean (%)	SD (%)	β[a]	SHP[b]	(Rank)
	AU	CN	FR	GM	HK	IT	JP	NL	SD	SW	UK					
Australia (AU)												1.05	7.07	0.94	0.071	(10)
Canada (CN)	0.60											0.88	5.78	0.99	0.057	(11)
France (FR)	0.37	0.46										1.19	6.29	1.00	0.102	(6)
Germany (GM)	0.34	0.42	0.69									1.09	6.26	0.91	0.086	(9)
Hong Kong (HK)	0.46	0.47	0.31	0.36								1.53	9.58	1.10	0.102	(6)
Italy (IT)	0.25	0.35	0.50	0.43	0.29							1.26	7.62	0.89	0.093	(8)
Japan (JP)	0.33	0.33	0.41	0.33	0.26	0.37						0.91	6.99	1.20	0.052	(12)
Netherlands (NL)	0.44	0.58	0.66	0.71	0.47	0.44	0.42					1.38	5.15	0.92	0.161	(1)
Sweden (SD)	0.44	0.49	0.49	0.54	0.39	0.44	0.39	0.54				1.71	7.28	1.08	0.159	(3)
Switzerland (SW)	0.38	0.46	0.61	0.67	0.34	0.35	0.41	0.70	0.49			1.13	5.40	0.85	0.107	(5)
United Kingdom (UK)	0.54	0.57	0.57	0.50	0.48	0.38	0.42	0.70	0.51	0.59		1.23	5.55	0.98	0.123	(4)
United States (US)	0.47	0.74	0.50	0.45	0.41	0.29	0.31	0.62	0.49	0.51	0.58	1.26	4.43	0.86	0.160	(2)

[a]β denotes the systematic risk (beta) of a country's stock market index measured against the world stock market index.
[b]SHP denotes the Sharpe performance measure, which is $(\bar{R}_i - R_f)/\sigma_i$ where R_i and σ_i are, respectively, the mean and standard deviation of returns to the ith market. Ranking of each market in terms of the Sharpe performance measure is provided in parentheses. The monthly risk-free interest rate, R_f, is 0.55 percent, which is the average monthly U.S. Treasury bill rate during the sample period 1980–2001.

Source: Returns on MSCI stock market indexes are from Datastream.

EXHIBIT 11.7

Risk Reduction:
Domestic versus
International
Diversification

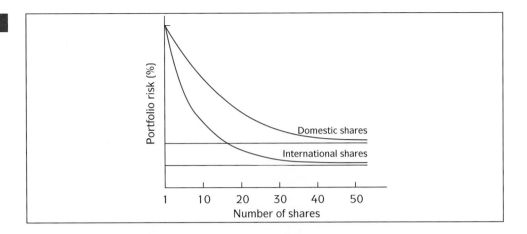

in the American dollar-based investors' optimal portfolio. This implies that the weak performance of the British pound against the American dollar should be responsible for the exclusion of the British market from the American investors' optimal portfolio. In contrast, the Swiss market is not included in the LC optimal international portfolio but is included in some national investors' (such as the German and Dutch) optimal portfolios. This inclusion must be due to a strong performance of the Swiss franc, rather than the Swiss stock market.

Having obtained optimal international portfolios, we can now evaluate the gains from holding these portfolios over purely domestic portfolios. We can measure the gains from holding international portfolios in two different ways: (1) the increase in the Sharpe performance measure, and (2) the increase in the portfolio return at the domestic-equivalent risk level. The increase in the Sharpe performance measure, ΔSHP, is given by the difference in the Sharpe ratio between the optimal international portfolio (OIP) and the domestic portfolio (DP), that is,

$$\Delta SHP = SHP(OIP) - SHP(DP) \tag{11.2}$$

ΔSHP represents the extra return per standard deviation risk accruing from international investment. On the other hand, the increase in the portfolio return at the "domestic-equivalent" risk level is measured by the difference in return between the domestic portfolio (DP) and the international portfolio (IP) that has the same risk as the domestic portfolio. This extra return, $\Delta \overline{R}$ accruing from international investment at

EXHIBIT 11.8

Selection of the
Optimal International
Portfolio

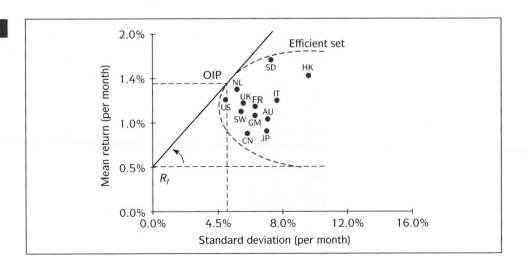

EXHIBIT 11.9 Composition of the Optimal International Portfolio by Investors' Domicile (Holding Period: 1980–2001)

Stock Market	From the Perspective of Investors Domiciled in												
	AU	CN	FR	GM	HK	IT	JP	NL	SD	SW	UK	US	LC[a]
Australia	0.1178												0.0122
Canada													
France													
Germany													
Hong Kong	0.0533	0.0331			0.0696		0.0447		0.0209			0.0161	0.0362
Italy		0.0262				0.0510			0.0380			0.0114	0.1105
Japan							0.0472						
Netherlands	0.2679	0.2853	0.6242	0.6193	0.3219	0.5541	0.4777	0.6081	0.4575	0.5508	0.4349	0.2996	0.1987
Sweden	0.3036	0.2392	0.3078	0.2541	0.3000	0.3546	0.3560	0.2571	0.2806	0.2618	0.3318	0.2645	0.3966
Switzerland			0.0195	0.0742				0.0776	0.0362	0.1813			
United Kingdom									0.0465		0.2098		0.0857
United States	0.2574	0.4162	0.0484	0.0523	0.3085	0.0403	0.0744	0.0573	0.1202	0.0061	0.0235	0.4084	0.1601
Total	1.0000	1.0000	1.0000	1.0000	1.0000	1.0000	1.0000	1.0000	1.0000	1.0000	1.0000	1.0000	1.0000
Risk-free rate (%)[b]	0.8145	0.6858	0.7447	0.4945	0.8005	0.9835	0.3486	0.5112	0.6902	0.3704	0.7651	0.5502	0.5502

[a]LC column provides the composition of optimal international portfolio without considering exchange rate changes.

[b]The risk-free rate denotes the average risk-free interest rate faced by investors domiciled in the corresponding country over the period 1980–2001. It is proxied by the one-month U.S. Treasury bill rate or eurocurrency interest rate.

the domestic-equivalent risk level, can be computed by multiplying ΔSHP by the standard deviation of the domestic portfolio, that is,

$$\Delta \overline{R} = (\Delta \text{SHP})(\sigma_{DP}) \tag{11.3}$$

Exhibit 11.10 presents both the measures of the gains from international investment from the perspective of each national investor. Let us first examine the results for American investors. As can be seen from the last row of the table, the optimal international portfolio has a mean return of 1.42 percent per month and a standard deviation of 4.51 percent, whereas the American domestic portfolio has a mean return of 1.26 percent and a standard deviation of 4.43 percent. The optimal international portfolio, thus, has a substantially higher return but a slightly higher risk than the domestic portfolio. As a result, the Sharpe performance measure increases from 0.161 to 0.193, a 20 percent increase. Alternatively, American investors can capture an extra return of 0.14 percent per month, or 1.68 percent per year, by holding an international portfolio at the domestic equivalent-risk, that is, at the standard deviation of 4.43 percent.

The gains from international portfolio diversification (IPD) are much larger for some national investors, especially for Australian, Canadian, Italian, and Japanese investors. Each of these national investors can increase the Sharpe ratio by more than 100 percent. Japanese investors, for instance, can increase the Sharpe ratio by nearly 300 percent or can capture an extra return of 9 percent per year at the Japan-equivalent risk level by holding their optimal international portfolio. Exhibit 11.10 indicates that the gains from IPD are relatively modest for investors from the Netherlands, Sweden, the United Kingdom, and the United States. Overall, the data presented in Exhibit 11.10 suggest that regardless of domicile and numeraire currency, investors can potentially benefit from IPD to a varying degree.

Analyses of gains from international portfolio divresification, such as we have presented in this chapter, are generally *ex post* in the sense that the risk-return characteristics are observed from the past. In application of these analytic methods, there is underlying assumption that historically observed returns, variances, and covariances are reasonable estimates of future (or expected) returns, variances, and covariances. To the extent that the past is not an accurate representation of the future, the resulting "estimation errors" in the data—when used to construct "optimal" international portfolios—may lead to inefficient (or suboptimal) allocation of funds.

Finally, much of the diversification gain from international investment stems from the less-than-perfect correlation of national industries and national indexes. For instance, Canada's resource industries, of which we have many, generate returns that are substantially different from—and not highly correlated with—returns on, say, industrial sectors in Japan or Italy. Beyond these cross-country industrial differences, however, another element of diversification in international investing stems from exchange rate variance and currency correlations. Since exchange rate movements tend to be random, they tend to dampen the benefits of the more fundamental (country or industrial) diversification. Therefore, the strategy of constructing an international equity portfolio while hedging foreign exchange risk allows the investor to emphasize (or capture the gains from) international industrial diversification while neutralizing exchange rate effects. In Appendix 11A, we outline in technical detail how to hedge exchange rate risk in an international portfolio.

EXHIBIT 11.10 Gains from International Diversification by Investor's Domicile (Monthly Returns: 1980–2001)

Investor's Domicile	Domestic Portfolio			Optimal International Portfolio			Gains from International Investment			
	Mean (%)	SD (%)	SHP	Mean (%)	SD (%)	SHP (%)	ΔSHP	(Δ%)[a]	ΔR(%)[b]	(%p.a.)[c]
Australia	1.25	5.72	0.076	1.76	4.67	0.202	0.126	(166)	0.72	(8.64)
Canada	0.96	5.12	0.054	1.54	4.16	0.205	0.151	(280)	0.77	(9.24)
France	1.40	5.93	0.110	1.76	5.24	0.194	0.084	(76)	0.50	(6.00)
Germany	1.14	5.85	0.111	1.59	5.02	0.218	0.107	(96)	0.63	(7.56)
Hong Kong	1.68	9.27	0.095	1.63	4.68	0.178	0.083	(87)	0.77	(9.24)
Italy	1.62	7.49	0.086	1.92	5.25	0.178	0.092	(107)	0.69	(8.28)
Japan	0.60	5.61	0.045	1.31	5.35	0.179	0.134	(298)	0.75	(9.00)
Netherlands	1.49	5.09	0.191	1.60	5.03	0.216	0.025	(13)	0.13	(1.56)
Sweden	2.06	7.26	0.188	1.85	4.82	0.241	0.053	(28)	0.38	(4.56)
Switzerland	1.12	4.89	0.154	1.51	5.20	0.219	0.065	(42)	0.32	(3.84)
United Kingdom	1.36	4.85	0.122	1.67	5.01	0.180	0.058	(48)	0.28	(3.36)
United States	1.26	4.43	0.161	1.42	4.51	0.193	0.032	(20)	0.14	(1.68)

[a]The number provided in parentheses represents the percentage increase in the Sharpe performance measure relative to that of the domestic portfolio, i.e., [ΔSHP/SHP(DP)] × 100, where ΔSHP denotes the difference in the Sharpe ratio between the optimal international portfolio and the domestic portfolio.
[b]This column provides the extra return accruing to the optimal international portfolio at the domestic-equivalent risk level.
[c]This column provides the annualized extra return accruing to the optimal international portfolio.

11.3 International Mutual Funds: Access to the World

Canadian investors can achieve international diversification quite easily through Canadian international mutual funds that now number well over 1,500. By investing in international mutual funds, Canadian investors can buy the funds in Canadian dollars and likewise receive foreign-source dividends, interest, and capital gains in Canadian dollars. The process is simple and convenient. For the Canadian investor, there is nothing "foreign" about the purchase of an international mutual fund besides the crucial fact that the securities in the fund are foreign. Professional managers establish the international portfolio strategy, and they look after diversification and portfolio transactions. The professional managers are in a position to deal with legal, institutional, and foreign-exchange matters that could be formidable to the individual investor. The 1,500+ Canadian international mutual funds offer a broad array of portfolios, including country funds, sector funds, as well as funds that focus on international growth or value or simply offshore indexes.

An investor adds foreign content to a portfolio with a view to enhancing performance—a combination of higher returns and lower risk. Returns and risk ought to be measured in the investor's home currency. How, then, have Canadian investors fared in their choice between domestic and foreign investments? As always, *ex post* assessment of performance depends on the time period that one looks at. For example, foreign funds served Canadian investors very well in the period 1991–2001 as the Canadian dollar fell steadily against foreign currencies, especially the American dollar. Then, the meltdown of 2002 hit all equities markets hard, which, like the crash of 1987, tends to make comparative *ex post* performance difficult to assess. Finally, in 2003, markets rallied strongly everywhere. Canadian investors and foreign investors in Canada were doubly blessed as the Canadian dollar also strengthened considerably.

Exhibit 11.11 provides risk-return profiles of a sample of Canadian international mutual funds. The returns are for the year 2003. The two risk measures are the conventional three-year standard deviation of monthly returns in Canadian dollars and the fund's beta. We also compute the Sharpe ratio for each fund. The table includes a set of international funds that do not include American shares and a set of funds that consist exclusively of American shares. For comparative reference, we note the performance of an all-Canadian fund.

It is clear from Exhibit 11.11 that the performance of Canadian equities was exceptional by world standards, reflecting the combination of positive returns on Canadian securities and the strengthening of the Canadian dollar. Insofar as the Canadian dollar rose substantially more against the American dollar than against non-American currencies, Canadian equities performance is correspondingly stronger against American equities than against non-American equities.

The Canadian performance is, indeed, so strong through the brief period covered by Exhibit 11.11 that to apply this statistical information to an optimal portfolio of international assets from the Canadian perspective would result in severe overweighting of Canadian shares. A bright past is seldom a true indicator of the relative rewards, risks, and covariances of the broader international set of assets. The recent *ex post* data are telling Canadian investors to keep their money at home. Nevertheless, Canadian investors are well advised to capture the *ex ante* diversification benefits that result from holding international assets.

EXHIBIT 11.11

International Mutual
Fund Performance
2003: Canadian Dollar
Returns

Fund	One-year Return	SD	Beta	Sharpe Ratio
Non-US Equities				
Bissett International	15.67	19.10	1.15	0.66
BMO International	4.60	16.65	1.05	0.10
BPI International Equity	10.96	17.12	1.05	0.46
CDA Global Stock (Templeton)	11.81	17.20	1.03	0.51
Centaur International Equity (TAL)	9.84	20.05	1.26	0.34
Clarington International Equity	21.36	24.08	1.41	0.76
Clarica Premier International	14.00	15.91	0.98	0.69
Genus International Equity	9.22	14.33	0.90	0.43
IA Credit Suisse Global Equity	6.39	15.95	0.97	0.21
Integra International Equity	10.85	17.63	0.98	0.45
Mawer World Investment	9.71	15.82	0.98	0.42
Average	**11.31**	**17.62**	**1.07**	**0.46**
US Equities				
AIC American Advantage	3.03	14.60	0.83	0.00
APEX US Equity	1.60	18.88	1.12	−0.07
Astra McLean Budden US Equity	4.43	18.48	1.11	0.08
BMO US Growth	3.48	15.54	0.92	0.03
Dynamic American Value	8.27	15.91	0.89	0.33
Evolution American	−7.66	17.27	0.98	−0.62
IA Ecfix US Equity (AGF)	1.38	21.77	0.96	−0.07
ING US Equity	−0.28	15.25	0.92	−0.22
Mavrix American Growth	6.95	21.39	1.14	0.18
RBC US Equity	5.81	15.11	0.89	0.19
TD US Equity	5.49	17.67	1.06	0.14
Average	**2.95**	**17.44**	**0.98**	**0.00**
Canada	**21.42**	**16.94**	**1.03**	**1.03**

Source: Globalfund.com.

Supplementary Material

In addition to international mutual funds, investors may achieve international portfolio diversification "at home" by investing in (1) country funds, (2) American depository receipts (ADRs), or (3) world equity benchmark shares (WEBS), without having to invest directly in foreign stock markets. In the next section, we discuss each of these instruments.

11.4 International Diversification through Country Funds

Recently, country funds have emerged as one of the most popular means of international investment in the United States as well as in other developed countries. As the name suggests, a country fund invests exclusively in shares of a single country. Using country funds, investors can

1. Speculate in a single foreign market with minimum costs.
2. Construct their own *personal* international portfolios using country funds as building blocks.
3. Diversify into *emerging markets* that are otherwise practically inaccessible.

Many emerging markets, such as India, Brazil, China, Russia, and Turkey, still remain largely segmented. As a result, country funds often provide international investors with the most practical, if not the only, way of diversifying into these largely inaccessible foreign markets.

The majority of country funds available, however, have a *closed-end* status. Like other closed-end funds, a **closed-end country fund (CECF)** issues a given number of shares that trade on the stock exchange of the host country as if the fund were an individual share by itself. Unlike shares of open-end mutual funds, shares of a closed-end country fund cannot be redeemed at the underlying net asset value set at the home market of the fund. Currently, about 30 countries offer CECFs, a partial list of which is provided in Exhibit 11.12. In the United States, the majority of CECFs are listed on the New York Stock Exchange, with a few listed on the American Stock Exchange.

Since the share value of a fund is set on an American stock exchange, it may very well diverge from the underlying net asset value (NAV) set in the fund's home market. The difference is known as a *premium* if the fund share value exceeds the NAV, or a *discount* in the opposite case. Exhibit 11.12 provides the magnitude of premiums/discounts for the sample CECFs. As indicated in the table, the average premium varies a great deal across funds, ranging from 63.17 percent (for the Korea Fund) to −24 percent (for the Brazil Fund). Like the Korea Fund, the Taiwan and Spain funds commanded large premiums, 37.89 percent and 21.57 percent, respectively. Like the Brazil Fund, the Mexico Fund traded at a steep discount, −21.14 percent on average. It was also observed that the fund premium/discount fluctuates widely over time. For instance, the Taiwan Fund premium varied between −25.27 percent and 205.39 percent. Most funds have traded at both a premium and a discount since their inception.[3] The behaviour of the fund premium/discount implies that the risk-return characteristics of a CECF can be quite different from those of the underlying NAV.

Cash flows from CECFs are generated by the underlying assets held outside the United States. But CECFs are traded in the United States and their market values, determined in the United States, often diverge from the NAVs. This "hybrid" nature of CECFs suggests that they may behave partly like American securities and partly like securities of the home market. To investigate this issue, consider the following "two-factor" market model:[4]

$$R_i = \alpha_i + \beta^{US}_i R_{US} + \beta^{HM}_i R_{HM} + e_i \tag{11.4}$$

where:

R_i = the return on the ith country fund,

R_{US} = the return on the American market index proxied by the Standard & Poor 500 Index,

R_{HM} = the return on the home market of the country fund,

β^{US}_i = the American beta of the ith country fund, measuring the sensitivity of the fund returns to the American market returns,

β^{HM}_i = the home market beta of the ith country fund, measuring the sensitivity of the fund returns to the home market returns, and

e_i = the residual error term.

Equation 11.4 is estimated for both the CECFs and their underlying net assets; that is, we run two regressions for each fund. In the first regression, the left-hand side (dependent) variable, R_i, is the return that American investors receive on the CECF share itself. In the second regression, the left-hand side variable is the return on the NAV. The estimation results are provided in Exhibit 11.12.

[3]A study by Bonser-Neal, Brauer, Neal, and Wheatley (1990) suggests that the country fund premium/discount reflects the barriers to direct portfolio investment in the home countries of the funds. They found that whenever these barriers were lowered, the fund premium declined.

[4]The returns to the home market, R_{HM}, employed in Equation 11.4 is, in fact, the "residual" obtained from regressing the home market returns on the American market returns. American investors who wish to diversify risk internationally will value exposure to the "pure" (or, orthogonal) foreign market risk, that is, β_{HM}.

EXHIBIT 11.12	American and Home Market Betas of Closed-End Country Funds and Their Net Asset Values							
Country	Average Fund Premium (%)	Fund Share Value			Net Asset Value			Sample Period
		β_{US}	β_{HM}	R^2	β_{US}	β_{HM}	R^2	
Australia	−14.77	0.62	0.48	0.13	0.25	0.81	0.60	1986.1–90.12
Brazil	−24.72	0.11	0.16	0.02	0.32	0.65	0.60	1988.4–90.12
Canada	−6.29	0.04	0.47	0.03	−0.19	0.29	0.11	1986.6–90.12
Germany	1.80	0.73	0.53	0.11	0.15	0.69	0.40	1986.7–90.12
India	−2.66	0.87	0.26	0.04	−0.27	0.66	0.40	1988.8–90.12
Italy	−12.49	0.89	0.68	0.21	0.13	0.57	0.28	1986.3–90.12
Korea	63.17	1.00	0.63	0.19	0.24	0.76	0.62	1985.1–90.12
Malaysia	−0.36	1.34	0.60	0.24	0.58	0.68	0.79	1987.6–90.12
Mexico	−21.14	0.99	0.53	0.13	0.33	0.75	0.62	1985.1–90.12
Spain	21.57	1.56	0.28	0.14	0.39	0.75	0.65	1988.7–90.12
South Africa	12.16	0.00	0.35	0.13	0.08	0.85	0.59	1985.1–90.12
Switzerland	−7.65	0.79	0.47	0.25	0.33	0.65	0.75	1987.8–90.12
Taiwan	37.89	1.46	0.39	0.26	0.19	0.40	0.13	1987.2–90.12
Thailand	−6.86	1.20	0.44	0.14	0.63	0.85	0.75	1988.2–90.12
U.K.	−16.55	1.04	0.62	0.36	0.55	0.73	0.37	1987.8–90.12
Average		0.84	0.46	0.16	0.25	0.67	0.51	

Source: E. Chang, C. Eun, and R. Kolodny, "International Diversification through Closed-End Country Funds," *Journal of Banking and Finance* (November 1995). Reprinted with permission of Elsevier Science.

Exhibit 11.12 shows that CECFs tend to have substantially higher American beta values than their underlying NAVs. The average American beta value is 0.84 for CECFs but is only 0.25 for the NAVs. On the other hand, the average home market beta is 0.46 for CECFs, which is compared with 0.67 for the NAVs. In the case of Korea, for example, the fund (underlying net assets) has an American beta of 1.00 (0.24) and a home market beta of 0.63 (0.76). In the case of Thailand, the fund (underlying net assets) has an American beta of 1.20 (0.63) and a home market beta of 0.44 (0.85). In other words, CECF returns are substantially more sensitive to the American market factor and less so to the home market factor than their corresponding NAVs. This implies that CECFs behave more like American securities in comparison with the NAVs.[5] However, the majority of CECFs retain significant home market betas, allowing American investors to achieve international diversification to a certain extent. Also noteworthy from the table is the fact that the coefficients of determination, R^2, tend to be quite low, 0.16 on average, for CECFs. This implies that CECFs are subject to significant *idiosyncratic* (or unique) risks that are related to neither the American nor the home market movements.

While CECFs behave more like American securities, they provide American investors with the opportunity to achieve international diversification at home without incurring excessive transaction costs. We now estimate the potential gains from international diversification using CECFs. Exhibit 11.13 provides the risk-return characteristics of 15 sample funds, as well as the American stock market index, during the sample period 1989.1–1990.12. It also presents the composition of the optimal international portfolio comprising CECFs and, for comparison purposes, the composition of the corresponding optimal portfolio comprising the NAVs.

The optimal portfolio consisting of CECFs dominates the American index in terms of risk-return efficiency; the Sharpe performance measure is 0.233 for the former and

---

[5]This finding is consistent with the Bailey and Lim (1992) study showing that CECFs act more like American securities than foreign stock market indexes.

| EXHIBIT 11.13 | Summary Statistics of the Weekly Returns for Closed-End Country Funds and Their Net Asset Values and the Compositions of Optimal Portfolios (in American Dollar Terms: 1989.1–1990.12) | | | | | | | |

Country	Country Fund Share			Net Asset Value			Optimal Portfolio	
	Mean (%)	SD (%)	Correlation with U.S.	Mean (%)	SD (%)	Correlation with U.S.	CECF (Weight)	NAV (Weight)
Australia	0.46	5.64	0.12	0.01	1.78	0.25	0.0033	0.0000
Brazil	0.73	6.31	−0.01	0.29	7.55	−0.02	0.1271	0.0023
Canada	0.14	4.91	−0.31	−0.19	1.98	−0.19	0.0660	0.0000
Germany	0.78	9.70	0.22	0.38	4.67	−0.11	0.0253	0.0000
India	0.36	5.93	0.18	0.15	3.92	−0.21	0.0750	0.0882
Italy	0.44	7.00	0.22	0.39	2.20	0.25	0.0000	0.1044
Korea	−0.37	6.79	0.25	0.00	2.91	0.08	0.0000	0.0000
Malaysia	0.72	7.89	0.35	0.37	3.21	0.29	0.0000	0.0000
Mexico	1.11	6.07	0.50	0.77	2.63	0.24	0.2427	0.6026
Spain	0.39	8.76	0.40	0.03	3.08	0.29	0.0000	0.0000
South Africa	0.43	4.00	−0.13	0.36	5.06	−0.03	0.2993	0.0954
Switzerland	0.27	4.50	0.46	0.20	2.48	0.36	0.0000	0.0000
Taiwan	0.57	7.42	0.31	−0.06	7.95	0.05	0.0000	0.0000
Thailand	0.71	8.42	0.29	0.50	5.14	0.23	0.0000	0.0000
U.K.	0.35	4.01	0.44	0.27	4.08	0.23	0.0424	0.0616
U.S. Index	0.18	2.06	1.00	0.18	2.06	1.00	0.1189	0.0454
						Total =	1.0000	1.0000
						Mean =	0.58%	0.58%
						SD =	2.49%	1.81%
						SHP =	0.233	0.320

Source: E. Chang, C. Eun, and R. Kolodny, "International Diversification through Closed-End Country Funds," *Journal of Banking and Finance* (October 1995). Reprinted with permission of Elsevier Science.

0.320 for the latter. This point can be seen clearly from Exhibit 11.14, which traces out the efficient sets, separately, for CECFs and NAVs.

The figure shows that the NAVs offer superior diversification opportunities compared with the CECFs. Consequently, those who can invest directly in foreign markets without incurring excessive costs are advised to do so. However, for the majority of investors without such opportunities, CECFs still offer a cost-effective way of diversifying internationally. Lastly, note that country funds from emerging markets receive significant

EXHIBIT 11.14
Efficient Sets: Country Funds versus Net Assets: 1989.1–1990.12

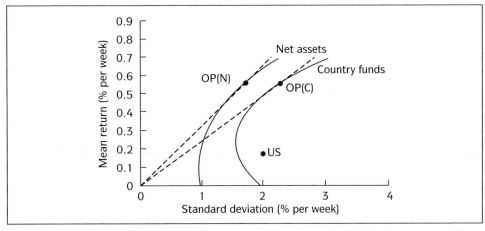

Note: OP(N) and OP(C) denote, respectively, the optimal portfolios comprising net assets and country funds. The efficient sets are illustrated by the dotted lines

weights in the optimal portfolio of CECFs. Specifically, the weight is 12.71 percent for the Brazil Fund, 7.50 percent for the India Fund, and 24.27 percent for the Mexico Fund. These emerging market funds, as a whole, receive about a 45-percent weight in the optimal CECF portfolio. This implies that CECFs from emerging markets can play an important role in expanding the investment opportunity set for international investors.

11.5 International Diversification with ADRs

www.adr.com/

This website managed by J.P. Morgan & Co. is a comprehensive source of information on American depository receipts.

Investors can achieve international diversification using American depository receipts (ADRs), as well as country funds. As explained in Chapter 8, ADRs represent receipts for foreign shares held in the American (depository) banks' foreign branches or custodians. Like closed-end country funds, ADRs are traded on American exchanges like domestic American securities. Consequently, investors can save transaction costs and also benefit from speedy and dependable disclosures, settlements, and custody services. The International Finance in Practice box on page 268, "Live Here, Invest Abroad," describes the virtues of investing via ADRs. It is noted that like American investors, British and European investors may achieve international diversification at home using global depository receipts (GDRs), which represent ownership claims on those foreign shares that are listed on the London Stock Exchange.

A few studies examined the potential benefits of international diversification with ADRs. Officer and Hoffmeister (1987) found that adding ADRs to a domestic portfolio had substantial risk reduction benefits. Including as few as four ADRs in a representative American stock portfolio reduced risk, measured by the standard deviation of returns, by as much as 25 percent without reducing the expected return. They also found that ADRs tend to have very low beta exposure to the American stock market. During the sample period 1973–1983, ADRs were found to have an average American beta of only 0.264.

Wahab and Khandwala (1993) found similar results. They reported that when investors hold an equally weighted portfolio of seven ADRs and the S&P 500, the annualized standard deviation of daily returns dropped from 30.2 percent (for a purely domestic portfolio) to 17.5 percent. They also reported that most of the nonsystematic risk of the portfolio was eliminated by adding only seven ADRs to the S&P 500. Adding ADRs beyond seven did not reduce the portfolio risk materially, regardless of portfolio weights.

Considering that the majority of ADRs are from such developed countries as Australia, Japan, and the United Kingdom, American investors have a limited opportunity to diversify into emerging markets using ADRs. However, in a few emerging markets like Mexico, investors can choose from several ADRs. In this situation, investors should consider the relative advantages and disadvantages of ADRs and CECFs as a means of international diversification. Compared with ADRs, CECFs are likely to provide more complete diversification. As shown previously, however, the potential gains from investing in them tend to be reduced by premiums/discounts.

11.6 International Diversification with WEBS

In April 1996, the American Stock Exchange (AMEX) introduced a class of securities called **World Equity Benchmark Shares (WEBS),** designed and managed by Barclays Global Investors. In essence, WEBS are exchange-traded open-end country funds that are designed to closely track foreign stock market indexes. Currently, there are 20 WEBS tracking the Morgan Stanley Capital International (MSCI) indexes for the following individual countries: Australia, Austria, Belgium, Brazil, Canada, France, Germany, Hong Kong, Italy, Japan, Korea, Malaysia, Mexico, the Netherlands, Singapore, Spain, Sweden, Switzerland, Taiwan, and the United Kingdom. The AMEX had previously introduced a similar security for the American market, Standard & Poor's Depository Receipts (SPDRs) known as "spiders," that is designed to track the S&P

www.ishares.com/

Provides extensive coverage of exchange traded funds, including WEBS.

500 Index. Using **exchange traded funds (ETFs)** like WEBS and spiders, investors can trade a whole stock market index as if it were a single share. Being open-end funds, WEBS trade at prices that are very close to their net asset values. In addition to single-country index funds, investors can achieve global diversification instantaneously just by holding shares of the S&P Global 100 Index Fund that is also trading on the AMEX with other WEBS.

A recent study by Khorana, Nelling, and Trester (1998) found that WEBS, indeed, track the underlying MSCI country indexes very closely. For example, the average correlation of daily returns between WEBS and the underlying country indexes is 0.97. They also found that the average correlation of WEBS with the S&P 500 Index is quite low, 0.22, which makes WEBS an excellent tool for international risk diversification. For those investors who desire international equity exposure, WEBS may well serve as a major alternative to such traditional tools as international mutual funds, ADRs, and closed-end country funds.

11.7 Why Home Bias in Portfolio Holdings?

As previously documented, investors can potentially benefit a great deal from international diversification. The actual portfolios that investors hold, however, are quite different from those predicted by the theory of international portfolio investment. Recently, various researchers, such as French and Porteba (1991), Cooper and Kaplanis (1994), Tesar and Werner (1993), and Glassman and Riddick (1993), documented the extent to which portfolio investments are concentrated in domestic equities.

Exhibit 11.15, which is adopted from Cooper and Kaplanis (1994), shows the extent of **home bias in portfolio holdings.** American investors, for instance, invested 98 percent of their funds in domestic equities as of 1987 when the American stock market accounted for only 36.4 percent of the world market capitalization value. Relatively speaking, French investors seem to invest more internationally—they put 35.6 percent of their funds in foreign equities and 64.4 percent in domestic equities. Considering, however, that the French share in the world market value is only 2.6 percent, French investors also display a striking degree of home bias in their portfolio holdings.

This home bias in actual portfolio holdings obviously runs counter to the strand of literature, including Grubel (1968), Levy and Sarnat (1970), Solnik (1974), Lessard (1976), and Eun and Resnick (1988), that collectively established a strong case for international diversification. This points to the following possibilities. First, domestic securities may provide investors with certain extra services, such as hedging against domestic inflation, that foreign securities do not. Second, there may be barriers, formal or informal, to investing in foreign securities that keep investors from realizing gains

EXHIBIT 11.15

The Home Bias in Equity Portfolios: December 1987

Country	Share in the World Market Value (%)	Proportion of Domestic Equities in the Portfolio (%)
France	2.6	64.4
Germany	3.2	75.4
Italy	1.9	91.0
Japan	43.7	86.7
Spain	1.1	94.2
Sweden	0.8	100.0
United Kingdom	10.3	78.5
United States	36.4	98.0
Total = 100.0		

Source: Ian Cooper and Evi Kaplanis, "Home Bias in Equity Portfolios, Inflation Hedging, and International Capital Market Equilibrium," *Review of Financial Studies* 7 (1994) pp. 45–60. Reprinted by permission of Oxford University Press.

Live Here, Invest Abroad

Global consumers, global investors. Americans' appetite for products from abroad only begins with French champagne, Swiss chocolate and Japanese televisions. American investors are flocking to buy stock in the foreign corporations that make such goods—and not only through the already well-publicized route of mutual funds. They are purchasing shares of individual companies in the form of American depository receipts, or ADRs.

ADRs of about 1,300 foreign firms trade on U.S. stock markets, with one ADR certificate equaling a given number of shares of stock. In 1993, total ADR trading volume on the New York and American exchanges and Nasdaq topped $200 billion, up from $94 billion in 1991 and $41 billion in 1988. With an average of 15 new ADRs a month, the trend shows no signs of topping out.

It's easy to comprehend the enthusiasm. Last year, Merrill Lynch's ADR Composite Index, which tracks 184 ADRs and is the only index of its kind, chalked up a 29.9 percent gain. That was far ahead of the 10.1 percent gain in the Standard & Poor's 500-stock index and just slightly below the average 30.2 percent return for international stock funds. Some ADRs enjoyed triple-digit returns. From March 1, 1993, to Feb. 28, 1994, for example, the ADR price of the Signet Group, the U.K.'s largest retailer of fine jewelry, surged 400 percent to $9.38.

Half a Dozen Winning ADRs

Of the 184 American depository receipts that trade on major U.S. exchanges, the six best performers over the year ended February 28 are listed below.

Company (Country)	Business	Recent Price	12-Month Price Change
Signet Group (Britain)	U.K./U.S. jewelry stores	$ 9.88	400.0%
Corimon (Venezuela)	Paints, chemicals, juices	15.50	189.4%
Fai Insurances (Australia)	Insurance	4.00	159.2%
Danka Business Sys. (Britain)	U.S./U.K. office equipment stores	43.13	143.6%
WPP Group (Britain)	Marketing/public relations	3.19	118.5%
Philips Electr. (Neth.)	Consumer electronics	27.75	108.4%

USN&WR—Basic data: Merrill Lynch International Quantitative Analysis

from international diversification. In what follows, we are going to examine possible reasons for the home bias in portfolio holdings.[6]

First, consider the possibility that investors face country-specific inflation risk due to the violations of purchasing power parity and that domestic equities may provide a hedging service against domestic inflation risk. In this case, investors who would like to hedge domestic inflation risk may allocate a disproportionate share of their investment funds to domestic equities, resulting in home bias. This, however, is not a likely scenario. Those investors who are averse to inflation risk are likely to invest in domestic risk-free bonds, rather than domestic equities, which tends to be a poor hedge against inflation.[7] In addition, a study by Cooper and Kaplanis (1994) rules out inflation hedging as a primary cause for home bias.

Second, the observed home bias may reflect institutional and legal restrictions on foreign investments. For example, many countries used to restrict foreigners' ownership share of domestic firms. In Finland, foreigners could own at most 30 percent of the shares outstanding of any Finnish firm. In Korea, foreigners' ownership proportion was restricted to 20 percent of any Korean firm. As a result, foreigners had to pay premiums for local shares, which might reduce the gains from investing in those restricted markets. At the same time, some institutional investors may not invest more than a

---

[6]For a survey of this issue, readers are referred to Uppal (1992).

[7]Fama and Schwert (1975) showed that common shares are a perverse hedge against domestic inflation in that returns to common shares are significantly negatively correlated with the inflation rate. In comparison, bond returns are positively correlated with the inflation rate.

"U.S. stocks are increasingly pricey and precarious," explains Mark Coler, publisher of the *Global Portfolio* (800-582-9854; $195 for a one-year trial subscription), an ADR newsletter that compiles brokerage reports but doesn't make its own recommendations. "Many foreign shares still have some big gains ahead as a global economic recovery takes hold."

To buy ADRs, you don't have to dial overseas; all it takes is a quick call to a broker. ADRs are issued by the U.S. banks that hold the underlying foreign shares in custody and are sold in U.S. dollars through brokers, just like stocks.

Watch the News

ADRs open the door to a new world, but staying abreast of currency fluctuations and economic and political developments is a must. When Mexico's top presidential candidate was assassinated last week, for example, the ADR price of Teléfonos de México, the national telephone company, dropped by more than 6 percent overnight.

Many foreign firms, moreover, tell shareholders—including those back home—as little as possible. About 70 percent of foreign companies offering ADRs choose not to file financial statements with the Securities and Exchange Commission. Executive pay, lines of business and insider trading thus remain mysteries, and shareholders rarely get prospectuses or quarterly income reports. As a result, these companies' ADRs trade on the "pink sheets" segment of the over-the-counter market, a realm exempt from the rules of the bigger exchanges.

Big Feet

Prices can be hard to track in that thinly traded part of the market, but that doesn't mean the companies are fly-by-nights or start-ups. Most pink-sheeted ADRs are big-foot entities like Nestlé, Mitsubishi and Deutsche Bank that simply reject the arduous process of conforming to U.S. standards.

For investors who want to learn more, Chicago-based Morningstar Inc., a publisher of mutual fund reports, plans a late April start-up, *Morningstar American Depository Receipts* (800-876-5005; biweekly; $35 for a three-month trial subscription). The report will probe 700 ADRs, including about 300 pink sheeters and all of the others, with up to 10 years of data, business summaries and market snapshots, as well as a list of the five mutual funds owning the greatest number of a company's shares.

Investors hungry for foreign fare sans stomachache can dine at foreign stock mutual funds. "Overseas funds probably won't see quite as much action this year, but the good ones are still likely to outperform the U.S. market," says Michael Stolper, publisher of the *Mutual Fund Monthly* newsletter (800-426-6502; $49 annually). Two that Stolper recommends are GAM International, (800) 426-4685, and Janus Worldwide, (800) 525-3713. GAM, a nine-year-old fund, has had an average annual return of 25.6 percent. Janus Worldwide had a 1993 return of 28.4 percent—champagne and chocolate performance by any measure.

certain fraction of their funds overseas under the so-called *prudent man rule*. For example, Japanese insurance companies and Spanish pension funds may invest at most 30 percent of their funds in foreign securities. These inflow and outflow restrictions may contribute to the home bias in actual portfolio holdings.

Third, extra taxes and transaction/information costs for foreign securities can inhibit cross-border investments, giving rise to home bias. Investors often have to pay withholding taxes on dividends from foreign securities for which they may or may not receive tax credits in their home country. Transaction costs can be higher for foreign securities, partly because many foreign markets are relatively thin and illiquid and partly because investment in foreign securities often involves transactions in foreign exchange markets. Moreover, as argued by Merton (1987), investors tend not to hold securities which they are not familiar with. To the extent that investors feel familiar with domestic securities, but not with foreign securities, they are going to allocate funds to domestic, but not to foreign, securities. It is even possible that some investors may not be fully aware of the potential gains from international investments. The International Finance in Practice box on page 270, "Going Abroad: The Attractions of Foreign Investment" provides a practical guide for individual investors interested in the benefits of international investments.

The observed home bias in asset holdings is likely to reflect a combination of some of the factors mentioned above. Considering the ongoing integration of international financial markets, coupled with the active financial innovations introducing new financial products, such as country funds and international mutual funds, home bias may be substantially mitigated in the near future.

Going Abroad: The Attractions of Foreign Investment

In general, the attraction of adding foreign securities to a portfolio is in the opportunity for diversification. You find assets abroad that you cannot find at home. To what extent is the foreign selection greater than the domestic? Well, Canada represents 2.5 percent of total world market capitalization. So, 97.5 percent of available assets are in other countries.

Special difficulties and risks arise when dealing in foreign shares and bonds. For one thing, there is the legitimate fear of the unknown. The foundation of good investment decisions is information, and access to dependable and relevant information tends to fade with distance. Then there are the problems associated with dealing in foreign currencies and foreign taxes, as well as foreign rules and regulations. All of this may seem forbidding. The question, as always in investing, is whether the potential gain is worth the effort. It generally is.

Foreign securities substantially expand the number and variety of assets that can be introduced into a portfolio. Consider that there are approximately 4,000 shares listed on the TSE, MSE, and the Canadian Venture Exchange. In comparison, there are 29,000 shares listed on exchanges around the world. So, for every Canadian stock available to a Canadian investor, seven shares are available abroad. The opportunity set expands even further when we bring in foreign bonds.

A portfolio is designed and constructed in view of expected return and risk. The attraction of foreign securities is *not* so much a matter of pursuing higher expected returns, but, rather, it is to achieve fuller diversification. The less-than-perfect correlation of the returns on domestic assets and foreign assets is all that is required to expand the set of return/risk combinations. At every level of expected return, risk is reduced through diversification. This expansion of the "efficient" set allows a portfolio to be designed with higher expected return per unit of risk. The smaller the domestic–foreign correlation, the more attractive are foreign shares in a portfolio.

Returns on foreign shares are less than perfectly correlated with returns on domestic shares for various reasons. Above all, some foreign shares are fundamentally different from anything that is available at home. For instance, Italian shoe companies are uniquely Italian. Even when we consider a foreign share that has a Canadian counterpart, the two are likely to have different price processes that result in diversification opportunities. For example, German banks and Canadian banks have different price responses to similar interest rate changes, not to mention that German and Canadian interest rates are not in perfect sync. As a result, holding Canadian *and* German banks can reduce risk at each level of expected return.

Another potential source of diversification is the exchange rate. A foreign asset is denominated in foreign currency. Even if the asset value is unchanged in terms of its home currency, holding that asset will result in a gain or loss for the Canadian investor if the exchange rate changes *vis-à-vis* the Canadian dollar. If the foreign currency appreciates, the Canadian investor captures a foreign exchange gain; if the foreign currency weakens, the investor incurs a foreign exchange loss.

If all the shares in the world marched to the same drummer, international diversification would be a fruitless exercise. If all securities are priced off the same "global index," a phenomenon which itself implies complete capital market integration, the effects of global diversification would then be built into all securities, foreign and domestic alike. An investor might as well stay at home. On the other hand, if capital markets around the world are not fully integrated, then differences among markets can be exploited through foreign investment.

The potential for fruitful, risk-reducing international diversification can be read directly from the correlations of, say, the TSE 300 and comparable indexes in other places, such as the S&P 500 in New York, FTSE in London, the CAC 40 in Paris, the Hang Seng in Hong Kong, and the All Ordinaries in Australia. A correlation coefficient of 1 indicates perfect correlation, and hence no diversification potential, whereas values less than 1 suggest that combining Canadian shares with that index or the shares within it would reduce risk. (See Table 11.1.)

TABLE 11.1	**Correlation Coefficients: Canadian Index versus Indexes in 11 Foreign Countries**

Monthly Data, January 1995 to December 2003

Country	Correlation Coefficient
United States	0.82
United Kingdom	0.73
France	0.66
Germany	0.65
Australia	0.61
Mexico	0.60
Hong Kong	0.57
Brazil	0.54
Singapore	0.53
Italy	0.45
Japan	0.37

A number of factors can make investing in foreign securities a bit more onerous than investing at home. High among these are informational problems, such as limited data on firms, differences in accounting and reporting practices, and the lack of performance benchmarks. In addition, some countries impose withholding taxes on interests and dividends paid to foreigners. Other countries, Canada among them, have tax-based impediments to foreign investments, such as the denial of RRSP eligibility beyond a certain limit of foreign investment.

Impediments to foreign investment seem bigger than they really are. For example, foreign transactions costs are not substantially greater than they are for domestic transactions. Taxes paid to foreign governments can usually be credited against the investor's tax at home. Information, especially for the major foreign companies or country indexes, is readily available. However, as discussed below, the foreign play can often be done very effectively through domestic vehicles, such as mutual funds—with professionals attending to information and analysis.

Many well-known foreign securities are readily available through brokers. Major Canadian brokers, including discount brokers, deal in all shares listed on North American exchanges. So, that provides direct access to the American shares and bonds. But what about destinations farther away, say, London, Paris, or Tokyo? Again, brokers can make arrangements. With substantial volume in these major exchanges and virtually no restrictions on foreign participation, Canadian brokers are only a few computer key strokes away from placing a direct order.

In addition, shares of major companies from outside of North America are often available in the form of American Depositary Receipts (ADRs). The ADR mechanism is simple and convenient. An offshore branch of a American bank purchases shares of a foreign company, say, Volvo in Sweden, and holds the shares in trust in its vault. American operations then issues a depositary receipt, a Volvo ADR, which is traded in the United States and beyond. An ADR is a security issued by an American bank in place of the foreign shares that it holds in trust. ADRs represent ownership in a foreign company. The value of the ADR is determined by the value of the underlying shares—a value relationship that is ensured by the fact that an investor can always trade in the ADR for a true share and hence eliminate any price discrepancy through arbitrage. The conveniences that ADRs provide include their denomination in American dollars, dividend flow through, tax management, and the bank's role as the custodian of the shares.

When dealing with direct purchases, the brokers' primary concerns are to do with liquidity and restrictions on trading in foreign markets. These concerns become increasingly serious with respect to more remote and unexplored markets. While Singapore and Rio are now well into the mainstream of global finance, one ought to be more circumspect in the case of, say, Kiev or Accra. Ukranian or Ghanaian shares are unlikely to be well researched. The markets are thin. Moreover, the currency risk is high. The Canadian investor will encounter substantial difficulty in direct purchases of securities in such remote markets.

In short, direct purchases are generally not the best route to foreign markets. For one thing, the Canadian investor is well advised to *diversify* foreign holdings. That can be especially challenging in terms of gathering information and executing transactions. Fortunately, most of the gain with little of the pain can be captured in other ways, such as through mutual funds with foreign content.

Mutual funds offer individual investors access to a variety of prefabricated portfolios with varying degrees and types of foreign content. For example:

Global funds invest in Canadian and non-Canadian shares.

International funds invest in non-Canadian shares only.

A *regional* fund invests in a specific geographic area, for example, Europe or Asia.

A *country* fund invests in a specific country, for example, the United States or Japan.

A *specialty* fund consists of shares in an industry group, such as telecommunications—with international diversification; for example, Nortel, Nokia, and France Telecom.

At the institutional level, the big players, such as insurance companies and pension funds, mimic foreign exposure—both its rewards and its risks—through derivatives. Through derivatives, the portfolio effects of foreign investment can be achieved through mimicry as opposed to direct purchase of foreign securities. Institutions often favour this approach, as it allows them to satisfy regulatory restrictions and yet have a significant foreign play with minimal capital commitment.

In summary, a world of opportunity beckons the wise investor. Adding foreign securities to the portfolio brings risk-reducing diversification along with a panorama of returns that are unavailable at home. The case for holding foreign securities is all the more compelling when one considers the full extent of most investors' undiversified exposure to the economic and financial idiosyncrasies of Canada. One's human capital and employment, house, tangible assets, pension, and bank account—the bulk of personal wealth—are all "domestic" assets. The investor's securities portfolio is virtually the only way to diversify within the broad portfolio of wealth.

Source: Excerpted fom D.J.S. Brean, "Going Abroad: The Attractions of Foreign Investment," in D.J.S Brean and John Hull, eds., *International Financial Research, Advisor's Guide Series*; Toronto: RMPublishing (2000).

SUMMARY

This chapter discusses the gains from international portfolio diversification, which emerged as a major form of cross-border investment in the 1980s, rivalling foreign direct investment by firms.

1. International portfolio investment (IPI) has been growing rapidly in recent years due to (a) the deregulation of financial markets, and (b) the introduction of such investment vehicles as international mutual funds, country funds, and internationally cross-listed shares, which allow investors to achieve international diversification without incurring excessive costs.

2. Investors diversify to reduce risk; the extent to which the risk is reduced by diversification depends on the covariances among individual securities making up the portfolio. Since security returns tend to covary much less across countries than within a country, investors can reduce portfolio risk more by diversifying internationally than purely domestically.

3. In a full-fledged risk-return analysis, investors can gain from international diversification in terms of "extra" returns at the "domestic-equivalent" risk level. Empirical evidence indicates that regardless of domicile and the numeraire currency used to measure returns, investors can capture extra returns when they hold their optimal international portfolios.

4. Foreign exchange rate uncertainty contributes to the risk of foreign investment through its own volatility as well as through its covariance with local market returns. Generally speaking, exchange rates are substantially more volatile than bond market returns but less so than stock market returns. This suggests that investors can enhance their gains from international diversification, especially in the case of bond investment, when they hedge exchange risk using, say, forward contracts.

5. American-based international mutual funds that investors actually held did provide investors with an effective global risk diversification. In addition, the majority of them outperformed the American stock market index in terms of the Sharpe performance measure. Closed-end country funds (CECFs) also provided American investors with an opportunity to achieve international diversification at home. CECFs, however, were found to behave more like American securities in comparison with their underlying net asset values (NAVs).

6. Despite sizable potential gains from international diversification, investors allocate a disproportionate share of their funds to domestic securities, displaying so-called home bias. Home bias is likely to reflect imperfections in the international financial markets, such as excessive transaction/information costs, discriminatory taxes for foreigners, and legal/institutional barriers to international investments.

KEY WORDS

closed-end country fund (CECF), 263
exchange traded funds (ETFs), 267
home bias in portfolio holdings, 270
optimal international portfolios, 251
Sharpe performance measure (SHP), 254
world beta, 254
World Equity Benchmark Shares (WEBS), 266

QUESTIONS

1. What factors are responsible for the recent surge in international portfolio investment?

2. Security returns are found to be less correlated across countries than within a country. Why can this be so?

3. Explain the concept of the world beta of a security.

4. Explain the concept of the Sharpe performance measure.

5. Explain how exchange rate fluctuations affect the return from a foreign market, measured in dollar terms. Discuss the empirical evidence on the effect of exchange rate uncertainty on the risk of foreign investment.

6. Would exchange rate changes always increase the risk of foreign investment? Discuss the condition under which exchange rate changes may actually reduce the risk of foreign investment.

7. Evaluate a home country's multinational corporations as a tool for international diversification.

8. Discuss the advantages and disadvantages of closed-end country funds (CECFs) relative to American depository receipts (ADRs) as a means of international diversification.

9. Why do you think closed-end country funds often trade at a premium or discount?

10. Why do investors invest the lion's share of their funds in domestic securities?

11. What are the advantages of investing via international mutual funds?

12. Discuss how the advent of the euro would affect international diversification strategies.

PROBLEMS

1. Suppose you are a euro-based investor who just sold the Microsoft shares that you had bought six months ago. You had invested 10,000 euros to buy Microsoft shares at $120 per share; the exchange rate was $1.50 per euro. You sold the shares at $135 per share and converted the dollar proceeds into euro at the exchange rate of $1.60 per euro. First, determine the profit from this investment in euro terms. Second, compute the rate of return on your investment in euro terms. How much of the return is due to the exchange rate movement?

2. Mr. James K. Silber, an avid international investor, just sold a share of Nestlé, a Swiss firm, for SF5,080. The share was bought for SF4,600 a year ago. The exchange rate is SF1.60 per dollar now and was SF1.78 per dollar a year ago. Mr. Silber received SF120 as a cash dividend immediately before the share was sold. Compute the rate of return on this investment in terms of American dollars.

3. In the above problem, suppose that Mr. Silber sold SF4,600, his principal investment amount, forward at the forward exchange rate of SF1.62 per dollar. How would this affect the dollar rate of return on this Swiss stock investment? In hindsight, should Mr. Silber have sold the Swiss franc amount forward or not? Why, or why not?

4. Japan Life Insurance Company invested $10,000,000 in pure-discount bonds when the exchange rate was 100 yen per dollar. The company liquidated the investment one year later for $10,650,000. The exchange rate turned out to be 120 yen per dollar at the time of liquidation. What rate of return did Japan Life realize on this investment in yen terms?

5. At the start of 2000, the annual interest rate was 6 percent in the United States and 2.8 percent in Japan. The exchange rate was 95 yen per dollar at the time. Mr. Jorus, manager of a Bermuda-based hedge fund, thought that the substantial interest advantage associated with investing in the United States relative to investing in Japan was not likely to be offset by the decline of the dollar against the yen. He thus concluded that it might be a good idea to borrow in Japan and invest in the United States. At the start of 2000, in fact, he borrowed ¥1,000 million for one year and invested in the United States. At the end of 2000, the exchange rate became 105 yen per dollar. How much profit did Mr. Jorus make in dollar terms?

6. From Exhibit 11.6, we obtain the following data in dollar terms:

Stock Market	Return (Mean)	Risk (SD)
United States	1.26% per month	4.43%
United Kingdom	1.23% per month	5.55%

The correlation coefficient between the two markets is 0.58. Suppose that you invest equally, that is, 50 percent in each of the two markets. Determine the expected return and standard deviation risk of the resulting international portfolio.[8] This problem can be solved using the spreadsheet MPTSolver.xls.

7. Suppose you are interested in investing in the stock markets of seven countries—Canada, France, Germany, Japan, Switzerland, the United Kingdom, and the United States. Specifically, you would like to solve for the optimal (tangency) portfolio comprising the above seven stock markets. In solving the optimal portfolio, use the input data (i.e., correlation coefficients, means, and standard deviations) provided in Exhibit 11.6. The risk-free interest rate is assumed to be 0.5 percent per month and you can take a short position in any stock market. What are the optimal weights for each of the seven stock markets? This problem can be solved using the MPTSolver.xls spreadsheet.

8. The HFS Trustees have solicited input from three consultants concerning the risks and rewards of an allocation to international equities. Two of them strongly favour such action, while the third consultant commented as follows:

"The risk reduction benefits of international investing have been significantly overstated. Recent studies relating to the cross-country correlation structure of equity returns during different market phases cast serious doubt on the ability of international investing to reduce risk, especially in situations when risk reduction is needed the most."

a. Describe the behaviour of cross-country equity return correlations which the consultant is referring to. Explain how that behaviour may diminish the ability of international investing to reduce risk in the short run.

   Assume the consultant's assertion is correct.

b. Explain why it might still be more efficient on a risk/reward basis to invest internationally, rather than only domestically, in the long run.

   The HFS Trustees have decided to invest in non-American equity markets and have hired Jacob Hind, a specialist manager, to implement this decision. He has recommended that an unhedged equities position be taken in Japan, providing the following comment and the table data to support his views:

   "Appreciation of a foreign currency increases the returns to an American dollar investor. Since appreciation of the Yen from 100¥/$US to 98¥/$US is expected, the Japanese stock position should not be hedged."

Market Rates and Hind's Expectations

	United States	Japan
Spot rate (yen per US$)	n/a	100
Hind's 12-month currency forecast (yen per US$)	n/a	98
1-year Eurocurrency rate (% per annum)	6.00	0.80
Hind's 1-year inflation forecast (% per annum)	3.00	0.50

   Assume that the investment horizon is one year and that there are no costs associated with currency hedging.

c. State and justify whether Hind's recommendation (not to hedge) should be followed. Show any calculations.

---

[8]The mean return on the portfolio is simply the weighted average of the returns on the individual securities that are included in the portfolio. The portfolio variance, on the other hand, can be computed using the following formula:

$$\text{Var}(R_p) = \Sigma_i \Sigma_j x_i x_j \sigma_{ij}$$

where x_i represents an investment weight for the ith security, and σ_{ij} denotes the variances and covariances among individual securities. In the case where the portfolio comprises two securities, its variance is computed as follows:

$$\text{Var}(R_p) = x_1^2 \sigma_1^2 + x_2^2 \sigma_2^2 + 2 x_1 x_2 \sigma_{12}$$

The standard deviation, of course, is the square root of the variance. It is also noted that the covariance σ_{ij} is related to the correlation coefficient ρ_{ij} via $\sigma_{ij} = \rho_{ij} \sigma_i \sigma_j$, where σ_i is the standard deviation of returns on the ith security.

CFA® PROBLEMS

9. Rebecca Taylor, an international equity portfolio manager, recognizes that an optimal country allocation strategy combined with an optimal currency strategy should produce optimal portfolio performance. To develop her strategies, Taylor produced the table below, which provides expected return data for the three countries and three currencies that she may invest in. The table contains the information she needs to make market strategy (country allocation) decisions and currency strategy (currency allocation) decisions.

Expected Returns for an American-Based Investor

Country	Local Currency Equity Returns	Exchange Rate Returns	Local Currency Eurodeposit Returns
Japan	7.0%	1.0%	5.0%
United Kingdom	10.5	−3.0	11.0
United States	8.4	0.0	7.5

a. Prepare a ranking of the three countries in terms of expected equity-market return premiums. Show your calculations.

b. Prepare a ranking of the three countries in terms of expected currency return premiums from the perspective of an American investor. Show your calculations.

c. Explain *one* advantage a portfolio manager obtains, in formulating a global investment strategy, by calculating both expected market premiums and expected currency premiums.

INTERNET EXERCISES

1. You would like to invest in the Mexican stock market and consider two alternative ways of investing in Mexico: (i) the Mexican closed-end country fund trading on the New York Stock Exchange, and (ii) the WEBS for Mexico trading on the American Stock Exchange. Their websites are:

   www.themexicofund.com

   www.ishares.com/international/Americas/MSCI Mexico Index Fund

   Study all the relevant information from the websites and evaluate the relative merits and demerits of the two securities for your Mexican investment. Which one would you prefer?

2. You would like to evaluate the performance of the seven major stock markets of the world—Canada, France, Germany, Japan, the Netherlands, the United Kingdom, and the United States—for the last five years. In doing so, you want to use the Sharpe ratio, providing a risk-adjusted performance measure. Compute this Sharpe performance measure for each of the seven markets using the data from the following website: www.msci.com. Briefly discuss your findings.

MINI CASE

Solving for the Optimal International Portfolio

Suppose you are a financial adviser and your client, who is currently investing only in the American stock market, is considering diversifying into the British stock market. At the moment, there are neither particular barriers nor restrictions on investing in the British stock market. Your client would like to know what kind of benefits can be expected from doing so. Using the data provided in problem 6, solve the following problems:

1. Graphically illustrate various combinations of portfolio risk and return that can be generated by investing in the American and British stock markets with different proportions. Two extreme proportions are (a) investing 100 percent in

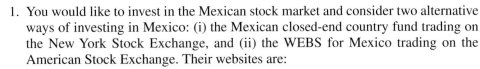

the United States with no position in the British market, and (b) investing 100 percent in the British market with no position in the American market.

2. Solve for the optimal international portfolio comprising the American and British markets. Assume that the monthly risk-free interest rate is 0.5 percent and that investors can take a short (negative) position in either market. This problem can be solved using the spreadsheet MPTSolver.xls.

3. What is the extra return that American investors can expect to capture at the American-equivalent risk level? Also trace out the efficient set. Appendix 11.B provides an example.

REFERENCES & SUGGESTED READINGS

Adler, Michael, and Bernard Dumas. "International Portfolio Choice and Corporation Finance: A Synthesis." *Journal of Finance* 38 (1983), pp. 925–84.

Bailey, Warren, and J. Lim. "Evaluating the Diversification Benefits of the New Country Funds." *Journal of Portfolio Management* 18 (1992), pp. 74–80.

Cooper, Ian, and Evi Kaplanis. "Home Bias in Equity Portfolios, Inflation Hedging, and International Capital Market Equilibrium," *Review of Financial Studies* 7 (1994), pp. 45–60.

Cumby, R., and J. Glen. "Evaluating the Performance of International Mutual Funds." *Journal of Finance* 45 (1990), pp. 497–521.

Errunza, Vihang, Ked Hogan, and Mao-Wei Hung. "Can the Gains from International Diversification Be Achieved without Trading Abroad?" *Journal of Finance* (1999), 2075–107.

Eun, Cheol, and Bruce Resnick. "Exchange Rate Uncertainty, Forward Contracts and International Portfolio Selection." *Journal of Finance* 43 (1988), pp. 197–215.

Eun, Cheol, and Bruce Resnick. "International Diversification of Investment Portfolios: U.S. and Japanese Perspectives." *Management Science* 40 (1994), pp. 140–61.

Eun, Cheol, and Bruce Resnick. "International Equity Investments with Selective Hedging Strategies." *Journal of International Financial Markets, Institutions and Money* 7 (1997), pp. 21–42.

Eun, Cheol, Richard Kolodny, and Bruce Resnick. "Performance of U.S.-Based International Mutual Funds." *Journal of Portfolio Management* 17 (1991), pp. 88–94.

French, K., and J. Poterba. "Investor Diversification and International Equity Markets." *American Economic Review* 81 (1991), pp. 222–26.

Glassman, Debra, and Leigh Riddick. "Why Empirical Portfolio Models Fail: Evidence That Model Misspecification Creates Home Asset Bias," unpublished manuscript, 1993.

Grubel, H. G. "Internationally Diversified Portfolios." *American Economic Review* 58 (1968), pp. 1299–1314.

Jorion, Philippe. "Asset Allocation with Hedged and Unhedged Foreign Stocks and Bonds." *Journal of Portfolio Management* 15 (Summer 1989), pp. 49–54.

Khorana, A., E. Nelling, and J. Trester. "The Emergence of Country Index Funds." *Journal of Portfolio Management* (Summer 1998), pp. 78–84.

Larsen, Glen, Jr., and Bruce Resnick. "Universal Currency Hedging for International Equity Portfolios under Parameter Uncertainty." *International Journal of Business* 4 (1999), pp. 1–17.

Larsen, Glen, Jr., and Bruce Resnick. "The Optimal Construction of Internationally Diversified Equity Portfolios Hedged against Exchange Rate Uncertainty." *European Financial Management* 6 (2000), pp. 479–514.

Longin, Francois, and Bruneo Solnik. "Is the Correlation in International Equity Returns Constant?: 1960–1990." *Journal of International Money and Finance* 14 (1995), pp. 3–26.

Officer, Dennis, and Ronald Hoffmeister. "ADRs: A Substitute for the Real Thing?" *Journal of Portfolio Management* (Winter 1987), pp. 61–65.

Roll, Richard. "The International Crash of 1987." *Financial Analyst Journal* 44 (1988), pp. 19–35.

Sener, T. "Objectives of Hedging and Optimal Hedge Ratios: U.S. vs. Japanese Investors." *Journal of Multinational Financial Management* 8 (1998), pp. 137–53.

Solnik, Bruno. "Why Not Diversify Internationally?" *Financial Analyst Journal* 20 (1974), pp. 48–54.

Tesar, L., and I. Werner. "Home Bias and High Turnover," unpublished manuscript, 1993.

Uppal, Raman. "The Economic Determinants of the Home Country Bias in Investors' Portfolios: A Survey." *Journal of International Financial Management and Accounting* 4 (1992), pp. 171–89.

Wahab, Mahmood, and Amit Khandwala. "Why Not Diversify Internationally with ADRs?" *Journal of Portfolio Management* (Winter 1993), pp. 75–82.

International Investment with Exchange Risk Hedging

In this appendix, we show how hedging the exchange rate risk in an international portfolio can enhance the risk-return efficiency of an internationally diversified portfolio of financial assets. We begin with return and variance of returns from the point of view of a Canadian dollar investor investing in individual foreign security i:

$$R_{i\$} = (1 + R_i)(1 + e_i) - 1 \qquad\qquad\text{(11A.1a)}$$
$$= R_i + e_i + R_i e_i \qquad\qquad\text{(11A.1b)}$$
$$\approx R_i - e_i. \qquad\qquad\text{(11A.1c)}$$

In equation (11A.1c), we ignore the cross-product term, $R_i e_i$, which is generally small, for discussion purpose. Consequently, the expected return to the Canadian dollar investor from investing in foreign security i can be approximated as:

$$\bar{R}_{i\$} \approx \bar{R}_i + \bar{e}_i \qquad\qquad\text{(11A.2)}$$

Also, we can express the variance of dollar returns from the ith foreign security as follows:

$$Var(R_{i\$}) = Var(R_i) + Var(e_i) + 2Cov(R_i, e_i) \qquad\qquad\text{(11A.3)}$$

Similarly, we can state the covariance between dollar returns from two different foreign securities as follows:

$$Cov(R_{i\$}, R_{j\$}) = Cov(R_i, R_j) + Cov(e_i, e_j) + Cov(R_i, e_j) + Cov(R_j, e_i) \qquad\text{(11A.4)}$$

Now, consider a simple exchange risk hedging strategy in which the Canadian dollar investor sells the expected foreign currency proceeds forward. In dollar terms, it amounts to exchanging the "uncertain" dollar return, $(1 + \bar{R}_i)(1 + e_i) - 1$, for the "certain" dollar return, $(1 + \bar{R}_i)(1 + f_i) - 1$, where $f_i = (F_i - S_i)/S_i$ is the forward exchange premium of the currency denominating security i. Although the expected foreign investment proceeds will be converted into Canadian dollars at the known forward exchange rate under this strategy, the unexpected foreign investment proceeds will have to be converted into Canadian dollars at the uncertain future spot exchange rate. The dollar rate of return under the hedging (H) strategy is thus given by

$$R_{i\$H} = [1 + \bar{R}_i](1 + f_i) + [R_i - \bar{R}_i](1 + e_i) - 1 \qquad\qquad\text{(11A.5a)}$$
$$= R_i + f_i + R_i e_i + \bar{R}_i(f_i - e_i) \qquad\qquad\text{(11A.5b)}$$

Since the third and fourth terms of equation (11A.5b) are likely to be small in magnitude, the expected hedged return for the Canadian dollar investor can be approximated as follows:

$$\bar{R}_{i\$H} \approx \bar{R}_i + f_i \qquad\qquad\text{(11A.6)}$$

Recall from the forward expectations parity discussion in Chapter 5 that f_i can be unbiased estimate of $\bar{e}_i$, i.e., $f_i \approx \bar{e}_i$. Comparison of equations (11A.1c) and (11A.6) thus indicates that the expected return to the Canadian dollar investor is approximately the same, whether the investor hedges the exchange rate risk in the investment or remains unhedged.

To the extent that the investor establishes an effective hedge to eliminate exchange rate uncertainty, the $Var(e_i)$ and $Cov(R_i, e_i)$ terms in equation (11A.3) will be close to zero. Similarly, the $Cov(e_i, e_j)$, $Cov(R_i, e_j)$, and $Cov(R_j, e_i)$ terms in equation (11A.4) will be close to zero. Consequently, given that f_i is a constant, it follows that

$$Var(R_{i\$H}) < Var(R_{i\$}), \text{ and}$$

$$Cov(R_{i\$H}, R_{j\$H}) < Cov(R_{i\$}, R_{j\$}).$$

It thus follows that the risk-return efficiency is likely to be superior if the investor hedges the exchange rate risk when investing internationally.

Solving for the Optimal Portfolio

Here, we explain how to solve for the optimal portfolio of risky securities when there exists a risk-free asset paying a certain risk-free interest rate, R_f. Once we assume that investors prefer more wealth to less and are averse to risk, we can solve for the "optimal" portfolio by maximizing the Sharpe ratio (SHPp) of the excess portfolio return to the standard deviation risk. In other words,

$$\text{Max SHPp} = [\bar{R}_p - R_f]/\sigma_p \tag{11B.1}$$

where $\bar{R}_p$ is the expected rate of return on the portfolio and σ_p is the standard deviation of the portfolio returns.

The expected portfolio return, $\bar{R}_p$, is just the weighted average of the expected returns to individual assets, $\bar{R}_i$, included in the portfolio, that is,

$$\bar{R}_p = \Sigma_i x_i \bar{R}_i \tag{11B.2}$$

where x_i denotes a fraction of wealth invested in the ith individual asset; the sum of fractions should add up to one, that is, $\Sigma_i x_i = 1$. The portfolio risk, σ_p, on the other hand, is related to the variances and covariances of individual asset returns as follows:

$$\sigma_p = [\Sigma_i \Sigma_j x_i x_j \sigma_{ij}]^{1/2} \tag{11B.3}$$

where σ_{ij} denotes the covariance of returns to the ith and jth assets. What is inside the bracket is the variance of portfolio return.

Now, let us consider a simple case where the portfolio includes only two risky assets, A and B. In this case, the risk and return of the portfolio will be determined as follows:

$$\bar{R}_p = x_A \bar{R}_A + x_B \bar{R}_B \tag{11B.4}$$

$$\sigma_p = [x_A^2 \sigma_A^2 + x_B^2 \sigma_B^2 + 2x_A x_B \sigma_{AB}]^{1/2} \tag{11B.5}$$

Suppose we now want to solve for the optimal portfolio using the two assets. We then first substitute Equations 11B.4 and 11B.5 in Equation 11B.1 and maximize SHPp with respect to the portfolio weights x's to obtain the following solution:

$$x_A = \frac{[\bar{R}_A - R_f]\sigma_B^2 - [\bar{R}_B - R_f]\sigma_{AB}}{[\bar{R}_A - R_f]\sigma_B^2 + [\bar{R}_B - R_f]\sigma_A^2 - [\bar{R}_A - R_f + \bar{R}_B - R_f]\sigma_{AB}}$$

$$x_B = 1 - x_A \tag{11B.6}$$

EXAMPLE Suppose we are trying to construct the optimal international portfolio using the American (US) and the Dutch (NL) stock market indexes. From Exhibit 11.4, we obtain the following data (in percentage per month) for the two stock markets:

$$\bar{R}_{US} = 1.26; \quad \sigma_{US}^2 = 19.62$$

$$\bar{R}_{NL} = 1.38; \quad \sigma_{NL}^2 = 26.52$$

$$\sigma_{US,NL} = \sigma_{US}\sigma_{NL}\rho_{US,NL} = (4.43)(5.15)(0.62) = 14.14$$

Using the monthly risk-free rate of 0.55 percent, we can substitute the given data into Equation 11B.6 to obtain

$$x_{US} =$$

$$\frac{(1.26 - 0.55)(26.52) - (1.38 - 0.55)(14.14)}{(1.26 - 0.55)(26.52) + (1.38 - 0.55)(19.62) - (1.26 - 0.55 + 1.38 - 0.55)(14.14)}$$

$$= 0.5319$$

$$x_{NL} = 1 - x_{US} = 1 - 0.5319 = 0.4681$$

The optimal international portfolio thus comprises 53.19 percent in the American market and 46.81 percent in the Dutch market. The expected return and risk of the optimal portfolio can be computed as follows:

$$\bar{R}_{OP} = (0.5319)(1.26\%) + (0.4681)(1.38\%) = 1.32\%$$

$$\sigma_{OP} = [(0.5319)^2 (19.62) + (0.4681)^2 (26.52) + 2(0.5319)(0.4681)(14.14)]^{1/2}$$

$$= 4.29\%$$

The Sharpe performance measure of the optimal international portfolio is 0.180 (= (1.32 − 0.55)/4.29), which is compared with the Sharpe measure of 0.160 for the American market. One can, thus, compute the extra return from holding the optimal international portfolio at the American domestic-equivalent risk level as follows:

$$\Delta R_{US} = (\Delta SHP)(\sigma_{US}) = (0.180 - 0.160)(4.43) = .089\%$$

or 1.07 percent per year.

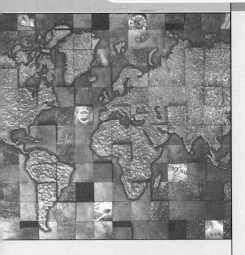

Foreign Exchange Exposure and Management

OUTLINE

Part Three is composed of three chapters covering the topics of economic, transaction, and translation exposure management, respectively.

CHAPTER 12 covers economic exposure, that is, the extent to which the value of the firm will be affected by unexpected changes in exchange rates. The chapter provides a way to measure economic exposure, discusses its determinants, and presents methods for managing and hedging economic exposure.

CHAPTER 13 covers the management of transaction exposure that arises from contractual obligations denominated in a foreign currency. Several methods for hedging this exposure are compared and contrasted. The chapter also includes a discussion of why an MNC should hedge, a debatable subject in the minds of both academics and practitioners.

CHAPTER 14 covers translation exposure or, as it is sometimes called, accounting exposure. Translation exposure refers to the effect that changes in exchange rates will have on the consolidated financial reports of an MNC. The chapter discusses, compares, and contrasts the various methods for translating financial statements denominated in foreign currencies and includes a discussion of managing translation exposure using funds adjustment and the pros and cons of using balance sheet and derivatives hedges.

Management of Economic Exposure

IN JANUARY 2003, the Canadian dollar exchange rate, that is, the number of Canadian dollars required to buy one American dollar in the spot market, was $1.575. By the end of the year 2003, the Canadian dollar had soared—or the American dollar had plummeted—to $1.300. Throughout the year the Canadian dollar appreciated more than 23 percent against the American dollar. That sharp change in the external value of the Canadian dollar, which was largely unexpected, had serious consequences for many Canadian firms. Some firms, such as those involved in exporting manufactured goods—for instance, automobiles or furniture—experienced a significant drop in their volume and profit on export sales. Other Canadian companies, especially those that import intermediate goods, enjoyed a windfall as their costs of production fell in Canadian dollar terms. Still other Canadian-based companies with foreign-source earnings saw the value of those earnings fall in line with the fall in the value of the of the American dollar. Toronto-based Four Seasons Hotels, for instance, reported a first-half 2003 net loss of $11 million compared with earnings of $26 million for the comparable period in 2002. The decline in Four Seasons' net earnings was attributed primarily to a foreign exchange loss which, according to the firm, "arose as a result of unprecedented movements in the American and Canadian dollars, British pound, and euro."

Changes in exchange rates may affect not only operating cashflows but also the dollar (home currency) values of assets and liabilities. A well-known example from Nova Scotia involves the finance of a bridge between Halifax and Dartmouth. In 1970, the Bridge Commission arranged loans from German and Swiss bankers to build the second of two bridges across the harbour. The loans—in fact, bonds denominated in German marks and Swiss francs—seemed attractive because of the low foreign interest rates. The Bridge Commission saved on interest expense and kept the tolls low. However, the subsequent and protracted drop in the value of the Canadian dollar against the German mark and the Swiss franc wiped out the interest cost advantage and added massively to the annual debt servicing costs. At its peak, the Bridge Commission's debt amounted to $125,000,000, nearly triple the total cost of construction for both harbour bridges.

Another classic illustration of the peril of facing currency exposure comes from Laker Airways, a British firm founded by Sir Freddie Laker, who pioneered the concept of mass-marketed, no-frills, low-fare air travel. Laker borrowed heavily in American dollars to finance acquisitions of aircraft, while the airline derived more than half its revenues in British pounds. As the American dollar appreciated against the British pound (and most other currencies) throughout the first half of the 1980s, the burden of servicing the dollar debts became overwhelming for Laker Airways, forcing it to default.

Effects on profits and corporate value that stem from changes in exchange rates, which are almost always unexpected, create "exchange rate risk." The unexpected nature of the exchange rate changes is crucial in the sense that an *expected* change would be built into the projections of profit and the value of, say, a firm's shares. We might ask, how do we know that the sharp appreciation of the Canadian dollar in 2003 was *unexpected*? The evidence is in the forward exchange rates that reveal traders' and financial institutions' views of what the exchange rate will be over ensuing months. In January 2003, for example, the 180-day forward rate was $1.59. If we consider this forward rate in January to be an informed forecast of what the exchange rate would be in June 2003, the forecast can then be compared with the actual exchange rate in June 2003. It turned out to be $1.37. The forward markets for foreign exchange were certainly not accurately forecasting the Canadian dollar appreciation of 2003.

The preceding examples suggest that exchange rate changes can systematically affect the value of the firm by influencing its operating cash flows as well as the domestic currency values of its assets and liabilities. In a study examining the exposure of American firms to currency risk, Jorion (1990) documented that a significant relationship exists between stock returns and the dollar's value. Recent studies, such as those by Choi and Prasad (1995), Simkins and Laux (1996), and Allayannis and Ofek (2001), also document that stock returns are sensitive to exchange rate movements.

Exhibit 12.1, drawn from the Simkins and Laux study, provides an estimate of American industries' market betas as well as the "forex" betas. The market and forex betas measure the sensitivities of an industry portfolio against the American stock market index and the dollar exchange rate index, respectively. As Exhibit 12.1 shows, the

EXHIBIT 12.1 Exchange Rate Exposure of American Industry Portfolios[a]	Industry	Market Beta[b]	Forex Beta[c]
	1. Aerospace	0.999	0.034
	2. Apparel	1.264	0.051
	3. Beverage	1.145	−0.437
	4. Building materials	1.107	0.604
	5. Chemicals	1.074	−0.009
	6. Computers, office equipment	0.928	0.248
	7. Electronics, electrical equipment	1.202	0.608*
	8. Food	1.080	−0.430
	9. Forest and paper products	1.117	0.445
	10. Furniture	0.901	1.217*
	11. Industrial and farm equipment	1.125	0.473
	12. Metal products	1.081	−0.440
	13. Metals	1.164	0.743*
	14. Mining and crude oil	0.310	−0.713
	15. Motor vehicles and parts	0.919	1.168*
	16. Petroleum refining	0.515	−0.746*
	17. Pharmaceuticals	1.124	−1.272*
	18. Publishing and printing	1.154	0.567
	19. Rubber and plastics	1.357	0.524
	20. Science, photo, and control equipment	0.975	−0.437*
	21. Cosmetics	1.051	0.417
	22. Textiles	1.279	1.831*
	23. Tobacco	0.898	−0.768*
	24. Toys, sporting goods	1.572	−0.660
	25. Transportation equipment	1.613	1.524*

[a]The market and forex (foreign exchange) betas are obtained from regressing the industry portfolio (monthly) returns, constructed from the *Fortune* 500 companies, on the American stock market index returns and the rate of change in the dollar exchange rate index over the sample period 1.1989–12.93.
[b]For every industry portfolio the market beta is statistically significant at the 1-percent level.
[c]The forex beta is significant for some industry portfolios and insignificant for others. Those forex betas that are significant at 10-percent or higher are denoted by (*).
Source: Betty Simkins and Paul Laux, "Derivatives Use and the Exchange Rate Risk of Investing in Large U.S. Corporations," Case Western Reserve University Working Paper (1996).

forex beta varies greatly across industry lines; it ranges from -1.272 for pharmaceuticals to 1.831 for textiles. A negative (positive) forex beta means that stock returns tend to move down (up) as the dollar appreciates. Out of the 25 industries studied, 10 were found to have significant exposure to exchange rate movements.

12.1 Three Types of Exposure

Before we turn to the important issue of how to measure and manage economic exposure, let us briefly discuss different types of exposure. It is conventional to classify foreign currency exposures into three types:

- Economic exposure
- Transaction exposure
- Translation exposure

www.stern.nyu.edu/
~igiddy/fxrisk.htm

Provides an overview of
exchange risk management
issues.

Economic exposure is defined as the extent to which the value of the firm is affected by unanticipated changes in exchange rates. Any anticipated changes in exchange rates would already be discounted and reflected in the firm's value. As we will discuss later in this chapter, changes in exchange rates can have a profound effect on the firm's competitive position in the world market and, thus, on its cash flows and market value.

Transaction exposure, a subject to be discussed in Chapter 13, is defined as the sensitivity of "realized" domestic currency values of the firm's contractual cash flows *denominated* in foreign currencies to unexpected exchange rate changes. Since settlements of these contractual cash flows affect the firm's domestic currency cash flows, transaction exposure is sometimes regarded as a short-term economic exposure. Transaction exposure arises from fixed-price contracting in a world where exchange rates change randomly.

On the other hand, **translation exposure,** which will be discussed in Chapter 14, refers to the potential that the firm's consolidated financial statements can be affected by changes in exchange rates. Consolidation involves translation of subsidiaries' financial statements from local currencies to the home currency. Consider a Canadian multinational firm that has subsidiaries in the United Kingdom and Japan. Each subsidiary will produce financial statements in local currency. To consolidate financial statements worldwide, the firm must translate the subsidiaries' financial statements in local currencies into the Canadian dollar, the home currency. As we will see later, translation involves many controversial issues. Resultant translation gains and losses represent the accounting system's attempt to measure economic exposure *ex post*. It does not provide a good measure of *ex ante* economic exposure.

In the remainder of this chapter, we focus on how to measure and manage economic exposure.

12.2 How to Measure Economic Exposure

Currency risk which refers to random changes in exchange rates, is not the same as currency exposure, which measures "what is at risk." Under certain conditions, a firm may not face any exposure at all, that is, nothing is at risk, even if exchange rates change randomly. Suppose your Canadian company maintains a vacation home for employees in the British countryside and the local price of this property always moves together with the pound price of the Canadian dollar. As a result, whenever the pound depreciates against the dollar, the local currency price of this property goes up by the same proportion. In this case, your company is not exposed to currency risk even if the pound/dollar exchange rate fluctuates randomly. The British asset your company owns has an embedded hedge against exchange risk, rendering the dollar price of the asset *insensitive* to exchange rate changes.

Consider an alternative situation in which the local (pound) price of your company's British asset barely changes. In this case, the dollar value of the asset will be highly *sensitive* to the exchange rate, since the former will change as the latter does. To the extent that the dollar price of the British asset exhibits "sensitivity" to exchange rate movements, your company is exposed to currency risk. Similarly, if your company's operating cash flows are sensitive to exchange rate changes, the company is again exposed to currency risk.

Exposure to currency risk, thus, can be properly measured by the *sensitivities* of (1) the future home currency values of the firm's assets (and liabilities), and (2) the firm's operating cash flows to random changes in exchange rates. The same point is illustrated by Exhibit 12.2; assets include the tangible assets (property, plant and equipment, inventory) as well as financial assets. Let us first discuss the case of asset exposure. For expositional convenience, assume that dollar inflation is nonrandom. Then, from the perspective of the Canadian firm that owns an asset in Britain, the exposure can be measured by the coefficient (b) in regressing the dollar value (P) of the British asset on the dollar/pound exchange rate (S).[1]

$$P = a + bS + e \tag{12.1}$$

where a is the regression constant and e is the random error term with mean zero, that is, $E(e) = 0$; $P = SP^*$, where P^* is the local currency (pound) price of the asset.[2] It is obvious from the above equation that the regression coefficient b measures the sensitivity of the dollar value of the asset (P) to the exchange rate (S). If the regression coefficient is zero, that is, $b = 0$, the dollar value of the asset is independent of exchange rate movements, implying no exposure. On the basis of the above analysis, one can say that *exposure is the regression coefficient*. Statistically, the **exposure coefficient, b**, is defined as follows:

$$b = \frac{\text{Cov}(P, S)}{\text{Var}(S)}$$

where Cov(P,S) is the covariance between the dollar value of the asset and the exchange rate, and Var(S) is the variance of the exchange rate.

EXHIBIT 12.2

Channels of Economic Exposure

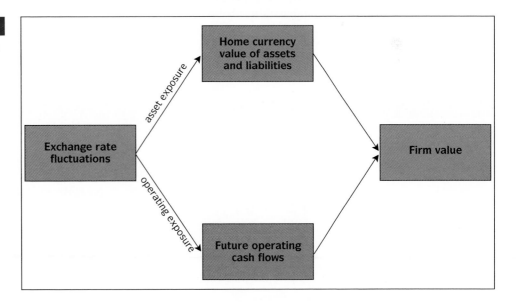

[1] Adler and Dumas (1984) first proposed this notion of currency exposure.

[2] In addition, the covariance between the random error (residual) term and the exchange rate is zero, that is, Cov(S,e) = 0, by construction.

Next, we show how to apply the exposure measurement technique using numerical examples. Suppose that a Canadian firm has an asset in Britain whose local currency price is random. For simplicity, let us assume that there are three possible states of the world, with each state equally likely to occur. The future local currency price of this British asset as well as the future exchange rate will be determined by the realized state of the world. First, consider Case 1, described in Panel A of Exhibit 12.3. Case 1 indicates that the local currency price of the asset (P^*) and the dollar price of the pound (S) are positively correlated so that depreciation (appreciation) of the pound against the dollar is associated with a declining (rising) local currency price of the asset. The dollar price of the asset on the future (liquidation) date can be $1,372, or $1,500 or $1,712, depending on the realized state of the world.

When we compute the parameter values for Case 1, we obtain $Cov(P,S) = 34/3$, $Var(S) = 0.02/3$, and thus $b = £1,700$. This pound amount, £1,700, represents the sensitivity of the future dollar value of the British asset to random changes in exchange rate. This finding implies that the Canadian firm faces a substantial exposure to currency risk. Note that the magnitude of the exposure is expressed in British pounds. For illustration, the computations of the parameter values for Case 1 are shown in Exhibit 12.4.

Next, consider Case 2. This case indicates that the local currency value of the asset is clearly negatively correlated with the Canadian dollar price of the British pound. In fact, the effect of exchange rate changes is exactly offset by movements of the local currency price of the asset, rendering the dollar price of the asset totally insensitive to exchange rate changes. The future dollar price of the asset will be uniformly $1,400 across the three states of the world. One, thus, can say that the British asset is effectively *denominated* in terms of the dollar. Although this case is clearly unrealistic, it shows that uncertain exchange rates or exchange risk does not necessarily constitute exchange exposure. Despite the fact that the future exchange rate is uncertain, the Canadian firm has nothing at risk in this case. Since the firm faces no exposure, no hedging will be necessary.

We now turn to Case 3, where the local currency price of the asset is fixed at £1,000. In this case, the Canadian firm faces a "contractual" cash flow that is *denominated* in pounds. This case, in fact, represents an example of the special case of economic exposure, transaction exposure. Intuitively, what is at risk is £1,000, that is, the exposure coefficient, b, is £1,000. Readers can confirm this by going through the same kind of computations as shown in Exhibit 12.4. Measurement of transaction exposure is, thus, very simple. The exposure coefficient, b, is the same as the magnitude of the contractual cash flow fixed in terms of foreign currency.

EXHIBIT 12.3

Measurement of Currency Exposure

State	Probability	P^*	S	$P(=SP^*)$	Parameters
A. Case 1					
1	1/3	£ 980	$1.40	$1,372	$Cov(P,S) = 34/3$
2	1/3	£1,000	$1.50	$1,500	$Var(S) = .02/3$
3	1/3	£1,070	$1.60	$1,712	$b = £1,700$
Mean			$1.50	$1,528	
B. Case 2					
1	1/3	£1,000	$1.40	$1,400	$Cov(P,S) = 0$
2	1/3	£ 933	$1.50	$1,400	$Var(S) = .02/3$
3	1/3	£ 875	$1.60	$1,400	$b = 0$
Mean			$1.50	$1,400	
C. Case 3					
1	1/3	£1,000	$1.40	$1,400	$Cov(P,S) = 20/3$
2	1/3	£1,000	$1.50	$1,500	$Var(S) = .02/3$
3	1/3	£1,000	$1.60	$1,600	$b = £1,000$
Mean			$1.50	$1,500	

EXHIBIT 12.4

Computations of Regression Parameters: Case 1

1. Computation of Means

$$\bar{P} = \sum_i q_i P_i = \frac{1}{3} (1{,}372 + 1{,}500 + 1{,}712) = 1{,}528$$

$$\bar{S} = \sum_i q_i S_i = \frac{1}{3} (1.40 + 1.50 + 1.60) = 1.50$$

2. Computation of Variance and Covariance

$$\mathrm{Var}(S) = \sum_i q_i (S_i - \bar{S})^2$$

$$= \frac{1}{3} [(1.40 - 1.50)^2 + (1.50 - 1.50)^2 + (1.60 - 1.50)^2]$$

$$= 0.02/3$$

$$\mathrm{Cov}(P,S) = \sum_i q_i (P_i - \bar{P})(S_i - \bar{S})$$

$$= \frac{1}{3} [(1{,}372 - 1{,}528) (1.40 - 1.50) + (1{,}500 - 1{,}528)$$

$$(1.50 - 1.50) + (1{,}712 - 1{,}528) (1.60 - 1.50)]$$

$$= 34/3$$

3. Computation of the Exposure Coefficient

$$b = \mathrm{Cov}(P,S)/\mathrm{Var}(S) = (34/3)/(0.02/3) = 1{,}700$$

Note: q_i denotes the probability for the ith state.

Once the magnitude of exposure is known, the firm can hedge the exposure simply by selling the exposure forward. In Case 3, where the asset value is fixed in terms of local currency, it is possible to completely eliminate the variability of the future dollar price of the asset by selling £1,000 forward. In Case 1, however, where the local currency price of the asset is random, selling £1,700 forward will not completely eliminate the variability of the future dollar price; there will be a residual variability that is independent of exchange rate changes.

On the basis of regression Equation 12.1, we can decompose the variability of the dollar value of the asset, Var(P), into two separate components: exchange rate–related and residual. Specifically,

$$\mathrm{Var}(P) = b^2 \mathrm{Var}(S) + \mathrm{Var}(e) \tag{12.2}$$

The first term on the right hand side of the equation, $b^2\mathrm{Var}(S)$, represents the part of the variability of the dollar value of the asset that is related to random changes in the exchange rate, whereas the second term, Var(e), captures the residual part of the dollar value variability that is independent of exchange rate movements.

The consequences of hedging the exposure by forward contracts are illustrated in Exhibit 12.5. Consider Case 1, where the firm faces an exposure coefficient (b) of £1,700. If the firm sells £1,700 forward, the dollar proceeds that the firm will receive are given by

$$\$1{,}700(F - S)$$

where F is the forward exchange rate and S is the spot rate realized on the maturity date. Note that for each pound sold forward, the firm receives a dollar amount equal to $(F - S)$. In Exhibit 12.5, the forward exchange rate is assumed to be $1.50, which is the same as the expected future spot rate. Thus, if the future spot rate turns out to be $1.40 under state 1, the dollar proceeds from the forward contract will be $170 = 1,700 (1.50 − 1.40). Since the dollar value (P) of the asset is $1,372 under state 1, the dollar value of the hedged position (HP) is $1,542 (= $1,372 + $170) under state 1.

Firms Feel the Pain of Peso's Plunge

Foreign-exchange traders and investors aren't the only Americans feeling the pain of the two-week plunge in the value of the Mexican peso.

For U.S. companies that are paid in pesos or that own substantial assets in Mexico, the recent 37% decline in the currency's value is a vivid example of just how quickly and substantially changes in the value of foreign currency can affect sales and profits.

And for the hundreds of companies that see Mexico as a ticket for expansion, the peso's fall is another reminder that foreign markets aren't anything like those at home. The Mexican financial crisis forces U.S. companies to "pay attention to the direction of the economy in any country they invest in," says Serge Ratmiroff, senior manager, international services, at Deloitte & Touche in Chicago.

The impact of the peso's fall on those that do business in the Mexican currency is striking. A U.S. company that sold widgets for 345 pesos early last month received about $100. Now, 345 pesos is valued at between $60 and $65. Meanwhile, as the value of the peso declines, prices of U.S. exports will rise, making them less affordable for Mexican buyers.

Ford Motor Co., for instance, said the peso's problems could dent its growth in exports to Mexico next year. Ford sent 27,000 to 28,000 vehicles to Mexico in 1994, up from a few hundred in 1992. It had hoped those sales would double over time with the aid of the North American Free Trade Agreement. But the auto maker's chairman and chief executive officer, Alexander Trotman, noted Tuesday that the cost of Ford autos "in peso terms has gone up enormously." Ford continues to build more than 200,000 vehicles a year in Mexico, but its Mexican output excludes such hot-sellers as the Mustang sports coupe, which is imported from the U.S. While wages should fall at its Mexican plants, at least in dollar terms, a spokesman said the company wouldn't see much gain from that because most of the parts used to assemble cars in Mexico actually are made in the U.S.

Other companies are feeling the impact immediately. Toy maker Mattel Inc. said yesterday that it will take an eight-cent-a-share charge for the fourth quarter because the peso's decline has reduced the value of its Mexican inventory and receivables. The charge means that despite a 35% jump in world-wide sales, Mattel's record earnings for the year will be on the "conservative" side of analysts' estimates.

Metalclad Corp., a Newport Beach, Calif., company with waste-oil recycling and landfill operations in Mexico, said the peso's plunge may wipe out its hopes for a profitable fiscal third quarter, ending Feb. 28. And Pilgrim's Pride, a Pittsburg, Texas, chicken producer, expects to take a substantial write-down for its first quarter ended Dec. 31, as it marks down its $120 million in assets in Mexico. A spokesman for Goodyear Tire & Rubber Co. in Akron, Ohio, said the company has "seen tire business fall off in Mexico because dealers don't want to sell the product at less than what they bought it for."

For many big U.S. companies, however, the swings are just another day in the currency markets. Mexico is a relatively small international market, though it accounts for about 9% of U.S. exports. Many companies say they do business in dollars or have otherwise hedged against currency changes, and won't feel any immediate financial impact. Further, those who manufacture there should see lower labor costs while some businesses, like trucking and hotels, contend they will benefit from increasing U.S. imports and tourism.

Still, some firms are putting expansion plans on hold and even large companies expect exports to Mexico to fall off this year as Mexican buyers adjust to the higher prices of U.S. goods. After all, that's part of Mexico's goal in letting the peso's value fall in relation to the dollar. "The whole purpose of what they're doing is to try to reduce the level of imports and increase Mexican exports," says Sidney Weintraub of the Center for Strategic and International Studies, a Washington think tank.

A drop in product sales to Mexico would be felt particularly in Texas, which exported about $20.38 billion in goods to its southern neighbor in 1993—nearly half the U.S. exports to Mexico. The state comptroller's office is predicting that exports will grow another 5% to 7% this year, but rise just 3% a year in 1996 and beyond, in part, because currency changes will curtail demand.

As shown in part A of Exhibit 12.5, the variance of the dollar value of the hedged position is only 392($)², whereas that of the unhedged position is 19,659($)². This result implies that much of the uncertainty regarding the future dollar value of the asset is associated with exchange rate uncertainty. As a result, once the exchange exposure is hedged, most of the variability of the dollar value of the asset is eliminated. The

EXHIBIT 12.5	**Future Quantities**	**State 1**	**State 2**	**State 3**	**Variance**

Future Quantities	State 1	State 2	State 3	Variance
A. Case 1 ($B_i = £1,700$)				
Local currency asset price (P^*)	980	1,000	1,070	
Exchange rate (S)	1.40	1.50	1.60	
Dollar value ($P = SP^*$)	1,372	1,500	1,712	19,659
Proceeds from forward contract	170	0	−170	
Dollar value of hedged position (HP)	1,542	1,500	1,542	392
B. Case 3 ($b = £1,000$)				
Local currency asset price (P^*)	1,000	1,000	1,000	
Exchange rate (S)	1.40	1.50	1.60	
Dollar value ($P = SP^*$)	1,400	1,500	1,600	6,667
Proceeds from forward contract	100	0	−100	
Dollar value of hedged position (HP)	1,500	1,500	1,500	0

EXHIBIT 12.5

Consequences of Hedging Currency Exposure

Note: In both cases, the forward exchange rate (F) is assumed to be $1.50/£. Proceeds from the forward contract are computed as $b(F - S)$. Recall that each of the three states is equally likely to happen, that is, $q_i = 1/3$ for each state.

residual variability of the dollar value of the asset that is independent of exchange rate changes, Var(e), is equal to 392($)^2$.

Let us now turn to Case 3 where the local currency price of the asset is fixed. In this case, complete hedging is possible in the specific sense that there will be no residual variability. As shown in part B of Exhibit 12.5, the future dollar value of the asset, which is totally dependent upon the exchange rate, has a variance of 6,667($)^2$. Once the firm hedges the exposure by selling £1,000 forward, the dollar value of the hedged position (HP) becomes nonrandom and is $1,500 across the three states of the world. Since the asset now has a constant dollar value, it is effectively *redenominated* in terms of the Canadian dollar.

12.3 Operating Exposure: Definition

While many managers understand the effects of random exchange rate changes on the dollar value of their firms' assets and liabilities denominated in foreign currencies, they often do not fully understand the effect of volatile exchange rates on operating cash flows. As the economy becomes increasingly globalized, more firms are subject to international competition. Fluctuating exchange rates can seriously alter the relative competitive positions of such firms in domestic and foreign markets, affecting their operating cash flows.

Unlike the exposure of assets and liabilities (such as accounts payable and receivable, loans denominated in foreign currencies, and so forth) that are listed in accounting statements, the exposure of operating cash flows depends on the effect of random exchange rate changes on the firm's competitive position, which is not readily measurable. This difficulty notwithstanding, it is important for the firm to properly manage **operating exposure** as well as **asset exposure.** In many cases, operating exposure may account for a larger portion of the firm's total exposure than contractual exposure. Formally, operating exposure can be defined as the *extent to which the firm's operating cash flows would be affected by random changes in exchange rates.*

12.4 Illustration of Operating Exposure

Before we discuss what determines operating exposure and how to manage it, it is useful to illustrate the exposure using a simple example. Suppose that a Canadian computer company, Newleaf Technologies of Kanata, Ontario, operates a wholly owned French subsidiary, Calais Computers, that assembles and sells Newleaf computers throughout Europe. Calais Computers imports microprocessors from Intel, at a cost of C$512 per unit. At the current exchange rate of C$1.60 per euro, each Intel microprocessor costs €320. Calais Computers hires French workers and sources all the other inputs locally. Calais faces a 50-percent income tax rate in the France.

Exhibit 12.6 summarizes projected operations for Calais Computers, assuming that the exchange rate will remain unchanged at C$1.60 per euro. The company expects to sell 50,000 units of personal computers per year at a selling price of €1,000 per unit. The unit variable cost is €650, which comprises €320 for the imported input and €330 for the locally sourced inputs. Needless to say, the euro price of the imported input will change as the exchange rate changes, which, in turn, can affect the selling price in the French market. Each year, Calais incurs fixed overhead costs of €4 million for rents, property taxes, and the like, regardless of output level. As the exhibit shows, the projected operating cash flow is €7,250,000 per year, which is equivalent to C$11,600,000 at the current exchange rate of C$1.60 per euro.

Now, consider the possible effect of a depreciation of the euro on the projected Canadian dollar operating cash flow of Calais Computers. Assume that the euro depreciates from C$1.60 to C$1.40 per euro. The dollar operating cash flow changes following a euro depreciation for a couple of reasons:

1. The **competitive effect:** A euro depreciation may affect operating cash flow in euros by altering the firm's competitive position in the marketplace.

2. The **conversion effect:** A given operating cash flow in euros will be converted into a lower dollar amount after the euro depreciation.

To get a feel of how the Canadian dollar operating cash flow may change as the exchange rate changes, consider the following cases with varying degrees of realism:

Case 1: No variables change, except the price of the imported input.

Case 2: The selling price as well as the price of the imported input changes, with no other changes.

Case 3: All the variables change.

In Case 1, illustrated in Exhibit 12.7, the unit variable cost of the imported input rises to €366 (= C$512/C$1.40) following the euro depreciation, with no other changes. Following the euro depreciation, the total variable costs become €34.8 million, lowering the firm's before-tax profit from €12.5 million (for the benchmark case) to €10.2 million. Considering that the firm faces a 50-percent income tax rate, depreciation of the euro will lower the net operating cash flow from €7.25 million (for the benchmark case) to €6.1 million. In terms of Canadian dollars, Calais' projected net operating cash flow changes from C$11.6 million to C$8.54 million as the exchange rate changes from C$1.60 per euro to C$1.40 per euro. Calais may be forced not to

EXHIBIT 12.6

Projected Operations for Calais Computers PLC: Benchmark Case (C$1.60/€)

Sales (50,000 units at €1,000/unit)	€50,000,000
Variable costs (50,000 units at €650/unit)[a]	32,500,000
Fixed overhead costs	4,000,000
Depreciation allowances	1,000,000
Net profit before tax	€12,500,000
Income tax (at 50%)	6,250,000
Profit after tax	6,250,000
Add back depreciation	1,000,000
Operating cash flow in pounds	€ 7,250,000
Operating cash flow in dollars	C$11,600,000

[a]The unit variable cost, €650, comprises €330 for the locally sourced inputs and €320 for the imported input, which is priced in Canadian dollars, i.e., C$512. At the exchange rate of C$1.60/€ the imported part costs €320.

EXHIBIT 12.7

Projected Operations
for Calais Computers
PLC: Case 1 (C$1.40/€)

Sales (50,000 units at €1,000/unit)	€50,000,000
Variable costs (50,000 units at €696/unit)	34,800,000
Fixed overhead costs	4,000,000
Depreciation allowances	1,000,000
Net profit before tax	€10,200,000
Income tax (at 50%)	5,100,000
Profit after tax	5,100,000
Add back depreciation	1,000,000
Operating cash flow in pounds	€ 6,100,000
Operating cash flow in dollars	C$ 8,540,000

raise the euro selling price because it faces a French competitor that manufactures similar products using only locally sourced inputs. An increase in selling price can potentially lead to a sharp decline in unit sales volume. Under this kind of competitive environment, Calais' costs are responsive to exchange rate changes, but the selling price is not. This asymmetry makes the firm's operating cash flow sensitive to exchange rate changes, giving rise to operating exposure.

In Case 2, which is analyzed in Exhibit 12.8, the selling price as well as the price of the imported input increases following the euro depreciation. In this case, Calais Computers does not face any serious competition in the French market and faces a highly inelastic demand for its products. Thus, Calais can raise the selling price to €1,143 (to keep the dollar selling price at C$1,600 after the euro depreciation) and still maintain the sales volume at 50,000 units. Computations presented in Exhibit 12.8 indicate that the projected operating cash flow actually increases to €9,675,000, which is equivalent to C$13,545,000. Compared with the benchmark case, the Canadian dollar operating cash flow is higher when the euro depreciates. This case shows that a euro depreciation need not always lead to a lower Canadian dollar operating cash flow.

We now turn to Case 3 where the selling price, sales volume, and the prices of both locally sourced and imported inputs change following the euro depreciation. In particular, we assume that both the selling price and the price of locally sourced inputs increase at the rate of 8 percent, reflecting the underlying inflation rate in France. As a result, the selling price will be €1,080 per unit and the unit variable cost of locally sourced inputs will be €356. Since the price of the imported input is €366, the combined unit variable cost will be €722. Facing an **elastic demand** for its products, sales volume declines to 40,000 units per year after the price increase. As Exhibit 12.9 shows, Calais's projected operating cash flow is €5.66 million, which is equivalent to C$7.924 million. The projected Canadian dollar cash flow under Case 3 is lower than that of the benchmark case by C$3.676 million.

Exhibit 12.10 summarizes the projected operating exposure effect of the euro depreciation on Calais Computers. For expositional purposes, it is assumed here that a

EXHIBIT 12.8

Projected Operations
for Calais Computers
PLC: Case 2 (C$1.40/€)

Sales (50,000 units at €1,143/unit)	€57,150,000
Variable costs (50,000 units at €696/unit)	34,800,000
Fixed overhead costs	4,000,000
Depreciation allowances	1,000,000
Net profit before tax	€17,350,000
Income tax (at 50%)	8,675,000
Profit after tax	8,675,000
Add back depreciation	1,000,000
Operating cash flow in pounds	€ 9,675,000
Operating cash flow in dollars	C$13,545,000

EXHIBIT 12.9

Projected Operations for Calais Computers PLC: Case 3 (C$1.40/€)

Sales (40,000 units at €1,080/unit)	€43,200,000
Variable costs (40,000 units at €722/unit)	28,880,000
Fixed overhead costs	4,000,000
Depreciation allowances	1,000,000
Net profit before tax	€ 9,320,000
Income tax (at 50%)	4,660,000
Profit after tax	4,660,000
Add back depreciation	1,000,000
Operating cash flow in pounds	€ 5,660,000
Operating cash flow in dollars	$ 7,924,000

EXHIBIT 12.10

Summary of Operating Exposure Effect of Pound Depreciation on Calais Computers

Variables	Benchmark Case	Case 1	Case 2	Case 3
Exchange rate (C$/€)	1.60	1.40	1.40	1.40
Unit variable cost (€)	650	696	696	722
Unit sales price (€)	1,000	1,000	1,143	1,080
Sales volume (units)	50,000	50,000	50,000	40,000
Annual cash flow (€)	7,250,000	6,100,000	9,675,000	5,660,000
Annual cash flow (C$)	11,600,000	8,540,000	13,545,000	7,924,000
Four-year present value (C$)[a]	33,118,000	24,382,000	38,671,000	22,623,000
Operating gains/losses (C$)[b]		−8,736,000	5,553,000	−10,495,000

[a]The discounted present value of dollar cash flows was computed over a four-year period using a 15-percent discount rate. A constant cash flow is assumed for each of four years.
[b]Operating gains or losses represent the present value of change in cash flows, which is due to pound depreciation, from the benchmark case.

change in exchange rate will have effects on the firm's operating cash flow for four years. The exhibit provides, among other things, the four-year present values of operating cash flows for each of the three cases as well as for the benchmark case. The proper discount rate for Calais' cash flow is assumed to be 15 percent. The exhibit also shows the operating gains or losses computed as the present value of changes in operating cash flows (over a four-year period) from the benchmark case that are due to the exchange rate change. In Case 3, for instance, the firm expects to experience an operating loss of C$10,495,000 due to the euro depreciation.

12.5 Determinants of Operating Exposure

Unlike contractual (i.e., transaction) exposure, which can readily be determined from the firm's accounting statements, operating exposure cannot be determined in the same manner. A firm's operating exposure is determined by (1) the structure of the markets in which the firm sources its inputs, such as labour and materials, and sells its products, and (2) the firm's ability to mitigate the effect of exchange rate changes by adjusting its markets, product mix, and sourcing.

To highlight the importance of market structure in determining operating exposure, consider a hypothetical company, Ford Mexicana, a subsidiary of Ford, which imports cars from the parent and distributes them in Mexico. If the dollar appreciates against the Mexican peso, Ford Mexicana's costs go up in peso terms. Whether this creates operating exposure for Ford critically depends on the structure of the car market in Mexico. For example, if Ford Mexicana faces competition from Mexican car makers whose peso costs did not rise, it will not be able to raise the peso price of imported Ford cars without risking a major reduction in sales. Facing a highly elastic demand for its products, Ford Mexicana cannot let the **exchange rate pass-through** the peso price.

As a result, an appreciation of the dollar will squeeze the profit of Ford Mexicana, subjecting the parent firm to a high degree of operating exposure.

In contrast, consider the case in which Ford Mexicana faces import competition only from other car makers like General Motors and Chrysler, rather than from local producers. Since peso costs of those other imported cars will be affected by a dollar appreciation in the same manner, the competitive position of Ford Mexicana will not be adversely affected. Under this market structure, the dollar appreciation is likely to be reflected in higher peso prices of imported cars pretty quickly. As a result, Ford will be able to better maintain its dollar profit, without being subject to a major operating exposure.

Generally speaking, a firm is subject to high degrees of operating exposure when *either* its cost *or* its price is sensitive to exchange rate changes. On the other hand, when *both* the cost *and* the price are sensitive or insensitive to exchange rate changes, the firm has no major operating exposure.

Given the market structure, however, the extent to which a firm is subject to operating exposure depends on the firm's ability to stabilize cash flows in the face of exchange rate changes. Even if Ford faces competition from local car makers in Mexico, for example, it can reduce exposure by starting to source Mexican parts and materials, which would be cheaper in dollar terms after the dollar appreciation. Ford can even start to produce cars in Mexico by hiring local workers and sourcing local inputs, thereby making peso costs relatively insensitive to changes in the dollar/peso exchange rate. In other words, the firm's flexibility regarding production locations, sourcing, and financial hedging strategy is an important determinant of its operating exposure to exchange risk.

Before we discuss how to hedge operating exposure, it is important to recognize that changes in nominal exchange rates may not always affect the firm's competitive position. This is the case when a change in exchange rate is exactly offset by the inflation differential. To show this point, let us again use the example of Ford Mexicana competing against local car makers. Suppose that the annual inflation rate is 4 percent in the United States and 15 percent in Mexico. For simplicity, we assume that car prices appreciate at the same pace as the general domestic inflation rate in both the United States and Mexico. Now, suppose that the dollar appreciates about 11 percent against the peso, offsetting the inflation rate differential between the two countries. This, of course, implies that purchasing power parity is holding.

Under this situation, the peso price of Ford cars appreciates by about 15 percent, which reflects a 4-percent increase in the dollar price of cars and an 11-percent appreciation of the dollar against the peso. Since the peso prices of both Ford, and locally produced cars rise by the same 15 percent, the 11 percent appreciation of the dollar will not affect the competitive position of Ford *vis-à-vis* local car makers. Ford, thus, does not have operating exposure.

If, however, the dollar appreciates by more than 11 percent against the peso, Ford cars will become relatively more expensive than locally produced cars, adversely affecting Ford's competitive position. Ford is, thus, exposed to exchange risk. Since purchasing power parity does not hold very well, especially in the short run, exchange rate changes are likely to affect the competitive positions of firms that are sourcing from different locations but selling in the same markets.

Before we move on, it would be useful to examine the relationship between exchange rate changes and the price adjustments of goods. Facing exchange rate changes, a firm may choose one of the following three pricing strategies: (1) pass the cost shock fully to its selling prices (complete pass-through), (2) fully absorb the shock to keep its selling prices unaltered (no pass-through), or (3) do some combination of the two strategies described above (partial pass-through). Import prices in the United States do not fully reflect exchange rate changes, exhibiting a partial pass-through phenomenon.

In a recent study, Yang (1997) investigated exchange rate pass-through in American manufacturing industries during the sample period 1980–1991 and found that the

EXHIBIT 12.11

Exchange Rate Pass-Through Coefficients for American Manufacturing Industries

Industry Code (SIC)	Industry	Pass-Through Coefficient
20	Food and kindred products	0.2485
22	Textile mill products	0.3124
23	Apparels	0.1068
24	Lumber and wood products	0.0812
25	Furniture and fixtures	0.3576
28	Chemicals and allied products	0.5312
30	Rubber and plastic products	0.5318
31	Leather products	0.3144
32	Stone, glass, concrete products	0.8843
33	Primary metal industries	0.2123
34	Fabricated metal products	0.3138
35	Machinery, except electrical	0.7559
36	Electrical and electronic machinery	0.3914
37	Transportation equipment	0.3583
38	Measurement instruments	0.7256
39	Miscellaneous manufacturing	0.2765
Average		0.4205

Source: Jiawen Yang. "Exchange Rate Pass-Through in U.S. Manufacturing Industries," *Review of Economics and Statistics* 79 (1997), pp. 95–104.

pricing behaviour of foreign exporting firms is generally consistent with partial pass-through. Exhibit 12.11, constructed on the basis of the Yang study, provides the pass-through coefficients for different industries; the coefficient would be 1 for complete pass-through and 0 for no pass-through. As can be seen from the exhibit, the pass-through coefficient ranges from 0.0812 for SIC 24 (lumber and wood products) to 0.8843 for SIC 32 (stone, glass, and concrete products). The average coefficient is 0.4205, implying that when the American dollar appreciates or depreciates by 1 percent, import prices of foreign products change, on average, by about 0.42 percent. It is noteworthy that partial pass-through is common but varies a great deal across industries. Import prices would be affected relatively little by exchange rate changes in industries with low product differentiation and, thus, high demand elasticities. In contrast, in industries with a high degree of product differentiation and, thus, low demand elasticities, import prices will tend to change more as the exchange rates change.

12.6 Managing Operating Exposure

As the economy becomes increasingly globalized, many firms are engaged in international activities, such as exports, cross-border sourcing, joint ventures with foreign partners, and establishing production and sales affiliates abroad. The cash flows of such firms can be quite sensitive to exchange rate changes. The objective of managing operating exposure is to stabilize cash flows in the face of fluctuating exchange rates.

Since a firm is exposed to exchange risk mainly through the effect of exchange rate changes on its competitive position, it is important to consider exchange exposure management in the context of the firm's long-term strategic planning. For example, in making such strategic decisions as choosing where to locate production facilities, where to purchase materials and components, and where to sell products, the firm should consider the currency effect on its overall future cash flows. Managing operating exposure is, thus, not a short-term tactical issue. The firm can use the following strategies for managing operating exposure:

1. Selecting low-cost production sites.
2. Flexible sourcing policy.

The Strong Yen and Toyota's Choice

Facing a strong yen in recent years that made Japanese exports more expensive, Toyota, Japan's biggest car maker, chose to shift production from Japan to U.S. manufacturing facilities, where the cost of production is lower. Toyota plans to boost U.S. production by about 50 percent by 1996 compared with 1993. Consequently, Toyota expects that its exports to the United States will decline by about 30 percent over the same period. The car maker also plans to double its production of engines at its Georgetown, Kentucky, plant. In addition to substantially boosting car production at its Georgetown factory, Toyota is also shifting production of all its pickup trucks sold in the United States from Japan to Fremont, California.

As a result, American-built vehicles will account for more than 60 percent of Toyota's U.S. sales in 1996 (about 800,000 units) compared with 46 percent in 1993. Toyota also will boost its exports from America to about 80,000 vehicles by 1996, an increase of about 60 percent from the 50,000 units exported in 1993. The company expects U.S. jobs will grow by 23 percent to 6,000 workers by 1996 at its Georgetown plant. At the same time, procurement of U.S. parts and materials will rise about 40 percent to $6.45 billion from $4.65 billion in 1993.

In addition to shifting production and sourcing to the United States, Toyota is using attractive lease deals to help close the price gap on imports. Since the company doesn't have to raise monthly leasing fees in step with the rising yen, the cars remain more attractive to U.S. consumers, although the company risks taking losses upon resale.

Although shifting production to the United States helps Toyota to get out of the dollar/yen problem and maintain its market share in the United States, it adds to the excess capacity problem of Toyota and leads to underutilization of domestic plants and job losses. A persistent strong yen can result in *hollowing out* of the Japanese economy, as some worry.

Source: Reprinted by permission of *The Wall Street Journal*, December 20, 1994, p. A11. © 1994 Dow Jones & Company, Inc. All Rights Reserved Worldwide.

3. Diversification of the market.
4. Product differentiation and R&D efforts.
5. Financial hedging.

Selecting Low-Cost Production Sites

When the domestic currency is strong or expected to become strong, eroding the competitive position of the firm, it can choose to locate production facilities in a foreign country where costs are low due to either the undervalued currency or underpriced factors of production. Recently, Japanese car makers, including Nissan and Toyota, have been increasingly shifting production to manufacturing facilities in both the United States and Canada in order to mitigate the negative effect of the strong yen on North American sales. German car makers, such as Daimler Benz and BMW, also decided to establish manufacturing facilities in North America for the same reason. A real-world example is provided by the International Finance in Practice box above, "The Strong Yen and Toyota's Choice."

Also, the firm can choose to establish and maintain production facilities in multiple countries to deal with the effect of exchange rate changes. Consider Toyota, which has manufacturing facilities in Canada, the United States, and Mexico, as well as Japan. Multiple manufacturing sites provide Toyota with a great deal of flexibility regarding where to produce, given the prevailing exchange rates. While the yen appreciated substantially against both the American and Canadian dollars, the Mexican peso depreciated against the North American currencies in recent years. Under this sort of exchange rate development, Toyota may choose to increase production in the United States, and especially in Mexico, in order to serve the American market. This is, in fact, how Nissan has reacted to the rising yen in recent years. Maintaining multiple manufacturing sites, however, may prevent the firm from taking advantage of economies of scale, raising its cost of production. The resultant higher cost can partially offset the advantages of maintaining multiple production sites.

Flexible Sourcing Policy

Even if the firm has manufacturing facilities only in the domestic country, it can substantially lessen the effect of exchange rate changes by sourcing from where input costs are low. In the early 1980s, when the dollar was very strong against most major currencies, multinational firms often purchased materials and components from low-cost foreign suppliers in order to keep themselves from being priced out of the market.

Facing the strong yen in recent years, many Japanese firms adopted the same practices. It is well known that Japanese manufacturers, especially in the car and consumer electronics industries, depend heavily on parts and intermediate products from such low-cost countries as Thailand, Malaysia, and China. The **flexible sourcing policy** need not be confined just to materials and parts. Firms can also hire low-cost guest workers from foreign countries instead of high-cost domestic workers in order to be competitive. For example, Japan Airlines is known to heavily hire foreign crews to stay competitive in international routes in the face of a strong yen.

Diversification of the Market

Another way of dealing with exchange exposure is **diversification of the market**—that is, geographically diversifying the firm's sales pattern. For example, Nova Chemicals Corporation, with global headquarters in Calgary, has markets throughout North America as well as in Europe and Asia for polystyrene and high-performance polymers. Reduced sales in, say, Japan due to a weakening yen would be partially offset by sales to Europe if the euro rose against the Canadian dollar as the yen weakened. Whenever exchange rates *vis-à-vis* the Canadian dollar are less then perfectly correlated—which virtually is always the case—then geographic diversification of sales has a risk-moderating effect.

It is sometimes argued that the firm can reduce currency exposure by diversifying across different business lines. The idea is that although each individual business may be exposed to exchange risk to some degree, the firm as a whole may not face a significant exposure. It is pointed out, however, that the firm should not get into new lines of business solely to diversify exchange risk because conglomerate expansion can bring about inefficiency and losses. Expansion into a new business should be justified in its own right.

R&D Efforts and Product Differentiation

Investment in R&D activities can allow the firm to maintain and strengthen its competitive position in the face of adverse exchange rate movements. Successful R&D efforts allow the firm to cut costs and enhance productivity. In addition, R&D efforts can lead to **product differentiation**—the introduction of new and unique products for which competitors offer no close substitutes. Since the demand for unique products tends to be highly inelastic (i.e., price insensitive), the firm would be less exposed to exchange risk. At the same time, the firm can strive to create a perception among consumers that its product is, indeed, different from those offered by competitors. Once the firm's product acquires a unique identity, its demand is less likely to be price sensitive.

Volvo, a Swedish automobile manufacturer, provides a good example here. The company has invested heavily in strengthening safety features of its cars and successfully established its reputation as the producer of safe cars. This reputation, reinforced by a focused marketing campaign, "Volvo for Life," helped the company carve out a niche among safety-minded consumers in highly competitive world automobile markets.

Financial Hedging

While not a substitute for the long-term, **operational hedging** approaches discussed above, **financial hedging** can be used to stabilize the firm's cash flows. For example, the firm can lend or borrow foreign currencies on a long-term basis. Or, the firm can use currency forward or options contracts and roll them over, if necessary. It is noted that existing financial contracts are designed to hedge against nominal, rather than real, changes in exchange rates. Since the firm's competitive position is affected by real changes in exchange rates, financial contracts can at best provide an approximate hedge against the firm's operating exposure. However, if operational hedges, which involve redeployment of resources, are costly or impractical, financial contracts can provide the firm with a flexible and economical way of dealing with exchange exposure.

Illustrated MINI CASE | Exchange Risk Management at Merck[3]

To examine how companies actually manage exchange risk exposure, we choose Merck & Co. Incorporated, a major American pharmaceutical company, and study its approach to overall exchange exposure management. While Merck's actual hedging decision reflects its own particular business situation, the basic framework for dealing with currency exposure can be informative for other firms.

Merck & Co. primarily develops, produces, and markets health-care pharmaceuticals. As a multinational company that operates in more than 100 countries, Merck had worldwide sales of $6.6 billion in 1989, and it controlled about a 4.7 percent market share worldwide. Merck's major foreign competitors are European firms and emerging Japanese firms. Merck is among the most internationally oriented American pharmaceutical companies, with overseas assets accounting for about 40 percent of the firm's total and with roughly 50 percent of its sales overseas.

As is typical in the pharmaceutical industry, Merck established overseas subsidiaries. These subsidiaries number about 70 and are responsible for finishing imported products and marketing in the local markets of incorporation. Sales are denominated in local currencies, and thus, the company is directly affected by exchange rate fluctuations. Costs are incurred partly in the American dollar for basic manufacturing and research and partly in terms of local currency for finishing, marketing, distribution, and so on. Merck found that costs and revenues were not matched in individual currencies mainly because of the concentration of research, manufacturing, and headquarters operations in the United States.

To reduce the currency mismatch, Merck first considered the possibility of redeploying resources in order to shift dollar costs to other currencies. The company, however, decided that relocating employees and manufacturing and research sites was not a practical and cost-effective way of dealing with exchange exposure. Having decided that operational hedging was not appropriate, Merck considered the alternative of financial hedging. Merck developed a five-step procedure for financial hedging:

1. Exchange forecasting.
2. Assessing strategic plan impact.
3. Hedging rationale.
4. Financial instruments.
5. Hedging program.

Step 1: Exchange Forecasting
The first step involves reviewing the likelihood of adverse exchange movements. The treasury staff estimates possible ranges for dollar strength or weakness over the five-year planning horizon. In doing so, the major factors expected to influence exchange rates, such as the American trade deficit, capital flows, the American budget deficit, and government policies regarding exchange rates, are considered. Outside forecasters are also polled on the outlook for the dollar over the planning horizon.

---

[3] This case is adopted from Lewent and Kearney (1990).

Step 2: Assessing Strategic Plan Impact

Once the future exchange rate ranges are estimated, cash flows and earnings are projected and compared under the alternative exchange rate scenarios, such as strong dollar and weak dollar. These projections are made on a five-year cumulative basis, rather than on a year-to-year basis because cumulative results provide more useful information concerning the magnitude of exchange exposure associated with the company's long-range plan.

Step 3: Deciding Whether to Hedge

In deciding whether to hedge exchange exposure, Merck focused on the objective of maximizing long-term cash flows and on the potential effect of exchange rate movements on the firm's ability to meet its strategic objectives. This focus is ultimately intended to maximize shareholder wealth. Merck decided to hedge for two main reasons. First, the company has a large portion of earnings generated overseas, while a disproportionate share of costs is incurred in dollars. Second, volatile cash flows can adversely affect the firm's ability to implement the strategic plan, especially investments in R&D that form the basis for future growth. To succeed in a highly competitive industry, the company needs to make a long-term commitment to a high level of research funding. But the cash flow uncertainty caused by volatile exchange rates makes it difficult to justify a high level of research spending. Management decided to hedge in order to reduce the potential effect of volatile exchange rates on future cash flows.

Step 4: Selecting the Hedging Instruments

The objective was to select the most cost-effective hedging tool that accommodated the company's risk preference. Among various hedging tools, such as forward currency contracts, foreign currency borrowing, and currency options, Merck chose currency options because it was not willing to forgo the potential gains if the dollar depreciated against foreign currencies as it has been doing against major currencies since the mid-eighties. Merck regarded option costs as premiums for the insurance policy designed to preserve its ability to implement the strategic plan.

Step 5: Constructing a Hedging Program

Having selected currency options as the key hedging vehicle, the company still had to formulate an implementation strategy regarding the term of the hedge, the strike price of the currency options, and the percentage of income to be covered. After simulating the outcomes of alternative implementation strategies under various exchange rate scenarios, Merck decided to (1) hedge for a multiyear period using long-dated options contracts, rather than hedge year-by-year, to protect the firm's strategic cash flows, (2) not use far out-of-money options to save costs, and (3) hedge only on a partial basis, with the remainder self-insured.

To help formulate the most cost-effective hedging program, Merck developed a computer-based model that simulated the effectiveness of various hedging strategies. Exhibit 12.12 provides an example of simulation results, comparing distributions of hedged and unhedged cash flows. Obviously, the hedged cash flow distribution has a higher mean and a lower standard deviation than the unhedged cash flow distribution. As we will discuss in Chapter 13, hedging may not only reduce risk but also increase cash flows if a reduced risk lowers the firm's cost of capital and tax liabilities. In this scenario, hedging is preferred to no hedging.

EXHIBIT 12.12

Cash Flows Unhedged versus Hedged

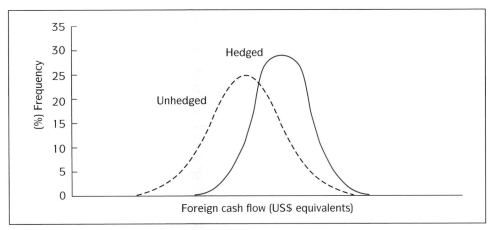

Source: J. Lewent and J. Kearney, "Identifying, Measuring, and Hedging Currency Risk at Merck." Reprinted with permission from the Bank of America *Journal of Applied Corporate Finance,* Winter 1990.

SUMMARY

In this chapter, we discussed how to measure and manage economic exposure to exchange risk. We also examined how companies manage currency risk in the real world.

1. Exchange rate changes can systematically affect the value of the firm by influencing the firm's operating cash flows as well as the domestic currency values of its assets and liabilities.

2. It is conventional to classify foreign currency exposure into three classes: economic exposure, transaction exposure, and translation exposure.

3. Economic exposure can be defined as the extent to which the value of the firm would be affected by unexpected changes in exchange rates. Transaction exposure is defined as the sensitivity of realized domestic currency values of the firm's contractual cash flows denominated in foreign currencies to unexpected exchange rate changes. Translation exposure, on the other hand, refers to the potential that the firm's consolidated financial statements can be affected by changes in exchange rates.

4. If the firm has an asset in a foreign country, its exposure to currency risk can be properly measured by the coefficient in regressing the dollar value of the foreign asset on the exchange rate. Once the magnitude of exposure is known, the firm can hedge the exposure simply by selling the exposure forward.

5. Unlike the exposure of assets and liabilities that are listed in accounting statements, operating exposure depends on the effect of random exchange rate changes on the firm's future cash flows, which are not readily measurable. Despite this difficulty, it is important to properly manage operating exposure, since operating exposure may account for a larger portion of the firm's total exposure than contractual exposure.

6. A firm's operating exposure is determined by (a) the structure of the markets in which the firm sources its inputs and sells its products, and (b) the firm's ability to mitigate the effect of exchange rate changes on its competitive position by adjusting markets, product mix, and sourcing.

7. Since a firm is exposed to exchange risk mainly via the effect of exchange rate changes on its competitive position, it is important to consider exchange exposure management in the context of the firm's overall long-term strategic plan. The

objective of exposure management is to stabilize cash flow in the face of fluctuating exchange rates.

8. To manage operating exposure, the firm can use various strategies, such as (a) choosing low-cost production sites, (b) maintaining flexible sourcing policy, (c) diversification of the market, (d) product differentiation, and (e) financial hedging using currency options and forward contracts.

KEY WORDS

asset exposure, *289*
competitive effect, *290*
conversion effect, *290*
diversification of the
  market, *296*
economic exposure, *284*
elastic demand, *291*

exchange rate pass-
  through, *292*
exposure coefficient, *285*
financial hedging, *296*
flexible sourcing
  policy, *296*
operating exposure, *289*

operational hedging, *296*
product
  differentiation, *296*
transaction
  exposure, *284*
translation
  exposure, *284*

QUESTIONS

1. How would you define economic exposure to exchange risk?

2. Explain the following statement: "Exposure is the regression coefficient."

3. Suppose that your company has an equity position in a French firm. Discuss the condition under which dollar/euro exchange rate uncertainty does not constitute exchange exposure for your company.

4. Explain the competitive and conversion effects of exchange rate changes on the firm's operating cash flow.

5. Discuss the determinants of operating exposure.

6. Discuss the implications of purchasing power parity for operating exposure.

7. General Motors exports cars to Spain, but the strong dollar against the euro hurts sales of GM cars in Spain. In the Spanish market, GM faces competition from Italian and French car makers, such as Fiat and Renault, whose operating currencies are the euro. What kind of measures would you recommend so that GM can maintain its market share in Spain?

8. What are the advantages and disadvantages to a firm of financial hedging of its operating exposure compared with operational hedges (such as relocating its manufacturing site)?

9. Discuss the advantages and disadvantages of maintaining multiple manufacturing sites as a hedge against exchange rate exposure.

10. Evaluate the following statement: "A firm can reduce its currency exposure by diversifying across different business lines."

11. Exchange rate uncertainty may not necessarily mean that firms face exchange risk exposure. Explain why this may be the case.

PROBLEMS

1. Suppose that you hold a piece of land in the city of London that you may want to sell in one year. As a Canadian resident, you are concerned with the Canadian dollar value of the land. Assume that if the British economy booms in the future, the land will be worth £2,000, and one British pound will be worth C$2.40. If the British economy slows down, on the other hand, the land will be worth less, say, £1,500, but the pound will be stronger, say, $2.50/£. You feel that the British economy will experience a boom with a 60-percent probability and a slowdown with a 40-percent probability.

a. Estimate your exposure (*b*) to the exchange risk.

b. Compute the variance of the dollar value of your property that is attributable to exchange rate uncertainty.

c. Discuss how you can hedge your exchange risk exposure and also examine the consequences of hedging.

2. A Canadian firm holds an asset in France and faces the following scenario:

	State 1	State 2	State 3	State 4
Probability	25%	25%	25%	25%
Spot rate	$1.20/€	$1.10/€	$1.00/€	$0.90/€
P^*	€1,500	€1,400	€1,300	€1,200
P	$1,800	$1,540	$1,300	$1,080

In the above table, P^* is the euro price of the asset held by the Canadian firm and P is the dollar price of the asset.

a. Compute the exchange exposure faced by the Canadian firm.

b. What is the variance of the dollar price of this asset if the Canadian firm remains unhedged against this exposure?

c. If the Canadian firm hedges against this exposure using a forward contract, what is the variance of the dollar value of the hedged position?

3. Suppose you are a British venture capitalist holding a major stake in an e-commerce start-up in Ottawa. As a British resident, you are concerned with the pound value of your Canadian equity position. Assume that if the Canadian economy booms in the future, your equity stake will be worth $1,000,000, and the exchange rate will be $1.40/£. If the Canadian economy experiences a recession, on the other hand, your Canadian equity stake will be worth $500,000, and the exchange rate will be $1.60/£. You assess that the Canadian economy will experience a boom with a 70-percent probability and a recession with a 30-percent probability.

a. Estimate your exposure to the exchange risk.

b. Compute the variance of the pound value of your Canadian equity position that is attributable to the exchange rate uncertainty.

c. How would you hedge this exposure? If you hedge, what is the variance of the pound value of the hedged position?

INTERNET EXERCISE

Coca-Cola, a well-known multinational company, derives about three-quarters of its revenue from overseas markets. It is, thus, highly likely that the company is exposed to currency risks. Investigate the company's exchange risk management policies and practices from its Annual Report (10-K) filed with the U.S. Securities and Exchange Commission (SEC), especially the "Financial Risk Management" section, which are available from the following website: www.edgar-online.com/bin/edgardoc/finSys_main.asp?dcn=0000021344-02-000011&nad=

How would you evaluate Coca-Cola's approach to exchange risk management?

MINI CASE

Economic Exposure of Calais Computers PLC

Consider Case 3 of Calais Computers PLC discussed in the chapter. Now, assume that the euro is expected to depreciate to $1.50 from the current level of $1.60 per pound. This implies that the euro cost of the imported part, that is, Intel's microprocessors, is €341 (=$512/$1.50). Other variables, such as the unit sales volume and the euro inflation rate, remain the same as in Case 3.

    a. Compute the projected annual cash flow in dollars.

    b. Compute the projected operating gains/losses over the four-year horizon as the discounted present value of change in cash flows, which is due to the pound depreciation, from the benchmark case presented in Exhibit 12.4.

    c. What actions, if any, can Calais take to mitigate the projected operating losses due to the euro depreciation?

REFERENCES & SUGGESTED READINGS

Adler, Michael, and Bernard Dumas. "Exposure to Currency Risk: Definition and Measurement." *Financial Management* (Spring 1984), pp. 41–50.

Allayannis, George, and Eli Ofek. "Exchange Rate Exposure, Hedging, and the Use of Foreign Currency Derivatives." *Journal of International Money and Finance* 20 (2001), pp. 273–96.

Bartov, Eli, and Gordon Bodnar. "Firm Valuation, Earnings Expectations, and the Exchange-Rate Exposure Effect." *Journal of Finance* 49 (1994), pp. 1755–85.

Choi, Jongmoo, and Anita Prasad. "Exchange Rate Sensitivity and Its Determinants: A Firm and Industry Analysis of U.S. Multinationals." *Financial Management* 23 (1995), pp. 77–88.

Dornbusch, Rudiger. "Exchange Rates and Prices." *American Economic Review* 77 (1987), pp. 93–106.

Dufey, Gunter, and S. L. Srinivasulu. "The Case for Corporate Management of Foreign Exchange Risk." *Financial Management* (Winter 1983), pp. 54–62.

Eaker, Mark. "The Numeraire Problem and Foreign Exchange Risk." *Journal of Finance* (May 1981), pp. 419–27.

Flood, Eugene, and Donald Lessard. "On the Measurement of Operating Exposure to Exchange Rates: A Conceptual Approach." *Financial Management* 15 (Spring 1986), pp. 25–36.

Glaum, M., M. Brunner, and H. Himmel. "The DAX and the Dollar: The Economic Exchange Rate Exposure of German Corporations." Working Paper, Europa-Universitat Viadrina, 1998.

Hekman, Christine R. "Don't Blame Currency Values for Strategic Errors." *Midland Corporate Finance Journal* (Fall 1986), pp. 45–55.

Jacque, Laurent. "Management of Foreign Exchange Risk: A Review Article." *Journal of International Business Studies* (Spring 1981), pp. 81–100.

Jorion, Philippe. "The Exchange-Rate Exposure of U.S. Multinationals." *Journal of Business* 63 (1990), pp. 331–45.

Lessard, Donald, and S. B. Lightstone. "Volatile Exchange Rates Can Put Operations at Risk." *Harvard Business Review* (July/August 1986), pp. 107–14.

Lewent, Judy, and John Kearney. "Identifying, Measuring and Hedging Currency Risk at Merck." *Journal of Applied Corporate Finance* (Winter 1990), pp. 19–28.

Pringle, John, and Robert Connolly. "The Nature and Causes of Foreign Currency Exposure." *Journal of Applied Corporate Finance* (Fall 1993), pp. 61–72.

Simkins, Berry, and Paul Laux. "Derivatives Use and the Exchange Rate Risk of Investing in Large U.S. Corporations." Working Paper, Case Western Reserve University (1996).

Wihlborg, Clas. "Economics of Exposure Management of Foreign Subsidiaries of Multinational Corporations." *Journal of International Business Studies* (Winter 1980), pp. 9–18.

Williamson, Rohan. "Exchange Rate Exposure and Competition: Evidence from the Automotive Industry." *Journal of Financial Economics* 59 (2001), pp. 441–75.

Yang, Jiawen. "Exchange Rate Pass-through in U.S. Manufacturing Industries." *Review of Economics and Statistics* 79 (1997), pp. 95–104.

Management of Transaction Exposure

AS DISCUSSED in Chapter 12, **transaction exposure** arises when a firm faces contractual cash flows that are fixed in a foreign currency. For example, suppose that CHC Helicopters of St John's, Newfoundland, a world leader in supply logistics to offshore oil rigs, has billed British Petroleum (BP) for services provided to BP's sites on the North Sea. CHC's invoice is for £1 million, due in three months.[1] When CHC Helicopters receives £1 million three months from now, it will convert these British pounds into Canadian dollars at the spot rate of exchange prevailing at that time. The future spot rate cannot be known in advance. Consequently, in dollar terms, the value of the settlement is uncertain. If the British pound appreciates (depreciates) against the Canadian dollar, the dollar receipt will be higher (lower). The uncertain end-result suggests that if CHC Helicopter does nothing to address this uncertainty, it is effectively speculating on the future course of the exchange rate. It is as if CHC is willing to take a bet that the British pound will appreciate against the Canadian dollar.

Consider another example. Say, Mitsubishi of Japan enters into a loan contract with the Swiss bank UBS that calls for payment of SF100 million for principal and interest in one year. To the extent that the yen/Swiss franc exchange rate is uncertain, Mitsubishi does not know how much yen will be required to buy SF100 million spot in one year's time. If the yen appreciates (depreciates) against the Swiss franc, a smaller (larger) yen amount will be needed to retire the SF-denominated loan.

These examples suggest that whenever a firm has foreign-currency-denominated receivables or payables, it is subject to transaction exposure, and the eventual settlements have the potential to affect the firm's cash flow position. Since modern firms are often involved in commercial and financial contracts denominated in foreign currencies, management of transaction exposure has become an important function of international financial management.

Unlike economic exposure, transaction exposure is well defined. Transaction exposure is simply the amount of foreign currency that is receivable or payable.

---

[1]There may be some question as to why CHC Helicopters would invoice BP in pounds, rather than in Canadian dollars. It is quite likely that the original contract was tendered by BP in a global competition that specified that settlement would be in British pounds.

This chapter focuses on alternative ways of hedging transaction exposure using various financial contracts and *operational techniques*:

Financial contracts:

- Forward market hedge
- Money market hedge
- Option market hedge
- Swap market hedge

Operational techniques:

- Choice of the invoice currency
- Lead/lag strategy
- Exposure netting

As we proceed to describe and illustrate various ways to address transaction exposure, it is useful to establish another specific business situation that gives rise to exposure. Let us say that Bombardier of Montreal exports commuter aircraft to Austrian Airlines. A payment of €10 million will be received by Bombardier in one year. Money market and foreign exchange rates relevant to the financial contracts that we will examine are:

Canadian interest rate	6.10 % per annum
European interest rate	9.00 % per annum
Spot exchange rate	$1.50/€
Forward exchange rate	$1.46/€

Let us now look at the various techniques for managing Bombardier's transactions exposure involving €10 million to be received one year from now.

13.1 Forward Market

www.gsm.uci.edu/~jorion/pachet/case.html

A case study by Prof. Philippe Jorion presents the situation of a company with transaction exposure to the Deutsche mark/dollar exchange rate.

Perhaps the most direct and popular way of hedging transaction exposure is by currency forward contracts or **forward market hedge**. Generally speaking, the firm may sell (buy) its foreign currency receivables (payables) forward to eliminate its exchange risk exposure. In the above example, in order to hedge foreign exchange exposure, Bombardier may simply sell forward its euros receivable, €10 million for delivery in one year, in exchange for a given amount of Canadian dollars. On the maturity date of the contract, Bombardier will have to deliver €10 million to the bank, which is the counterparty of the contract, and, in return, take delivery of C$14.6 million (C$1.46 × 10 million), regardless of the spot exchange rate that may prevail on the maturity date. Bombardier will, of course, use the €10 million that it is going to receive from Austrian Airways to fulfill the forward contract. Since Bombardier's euro receivable is exactly offset by the euro payable (created by the forward contract), the company's net euro exposure becomes zero.

Since Bombardier is assured of receiving a given dollar amount, $14.6 million, from the counterparty of the forward contract, the dollar proceeds from this European sale will not be affected at all by future changes in the exchange rate. This point is illustrated in Exhibit 13.1. Once Bombardier enters into the forward contract, exchange rate uncertainty becomes irrelevant for Bombardier. Exhibit 13.1 also illustrates how the dollar proceeds from the European sale will be affected by the future spot exchange rate when exchange exposure is not hedged. The exhibit shows that the dollar proceeds under the forward hedge will be higher than those under the unhedged position if the future spot exchange rate turns out to be less than the forward rate, that is, $F = \$1.46/€$, and the opposite will hold if the future spot rate becomes higher than the forward rate. In the latter case, Bombardier forgoes an opportunity to benefit from a strong euro.

Suppose that on the maturity date of the forward contract, the spot rate turns out to be $1.40/€, which is less than the forward rate, $1.46/€. In this case, Bombardier would have received C$14.0 million, rather than C$14.6 million, had it not entered into the

EXHIBIT 13.1

Dollar Proceeds from the European Sale: Forward Hedge versus Unhedged Position

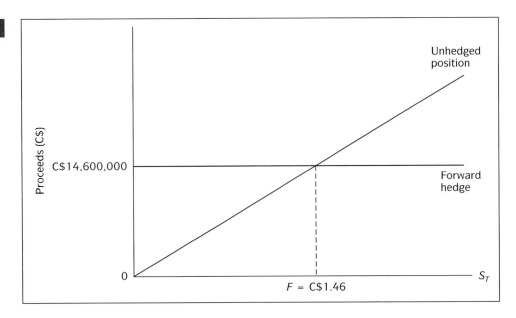

forward contract. Thus, one can say that Bombardier gained C$0.6 million from forward hedging. Needless to say, Bombardier will not always gain in this manner. If the spot rate is, say, C$1.50/€ on the maturity date, then Bombardier could have received C$15.0 million by remaining unhedged. Thus, one can say *ex post* that forward hedging cost Bombardier $0.40 million.

The gains and losses from forward hedging can be illustrated as in Exhibits 13.2 and 13.3. The gain/loss is computed as follows:

$$\text{Gain} = (F - S_T) \times \text{€10 million} \tag{13.1}$$

Obviously, the gain will be positive as long as the forward exchange rate is greater than the spot rate on the maturity date, that is, $F > S_T$, and the gain will be negative (that is, a loss will result) if the opposite holds. As Exhibit 13.3 shows, the firm theoretically can gain as much as C$14.6 million when the euro becomes worthless, which, of course, is unlikely, whereas there is no limit to possible losses.

It is important, however, to note that the above analysis is *ex post* in nature and that no one can know for sure what the future spot rate will be beforehand. The firm must decide whether to hedge or not to hedge *ex ante*. To help the firm decide, it is useful to consider the following three alternative scenarios:

1. $\bar{S}_T \approx F$
2. $\bar{S}_T < F$
3. $\bar{S}_T > F$

where $\bar{S}_T$ denotes the firm's expected spot exchange rate for the maturity date.

Under the first scenario, where the firm's expected future spot exchange rate, $\bar{S}_T$, is about the same as the forward rate, F, the "expected" gains or losses are approximately zero. But forward hedging eliminates exchange exposure. In other words, the firm can eliminate foreign exchange exposure without sacrificing any expected Canadian dollar proceeds from the foreign sale. Under this scenario, the firm would be inclined to hedge as long as it is averse to risk. Note that this scenario becomes valid when the forward exchange rate is an unbiased predictor of the future spot rate.[2]

---

[2]As mentioned in Chapter 5, the forward exchange rate will be an unbiased predictor of the future spot rate if the exchange market is informationally efficient and the risk premium is not significant. Empirical evidence indicates that the risk premium, if it exists, is generally not very significant. Unless the firm has private information that is not reflected inthe forward rate, it would have no reason for disagreeing with the forward rate.

Spot Exchange Rate on the Maturity Date (S_T)	Receipts from the British Sale		Gains/Losses from Hedge[b]
	Unhedged Position	Forward Hedge	
C$1.30	C$13,000,000	C$14,600,000	C$1,600,000
C$1.40	C$14,000,000	C$14,600,000	C$ 600,000
C$1.46[a]	C$14,600,000	C$14,600,000	0
C$1.50	C$15,000,000	C$14,600,000	−C$ 400,000
C$1.60	C$16,000,000	C$14,600,000	−C$1,400,000

[a]The forward exchange rate (F) is C$1.46/€
[b]The gains/losses are computed as the proceeds under the forward hedge minus the proceeds from the unhedged position at the various spot exchange rates on the maturity date.

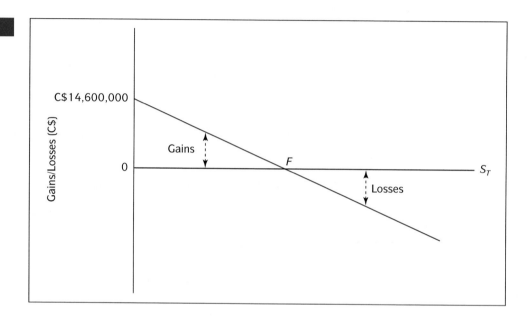

Under the second scenario, where the firm's expected future spot exchange rate is less than the forward rate, the firm expects a positive gain from forward hedging. Since the firm expects to increase the Canadian dollar proceeds while eliminating exchange exposure, it would be even more inclined to hedge under this scenario than under the first scenario. The second scenario, however, implies that the firm's management dissents from the market's consensus forecast of the future spot exchange rate as reflected in the forward rate.

Under the third scenario, on the other hand, where the firm's expected future spot exchange rate is more than the forward rate, the firm can eliminate exchange exposure via the forward contract only at the cost of reduced expected Canadian dollar proceeds from the foreign sale. Thus, Bombardier would be less inclined to hedge under this scenario, other things being equal. Despite lower expected Canadian dollar proceeds, however, the firm may still end up hedging. Whether Bombardier actually hedges or not depends on the degree of risk aversion; the more risk averse the firm is, the more likely it is to hedge. From the perspective of a hedging firm, the reduction in the expected Canadian dollar proceeds can be viewed implicitly as an "insurance premium" paid for avoiding the hazard of exchange risk.

Bombardier can use a currency futures contract, rather than a forward contract, to hedge. However, a futures contract is not as suitable as a forward contract for the purpose of hedging for two reasons. First, unlike forward contracts that are tailor made to the firm's specific needs, futures contracts are standardized instruments in terms of contract size, delivery date, and so forth. In most cases, therefore, the firm can only hedge approximately. Second, due to the marking-to-market property, there are interim cash flows prior to the maturity date of the futures contract that may have to be invested at uncertain interest rates. As a result, exact hedging again would be difficult.

13.2 Money Market Hedge

Transaction exposure can also be hedged by lending and borrowing in the domestic and foreign money markets—that is, **money market hedge**. Generally speaking, the firm may borrow (lend) in foreign currency to hedge its foreign currency receivables (payables), thereby matching its assets and liabilities in the same currency. Again using the same example presented above, Bombardier can eliminate the exchange exposure arising from the European sale by first borrowing in euros, then converting the loan proceeds into Canadian dollars, which then can be invested at the dollar interest rate. On the maturity date of the loan, Bombardier will use the euro receivable to pay off the euro loan. If Bombardier borrows a particular euro amount so that the maturity value of this loan becomes exactly equal to the euro receivable from the European sale, Bombardier's net euro exposure is reduced to zero, and Bombardier will receive the future maturity value of the dollar investment.

The first important step in money market hedging is to determine the amount of euros to borrow. Since the maturity value of borrowing should be the same as the euro receivable, the amount to borrow can be computed as the discounted present value of the euro receivable, that is, €10 million/(1.09) = €9,174,312. When Bombardier borrows €9,174,312, it then has to repay €10 million in one year, which is equivalent to its euro receivable. The step-by-step procedure of money market hedging can be illustrated as follows:

Step 1: Borrow €9,174,312 in Europe

Step 2: Convert €9,174,312 into $13,761,468 at the current spot exchange rate of C$1.50/€

Step 3: Invest C$13,761,468 in Canadian Treasury bills.

Step 4: Collect €10 million from Austrian Airways and use it to repay the euro loan.

Step 5: Receive the maturity value of the dollar investment, that is, C$14,600,918 = C$13,761,468(1.061), which is the guaranteed Canadian dollar proceeds from the European sale.

Exhibit 13.4 provides a cash flow analysis of money market hedging. The table shows that the net cash flow is zero at the present time, implying that, apart from possible transaction costs, the money market hedge is fully self-financing. The table also clearly shows how the 10 million euro receivable is exactly offset by the 10 million euro payable (created by borrowing), leaving a net cash flow of C$14,600,918 on the maturity date.[3]

	EXHIBIT 13.4 **Cash Flow Analysis of a Money Market Hedge**	Transaction	Current Cash Flow	Cash Flow at Maturity
		1. Borrow euros	£ 9,174,312	−£10,000,000
		2. Buy dollar spot	C$13,761,468	
		with euros	−£ 9,174,312	
		3. Invest in Canadian TBs	−C$13,761,468	C$14,600,918
		4. Collect euro receivable		£10,000,000
		Net cash flow	0	C$14,600,918

---

[3]In the case where the firm has an account payable denominated in euro, the money market hedge calls for borrowing in Canadian dollars, buying euro spot, and investing at the euro interest rate.

Managing Currency Exposure: The Perspective of a Bank

Our extensive example of Bombardier's purchase of a forward contract illustrates the arrangement from Bombardier's perspective. Bombardier starts the process by contacting a bank. Once the forward contract is established, the bank has taken on the risk that Bombardier had faced.

Banks, however, are not in the business of taking large speculative positions on foreign currencies. The foreign exchange desk of a bank is there to serve its clients. When a bank makes a forward foreign exchange commitment to a customer, the bank typically tries to quickly neutralize the exposure that it has taken on. This note illustrates how this is done. The setting is a Canadian firm that purchases American dollars six months forward from a Canadian bank.

All forward foreign currency transactions are done by banks. More than 95 percent of all foreign currency transactions are done *within* banks. Thus, banks are foreign exchange *brokers* to the industrial and commercial world. The foreign exchange desks of banks are not in the business of speculating, that is, taking exposed positions on foreign currencies.

A typical transaction that a bank might encounter in dealing with a customer looks like this: Someone phones the bank to enquire about *buying* one million American dollars six months from now. Perhaps it is a Canadian company retiring an American dollar-denominated corporate bond.

The bank's customer wants US$1,000,000 six months forward.

Today, June 1, the six-month *forward* rate is 0.7500. Of course, this is in American dollars per Canadian dollar.

The bank officer at the foreign exchange desk says, "O.K., one million December American dollars at 0.7500. That will be 1,333,333 Canadian dollars. Done!"

The customer's problem is solved.

Now, the bank has a problem. The bank is *short* American dollars. The bank must provide US$1,000,000 six months from now. The bank is exposed.

How does the bank manage *its* risk?

Immediately, the bank will reverse its American dollar forward position by an offsetting transaction in the spot market. The bank will immediately *buy* US$1,000,000 spot.

Why wouldn't the bank make an offsetting transaction in the *forward* market—that is, why wouldn't it commit to *buy* US$1,000,000 in December? That is a rhetorical question. The bank would if it could. Imagine if the officer at the foreign exchange desk had simultaneous calls from two customers, one looking to *buy* US$1,000,000 in December and one wanting to *sell* the same amount at the same time. Of course, these two offsetting transactions would cancel each other out from the bank's perspective, and the bank would simply—and profitably—capture the bid-ask spread. Pure brokerage.

However, things are seldom that simple. The bank must *manage* its brokerage operations. That is the bank's skill.

The *spot* market is much more liquid and generally presents substantially smaller spreads than the *forward* market. So, the bank can more easily and more readily sell American dollars in the *spot* market.

Now, let us say that the *forward* exchange rate (expressed in American dollars per Canadian dollar) is greater than the *spot* exchange rate.

spot:	0.7450	Now, June
forward:	0.7500	December

In the back of your mind—but not too far back—you should be asking yourself what this forward premium implies for (1) the expected future spot rate, and (2) the United States–Canada interest differential. The latter will soon become important.

The bank pays C$1,342,282 for US$1,000,000. This is a *spot* transaction.

After the offsetting transaction in the *spot* market (establishing a *long* position in the American dollar to offset the *short* forward position), the remaining net exposure is to the United States–Canada interest differential. That is foreign interest rate exposure. The bank can swap that risk away with a United States–Canada interest rate swap. The transactional cost of the United States–Canada interest rate swap is the cost of insurance for the remaining bit of risk. The swap assures the bank of receiving a flow of Canadian dollar interest despite the fact that it holds American dollars on account.

The maturity value of the dollar investment from the money market hedge turns out to be nearly identical to the dollar proceeds from forward hedging. This result is no coincidence. Rather, this is due to the fact that the interest rate parity (IRP) condition is approximately holding in our example. If the IRP is not holding, the dollar proceeds

The bank's three transactions can be illustrated with a simple diagram:

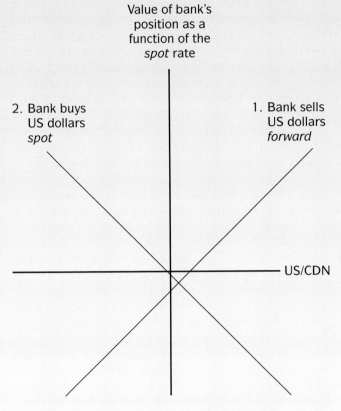

Value of bank's position as a function of the *spot* rate

2. Bank buys US dollars *spot*

1. Bank sells US dollars *forward*

US/CDN

After Steps 1 and 2, that is, after the bank offsets its *forward* short position with a *spot* long, the remaining net exposure is to the United States–Canada interest differential for six months. The bank will swap that risk away with a United States–Canada interest rate swap.

In the diagram, the intersection of the two axes is the *spot* rate. A little to the right is the *forward* rate. The bank's exposure due to the first transaction is represented by an upward sloping 45-degree line passing through the *forward* rate. Why is the line sloping upward? Well, if the exchange rate (expressed as US$/C$) increases, it would take fewer Canadian dollars to buy the requisite US$1,000,000. Unhedged, the bank's value (on the vertical axis) would increase if US$/C$ increases, that is, if the Canadian dollar appreciates. The second (offsetting) transaction requires a downward sloping 45-degree line passing through the *spot* rate. The third transaction, the *swap*, eliminates the exposure associated with the gap between the *spot* and *forward* rates.

Finally, there is another way that the bank could handle its exposure to the exchange rate risk that it incurs in its function as a forward exchange broker.

The key point is that the bank must deliver US$1,000,000 in December, for which it will receive C$1,333,333. The C$1,333,333 is secure. The issue for the bank is how to structure the future delivery of US$1,000,000 while avoiding exchange rate risk.

Buying American dollars *spot* gets rid of most of the foreign exchange risk. However, buying the full US$1,000,000 may be overkill. The American-interest flow on the securities that the bank purchases with those funds leaves residual exchange rate risk associated with the American-interest that accrues between now and December.

Instead of buying US$1,000,000, the bank could purchase December American discount bonds in the amount of US$1,000,000/$(1 + r_{US}/2)$ where r_{US} is the yield on the discount bonds. In other words, the bank purchases riskless securities today that retire in December with a liquidation value of US$1,000,000.

Say r_{US} equals 5 percent. Then, US$1,000,000 / $(1 + r_{US}/2)$ equals US$975,610.

The purchase today of December American discount bonds in the amount of US$975,610 will result in US$1,000,000 in December.

In this way, the bank establishes its own "money market" hedge on its American-forward obligation.

What would determine whether the bank ought to "over-borrow" the full US$1,000,000 and swap the American-interest into Canadian dollars as opposed to buying US$975,610 of December American discount bonds? This type of decision generally turns on such considerations such as whether the bank has a substantial swap book that would make it easy (and cheap) to swap American interest into Canadian or whether the bank is heavily involved in the American discount securities market, in which case it may have an operational advantage in that market.

All in all, the difference between the two approaches is likely to be small. The advantage of purchasing American discount bonds is that it is neater and it reduces the bank's capital commitment.

Keep in mind that the bank is essentially operating as a broker in the forward market, and hence it ought to take advantage of any internal administrative efficiencies that it may have in managing its own risk.

from money market hedging will not be the same as those from forward hedging. As a result, one hedging method will dominate another. In a competitive and efficient world financial market, however, any deviations from IRP are not likely to persist.

13.3 Options Market Hedge

One possible shortcoming of both forward and money market hedges is that these methods completely eliminate exchange exposure. Consequently, the firm has to forgo the opportunity to benefit from favourable exchange rate changes. To elaborate on this point, let us assume that the spot exchange rate turns out to be C$1.60 per euro on the maturity date of the forward contract. In this instance, forward hedging would cost Bombardier C$1.4 million in terms of forgone dollar receipts (see Exhibit 13.2). If Bombardier had, indeed, entered into a forward contract, it would regret its decision to do so. With its euro receivable, Bombardier ideally would like to protect itself only if the euro weakens, while retaining the opportunity to benefit if the euro strengthens. Currency options provide such a *flexible* "optional" hedge against exchange exposure. Generally speaking, the firm may buy a foreign currency call (put) option to hedge its foreign currency payables (receivables), which is known as **options market hedge**.

To show how the options hedge works, suppose that in the over-the-counter market Bombardier purchased a put option on 10 million euros with an exercise price of C$1.46 and a one-year expiration. Assume that the option premium (price) was C$0.02 per euro. Bombardier thus paid C$200,000 (= C$0.02 × 10 million) for the option. This transaction provides Bombardier with the right, but not the obligation, to sell up to €10 million for C$1.46/€, regardless of the future spot rate.

Now, assume that the spot exchange rate turns out to be C$1.30 on the expiration date. Since Bombardier has the right to sell each euro for C$1.46, it will certainly exercise its put option on the euro and convert €10 million into C$14.6 million. The main advantage of options hedging is that the firm can decide whether to exercise the option based on the realized spot exchange rate on the expiration date. Recall that Bombardier paid C$200,000 upfront for the option. Considering the time value of money, this upfront cost is equivalent to C$212,200 (= C$200,000 × 1.061) as of the expiration date. This means that under the options hedge, the net dollar proceeds from the European sale become C$14,387,800:

$$C\$14,387,800 = C\$14,600,000 - C\$212,200$$

Since Bombardier is going to exercise its put option on the euro whenever the future spot exchange rate falls below the exercise rate of C$1.46, it is assured of a "minimum" dollar receipt of C$14,387,800 from the European sale.

Next, consider an alternative scenario where the euro appreciates against the Canadian dollar. Assume that the spot rate turns out to be C$1.60 per euro on the expiration date. In this event, Bombardier would have no incentive to exercise the option. It will, rather, let the option expire and convert €10 million into C$16 million at the spot rate. Subtracting C$212,200 for the option cost, the net dollar proceeds will become C$15,787,800 under the option hedge. As suggested by these scenarios, the options hedge allows the firm to *limit the downside risk while preserving the upside potential*. The firm, however, has to pay for this flexibility in terms of the option premium. There rarely exist free lunches in finance! Note that neither the forward nor the money market hedge involves any upfront cost.

Exhibit 13.5 provides the net Canadian dollar proceeds from the European sale under options hedging for a range of future spot exchange rates. The same results are illustrated in Exhibit 13.6. As Exhibit 13.6 shows, the options hedge sets a "floor" for the Canadian dollar proceeds. The future Canadian dollar proceeds will be at least C$14,387,800 under the option hedge. Bombardier, thus, can be said to have an insurance policy against the exchange risk hazard; the upfront option cost, C$200,000, Bombardier incurred can be regarded as an insurance premium. When a firm has an account payable, rather than a receivable, in terms of a foreign currency, the firm can set a "ceiling" for the future dollar cost of buying the foreign currency amount by buying a call option on the foreign currency amount.

EXHIBIT 13.5

Dollar Proceeds from
Options Hedge

Future Spot Exchange Rate (S_T)	Exercise Decision	Gross Dollar Proceeds	Option Cost	Net Dollar Proceeds
C$1.30	Exercise	C$14,600,000	C$212,200	C$14,387,800
C$1.40	Exercise	C$14,600,000	C$212,200	C$14,387,800
C$1.46	Neutral	C$14,600,000	C$212,200	C$14,387,800
C$1.50	Not exercise	C$15,000,000	C$212,200	C$14,787,800
C$1.60	Not exercise	C$16,000,000	C$212,200	C$15,787,800

Note: The exercise exchange rate (E) is C$1.46 in this example.

EXHIBIT 13.6

Dollar Proceeds from
the European Sale:
Option versus Forward
Hedge

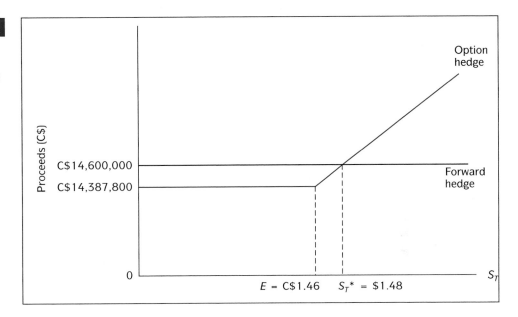

Exhibit 13.6 also compares the dollar proceeds from forward and options hedges. As indicated in the exhibit, the options hedge dominates the forward hedge for future spot rates greater than C$1.48 per euro, whereas the opposite holds for spot rates lower than C$1.48 per euro. Bombardier will be indifferent between the two hedging methods at the "break-even" spot rate of C$1.48 per euro.

The break-even spot rate, which is useful for choosing a hedging method, can be determined as follows:

$$C\$(10,000,000)S_T - C\$212,200 = C\$14,600,000$$

By solving the equation for S_T, we obtain the break-even spot rate, $S_T^* = C\$1.48$. The break-even analysis suggests that if the firm's expected future spot rate is greater (less) than the break-even rate, then the options (forward) hedge might be preferred.

Unlike the forward contract, which has only one forward rate for a given maturity, there are multiple exercise exchange rates (prices) for the options contract. In the preceding discussion, we worked with an option with an exercise price of C$1.46. Considering that Bombardier has a euro receivable, it is tempting to think that it would be a good idea for Bombardier to buy a put option with a higher exercise price, thereby increasing the minimum dollar receipt from the European sale. But it becomes immediately clear that the firm has to pay for it in terms of a higher option premium. Again, there is no free lunch. Choice of the exercise price for the options contract ultimately depends on the extent to which the firm is willing to bear exchange risk. For instance, if the firm's objective is only to avoid very unfavourable exchange rate changes (that is, a major depreciation of the euro in Bombardier's example), then it should consider buying an out-of-money put option with a low exercise price, saving option costs. The three alternative hedging strategies are summarized in Exhibit 13.7.

EXHIBIT 13.7	Bombardier's Alternative Hedging Strategies: A Summary	
Strategy	Transactions	Outcomes
Forward market hedge	1. Sell €10,000,000 forward for dollars now. 2. In one year, receive €10,000,000 rate from the European client and deliver it to the counterparty of the forward contract.	Assured of receiving C$14,600,000 in one year; future spot exchange becomes irrelevant.
Money market hedge	1. Borrow €9,174,312 and buy C$13,761,468 spot now. 2. In one year, collect €10,000,000 from the European client and pay off the euro loan using the amount.	Assured of receiving C$13,761,468 now or C$14,600,918 in one year; future spot exchange rate becomes irrelevant.
Options market hedge	1. Buy a put option on €10,000,000 for an upfront cost of C$200,000. 2. In one year, decide whether to exercise the option upon observing the prevailing spot exchange rate.	Assured of receiving at least C$14,387,800 or more if the future spot exchange rate exceeds the exercise exchange rate; Bombardier controls the downside risk while retaining the upside potential.

13.4 Cross-Hedging Minor Currency Exposure

If a firm has receivables or payables in major currencies, such as the euro, British pound, or Japanese yen, it can easily use forward, money market, or options contracts to manage its exchange risk exposure. In contrast, if the firm has positions in minor currencies, such as the Korean won, Thai bath, or Czech koruna, it may be either very costly or impossible to use financial contracts in these currencies. This is because the financial markets of the developing countries are relatively underdeveloped and often highly regulated. Facing this situation, the firm may consider using **cross-hedging** techniques to manage its minor currency exposure. Cross-hedging involves hedging a position in one asset by taking a position in another asset.

Suppose a Canadian firm has an account receivable in Korean won and would like to hedge its won position. If there were a well-functioning forward market in won, the firm would simply sell the won receivable forward. But the firm finds it impossible to do so. However, since the won/Canadian dollar exchange rate is highly correlated with the yen/dollar exchange rate, the Canadian firm may sell a yen amount, which is equivalent to the won receivable, forward against the Canadian dollar thereby cross-hedging its won exposure. Obviously, the effectiveness of this cross-hedging technique would depend on the stability and strength of the won/yen correlation. A study by Aggarwal and Demaskey (1997) indicates that Japanese yen derivative contracts are fairly effective in cross-hedging exposure to minor Asian currencies, such as the Indonesian rupiah, Korean won, Philippine peso, and Thai bath. Likewise, German mark derivatives can be effective in cross-hedging exposures in some Central and East European currencies, such as the Czech koruna, Estonian kroon, and Hungarian forint.

Another study by Benet (1990) suggests that commodity futures contracts may be used effectively to cross-hedge some minor currency exposures. Suppose the Canadian dollar price of the Mexican peso is positively correlated to the world oil price. Note that Mexico is a major exporter of oil, accounting for roughly 5 percent of the world market share. Considering this situation, a firm may use oil futures contracts to manage its peso exposure. The firm can sell (buy) oil futures if it has peso receivables (payables). In the same vein, soybean and coffee futures contracts may be used to cross-hedge a Brazilian real exposure. Again, the effectiveness of this cross-hedging technique would depend on the strength and stability of the relationship between the exchange rate and the commodity futures prices.

13.5 Hedging Contingent Exposure

In addition to providing a flexible hedge against exchange exposure, options contracts can also provide an effective hedge against what might be called **contingent exposure**. Contingent exposure refers to a situation in which the firm may or may not be subject to exchange exposure. Let us consider an example from the perspective of an American firm with Canadian dollar transaction exposure. Suppose General Electric (GE) is bidding on a hydroelectric project in Quebec. If the bid is accepted, which will be known in three months, GE is going to receive C$100 million to initiate the project. Since GE may or may not face exchange exposure depending on whether its bid will be accepted, it faces a typical contingent exposure situation.[4]

It is difficult to deal with contingent exposure using traditional hedging tools, such as forward contracts. Suppose that GE sold C$100 million forward to hedge the contingent exposure. If GE's bid is accepted, then GE will have no problem because it will have C$100 million to fulfill the forward contract. However, if the bid is rejected, GE now faces an unhedged short position in Canadian dollars. Clearly, a forward contract does not provide a satisfactory hedge against contingent exposure. A "do-nothing" policy does not guarantee a satisfactory outcome either. The problem with this policy is that if GE's bid is accepted, the firm ends up with an unhedged long position in Canadian dollars.

An alternative approach is to buy a three-month put option on C$100 million. In this case, there are four possible outcomes:

1. The bid is accepted, and the spot exchange rate turns out to be less than the exercise rate: In this case, the firm will simply exercise the put option and convert C$100 million at the exercise rate.

2. The bid is accepted, and the spot exchange rate turns out to be greater than the exercise rate: In this case, the firm will let the put option expire and convert C$100 million at the spot rate.

3. The bid is rejected, and the spot exchange rate turns out to be less than the exercise rate: In this case, although the firm does not have Canadian dollars, it will exercise the put option and make a profit.

4. The bid is rejected, and the spot rate turns out to be greater than the exercise rate: In this case, the firm will simply let the put option expire.

The above scenarios indicate that when the put option is purchased, each outcome is adequately covered; the firm will not be left with an unhedged foreign currency position. Again, it is stressed that the firm has to pay the option premium upfront. The preceding discussion is summarized in Exhibit 13.8.

13.6 Hedging Recurrent Exposure with Swap Contracts

Firms often have to deal with a "sequence" of accounts payable or receivable in terms of a foreign currency. Such recurrent cash flows in a foreign currency can best be hedged using a currency swap contract, which is an agreement to exchange one currency for another at a predetermined exchange rate, that is, the swap rate, on a sequence of future dates. As such, a swap contract is like a portfolio of forward

---

[4]These days, it is not unusual for the exporter to let the importer choose the currency of payment. For example, in the Bombardier case, Bombardier may allow Austrian Airways to pay either C$15 million or €10 million. To the extent that Bombardier does not know in advance which currency it is going to receive, it faces a contingent exposure. Given the future spot exchange rate, Austrian Airways will choose to pay with a cheaper currency. It is noteworthy that in this example, Bombardier provides Austrian Airways with a free option to buy up to C$15 million using euros (which is equivalent to an option to sell euros for dollars) at the implicit exercise rate of C$1.50/€.

EXHIBIT 13.8

Contingent Exposure Management: The Case of GE Bidding for a Quebec Hydro-electric Project

Alternative Strategies	Bid Outcome	
	Bid Accepted	Bid Rejected
Do nothing	An unhedged long position in C$100 million	No exposure
Sell C$ forward	No exposure	An unhedged short position in C$100 million
Buy put option on C$[a]	If the future spot rate becomes less than the exercise rate, $(S_T < E)$	
	Convert C$100 million at the exercise price	Exercise the option and and make a profit
	If the future spot rate becomes greater than the exercise rate, $(S_T > E)$	
	Let the option expire and convert C$100 million at the spot exchange rate	Simply let the option expire

[a]If the future spot rate turns out to be equal to the exercise price, that is, $S_T = E$, GE will be indifferent between (i) exercising the option and (ii) letting the option expire and converting C$100 million at the spot rate.

contracts with different maturities. Swaps are very flexible in terms of amount and maturity; the maturity can range from a few months to 20 years.

Suppose that Bombardier is scheduled to deliver an aircraft to Austrian Airways at the beginning of each year for the next five years, starting in 2004. Austrian Airways, in turn, is scheduled to pay €10,000,000 to Bombardier on December 1 of each year for five years, starting in 2004. In this case, Bombardier faces a sequence of exchange risk exposures. As previously mentioned, Bombardier can hedge this type of exposure using a swap agreement by which Bombardier delivers €10,000,000 to the counterparty of the contract on December 1 of each year for five years and takes delivery of a predetermined dollar amount each year. If the agreed swap exchange rate is $1.50/€, then Bombardier will receive $15 million each year, regardless of the future spot and forward rates. Note that a sequence of five forward contracts would not be priced at a uniform rate, $1.50/€; the forward rates will be different for different maturities. In addition, longer-term forward contracts are not readily available.

13.7 Hedging through Invoice Currency

While such financial hedging instruments as forward, money market, swap, and options contracts are well known, **hedging through invoice currency**—an operational technique—has not received much attention. The firm can *shift, share,* or *diversify* exchange risk by appropriately choosing the currency of invoice. For instance, if Bombardier invoices C$15 million, rather than €10 million for the sale of the aircraft, then it does not face exchange exposure anymore. Note, however, that the exchange exposure has not disappeared; it has merely shifted to the European importer. Austrian Airways now has an account payable denominated in Canadian dollars.

Instead of shifting the exchange exposure entirely to Austrian Airways, Bombardier can share the exposure with Austrian Airways by, for example, invoicing half of the bill in Canadian dollars and the remaining half in euros, that is, C$7.5 million and €5 million. In this case, the magnitude of Bombardier's exchange exposure is reduced by half. As a practical matter, however, the firm may not be able to use risk shifting or sharing as much as it wishes to for fear of losing sales to competitors. Only an exporter with substantial market power can use this approach. In addition, if the currencies of both the exporter and the importer are not suitable for settling international trade, neither party can resort to risk shifting/sharing to deal with exchange exposure.

The firm can diversify exchange exposure to some extent by using currency basket units, such as the SDR, as the invoice currency. Often, multinational corporations and sovereign entities are known to float bonds denominated either in the SDR or in the ECU prior to the introduction of the euro. For example, the Egyptian government charges for the use of the Suez Canal using the SDR. Obviously, these currency baskets are used to reduce exchange exposure. As previously noted, the SDR now comprises four individual currencies, the American dollar, the euro, the Japanese yen, and the British pound. Because the SDR is a portfolio of currencies, its value should be substantially more stable than the value of any individual constituent currency. Currency basket units can be a useful hedging tool, especially for long-term exposure for which no forward or options contracts are readily available. The International Finance in Practice box on page 316 "The LCBO and Foreign Exchange Risk Management" shows how companies deal with exchange risk exposure using various operational techniques.

13.8   Hedging via Lead and Lag

Another operational technique the firm can use to reduce transaction exposure is leading and lagging foreign currency receipts and payments. To "lead" means to pay or collect early, and to "lag" means to pay or collect late. The firm would like to lead soft currency receivables and lag hard currency receivables to avoid the loss from depreciation of the soft currency and benefit from the appreciation of the hard currency. For the same reason, the firm will attempt to lead the hard currency payables and lag soft currency payables.

To the extent that the firm can effectively implement the **lead/lag strategy**, the transaction exposure the firm faces can be reduced. However, a word of caution is in order. Suppose, concerned with the likely depreciation of the euro, Bombardier would like Austrian Airways to prepay €10 million. Bombardier's attempt to lead the euro receivable may encounter difficulties. First of all, Austrian Airways would like to lag this payment, which is denominated in the soft currency (the euro), and thus has no incentive to prepay unless Bombardier offers a substantial discount to compensate for the prepayment. This, of course, reduces the benefits of collecting the euro receivable early. Second, pressing Austrian Airways for prepayment can hamper future sales efforts by Bombardier. Third, to the extent that the original invoice price, €10 million, incorporates the expected depreciation of the euro, Bombardier is already partially protected against the depreciation of the euro.

The lead/lag strategy can be employed more effectively to deal with intrafirm payables and receivables, such as material costs, rents, royalties, interests, and dividends, among subsidiaries of the same multinational corporation. Since managements of various subsidiaries of the same firm are presumably working for the good of the entire firm, the lead/lag strategy can be applied more aggressively.

13.9   Exposure Netting

In 1984, Lufthansa, a German airline, signed a contract to buy US$3 billion worth of aircraft from Bombardier and entered into a forward contract to purchase US$1.5 billion forward for the purpose of hedging against the expected appreciation of the dollar against the German mark. This decision, however, suffered from a major flaw: A significant portion of Lufthansa's cash flows was also American dollar-denominated. As a result, Lufthansa's net exposure to the exchange risk might not have been significant. Lufthansa had a so-called natural hedge. In 1985, the American dollar depreciated

The LCBO and Foreign Exchange Risk Management

The Liquor Control Board of Ontario (LCBO) is the single largest importer of wines, spirits, and beer in the world. In 2003, the LCBO imported liquor worth more than C$800 million. These imports come from many sources. Wines come from Australia, Chile, France, Italy, the United States, and several other warm countries. Ireland, Sweden, and the United Kingdom are important providers of spirits. Jamaica sends us strong rum.

The LCBO's foreign exchange exposure creates a complex risk management problem. When the Canadian dollar rises or falls, it does not move to the same degree against all currencies. The LCBO is exposed to risk from a variety of foreign exchange movements.

The LCBO has devised a method to simplify its currency dealings with foreign suppliers of wines and spirits. First, the LCBO makes known to agents that the LCBO deals only in a small number of foreign currencies—primarily the American dollar and the Euro. For suppliers from the United States or Europe, this is not an issue. On the other hand, agents for Chilean wine or Swedish vodka must quote prices to the LCBO either in American dollars or euros—or perhaps Canadian dollars. This pushes foreign exchange transactional exposure (between, say, the Swedish krone and the Canadian dollar) on to suppliers of wines and spirits from countries other than the United States or Europe. This is a policy that only a very large importer could sustain.

The second feature of the LCBO's exchange risk management takes the form of "announced exchange rates" for purchases of imported wines and spirits. Again, this arrangement is workable because the LCBO is an important customer for its suppliers. The LCBO announces exchange rates that it will apply in processing invoices in foreign currencies over the subsequent quarter. For example, in July 2004, the LCBO announced that it will process all Euro-denominated invoices received in August, September, and October at C$1.65/€. The LCBO orders a shipment of wine from a French supplier at an invoice price of, say, €100,000 specified at the time of the order. The supplier accepts the LCBO's "offer exchange rate" scheme. Compared with what the French supplier would receive in euro if he were to take payment in Canadian dollars on the spot market at the time of delivery, under the LCBO "offer exchange rate" scheme, a change in the exchange rate between the time of the order and the time of delivery results in a foreign exchange *gain* (recorded in euro) for the exporter if the Canadian dollar appreciates against the euro or a foreign *loss* if the Canadian dollar depreciates.

Finally, during each three-month span of its "announced rates" the LCBO protects itself with forward contracts and foreign exchange options. The policy is to hedge approximately 50 percent of the exposure.

substantially against the mark and, as a result, Lufthansa experienced a major foreign exchange loss from settling the forward contract. This episode shows that when a firm has both receivables and payables in a given foreign currency, it should consider hedging only its *net* exposure.

So far, we have discussed exposure management on a currency-by-currency basis. In reality, a typical multinational corporation is likely to have a portfolio of currency positions. For instance, a Canadian firm may have an account payable in euros and, at the same time, an account receivable in Swiss francs. Considering that the euro and Swiss franc move against the dollar almost in lockstep, the firm can just wait until these accounts become due and then buy euros spot with Swiss francs. It can be wasteful and unnecessary to buy euros forward and sell Swiss francs forward. In other words, if the firm has a portfolio of currency positions, it makes sense to hedge residual exposurem, rather than hedge each currency position separately.

If the firm would like to apply **exposure netting** aggressively, it helps to centralize the firm's exchange exposure management function in one location. Many multinational corporations are using a **reinvoice centre**, a financial subsidiary, as a mechanism for centralizing exposure management functions. All the invoices arising from intrafirm transactions are sent to the reinvoice centre, where exposure is netted. Once the residual exposure is determined, then foreign exchange experts at the centre determine optimal hedging methods and implement them.

13.10 Should the Firm Hedge?

We have discussed how the firm can hedge exchange exposure if it wishes. We have not discussed whether the firm should try to hedge to begin with. As can be seen from the International Finance in Practice box on page 318, "To Hedge or Not to Hedge," there hardly exists a consensus on whether the firm should hedge. Some would argue that exchange exposure management at the corporate level is redundant when shareholders can manage the exposure themselves. Others would argue that what matters in the firm valuation is only systematic risk; corporate risk management may only reduce the total risk. These arguments suggest that corporate exposure management would not necessarily add to the value of the firm.

While the above arguments against corporate risk management may be valid in a "perfect" capital market, one can make a case for it based on various market imperfections:

1. Information asymmetry: Management knows about the firm's exposure position much better than shareholders. Thus, the management of the firm, not its shareholders, should manage exchange exposure.

2. Differential transaction costs: The firm is in a position to acquire low-cost hedges; transaction costs for individual shareholders can be substantial. Also, the firm has hedging tools like the reinvoice centre that are not available to shareholders.

3. Default costs: If default costs are significant, corporate hedging would be justifiable because it will reduce the probability of default. Perception of a reduced default risk, in turn, can lead to a better credit rating and lower financing costs.

4. Progressive corporate taxes: Under progressive corporate tax rates, stable before-tax earnings lead to lower corporate taxes than volatile earnings with the same average value. This happens because under progressive tax rates, the firm pays more taxes in high-earning periods than it saves in low-earning periods.

The last point merits elaboration. Suppose the country's corporate income tax system is such that a tax rate of 20 percent applies to the first C$10 million of corporate earnings and a 40-percent rate applies to any earnings exceeding C$10 million. Firms thus face a simple progressive tax structure. Now consider an exporting firm that expects to earn C$15 million if the dollar depreciates, but only C$5 million if the dollar appreciates. Let us assume that the dollar may appreciate or depreciate with equal chances. In this case, the firm's expected tax will be C$2.5 million:

$$\text{Expected tax} = \tfrac{1}{2}[(0.20)(\text{C\$5,000,000})] + \tfrac{1}{2}[(0.20)(\text{C\$10,000,000})$$
$$+ (0.40)(\text{C\$5,000,000})]$$
$$= \text{C\$2,500,000}$$

Now, consider another firm, B, that is identical to firm A in every respect except that, unlike firm A, firm B aggressively and successfully hedges its risk exposure and, as a result, it can expect to realize certain earnings of C$10,000,000, the same as firm A's expected earnings. Firm B, however, expects to pay only C$2 million as taxes. Obviously, hedging results in a C$500,000 tax saving. Exhibit 13.9 illustrates this situation.

While not every firm is hedging exchange exposure, many firms are engaged in hedging activities, suggesting that corporate risk management is relevant to maximizing the firm's value. To the extent that for various reasons, shareholders themselves cannot properly manage exchange risk, the firm's managers can do it for them, contributing to the firm's value. Some corporate hedging activities, however, might be motivated by managerial objectives; managers may want to stabilize cash flows so that the risk to their human capital can be reduced.

INTERNATIONAL FINANCE
IN PRACTICE

To Hedge or Not to Hedge

"Most value-maximising firms do not hedge." Thus Merton Miller and Christopher Culp, two economists at the University of Chicago, said in a recent article[1] about Metallgesellschaft, a firm that saw its value plunge after its oil-price hedging strategy came a cropper. Yet the vast majority of firms that use derivatives do so to hedge. Last year's survey of big American non-financial companies by the Wharton School and Chase Manhattan bank found that, of those firms that used derivatives (about one-third of the sample), some 75% said they did so to hedge commitments. As many as 40% of the derivatives users said they sometimes took a view on the direction of markets, but only 8% admitted to doing so frequently.

To justify speculation, managers ought to have good reason to suppose that they can consistently outwit firms for which playing the financial markets is a core business. Commodity businesses, such as oil or grain companies taking positions on the direction of their related commodity markets, may have such reason, but non-financial firms taking bets on interest rates or foreign-exchange rates almost certainly do not—though some claim to make a profit on it. But why might hedging be wrong?

In the 1950s, Merton Miller and Franco Modigliani, another financial economist, demonstrated that firms make money only if they make good investments—the kind that increase their operating cash flows. Whether those investments are financed through debt, equity or retained earnings is irrelevant. Different methods of financing simply determine how a firm's value is divided between its various sorts of investors (e.g., shareholders or bondholders), not the value itself. This surprising insight helped win each of them a Nobel prize. If they are right, it has crucial implications for hedging. For if methods of financing and the character of financial risks do not matter, managing them is pointless. It cannot add to the firm's value; on the contrary, as derivatives do not come free, using them for hedging might actually lower that value. Moreover, as Messrs Miller and Modigliani

showed, if investors want to avoid the financial risks attached to holding shares in a firm, they can diversify their portfolio of holdings. Firms need not manage their financial risks; investors can do it for themselves.

In recent years, other academics have challenged the Miller-Modigliani thesis—at least in its pure form—and demonstrated that hedging can sometimes add value. That is because firms may be able to manage certain risks internally in ways that cannot be replicated by outside investors. Some investors may not want, or be able, to hold diversified share portfolios (for instance, if the firm is family-owned). It may be possible to use derivatives to reduce profits in good years and raise them in bad years in order to cut the firm's average tax bill. Hedging can also be used to prevent the firm getting into financial difficulties, or even going bust.

Recently, another view has been winning converts. According to Kenneth Froot, David Sharfstein and Jeremy Stein, three Boston-based economists, firms should hedge to ensure they always have sufficient cash flow to fund their planned investment programme.[2] Otherwise some potentially profitable investments may be missed because of inefficiencies in the bond and equity markets that prevent the firm raising the funds, or the reluctance of managers to tap these markets when internal cash is tight. Merck, an American pharmaceuticals firm, has helped to pioneer the use of derivatives to ensure that investment plans—particularly in R&D—can always be financed. In a paper explaining the firm's strategy, Judy Lewent and John Kearney observed that "our experience, and that of the [drugs] industry in general, has been that cash-flow and earnings uncertainty caused by exchange-rate volatility leads to a reduction in research spending."[3]

Though apparently simple, such a strategy has some intriguing implications. As Messrs Froot, Scharfstein and Stein point out, the factors that cause cash flow to fall below expectations may also cut the number of

A study by Allayannis and Weston (2001) provides direct evidence on the important issue of whether hedging actually adds to the value of the firm. Specifically, they examine whether firms with currency exposure that use foreign currency derivative contracts, such as currency forward and options, increase their valuation. The authors find that American firms that face currency risk and use currency derivatives for hedging have, on average, about 5 percent higher value than firms that do not use currency derivatives. For firms that have no direct foreign involvement but may be exposed to exchange rate movements via export/import competition, they find a small hedging valuation premium. In addition, they find that firms that stop hedging experience a decrease in firm valuation compared with those firms that continue to hedge. Their study thus clearly suggests that corporate hedging contributes to firm value.

318

profitable investment opportunities, so lessening the need to hedge. For instance, an oil company's cash flow may suffer due to a fall in oil prices. However, that fall in prices also reduces the value of investing in developing new oil fields. With fewer profitable projects to invest in, the firm will need less cash to finance investment.

All about Cash Flow

Rene Stulz, an economist at Ohio State University, sees even more powerful implications.[4] He says that there are only a couple of good reasons why a firm should hedge. One is to cut its tax bills, which is likely to happen only if the firm's profits tend to yo-yo between lower and higher tax bands. The other one is being unable to get cash when it needs it, or facing a serious risk of running short. By this rule, reckons Mr. Stulz, a firm with little debt or with highly-rated debt has no need to hedge, as the risk of it getting into financial trouble is tiny. If he is right, many of America's biggest hedgers—including some of those that have revealed losses on derivatives, such as Procter & Gamble—may be wasting their energies, or worse. By contrast, Mr. Stulz thinks that if a firm is highly geared, hedging can boost its value significantly. Indeed, during the leveraged buy-out craze of the 1980s, when firms were taken over by buying off shareholders and loading up on debt, tough risk-management requirements were standard in any borrowing arrangement.

Messrs. Culp and Miller, of the University of Chicago, take this argument a step further in defending the management of Metallgesellschaft from some of the wilder accusations of recklessness (a matter that is now before the American courts). Instead of analysing the firm's hedging strategy (which involved selling oil for up to ten years ahead and hedging this exposure with futures contracts) in terms of its effectiveness in reducing risk, Messrs. Culp and Miller argue that the company had no need to reduce its risk-exposure because it had no reason to suppose it could not get hold of cash if needed. After all, the mighty Deutsche Bank, as its principal creditor and controlling shareholder, was behind the firm,

ensuring that it could not go bust; and, as it turned out, it did not. Rather, the aim of the hedging strategy was to exploit what Metallgesellschaft thought was its superior understanding of the relationship between spot prices and futures prices—risky but not obviously foolish.

Not everyone agrees that firms with little debt should not hedge. Myron Scholes, an economist at Stanford University, reaches the opposite conclusion: firms with little debt could reduce their riskiness by hedging, and so be able to borrow more and rely less on equity. Equity can be expensive compared with debt; it is inherently riskier, offering no guaranteed payout, so investors require a higher average return on it than they do on bonds. Ultimately, through risk-reducing hedging and borrowing, more firms might be able to remain (or become) privately owned, reckons Mr. Scholes. But to do this well, managers will need a very good understanding of the risks to which their firm is exposed, and of opportunities to hedge.

However, the way firms typically use derivatives to reduce the cost of capital is different from that described above. Rather than hedge and borrow more, they substitute for traditional debt a hybrid of bonds and options and/or futures that will pay off in certain circumstances, thus lowering capital costs. This is speculation dressed up as prudence, because if events take an unexpected turn, capital costs go up by at least the cost of the options.

[1]"Hedging in the Theory of Corporate Finance: A Reply to Our Critics." By Christopher Culp and Merton Miller. *Journal of Applied Corporate Finance*; Spring 1995.

[2]"A Framework for Risk Management." By Kenneth Froot, David Scharfstein and Jeremy Stein. *Harvard Business Review*; November 1994.

[3]"Identifying, Measuring and Hedging Currency Risk at Merck." By Judy Lewent and John Kearney. In *The New Corporate Finance*, edited by Donald Chew, McGraw-Hill; 1993.

[4]"Rethinking Risk Management" By Rene Stulz. Ohio State University working paper; 1995.

Source: *The Economist*, February 10, 1996, pp. PS10–12. © 1996 The Economist Newspaper Group, Inc. Reprinted with permission.

13.11　What Risk Management Products Do Firms Use?

In a recent survey, Jesswein, Kwok, and Folks (1995) documented the extent of knowledge and use of foreign exchange risk management products by American corporations. On the basis of a survey of *Fortune* 500 firms, they found that the traditional forward contract is the most popular product. As Exhibit 13.10 shows, about 93 percent of respondents of the survey used forward contracts. This old, traditional instrument has not been supplanted by recent "fancy" innovations. The next commonly used instruments are foreign currency swaps (52.6 percent) and over-the-counter currency options (48.8 percent). Such recent innovations as compound options (3.8 percent) and lookback options (5.1 percent) are among the least extensively used instruments. These

EXHIBIT 13.9

Tax Savings from
Hedging Exchange
Risk Exposure

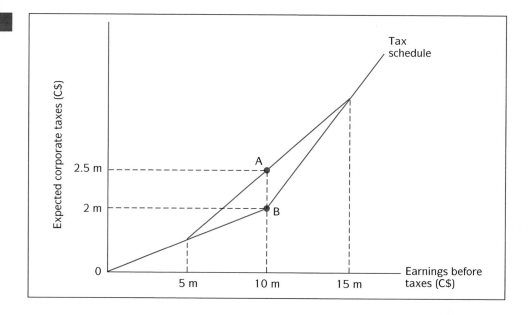

EXHIBIT 13.10

A Survey of Knowledge
and Use of Foreign
Exchange Risk
Management Products[a]

Type of Product	Heard of (Awareness)	Used (Adoption)
Forward contracts	100.0%	93.1%
Foreign currency swaps	98.8	52.6
Foreign currency futures	98.8	20.1
Exchange-traded currency options	96.4	17.3
Exchange-traded futures options	95.8	8.9
Over-the-counter currency options	93.5	48.8
Cylinder options	91.2	28.7
Synthetic forwards	88.0	22.0
Synthetic options	88.0	18.6
Participating forwards, etc.	83.6	15.8
Forward exchange agreements, etc.	81.7	14.8
Foreign currency warrants	77.7	4.2
Break forwards, etc.	65.3	4.9
Compound options	55.8	3.8
Lookback options, etc.	52.1	5.1
Average across products	84.4%	23.9%

[a]The products are ranked by the percentages of respondents who have heard of products. There are 173 respondents in total.
Source: Kurt Jesswein, Chuck Kwok, and William Folks, Jr., "Corporate Use of Innovative Foreign Exchange Risk Management Products," *Columbia Journal of World Business* (Fall 1995).

findings seem to indicate that most American firms meet their exchange risk management needs with forward, swap, and options contracts.

The Jesswein, Kwok, and Folks survey also shows that among the various industries, the finance/insurance/real estate industry stands out as the most frequent user of exchange risk management products. This finding is not surprising. This industry has more finance experts who are skillful at using derivative securities. In addition, this industry handles mainly financial assets, which tend to be exposed to exchange risk. The survey further shows that the corporate use of foreign exchange risk management products is positively related to the firm's degree of international involvement. This finding is not surprising either. As the firm becomes more internationalized through cross-border trade and investments, it is likely to handle an increasing amount of foreign currencies, giving rise to a greater demand for exchange risk hedging.

SUMMARY

1. The firm is subject to a transaction exposure when it faces contractual cash flows denominated in foreign currencies. Transaction exposure can be hedged by financial contracts, such as forward, money market, and options contracts, as well as by such operational techniques as the choice of invoice currency, lead/lag strategy, and exposure netting.

2. If the firm has a foreign-currency-denominated receivable (payable), it can hedge the exposure by selling (buying) the foreign currency receivable (payable) forward. The firm can *expect* to eliminate the exposure without incurring costs as long as the forward exchange rate is an unbiased predictor of the future spot rate. The firm can achieve equivalent hedging results by lending and borrowing in the domestic and foreign money markets.

3. Unlike forward and money market hedges, currency options provide flexible hedges against exchange exposure. With the options hedge, the firm can limit the downside risk while preserving the upside potential. Currency options also provide the firm with an effective hedge against contingent exposure.

4. The firm can shift, share, and diversify exchange exposure by appropriately choosing the invoice currency. Currency basket units, such as the SDR and ECU, can be used as an invoice currency to partially hedge long-term exposure for which financial hedges are not readily available.

5. The firm can reduce transaction exposure by leading and lagging foreign currency receipts and payments, especially among its own affiliates.

6. When a firm has a portfolio of foreign currency positions, it makes sense only to hedge the residual exposure, rather than hedging each currency position separately. The reinvoice centre can help implement the portfolio approach to exposure management.

7. In a perfect capital market where shareholders can hedge exchange exposure as well as the firm, it is difficult to justify exposure management at the corporate level. In reality, capital markets are far from perfect, and the firm often has advantages over the shareholders in implementing hedging strategies. There, thus, exists room for corporate exposure management to contribute to the firm value.

KEY WORDS

contingent exposure, *313*
cross-hedging, *312*
exposure netting, *316*
forward market
    hedge, *304*

hedging through invoice
    currency, *314*
lead/lag strategy, *315*
money market
    hedge, *307*

options market
    hedge, *310*
reinvoice centre, *316*
transaction
    exposure, *303*

QUESTIONS

1. How would you define *transaction exposure*? How is it different from economic exposure?

2. Discuss and compare hedging transaction exposure using the forward contract versus money market instruments. When do alternative hedging approaches produce the same result?

3. Discuss and compare the costs of hedging by forward contracts and options contracts.

4. What are the advantages of a currency options contract as a hedging tool compared with the forward contract?

5. Suppose your company has purchased a put option on the euro to manage exchange exposure associated with an account receivable denominated in that currency. In this case, your company can be said to have an "insurance" policy on its receivable. Explain in what sense this is so.

6. Recent surveys of corporate exchange risk management practices indicate that many American firms simply do not hedge. How would you explain this result?

7. Should a firm hedge? Why, or why not?

8. Using an example, discuss the possible effect of hedging on a firm's tax obligations.

9. Explain *contingent exposure* and discuss the advantages of using currency options to manage this type of currency exposure.

10. Explain cross-hedging and discuss the factors determining its effectiveness.

PROBLEMS

The spreadsheet TRNSEXP.xls may be used in solving parts of problems 2, 3, 4, and 6.

1. Celestica of Toronto sold an advanced computer system to the Max Planck Institute in Germany on credit and invoiced €10 million payable in six months. Currently, the six-month forward exchange rate is C$1.50/€ and the foreign exchange adviser for Cray Research predicts that the spot rate is likely to be C$1.42/€ in six months.

   a. What is the expected gain/loss from a forward hedge?

   b. If you were the financial manager of Celestica, would you recommend hedging this euro receivable? Why, or why not?

   c. Suppose the foreign exchange adviser predicts that the future spot rate will be the same as the forward exchange rate quoted today. Would you recommend hedging in this case? Why, or why not?

2. RIM of Waterloo purchased computer chips from NEC, a Japanese electronics concern, and was billed ¥250 million payable in three months. Currently, the spot exchange rate is ¥105/C$, and the three-month forward rate is ¥100/C$. The three-month money market interest rate is 8 percent per annum in Canada and 7 percent per annum in Japan. The management of RIM decided to use a money market hedge to deal with this yen account payable.

   a. Explain the process of a money market hedge and compute the Canadian dollar cost of meeting the yen obligation.

   b. Conduct a cash flow analysis of the money market hedge.

3. You plan to visit Geneva, Switzerland, in three months to attend an international business conference. You expect to incur a total cost of SF5,000 for lodging, meals, and transportation during your stay. As of today, the spot exchange rate is C$1.10/SF and the three-month forward rate is C$1.13/SF. You can buy the three-month call option on SF with an exercise price of C$1.14/SF for the premium of C$0.05 per SF. Assume that your expected future spot exchange rate is the same as the forward rate. The three-month interest rate is 6 percent per annum in Canada and 4 percent per annum in Switzerland.

   a. Calculate your expected dollar cost of buying SF5,000 if you choose to hedge by a call option on SF.

   b. Calculate the future dollar cost of meeting this SF obligation if you decide to hedge using a forward contract.

   c. At what future spot exchange rate will you be indifferent between the forward and option market hedges?

   d. Illustrate the future dollar cost of meeting the SF payable against the future spot exchange rate under both the options and forward market hedges.

4. Bombardier just signed a contract to sell aircraft to Air France. Air France will be billed €20 million payable in one year. The current spot exchange rate is C$1.05/€

and the one-year forward rate is C$1.10/€. The annual interest rate is 6 percent in Canada and 5 percent in France. Bombardier is concerned with the volatile exchange rate between the dollar and the euro and would like to hedge exchange exposure.

   a. It is considering two hedging alternatives: sell the euro proceeds from the sale forward or borrow euros from Crédit Lyonnaise against the euro receivable. Which alternative would you recommend? Why?

   b. Other things being equal, at what forward exchange rate would Bombardier be indifferent between the two hedging methods?

5. Suppose that Kitchener Machinery sold a drilling machine to a Swiss firm and gave the Swiss client a choice of paying either C$10,000 or SF9,000 in three months.

   a. In the example, Kitchener Machinery effectively gave the Swiss client a free option to buy up to C$10,000 using Swiss francs. What is the "implied" exercise exchange rate?

   b. If the spot exchange rate turns out to be C$1.08/SF, which currency do you think the Swiss client will choose to use for payment? What is the value of this free option for the Swiss client?

   c. What is the best way for Kitchener Machinery to deal with exchange exposure?

6. The Bay of Fundy Cruise Company (BofC) purchased a ship from Mitsubishi Heavy Industry for 500 million yen payable in one year. The current spot rate is ¥100/C$, and the one-year forward rate is 110/C$. The annual interest rate is 5 percent in Japan and 8 percent in Canada. BofC can also buy a one-year call option on yen at the strike price of C$0.01 per yen for a premium of 0.014 cents per yen.

   a. Compute the future dollar costs of meeting this obligation using the money market and forward hedges.

   b. Assuming that the forward exchange rate is the best predictor of the future spot rate, compute the expected future dollar cost of meeting this obligation when the option hedge is used.

   c. At what future spot rate do you think BofC may be indifferent between the option and forward hedge?

7. Airbus sold an A400 aircraft to Air Canada and billed C$30 million payable in six months. Airbus is concerned about the euro proceeds from international sales and would like to control exchange risk. The current spot exchange rate is C$1.50/€, and the six-month forward exchange rate is C$1.575/€. Airbus can buy a six-month put option on Canadian dollars with a strike price of €0.65/C$ for a premium of €0.02 per Canadian dollar. Currently, the six-month interest rate is 5 percent in the euro zone and 6 percent in Canada.

   a. Compute the guaranteed euro proceeds from the sale to Air Canada if Airbus decides to hedge using a forward contract.

   b. If Airbus decides to hedge using money market instruments, what action does Airbus need to take? What would be the guaranteed euro proceeds from the sale in this case?

   c. If Airbus decides to hedge using put options on Canadian dollars, what would be the "expected" euro proceeds from the sale? Assume that Airbus regards the current forward exchange rate as an unbiased predictor of the future spot exchange rate.

   d. At what future spot exchange do you think Airbus will be indifferent between the option and money market hedge?

INTERNET EXERCISE

BankWare, an Ottawa-based company specializing in banking-related softwares, exported its software for automatic teller machines (ATM) to Oslo Commerce Bank, which is trying to modernize its operation. Facing competition from European software vendors, BankWare decided to bill the sales in the client's currency, Norwegian krone 500,000, payable in one year. Since there are no active forward currency markets for the Norwegian currency, BankWare is considering selling a euro or British pound amount forward for cross-hedging purpose. Assess the hedging effectiveness of selling the euro versus pound amount forward to cover the company's exposure to the Norwegian currency. In solving this problem, consult exchange rate data available from the following website: www.pacific.commerce.ubc.ca/xr/

REFERENCES & SUGGESTED READINGS

Aggarwal, R., and A. Demaskey. "Cross-Hedging Currency Risks in Asian Emerging Markets Using Derivatives in Major Currencies." *Journal of Portfolio Management* (Spring 1997), pp. 88–95.

Allayannis, George, and James Weston. "The Use of Foreign Currency Derivatives and Firm Market Value." *Review of Financial Studies* 14 (2001), pp. 243–76.

Aubey, R., and R. Cramer. "Use of International Currency Cocktails in the Reduction of Exchange Rate Risk." *Journal of Economics and Business* (Winter 1977), pp. 128–34.

Benet, B. "Commodity Futures Cross-Hedging of Foreign Exchange Exposure." *Journal of Futures Markets* (Fall 1990), pp. 287–306.

Beidelman, Carl, John Hillary, and James Greenleaf. "Alternatives in Hedging Long-Date Contractual Foreign Exchange Exposure." *Sloan Management Review* (Summer 1983), pp. 45–54.

Dufey, Gunter, and S. Srinivasulu. "The Case for Corporate Management of Foreign Exchange Risk." *Financial Management* (Winter 1983), pp. 54–62.

Folks, William. "Decision Analysis for Exchange Risk Management." *Financial Management* (Winter 1972), pp. 101–12.

Giddy, Ian. "The Foreign Exchange Option as a Hedging Tool." *Midland Corporate Finance Journal* (Fall 1983), pp. 32–42.

Jesswein, Kurt, Chuck C. Y. Kwok, and William Folks, Jr. "Corporate Use of Innovative Foreign Exchange Risk Management Products." *Columbia Journal of World Business* (Fall 1995), pp. 70–82.

Khoury, Sarkis, and K. H. Chan. "Hedging Foreign Exchange Risk: Selecting the Optimal Tool." *Midland Corporate Finance Journal* (Winter 1988), pp. 40–52.

Smithson, Charles. "A LEGO Approach to Financial Engineering: An Introduction to Forwards, Futures, Swaps and Options." *Midland Corporate Finance Journal* (Winter 1987), pp. 16–28.

Stulz, Rene, and Clifford Smith. "The Determinants of Firms' Hedging Policies." *Journal of Financial and Quantitative Analysis* (December 1985), pp. 391–405.

CHAPTER 14

Management of Translation Exposure

CORPORATE ACCOUNTS—including the income statement, balance sheet, cash flow statement, and statement of changes in financial position—present a detailed picture of the firm's financial structure and income flow. The balance sheet is a detailed list of assets and liabilities. It is like is a snapshot. For a moving picture, we have the income statement with its report of revenues and costs and, ultimately, net income. The statement of changes in financial position identifies where the firm's cash comes from and where it goes.

For a strictly domestic firm, the line items in the corporate accounts are expressed in only one currency, for example, in the Canadian dollar for Canadian firms. Changes in the exchange rate obviously have no direct impact on the corporate accounts of a purely domestic firm. However, when a Canadian firm has assets and liabilities as well as revenues, costs and profits abroad, these items are first denominated locally—that is, in the foreign country—in a *foreign* currency. The Canadian parent company of a foreign branch or subsidiary is then required to *translate* the financial values denominated in foreign currency into Canadian dollar values. Changes in the exchange rate result in changes in translated values.

The accounting exercise of translating foreign currency values into values expressed in the home-country currency is referred to as *consolidation*. Consolidation is meant to produce accurate and relevant values of offshore corporate assets, liabilities, and operations.

A simple example illustrates the mechanics of foreign currency translation. Four Seasons Hotel, based in Toronto, owns and operates a hotel in Paris on the exquisite Avenue Georges V. The hotel property is valued in euro at €100 million. Four Seasons has arranged a €70 million mortgage on the property, held by Banque Paribas. Net equity is €30 million. Let us say that on December 31, 2003, the C$/€ exchange rate is C$1.50 = €1. A year later, on December 31, 2004, following a strengthening of the euro against the Canadian dollar, the exchange rate has moved to C$1.70 = €1. The table below shows the impact of the change in the exchange rate on the Canadian dollar value of the asset, the liability, and the equity.

	Euro	C$1.50 = €1	C$1.70 = €1	Change (C$)
Hotel Property (an asset)	€100 m	C$150 m	C$170 m	C$20 m (+)
Mortgage (a liability)	€70 m	C$105 m	C$119 m	C$14 m (−)
Equity	€30 m	C$45 m	C$51 m	C$6 m (+)

From the perspective of Four Seasons in Toronto, the Canadian dollar value of the Paris property has risen by C$20 million as a result of the appreciation of the euro. This is a gain from the Canadian perspective (hence the plus sign). On the other hand, the Canadian dollar value of the mortgage owed to Banque Paribas has risen by C$14 million. This is a loss to Four Seasons (Toronto). Finally, Four Season's equity in the Paris hotel has risen by C$6 million, which, of course, represents the net gain to Four Seasons (Toronto) as a result of the change in the exchange rate.

These changes in the Canadian dollar values of euro-denominated assets, liabilities, and equity illustrate the fundamental principle of translation exposure and the effects of translation. Being long in an asset in a foreign currency—for example, Four Seasons' ownership of the hotel property in Paris—gives rise to a foreign exchange gain when the foreign currency appreciates. On the other hand, a liability—or being "short" a financial asset—such as the mortgage at Paribas, results in a foreign exchange loss if the foreign currency appreciates.

The reverse of these principles is equally true. Being long in an asset in a foreign currency results in a foreign exchange loss when the foreign currency depreciates, that is, when the Canadian dollar appreciates. On the other hand, having a liability—or being "short" a financial asset—results in a foreign exchange gain if the foreign currency depreciates.

The rule of thumb is that an investor always wants to be long in assets denominated in an appreciating foreign currency.

These translation effects of changes in the exchange rate do not affect Four Seasons' Paris-based operations. Nor does it seem reasonable or appropriately conservative, as accountants would want us to be, to "recognize" these foreign exchange gains immediately as part of income for the year. We will return to this point in a moment.

Let us consider some shorter-term balance sheet items and cash flows associated with Four Seasons' hotel operations in Paris. Let us say that Current Assets—cash, inventory, receivables—are €8 million, Current Liabilities are €6 million and over the year the hotel on Georges V generated after-tax income of €15 million. What do we make of these euro numbers as translated into Canadian dollars in the parent's accounts kept in Toronto?

	Euro	**C\$1.50 = €1**	**C\$1.70 = €1**	**Change (C\$)**
Current Assets	€ 8 m	C\$12 m	\$13.6 m	\$1.6 m (+)
Current Liabilities	€ 6 m	C\$ 9 m	\$10.2 m	\$1.2 m (−)
Net Income	€ 12 m	C\$18 m	\$20.4 m	\$2.4 m (+)

These particular items—Current Assets, Current Liabilities, and Net Income—are affected by the appreciation of the euro in a similar fashion to the hotel property, mortgage, and equity discussed above. However, Current Assets, Current Liabilities, and Net Income are much "closer to cash" than is the case for the hotel, the mortgage, or equity. The impact of the appreciation of the euro on the Canadian dollar value on each of these items close to cash is less likely to be reversed by a euro depreciation before they leave the cash cycle. When Four Seasons (Toronto) reports its consolidated worldwide income for 2004 in Canadian dollar terms, foreign exchange gains or losses on near cash items are more appropriately included in the consolidated "bottom line" figure.

It is less relevant to include foreign exchange gains or losses on longer-term assets and liabilities in Four Seasons' consolidated, translated worldwide income figure for 2004. Consider the hotel property and the mortgage. In view of the substantial random element in foreign exchange rate movements, the rise in the euro against the Canadian dollar in 2004 could well be reversed over subsequent years. If foreign exchange gains and losses on long-lived assets and liabilities are annually (or quarterly) translated and consolidated in the parent company's worldwide net income figure, the random variance of the exchange rate over the life of these long-lived assets or liabilities could introduce substantial year-to-year variance in the net income of the firm.

Professional accounting organizations, which develop and oversee accounting regulations, such as the Canadian Institute of Chartered Accounts (CICA), are acutely aware of the need for accurate and relevant translated accounting statements for the foreign operations of Canadian-based multinational enterprises. They are also aware that random year-over-year variance resulting from foreign exchange rate variance can compromise the accuracy, stability, and usefulness of corporate accounts. The CICA in Canada, like the Financial Accounting Standards Board (FASB) in the United States and comparable groups elsewhere, address the issue in similar but not identical ways. We will briefly outline key features of the Canadian approach.

14.1 Translation Methods

Foreign Operations

www.cica.ca
The web page of the Canadian Institute of Chartered Accountants.

The *CICA Handbook* Section 1650 contains recommendations on procedure and accounting policy in regard to foreign operations of Canadian companies. Section 1650 begins by defining and categorizing foreign operations. Foreign operations can take the form of a subsidiary, division, or branch of a Canadian company or a cooperative joint venture with a foreign company. Foreign operations involve business activities that are made and recorded in a currency other than the Canadian dollar. Foreign operations are divided into two categories:

An **integrated foreign operation** is financially or operationally interdependent with the Canadian parent company such that exposure to exchange rate changes is similar to the exposure which would exist had the transactions of the foreign operation been undertaken directly by the Canadian parent. On the other hand, a **self-sustaining foreign operation** is a foreign operation that is financially and operationally independent of the Canadian company such that the exposure to exchange rate changes is limited to the Canadian company's net investment in the foreign operation.

For purposes of our focus on managerial implications of these distinctions, an offshore branch of a Canadian bank, such as the Bank of Nova Scotia's branch in London, England, is typical of an integrated foreign operation. The London banking operations of the Bank of Nova Scotia require the capital base, the security and information base, the Canadian regulatory structure, and the direct and immediate managerial guidance that Canadian headquarters provides. On the other hand, a typical self-sustaining foreign operation is an offshore corporate arrangement that a manufacturing firm, such as Magna International of Aurora, Ontario, has with it subsidiary in Steyr, Austria. Magna (Austria) is financially and operationally independent of the parent Canadian company such that the exposure to exchange rate changes is limited to Magna's net investment in the European operations.

Two Approaches to Translation: Current Rate Method and the Temporal Approach

The Canadian approach to foreign currency translation calls for the application of one of two alternative approaches: either the **current rate method** or the **temporal approach**.

The current rate method is widely used around the world today. Under this method, all items in financial statements are translated at the *current* exchange rate with few exceptions. Line items include:

- *Assets and liabilities*. All assets and liabilities are translated at the current rate of exchange, that is, the rate of exchange in effect on the day the balance sheet is prepared.

- *Income statement items*. All items, including depreciation and cost of goods sold, are translated at either the actual exchange rate on the dates that the various revenues, expenses, gains, and losses were incurred or at an appropriately weighted average exchange rate for the period.

- *Distributions*. Dividends paid are translated at the exchange rate in effect on the date of payment.

- *Equity items*. Common shares and paid-in capital accounts are recorded at historical rates. Year-end retained earnings consist of the original beginning-of-year retained earnings plus or minus any income or loss for the year.

The current rate method has features that are important both for the consistency of international accounting and for corporate financial management. Above all, gains or losses resulting from translation are not included in the calculation of consolidated net income. Instead, they are reported in a separate reserve account on the consolidated balance sheet with such a title as **cumulative translation adjustment**. If a foreign subsidiary is later sold or liquidated, gains or losses that have accumulated in this account are reported as one component of the total gain or loss on sale or liquidation. By keeping translation gains and losses separate, the current rate method offers accounting information to management, shareholders, and creditors concerning income and performance in foreign operations that is not confounded with nonbusiness gains or losses due to exchange rate changes.

Under the current rate method, gains or losses on translation flow to a reserve account. They do not end up year-to-year in the income statement. As a result, reported earnings do not suffer variance due to foreign exchange translation gains or losses.

The current rate method ensures that relative proportions of individual balance sheet items in the (translated) financial statements of foreign operations are not distorted by foreign exchange gains and losses. Important managerial signals, such as the profit margin, the current ratio or the debt-to-equity ratio for foreign operations, remain as they are in the foreign currency. Perhaps the main shortcoming of the current rate method is that it compromises the accounting convention (called the **conservative principle**) of recording balance sheet items at historical cost. For example, foreign assets purchased with dollars and then recorded on the subsidiary's statements at their foreign currency historical cost are translated back into dollars at a different rate. Consequently such assets are reported in the consolidated statement (in dollars) at something other than their historical Canadian dollar cost.

Temporal Method

Under the temporal method, specific assets and liabilities are translated at exchange rates that correspond to the time the asset was acquired or the liability was incurred. The temporal method ensures that income-generating assets, such as inventory and net plant and equipment, are restated regularly to reflect their market value. The main tenets of the temporal method are:

- *Monetary assets*, such as cash, marketable securities, accounts receivable, and long-term receivables, as well as monetary liabilities, such as current liabilities and long-term debt, are translated at current exchange rates.

- *Nonmonetary assets and liabilities*, such as inventory and fixed assets, are translated at historical exchange rates.

- *Income statement items* are translated at the average exchange rate for the period. Exceptions include the noncash expense of depreciation and cost of goods sold that are directly associated with nonmonetary assets and liabilities; these items are translated at their historical rates.

- *Distributions*. Dividends paid are translated at the exchange rate in effect on the date of payment.

- *Equity items*. Common shares and paid-in capital accounts are recorded at historical rates. Year-end retained earnings consist of the original beginning-of-year retained earnings plus or minus any income or loss for the year, plus or minus any imbalance from translation.

Under the temporal method, gains or losses resulting from translation are carried directly to current consolidated income. Unlike the current rate method, these gains or losses do not go to an equity reserve account. Under the temporal method, then, foreign exchange gains and losses arising from translation introduce volatility of consolidated earnings. However, the volatility is damped to the extent that many items in the temporal approach are translated at their historical rates.

The advantage of the temporal method of translation is that foreign nonmonetary assets are recorded at their original cost in the consolidated statement. This is consistent the conservative accounting convention of "original cost treatment" of assets as they appear in the accounts of the parent firm. In practice, however, if some foreign

<table>
<tr>
<td>

EXHIBIT 14.1

Salient Economic Factors for Determining the Functional Currency

</td>
<td>

The **reporting currency** is defined as the currency in which the MNC prepares its consolidated financial statements. That currency is usually the currency in which the parent firm keeps its books, which, in turn, is usually the currency of the country in which the parent is located and conducts most of its business.

Cash Flow Indicators
Foreign Currency: Foreign entity's cash flows are primarily in foreign currency, and they do not directly affect the parent firm's cash flows.
Parent's Currency: Foreign entity's cash flows directly affect the parent's cash flows and are readily available for remittance to the parent firm.

Sales Price Indicators
Foreign Currency: Sales prices for the foreign entity's products are generally not responsive on a short-term basis to exchange rate changes but are determined more by local competition.
Parent's Currency: Sales prices for the foreign entity's products are responsive on a short-term basis to exchange rate changes, where sales prices are determined through worldwide competition.

Sales Market Indicators
Foreign Currency: There is an active local sales market for the foreign entity's products.
Parent's Currency: The sales market is primarily located in the parent's country or sales contracts are denominated in the parent's currency.

Expense Indicators
Foreign Currency: Factor of production costs of the foreign entity are primarily local costs.
Parent's Currency: Factor of production costs for the foreign entity are primarily, and on a continuing basis, costs for components obtained from the parent's country.

Financing Indicators
Foreign Currency: Financing of the foreign entity is primarily denominated in the foreign currency and the debt service obligations are normally handled by the foreign entity.
Parent's Currency: Financing of the foreign entity is primarily from the parent, with debt service obligations met by the parent, or the debt service obligations incurred by the foreign entity are primarily made by the parent.

Intercompany Transactions and Arrangements Indicators
Foreign Currency: There is a low volume of intercompany transactions and a minor inter-relationship of operations between the foreign entity and the parent. However, the foreign entity may benefit from competitive advantages of the parent, such as patents or trademarks.
Parent's Currency: There is a large volume of intercompany transactions and an extensive inter-relationship of operations between the foreign entity and the parent. Moreover, if the foreign entity is only a shell company for carrying accounts that could be carried on the parent's books, the functional currency would generally be the parent's currency.

</td>
</tr>
</table>

Source: Excerpted from *Foreign Currency Translation, Statement of Financial Accounting Standards No. 52,* Paragraph 42, Financial Accounting Standards Board, Stamford, CT. Used by permission.

accounts are translated at one (historical) foreign exchange rate, while others are translated at different rates, the resulting translated balance sheet will not balance. Hence there is a need for a "plug" to remove what has been called the *dangling debit or credit.* The economic or managerial nature of the gain or loss represented by the "plug" is open to question.

EXHIBIT 14.2	Foreign-Currency Translation Methods Used in Other Major Developed Countries

Japan

Receivables and payables in foreign currencies must be translated into yen at the end of the accounting period. Both translation gains or losses and realized foreign exchange gains or losses are treated as taxable income or loss and flow through earnings. Historical exchange rates that existed at the transaction date are generally used to record revenue, costs, and expenses resulting from foreign currency transactions.

Short-term foreign currency receivables and payables are translated at the prevailing year-end rate. Long-term foreign currency receivables and payables are translated at the historical rate, except in unusual circumstances. Securities, inventories, and fixed assets are translated at the rate in effect when they were acquired (historical rate).

Any change in the method of translating foreign currencies requires prior approval by tax regulators.

Germany

As of year-end 1992, a common treatment of foreign-currency translation had not been implemented. All translation methods are, in principle, acceptable.

A broad variety of practices are followed, including the (1) current/noncurrent, (2) monetary/nonmonetary, (3) temporal, (4) closing, and (5) current rate methods. Some companies flow translation gains or losses through shareholders' equity, while others flow the impact of foreign-currency translation through the profit and loss account.

France

Many different methods of foreign-currency translation are followed.

GROUP ACCOUNTS:

Most companies appear to use the closing exchange rate for balance sheet translations (translation gains and losses impact shareholders' equity) and the average exchange rate for the income statement.

Differences between income statement and balance sheet translation gains and losses (if different exchange rates are used) would flow through shareholders' equity.

INDIVIDUAL ACCOUNTS:

Detailed rules govern foreign-currency translation in individual company accounts. These give rise to long-term deferred charges and credits.

Unsettled monetary assets and liabilities denominated in a foreign currency must be restated to their closing value at the balance sheet date. Foreign exchange gains are recorded as long-term deferred credits and released when the account is settled.

Foreign exchange losses result in the following entries: (1) The original account is adjusted and a deferred charge appears on the balance sheet; (2) a balance sheet provision is set up, and the income statement is debited.

Foreign-currency translation policies may differ. Some firms only provide against unrealized foreign exchange losses if they exceed unrealized foreign exchange gains. These deferred exchange gains and losses could be offset against each other with the difference applied to the risk provision.

Italy

REALIZED GAINS AND LOSSES:

Income, receipts, and expenditures in foreign currency are translated at the exchange rates that existed on the transaction date. These realized gains and losses flow through the income statement.

UNREALIZED GAINS AND LOSSES:

The average exchange rate of the last month of the accounting period is used for foreign-currency translation. Items denominated in foreign currency are originally recorded at the exchange rate that existed on the transaction date.

Unrealized foreign currency translation gains and losses flow through a special provision, impacting shareholders' equity.

United Kingdom

Foreign-currency translation adjustments are disclosed for both individual and group (consolidated) accounts. In cases of consolidation, companies prepare a set of translation accounts for (1) the individual firms within the group, and (2) the group as a whole.

INDIVIDUAL COMPANY:

Foreign-currency transactions are generally translated into the home currency of each company using the average rate method. Nonmonetary assets are not restated.

Currency differences flow through the profit and loss account (separately from ongoing businesses) and are shown as discontinued operations. Exchange rate gains and losses related to foreign currency hedging pass through reserves.

GROUP ACCOUNTS:

The average rate/net investment method is commonly used, although the temporal method is also acceptable. Consolidated accounts are prepared in the currency in which the parent company is based.

Investments in the foreign enterprises are represented by the net worth held by the parent. Exchange rate gains or losses that impact the group accounts pass through reserves, with no impact on the group profit and loss account.

Source: © 1993 by Goldman Sachs.

Which Method in Canada: Current Rate or Temporal?

The *CICA Handbook* Section 1650 outlines the advantages and disadvantages of both the *current rate method* and the *temporal method* of translation for consolidation. The ultimate objective of translation is to express financial statements of the foreign operation in Canadian dollars in a manner which best reflects the reporting enterprise's exposure to exchange rate changes. The recommended approach depends on the circumstances.

For *integrated* foreign operations, such as an offshore *branch*, the Canadian parent company's exposure to exchange rate changes is similar to the exposure which would exist had the transactions and activities of the foreign operation been undertaken by the parent company. Therefore, financial statements of foreign operations should be consistent with the measurement of domestic transactions and operations. The translation method that best achieves this objective is the temporal method because it uses the Canadian dollar as the unit of measure.

For *self-sustaining* foreign operations, such as an off-shore *subsidiary*, the Canadian parent company's exposure to exchange rate changes is limited to its net investment in the foreign operation. Therefore, accounting for such operations as if they were transacted in Canadian dollars is less relevant than measuring the overall effect of changes in the exchange rate on the net investment in such operations. The financial statements of self-sustaining foreign operation should be expressed in a way that does not change the financial results and relationships of the foreign operation. The translation method that best achieves this objective is the current rate method because it uses the currency of the foreign operation as the unit of measure.

For **foreign currency transactions**, the objective of translation is to express such transactions in a manner that achieves consistency with the accounting treatment for domestic transactions. Since domestic transactions are automatically measured in Canadian dollars, the Canadian dollar is the appropriate unit of measure for foreign currency transactions. Accordingly, the temporal method should be used to translate foreign currency transactions.

Illustrated MINI CASE

Consolidation of Accounts According to the CICA Handbook Section 1650: The Maple Corporation

We use a mini case to illustrate consolidating the balance sheet of an MNC according to *CICA Handbook* Section 1650. The basic information in Exhibit 14.3 shows the unconsolidated balance sheets for Maple Corporation, a Canadian parent firm, and its two wholly owned affiliates located in Mexico and Spain. Maple Corp. is a Manitoba-based manufacturer of wooden furniture. The Mexican manufacturing affiliate has been established to cater to the Mexican market, which is expected to expand rapidly under NAFTA. Similarly, the Spanish manufacturing affiliate was established to handle demand in the European Union. The functional currency of the Mexican affiliate is the peso, and the euro is the functional currency for the Spanish affiliate. The reporting currency is the Canadian dollar. The initial exchange rates assumed in the example are: C$1 = Ps10 = €1.10 = SF1.50.

The nonconsolidated balance sheets and the footnotes to the statements indicate that the Mexican affiliate owes the parent firm Ps3,000,000, which is carried on the parent's books as a $300,000 accounts receivable at the current exchange rate of Ps10.00/$1. The $2,200,000 investment of the parent firm in the Mexican affiliate is the translated amount of Ps22,000,000 of equity on the Mexican affiliate's books. Similarly, the $1,660,000 investment of the parent in the Spanish affiliate is the translated amount of €1,826,000 of equity on the Spanish affiliate's books. The footnotes also show that the Spanish affiliate has a SF375,000 loan outstanding from a Swiss bank, translated at SF1.3636/€1, and carried at €275,000 as part of its €1,210,000 of notes payable.

EXHIBIT 14.3	**Nonconsolidated Balance Sheet for Maple Corporation and Its Mexican and Spanish Affiliates, December 31, 2004** (in 000 Currency Units)		
	Maple Corp. (Parent)	**Mexican Affiliate**	**Spanish Affiliate**
Assets			
Cash	$ 950	Ps 6,000	€ 825
Accounts receivable	1,750[a]	9,000	1,045
Inventory	3,000	15,000	1,650
Investment in Mexican affiliate	2,200[b]	—	—
Investment in Spanish affiliate	1,660[c]	—	—
Net fixed assets	9,000	46,000	4,400
Total assets	$18,560	Ps 76,000	€7,920
Liabilities and Net Worth			
Accounts payable	$ 1,800	Ps 10,000	€1,364
Notes payable	2,200	17,000	1,210[d]
Long-term debt	7,110	27,000	3,520
Common shares	3,500	16,000	1,320[c]
Retained earnings	3,950	6,000	506[c]
Total liabilities and net worth	$18,560	Ps 76,000	€7,920

[a]The parent firm is owed Ps3,000,000 by the Mexican affiliate. This sum is included in the parent's accounts receivable as $300,000. The remainder of the parent's (Mexican affiliate's) accounts receivable (payable) are denominated in dollars (pesos).

[b]The Mexican affiliate is wholly owned by the parent firm. It is carried on the parent firm's books at $2,200,000. This represents the sum of the common shares (Ps16,000,000) and retained earnings (Ps6,000,000) on the Mexican affiliate's books, translated at Ps10/$1.

[c]The Spanish affiliate is wholly owned by the parent firm. It is carried on the parent firm's books at $1,660,000. This represents the sum of the common shares (€1,320,000) and the retained earnings (€506,000) on the Spanish affiliate's books, translated at €1.10/$1.

[d]The Spanish affiliate has outstanding notes payable of SF375,000 (÷ SF1.3636/€1 = €275,000) from a Swiss bank. This loan is carried on the Spanish affiliate's books as part of the €1,210,000 = €275,000 + €935,000.

Exhibit 14.4 shows the process of consolidating the balance sheets for Maple Corp. and its affiliates. Note that *both* intracompany debt *and* investment net out in the consolidation. That is, the Ps3,000,000 owed by the Mexican affiliate to the parent is not reflected in the consolidated accounts receivable nor in the accounts payable. When this debt is eventually paid, in effect, it will be the same as taking money out of one company pocket and putting it into another. In a similar vein, the investment of the parent in each affiliate cancels with the net worth of each affiliate. The parent owns the affiliates, and, in turn, the shareholders' investment represents ownership of the parent firm. In this manner, the shareholders own the entire MNC.

The consolidation presented in Exhibit 14.4 is rather simplistic. It is nice and neat from the standpoint that the consolidated balance sheet, in fact, balances. That is, total assets equal total liabilities and net worth. In the example, it is implied that the current exchange rates used are the same as those used when the affiliates were originally established; that is, they have not changed from that time. Thus, the example is not very realistic, even though it properly presents the mechanics of the consolidation process under CICA rules. After all, the central purpose of a translation method is to deal in some systematic way with exchange rate *changes*.

To determine the effect that exchange rate changes will have on the consolidated balance sheet of an MNC, it is useful to prepare a translation exposure report. A **translation exposure report** shows, for each account that is included in the consolidated balance sheet, the amount of foreign exchange exposure that exists for each foreign currency in which the MNC has exposure. Continuing with our example of Maple Corp. and its affiliates, we know from Exhibit 14.3 that the MNC has foreign

	Maple Corp. (Parent)	Mexican Affiliate	Spanish Affiliate	Consolidated Balance Sheet
EXHIBIT 14.4 — Consolidated Balance Sheet for Maple Corporation and Its Mexican and Spanish Affiliates, December 31, 2004 (in $000): Pre-Exchange Rate Change				
Assets				
Cash	$ 950	$ 600	$ 750	$ 2,300
Accounts receivable	1,450ª	900	950	3,300
Inventory	3,000	1,500	1,500	6,000
Investment in Mexican affiliation	—ᵇ	—	—	—
Investment in Spanish affiliation	—ᶜ	—	—	—
Net fixed assets	9,000	4,600	4,000	17,600
Total assets				$29,200
Liabilities and Net Worth				
Accounts payable	$1,800	$ 700ª	$1,240	$ 3,740
Notes payable	2,200	1,700	1,100ᵈ	5,000
Long-term debt	7,110	2,700	3,200	13,010
Common shares	3,500	—ᵇ	—ᶜ	3,500
Retained earnings	3,950	—ᵇ	—ᶜ	3,950
Total liabilities and net worth				$29,200

ª$1,750,000 − $300,000 (= Ps3,000,000/(Ps10.00/$1.00)) intracompany loan = $1,450,000.
ᵇ·ᶜThe investment in the affiliates cancels with the net worth of the affiliates in the consolidation.
ᵈThe Spanish affiliate owes a Swiss bank SF375,000 (÷ SF1.3636/€1.00 = €275,000). This is carried on the books as part of the €1,210,000 = €275,000 + €935,000. €1,210,000/(€1.10/$1.00) = $1,100,000.

exchange exposure from the Mexican peso, euro, and Swiss franc. A change in any one of these currency exchange rates versus the reporting currency will have an effect on the consolidated balance sheet if there exists a net translation exposure for that currency.

Exhibit 14.5 presents the translation exposure report for Maple Corp. The report shows, for each exposure currency, the amount of exposed assets and exposed liabilities denominated in that currency, and the net difference, or net exposure. For the Mexican peso the net exposure, a positive Ps25,000,000; for the euro, a positive €2,101,000; and for the Swiss franc, a negative SF375,000. A positive net exposure means there are more exposed assets than liabilities, and *vice versa* for negative net exposure. When the exchange rate of an exposure currency depreciates against the reporting currency, exposed assets fall in translated value by a greater (smaller) amount than exposed liabilities if there is positive (negative) net exposure. Analogously, when an exposure currency appreciates against the reporting currency, exposed assets increase in translated value by a smaller (greater) amount than exposed liabilities if there is negative (positive) net exposure. Consequently, the consolidation process will not result in a consolidated balance sheet that balances after an exchange rate change.

To show the effect on the consolidation process after an exchange rate change, let us perform the consolidation of the nonconsolidated balance sheets from Exhibit 14.3 once again, assuming this time that exchange rates have changed from $1 = Ps10 = €1.10 = SF1.50 to $1 = Ps10 = €1.1786 = SF1.50. We are assuming that only the euro has changed (depreciated) versus all other currencies in order to keep the example simple so as to better decipher the effect of an exchange rate change.

To get an overview of the effect of the exchange rate change, recall from Exhibit 14.5 that there is a positive net exposure of €2,101,000. This implies that after the 6.67 percent depreciation from €1.1000/$1 to €1.1786/$1, the exposed assets

EXHIBIT 14.5 **Translation Exposure Report for Maple Corporation and Its Mexican and Spanish Affiliates, December 31, 2004** (in 000 Currency Units)		Mexican Peso	Euro	Swiss Franc
	Assets			
	Cash	Ps 6,000	€ 825	SF 0
	Accounts receivable	9,000	1,045	0
	Inventory	15,000	1,650	0
	Net fixed assets	46,000	4,400	0
	Exposed assets	Ps 76,000	€ 7,920	SF 0
	Liabilities			
	Accounts payable	Ps 7,000	€ 1,364	SF 0
	Notes payable	17,000	935	375
	Long-term debt	27,000	3,520	0
	Exposed liabilities	Ps 51,000	€ 5,819	SF 375
	Net exposure	Ps 25,000	€ 2,101	(SF375)

denominated in euros will have fallen in translated value by $127,377 more than the exposed liabilities denominated in euros. This can be calculated as follows:

$$\frac{\text{Net exposure currency } i}{S_{new}(i/\text{reporting})} - \frac{\text{Net exposure currency } i}{S_{old}(i/\text{reporting})}$$

$$= \text{Reporting currency imbalance.}$$

For our example,

$$\frac{€2,101,000}{€1.1786/\$1} - \frac{€2,101,000}{€1.1000/\$1} = -\$127,377$$

EXHIBIT 14.6	**Consolidated Balance Sheet for Maple Corporation and Its Mexican and Spanish Affiliates, December 31, 2004 (in $000): Post-Exchange Rate Change**			
	Maple Corp. (Parent)	Mexican Affiliate	Spanish Affiliate	Consolidated Balance Sheet
Assets				
Cash	$ 950	$ 600	$ 700	$ 2,250
Accounts receivable	1,450[a]	900	887	3,237
Inventory	3,000	1,500	1,400	5,900
Investment in Mexican affiliate	—[b]	—	—	—
Investment in Spanish affiliate	—[c]	—	—	—
Net fixed assets	9,000	4,600	3,733	17,333
Total Assets				$28,720
Liabilities and Net Worth				
Accounts payable	$1,800	$ 700[a]	$1,157	$ 3,657
Notes payable	2,200	1,700	1,043[d]	4,943
Long-term debt	7,110	2,700	2,987	12,797
Common shares	3,500	—[b]	—[c]	3,500
Retained earnings	3,950	—[b]	—[c]	3,950
CTA	—	—	—	(127)
Total liabilities and net worth				$28,720

[a]$1,750,000 − $300,000 (= Ps3,000,000/(Ps10/$1)) intracompany loan = $1,450,000.
[b, c]Investment in affiliates cancels with the net worth of the affiliates in the consolidation.
[d]The Spanish affiliate owes a Swiss bank SF375,000 (÷ SF1.2727/€1.00 = €294,649). This is carried on the books, after the exchange rate change, as part of €1,229,649 = €294,649 + €935,000. €1,229,649/(€1.1786/$1) = $1,043,313.

In other words, the net translation exposure of €2,101,000 in dollars is currently $1,910,000 when translated at the current exchange rate of €1.1000/$1. A 6.67 percent depreciation of the euro to €1.1786/$1 will result in a translation loss of $127,377 = €2,101,000 ÷ 1.1000 × 0.0667.

Exhibit 14.6 shows the consolidation process and consolidated balance sheet for Maple Corporation and its two foreign affiliates after the depreciation of the euro. Note that the values for the accounts are the same as in Exhibit 14.4 for the parent firm and the Mexican affiliate. However, the values of the accounts of the Spanish affiliate are different because of the exchange rate change. In order for the consolidated balance sheet to now balance, it is necessary to have a "plug" equity account with a balance of −$127,377. This special equity account is referred to as the cumulative translation adjustment account, or CTA account. The balance of this account at any time represents the accumulated total of all past translation adjustments. The *CICA Handbook* Section 1650 handles the effect of exchange rate changes as an adjustment to equity, rather than as an adjustment to net income, because exchange rate changes have an indirect effect on the net investment that may be realized upon sale or liquidation. Prior to sale or liquidation, that effect is so uncertain and remote as to require that translation adjustments arising currently should not be reported as part of operating results.

14.2 Management of Translation Exposure

Translation Exposure versus Transaction Exposure

In Chapter 13, we discussed transaction exposure and ways to manage it. It is interesting to note that some items that are a source of transaction exposure are also a source of translation exposure, and some are not. Exhibit 14.7 presents a transaction exposure report for Maple Corp. and its two affiliates. Items that create transaction exposure are receivables or payables that are denominated in a currency other than the currency in which the unit transacts its business, or cash holdings denominated in a foreign currency. From the exhibit, it can be seen that the parent firm has two sources of transaction exposure. The Ps3,000,000 accounts receivable the parent holds on the Mexican affiliate is also a transaction exposure, but it is not a translation exposure because of the netting of intracompany payable and receivables. The SF375,000 notes payable the Spanish affiliate owes the Swiss bank is both a transaction and a translation exposure.

It is, generally, not possible to eliminate both translation and transaction exposure. In some cases, the elimination of one exposure will also eliminate the other. But in other cases, the elimination of one exposure actually creates the other. Since transaction exposure involves real cash flows, we believe it should be considered the most important of the two. That is, one would not want to create transaction exposure at the expense of minimizing or eliminating translation exposure. As previously noted, the translation process has no direct effect on reporting currency cash flows and will only have a realizable effect on net investment upon the sale or liquidation of the assets.

Maple Corporation and its affiliates can take certain measures to reduce its transaction exposure and to simultaneously reduce its translation exposure. The parent

EXHIBIT 14.7

Transaction Exposure Report for Maple Corporation and Its Mexican and Spanish Affiliates, December 31, 2004

Affiliate	Amount	Account	Translation Exposure
Parent	Ps3,000,000	Accounts receivable	No
Spanish	SF375,000	Notes payable	Yes

firm can request payment of the Ps3,000,000 owed to it by the Mexican affiliate. The Spanish affiliate has enough cash to pay off the SF375,000 loan to the Swiss bank. If these steps are taken, all transaction exposure for the MNC will be eliminated. Moreover, translation exposure will be reduced. This can be seen from Exhibit 14.8, which presents a revision of Exhibit 14.5, the translation exposure report for Maple Corporation and its affiliates. Exhibit 14.8 shows that there is no longer any translation exposure associated with the Swiss franc. The exhibit shows that the net exposure has been reduced from Ps25,000,000 to Ps22,000,000 for the peso and from €2,101,000 to €1,826,000 for the euro.

Hedging Translation Exposure

Exhibit 14.8 indicates that there is still considerable translation exposure with respect to changes in the exchange rate of the Mexican peso and the euro against the Canadian dollar. There are two methods for dealing with this remaining exposure if one feels compelled to attempt to control accounting changes in value of net investment. These methods are a balance sheet hedge or a derivatives hedge.

Balance Sheet Hedge

Note that translation exposure is not entity specific; rather, it is currency specific. Its source is a mismatch of net assets and net liabilities denominated in the same currency. A **balance sheet hedge** eliminates the mismatch. Using the euro as an example, Exhibit 14.8 shows that there are €1,826,000 more exposed assets than liabilities. If the Spanish affiliate, or more practically the parent firm or the Mexican affiliate, had €1,826,000 more liabilities, or less assets, denominated in euros, there would not be any translation exposure with respect to the euro. A perfect balance sheet hedge would have been created. A change in the €/$ exchange rate would no longer have any effect on the consolidated balance sheet since the change in value of the assets denominated in euros would completely offset the change in value of the liabilities denominated in euros. Nevertheless, if the parent firm or the Mexican affiliate increased its liabilities through, say, euro-denominated borrowings to affect the balance sheet hedge, it would simultaneously be creating transaction exposure in the euro, if the new liability could not be covered from euro cash flows generated by the Spanish affiliate.

Derivatives Hedge

According to Exhibit 14.5, we determined that when the net exposure for the euro was €2,101,000, a depreciation from €1.1000/$ to €1.1786/$ would create a loss of shareholders' equity equal to $127,377. According to the revised translation exposure report shown as Exhibit 14.8, the same depreciation in the euro will result in an equity loss of $110,704, still a sizable amount. (The calculation of this amount is left as an exercise for the reader.) Management could use a derivative product, such as a forward contract, to attempt to hedge this potential loss. We use the word "attempt" because as

---

EXHIBIT 14.8

Revised Translation Exposure Report for Maple Corporation and Its Mexican and Spanish Affiliates, December 31, 2004 (in 000 Currency Units)

	Mexican Peso	Euro	Swiss Franc
Assets			
Cash	Ps 3,000	€ 550	SF0
Accounts receivable	9,000	1,045	0
Inventory	15,000	1,650	0
Net fixed assets	46,000	4,400	0
Exposed assets	Ps 73,000	€7,645	SF0
Liabilities			
Accounts payable	Ps 7,000	€1,364	SF0
Notes payable	17,000	935	0
Long-term debt	27,000	3,520	00
Exposed liabilities	Ps 51,000	€5,819	SF0
Net exposure	Ps 22,000	€1,826	SF0

the following example demonstrates, using a **derivatives hedge** to control translation exposure really involves speculation about foreign exchange rate changes.

EXAMPLE 14.1 Hedging Translation Exposure with a Forward Contract To see how a forward contract can be used to hedge the $110,704 potential translation loss in equity, assume that the forward rate coinciding with the date of the consolidation is €1.1393/$1. If the expected spot rate on the consolidation date is forecast to be €1.1786/$1, a forward sale of €3,782,468 will "hedge" the risk:

$$\frac{\text{Potential translation loss}}{F(\text{reporting/functional}) - \text{Expected}[S(\text{reporting/functional})]}$$

= forward contract position in functional currency,

$$\frac{\$110,704}{1/(€1.1393/\$1) - 1/(€1.1786/\$1)} = €3,782,468$$

The purchase of €3,782,468 at the expected spot price will cost $3,209,289. The delivery of €3,782,468 under the forward contract will yield $3,319,993, for a profit of $110,704. If everything goes as expected, the $110,704 profit from the forward hedge will offset the equity loss from the translation adjustment. Note, however, that the hedge will not provide a certain outcome because the size of the forward position is based on the expected future spot rate. Consequently, the forward position taken in euros is actually a speculative position. If the realized spot rate turns out to be less than €1.1393/$1, a loss from the forward position will result. Moreover, the hedging procedure violates the hypothesis that the forward rate is an unbiased predictor of the future spot rate.

Translation Exposure versus Operating Exposure

As noted, an unhedged depreciation in the euro will result in an equity loss. Such a loss, however, would only be a paper loss. It would not have any direct effect on reporting currency cash flows. Moreover, it would only have a realizable effect on net investment in the MNC if the affiliate's assets were sold or liquidated. However, as was discussed in Chapter 12, the depreciation of the local currency may, under certain circumstances, have a favourable operating effect. A currency depreciation may, for example, allow the affiliate to raise its sales price because the prices of imported competitive goods are now relatively higher. If costs do not rise proportionately and unit demand remains the same, the affiliate would realize an operating profit as a result of the currency depreciation. It is such substantive issues as these, which result in realizable changes in operating profit, that management should concern itself with.

14.3 Empirical Analysis of a Change in Accounting for Translation Gains and Losses

Garlicki, Fabozzi, and Fonfeder (1987) tested a sample of American MNCs to determine if there was a change in value when the firms were required to switch their methods for accounting for translation gains and losses. The old system (FASB 8) called for recognizing translation gain or loss immediately in net income. The replacement system (FASB 52) called for translation gains and losses to be recognized in the cumulative translation adjustment account on the balance sheet. Consequently, the change in the translation process had an effect on reported earnings. "Despite the impact of the change . . . on reported earnings, the actual cash flow of multinationals would not be

The Shell Case

Measurement of translation gains and losses is an accounting exercise. It is generally considered to have relatively little managerial significance. Management, as well as investors and creditors, ought to be able to "see through" the effects of translation changes in recorded values. Informed and interested analysts likewise ought to be able to distinguish mere accounting entries from real value-relevant changes in cash flows

Translation can become more relevant for management when it influences other real processes, such as tax calculations. Whereas a company's tax liability must be determined with regard for generally accepted accounting principles, such principles can be obscured through translation, for example, in determining the cost of funds borrowed from foreign sources. A famous tax/accounting case involving Shell Canada is especially interesting in this respect, not least for being very contentious. The Shell Canada case moved through various levels of the courts, ultimately arriving at the Supreme Court of Canada. The Supreme Court decided in favour of Shell. The decision was shaped largely by the judges' view that it was not the Supreme Court's responsibility to disentangle a complex international corporate borrowing arrangement. This note reviews the case.

In 1988, Shell Canada structured an international financing arrangement that resulted in substantial savings of Canadian corporate tax. Shell was able to convert translation losses on foreign borrowing into tax deductions in Canada.

Shell Canada borrowed New Zealand dollars at a time New Zealand was experiencing high inflation and high nominal interest rates. Shell immediately swapped the New Zealand funds for American dollars and simultaneously structured a series of forward contracts to buy back New Zealand funds in order to service and retire the debt over the ensuing five years. When it reported its Canadian tax liability, Shell claimed interest deductions based on the New Zealand interest rate which included a substantial "inflation" component. The inflated New Zealand interest rate resulted in interest deductions that exceeded deductions that would have applied to money borrowed in American or Canadian dollars. In addition, the steadily weakening New Zealand dollar against the American dollar (built into the forward exchange rate) allowed Shell eventually to realize a substantial foreign exchange gain that enjoyed preferential tax treatment in Canada.

When Shell Canada filed its corporate tax return, Revenue Canada disallowed the portion of the interest deduction that represented the difference between the interest rate on the New Zealand debt and the market rate of interest on a comparable American dollar loan. In the opinion of the Canadian tax authorities, Shell's borrowing in New Zealand dollars together with the array of forward contracts was a merger of two contracts into one—a borrowing contract and the swap-plus-forward-purchase—which, in effect, created a borrowing of American funds and future obligations to pay interest in American funds. Revenue Canada also treated Shell Canada's foreign exchange gain on the transaction as a gain on income account as opposed to a (tax-preferred) capital gain.

On appeal to the Tax Court of Canada, Shell Canada successfully reversed the assessment. In turn, the Minister of Revenue appealed the Tax Court's decision to the Federal Court of Appeal and won on behalf of Revenue Canada.

Finally, Shell Canada took the case to the Supreme Court on appeal. In June 1999, The Supreme Court allowed the appeal of Shell Canada and dismissed the cross-appeal of the Minister of Revenue. Shell won.

The Shell Case illustrates international tax arbitrage. The deliberations and testimony in the Shell Case accentuate the ambiguity of the translated cost of money borrowed in a foreign currency.

affected *if managers were not making suboptimal decisions based on accounting rather than economic considerations under Statement 8.* In such circumstances, the mandated switch . . . should not change the value of the firm."

The researchers tested their hypothesis concerning a change in value on the initial exposure draft date and on the date FASB 52 was adopted. They found that there was no significant positive reaction to the change or perceived change in the foreign currency translation process. The results suggest that market agents do not react to cosmetic earnings changes that do not affect value. Other researchers have found similar results when investigating other accounting changes that had only a cosmetic effect on earnings. The results underline the futility of attempting to manage translation gains and losses.

SUMMARY

In this chapter, we have discussed the nature and management of translation exposure. Translation exposure relates to the effect that an unanticipated change in exchange rates will have on the consolidated financial reports of an MNC.

1. The four recognized methods for consolidating the financial reports of an MNC include the current/noncurrent method, the monetary/nonmonetary method, the temporal method, and the current rate method.

2. An example comparing and contrasting the four translation methods was presented under the assumptions that the foreign currency had appreciated and depreciated. It was noted that under the current rate method the gain or loss due to translation adjustment does not affect reported cash flows, as it does with the other three translation methods.

3. In implementing the *CICA Handbook* Section 1650, the functional currency of the foreign entity must be translated into the reporting currency in which the consolidated statements are reported. The local currency of a foreign entity may not always be its functional currency. If it is not, the temporal method of translation is used to remeasure the foreign entity's books into the functional currency. The current rate method is used to translate from the functional currency to the reporting currency. In some cases, a foreign entity's functional currency may be the same as the reporting currency, in which case translation is not necessary.

4. Foreign currency translation methods used in other major developed countries were briefly summarized in Exhibit 14.2. As the exhibit shows, a broad variety of methods are used in practice.

5. A mini case illustrating the translation process of the balance sheet of a parent firm with two foreign wholly owned affiliates according to the *CICA Handbook* Section 1650 was presented. This was done assuming that the foreign exchange rates had not changed since the inception of the businesses and, again, after an assumed change to more thoroughly show the effects of balance sheet consolidation under the *CICA Handbook* Section 1650. When a net translation exposure exists, a cumulative translation adjustment account is necessary to bring balance to the consolidated balance sheet after an exchange rate change.

6. Two ways to control translation risk were presented: a balance sheet hedge and a derivatives "hedge." Since translation exposure does not have an immediate direct effect on operating cash flows, its control is relatively unimportant in comparison to transaction exposure, which involves potential real cash flow losses. Since it is, generally, not possible to eliminate both translation and transaction exposure, it is more logical to effectively manage transaction exposure, even at the expense of translation exposure.

KEY WORDS

balance sheet hedge, *336*
conservative principle, *328*
cumulative translation adjustment (CTA), *328*
current rate method, *327*
derivatives hedge, *337*
foreign currency transaction, *331*
integrated foreign operation, *327*
reporting currency, *329*
self-sustaining foreign operation, *327*
temporal approach, *327*
translation exposure report, *332*

QUESTIONS

1. Explain the difference in the translation process between the current rate method and the temporal method.

2. How are translation gains and losses handled differently according to the current rate method in comparison with the other method, that is, the temporal method?

3. Identify instances under the *CICA Handbook* (Section 1650) when a foreign entity's functional currency would be the same as the parent firm's currency.

4. Describe the remeasurement and translation process under the *CICA Handbook* (Section 1650) of translating into the reporting currency the books of a wholly owned affiliate that keeps its books in the local currency of the country in which it operates, which is different from its functional currency.

5. It is, generally, not possible to completely eliminate both translation exposure and transaction exposure. In some cases, the elimination of one exposure will also eliminate the other. But in other cases, the elimination of one exposure actually creates the other. Discuss which exposure might be viewed as the most important to effectively manage, if a conflict between controlling both arises. Also, discuss and critique the common methods for controlling translation exposure.

INTERNET EXERCISE

Ford Motor Company manufactures and sells motor vehicles worldwide. Through their worldwide operations, they are exposed to all types of foreign currency risk. Their website is www.ford.com. Go to this website and access their 2003 annual report. Scroll through the report until you find the section "Quantitative and Qualitative Disclosures about Market Risk" on page 62. In the subsection titled "Foreign Currency Risk" is a discussion of how Ford uses VAR analysis (see Chapter 6 of the text) in evaluating foreign currency exposure for hedging. Note from the discussion that Ford includes transaction exposure in the analysis but does not include translation exposure. This is consistent with the discussion in the chapter mentioning that the translation process does not have a direct effect on reporting currency cash flows and will only have a realizable effect on net investment upon the sale or liquidation of exposed assets.

MINI CASE

Sundance Sporting Goods, Inc.

Sundance Sporting Goods, Inc., is an American manufacturer of high-quality sporting goods—principally golf, tennis, and other racquet equipment, and also lawn sports, such as croquet and badminton—with administrative offices and manufacturing facilities in Chicago, Illinois. Sundance has two wholly owned manufacturing affiliates, one in Mexico and the other in Canada. The Mexican affiliate is located in Mexico City and services all of Latin America. The Canadian affiliate is in Toronto and serves only Canada. Each affiliate keeps its books in its local currency, which is also the functional currency for the affiliate. The current exchange rates are: $1 = C$1.25 = Ps3.30 = A1 = ¥105 = W800. The nonconsolidated balance sheets for Sundance and its two affiliates appear in the accompanying table.

You joined the International Treasury division of Sundance six months ago after spending the last two years studying for your MBA degree. The corporate treasurer has asked you to prepare a report analyzing all aspects of the translation exposure faced by Sundance as an MNC. She has also asked you to address in your analysis the relationship between the firm's translation exposure and its transaction exposure. After performing a forecast of future spot rates of exchange, you decide that you must do the following before any sensible report can be written.

a. Using the current exchange rates and the nonconsolidated balance sheets for Sundance and its affiliates, prepare a consolidated balance sheet for Sundance.

b. i. Prepare a translation exposure report for Sundance Sporting Goods, Inc., and its two affiliates.

   ii. Using the translation exposure report you have prepared, determine if any reporting currency imbalance will result from the change in exposure currency exchange rates. Your forecast is that exchange rates will change from $1 = C$1.25 = Ps3.30 = A1 = ¥105 = W800 to $1 = C$1.30 = Ps3.30 = A1.03 = ¥105 = W800.

c. Prepare a second consolidated balance sheet for the MNC using the exchange rates you expect in the future. Determine how any reporting currency imbalance will affect the new consolidated balance sheet for the MNC.

d. i. Prepare a transaction exposure report for Sundance and its affiliates. Determine if any transaction exposures are also translation exposures.

   ii. Investigate what Sundance and its affiliates can do to control its transaction and translation exposures. Determine if any of the translation exposure should be hedged.

Nonconsolidated Balance Sheet for Sundance Sporting Goods, Inc. and Its Mexican and Canadian Affiliates, December 31, 2002
(in 000 currency units)

	Sundance, Inc. (Parent)	Mexican Affiliate	Canadian Affiliate
Assets			
Cash	US$ 1,500	Ps 1,420	C$ 1,200
Accounts receivable	2,500[a]	2,800[e]	1,500[f]
Inventory	5,000	6,200	2,500
Investment in Mexican affiliate	2,400[b]	—	—
Investment in Canadian affiliate	3,600[c]	—	—
Net fixed assets	12,000	11,200	5,600
Total assets	US$27,000	Ps21,620	C$10,800
Liabilities and Net Worth			
Accounts payable	US$ 3,000	Ps 2,500[a]	C$ 1,700
Notes payable	4,000[d]	4,200	2,300
Long-term debt	9,000	7,000	2,300
Common shares	5,000	4,500[b]	2,900[c]
Retained earnings	6,000	3,420[b]	1,600[c]
Total liabilities and net worth	US$27,000	Ps21,620	C$10,800

[a]The parent firm is owed Ps1,320,000 by the Mexican affiliate. This sum is included in the parent's accounts receivable as US$400,000, translated at Ps3.30/US$1. The remainder of the parent's (Mexican affiliate's) accounts receivable (payable) are denominated in dollars (pesos).

[b]The Mexican affiliate is wholly owned by the parent firm. It is carried on the parent firm's books at US$2,400,000. This represents the sum of the common shares (Ps4,500,000) and retained earnings (Ps3,420,000) on the Mexican affiliate's books, translated at Ps3.30/US$1.

[c]The Canadian affiliate is wholly owned by the parent firm. It is carried on the parent firm's books at US$3,600,000. This represents the sum of the common shares (C$2,900,000) and the retained earnings (C$1,600,000) on the Canadian affiliate's books, translated at C$1.25/$1.

[d]The parent firm has outstanding notes payable of ¥126,000,000 due a Japanese bank. This sum is carried on the parent firm's books as US$1,200,000, translated at ¥105/$1. Other notes payable are denominated in American dollars.

[e]The Mexican affiliate has sold on account A120,000 of merchandise to an Argentine import house. This sum is carried on the Mexican affiliate's books as Ps396,000, translated at A1/Ps3.30. Other accounts receivable are denominated in Mexican pesos.

[f]The Canadian affiliate has sold on account W192,000,000 of merchandise to a Korean importer. This sum is carried on the Canadian affiliate's books as CD300,000, translated at W800/CD1.25. Other accounts receivable are denominated in Canadian dollars.

REFERENCES & SUGGESTED READINGS

Arpan, J. S., and L. H. Radenbaugh. *International Accounting and Multinational Enterprises,* 2nd ed. New York: Wiley, 1985.

Coopers & Lybrand. *Foreign Currency Translation and Hedging.* New York: Coopers & Lybrand, February 1994.

Financial Accounting Standards Board. *Accounting for the Translation of Foreign Currency Transactions and Foreign Currency Financial Statements, Statement of Financial Accounting Standards No. 8,* Stamford, CT: Financial Accounting Standards Board, October 1975.

Financial Accounting Standards Board. *Foreign Currency Translation, Statement of Financial Accounting Standards No. 52.* Stamford, Conn.: Financial Accounting Standards Board, December 1981.

Garlicki, T. Dessa, Frank J. Fabozzi, and Robert Fonfeder. "The Impact of Earnings under FASB 52 on Equity Returns." *Financial Management* 16 (1987), pp. 36–44.

Haried, Andrew A., Leroy F. Imdieke, and Ralph E. Smith. *Advanced Accounting,* 6th ed. New York: Wiley, 1994.

Napolitano, Gabrielle. *International Accounting Standards: A Primer.* New York: Goldman, Sachs & Co., November 24, 1993.

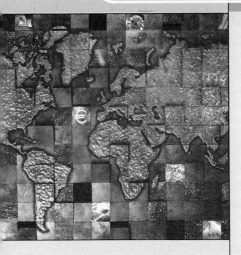

Financial Management of the Multinational Firm

Part Four covers topics on financial management practices for the MNC.

CHAPTER 15 discusses why multinational corporations (MNCs) make capital expenditures in productive capacity in foreign lands, rather than just producing domestically and then exporting to overseas markets.

CHAPTER 16 deals with the international capital structure and the cost of capital of an MNC. An analytical argument is presented showing that the firm's cost of capital is lower when its shares trade internationally and if debt capital is sourced internationally.

CHAPTER 17 presents the adjusted present value (APV) framework of Donald Lessard that is useful for the parent firm in analyzing a capital expenditure in foreign operations.

CHAPTER 18 covers issues in cash management for the MNC. The chapter shows that if an MNC establishes a centralized cash depository and a multilateral system, the number of foreign cash flow transactions can be reduced, saving it money and giving it better control of its cash.

CHAPTER 19 provides a brief introduction to trade financing and countertrade. An example of a typical foreign trade transaction explains the three primary documents that are used in trade financing: letter of credit, time draft, and bill of lading.

CHAPTER 20 on the international tax environment opens with a discussion of the theory of taxation. Different methods of taxation are considered, and income tax rates in select countries are compared.

CHAPTER 21 provides an introduction to corporate governance issues and discusses how corporate governance structure affects corporate decision-making procedures and shareholder welfare in different countries.

CHAPTER 15

Foreign Direct Investment and Cross-Border Acquisitions

MCCAIN FOODS of tiny Florenceville, New Brunswick, has 55 plants on six continents. One out of every three French fries in the world is produced by McCain. When McCain sets up operations in, say, the United States to wash, slice, freeze, package, and distribute French fries throughout the United States, McCain is involved in **foreign direct investment (FDI)**. Foreign direct investment refers to corporate investment when the corporation that makes the investment is foreign owned. Foreign direct investment is done by multinational enterprise.

Canadian firms have a substantial global presence through foreign direct investment (Exhibit 15.1). Alcan, the aluminum giant with corporate headquarters in Toronto, is an excellent example. Alcan has total assets worldwide of US$20 billion—half in Canada, half abroad. Alcan employs 11,000 people in Canada and 26,000 abroad. Alcan bauxite mines or smelting plants in Europe, Asia, and Latin America operate with technology and management that is centred in Canada.

The Bank of Montreal (BMO) has major retail banking operations in mid-west United States, which BMO conducts through its wholly subsidiary, the Harris Bank. Magna International based in Aurora, Ontario, is a major parts supplier to the North American automobile industry. Magna also has plants throughout Europe, Asia, and Latin America to serve the global automobile industry. The Bata Shoe Company, with headquarters in Batawa, Ontario, has manufacturing plants and retail facilities in 50 countries. The list of examples of foreign direct investment by Canadian firms includes Bell Canada Enterprises, Nortel, Irving Oil, Falconbridge, Four Seasons Hotels, Seagrams, and many others.

Canada, of course, is also host to a great deal of foreign direct investment from other countries (Exhibit 15.2). Foreign-owned companies, such as British Petroleum (BP), Coca-Cola, General Foods, General Motors, General Electric, Honda, Nestlé, and Weyerhaeuser, have plants and operations throughout Canada.

Foreign direct investment implies a substantial degree of ownership and control of operations in the host country. Honda, for example, with two manufacturing plants in Alliston, Ontario, is 100 percent owned by the parent company in Japan. Honda (Canada) answers to corporate headquarters in Japan.

The benefits from foreign direct investment are economically important. Foreign direct investment generally comes as a package of capital, technology, and managerial know-how—in production, marketing, finance, human resources—as well as patents and trade marks. Inbound FDI brings that package to the host country, adding to productive capital, creating employment and often introducing advanced technology. Outbound FDI, such as Barrick's gold operations in Australia or Peru, reflects the profitable pursuit of investment opportunities by Canadian firms. McCain Foods would be severely constrained if it produced and sold French fries only in Canada.

Foreign direct investment is a facet of the globalization of industry. Over the past decade, FDI has grown more rapidly, indeed almost twice as fast as international trade. In fact, more than 80 percent of international trade in manufactured goods takes place

EXHIBIT 15.1

Canada's Largest Home-Based Transnational Corporations (millions of Canadian dollars and number)

Company	Industry	Sales	Employees
Industrial			
Onex Corp.	Diversified	24,531	97,300
Seagram's	Beverages	23,090	—
George Weston	Food	23,344	—
Canadian Pacific	Diversified	16,102	45,521
Bombardier Inc.	Aircraft manufacturing	16,101	56,000
Magna International	Motor Vehicles	15,608	—
Celestica	Electrical and electronic equipment	14,478	30,000
Alcan	Metals	13,581	53,000
Quebecor	Publishing and printing	10,915	52,000
Petro-Canada	Petroleum	9,372	4,024
Noranda	Metals	6,957	—
Alberta Energy	Petroleum	6,315	—
Nova Chemicals	Chemicals	5,814	4,700
Abitii-Consolidated	Paper	5,677	—
Tertiary			
Nortel Networks	Telecommunications	44,946	94,500
Transcanada Pipelines	Electricity, gas, and water	21,156	2,663
BCE	Telecommunications	18,094	75,000
Empire Company Ltd.	Trade	11,164	—
Air Canada	Transport and storage	9,283	31,560
Westcoast Energy	Electrcity, gas, and water	8,955	5,455
CN	Transport and storage	5,446	22,547
Canadian Tire	Trade	5,208	—
Laidlaw	Transport and storage	4,295	94,900
Teleglobe	Telecommunications	4,256	5,295
Rogers Communication	Telecommunications	3,504	12,700
Atco	Electricity, gas, and water	3,076	
Aliant	Telecommunications	2,274	10,486
Transat A.T.	Transport and storage	1,923	2,400
Extendicare	Other services	1,807	38,800

Finance and Insurance		Assets	Employees
Royal Bank of Canada	Finance	294,054	49,232
Canadian Imperial Bank of Commerce	Finance	267,702	45,998
The Toronto-Dominion Bank	Finance	264,818	28,001
The Bank of Nova Scotia	Finance	253,171	47,668
Bank of Montreal	Finance	233,396	33,400
Manulife Financial Corporation	Insurance	114,460	28,000
Caisse Centrale Desjardins	Finance	76,117	48,000
National Bank of Canada	Finance	75,827	16,616
Power Corporation of Canada	Insurance	60,182	—
Great-West Lifeco	Insurance	55,479	—
Canada Life Financial Corporation	Insurance	54,650	—
Sun Life Financial Services of Canada	Insurance	10,209	11 222

Sources: *The Banker's Almanac*, 2001 (London, Reed Information Services Ltd., 2001); *Classic Ratings Database*, 2001 (New York, McGraw-Hill Companies, 2001); *Thomson Financial Piranhaweb* (http://www.piranha web.com); *Who Owns Whom, 2000* (London, Dun and Bradstreet Ltd., 2000); *Global Researcher—Worldscope Database* (CD-Rom) June 2001; *Wright Company Analysis* (http://profiles.wisi.com/); various company websites.

within multinational enterprise, for example, from subsidiary to parent. Much of the enormous back-and-forth trade between Ontario and Michigan in the integrated North American automobile sector is *intrafirm* trade within Ford, GM, and Daimler-Chrysler.

EXHIBIT 15.2   Largest Foreign Investments in Canada (millions of Canadian dollars and number)

Company	Host Economy	Industry	Sales	Employees
A. Industrial				
Imperial Oil Ltd	United States	Petroleum	17,829	6,704
Sara Lee Corporation of Canada Ltd	United States	Food	17,511	265
Weyerhaeuser Company Ltd	United States	Wood and wood products	12,262	6,000
Shell Canada Ltd	Netherlands/ United Kingdom	Petroleum	8,100	3,392
Adm Agri-Industries Ltd	United States	Food	5,440	17,000
Meritor Automotive Canada Inc	United States	Motor vehicles	4,450	1,000
Canadian Ultramar Ltd	United States	Petroleum	4,321	
General Motors of Canada Ltd	United States	Motor vehicles	3,621	24,000
Imperial tobacco Canada Ltd	United Kingdom	Tobacco	3, 583	2,000
Medis-Health & Pharmaceutical Services Inc	United States	Pharmaceuticals	2,977	1,800
Danka Canada Inc	United Kingdom	Electrical and electronic equip.	2,496	100
Rexel Canada Inc	France	Electrical and electronic equip.	2,467	4,200
DaimierChrysler Canada Inc	Germany	Motor vehicles	2,459	16,300
Bowater Canada Inc	United States	Paper	2,312	
Allied Domecq Canada Ltd	United States	Beverages	2,230	
B. Tertiary				
Hewlett-Packard (Canada) Ltd	United States	Trade	18,000	1,505
UAP Inc	United States	Trade	6,614	5,300
Sears Canada Inc	United States	Trade	6,131	42,000
Canada Safeway Ltd	United States	Trade	4,942	500
Sodexho Marriott Services Canada Ltd	United States	Restaurants	4,502	5,000
Field Aviation Company Inc	United Kingdom	Transport and storage	4,055	60,000
Wal-Mart Canada Inc	United States	Trade	3,763	40,000
Cargill Ltd	United States	Transport and storage	3,700	4,700
Mitsui & Co (Canada) Ltd	Japan	Other services	3,414	104
Great Atlantic and Pacific Tea Company Ltd	Germany	Trade	3,202	20,000
Giants Travel Ltd	United States	Tourism	3,000	
Philip Services Corp.	United States	Waste management	2,977[a]	13,000[a]
Costco Canada Inc	United States	Trade	2,821	7,000
Westburne Inc	France	Trade	2,467[b]	5,256[b]
McDonald's Restaurants of Canada Ltd	United States	Restaurants	2,000	60,000

Company	Host Economy	Industry	Assets	Employees
C. Finance and Insurance				
HSBC Bank of Canada	United Kingdom	Finance	29,438	6,000
Citibank Canada	United States	Finance	11,160	1,240
Societe Generale	France	Finance	4,391[c]	120[c]
ABN AMRO Bank Canada	Netherlands	Finance	3,298	180
BNP Paribas	France	Finance	3,291	
Bank of Tokyo-Mitsubishi	Japan	Finance	3,022[c]	
The Chase Manhattan Bank of Canada	United States	Finance	2,255[d]	45[d]
Banca Commerciale Italiana of Canada	Italy	Finance	1,429	300
National Bank of Greece	Greece	Finance	541	241
Korea Exchange Bank of Canada	Republic of Korea	Finance	382[c]	77[c]
The Bank of East Asia	Hong Kong, China	Finance	305	72
Bank of China	China	Finance	249	59
State Bank of India	India	Finance	145[c]	36[c]
CTC Bank of Canada	Taiwan, Province of China	Finance	61	18

Sources: *The Banker's Almanac*, 2001 (London, Reed Information Services Ltd., 2001); *Classic Ratings Database*, 2001 (New York, McGraw-Hill Companies, 2001); *Thomson Financial Piranhaweb* (http://www.piranha web.com); *Who Owns Whom, 2000* (London, Dun and Bradstreet Ltd., 2000); *Global Researcher—Worldscope Database* (CD-Rom) June 2001; *Wright Company Analysis* (http://profiles.wisi.com/); various company websites.

In this chapter, we investigate why companies decide to undertake FDI as opposed to the alternative of exporting their products and services. We quickly see that in some cases FDI is virtually the only option to penetrate foreign markets. Four Seasons Hotels cannot export its hotel business. Likewise Barrick goes where the gold is. Like all corporate investment, FDI is motivated by the search for new and expanded markets or by the opportunity to produce more efficiently with the use of foreign resources, such as lower-cost labour.

We will look closely at an increasing popular mode of FDI, namely, **cross-border mergers and acquisitions**. For example, CN, Canada's national railway, recently acquired Illinois Central and Wisconsin Central Railways as part of CN's strategy to reshape itself from an east-west one-country railway to a continental transportation system. In the financial sector, ManuLife of Toronto acquired John Hancock of Boston to form the second largest life insurance company in North America. Such cross-border mergers and acquisitions reflect corporate strategy along with substantial international financial reorganization.

In the latter part of the chapter, we introduce an investment perspective that is unique to foreign direct investment—*political risk*. Once a corporation establishes facilities in a foreign country, its operations are subject to the "rules of the game" set by the host country. Political risk ranges from unexpected restrictions on repatriation of foreign earnings to outright confiscation of corporate assets. It is essential to the security and welfare of the corporation to effectively assess and manage political risk. Before we turn to corporate issues, however, let us briefly review global trends in foreign direct investment.

15.1 Global Trends in FDI

The recent trends in **FDI flows** are presented in Exhibit 15.3 and Exhibit 15.4. FDI flows represent new additions to the existing stock of FDI. During the six-year period 1997–2002, total annual worldwide FDI flows amounted to about $830 billion on average. As can be expected, several developed countries are the dominant sources of FDI *outflows*. The United States, on average, invested about $139 billion per year overseas, closely followed by the United Kingdom, which invested about $135 billion per year. France, Germany, and the Netherlands also invested heavily overseas, each exceeding $45 billion per year. After these "big five" come Spain, Canada, Japan, Switzerland, Sweden, and Italy. The developed countries account for about 90 percent of the total worldwide FDI outflows during this five-year period. This implies that multinational corporations (MNCs) domiciled in these countries should have certain comparative advantages in FDI.

Exhibits 15.3 and 15.4 also show FDI *inflows* by country. During the five-year period 1997–2002, the United States received the largest amount of FDI inflows, $202 billion per year on average, among all countries. The next most popular destinations of FDI flows were the United Kingdom, Germany, China, France, the Netherlands, Canada, Spain, and Mexico. These nine countries account for about 60 percent of the total worldwide FDI inflows, suggesting these countries must have locational advantages for FDI over other countries. In contrast to its substantial role as an originating country of FDI outlfows, Japan plays a relatively minor role as a host of FDI inflows; Japan received only $6.7 billion worth of FDI, on average, per year during the period 1997–2002, reflecting a variety of legal, economic, and cultural barriers to foreign investment in Japan. It is noted that FDI flows declined in 2002, reflecting a slowdown of the world economy.

It is noteworthy that FDI flows into China have dramatically increased in recent years. The amount of inflow increased from $3.5 billion in 1990 to 52.7 billion in 2002. By 1993, China had emerged as the second most important host country for FDI, trailing only the United States. China not only by lower labour and material costs but also to preempt the entry of rivals into China's potentially huge market.

Among the developing countries, Mexico is another country that experienced substantial FDI inflows, $15 billion on average per year. It is well known that MNCs invest in Mexico, a low-cost country, to serve the North American as well as Mexican

EXHIBIT 15.3		Foreign Direct Investment—Outflows (Inflows) in Billions of Dollars					
Country	1997	1998	1999	2000	2001	2002	Annual Average
Australia	5.9	2.5	3.0	5.1	11.2	14.0	7.0
	(8.6)	(6.6)	(5.7)	(12.0)	(4.1)	(6.9)	(7.3)
Canada	22.0	26.6	15.6	47.5	35.5	20.6	28.0
	(11.5)	(16.5)	(24.4)	(66.6)	(27.5)	(28.8)	(29.2)
China	2.6	1.6	1.8	0.9	1.8	52.7	10.2
	(44.2)	(45.5)	(40.3)	(40.8)	(46.8)	(2.8)	(36.7)
France	35.6	40.6	120.6	175.5	82.8	51.5	84.4
	(23.2)	(28.0)	(47.1)	(42.9)	(52.6)	(62.5)	(42.7)
Germany	40.3	86.6	109.5	49.3	43.3	38.0	61.2
	(9.6)	(19.9)	(54.8)	(195.1)	(31.8)	(24.5)	(56.0)
Italy	10.2	12.1	6.7	12.3	21.5	14.5	12.9
	(3.7)	(2.6)	(6.9)	(13.4)	(14.9)	(17.1)	(9.8)
Japan	26.0	24.2	22.7	31.6	38.1	9.3	25.3
	(3.2)	(3.2)	(12.7)	(8.3)	(6.2)	(31.5)	(10.9)
Mexico	1.1	1.4	1.5	1.0	3.7	13.6	3.7
	(12.8)	(10.2)	(12.5)	(14.7)	(24.7)	(1.0)	(12.7)
Netherlands	21.5	38.3	57.7	71.3	44.0	29.2	43.7
	(9.4)	(31.9)	(41.3)	(52.5)	(50.5)	(26.3)	(34.8)
Spain	12.5	18.4	42.1	54.7	27.8	21.2	29.5
	(6.4)	(11.3)	(15.8)	(37.5)	(21.8)	(18.5)	(18.6)
Sweden	12.6	22.5	21.9	40.6	7.2	11.1	19.3
	(10.9)	(19.4)	(60.9)	(23.4)	(12.7)	(10.9)	(23.0)
Switzerland	16.7	17.4	33.3	42.7	16.3	9.3	22.6
	(4.9)	(3.7)	(11.7)	(16.3)	(10.0)	(11.8)	(9.7)
United Kingdom	63.6	114.2	201.4	253.9	39.5	24.9	116.3
	(37.0)	(63.1)	(87.9)	(116.6)	(53.8)	(39.7)	(66.4)
United States	110.0	132.8	174.6	164.9	113.9	30.0	121.0
	(109.3)	(193.4)	(283.4)	(300.9)	(124.4)	(120.0)	(188.6)
World	475.1	648.9	1,042.1	1,379.5	620.7	651.2	802.9
	(464.3)	(643.9)	(1,088.3)	(1,491.9)	(735.1)	(647.4)	(845.2)

Source: Adapted from *World Investment Report 2002*, UNCTAD.

markets. Similarly, in Europe, MNCs invested heavily, $18.6 billion per year, in Spain where the costs of production are relatively low compared with other European countries, such as France and Germany. Most likely, MNCs also invest in Spain to gain a foothold in the huge single market of the European Union.

Now, let us turn our attention to **FDI stocks,** which are the accumulation of previous FDI flows. The overall cross-border production activities of MNCs are best captured by FDI stocks. Exhibit 15.5 provides a summary of FDI stocks, both outward and inward, by country. The total worldwide FDI stock, which was about $514 billion in 1980, rose to $7,123 billion in 2002. In the case of Canada, FDI outward stock rose tenfold from $22.6 billion in 1980 to $273.7 billion in 2002. Canada ranks with the United States, the United Kingdom, Germany, Japan, the Netherlands, France, and Switzerlandas the source of the most outward FDI. For FDI inward stock, on the other hand, the United States, China, the United Kingdom, Germany, France, and the Netherlands are the most important hosts. Exhibit 15.6 shows the direction of FDI stocks among the three major economic centres, that is, the United States, the European Union, and Japan. Clearly, much of the FDI stocks are concentrated in these three major economic centres.

EXHIBIT 15.4

Average Foreign Direct Investments per Year during 1997–2002
(Billions of Dollars)

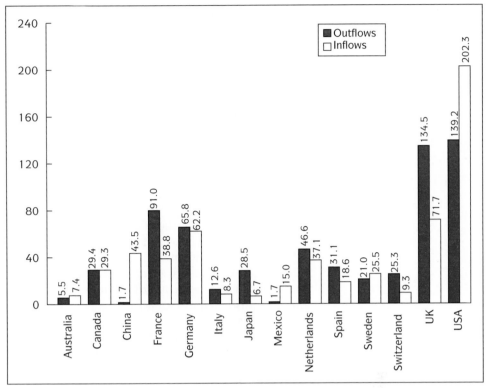

Source: Adapted from *World Investment Report 2002,* UNCTAD.

Exhibit 15.5 shows that in 1980, the stock of FDI in Canada was more than twice the stock of Canadian direct investment abroad. By 1990, the inward and outward stocks of FDI were almost equal. Today, the stock of Canadian FDI in other countries is more than twice the stock of FDI in Canada. This rapid and remarkable reversal of Canada's FDI position reflects, in part, the aggressive pursuit of offshore investment opportunities by Canadian firms, such as Alcan, Bombardier, Canfor, Domtar, and firms all the way through the industrial alphabet. On the other hand, these figures may also prompt the disturbing suggestion that Canada has become a less attractive destination for foreign capital.

15.2 Why Do Firms Invest Overseas?

Why do firms locate production overseas, rather than exporting from the home country or licensing production to a local firm in the host country? In other words, why do firms seek to extend corporate *control* overseas by forming multinational corporations? Unlike the theory of international trade or the theory of international portfolio investment, we do not have a well-developed, comprehensive theory of FDI. But several theories can shed light on certain aspects of the FDI phenomenon. Most explanations, in one way or another, involve *market imperfections,* in product, factor, or capital markets as the key motivating forces driving FDI.

In what follows, we discuss some of the key factors that are important in firms' decisions to invest overseas:

- Trade barriers
- Imperfect labour market
- Intangible assets
- Vertical integration

- Product life cycle
- Shareholder diversification services

Trade Barriers

Tariffs, which are essentially taxes on imports imposed by the destination nation, are among the oldest and most venerable restrictions on trade. Rather than paying the tariff on exported goods, foreign companies would often opt to set up production facilities to serve the market protected by tariff. For example, an American company that faced tariffs on goods destined for, say, Canada, would often choose to "jump the tariff wall" by setting up production facilities in Canada. Indeed, Canada has a long history of attracting such foreign direct investment.

When a foreign firm would produce just for the Canadian market, that firm—say in household durables, such as General Electric (Canada) or Westinghouse (Canada)—would be forced into smaller and less efficient production runs in Canada than in the home country. Canada's tariff barriers were recognized long ago as a source of industrial inefficiency in Canada, especially in manufacturing. Canada came to be known as a "branch plant" economy.

A recent example in Canada where tariffs, indeed, induced FDI involves the automobile sector. A 6-percent tariff on imported finished vehicles from outside of North America was a major reason for Honda and Toyota of Japan to build manufacturing plants in Canada.

Fortunately, over the past 50 years, import tariffs have been cut dramatically. Indeed, for all practical purposes, Canada no longer imposes tariffs on imports, especially on

EXHIBIT 15.5

Foreign Direct Investment—Outward (Inward) Stocks in Billions of Dollars

Country	1980	1985	1990	1995	2002
Australia	2.3	6.7	30.1	41.3	91.2
	(13.2)	(25.0)	(75.8)	(104.2)	(128.7)
Canada	22.6	40.9	78.9	110.4	273.7
	(54.2)	(64.7)	(113.1)	(116.8)	(221.5)
China	0.0	0.1	2.5	17.3	447.9
	(0.0)	(3.4)	(14.1)	(129.0)	(35.5)
France	23.6	37.1	110.1	200.9	652.1
	(22.6)	(33.4)	(86.5)	(162.4)	(401.3)
Germany	43.1	59.9	151.6	235.0	577.8
	(36.6)	(36.9)	(111.2)	(134.0)	(451.6)
Italy	7.3	16.3	56.1	86.7	194.5
	(8.9)	(18.9)	(58.0)	(64.7)	(126.5)
Japan	19.6	43.9	201.4	305.5	331.6
	(3.3)	(4.7)	(9.9)	(17.8)	(59.6)
Mexico	0.1	0.5	0.6	2.7	12.0
	(9.0)	(14.8)	(27.9)	(61.3)	(140.0)
Netherlands	42.1	47.8	109.1	158.6	355.6
	(19.2)	(24.9)	(73.7)	(102.6)	(314.6)
Spain	1.2	2.1	14.9	34.3	216.1
	(5.1)	(8.9)	(66.3)	(128.9)	(217.8)
Sweden	5.6	12.4	49.5	61.6	145.4
	(3.6)	(5.1)	(12.5)	(32.8)	(110.5)
Switzerland	21.5	21.4	65.7	108.3	297.6
	(8.5)	(10.1)	(33.7)	(43.1)	(118.1)
United Kingdom	80.4	100.3	230.8	319.0	1,033.0
	(63.0)	(64.0)	(218.0)	(244.1)	(638.6)
United States	220.2	251.0	435.2	705.6	1,775.1
	(83.0)	(184.6)	(394.9)	(564.6)	(1,572.6)
World FDI Stock	514.2	679.4	1,667.6	2,657.9	7,123.0

Source: Adapted from various issues of *World Investment Report*, UNCTAD.

EXHIBIT 15.6 FDI Stock among Triad Members and Their Clusters (Billions of Dollars)[a]

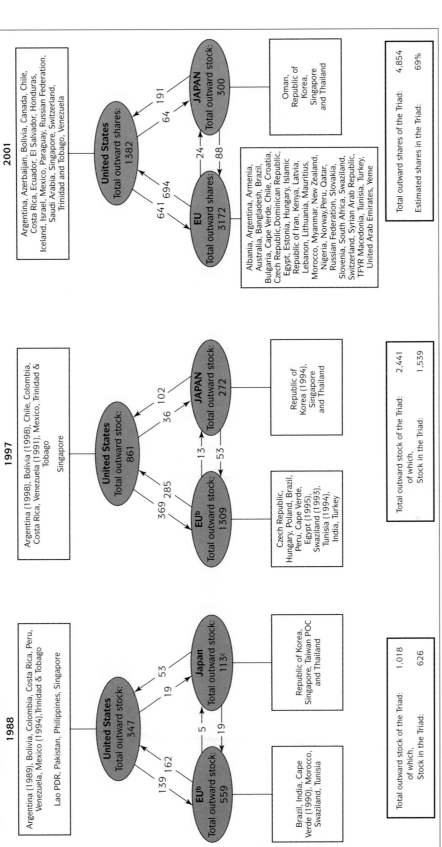

[a] The host countries in which the Triad member accounts for at least 30 percent of total FDI inflows during a three-year period in the latter half of the 1980s/beginning of the 1990s or total inward FDI stock in 1988 are selected for the 1988 chart; and at least 30 percent of total FDI inflows during a three-year period in the mid-1990s or total inward FDI stock in 1997 for the 1997 chart. In cases where data are available for years other than those stated in the respective charts, those years are indicated in parentheses.

[b] Includes Austria (1996 instead of 1997), Denmark (1996 instead of 1997), Finland (1991 instead of 1988, and 1996 instead of 1997), Germany (1996 instead of 1997), Italy, Netherlands (1996 instead of 1997), Sweden (1996 instead of 1997), and United Kingdom that account for more than 90 percent of the EU outward stock. Denmark is not included for 1988 due to unavailability of data.

[c] Cumulative flows on a balance-of-payment basis since 1968.

Source: UNCTAD, FDI/TNC database.

goods from our largest trading partner, the United States. The Free Trade Agreement with the United States followed by the North American Free Trade Agreement (NAFTA), which includes Mexico, set up an agenda to virtually eliminate tariffs among the NAFTA member countries.

The same story applies throughout most of the world. Trade among the 25 member states of the European Union crosses old borders tariff-free.

Tariff barriers have been largely dismantled, except in two particularly troublesome areas, agriculture and textiles. The remaining tariffs that affect these sectors, such as American tariffs on sugar or Europe's tariffs on textiles, create serious difficulties for the developing nations, as it denies markets for the labour-intensive, relatively low-skill production in which they have distinct comparative advantage.

Trade barriers can also arise *naturally* from transportation costs. Such products as mineral ore and cement that are bulky, relative to their economic values, may not be suitable for exporting because high transportation costs will substantially reduce profit margins. In these cases, FDI can be made in the foreign markets to reduce transportation costs.

Imperfect Labour Market

Suppose Samsung, a Korean conglomerate, would like to build production facilities for its consumer electronics products to serve the North American markets. Samsung could locate its production facilities anywhere in North America if the firm is concerned only with circumventing trade barriers imposed by NAFTA. Samsung chose to locate its production facilities in northern Mexico, rather than in Canada or the United States, mainly because it wanted to take advantage of the lower costs of labour in Mexico.

Labour services in a country can be severely underpriced relative to its productivity because workers are not allowed to freely move across national boundaries to seek higher wages. Among all factor markets, the labour market is the most imperfect. Severe imperfections in the labour market lead to persistent wage differentials among countries. Exhibit 15.7 provides the hourly labour costs in the manufacturing sector for selected countries in 2001. Compared with Germany, hourly compensation for factory workers is about $12 less in Spain. The hourly compensation is only $1.70 in Mexico, compared with $20.67 in the United States.

EXHIBIT 15.7

Labour Costs around the Globe (2001)

Country	Average Hourly Cost (US$)
Germany	23.04
United States	20.67
Belgium	20.25
Japan	19.52
Sweden	18.41
France	16.70
United Kingdom	15.75
Canada	15.70
Italy	14.51
Australia	13.22
Spain	10.94
Israel	10.54
Korea	7.53
Hong Kong	5.47
Taiwan	5.44
Mexico	1.70
Philippines	0.66
China	0.60
Indonesia	0.22

Source: *The Economist* Intelligence Unit

When workers are not mobile because of immigration barriers, firms themselves move to the workers in order to benefit from lower-cost labour. This is one of the main reasons MNCs move production to such countries as Mexico, China, and India or to Thailand, Malaysia, and Indonesia, where labour costs are low relative to worker productivity.

Intangible Assets

Coca-Cola has invested in bottling plants all over the world, rather than, say, licensing local firms to produce Coke. Coca-Cola chose FDI as a mode of entry into foreign markets for an obvious reason—it wanted to protect the formula for its famed soft drink. If Coca-Cola licenses a local firm to produce Coke, it has no guarantee that the secrets of the formula will be maintained. Once the formula is leaked to other local firms, they may come up with similar products, which will hurt Coca-Cola's sales. In the 1960s, in a famous example, Coca-Cola, faced strong pressure from the Indian government to reveal the Coke formula as a condition for continued operations in India. Instead of revealing the formula, Coca-Cola chose to withdraw from India.[1]

MNCs may undertake overseas investment projects in a foreign country despite the fact that local firms may enjoy inherent advantages. This implies that MNCs have significant advantages over local firms. The basis of the advantages that MNCs hold are generally referred to as their **intangible asset**. Examples include technological, managerial, and marketing know-how, superior R&D capabilities, and brand power. These intangible assets are often hard to package and sell to foreigners. In addition, the property rights in intangible assets are difficult to establish and protect, especially in foreign countries where legal recourse may not be readily available. As a result, firms may find it more profitable to establish foreign subsidiaries and capture returns directly by *internalizing* transactions in these assets. The internalization theory helps explain why MNCs often dominate local firms. Imagine how difficult it would be for a new Canadian firm to outperform L'Oreal, Sony, or Microsoft or, conversely how difficult it is for firms abroad to go head-to-head with McCains, Seagrams, or Barrick.

A strand of literature, including Caves (1982) and Magee (1977), places special emphasis on the role of market imperfections for intangible assets in motivating firms to undertake FDI. According to the **internalization theory** of FDI, firms that have intangible assets with a *public good* property tend to invest directly in foreign countries in order to use these assets on a larger scale and, at the same time, avoid the misappropriations of intangible assets that may occur while transacting in foreign markets through a market mechanism.[2]

Vertical Integration

Suppose Royal Dutch Shell purchases a significant portion of crude oil for its refinery facilities from a Saudi oil company that owns the oil fields. In this situation, Royal Dutch Shell can experience a number of problems. For example, Royal Dutch Shell, the downstream firm, would like to hold the crude oil price down, whereas the Saudi oil company, an upstream firm, would like to push the price up. If the Saudi company has stronger bargaining power, Royal Dutch Shell may be forced to pay a higher price than it would like to, adversely affecting the firm's profits. As the world's demand for refined oil fluctuates, one of the two firms is likely to bear more risk than the other. The conflict between the upstream and downstream firms can be resolved, however, if the two firms form a vertically integrated firm. Obviously, if Royal Dutch Shell controls the oil fields, the problems will disappear.

Generally speaking, MNCs undertake FDI in countries where inputs are available in order to secure their supply at a stable price. Furthermore, if MNCs have significant

---

[1]Coca-Cola re-entered the Indian market as India gradually liberalized its economy, improving the climate for foreign investments.

[2]Examples of public goods include public parks, lighthouses, and radio/TV broadcasting services. Once these goods are produced, it is difficult to preclude the public from using them, whether they are paying or not.

control over the input market, this creates a barrier to entry to the industry. Many MNCs involved in extractive/natural resources industries directly own oil fields, mine deposits, and forests for these reasons. Likewise, MNCs in manufacturing and processing often find it profitable to locate facilities near the natural resources in order to save transportation costs. It would be costly to bring bulky bauxite ore to the home country and then extract the aluminum.

Although the majority of vertical FDIs are *backward* in that FDI involves an industry abroad that produces inputs for MNCs, foreign investments can take the form of *forward* vertical FDI when they involve an industry abroad that sells an MNC's outputs. As is well known, American car makers found it difficult to market their products in Japan. This is partly because most car dealers in Japan have a long and close business relationship with the Japanese car makers and are reluctant to carry foreign imports. To overcome this problem, American car makers began to build their own network of dealerships in Japan to help sell their cars. This is an example of forward vertical FDI.

Product Life Cycle

It is often obvserved that firms undertake FDI at a particular stage in the life cycle of the products that they initially introduced. Throughout the 20th century, the majority of new products, such as computers, televisions, and mass-produced cars, were developed in industrialized nations and first marketed at home. According to **product life-cycle theory,** when firms first introduce new products, they choose to keep production facilities at home, close to customers. In the early stage of the product life cycle, the demand for the new product is relatively insensitive to the price, and thus, the pioneering firm can charge a relatively high price. At the same time, the firm can continuously improve the product on the basis of feedback from its customers at home.

As demand for the new product develops in foreign countries, the pioneering firm begins to export to those countries. As the foreign demand for the product continues to grow, the pioneering firm, as well as foreign firms, may be induced to start production in foreign countries to serve local markets. As the product becomes standardized and mature, it becomes important to cut the cost of production to stay competitive. A foreign producer operating in a low-cost country has an advantage in world markets. They export. Likewise, the pioneering firm has an incentive to set up operations in the lost-cost country. In other words, FDI takes place when the product reaches maturity and cost becomes an important consideration. FDI can, thus, be interpreted as a *defensive* move to maintain the firm's competitive position against its domestic and foreign rivals. The International Finance in Practice box "Linear Sequence in Manufacturing: Singer & Company" provides an interesting historical example supporting the product life-cycle view of FDI.

Product life-cycle theory predicts that over time, most manufactured products, such as laptop computers today, become standardized commodities, and the production gravitates to the places whery they can be manufactured at the lowest cost. The advanced countries that first developed and manufactured the products, often for export, switch to becoming importers of the product. The dynamic changes in the international trade pattern are illustrated in Exhibit 15.8. The prediction of the product life-cycle theory is consistent with the pattern of dynamic changes observed for many products. For instance, personal computers (PCs) were first developed by American firms (such as IBM and Apple Computer) and exported to overseas markets. As PCs became a standardized commodity, however, the United States became a net importer of PCs from foreign producers based in such countries as Japan, Korea, and Taiwan, as well as foreign subsidiaries of American firms.

It should be pointed out that life cycle theory was developed in the 1960s when the United States was the unquestioned leader in R&D capabilities and product innovations. Increasingly, product innovations are taking place in a broader global arena and

Linear Sequence in Manufacturing: Singer & Company

Singer was one of the first United States–based companies that internationalized its operations. In August 1850, I.M. Singer invented a sewing machine and established I.M. Singer & Company in New York in 1851 to manufacture and sell the machines in the United States. To protect this innovative product, Singer had applied for and obtained domestic and some foreign patents by 1851. Until 1855, the company concentrated on fine-tuning its operations in the domestic market.

The first step towards internationalizing took place in 1855, when Singer & Co. sold its French patent for the single thread machine to a French merchant for a combination of lump-sum payment and royalties. This proved to be a bad experience for Singer as the French merchant was reluctant to pay royalties and handled competitors' products, leading to disputes and discouraging Singer from selling foreign patents to independent businesspersons. By 1856, Singer stopped granting territorial rights to independents in the domestic market due to bad experiences and began establishing its own sales outlets. Independent agents were not providing user instructions to buyers and failed to offer servicing. They were also reluctant to risk their capital by providing instalment payments as well as carrying large inventories.

Learning from its domestic problems, Singer used franchised agents as a mode of entry abroad; they sold and advertised the company's product in a given region. By 1858, Singer had independent businesspersons as foreign agents in Rio de Janeiro and elsewhere. Between September 1860 and May 1861, the company exported 127 machines to agents in Canada, Cuba, Curacao, Germany, Mexico, Peru, Puerto Rico, Uruguay, and Venezuela. Due to its domestic experience, Singer sped up the linear sequence, sometimes simultaneously using both franchised agents and its own sales outlets.

Singer also started extending its policy of establishing sales outlets to foreign markets. By 1861, it had salaried representatives in Glasgow and London. They established additional branches in England, to each of which the machines were sold on commission. By 1862, Singer was facing competition in England from imitators. Foreign sales of Singer machines increased steadily as the company was able to sell machines abroad at prices lower than in the United States because of the undervaluation of the dollar. In 1863, Singer opened a sales office in Hamburg, Germany, and later in Sweden. By 1866, the European demand for Singer machines surpassed supplies and competitors were taking advantage of Singer's inability to supply the machines. After the Civil War, the United States currency appreciated; at the same time, wages in the United States began to rise, increasing manufacturing costs and affecting firms' international competitiveness. As a result, some United States firms started establishing factories abroad.

In 1868, Singer established a small assembly factory in Glasgow, with parts imported from the United States. The venture proved to be successful and, by 1869, Singer decided to import tools from the United States to manufacture all parts in Glasgow. By 1874, partly due to the recession at home, Singer was selling more than half of its output abroad. Then, Singer started replacing locally financed independent agents with salaried-plus-commission agents. By 1879, its London regional headquarters had 26 offices in the United Kingdom and one each in Paris, Madrid, Brussels, Milan, Basel, Capetown, Bombay, and Auckland.

By the 1880s, the company had a strong foreign sales organization, with the London regional headquarters taking the responsibility for sales in Australia, Asia, Africa, the southern part of South America, the United Kingdom, and a large part of the European continent. The Hamburg office was in charge of northern and middle Europe, while the New York office looked after sales in the Caribbean, Mexico, the northern part of South America and Canada. By 1881, the capacity in Singer's three factories in Glasgow was insufficient to meet demand. Therefore, in 1882, Singer established a modern plant in Kilbowie near Glasgow with the latest United States machine tools and with a capacity equivalent to that of its largest factory in the United States. In 1883, Singer set up manufacturing plants in Canada and Australia. Through experience, Singer learned that it could manufacture more cost effectively in Scotland than in the United States for sales in Europe and other markets.

Source: *World Investment Report 1996*, UNCTAD, p. 77.

new products are introduced simultaneously in many advanced countries. Production facilities may be located in multiple countries from the inception of a new product. The international system of production is becoming too complicated to be explained by a simple version of the product life-cycle theory.

EXHIBIT 15.8

The Product Life Cycle

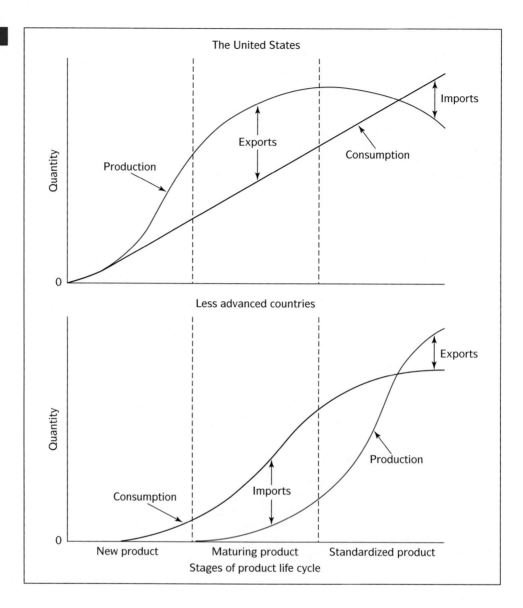

Shareholder Diversification Services

If investors cannot effectively diversify their portfolio holdings internationally because of barriers to cross-border capital flows, firms may be able to provide their shareholders with indirect diversification services by making direct investments in foreign countries. When a firm holds assets in many countries, the firm's cash flows are internationally diversified. Thus, shareholders of the firm can indirectly benefit from international diversification even if they are not directly holding foreign shares. Capital market imperfections, thus, may motivate firms to undertake FDI.

Although shareholders of MNCs may indirectly benefit from corporate international diversification, it is not clear that firms are motivated to undertake FDI for the purpose of providing shareholders with diversification services. Considering the fact that many barriers to international portfolio investments have been dismantled in recent years, enabling investors to diversify internationally by themselves, capital market imperfections as a motivating factor for FDI are likely to become less relevant.

15.3 Cross-Border Mergers and Acquisitions

Foreign direct investment can take place either through **greenfield investments**, which involve building new production facilities in a foreign country, or through *cross-border mergers and acquisitions,* which involve combining with or buying existing foreign businesses. In recent years, a growing portion of FDI has taken the form of cross-border mergers and acquisitions, accounting for more than 50 percent of FDI flows in terms of dollar amount. In 1998, for instance, British Petroleum purchased Amoco, an American oil company, for $55 billion. Daimler-Benz of Germany acquired Chrysler, the third-largest American car company, for $40.5 billion. And Hoechst, a major German pharmaceutical company, acquired Rhone-Poulenc SA (Life Sciences), a French company, for $21.2 billion. To top it all, Vodafone, a British telecommunication company, paid $203 billion to acquire Mannesmann, a major German company, in 2000. Exhibit 15.9 lists major cross-border mergers and acquisition (M&A) deals that were consummated during 1996–2001. The rapid increase in cross-border M&A deals can be attributed to the ongoing liberalization of capital markets and the integration of the world economy.

Firms may be motivated to engage in cross-border M&A deals to bolster their competitive positions in the world market by acquiring special assets from other firms or using their own assets on a larger scale. As a mode of FDI entry, cross-border M&As offer two key advantages over greenfield investments: speed and access to proprietary assets. A recent United Nations study aptly discusses why firms choose M&As as a mode of investment.

Mergers and acquisitions are a popular mode of investment for firms wishing to protect, consolidate and advance their global competitive positions, by selling off divisions that fall outside the scope of their core competence and acquiring strategic assets that enhance their competitiveness. For those firms, "ownership" assets acquired from another firm, such as technical competence, established brand names, and existing supplier networks and distribution systems, can be put to immediate use towards better serving global customers, enhancing profits, expanding market share and increasing corporate competitiveness by employing international production networks more efficiently.[3]

The International Finance in Practice box "DaimlerChrysler: The First Global Car Colossus," page 358, provides a real-world example involving the merger deal between Daimler, a German car company, and Chrysler, the third-largest American car maker. As mentioned in the box, the combined company expects to cut costs by as much as $3 billion annually and fill product and geographic gaps. Anticipating the synergistic gains, share prices of both companies rose upon the announcement of a $40.5-billion deal.

Cross-border acquisitions of businesses are a politically sensitive issue, as most countries prefer to retain local control of domestic firms. As a result, although countries may welcome greenfield investments, as they are viewed as representing new investment and employment opportunities, foreign firms' bids to acquire domestic firms are often resisted and sometimes even resented. Whether or not cross-border acquisitions produce **synergistic gains** and how such gains are divided between acquiring and target firms are, thus, important issues from the perspective of shareholder welfare and public policy. Synergistic gains are obtained when the value of the combined firm is greater than the stand-alone valuations of the individual (acquiring and target) firms.[4] If cross-border acquisitions generate synergistic gains and both the acquiring and target shareholders gain wealth at the same time, one can argue that

---

[3]Source: *World Investment Report 1996,* UNCTAD, p. 7.

[4]Synergistic gains may arise if the combined companies can save on the costs of production, marketing, distribution, and R&D and redeploy the combined assets to the highest-value projects.

DaimlerChrysler:
The First Global Car Colossus

By Bill Vlasic.

The champagne was on ice at the Dorchester Hotel in London. Earlier in the day on May 6, the board of Chrysler Corp. and the management board of Daimler Benz approved a historic merger, creating a $130 billion automotive colossus known as DaimlerChrysler AG. The chief executives of two of the world's largest auto makers, Chrysler's Robert J. Eaton and Daimler's Jürgen Schrempp, strode across the room and sealed the largest merger in automotive history—and the third-largest deal ever—with a handshake. The mood was electric as the assembled executives prepared to pop the cork on a pact that would send shock waves around the world. "Both men were enormously energized," says a source close to the deal.

And why not? It looks like a marriage made in automotive heaven. In one bold stroke, the pending merger of Daimler and Chrysler dramatically changes the landscape of the global auto industry. By combining forces, Daimler, Germany's biggest industrial concern, and Chrysler, America's No. 3 carmaker, bring a range of hot-selling models and formidable financial muscle under one garage roof. Simply said, DaimlerChrysler is set to transform the way the auto industry operates worldwide.

The megadeal, which was set to be formally announced on May 7, unites two of the world's most profitable auto companies—with combined 1997 net earnings of $4.6 billion. And if ever a merger had the potential for that elusive quality—synergy—this could be the one. Mercedes-Benz passenger cars are synonymous with luxury and sterling engineering. Chrysler is renowned for its low-cost production of trucks, minivans, and sport-utility vehicles. Chrysler is almost wholly domestic, and Mercedes is increasing global sales—albeit within the confines of the luxury-car market. By spreading Chrysler's production expertise to Daimler operations and merging both product-development forces, the new company could cut costs by up to $3 billion annually—including $1.1 billion in purchasing costs, analysts say.

But DaimlerChrysler is about more than cutting costs and filling product and geographic gaps. It's about the emergence of a new category of global carmaker at a critical moment in the industry—when there is plant capacity to build at least 15 million more vehicles each year than will be sold. And overcapacity is expected to balloon to 18.2 million vehicles by 2002 as Asia continues to decline, predicts Standard & Poor's DRI, a division of The McGraw-Hill Companies. Consolidation is inevitable; from about 40 auto companies now, to about 20 in the next century, says DRI analyst Sam Fiorani.

DaimlerChrysler, then, may be the first member of the 21st century 20. "The Mercedes-Chrysler deal sanctions the concept of auto mergers and is a major catalyst for more," says Joseph S. Phillippi, auto analyst for Lehman Brothers Inc. Eaton, in an Apr. 27 interview with *Business Week,* predicted that Western auto makers with the wherewithal would snap up the troubled auto makers of South Korea and Southeast Asia. General Motors Corp., for example, is considering a big stake in Korea's beleaguered Daewoo. In Europe, auto makers such as Volvo, Fiat, PSA (Peugeot/Citröen), and Renault are ripe for takeover.

DaimlerChrysler will have the wherewithal. It will have $130 billion in annual sales and assets totaling $120 billion. It will have factories on four continents.

Indeed, both partners were giants in their own right. So why merge? Top executives at the two companies came to realize that if they continue to go it alone, their companies could survive as strong regional players—but might be forced onto the shoulder in a global industry. "There are world forces at work that are driving consolidation," Eaton said in the April interview. "Two factors are huge: the worldwide excess capacity in autos and the Asian economic crisis."

Eaton and Schrempp hatched their stunning plan in secret meetings over the past nine months in Germany and Detroit. Daimler was represented by Goldman, Sachs & Co. and Deutsche Bank, while CS First Boston represented Chrysler. The estimated $40 billion deal is being financed by a stock swap of two Chrysler shares for every one Daimler share. It will leave Chrysler shareholders with 43% of the combined entity, while Daimler stockholders control 57%, say sources familiar with the deal. That will make DaimlerChrysler a German company for tax and accounting benefits, these sources say.

But the company will have dual headquarters. A cross-border acquisitions are mutually beneficial and, thus, should not be thwarted both from national and global perspectives.

Synergistic gains may or may not arise from cross-border acquisitions, depending on the motives of the acquiring firms. In general, gains will result when the acquirer is

source close to Daimler says that Daimler and Chrysler headquarters will remain in Stuttgart and Auburn Hills, Mich., for some time to come. "Can you imagine Daimler leaving Stuttgart? Can you imagine Chrysler leaving Detroit?" It will also have co-CEOS—to start. After three years, however, Eaton is expected to retire, allowing Schrempp to take full control, say sources familiar with the arrangement.

Investors immediately applauded—pushing Chrysler shares up 7⅜ to 48¹³⁄₁₆ on May 6. "Chrysler has the trucks, vans, and SUVS, and Daimler has the luxury cars," says Seth M. Glickenhaus of Glickenhaus & Co., an investment firm that holds 8 million Chrysler shares. "There are enormous synergies in product."

One of the biggest opportunities is for the paired company to plunge into new markets that neither could assay alone. Neither has much of a presence in Latin America or Asia, although Daimler does sell heavy trucks there. Chrysler's inexpensive small cars will give Daimler a vehicle to drive into emerging markets. "With our [upscale] product portfolio, we will never be a mass marketer," says a source close to Daimler. "There are some markets where [Mercedes] will never be able to have an impact."

The first venture of the new merged company likely will be a barebones little car, smaller than Chrysler's subcompact Neon model, to sell in Asia and Latin America. "We would like a sub-Neon vehicle for the international market," says Eaton. "We started looking at projects four years ago, and it's something we're looking at harder now." Ironically, such a car may be powered by engines to be made in Brazil in a joint venture between Chrysler and BMW—Mercedes' archival in Germany. BMW declines to comment on the DaimlerChrysler union.

Indeed, most rivals are too stunned to react. Both Ford and GM declined to comment. On the other hand, many industry watchers immediately questioned whether the enormously divergent cultures of Auburn Hills and Stuttgart won't get in the way of all that synergy. "I can't imagine two more different cultures," says Furman Selz auto analyst Maryann N. Keller.

Chrysler's brushes with bankruptcy forged a culture dedicated to speedy product development, lean operations, and flashy design. Daimler remains a buttoned-down, engineering-driven bureaucracy known for conservatively styled products. "The reaction here is shock, excitement, enthusiasm, and concern," says one Chrysler exec.

Schrempp and Eaton are certainly an odd couple. Eaton, 58, is a Kansas-born engineer who worked his way up the ranks at GM before replacing Lee Iacocca as Chrysler chairman in 1993. His soft-spoken manner belies his reputation as a savvy manager. When he took the job at Chrysler, Motown observers expected that his rival, Robert A. Lutz, would bolt. Yet Eaton and Lutz came together to drive Chrysler to record sales and profits. Lutz, 66, now vice-chairman, is expected to retire soon.

Schrempp, who once trained as an auto mechanic, is also an engineer who climbed the corporate ladder to become CEO in 1995 after 28 years with Daimler. After he won the top post, he forced out his rival for the job, Helmut Werner, who had engineered a turnaround with hot products, like the M-class sport utility vehicles and SLK roadster, and youthful, irreverent marketing.

Can Chrysler and Mercedes live together? It could be tough because they will want to protect their vastly different brands. The Mercedes network "is not the kind of distribution system that Chrysler wants or needs, or even could use," says Keller. Nor is it likely that a Mercedes sedan will one day roll down a Chrysler line. "People buy Mercedes because they think they're made by guys in white coats," says Keller. "That image better not be contaminated by the idea that it's being built by a bunch of guys in Indiana."

So how will Chrysler and Mercedes help each other without losing their identities? Chrysler's slowly improving quality could take a quantum leap forward with help from Daimler engineers. And Daimler's diesel engines, for example, could help Chrysler in its efforts to sell subcompacts and minivans in Europe and elsewhere. Chrysler, for its part, has the industry's best supplier relations, while Daimler still relies on strong-arm techniques to get lower prices from its suppliers. Together, they can save on warehousing and logistics for cars and spare parts in both Europe and the U.S. They also can jointly make internal components like air-conditioning systems and door latches and pool their resources in developing basic technology.

Well before anyone knows if DaimlerChrysler is a success, however, its very existence could reshape the industry. Look for auto makers to scramble for partners to ensure survival as one of the 21st century 20. How that plays out is anybody's guess. "The odd man out here seems to be the Japanese," says Phillippi of Lehman Brothers. "Nissan and Honda in particular have only two legs to stand on: North America and Japan." That won't be enough in this race.

Source: *Business Week,* May 18, 1998, pp. 40–43. Reprinted with permission.

---

motivated to take advantage of the market imperfections mentioned earlier. In other words, firms may decide to acquire foreign firms to take advantage of mispriced factors of production and to cope with trade barriers.

As previously mentioned, imperfections in the market for *intangible assets* can also

EXHIBIT 15.9   Top 40 Cross-Border M&A Deals Completed during 1996–2001

No	Year	Deal Value ($ Billion)	Acquiring Company	Home Economy	Industry of the Acquiring Company	Acquired Company	Host Economy	Industry of the Acquired Company
1	2000	202.8	Vodafone AirTouch PLC	United Kingdom	Radiotelephone communications	Mannesmann AG	Germany	Radiotelephone communications
2	1999	60.3	Vodafone Group PLC	United Kingdom	Telecommunications	AirTouch Communications	United States	Telecommunications
3	1998	48.2	British Petroleum Co PLC(BP)	United Kingdom	Oil and gas; petroleum refining	Amoco Corp	United States	Oil and gas; petroleum refining
4	2000	46.0	France Telecom SA	France	Telephone communications, except radiotelephone	Orange PLC (Mannesmann AG)	United Kingdom	Telephone communications, except radiotelephone
5	1998	40.5	Daimler-Benz AG	Germany	Transportation equipment	Chrysler Corp	United States	Transportation equipment
6	2000	40.4	Vivendi SA	France	Water supply	Seagram Co Ltd	Canada	Motion picture and video tape production
7	1999	34.6	Zeneca Group PLC	United Kingdom	Drugs	Astra AB	Sweden	Drugs
8	1999	32.6	Mannesmann AG	Germany	Metal and metal products	Orange PLC	United Kingdom	Telecommunications
9	2001	29.4	VoiceStream Wireless Corp	United States	Radiotelephone communications	Deutsche Telekom AG	Germany	Radiotelephone communications
10	2000	27.2	BP Amoco PLC	United Kingdom	Petroleum refining	ARCO	United States	Petroleum refining
11	2000	25.1	Unilever PLC	United Kingdom	Creamery butter	Bestfoods	United States	Dried fruits, vegetables, and soup mixes
12	1999	21.9	Rhone-Poulenc SA	France	Chemicals and allied products	Hoechst AG	Germany	Chemicals and allied products
13	2000	19.4	Zurich Allied AG	Switzerland	Life insurance	Allied Zurich PLC	United Kingdom	Life insurance
14	1998	18.4	Zurich Versicherungs GmbH	Switzerland	Insurance	BAT Industries PLC-Financial	United Kingdom	Insurance
15	2000	16.5	UBS AG	Switzerland	Banks, non–American chartered	PaineWebber Group Inc	United States	Security brokers, dealers and flotation companies
16	2000	14.4	Vodafone AirTouch PLC	United Kingdom	Radiotelephone communications	Airtel SA	Spain	Radiotelephone communications
17	2001	13.8	Viag Interkom GmbH & Co	Germany	Telephone communications, except radiotelephone	British Telecommunications PLC	United Kingdom	Telephone communications, except radiotelephone
18	1999	13.6	Deutsche Telekom AG	Germany	Telecommunications	One 2 One	United Kingdom	Telecommunications
19	2000	13.5	Credit Suisse First Boston	United States	Security brokers, dealers, and flotation companies	Donaldson Lufkin & Jenrette	United States	Commodity contracts brokers and dealers
20	1999	13.2	Repsol SA	Spain	Oil and gas; petroleum refining	YPF SA	Argentina	Oil and gas; petroleum refining
21	1999	12.6	Scottish Power PLC	United Kingdom	Electric, gas, and water distribution	PacifiCorp	United States	Electric, gas, and water distribution
22	2001	12.5	Banacci	Mexico	Commercial banks	Citigroup Inc	United States	Commercial banks
23	2001	12.5	Fortis(NL)NV	Netherlands	Life insurance	Fortis (B)	Belgium	Life insurance
24	2000	11.8	Cap Gemini SA	France	Business consulting services, nec	Ernst & Young-Consulting Bus.	United States	Business consulting services, nec
25	2001	11.5	Billiton PLC	United Kingdom	Miscellaneous metal ores	BHP Ltd	Australia	Steel works, blast furnaces, and rolling mills
26	2001	11.2	AXA Financial Inc	United States	Life insurance	AXA Group(AXA-UAP)	France	Life insurance
27	2001	11.1	De Beers Consolidated Mines	South Africa	Miscellaneous nonmetallic minerals, except fuels	DB Investments	United Kingdom	Investors
28	2000	11.1	HSBC Holdings PLC	United Kingdom	Banks, non–American chartered	Credit Commercial deFrance	France	Banks, non–American chartered
29	2000	11.0	NTL Inc	United States	Cable and other pay television services	CWC ConsumerCo	United Kingdom	Telephone communications, except radiotelephone
30	1998	10.9	Texas Utilities Co	United States	Electric, gas, and water distribution	Energy Group PLC	United Kingdom	Electric, gas, and water distribution
31	1999	10.8	Wal-Mart Stores (UK) Ltd	United Kingdom	Investment and commodity firms, dealers, exchanges	ASDA Group PLC	United Kingdom	Retail trade-food stores
32	2000	10.8	Aegon NV	Netherlands	Insurance	TransAmerica Corp	United States	Insurance
33	2001	10.5	Ralston Purina Co	United States	Dog, cat, and pet food	Nestlé SA	Switzerland	Food and beverages
34	1998	10.2	Universal Studios Inc	United States	Motion picture production and distribution	PolyGram NV(Phillips Electrn)	Netherlands	Electronic and electrical equipment
35	1998	10.2	Roche Holding AG	Switzerland	Drugs	Corange Ltd	Bermuda	Drugs
36	2000	10.2	Telefonica SA	Spain	Telephone communications, except radiotelephone	Telecommunications de Sao Paulo	Brazil	Telephone communications, except radiotelephone
37	1999	10.1	Global Crossing Ltd	Bermuda	Telecommunications	Frontier Corp	United States	Telecommunications
38	1999	9.8	ABB AG	Switzerland	Electronic and electrical equipment	ABB AB	Sweden	Electronic and electrical equipment
39	2001	9.8	AT&T Wireless Group	United States	Radiotelephone communications	NTT DoCoMo Inc	Japan	Telephone communications, except radiotelephone
40	2000	9.4	BellSouth GmbH (KPN, BellSouth)	Netherlands	Telephone communications, except radiotelephone	E-Plus Mobilfunk GmbH (Otelo)	Germany	Radiotelephone communications

Source: *World Investment Report*, various issues.

play a major role in motivating firms to undertake cross-border acquisitions. According to the internalization theory, a firm with intangible assets that have a public good property, such as technical and managerial know-how, may acquire foreign firms as a platform for using its special assets on a larger scale and, at the same time, avoid the misappropriation that may occur while transacting in foreign markets through a market mechanism. Cross-border acquisitions may also be motivated by the acquirer's desire to acquire and internalize the target firm's intangible assets. In this *backward-internalization* case, the acquirer seeks to create wealth by appropriating the rent generated from the economy of scale obtained from using the target's intangible assets on a global basis. The internalization, thus, may proceed *forward* to internalize the acquirer's assets, or *backward* to internalize the target's assets.

Morck and Yeung (1992) investigate the effect of international acquisitions on the share prices of American firms. They show that American acquiring firms with information-based intangible assets experience a significantly positive share price reaction upon foreign acquisition. This is consistent with the findings of their earlier work (1991) that the market value of the firm is positively related to its multinationality because of the firm's intangible assets, such as R&D capabilities, with public good nature. It is not the multinationality *per se* that contributes to the firm's value. Their empirical findings support the (forward-) internalization theory of FDI.

Eun, Kolodny, and Scheraga (1996), on the other hand, directly measure the magnitude of shareholders' gains from cross-border acquisitions, using a sample of major foreign acquisitions of American firms that took place during the period 1979–1990. Their findings are summarized in Exhibit 15.10. First, the exhibit shows that American target shareholders realized significant wealth gains, $103 million on average, regardless of the nationality of the acquirers. Second, the wealth gains to foreign acquiring shareholders, however, varied greatly across the acquiring countries. Shareholders of British acquirers experienced significant wealth reduction, −$123 million on average, whereas Japanese shareholders experienced major wealth increases, $228 million on average. Canadian acquisitions of American firms produced modest wealth increases for their shareholders, $15 million, on average.

Third, cross-border acquisitions are generally found to be synergy-generating corporate activities. Shareholders of the "paired" sample of American targets and foreign acquirers experienced positive combined wealth gains, $68 million, on average. Synergistic gains, however, vary a great deal across acquiring countries. Japanese acquisitions generated large combined gains, $398 million, on average, which were shared by target shareholders (43 percent) and acquiring shareholders (57 percent).[5] In contrast, British acquisitions produced a somewhat negative combined wealth gain, −$28 million, on average, and caused a wealth transfer from acquiring to target shareholders.

Eun, Kolodny, and Scheraga argue that the significant gains for Japanese acquirers can be attributed to the successful internalization of the R&D capabilities of their targets, which have a much higher R&D intensity, on average, than the targets of acquirers from other countries. Thus, the desire to "backward" internalize the target's intangible assets appears to be an important driving force for Japanese acquisition programs in the United States. This supports the backward-internalization hypothesis.[6] In the case of British acquisitions, the average combined wealth gain was negative, and the acquiring shareholders lost substantial wealth. It, thus, appears that the managers of British firms often undertook negative net present value (NPV) projects when they acquired American firms. It is well known that corporate acquisitions can be driven by

---

[5]This result is quite different from the findings of studies of domestic acquisitions showing that target shareholders capture the lion's share of synergistic gains.

[6]Japanese acquirers themselves are highly R&D intensive. This suggests that Japanese acquisitions of American firms may generate technological synergies and that Japanese firms may be capable of using American target firms' technical know-how.

Reebok laces up CCM deal
Venerable brand now U.S. owned
Hockey's growth appeals to buyer

By Bill Vlasic.

The American shoe company named for an African gazelle is now in the hockey business. Reebok International Ltd., announced plans yesterday to acquire Montreal-based hockey equipment manufacturer Hockey Company Holdings Inc. in a deal valued at $436 million. The transaction marks the sale of the last of Canada's leading hockey equipment brands to a big U.S. sporting goods maker and lengthens Reebok's reach into the continent's major sports leagues.

Hockey Co., which makes apparel and equipment under the CCM, Jofa and Koho brands, had sales of $239.9 million last year for a profit of $18.6 million. The deal will give Massachusetts-based Reebok, the second largest U.S. athletic-shoe maker, the long-term rights to supply game jerseys to the NHL's 30 teams, as well as the Canadian Hockey League and American Hockey League. Hockey Co. also makes replica jerseys for sale to the public.

Hockey Co.'s leading investors have agreed to Reebok's cash offer of $21.25 a share. The offer is for $204 million (U.S) plus $125 million assumed debt.

Reebok spokesperson John Frascotti cited hockey's increasing popularity as a reason to get into business.

"At the youth level, college level and professional level, the sport is really an appealing sport because it is captivating to both play and watch," he said. Last year Hockey Co. claimed, in a prospectus filed with Canadian securities officials, that hockey was the second-fastest growing sport in the United States, with 2.2 million participants in 2001.

Analyst Phil Yockey sees the trend, too. "Hockey is bigger than it's ever been," said Yockey, president of When2Trade of St. Louis. "Globally, soccer and hockey are where the growth is. I don't think they're going to expand any more baseball teams or football teams."

Yockey said the deal could bump Reebok's stock 10 per cent over the next year.

But that growth might depend, in part, on the outcome of the NHL's current labour negotiations, which some believe could lead to a players strike or lock-out in the 2004-05 season.

With the announcement yesterday, Reebok appears to be breaking away from Nike, which made its foray into the hockey business 10 years ago when it bought Canstar Sports Inc., maker of Bauer and Cooper skates,

for $546 million. The Bauer name dates back to 1930. In June, 2003, when Hockey Co. went public, the company claimed to have a 30 per cent share of the worldwide market for hockey equipment and apparel in 2001, with its closest competitor, Bauer Nike Hockey Inc., at 19 per cent. Hockey Co. also claims that as of late 2002, 99 per cent of NHL players used at least one piece of its gear.

Hockey Co. maintains three manufacturing facilities in the Montreal area, one in Sweden, one in Finland and a U.S. sales and distribution office, and employs, 1,300 worldwide, about 1,000 of whom work in Canada. Though he praised Hockey Co.'s management, Frascotti said he did not know if the takeover will affect its operations. "We think they have done a wonderful job in the last four, five years," he said. "We haven't gone down the path of looking for operations synergies in terms of figuring out at this stage how these organizations will dovetail. . . . We have a lot of confidence in the management team at the Hockey Company."

When Nike acquired Canstar, it promised little would change at Montreal-based company, but workforces at Canadian plants have seen cuts. More than 130 employees lost their jobs in January when regular production ceased at the Cambridge hockey stick plant. Ten to 14 employees remain but the plant is expected to fully close at the end of this month. The Mississauga goalie equipment plant and its 33 employees will stop production some time in the fall. And the St. Jerome, Que., plant is expected to lose 118 of its current 220 workers in July.

But Hockey Co. president and CEO Matt O'Toole said he does not expect the proposed takeover by Reebok to result in cuts. "I think one of the exciting things about the acquisition is it's really not based on cost reduction . . . but much more (on) growth opportunities to bring the Reebok brand name into hockey," he said. "It's business as usual for us here."

CCM, the Canadian Cycle and Motor Co., opened its doors in Weston in September, 1899. But shortly after, as the bicycle market in Canada declined, CCM stared making skates. The CCM Tackaberry (Tacks) hockey skate has been a favourite of hockey players since 1937.

Source: *Toronto Star,* Saturday, April 9, 2004.

EXHIBIT 15.10	Average Wealth Gains from Cross-Border Acquisitions: Foreign Acquisitions of American Firms					
Country of Acquirer	Number of Cases	R&D/Sales (%)		Average Wealth Gains (in Million US$)		
		Acquirer	Target	Acquirer	Target	Combined
Canada	10	0.21	0.65	14.93	85.59	100.53
Japan	15	5.08	4.81	227.83	170.66	398.49
U.K.	46	1.11	2.18	−122.91	94.55	−28.36
Other	32	1.63	2.80	−47.46	89.48	42.02
All	103	1.66	2.54	−35.01	103.19	68.18

Source: Reprinted from *Journal of Banking and Finance* 20, C. Eun, R. Kolodny, and C. Scheraga, "Cross-Border Acquisitions and Shareholder Wealth: Tests of the Synergy and Internalization Hypotheses," pp. 1559–1582, ©1996 with kind permission from Elsevier Science-NL, Sara Burgerhartstreet 25, 1055 KV Amsterdam, The Netherlands.

managers who pursue growth and diversification at the expense of shareholders' interests. As Jensen points out (1986), managers may benefit by expanding the firm beyond the size that maximizes shareholder wealth for various reasons.[7]

15.4 Political Risk and FDI

In assessing investment opportunities in a foreign country, it is important for a parent firm to take into consideration the risk arising from the fact that investments are located in a foreign country. A sovereign country can take various actions that may adversely affect the interests of MNCs. In this section, we are going to discuss how to measure and manage **political risk,** which refers to the potential losses to the parent firm resulting from adverse political developments in the host country. Political risks range from the outright expropriation of foreign assets to unexpected changes in the tax laws that hurt the profitability of foreign projects.

Political risk that firms face can differ in terms of the incidence as well as the manner in which political events affect them. Depending on the incidence, political risk can be classified into two types:

1. *Macro-risk,* where all foreign operations are affected by adverse political developments in the host country.
2. *Micro-risk,* where only selected areas of foreign business operations or particular foreign firms are affected.

The communist victory in China in 1949 is an example of macro-risk, whereas the predicament of Enron in India, which we will discuss shortly, is an example of micro-risk.

Depending on the manner in which firms are affected, political risk can be classified into three types:

1. *Transfer risk,* which arises from uncertainty about cross-border flows of capital, payments, know-how, and the like.
2. *Operational risk,* which is associated with uncertainty about the host country's policies affecting the local operations of MNCs.
3. *Control risk,* which arises from uncertainty about the host country's policy regarding ownership and control of local operations.

Examples of transfer risk include the unexpected imposition of capital controls, inbound or outbound, and withholding taxes on dividend and interest payments. Examples for operational risk, on the other hand, include unexpected changes in environmental policies, sourcing/local content requirements, minimum wage law, and restriction on access

[7]For example, managers' payments are often positively related to the size of the assets they control, not just profits.

to local credit facilities. Lastly, examples of control risk include restrictions imposed on the maximum ownership share by foreigners, mandatory transfer of ownership to local firms over a certain period of time (fade-out requirements), and the nationalization of local operations of MNCs.

Recent history is replete with examples of political risk. As Mao Ze-dong took power in China in 1949, his communist government nationalized foreign assets with little compensation. The same happened again when Castro took over Cuba in 1960. Even in a country controlled by a noncommunist government, strong nationalist sentiments can lead to the expropriation of foreign assets. For example, when Gamal Nasser seized power in Egypt in the early 1950s, he nationalized the Suez Canal, which had been controlled by British and French interests. Politically, this move was immensely popular throughout the Arab world. The International Finance in Practice box "Stories Past and Present" on page 366 provides other historical examples showing how foreign investments can be decimated by nationalistic actions in a host country.

As Exhibit 15.11 shows, the frequency of expropriations of foreign-owned assets peaked in the 1970s, when as many as 30 countries were involved in expropriations each year. Since then, however, expropriations have dwindled to practically nothing. This change reflects the popularity of *privatization,* which, in turn, is attributable to widespread failures of state-run enterprises and mounting government debts around the world.

This, however, does not mean that political risk is a thing of the past. In 1992, the Enron Development Corporation, a subsidiary of the Houston-based energy company, signed a contract to build the largest-ever power plant in India, requiring a total investment of $2.8 billion. Severe power shortages have been one of the bottlenecks hindering India's economic growth. After Enron had spent nearly $300 million, the project was cancelled by Hindu nationalist politicians in the state of Maharashtra where the plant was to be built. Subsequently, Maharashtra invited Enron to renegotiate its contract. If Enron had agreed to renegotiate, it may have had to accept a lower profitability for the project. The lack of an effective means of enforcing contracts in a foreign country is a major source of political risk associated with FDI.

Political risk is not easy to measure. Difficult as it may be, MNCs still have to measure political risk for foreign projects under consideration. Experts of political risk analysis evaluate, often subjectively, a set of key factors, such as:

- *The host country's political and government system:* Whether the host country has political and administrative infrastructure, that allow for effective and streamlined policy decisions has important implications for political risk. If a country has too many political parties and frequent changes in government (Italy, for example), government policies may become inconsistent and discontinuous, creating political risk.

- *Track records of political parties and their relative strength:* Examination of the ideological orientations and historical track records of political parties would reveal a great deal about how they would run the economy. If a party has a strong nationalistic ideology and/or socialist beliefs, it may implement policies that are detrimental to foreign interests. On the other hand, a party that subscribes to a liberal and market-oriented ideology is not very likely to take actions to damage the interests of foreign concerns. If the former party is more popular than the latter party and, thus, more likely to win the next general election, MNCs will face more political risk.

- *Integration into the world system:* If a country is politically and economically isolated and segmented from the rest of the world, it would be less willing to observe the rules of the game. North Korea, Iraq, Libya, and Cuba are examples. If a country is a member of a major international organization, such as the EU, OECD, and WTO, it is more likely to abide by the rules of the game, reducing political risk. In the same vein, as China joins the World Trade Organization (WTO), MNCs operating in China may face less political risk.

EXHIBIT 15.11

Frequency of
Expropriations of
Foreign-Owned Assets

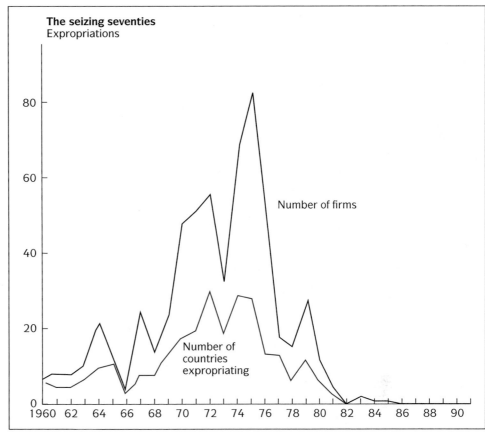

Source: *The Economist,* March 27, 1993, p. 19. ©1993 The Economist Newspaper Group, Inc. Reprinted with permission.

- *The host country's ethnic and religious stability:* As can be seen from recent civil war in Bosnia, domestic peace can be shattered by ethnic and religious conflicts, causing political risk for foreign business. Additional examples are provided by Nigeria, Rwanda, Northern Ireland, Turkey, Israel, and Sri Lanka.

- *Regional security:* Real and potential aggression from a neighbouring country is obviously a major source of political risk. Kuwait is a recent example. Such countries as South Korea and Taiwan may potentially face the same risk, depending on the future course of political developments in East Asia. Israel and its Arab neighbours still face this risk as well.

- *Key economic indicators:* Often, political events are triggered by economic situations. Political risk, thus, is not entirely independent of economic risk. For example, persistent trade deficits may induce a host country's government to delay or stop interest payments to foreign lenders, erect trade barriers, or suspend the convertibility of the local currency, causing major difficulties for MNCs. Severe inequality in income distribution (for example, in many Latin American countries) and deteriorating living standards (as in Russia after the collapse of the Soviet Union) can cause major political disturbances. Argentina's protracted economic recession and the eventual collapse of the peso–dollar parity led to the freezing of bank deposits, street riots, and three changes of the country's presidency in as many months in 2002.

MNCs may use in-house experts to do the analysis. But often, MNCs use outside experts who provide professional assessments of political risks in different countries. For example, Morgan Stanley offers an in-depth analysis of country/political risks

INTERNATIONAL FINANCE
IN PRACTICE

Stories Past and Present

An old story: Brazilian Tramways

The first electric trams in Brazil were built in 1891 by Thomson-Houston Company of Lynn, Massachusetts, which the following year became the General Electric Company. GE went on to build most of the early electric lines in Brazil and throughout Latin America, often retaining ownership. Other players soon entered the field, and, by 1907, a Canadian group had created South America's first great tramway empire, holding most of the lines in Rio de Janeiro and São Paulo as well as an assortment of telephone, gas, and water companies. The Canadians were bitterly and publicly opposed by a powerful Brazilian family, the Guinles, who also sought control of utilities in the major cities. The dispute profoundly affected the attitudes of Brazilians toward foreign-owned tramways. As a result of street riots and large-scale destruction of equipment in the city of Salvador, the Canadians curtailed their expansion efforts and in 1912 consolidated their assets into Brazilian Traction, Light & Power.

American & Foreign Power, the GE affiliate, eventually joined the fray and acquired 333 utilities in Brazil alone, with tramway systems in 13 Brazilian cities. By 1933, however, rising anti-Yankee sentiment led to freezing of tram fares at their 1909 level. A number of small companies shut down. Others switched to closed cars to increase fare collections. These cars were distinctly unpopular with riders because of the heat (and perhaps because of the better fare collection).

Still, on the eve of World War II, North American companies operated roughly two-thirds of Brazil's tramway systems. The lethal combination of parts shortages, increased hydroelectric power costs, and the effect of inflation on fixed fares led companies to cut back on service and, in some cases, to leave the business. In 1947, Brazilian Traction sold its São Paulo system to the municipal transport board, which then proceeded to raise fares by 250%. Rioting citizens pleaded for the foreigners and low rates. But, by 1950, a new president had vowed to rid Brazil of foreign corporations. AFP and most other foreign investors were quite willing by this point to sell their unprofitable tram systems to the Brazilians. By 1960, only Brazilian Traction's Rio system remained foreign owned; this last holdout went the way of the rest when it was acquired by the state in January 1965.

A recent story: Bangkok Toll Road

To help relieve Bangkok's horrible traffic congestion, a Japanese-led consortium was granted a 30-year concession to build a 12-mile toll road in the city. Just as part of the road was about to be opened in 1993, the Thai Expressway and Rapid Transit Authority (ETA) balked at the 30-baht toll that had been specified in the contract. Hesitating to absorb the proposed 10-baht toll reduction, the private consortium delayed opening the completed sections of road, and it halted further construction when its lenders suspended credit. Claiming to fear riots on the part of frustrated motorists who were angered at being unable to use the expressway, the ETA obtained a court order to force the road open and insisted on reopening negotiations to settle this and a number of other outstanding issues. Kumagai Gumi, the lead investor, reportedly with more than $100 million exposure, and its bankers, with still more at stake, cried foul, publicly accusing the Thai government of nationalizing the project. Eventually, Kumagai sold its 65% interest. And all this occurred in a country that is viewed as being very hospitable to foreign direct investment.

Source: Reprinted by permission of *Harvard Business Review.* From "Is Foreign Infrastructure Still Risky?" by Louis T. Wells and Eric S. Gleason, Sept./Oct. 1995. ©1995 by the President and Fellows of Harvard College; all rights reserved.

using a variety of data sources, including government and private sector publications, statistics provided by international organizations, newspaper articles, and on-site due diligence in countries with government officials and the private sector. Exhibits 15.12 and 15.13 provide such an analysis for two countries, South Korea and Hungary, both of which became full-fledged democracies in the last decade.

www.euromoney.com/index.html

Provides data and articles from *Euromoney.*

Euromoney also provides such an assessment twice a year.[8] As Exhibit 15.14 shows, *Euromoney* provides country ratings by political risk, credit rating, economic performance, and other factors. It also provides the overall country risk ranking based on an opinion poll of economists and political analysts, plus market data and debt figures. **Country risk** is a broader measure of risk than political risk, as the former encompasses political risk, credit risk, and other economic performances. As of 2002, such

---

[8]Each year, *Euromoney* publishes its country risk ranking in the March and September issues.

EXHIBIT 15.12	Political Risk Analysis: South Korea

Moody's: A1; S&P: A+, Economist Intelligence Unit Rating: B, Political Risk: C

Strengths	Weaknesses

Political

- Strong democratic institutions
- Member of OECD and WTO
- Barriers to foreign investment have been removed

- Regional tensions within the country and *vis-à-vis* North Korea
- Political flux likely to inhibit economic policy initiatives
- Difficult labour relations
- Business : political collusion ("chaebol" conglomerates)
- Anti-Western sentiment among students

Economic

- Solid economic growth
- Low inflation
- Prudent fiscal management
- Strong manufacturing sector/diversified exports
- Continuing appreciation of the won against the American dollar
- Current Account surplus/expanding foreign exchange reserves
- China is Korea's largest export market
- Favourable debt profile

- Lacks natural resources and oil
- Requires further financial sector reform

Key Ratios (%)	1999	2000	2001	2002	2003	2004	2005
Real GDP Growth (%/yr)	9.4	8.5	3.8	6.9	3.1	6.4	4.7
Inflation (%/yr)	0.8	2.3	4.1	2.8	3.5	3.0	2.5
External Debt/Exports (%)	78	61	61	62	55	49	45
Debt Service Ratio	24.9	11.5	14.2	7.6	6.2	5.4	5.5
Current Account Balance/GDP (%)	6.7	3.2	2.4	1.4	2.5	6.0	5.0
Budget Balance/GDP (%)	−2.5	1.1	1.2	3.3	1.1	1.2	1.2

Source: IFS, World Bank Debt Tables, IIF, Monthly Statistical Bulletin of the Bank of Korea, Morgan Stanley Credit Research.

South Korea's economy is one of the most dynamic in the world. Economic fundamentals remain strong, and a well-developed industry geared toward exports has made South Korea's economy one of the fastest growing in the world during the past decade. Exports are diversified and competitive, and foreign portfolio investment has increased greatly following recent financial deregulation and easing of foreign exchange controls. Sound fiscal policy is evidenced by budget surpluses; unemployment is low; and, by developing country standards, inflation is moderate. External debt at US$145 billion, or 40 percent of export earnings, and the debt service ratio of 20 percent are very favourable. The country's few weaknesses include a lack of natural resources, dependence on imported oil, and a financial system that needs to be deregulated, modernized, and brought to world standards. The development of the financial sector is a requirement for the further development of the domestic economy and export sector and more effective macroeconomic management.

It is in the political area that the greatest risks lie. Despite great progress (a smooth transition to democracy through presidential elections), at times, the political climate is uncertain, as South Korea is still a young democracy and the main opposition party is radical. Anti-Western sentiment is prevalent among students and some labour demonstrators. Labour relations have been difficult, with major strikes occurring every spring. The military threat from North Korea remains troubling and has re-emerged as a global concern. The financial and social cost of a prospective reunification can be great. Finally, per-capita income is still well below that of the developed countries.

countries as Switzerland, Norway, Luxembourg, and Denmark were considered practically free of political risk. In contrast, such countries as Israel, China, India, Mexico, and Brazil were rated as having substantial political risk, while such countries as Argentina, Indonesia, Russia, and Yugoslavia were rated as among the most politically risky countries. Exhibit 15.14 shows that the ranking of countries by political risk closely coincides with that by overall country risk.

Canada's National Policy Framework Concerning FDI

Since 1985, the basic legal framework for foreign investment in Canada is provided by *The Investment Canada Act* which replaced the more restrictive *Foreign Investment Review Act*. As of October 2001, the main features of the national FDI regime include the following:

Admission and establishment: Canada has a formal investment review process. Any investment by a non-Canadian to establish a new enterprise, regardless of size, or to acquire direct control of any existing business with assets of at least $200 million or in an activity that is identified as being "culturally sensitive" must be notified to Investment Canada. Notification is also required when a foreign company plans to acquire indirect control of any existing Canadian business with assets over C$50 million. Investment in some activities is covered by special legislation. For example the banking industry is governed by the *Bank Act*. Amendments to the *Bank Act* in 1992, 1997, and 1999 have facilitated foreign bank operations, and since 1999, foreign banks are permitted to open branches in Canada. The *Broadcast Act* covers foreign investment in radio, television, and broadcasting.

Ownership and control: There are no general ownership and control limitations but some foreign ownership restrictions exist in specific sectors, such as commercial aviation (25 percent foreign ownership), energy and mining (foreign investors cannot be majority owners of uranium mines), telecommunications, and fishing, (49 percent). There are no overall limitations on foreign ownership with regard to privatization.

Incentives: Canada offers a wide array of incentives at the federal and provincial levels. Municipal governments, however, are prohibited from offering tax incentives. The incentives are designed mainly to encourage research and development and promote regional economies. They are available to any qualifying investor, whether Canadian or foreign. Generally, incentives are not oriented toward the promotion of exports. Incentives may take the form of grants, loans, loan guarantees, venture capital, or tax credits.

Let us now turn to the issue of how to manage political risk. First, MNCs can take a conservative approach to foreign investment projects when faced with political risk. When a foreign project is exposed to political risk, the MNC can explicitly incorporate political risk into the capital budgeting process and adjust the project's NPV accordingly. The firm may do so either by reducing expected cash flows or by increasing the cost of capital. The MNC may undertake the foreign project only when the adjusted NPV is positive. It is important here to recognize that political risk may be diversifiable to some extent. Suppose that an MNC has assets in, say, 30 different countries. Since the political risks in different countries may not be positively correlated, the political risk associated with a single country may be diversifiable to some extent. To the extent that political risk is diversifiable, a major adjustment to the NPV may not be necessary. This consideration also suggests that MNCs can use geographic diversification of foreign investments as a means of reducing political risk. Put simply, do not put all your eggs in one basket.

Second, once an MNC decides to undertake a foreign project, it has various options to minimize exposure to political risk. For example, an MNC can form a joint venture with a local company. If the project is partially owned by a local company, the foreign government may be less inclined to expropriate it, since that would hurt the local company as well as the MNC. The MNC may also consider forming a consortium of international companies to undertake the foreign project. In this case, the MNC can reduce its exposure to political risk and, at the same time, make expropriation more costly to

| **EXHIBIT 15.13** | **Political Risk Analysis: Hungary** |

Moody's: Ba1; S&P: BB, Economic Intelligence Unit Rating: B; Political Risk: B

Strengths	**Weaknesses**
Political	
• New member of the European Union (2004)	• Centre-left ruling coalition put low priority on economic reforms
• Reform-oriented finance minister	• Central bank and government in frequent conflict
• Ethnically homogeneous	• Inefficient middle-rank government officials
• Labour supports reform	
Economic	
• New member of European Unnion	• Problems in meeting Euro criteria—Euro entry unlikely before 2010
• Commitment to pre-Euro convergence program	• Inflation rising and running above EU average
• Investment sentiment strong	• External debt and debt service ratio rising
• Tourism, a major sector, expected to grow	• Companies are financially weak
• Europe is largest export market	• Excess industrial capacity
	• Requires further financial sector reform
	• Declining population

Key Ratios (%)	1999	2000	2001	2002	2003	2004	2005
Real GDP Growth (%/yr)	4.2	5.2	3.8	3.5	2.9	3.3	3.9
Inflation (%/yr)	10.0	9.8	9.2	5.3	4.7	7.5	4.7
External Debt/Exports (%)	94	83	77	76	81	82	82
Debt Service Ratio	23	22	35	18	16	17	19
Current Account Balance/GDP (%)	−2.5	−3.9	−1.7	−2.7	−5.5	−6.2	−5.2
Budget Balance/GDP (%)	−3.2	−3.0	−0.5	−5.5	−2.2	−1.1	0.2

Source: IFS, World Bank Debt Tables, IIF, National Bank of Hungary, Morgan Stanley Credit Research.

Hungary is unique among former Eastern Bloc countries—including Poland, Czechoslovakia, Bulgaria and Romania—for having made a relatively smooth transition to a market economy following the collapse of the Soviet Union without splitting up (as did Czechoslovakia) or encountering internal strife as in Poland. Hungary's transition to a multiparty democracy was completed with general elections in 1990. This country of 10 million people enjoys relative stability in a region torn by ethnic violence.

The most significant recent political and economic initiative by Hungary is its accession to the European Union on May 1, 2004, along with Poland, the Czech Republic, and seven smaller states. The economic prerequisites to join the EU, including liberalization of trade and investment as well as commitment to pre-euro convergence criteria (to low maximum levels of interest rates, inflation and deficits) will, in the long run, strengthen Hungary's industrial position. In the continuing transition to an efficient and stable economy, however, the country faces serious challenges. The political machinery is still burdened by the attitudes and influence of <u>apparatchiks</u> of the old regime. Conflict between the central bank (monetary policy and exchange rate management) and the government (fiscal policy and regulation) slows the program for constructive market reform. Dependency on Europe as the primary export destination—with Europe experiencing slow growth—is related to chronic unemployment, persistent current account deficits, increases in foreign borrowing, and a rising debt-service ratio.

Hungary's economic transformation and resilience in the post-Soviet era is impressive. The process of economic reform, is aimed at a dynamic private sector, restructured state sector, and liberalized trade. The private sector now represents 45 percent of GDP, from only 10 percent in 1989. Trade and cross-border investment policies have been liberalized to the EU standard.

EXHIBIT 15.14

Country Risk Rankings

Rank	Country	Country Risk	Political Risk	Economic Performance	Credit Rating
	Weighting:	100.00	25.00	25.00	10.00
1	Luxembourg	99.78	24.93	25.00	10.00
2	Switzerland	98.51	24.95	23.59	10.00
3	Norway	97.67	25.00	22.70	10.00
4	Denmark	95.99	24.62	21.74	9.79
5	United States	95.15	24.13	21.02	10.00
6	Sweden	94.12	24.19	20.37	9.58
7	Finland	93.81	24.62	19.22	10.00
8	Netherlands	93.60	24.42	19.20	10.00
9	Ireland	93.20	23.80	19.48	10.00
10	Austria	93.04	24.04	19.02	10.00
11	United Kingdom	92.70	24.17	18.56	10.00
12	France	92.37	24.21	18.19	10.00
13	Germany	91.95	24.07	17.90	10.00
14	Canada	91.87	24.29	17.82	9.79
15	Belgium	91.00	23.23	18.55	9.38
16	Australia	90.39	23.13	18.56	8.96
17	Singapore	90.24	23.25	18.84	9.79
18	Japan	88.68	21.50	19.26	8.75
19	Spain	88.59	23.06	16.02	9.58
20	Italy	88.48	22.84	16.50	9.17
21	Iceland	86.75	20.40	18.59	7.92
22	New Zealand	86.69	22.35	15.44	8.96
23	Bermuda	85.79	22.04	19.80	8.96
24	Portugal	84.95	22.16	13.69	9.17
25	Taiwan	82.60	21.14	15.31	8.13
34	South Korea	69.46	18.34	12.60	6.46
35	Hungary	69.25	17.79	10.57	6.25
38	Israel	68.67	15.99	12.22	6.46
39	Saudi Arabia	65.78	15.66	9.80	4.38
40	Czech Republic	65.64	17.53	10.47	5.83
42	Poland	64.60	16.40	9.09	5.63
43	Chile	64.49	16.76	9.77	6.04
50	Mexico	60.81	15.09	9.10	4.58
52	South Africa	59.06	14.94	8.98	4.58
58	China	56.39	16.97	9.39	5.83
59	Thailand	56.28	14.73	8.77	4.38
61	India	55.10	14.79	7.63	3.13
67	Egypt	50.28	12.05	6.43	3.96
74	Iran	46.38	12.03	6.61	1.88
75	Vietnam	46.09	11.12	7.12	2.29
76	Russia	45.03	11.74	8.26	2.50
80	Turkey	43.76	8.12	6.39	1.25
83	Brazil	42.62	9.13	7.25	1.67
96	Indonesia	37.45	6.88	5.70	0.83
129	Yugoslavia	29.65	3.60	5.10	0.00
146	Argentina	27.13	2.56	4.42	0.21
159	Nigeria	24.47	6.57	4.72	0.00
169	Zimbabwe	22.30	2.52	0.05	0.00
182	Cuba	13.31	4.36	7.78	0.00
185	North Korea	1.38	0.00	0.22	0.00

Source: *Euromoney*, September 2002.

the host government. Understandably, the host government may not wish to take action that antagonizes many countries at the same time. Alternatively, MNCs can use local debt to finance the foreign project. In this case, the MNC has an option to repudiate its debt if the host government takes action to hurt its interests.

Third, MNCs may purchase insurance against the hazard of political risk. Such insurance policies, which are available in many advanced countries, are especially useful to small firms that are less well equipped to deal with political risk on their own. In Canada, the **Export Development Corporation** (EDC), a federally owned organization, offers insurance against (1) the inconvertibility of foreign currencies, (2) expropriation of Canadian-owned assets overseas, (3) destruction of Canadian-owned physical properties due to war, revolution, and other violent political events in foreign countries, and (4) loss of business income due to political violence. EDC's primary goal in respect of FDI is to support Canadian private investments in the economies of developing countries. Alternatively, MNCs may also purchase tailor-made insurance policies from private insurers, such as Lloyd's of London.

When the political risk faced by an MNC can be fully covered by an insurance contract, the MNC can subtract the insurance premium from the expected cash flows from the project in computing its NVP. The MNC then can use the usual cost of capital, which would be used to evaluate domestic investment projects, in discounting the expected cash flows from foreign projects. Lastly, it is pointed out that many countries have concluded bilateral or multilateral investment protection agreements, effectively eliminating most political risk. As a result, if an MNC invests in a country that signed the investment protection agreement with the MNC's home country, it need not be overly concerned with political risk.

One particular type of political risk that MNCs and investors may face is corruption associated with the abuse of public offices for private benefits. Investors may often encounter demands for bribes from politicians and government officials for contracts and smooth bureaucratic processes. If companies refuse to make *grease payments*, they may lose business opportunities or face difficult bureaucratic red tape. If companies pay, on the other hand, they may risk violating laws or being embarrassed when the payments are discovered and reported in the media. Corruption can be found anywhere in the world. But it is a much more serious problem in many developing and transition economies, where the state sector is large, democratic institutions are weak, and the press is often muzzled. In 1997, the OECD also adopted a treaty to criminalize the bribery of foreign officials by companies. Bribery, thus, is both morally and legally wrong for companies from most of the developed countries. Another particular risk that companies may face is extortion demands from Mafia-style criminal organizations. For example, the majority of companies in Russia are known to have paid extortion demands. To deal with this kind of situation, it is important for companies to hire people who are familiar with local operating environments, strengthen local support for the company, and enhance physical security measures.

SUMMARY

This chapter discusses various issues associated with foreign direct investments (FDI) by MNCs, which play a key role in shaping the nature of the emerging global economy.

1. Firms become *multinational* when they undertake FDI. FDI may involve either the establishment of new production facilities in foreign countries or acquisitions of existing foreign businesses.

2. During the recent five-year period 1997–2002, total annual worldwide FDI flows amounted to about $830 billion on average. The United States is the largest recipient, as well as initiator, of FDI. Besides the United States, France, Germany, the Netherlands, and the United Kingdom are the leading sources of FDI outflows,

whereas the United Kingdom, China, France, Germany, and the Netherlands are the major destinations for FDI in recent years.

3. Most existing theories of FDI put emphasis on various market imperfections, that is, imperfections in product, factor, and capital markets, as the key motivating forces driving FDI.

4. The *internalization* theory of FDI holds that firms that have intangible assets with a public good property tend to invest directly in foreign countries in order to use these assets on a larger scale and, at the same time, avoid the misappropriations that may occur while transacting in foreign markets through a market mechanism.

5. According to the product life-cycle theory, when firms first introduce new products, they choose to produce at home, close to their customers. Once the product becomes standardized and mature, it becomes important to cut production costs to stay competitive. At this stage, firms may set up production facilities in low-cost foreign countries.

6. In recent years, a growing portion of FDI has taken the form of cross-border acquisitions of existing businesses. *Synergistic* gains may arise if the acquirer is motivated to take advantage of various market imperfections.

7. Imperfections in the market for intangible assets, such as R&D capabilities, may play a key role in motivating cross-border acquisitions. The internalization may proceed *forward* to internalize the acquirer's intangible assets or *backward* to internalize the target's intangible assets.

8. In evaluating political risk, experts focus their attention on a set of key factors, such as the host country's political/government system, historical records of political parties and their relative strengths, integration of the host country into the world political/economic system, the host country's ethnic and religious stability, regional security, and key economic indicators.

9. In evaluating a foreign investment project, it is important for the MNC to consider the effect of political risk, as a sovereign country can change the *rules of the game.* The MNC may adjust the cost of capital upward or lower the expected cash flows from the foreign project. Or the MNC may purchase insurance policies against the hazard of political risks.

KEY TERMS

country risk, *366*
cross-border mergers and acquisitions, *347*
Export Development Corporation (EDC), *371*

FDI flows, *347*
FDI stocks, *348*
foreign direct investments (FDI), *344*
greenfield investment, *357*
intangible assets, *353*

internalization theory, *353*
political risk, *363*
product life-cycle theory, *354*
synergistic gains, *357*

QUESTIONS

1. Recently, many foreign firms from both the developed and the developing countries acquired high-tech American firms. What has motivated these firms to acquire American firms?

2. Japanese MNCs, such as Toyota, Toshiba, and Matsushita, made extensive investments in Southeast Asian countries, such as Thailand, Malaysia, and Indonesia. What forces are driving Japanese investments in this region?

3. Since NAFTA was established, many Asian firms, especially those from Japan and Korea, have made extensive investments in Mexico. Why do you think these Asian firms decided to build production facilities in Mexico?

4. How would you explain the fact that China emerged as the second most important recipient of FDI after the United States in recent years?

5. Explain the internalization theory of FDI. What are the strengths and weaknesses of the theory?

6. Explain product life-cycle theory of FDI. What are the strengths and weaknesses of the theory?

7. Why do you think the host country tends to resist cross-border acquisitions, rather than greenfield investments?

8. How would you incorporate political risk into the capital budgeting process of foreign investment projects?

9. Explain and compare forward versus backward internalization.

10. It has been ovserved that the profitability of Canadian FDI in the United States is significantly lower than the profitability of American investments in Canada. What factors might account for this difference?

11. Define *country risk*. How is it different from political risk?

12. What are the advantages and disadvantages of FDI as compared with a licensing agreement with a foreign partner?

13. What operational and financial measures can an MNC take to minimize the political risk associated with a foreign investment project?

14. Study the experience of Enron in India and discuss what we can learn from it for the management of political risk.

15. Discuss the different ways political events in a host country may affect local operations of an MNC.

16. What factors would you consider in evaluating the political risk associated with making FDI in a foreign country.

INTERNET EXERCISE

You are hired as a political consultant for General Motors Company, which is considering building automobile plants in three countries: Brazil, China, and Poland. Choose a country and analyze the political risk of investing in that country. In doing so, utilize such websites as: www.odci.gov/cia/publications/factbook, or any other relevant Internet resources. You may prepare a final report to GM using a similar format to Exhibit 15.12.

MINI CASE

Enron versus Bombay Politicians*

On August 3, 1995, the Maharashtra state government dominated by the nationalist, right-wing Bharatiya Janata Party (BJP), abruptly cancelled Enron's $2.9 billion power project in Dabhol, located south of Bombay, the industrial heartland of India. This came as a huge blow to Rebecca P. Mark, the chairman and chief executive of Enron's international power unit, who spearheaded the Houston-based energy giant's international investment drive. Upon the news release, Enron's share price fell immediately by about 10 percent to US$33½. Mark sprang to action to resuscitate the deal with the Maharashtra state, promising concessions. This effort, however, was met with scorn from BJP politicians. Enron's Dabhol debacle cast a serious doubt on the company's aggressive global expansion strategy, involving some $10 billion in projects in power plants and pipelines spanning across Asia, South America, and the Middle East.

Enron became involved in the project in 1992 when the new reformist government of the Congress Party (I), led by Prime Minister Narasimha Rao, was keen on

---

*The depiction of political risk in this mini-case remains relevant despite the subsequent and infamous collapse of Enron and the change in the Indian political scene.

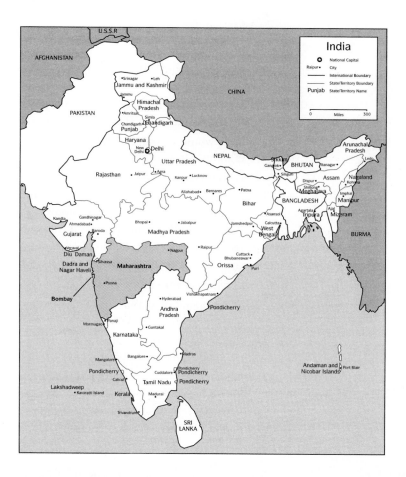

attracting foreign investment in infrastructure. After meeting with the Indian government officials visiting Houston in May, Enron dispatched executives to India to hammer out a "memorandum of understanding" in just 10 days to build a massive 2,015-megawatt Dabhol power complex. New Delhi placed the project on a fast track and awarded it to Enron without competitive bidding. Subsequently, the Maharashtra State Electricity Board (MSEB) agreed to buy 90 percent of the power Dabhol would produce. Two other American companies, General Electric (GE) and Bechtel Group, agreed to join Enron as partners for the Dabhol project.

In the process of structuring the deal, Enron made a profound political miscalculation: It did not seriously take into consideration a rising backlash against foreign investments by an opposition coalition led by the BJP. During the state election campaign in early 1995, the BJP called for a re-evaluation of the Enron project. Jay Dubashi, the BJP's economic advisor, said that the BJP would review all foreign investments already in India, and "If it turns out that we have to ask them to go, then we'll ask them to go." Instead of waiting for the election results, Enron rushed to close the deal and began construction, apparently believing that a new government would find it difficult to unwind the deal when construction was already under way. Enron was not very concerned with local political sentiments. Enron fought to keep the contract details confidential, but a successful lawsuit by a Bombay consumer group forced the company to reveal the details: Enron would receive 7.4 cents per kilowatt-hour from MSEB and Enron's rate of return would be 23 percent, far higher than 16 percent over the capital cost that the Indian government guaranteed to others. Critics cited the disclosure as proof that Enron had exaggerated project costs to begin with and that the deal might have involved corruption.

The BJP won the 1995 election in Maharashtra state and fulfilled its promise. Manohar Joshi, the newly elected Chief Minister of Maharashtra, who campaigned on a pledge to "drive Enron into the sea," promptly cancelled the project, citing inflated project costs and too high electricity rates. This pledge played well with Indian voters with visceral distrust of foreign companies since the British colonial era. (It helps to recall that India was first colonized by a foreign company, the British East India Company.) By the time the project was cancelled, Enron already had invested some $200 million. Officials of the Congress Party who championed the Dabhol project in the first place did not come to the rescue of the project. The BJP criticized the Congress Party, rightly or wrongly, for being too corrupt to reform the economy and too cozy with business interests. In an effort to pressure Maharashtra to reverse its decision, Enron "pushed like hell" the U.S. Energy Department to make a statement in June 1995 to the effect that cancelling the Enron deal could adversely affect other power projects. The statement only compounded the situation. The BJP politicians immediately criticized the statement as an attempt by Washington to bully India.

After months of nasty exchanges and lawsuits, Enron and Maharashtra negotiators agreed to revive the Dabhol project. The new deal requires that Enron cut the project's cost from $2.9 billion to $2.5 billion, lower the proposed electricity rates, and make a state-owned utility a new 30 percent partner of the project. A satisfied Chief Minister Joshi stated: "Maharashtra has gained tremendously by this decision." Enron needed to make a major concession to demonstrate that its global power projects are still on track. The new deal led Enron to withdraw a lawsuit seeking $500 million in damages from Maharashtra for the cancellation of the Dabhol project.

Discussion Points

1. Discuss the chief mistakes that Enron made in India.
2. Discuss what Enron might have done differently to avoid its predicament in India.

REFERENCES & SUGGESTED READINGS

Aharoni, Yair. "The Foreign Investment Decision Process." *Harvard Business School,* 1966.

Caves, Richard. *Multinational Enterprise and Economic Analysis.* Cambridge, MA: Harvard University Press, 1982.

Doukas, John, and Nicholas Travlos. "The Effect of Corporate Multinationalism on Shareholders' Wealth: Evidence from International Acquisitions." *Journal of Finance* 43 (1988), pp. 1161–75.

Dunning, John. *Economic Analysis and the Multinational Enterprise.* New York: Praeger, 1975.

The Economist. "Multinationals, a Survey." (March 27, 1993), pp. 4–20.

Dunning, John H. "Location and the Multinational Enterprise: A Neglected Factor." *Journal of International Business Studies* 29 (1998), pp. 45–66.

Eun, C., R. Kolody, and C. Scheraga. "Cross-Border Acquisitions and Shareholder Wealth: Tests of Synergy and Internalization Hypotheses." *Journal of Banking and Finance* 20 (1996), pp. 1559–82.

Harris, Robert, and David Ravenscraft. "The Role of Acquisitions in Foreign Direct Investment: Evidence from the U.S. Stock Market." *Journal of Finance* 46 (1991), pp. 825–44.

Hejazi, Walid. "Canada's FDI experience: What Kind of Host Are We?" *Policy Options/Options Politiques.* Montreal: The Institute for Research on Public Policy, April 2004.

Hejazi, Walid and Peter Pauly. "Motivations for FDI and Domestic Capital Formation." *Journal of International Business Studies* 34 (2002), pp. 282–89.

Hymer, Stephen. *The International Operations of National Firms: A Study of Direct Foreign Investment.* Cambridge, MA: MIT Press, 1976.

Jensen, Michael. "The Takeover Controversy: Analysis and Evidence." *Midland Corporate Finance Journal* 5 (1986), pp. 1–27.

Kang, Jun-Koo. "The International Market for Corporate Control: Mergers and Acquisitions of U.S. Firms by Japanese Firms." *Journal of Financial Economics* 35 (1993), pp. 345–71.

Kindleberger, Charles. *American Business Abroad.* New Haven, CT: Yale University Press, 1969.

Kobrin, Stephen. "Political Risk: A Review and Reconsideration." *Journal of International Business Studies* 10 (1979), pp. 67–80.

Lessard, Donald R. "Incorporating Country Risk in the Valuation of Offshore Projects." 9, No. 3., (1996) *Journal of Applied Corporate Finance,* pp. 52–63.

Mandel, Robert. "The Overseas Private Investment Corporation and International Investment." *Columbia Journal of World Business* 19 (1984), pp. 89–95.

Magee, Stephen. "Information and the Multinational Corporation: An Appropriability Theory of Direct Foreign Investment." In Jagdish N. Bhagwati (ed.), *The New International Economic Order.* Cambridge, MA: MIT Press, 1977.

Morck, Randall, and Bernard Yeung. "Why Investors Value Multinationality." *Journal of Business* 64 (1991), pp. 165–87.

——. "Internalization: An Event Study Test." *Journal of International Economics* 33 (1992), pp. 41–56.

Ragazzione, Giorgio. "Theories of Determinants of Direct Foreign Investment." *IMF Staff Papers* 20 (1973), pp. 471–98.

Rugman, Alan. "Internalization Is Still a General Theory of Foreign Direct Investment." *Weltwirtschaftliche Archiv.* 121 (1985), pp. 570–76.

Rummel, R. J., and David Heenan. "How Multinationals Analyze Political Risk." *Harvard Business Review* 56 (1978), pp. 67–76.

The Transnational Corporations Journal, published in three issues per year by *The UN Centre on Transnationals* (Geneva) is a rich source of information on foreign direct investment.

The World Investment Report, Geneva: UNCTAD (United Nations Conference on Trade and Development), annual.

Vernon, Raymond. "The Product Cycle Hypothesis in a New International Environment." *Oxford Bulletin of Economics and Statistics* 41 (1979), pp. 255–67.

CHAPTER 16

International Capital Structure and the Cost of Capital

CAPITAL STRUCTURE refers to the right-hand side of the corporate balance sheet. A company's capital structure is a description of how that company is financed—how much debt and how much equity. Corporate decisions on capital structure generally involve adjusting the debt–equity ratio so as minimize the overall cost of capital. Whereas debt tends to be relatively cheap with interest payments that are tax deductible, equity is generally more costly. However, since a firm cannot raise low-cost debt without having an equity base, the choice of the optimal debt–equity ratio can be a complex problem involving interest and tax rates, business and financial risk, and equity market conditions.

This chapter deals with international aspects of capital structure and the cost of capital. The main theme is that modern corporations look beyond their national borders and outside their domestic financial markets to raise capital. For several substantial reasons discussed in this chapter, going abroad for capital can provide significant benefits in the form of expanded access to capital and lower capital costs. A lower cost of capital enhances corporate value. Furthermore, since the cost of capital is the cut-off or "hurdle rate" in investment decisions, a lower cost of capital can make otherwise unattractive projects attractive.

There is a close connection between the corporate themes of the chapter and the global phenomenon of *capital market integration*. Capital market integration refers to the increasing ease of accessing capital from other countries. As we saw in Chapter 8 on international equity markets and in Chapter 11 on international portfolio investment, corporate bonds and shares of foreign companies are readily accessible to investors virtually anywhere in the world. Impediments and costs to purchasing foreign securities are much less onerous than they once were. When investors and corporations buy or sell securities in other countries, they are part of the process of international capital market integration.

If international capital markets were completely integrated, it would not matter whether firms raised capital from domestic or foreign sources, since the cost of capital would be equalized across countries. Just as a high degree of competition in, say, the market for produce means that you do not have to run all over town to find the best price for lettuce—and so you can confidently shop at your local green grocer—a truly integrated international capital market would reflect global competition for capital, and hence, local capital costs would equal global capital costs. However, barriers to cross-border capital flows including incompatible regulations, costly information, and foreign exchange risk can cause segmentation in the markets. If capital markets are segmented to some degree, firms may be able to create value for their shareholders by issuing securities in foreign as well as domestic markets.

Cross-listing a firm's shares on both domestic and foreign stock exchanges is an effective way for a firm to counteract the negative effects of market segmentation. This is essentially "internationalizing" capital structure. Many Canadian firms, including Alcan, Bombardier, CN, Domtar, Nortel, and TD Bank, that are listed on the Toronto Stock Exchange are also listed on the New York Stock Exchange or NASDAQ. Large global firms, such as IBM, Sony, and British Petroleum, are simultaneously listed and traded on the New York, London, and Tokyo stock exchanges. By internationalizing its share ownership structure, a firm can potentially increase its share price and lower its cost of capital.

In this chapter, we examine various implications of internationalizing the capital structure for the firm's market value and cost of capital. We look at existing restrictions on foreign ownership of domestic firms and their effects on the corporate cost of capital. We are ultimately concerned with the ability of a multinational corporation (MNC) to obtain capital at the lowest possible cost so that it can profitably expand its capital expenditure program and enhance shareholder wealth. We begin the chapter with a review of cost of capital concepts and basic asset pricing theory.

16.1   Cost of Capital

The **cost of capital** is the minimum rate of return an investment project must generate in order to pay its financing costs. If the return on an investment project is just equal to the cost of capital, undertaking the project will leave the firm's value unaffected. When a firm identifies and undertakes an investment project that generates a return exceeding its cost of capital, the firm's value will increase. It is, thus, important for a value-maximizing firm to try to lower its cost of capital.

When a firm has both debt and equity in its capital structure, its financing cost can be represented by the **weighted average cost of capital.** It can be computed by weighting the after-tax borrowing cost of the firm and the cost of equity capital, using the capital structure ratio as the weight. Specifically,

$$K = (1 - \lambda)K_l + \lambda (1 - \tau)i \qquad \qquad (16.1)$$

where:

K = weighted average cost of capital,

K_l = cost of equity capital for a levered firm,

i = before-tax cost of debt capital (i.e., borrowing),

τ = marginal corporate income tax rate, and

λ = debt-to-total-market-value ratio.

In general, both K_l and i increase as the proportion of debt in the firm's capital structure increases. At the optimal combination of debt and equity financing, however, the weighted average cost of capital (K) will be the lowest. Firms may have an incentive to use debt financing to take advantage of the tax-deductibility of interest payments. In most countries, interest payments are tax deductible, unlike dividend payments. Debt financing, however, must be balanced against possible bankruptcy costs associated with higher debt. A trade-off between the tax advantage of debt and potential bankruptcy costs is, thus, a major factor in determining optimal capital structure.

Optimal capital structure is important, since maximizing shareholder wealth implies financing new capital expenditures up to the point where the marginal return on invested capital equals the cost of capital. Policy that lowers the firm's cost of capital will increase profitable capital expenditures that the firm takes on and increase shareholder wealth. Internationalizing the firm's cost of capital is one such policy.

Exhibit 16.1 illustrates this point. The value-maximizing firm would undertake an investment project as long as the internal rate of return on the project exceeds the firm's

EXHIBIT 16.1

The Firm's Investment Decision and the Cost of Capital

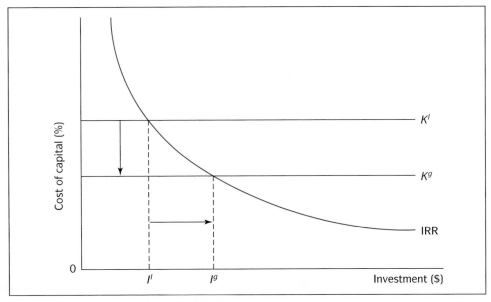

Note: K^l and K^g represent, respectively, the cost of capital under local and international capital structures; IRR represents the internal rate of return on investment projects; I^l and I^g represent the optimal investment outlays under the alternative capital structures.

cost of capital. When investment projects are ranked in descending order in terms of internal rate of return (IRR), the firm faces a negatively sloped IRR schedule, as depicted in the exhibit. The firm's optimal capital expenditure is determined at the point where the IRR schedule intersects the cost of capital.

Now, suppose that the firm's cost of capital can be reduced from K^l under the local capital structure to K^g under an internationalized capital structure. The firm can then increase its profitable investment outlay from I^l to I^g, contributing to the firm's value. It is important, however, to note that a reduced cost of capital increases the firm's value not only through increased investments in new projects but also through revaluation of the cash flows from existing projects.

16.2 Cost of Capital in Segmented versus Integrated Markets

The main difficulty in computing the financing cost (K) of a firm is related to the cost of equity capital (K_e). The cost of equity capital is the expected return on the firm's shares that investors require. This return is typically estimated using the **Capital Asset Pricing Model (CAPM).** The CAPM states that the equilibrium expected rate of return on a share (or more generally any security) is a linear function of the systematic risk inherent in the security. Specifically, the CAPM-determined expected rate of return for the ith security is:

$$\bar{R}_i = R_f + (\bar{R}_M - R_f)\beta_i \tag{16.2}$$

where R_f is the risk-free rate of return and $\bar{R}_M$ is the expected return on the **market portfolio,** the market-value-weighted portfolio of all assets. **Beta,** β_i, is a measure of systematic risk inherent in security i. **Systematic risk** is the nondiversifiable market risk of an asset. The CAPM equation shows that the required return of security i, $\bar{R}_i$, increases in β_i. The greater the market risk, the greater is the required return. Beta is calculated as $Cov(R_i,R_M)/Var(R_M)$, where $Cov(R_i,R_M)$ is the covariance of future returns between security i and the market portfolio and $Var(R_M)$ is the variance of returns of the market portfolio.

Now, suppose that international financial markets are segmented and, as a result, investors can only diversify domestically. In this case, the market portfolio (M) in the CAPM formula would represent the domestic market portfolio, proxied by S&P/TSX in Canada. The relevant risk measure in pricing assets is beta measured against the domestic market portfolio. In segmented capital markets, the same future cash flows are likely to be priced differently across countries, as they would be viewed as having different systematic risks by investors from different countries.

On the other hand, suppose international financial markets are fully integrated and, consequently, investors can diversify internationally. In this case, the market portfolio in the CAPM ought to be the "world" market portfolio comprising all assets in the world. The relevant risk measure then is beta measured against the world market portfolio. In integrated international financial markets, the same future cash flows are priced in the same way everywhere. Investors require, on average, lower expected returns on securities under integration than under segmentation because they can diversify risk more efficiently under integration.

EXAMPLE 16.1 **A Numerical Illustration** Suppose the domestic Canadian beta of Barrick, the Toronto based gold company, is 1.2. This Canadian beta for Barrick is estimated in a regression of the returns on Barrick shares on the returns of the S&P/TSX, the Toronto index. In addition, let us say that the expected return on the S&P/TSX is 12 percent and the Canadian risk-free interest rate, proxied by the Canadian Treasury Bill rate, is 4 percent. If Canadian capital markets are segmented from the rest of the world, the expected return on Barrick shares is determined as follows:

$$R_{BAR}^{CAN} = R_f^{CAN} + (R_{TSX}^{CAN} - R_f^{CAN})\, \beta_{BAR}^{CAN}$$

$$= 4 + (12 - 4)\, 1.2 = 13.6$$

In view of the Canadian systematic risk of Barrick, Canadian investors require 13.6 percent return on their investment in Barrick shares.

Suppose now that Canadian capital markets are integrated with the rest of the world. For all practical purposes, it enough to say that Canadian and American capital markets are integrated. In this situation, American investors can hold Barrick shares. American investors would be concerned with Barrick's beta as estimated in a regression of Barrick shares on the returns of the S&P 500, the New York index. Say, this American beta for Barrick is 1.0. Say, the expected return on the S&P 500 is 13 percent and the American risk-free interest rate, proxied by the U.S. Treasury Bill rate, is 4 percent. Then, the American valuation of Barrick is:

$$R_{BAR} = R_f + (R_{NYSE}^{US} - R_f^{US})\, \beta_{BAR}^{US}$$

$$= 4 + (13 - 4)\, 1.0 = 13$$

American investors would accept a lower return on Barrick shares than Canadian investors. American investors would bid up the price of Barrick shares.

As a matter of fact, Barrick is listed on both the Toronto Stock Exchange (ABX.TO) and the New York Stock Exchange (ABX).

Obviously, the integration or segmentation of international financial markets has major implications for determining the cost of capital. However, empirical evidence on the issue is less than clear-cut. Increasingly, such researchers as Harvey (1991) and Chan, Karolyi, and Stulz (1992) find it difficult to reject the international version of the

CAPM, suggesting that international financial markets are integrated, rather than segmented. Other researchers, including French and Poterba (1991), however, have documented that investors actually diversify internationally only to a limited extent, suggesting that international financial markets should be more segmented than integrated. In a study examining the integration of the Canadian and American stock markets, Mittoo (1992) has found that Canadian shares cross-listed on American exchanges are priced in an integrated market and that segmentation is predominant for those Canadian shares that are not cross-listed.

These studies suggest that international financial markets are certainly not segmented anymore but still are not fully integrated. If international financial markets are less than fully integrated, which is likely to be the case, there can be systematic differences in the cost of capital among countries.

16.3 Does the Cost of Capital Differ among Countries?

It is often argued that Canadian and American firms labour under the burden of heavier capital costs relative to foreign rivals, especially in Japan and Germany. This argument, of course, implies that capital markets are less than fully integrated. It would be useful to directly compare the cost of capital across countries to see if the argument has any merit.

McCauley and Zimmer (1994) provide a direct comparison of the cost of capital among four major countries, Germany, Japan, the United Kingdom, and the United States. They first estimate the costs of debt and equity capital and then compute the cost of funds as the weighted average cost of capital using the capital structure in each country as the weight. They compute the cost of capital in real terms after adjusting for the inflation rate. In their study, the cost of debt is measured as the real after-tax rate of interest faced by nonfinancial corporate borrowers. In estimating the cost of equity, McCauley and Zimmer first determine true economic earnings adjusting for various distortions, such as depreciation, inventory profits, and cross-holdings of shares, and compare those internationally comparable earnings with the respective national market capitalizations.

The estimated debt and equity costs they compute are presented in Exhibits 16.2 and 16.3, respectively. As Exhibit 16.2 shows, prior to 1982, real debt costs were often negative and divergent among countries, reflecting the distortions of inflation. Since then, debt costs have become similar for American, Japanese, and British firms. German firms apparently enjoyed a lower cost of debt during the period 1982–1988. Exhibit 16.3 shows that Japanese firms clearly enjoyed a lower cost of equity capital than the other three countries, especially during the period 1986–1989. It is noteworthy, however, that the costs of equity of the four countries have converged in the 1990s.

Exhibit 16.4 shows the trend in the capital structure as measured by the debt-to-equity value ratio in each of the four countries. Clearly, Germany and Japan have higher debt ratios than the United States and the United Kingdom. There are a few reasons for the higher debt ratios for German and Japanese firms. First, historically, the banking sector in both countries has played a much more important role in corporate financing than stock markets. Second, both German and Japanese firms could carry high levels of debt without seriously exposing themselves to default risks since banks, which often belong to the same business concern or *keiretsu,* frequently hold bonds as well as shares of these firms. This tends to reduce the agency problems (or conflict of interest) between bondholders and shareholders.[1] German and Japanese firms,

---

[1] Evidence, summarized in Stulz (1996), indicates that the agency costs of managerial discretion are lower in Japan than in the United States. This implies that Japanese managers are less likely to undertake unprofitable investment projects at the expense of existing shareholders. Unless closely monitored by shareholders, the management may pursue corporate empire building for its own interests. Stulz argues that if agency costs are indeed lower in Japan, then the cost of capital can be lower in Japan than the United States, even if international financial markets are integrated.

EXHIBIT 16.2

Effective Real After-Tax Cost of Debt

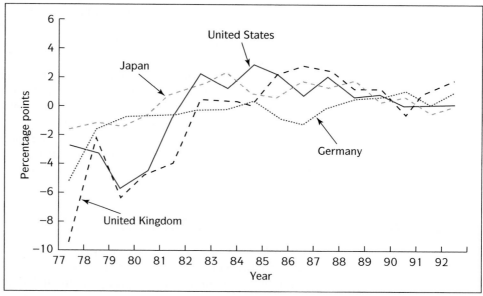

Source: Robert McCauley and Steven Zimmer, "Exchange Rates and International Differences in the Cost of Capital," in Y. Amihud and R. Levich (eds.), *Exchange Rates and Corporate Performance* (Burr Ridge, Ill.: Irwin, 1994).

EXHIBIT 16.3

Cost of Equity

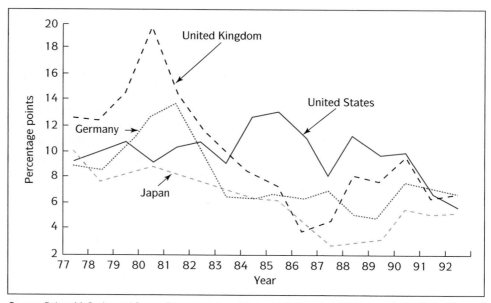

Source: Robert McCauley and Steven Zimmer, "Exchange Rates and International Differences in the Cost of Capital," in Y. Amihud and R. Levich (eds.), *Exchange Rates and Corporate Performance* (Burr Ridge, Ill.: Irwin, 1994).

however, "deleveraged" substantially in recent years, whereas the capital structure of American and British firms stayed relatively stable through time.

The cost of funds (that is, the weighted average cost of capital) advantage enjoyed by Japanese and German firms are evident from Exhibit 16.5. The German firms' advantage stemmed mostly from low-cost, short-term debts, whereas the Japanese firms' advantage arose from both low debt and equity costs. Exhibit 16.5, however, also shows the differential cost of funds among countries diminishing in the 1990s.

In perfect markets, firms would be indifferent between raising funds abroad or at home. When markets are imperfect, however, international financing can lower the

EXHIBIT 16.4

Debt-to-Equity Value Ratios

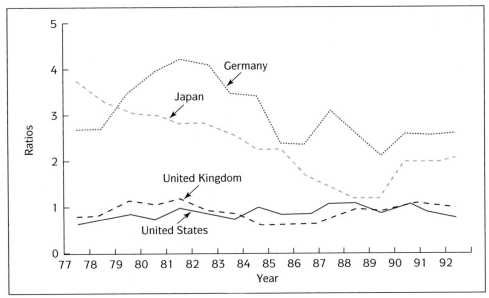

Source: Robert McCauley and Steven Zimmer, "Exchange Rates and International Differences in the Cost of Capital," in Y. Amihud and R. Levich (eds.), *Exchange Rates and Corporate Performance* (Burr Ridge, Ill.: Irwin, 1994).

EXHIBIT 16.5

Real After-Tax Cost of Funds

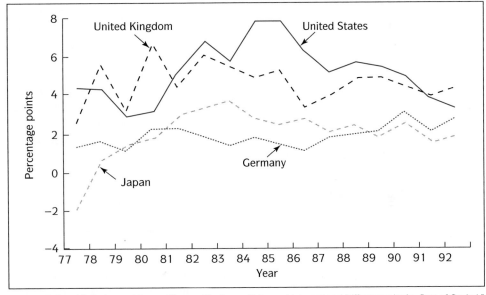

Source: Robert McCauley and Steven Zimmer, "Exchange Rates and International Differences in the Cost of Capital," in Y. Amihud and R. Levich (eds.), *Exchange Rates and Corporate Performance* (Burr Ridge, Ill.: Irwin, 1994).

firm's cost of capital. In Chapter 7, for example, we saw that Eurobond financing was typically a less expensive form of debt financing than domestic bond financing. We continue with this line of thinking in this chapter, where we explore ways of lowering the cost of equity capital through internationalizing the firm's ownership structure. Let us first examine the historical experiences of one firm, Novo Industri, that has successfully internationalized its cost of capital by cross-border listings.

Illustrated MINI CASE | Novo Industri

www.novo.dk/

The homepage of Novo
provides basic information
about the company.

Novo Industri A/S is a Danish multinational corporation that controls about 50 percent of
the world industrial enzyme market. The company also produces health-care products,
including insulin. On July 8, 1981, Novo listed its shares on the New York Stock
Exchange, thereby becoming the first Scandinavian company to directly raise equity capital in the United States.

In the late 1970s, Novo management decided that in order to finance the planned
future growth of the company, it had to tap into international capital markets. Novo could
not expect to raise all the necessary funds exclusively from the Danish stock market,
which is relatively small and illiquid. In addition, Novo management felt that the company
faced a higher cost of capital than its main competitors, such as Eli Lilly and Miles Lab,
because of the segmented nature of the Danish stock market.

Novo, thus, decided to internationalize its cost of capital in order to gain access to additional sources of capital and, at the same time, lower its cost of capital. Initially, Novo
increased the level of financial and technical disclosure, followed by Eurobond issue and
the listing of its shares on the London Stock Exchange in 1978. In pursuing its goals further, Novo management decided to sponsor an American depository receipt (ADR) so that
American investors could invest in the company's shares using American dollars, rather
than Danish kroners. Morgan Guarantee issued the ADR shares, which began trading in
the over-the-counter (OTC) market in April 1981. On July 8, 1981, Novo sold 1.8 million
ADR shares, raising Dkr 450 million, and, at the same time, listed its ADR shares on the
New York Stock Exchange. The chronology of these events is provided in Exhibit 16.6.

As can be seen from Exhibit 16.7, Novo's share price reacted very positively to the
American listing. Other Danish shares, though, did not experience comparable price
increases. The sharp increase in Novo's share price indicates that the stock became fully
priced internationally upon American listing. This, in turn, implies that the Danish stock
market was, indeed, segmented from the rest of the world. From the experiences of Novo,
we can derive the following lesson: *Firms operating in a small, segmented domestic capital market can gain access to new capital and lower the cost of capital by listing their
shares on large, liquid capital markets, such as the New York and London Stock
Exchanges.*

EXHIBIT 16.6

**Process of
Internationalizing the
Capital Structure: Novo**

1977:	Novo increased the level of its financial and technical disclosure in both Danish and English versions. Grieveson, Grant and Co, a British stock brokerage firm, started to follow Novo's shares and issued the first professional security analyst report in English. Novo's share price: DKr200–225.
1978:	Novo raised $20 million by offering convertible Eurobond, underwritten by Morgan Grenfell. Novo listed on the London Stock Exchange.
1980 April:	Novo organized a marketing seminar in New York City promoting its share to American investors.
1980 December:	Novo's share price reached DKr600 level; P/E ratio rose to around 16.
1981 April:	Novo ADRs were listed on NASDAQ (5 ADRs = one share) Morgan Guaranty Trust Co. served as the depository bank.
1981 July:	Novo listed on NYSE. Novo share price reached DKr1400. Foreign ownership increased to over 50 percent of the shares outstanding. American institutional investors began to hold Novo shares.

Source: Arthur Stonehill and Kare Dullum, *Internationalizing the Cost of Capital,* New York: John Wiley & Sons,
1982.

EXHIBIT 16.7

Novo B's Share Prices Compared to Stock Market Indexes

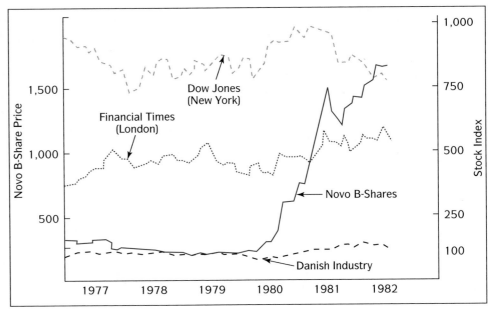

Source: Arthur I. Stonehill and Kare B. Dullum, *Internationalizing the Cost of Capital: The Novo Experience and National Policy Implications,* John Wiley & Sons, 1982, p. 73. Note that Novo A shares are nontradable shares held by the Novo Foundation. Reprinted with permission.

16.4 Cross-Border Listings of Shares

As we have seen from the case of Novo Industri, firms can potentially benefit from cross-border listings. As a result, cross-border listings of shares have become quite popular among major corporations. Exhibit 16.8 shows the extent of cross-border listings on major stock exchanges. The largest contingent of foreign shares (531 companies at the end of 1995) are listed on the London Stock Exchange. These 531 listings, together with several hundred unlisted foreign issues, accounted for 54 percent of London's average daily turnover of $4.5 billion in 1995. American exchanges attracted the next largest contingent of foreign shares with 247 on the New York Stock Exchange (NYSE) and 362 on NASDAQ. Exhibit 16.9 provides a partial list of overseas shares that are listed on the NYSE.

Generally speaking, a company can benefit from cross-border listings of its shares in the following ways:

1. The company can expand its potential investor base, which will lead to a higher share price and a lower cost of capital.

2. Cross-listing creates a secondary market for the company's shares, which facilitates raising new capital in foreign markets.[2]

3. Cross-listing can enhance the liquidity of the company's share.

4. Cross-listing enhances the visibility of the company's name and its products in foreign marketplaces.

---

[2]Chaplinsky and Ramchand (1995) report that compared with exclusively domestic offerings, global equity offerings enable firms to raise capital at advantageous terms. In addition, they report that the negative share price reaction that equity issue often elicits is reduced if firms have a foreign tranche in their offer.

EXHIBIT 16.8		Distribution of Listings of Foreign Shares on Major Stock Exchanges				
	1998 Total	Foreign	Number of Foreign Companies			
Stock Exchange	Turnover ($ Billions)	Turnover as % of Total	1986	1990	1995	1998
New York	7,345	8.5	59	96	247	392
NASDAQ	5,820	3.4	244	256	362	441
London	2,999	54.4	584	613	531	522
Tokyo	867	0.1	52	125	77	52
Paris	615	1.5	195	226	194	178
Frankfurt	1,578	2.3	181	234	235	235
Taiwan	464	0.0	0	0	0	0
Zurich	713	5.2	194	234	233	193
Osaka	250	0.0	0	0	0	0
Madrid	676	0.0	0	2	4	5
Seoul	160	0.0	0	0	0	0
Toronto	322	0.3	51	66	62	49

Sources: G. Andrew Karolyi, "What Happens to Stocks That List Shares Abroad? A Survey of Evidence and Its Managerial Implications," University of Western Ontario Working Paper, 1996. London Stock Exchange Fact File, 1999.

EXHIBIT 16.9	Foreign Firms Listed on the New York Stock Exchange (Selected)
Country	Firms
Australia	Broken Hill Prop., Cole Myers, FAI, News Corporation, Western Mining, Westpac
Brazil	Aracruz Celulose, Gerdau, Telebras, Unibanco
Canada	Alcan Aluminum, Avalon, Barrick, CN, Domtar, Mitel, Northern Telecom, Seagram
China	China Eastern Airlines, Hauneng Power International, Shanghai Petrochemical
Finland	Metso Corp., Nokia Corp., UPM-Kymmene
France	Elf Acquitaine, France Telecom, Rhone Poulenc, Thomson Multimedia, TOTALFina
Germany	Celanese, Deutsche Telecom, DaimlerChrysler, Hoechst, SAP, VEBA
Italy	Benetton, Fiat, Luxottica, Montedison, Telecom Italia
Japan	Canon, Fuji Photo Film, Japan Air Lines, Kirin Brewery, Kubota, Mitsui Co., NEC, Nissan Motor, Sanyo Electric, Sony, Toyota Motor
Korea	Korea Electric Power, Korea Telecom, Pohang Iron & Steel, SK Telecom
Mexico	Cemex, Impresas ICA, Grupo Televisa, Telefonos de Mexico, Vitro
Netherlands	Aegon, KLM, Philips, Polygram, Royal Dutch Petrol., Unilever, ABN AMRO Holdings
Russia	Tatnet, Rostelecom, Vimpel-Communications
South Africa	ASA Limited
Spain	Banco Bilbao, Banco Central, Banco Santan., Emprosa National, Repsol, Telefon. Nac.
United Kingdom	Attwoods, Barclays, Bass Public, Beazer, BET, British Airways, British Gas, British Petrol., British Steel, British Telecom., Cable & Wireless, Glaxo, Grand Met

Source: *NYSE Factbook,* 1999.

5. Cross-listed shares may be used as the "acquisition currency" for taking over foreign companies.

6. Cross-listing may improve the company's corporate governance and transparency.

The last point deserves detailed discussion here. Consider a company in a country where shareholders' rights are not well protected and controlling shareholders (e.g., founding families and large shareholders) derive substantial private benefits, such as, inflated salaries, bonuses, and even thefts, from controlling the company. Once the company cross-lists its shares on the New York Stock Exchange (NYSE), London

Stock Exchange (LSE), or other foreign exchanges that impose stringent disclosure and listing requirements, controlling shareholders may not be able to continue to divert company resources to their private benefit. As argued by Doidge, Karolyi, and Stulz (2001), in spite of the "inconveniences" associated with a greater public scrutiny and enhanced transparency, controlling shareholders may choose to cross-list the company shares overseas, as it can be ultimately in their best interests to bond themselves to "good behaviour" and to be able to raise funds to undertake profitable investment projects (thereby increasing share prices). This implies that if a foreign company does not need to raise capital, it may not choose to pursue foreign listings so that controlling shareholders can continue to extract private benefits from the company. The study by Doidge et al. shows that other things being equal, those foreign companies that are listed on American exchanges are valued nearly 17 percent higher, on average, than those that are not, reflecting investors' recognition of the enhanced corporate governance associated with American listings. Since the London Stock Exchange also imposes stringent disclosure and listing requirements, foreign firms cross-listed on the exchange may also experience positive revaluation due to the effect of enhanced corporate governance.[3]

Despite these potential benefits, not every company seeks overseas listings because of the costs.

1. It can be costly to meet the disclosure and listing requirements imposed by the foreign exchange and regulatory authorities.

2. Once a company's shares are traded in overseas markets, there can be volatility spillover from those markets.

3. Once a company's shares are made available to foreigners, they might acquire a controlling interest and challenge the domestic control of the company.

Disclosure requirements appear to be the most significant barrier to overseas listings. For example, adaptation to American accounting rules, which is required by the U.S. Security and Exchange Commission (SEC), is found to be the most onerous barrier facing foreign companies that consider NYSE listings. According to a German survey conducted by Glaum and Mandler (1996), one-third of the German sample firms are, in principle, interested in American listings but view the required adaptation of financial statements to the American Generally Accepted Accounting Principles (US-GAAP) as a major obstacle. Daimler-Benz, a German firm listed on the NYSE, employs US-GAAP as well as German accounting law and publishes two versions of consolidated financial statements with different reported earnings.[4] As can be seen from Exhibit 16.10, the company's net earnings were positive by German accounting rules but negative by American rules in 1993 and 1994. In light of the costs and benefits of overseas listings, a foreign listing should be viewed as an investment project to be undertaken if it is judged to have a positive net present value (NPV) and, thus, adds to the firm's value.

In an extensive survey of the literature on the corporate decision to cross-list shares, Karolyi (1996) reports that (1) the share price reacts favourably to cross-border listings; (2) the total postlisting trading volume increases on average, and, for many issues, home-market trading volume also increases; (3) liquidity of trading in shares improves overall; (4) the share's exposure to domestic market risk is significantly reduced and is

---

[3]As Dahya, McConnell, and Travlos (2002) point out, the standard of corporate governance has been raised significantly in the United Kingdom since the "Cadbury Committee" issued the *Code of Best Practice* in 1992, recommending that corporate boards include at least three outside directors and that the positions of chairman and CEO be held by different individuals.

[4]Unlike American and Canadian accounting rules, German accounting rules are driven by tax considerations and creditor protection. For this reason, prudence, not a true and fair view, is the dominant accounting principle. German managers are granted broad discretion in accounting policy, and they try to achieve income smoothing.

INTERNATIONAL FINANCE
IN PRACTICE

The U.S. Welcomes the Alien Invasion

Last year 7.5% of the $2.25 trillion worth of shares traded on the New York Stock Exchange (NYSE) came in the form of American depository receipts (ADRs). This percentage is likely to be even higher this year, helped by new issues from foreign companies, which are expected to surpass the record of 37 new listings set during 1993.

In addition to the NYSE's ADRs, a steady stream of depository receipts (DRs) trade over-the-counter, are listed on other exchanges such as Amex and Nasdaq, or are privately placed under Rule 144A and trade on the Portal system.

The depository receipts marketplace is becoming truly global. Until the late 1980s most DRs represented shares of European companies, but today investors in the United States can place orders domestically for dollar-denominated shares from countries as diverse as Chile, China, India and Mexico.

Investment bankers report the busiest schedule of offerings that they have ever seen in the depository receipts business, although volatility in many emerging markets has caused some concern among underwriters.

European DR issuance is being primarily driven by privatization programmes, notably those being implemented by France and Italy. In Asia, companies from mainland China and Hong Kong need capital to expand against a backdrop of runaway economic growth. And in Latin America the passage of the North American Free Trade Agreement (NAFTA) is expected to spur issuance from Mexico, while a dozen Chilean companies have plans to launch DRs this year. In addition, 1994 should witness the first DRs from countries including Sri Lanka, Pakistan, Peru and Uruguay.

The issuing companies are attracted by the growing demand for international equities in the form of ADRs from investors in the United States, accompanied by European and Asian demand for DRs that trade on exchanges outside the US—often referred to as global depository receipts.

Some companies urgently need to raise fresh capital in quantities unavailable at home. Others simply wish to broaden their investor base, and are being persuaded to set up an ADR programme without raising fresh capital.

But both groups have realized that in the global competition for capital those companies that broaden their investor base by actively courting the foreign investor stand a better chance of achieving a strong share price, and will be in a better position to raise capital as and when needed.

The message is clear. An ADR programme is becoming a necessity in order to gain full access to the US investor. And as the range of foreign shares available in depository receipt form grows many US investors may feel that there is even less of an incentive to hunt for stocks in overseas markets. This effect is magnified by the fact that issuance of depository receipts usually generates a great deal of research and broker interest, and pushes a company's story to the forefront of the many thousands seeking the attention of investors.

There are a range of options available to foreign companies wishing to access the depository receipt market. The simplest is the so-called level-one ADR, which entails setting up a programme under which existing domestic shares can be switched into DR form upon demand and trade over-the-counter. Similarly, level-two programmes

---

EXHIBIT 16.10

Daimler-Benz's Net Profit/Loss (DM bn): German versus American Accounting Rules

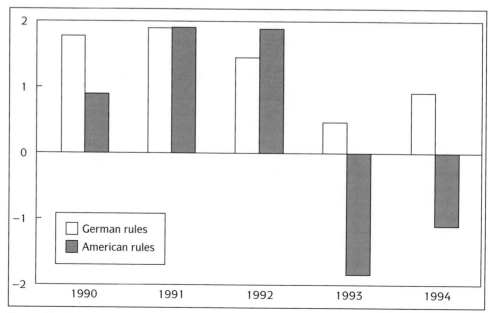

Source: *The Economist,* May 20, 1995.

388

may be set up under which existing shares can be transformed into DRs—but this time listed on an exchange.

Level-one and level-two programmes lack the benefits which come from the excitement created in the market by an offering of new stock. Nonetheless bankers do not feel that a company should ignore the market if it has no immediate capital-raising needs. "A level-one programme gives companies the chance to stand out," says Joseph Velli, an executive vice-president at Bank of New York, "and helps generate research product and broker interest."

UK companies such as Guinness and Tesco have built up a following by allowing existing shares to trade over-the-counter in the United States in the form of depository receipts. And more recently Telecommunicacoes Brasileiras (Telebras) has also successfully broadened its shareholder base with a level-one programme.

However, the majority of new depository receipt programmes do involve capital-raising. Until the 1980s this typically involved a European company selling ADRs to investors in the United States. But with Latin American and Asian companies doing more offerings, this is increasingly via a global depository receipt (GDR) offering which can tap simultaneously into investor demand from the US, Europe and Asia. Regardless of the terminology, both ADRs and GDRs represent the same basic structure of dollar-denominated securities.

Where capital is being raised, the major decisions a company has to make are whether to place stock privately under 144A or make a public offering; and, if the latter, where to list the depository receipts.

Currently there is a clear trend away from 144A issues toward full registration with the Securities and Exchange Commission.

"Even with a 144A placement, there is still a great deal of disclosure, the same roadshow, and a lot of work leading up to the offering," comments Bill Treut, who heads ADR sales for Latin American at Citibank.

Companies have realized that the accounting reconciliation problem is not as daunting a task as they previously thought. These factors have convinced many of them that it makes sense to take the extra steps needed to do a public offering.

"For particular reasons," Treut says, "some companies feel they have a limited window of opportunity" and can take advantage of the speed of the 144A process. "But without those special factors, the definite trend is toward full registration."

In 1991, $2.29 billion was raised via 144A placements; this rose to $3.83 billion in 1992, but fell back to $2.14 billion last year. Meanwhile, total capital raised via all DRs during 1993 was $9.54 billion, up from $5.26 billion in 1992, and $4.61 billion in 1991. That was preceded by three relatively quiet years in the wake of 1987, when $4.59 billion was raised.

One drawback with 144A placements is that they narrow the institutional investor base down to qualified institutional buyers (QIBs), and totally exclude the retail sector and smaller institutions. Second, liquidity is often not very good on the Portal secondary market trading system, so even the QIBs feel more comfortable buying public stock offerings.

The global trend toward harmonization of accounting standards is also having the effect of bringing more and more foreign companies closer to US accounting principles. This is putting foreign companies in a position where taking the step toward SEC filing for a public ADR issue is less of a challenge.

Source: Michael Marray, *Euromoney,* April 1994, pp. 61–63. Adapted with permission.

associated with only a small increase in global market risk; (5) cross-border listings resulted in a net reduction in the cost of equity capital of 114 basis points on average; and (6) stringent disclosure requirements are the greatest impediment to cross-border listings. A recent study by Miller (1999) also confirms that dual listing can mitigate barriers to international capital flows, resulting in a higher share price and a lower cost of capital. Considering these findings, cross-border listings of shares seem to have been, on average, positive NPV projects.

Supplementary Material

16.5   Capital Asset Pricing under Cross-Listings

To fully understand the effects of international cross-listings, it is necessary to understand how assets will be priced under the alternative capital market regimes. In this section, we discuss an **International Asset Pricing Model (IAPM)** in a world in which some assets are internationally tradable, while others are not. For ease of discussion, we will assume that cross-listed assets are **internationally tradable assets**, while all other assets are **internationally nontradable assets.**

It is useful for our purpose to recalibrate the CAPM formula. Noting the definition of beta, the CAPM Equation 16.2 can be restated as:

$$\overline{R}_i = R_f + [(\overline{R}_M - R_f)/Var(R_M)]Cov(R_i, R_M) \tag{16.3}$$

For our purposes it is best to define $[(\overline{R}_M - R_f)/Var(R_M)]$ as equal to $A^M M$, where A^M is a **measure of aggregate risk aversion** of all investors and M is the aggregate market value of the market portfolio. With these definitions, Equation 16.3 can be restated as:

$$\overline{R}_i = R_f + A^M M Cov(R_i, R_M) \tag{16.4}$$

Equation 16.4 indicates that, given investors' aggregate risk-aversion measure, the expected rate of return on an asset increases as the asset's covariance with the market portfolio increases.

Before we introduce the IAPM with cross-listing, however, let us first discuss the asset pricing mechanism under complete segmentation and integration as benchmark cases. Suppose that there are two countries in the world, the domestic country and the foreign country. In a **completely segmented capital market** where no assets are internationally tradable, they will be priced according to their respective **country systematic risk.** For domestic country assets, the expected asset return is calculated as:

$$\overline{R}_i = R_f + A^D D Cov(R_i, R_D) \tag{16.5}$$

and for foreign country assets, the expected asset return is calculated as:

$$\overline{R}_g = R_f + A^F F Cov(R_g, R_F) \tag{16.6}$$

where $\overline{R}(\overline{R}_g)$ is the current equilibrium expected return on the ith (gth) domestic (foreign) asset, R_f is the risk-free rate of return that is assumed to be common to both domestic and foreign countries, $A^D(A^F)$ denotes the risk-aversion measure of domestic (foreign) investors, $D(F)$ denotes the aggregate market value of all domestic (foreign) securities, and $Cov(R_i, R_D)[Cov(R_g, R_F)]$ denotes the covariance between the future returns on the ith (gth) asset and returns on the **domestic (foreign) country market portfolio.**

By comparison, in **fully integrated world capital markets** where all assets are internationally tradable, each asset will be priced according to the **world systematic risk.** For both domestic and foreign country assets:

$$\overline{R}_i = R_f + A^W W Cov(R_i, R_W) \tag{16.7}$$

where A^W is the aggregate risk-aversion measure of world investors, W is the aggregate market value of the **world market portfolio** that comprises both the domestic and foreign portfolios, and $Cov(R_i, R_W)$ denotes the covariance between the future returns of the ith security and the world market portfolio.

As we will see shortly, the asset pricing relationship becomes more complicated in **partially integrated world financial markets** where some assets are internationally tradable (that is, those that are cross-listed), while others are nontradable.

To tell the conclusion first, internationally tradable assets will be priced *as if* world financial markets were completely integrated. Regardless of the nationality, a tradable asset will be priced solely according to its world systematic risk as described in Equation 16.7. Nontradable assets, on the other hand, will be priced according to a world systematic risk, reflecting the spillover effect generated by the traded assets, as well as a country-specific systematic risk. Due to the **pricing spillover effect,** nontradable assets will *not* be priced as if world financial markets were completely segmented.

For nontradable assets of the domestic country, the pricing relationship is given by

$$\bar{R}_i = R_f + A^W W Cov^*(R_i, R_W) + A^D D[Cov(R_i, R_D) - Cov^*(R_i, R_D)] \qquad \textbf{(16.8)}$$

where $Cov^*(R_i, R_D)$ is the *indirect* covariance between the future returns on the ith nontradable asset and the domestic country's market portfolio that is induced by tradable assets. Formally,

$$Cov^*(R_i, R_D) = \sigma_i \sigma_D \rho_{iT} \rho_{TD} \qquad \textbf{(16.9)}$$

Where σ_i and σ_D are, respectively, the standard deviations of returns of the ith asset and the domestic country's market portfolio; ρ_{iT} is the correlation coefficient between the ith nontradable asset and portfolio T of tradable assets, and ρ_{TD} is the correlation coefficient between the returns of portfolio T and the domestic country's market portfolio. Similarly, $Cov^*(R_i, R_W)$ is the *indirect* covariance between the ith nontradable asset and the world market portfolio. Nontradable assets of the foreign country will be priced in an analogous manner; thus, it is necessary to concentrate only on the pricing of nontradable assets in the domestic country.

Equation 16.8 indicates that nontradable assets are priced according to: (1) the **indirect world systematic risk**, $Cov^*(R_i, R_W)$, and, (2) the *pure* domestic systematic risk, $Cov(R_i, R_D) - Cov^*(R_i, R_D)$, which is the domestic systematic risk, net of the part induced by tradable assets. Despite the fact that nontradable assets are traded only within the domestic country, they are priced according to an indirect world systematic risk as well as a country-specific systematic risk. This partial international pricing of nontradable assets is due to the pricing spillover effect generated by tradable assets.

Although nontradable assets are exclusively held by domestic (local) investors, they are priced partially internationally, reflecting the spillover effect generated by tradable assets. As can be inferred from Equation 16.8, nontradable assets will not be subject to the spillover effect and, thus, be priced solely domestically only if they are not correlated at all to tradable assets. This, of course, is not a likely scenario. The pricing model also implies that if the domestic and foreign market portfolios can be exactly replicated using tradable assets, all nontradable, as well as tradable, assets will be priced fully internationally as if world financial markets were completely integrated.

The IAPM has a few interesting implications. First, international listing (trading) of assets in otherwise segmented markets directly integrates international capital markets by making these assets tradable. Second, firms with nontradable assets essentially get a **free ride** with firms with tradable assets in the sense that the former indirectly benefit from international integration in terms of a lower cost of capital and higher asset prices, without incurring any associated costs. Appendix 16A makes this point clear using numerical simulations.

The asset pricing model with nontraded assets demonstrates that the benefits from partial integration of capital markets can be transmitted to the entire economy through the pricing spillover effect. The pricing spillover effect has an important policy implication: *To maximize the benefits from partial integration of capital markets, a country should choose to internationally cross-list those assets that are most highly correlated with the domestic market portfolio.*

Consistent with the theoretical analyses presented above, many firms have indeed experienced a reduction in the cost of capital when their shares were listed on foreign markets. In their study of foreign shares listed on American stock exchanges, Alexander, Eun, and Janakiramanan (1988) found that foreign firms from such countries as Australia and Japan experienced a substantial reduction in the cost of capital. Canadian firms, in contrast, experienced a rather modest reduction in the cost of capital upon American listings, probably because Canadian markets were more integrated with American markets than with other markets when American listings took place.

16.6   The Effect of Foreign Equity Ownership Restrictions

While companies have incentives to internationalize their ownership structure to lower the cost of capital and increase their market values, they may be concerned, at the same time, with possible loss of corporate control to foreigners. Consequently, governments in both the developed and the developing countries often impose restrictions on the maximum percentage ownership of local firms by foreigners. In such countries as India, Mexico, and Thailand, foreigners are allowed to purchase no more than 49 percent of the outstanding shares of local firms. These countries want to make sure that foreigners do not acquire majority stakes in local companies. France and Sweden once imposed an even tighter restriction of 20 percent. In Korea, foreigners were allowed to own only 20 percent of the shares of any local firm until recently.

In Switzerland, a local firm can issue two different classes of equity shares, bearer shares and registered shares. Foreigners are often allowed to purchase only bearer shares. In a similar vein, Chinese firms issue A shares and B shares, and foreigners are allowed to hold only B shares. Exhibit 16.11 lists examples of historical restrictions on foreign ownership of local firms for various countries. Obviously, these restrictions are imposed as a means of ensuring domestic control of local firms, especially those that are considered strategically important to national interests.[5]

Pricing-to-Market Phenomenon

Suppose that foreigners, if allowed, would like to buy 30 percent of a Korean firm, but they are constrained to purchase at most 20 percent due to ownership constraints imposed on foreigners. Because the constraint is effective in limiting desired foreign ownership, foreign and domestic investors may face different market share prices. In other words, shares can exhibit a dual pricing or **pricing-to-market (PTM) phenomenon** due to legal restrictions imposed on foreigners.

EXHIBIT 16.11	Restrictions on Equity Ownership by Foreigners: Historical Examples
Country	**Restrictions on Foreigners**
Australia	10% in banks, 20% in broadcasting, and 50% in new mining ventures.
Canada	20% in broadcasting, and 25% in bank/insurance companies.
China	Foreigners are restricted to B shares; only locals are eligible for A shares.
France	Limited to 20%.
India	Limited to 49%.
Indonesia	Limited to 49%.
Mexico	Limited to 49%.
Japan	Maximum of 25–50% for several major firms; acquisition of over 10% of a single firm subject to approval of the Ministry of Finance.
Korea	Limited to 20%.
Malaysia	20% in banks and 30% in natural resources.
Norway	0% in pulp, paper, and mining, 10% in banks, 20% in industrial and oil shares, and 50% in shipping companies.
Spain	0% in defence industries and mass media. Limited to 50% for other firms.
Sweden	20% of voting shares and 40% of total equity capital.
Switzerland	Foreigners can be restricted to bearer shares.
U.K.	Government retains the veto power over any foreign takeover of British firms.

Source: Various publications of Price Waterhouse.

---

[5]Stulz and Wasserfallen (1995) suggest a theoretical possibility that firms may impose restrictions on foreigners' equity ownership to maximize their market values. They argue that when domestic and foreign investors have differential demand functions for a firm's shares, the firm can maximize its market value by discriminating between domestic and foreign investors.

Illustrated MINI CASE | **Nestlé**

The majority of publicly traded Swiss corporations have up to three classes of common shares: (1) registered shares, (2) voting bearer shares, and (3) nonvoting bearer shares. Until recently, foreigners were not allowed to buy registered shares; they were only allowed to buy bearer shares. Registered shares were made available only to Swiss nationals.

In the case of Nestlé, a well-known Swiss multinational corporation that derives more than 95 percent of its revenue from overseas markets, registered shares accounted for about 68 percent of the votes outstanding. This implies that it was practically impossible for foreigners to gain control of the firm. On November 17, 1988, however, Nestlé announced that the firm would lift the ban on foreigners buying registered shares. The announcement was made after the Zurich Stock Exchange closed.

Nestlé's board of directors mentioned two reasons for lifting the ban on foreigners. First, despite the highly multinational nature of its business activities, Nestlé maintained a highly nationalistic ownership structure. At the same time, Nestlé made high-profile cross-border acquisitions, such as Rowntree (the United Kingdom) and Carnation (the United States). Nestlé's practices, thus, were criticized as unfair and incompatible with free-market principles. The firm needed to remedy this situation. Second, Nestlé realized that the ban against foreigners holding registered shares had the effect of increasing its cost of capital, negatively affecting its competitive position in the world market.

As Exhibit 16.12 illustrates, prior to the lifting of the ban on foreigners, (voting) bearer shares traded at about twice the price of registered shares. The higher price for bearer shares suggests that foreigners desired to hold more than they were allowed to in the absence of ownership restrictions imposed on them. When the ban was lifted, however, prices of the two types of shares immediately converged; the price of bearer shares declined by about 25 percent, whereas that of registered shares increased by about 35 percent. Because registered shares represented about two-thirds of the total number of voting shares, the total market value of Nestlé increased substantially when it fully internationalized its ownership structure. This, of course, means that Nestlé's cost of equity capital declined substantially.

www.nestle.com/

The homepage of Nestlé provides basic information about the company.

EXHIBIT 16.12

Price Spread between Bearer and Registered Shares of Nestlé

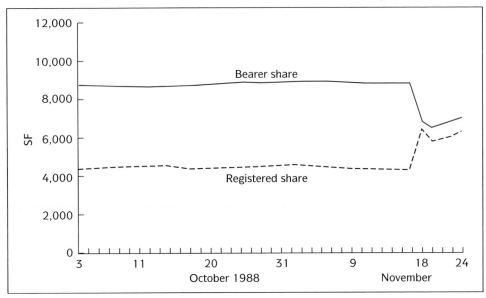

Source: *Financial Times,* November 26, 1988, p. 1. Adapted with permission.

Hietala (1989) documented the PTM phenomenon in the Finnish stock market. Finnish firms used to issue restricted and unrestricted shares, with foreigners allowed to purchase only unrestricted shares. Unrestricted shares accounted for at most 20 percent of the total number of shares of any Finnish firm. Because of this legal restriction, if foreigners desired to hold more than 20 percent of a Finnish firm, dual pricing could result. Indeed, Hietala found that most Finnish firms exhibited the PTM phenomenon, with unrestricted shares trading at roughly a 15-percent to 40-percent premium relative to restricted shares. Recently, Finland completely abolished restrictions imposed on foreigners.

Supplementary Material

Asset Pricing under Foreign Ownership Restrictions

In this section, we formally investigate how equilibrium asset prices are determined when foreigners are subject to ownership restrictions on the maximum proportionate ownership of domestic firms. As before, we assume that there are two countries in the world, the domestic country and the foreign country. For simplicity, we assume that the foreign country imposes an ownership constraint on investors from the domestic country but that the domestic country does not impose any constraints on investors from the foreign country. Consequently, domestic country investors are restricted to holding at most a certain percentage of the shares of any foreign firms, whereas foreign country investors are not restricted in any way from investing in the domestic country.

Since we assume that there are no investment restrictions on domestic shares, both domestic and foreign country investors face the same price for the same domestic asset, which equals the perfect capital market price. As far as domestic assets are concerned, the law of one price prevails. For foreign shares, however, the PTM phenomenon applies.

Specifically, domestic country assets will be priced according to Equation 16.7, the fully integrated world capital market's IAPM. Foreign shares will be priced differently, depending upon whether the investor is from the foreign or domestic country. Investors from the domestic country will pay a premium above and beyond the *perfect market price* that would prevail in the absence of restrictions, whereas investors from the foreign country will receive a discount from the perfect market price. This implies that the domestic country investors would require a lower return on foreign country shares than the foreign country investors.

Eun and Janakiramanan (1986) offer the following solutions for the equilibrium rates of return for foreign asset i from the domestic and the foreign country investors' perspectives, respectively:

$$\bar{R}_i^d = R_f + A^W W Cov(R_i, R_W) - (A^W W - \delta A^D D)[Cov(R_i, R_F) - Cov(R_i, R_S)] \quad \textbf{(16.10)}$$

$$\bar{R}_i^f = R_f + A^W W Cov(R_i, R_W) + [(1 - \delta)A^D D - A^W W]$$
$$[Cov(R_i, R_F) - Cov(R_i, R_S)] \quad \textbf{(16.11)}$$

where δ represents the fraction of the ith foreign firm that domestic country investors as a whole are allowed to own. In the above equations, portfolio S refers to the **substitution portfolio,** which is the portfolio of domestic country assets that is most highly correlated with the foreign market portfolio F. Portfolio S can thus be regarded as the domestic country investors' best *home-made* substitute for the foreign market portfolio F.

According to the above model, the equilibrium rates of return depend critically on (1) the severity of the ownership constraint (δ), and (2) the ability of domestic country investors to replicate the foreign market portfolio using their domestic assets, which is measured by the **pure foreign market risk**, $Cov(R_i,R_F) - Cov(R_i,R_S)$. In the special case where portfolio S is a perfect substitute for the foreign market portfolio F, we have $Cov(R_i,R_F) = Cov(R_i,R_S)$. In this event, the foreign asset will be priced as if world capital markets are fully integrated from both the domestic and foreign investors' perspectives, even though an ownership constraint is in force. In general, however, domestic country investors will pay premiums for foreign assets (that is, accept a lower rate of return than the perfect capital market rate) to the extent that they cannot precisely replicate the foreign market portfolio using domestic assets. Foreign country investors, on the other hand, will get a discount (that is, receive a higher rate than the perfect capital market rate).

EXAMPLE | **16.2** | **A Numerical Illustration**   To illustrate the effect of foreign ownership restrictions on the firm's cost of equity capital, we conduct a numerical simulation using the model economy described in Exhibit 16.13.

Exhibit 16.13 provides the standard deviations and correlation matrix of our model economy. Firms D1 to D4 belong to the domestic country and firms F1 to F4 belong to the foreign country. For simplicity, the correlation matrix reflects the stylized fact that asset returns are typically less correlated between countries than within a country; the pairwise correlation is uniformly assumed to be 0.50 within a country and 0.15 between countries. Both domestic and foreign investors are assumed to have the same aggregate risk-aversion measure, and the risk-free rate is assumed to be 9 percent.

Exhibit 16.14 considers the case in which the foreign country imposes a 20-percent ownership constraint ($\delta_F = 20$ percent), whereas the domestic country does not impose any constraint on foreign investors. In this case, domestic country assets are priced as if the capital markets were completely integrated. Foreign country assets, however, are priced to market.

In general, the exhibit shows that the firm's cost of capital tends to be higher under the 20-percent ownership constraint than under complete integration. This implies that restricting foreign equity ownership in a firm will have a negative effect on the firm's cost of equity capital. For comparison purposes, we again provide the results obtained under complete segmentation and integration. Specifically, consider foreign firm F1. The exhibit shows that with the 20 percent ownership constraint, the firm's cost of capital is 22.40 percent, which is computed as a weighted average of the required returns by the domestic and foreign country investors in F1. Note that in the absence of the restriction, the firm's cost of capital would have been substantially lower, 19.03 percent. It is also noteworthy that when the PTM phenomenon prevails, the firm's cost of capital depends on which investors, domestic or foreign, supply capital. The exhibit also provides the case where both the domestic and foreign countries impose restrictions at the 20 percent level, that is, $\delta_D = 20\%$ and $\delta_F = 20\%$. Interpretation of this case is left to the readers.

EXHIBIT 16.13			Description of the Model Economy							
					Correlation Matrix					
Firm	Expected Future Share Price ($)	Standard Deviation of Share Price ($)	D2	D3	D4	F1	F2	F3	F4
D1	100	16	0.50	0.50	0.50	0.15	0.15	0.15	0.15
D2	100	20		0.50	0.50	0.15	0.15	0.15	0.15
D3	100	24			0.50	0.15	0.15	0.15	0.15
D4	100	28				0.15	0.15	0.15	0.15
F1	100	18					0.50	0.50	0.50
F2	100	22						0.50	0.50
F3	100	26							0.50
F4	100	30							

Note: Firms D1 to D4 are from the domestic country, whereas firms F1 to F4 are from the foreign country. The risk-free interest rate is assumed to be 9 percent. The domestic and foreign country investors are assumed to have the same aggregate (absolute) risk-aversion measure.

EXHIBIT 16.14

International Capital Market Equilibria: The Effect of Foreign Equity Ownership Restrictions

		σ-constraint			
Asset	Complete Segmentation	$\delta_D = 20\%$ $\delta_F = 20\%$	$\delta_F = 20\%$	Complete Integration
A. Equilibrium Asset Prices ($)[a]				
D1	81.57	83.04/87.45	85.25	85.25
D2	78.53	80.45/86.22	83.34	83.34
D3	75.30	77.75/85.07	81.41	81.41
D4	71.88	74.86/83.82	79.34	79.34
F1	79.19	86.91/81.12	87.86/80.16	84.01
F2	75.87	85.66/78.31	86.87/77.11	81.99
F3	72.34	84.50/75.38	85.92/73.96	79.94
F4	68.62	83.24/72.28	84.90/70.62	77.76
B. Cost of Equity Capital (%)				
D1	22.59	19.15	17.30	17.30
D2	27.34	22.54	19.99	19.99
D3	32.80	26.24	22.84	22.84
D4	39.12	30.46	26.04	26.04
F1	26.28	21.54	22.40	19.03
F2	31.80	25.34	26.48	21.97
F3	38.24	39.96	32.82	25.09
F4	45.73	47.95	38.85	28.60

[a]The two figures indicate the asset prices for domestic/foreign country investors, respectively.

16.7 The Financial Structure of Subsidiaries

A problem faced by financial managers of multinational corporations is how to determine the financial structure of foreign subsidiaries. There are essentially three different approaches to determining the subsidiary's financial structure:

1. Conform to the parent company's norm.

2. Conform to the local norm of the country where the subsidiary operates.

3. Vary judiciously to capitalize on opportunities to lower taxes, reduce financing costs and risks, and take advantage of various market imperfections.

Which approach to take depends largely on the extent to which the parent company is responsible for the subsidiary's financial obligations. When the parent is fully responsible for the subsidiary's obligations, the independent financial structure of the subsidiary is irrelevant; it is the parent's overall financial structure that becomes relevant. When the parent is legally and morally responsible for the subsidiary's debts, potential creditors will examine the parent's overall financial conditions, not the subsidiary's.

When, however, the parent company is willing to let its subsidiary default, or the parent's guarantee of its subsidiary's financial obligations becomes difficult to enforce across national borders, the subsidiary's financial structure becomes relevant. In this case, potential creditors will examine the subsidiary's financial conditions closely to assess default risk. As a result, the subsidiary should choose its own financial structure to reduce default risk and, thus, financing costs.

In reality, the parent company cannot let its subsidiary default on its debts without expecting its worldwide operations to be hampered in one way or another. Default by a subsidiary can deplete the parent's reputational capital, possibly increase its own cost of capital, and certainly make it difficult to undertake future projects in the country where default occurred. Various surveys, including one by Robert Stobaugh, strongly suggest that parent firms of MNCs, indeed will not allow their subsidiaries to default, regardless of circumstances.

An immediate implication of the parent's legal and moral obligation to honour its subsidiary's debts is that the parent should monitor its subsidiary's financial conditions closely and make sure that the firm's overall financial conditions are not adversely affected by the subsidiary's financial structure. What really matters is the marginal impact that the subsidiary's financial structure may have on the parent's worldwide financial structure. The subsidiary's financial structure should be chosen so that the parent's overall cost of capital can be minimized.

In light of the above discussion, neither the first nor the second approach to determining the subsidiary's financial structure can be deemed appropriate. The first approach, which calls for replicating the parent's financial structure, is not necessarily consistent with minimizing the parent's overall cost of capital. Suppose the subsidiary can locally borrow at a subsidized interest rate because the host government is eager to attract foreign investments. In this situation, the subsidiary should borrow locally and exploit the lower interest rate, even if this means that the subsidiary's debt ratio will exceed the parent's norm. If deemed necessary, the parent can simply lower its own debt ratio. In other words, the distribution of debt between the parent and the subsidiary can be adjusted to take advantage of the subsidized loans. Also, in a special case where the subsidiary is operating in a country that regulates its financial structure, it would be difficult to replicate the parent's norm even if that were desirable.

The second approach calls for adopting the local financing norm. In essence, the approach is based on "When in Rome, do as the Romans do." By following the local norm, the firm can reduce the chance of being singled out for criticism. This approach makes sense only when the parent is not responsible for the subsidiary's obligations and the subsidiary has to depend on local financing due to, say, segmentation of financial markets. Otherwise, it does not make much sense. Suppose each foreign subsidiary conforms to the local financing norm, which reflects the host country's cultural, economic, and institutional environments. Then, the parent firm's worldwide financial structure will be determined strictly in a "residual" manner. The overall financial structure so determined is not likely to be the optimal one that minimizes the parent's overall cost of capital. When the host country's norm reflects, for example, the immature nature of local financial markets, a subsidiary of the MNC with ready access to global financial markets should not slavishly follow the local norm. Doing so means that the MNC gives up its advantage in terms of a lower cost of capital.

This brings us to the third approach, which appears to be the most reasonable and consistent with the goal of minimizing the firm's overall cost of capital. The subsidiary should take advantage of subsidized loans as much as possible whenever available. It should also take advantage of tax deductions of interest payments by borrowing more heavily than is implied by the parent's norm when the corporate income tax rate is higher in the host country than in the home country, unless foreign tax credits are useful.

Apart from the tax factor, political risk is another factor that should be considered in choosing the method of financing the subsidiary. Political risk generally favours local financing over the parent's direct financing. The parent company can renounce the subsidiary's local debt in the event that the subsidiary's assets are expropriated. When the subsidiary is financed by local creditors and shareholders, the chance of expropriation itself can be lowered. When a subsidiary is operating in a developing country, financing from such international development agencies as the World Bank and International Finance Corporation will lower political risk. When the choice is between external debt and equity financing, political risk tends to favour the former. This is the case because the host government tolerates repatriation of funds in the form of interest much better than dividends.

To summarize, since the parent company is responsible, legally and/or morally, for its subsidiary's financial obligations, it has to decide the subsidiary's financial structure considering the latter's effect on the parent's overall financial structure. The subsidiary, however, should be allowed to take advantage of any favourable financing opportunities available in the host country because that is consistent with the goal of minimizing the overall cost of capital of the parent. If necessary, the parent can adjust its own financial structure to bring about the optimal overall financial structure.

SUMMARY

In this chapter, we have discussed the cost of capital for a multinational firm. Reflecting the trend toward more liberalized and deregulated financial markets, major corporations of the world are internationalizing their capital structure by allowing foreigners to hold their shares and debts.

1. International comparison of the cost of funds indicates that while the costs of funds are converging among major countries in recent years, international financial markets are less than fully integrated. This suggests that firms can increase their market values by judiciously raising capital overseas.

2. When a firm is operating in a segmented capital market, it can reduce the negative effects by cross-listing its shares on foreign stock markets, thereby making the shares internationally tradable.

3. A firm can benefit from international cross-listings in terms of (a) a lower cost of capital and a higher share price, and (b) access to new sources of capital.

4. When a firm's shares are cross-listed on foreign exchanges in an otherwise segmented capital market, the shares will be priced according to the world systematic risk as if international capital markets were fully integrated. Internationally nontradable assets will be priced according to a country-specific systematic risk and an indirect world systematic risk, reflecting the pricing spillover effect generated by internationally tradable assets.

5. Although the trend is toward more liberal world financial markets, many countries still maintain restrictions on investment by foreigners, especially the maximum percentage ownership of a local firm by foreigners. Under an ownership constraint, foreign and domestic country investors may face different share prices,

resulting in the pricing-to-market (PTM) phenomenon. PTM generally raises the firm's overall cost of capital.

6. The parent company should decide the financing method for its own subsidiary with a view to minimizing the parent's overall cost of capital. To the extent that the parent is responsible for its subsidiary's financial obligations, the subsidiary's own financial structure is irrelevant.

KEY WORDS

beta, *379*
Capital Asset
   Pricing Model
   (CAPM), *379*
capital structure, *377*
completely segmented
   capital market, *390*
cost of capital, *378*
country systematic
   risk, *390*
domestic (foreign)
   country market
   portfolio, *390*
free ride, *391*
fully integrated world
   capital markets, *390*

indirect world systematic
   risk, *391*
International Asset Pricing
   Model (IAPM), *389*
internationally
   nontradable asset, *390*
internationally tradable
   asset, *390*
market portfolio, *379*
measure of aggregate risk
   aversion, *390*
partially integrated
   world financial
   markets, *390*

pricing spillover
   effect, *390*
pricing-to-market (PTM)
   phenomenon, *392*
pure foreign market
   risk, *395*
substitution portfolio, *394*
systematic risk, *379*
weighted average cost of
   capital, *378*
world market
   portfolio, *390*
world systematic risk, *390*

QUESTIONS

1. Suppose that your firm is operating in a segmented capital market. What actions would you recommend to mitigate the negative effects?

2. Explain why and how a firm's cost of capital may decrease when the firm's shares are cross-listed on foreign stock exchanges.

3. Explain the pricing *spillover effect.*

4. In what sense do firms with nontradable assets get a *free ride* from firms whose securities are internationally tradable?

5. Define and discuss *indirect world systematic risk.*

6. Discuss how the cost of capital is determined in segmented versus integrated capital markets.

7. Suppose there exists a nontradable asset with a perfect positive correlation with a portfolio *T* of tradable assets. How will the nontradable asset be priced?

8. Discuss what factors motivated Novo Industri to seek American listing of its shares. What lessons can be derived from Novo's experiences?

9. Discuss foreign equity ownership restrictions. Why do you think countries impose these restrictions?

10. Explain the *pricing-to-market phenomenon.*

11. Explain how the premium and discount are determined when assets are priced to market. When would the law of one price prevail in international capital markets even if foreign equity ownership restrictions are imposed?

12. Under what conditions will the foreign subsidiary's financial structure become relevant?

13. Under what conditions would you recommend that the foreign subsidiary conform to the local norm of financial structure?

PROBLEMS

Answer problems 1–3 based on the stock market data given by the following table:

| | **Correlation Coefficients** | | | | |
	Telmex	Mexico	World	SD(%)	$\bar{R}$(%)
Telmex	1.00	.90	0.60	18	?
Mexico		1.00	0.75	15	14
World			1.00	10	12

The above table provides the correlations among Telmex, a telephone/ communication company located in Mexico, the Mexican stock market index, and the world market index, together with the standard deviations (SD) of returns and the expected returns ($\bar{R}$). The risk-free rate is 5 percent.

1. Compute the domestic country beta of Telmex as well as its world beta. What do these betas measure?

2. Suppose the Mexican stock market is segmented from the rest of the world. Using the CAPM paradigm, estimate the equity cost of capital of Telmex.

3. Suppose now that Telmex has made its shares tradable internationally via cross-listing on NYSE. Again using the CAPM paradigm, estimate Telmex's equity cost of capital. Discuss the possible effects of international pricing of Telmex shares on the share prices and the firm's investment decisions.

INTERNET EXERCISE

You are the controlling shareholder of Taiwan-based Dragon Semicon, a company with a strong growth potential. In order to fund future growth, you are considering listing the company shares either on the New York or the London stock exchange. Visit the websites of the two exchanges to find out and compare their listing and disclosure requirements for foreign companies.

REFERENCES & SUGGESTED READINGS

Adler, Michael. "The Cost of Capital and Valuation of a Two-Country Firm." *Journal of Finance* 29 (1974), pp. 119–32.

Alexander, Gordon, Cheol Eun, and S. Janakiramanan. "Asset Pricing and Dual Listing on Foreign Capital Markets: A Note." *Journal of Finance* 42 (1987), pp. 151–58.

———. "International Listings and Stock Returns: Some Empirical Evidence." *Journal of Financial and Quantitative Analysis* 23 (1988), pp. 135–51.

Bailey, Warren, and Julapa Jagtiani. "Foreign Ownership Restrictions and Stock Prices in the Thai Market." *Journal of Financial Economics* 36 (1994), pp. 57–87.

Black, Fisher. "International Capital Market Equilibrium with Investment Barriers." *Journal of Financial Economics* 1 (1974), pp. 337–52.

Chan, K. C., Andrew Karolyi, and Rene Stulz. "Global Financial Markets and the Risk Premium on U.S. Equity." *Journal of Financial Economics* 32 (1992), pp. 137–67.

Chaplinsky, Susan, and Latha Ramchand. "The Rationale for Global Equity Offerings." University of Virginia Working Paper, 1995.

Cohn, Richard, and John Pringle. "Imperfections in International Financial Markets: Implications for Risk Premia and the Cost of Capital to Firms." *Journal of Finance* 28 (1973), pp. 59–66.

Dahya, J., J. McConnell, and N. Travlos. "The Cadbury Committee, Corporate Performance, and Top Management Turnover." *Journal of Finance* 57 (2002), pp. 461–83.

Doidge, Craig, Andrew Karolyi, and Rene Stulz. "Why Are Foreign Firms Listed in the U.S. Worth More?" Ohio State University Working Paper, 2001.

Errunza, Vihang, and Etienne Losq. "International Asset Pricing under Mild Segmentation: Theory and Test." *Journal of Finance* 40 (1985), pp. 105–24.

Eun, Cheol, and S. Janakiramanan. "A Model of International Asset Pricing with a Constraint on the Foreign Equity Ownership." *Journal of Finance* 41 (1986), pp. 897–914.

French, K., and J. Poterba. "Investor Diversification and International Equity Markets." *American Economic Review* 81 (1991), pp. 222–26.

Harvey, Campbell. "The World Price of Covariance Risk." *Journal of Finance* 46 (1991), pp. 111–57.

Hietala, Pekka. "Asset Pricing in Partially Segmented Markets: Evidence from the Finnish Markets." *Journal of Finance* 44 (1989), pp. 697–718.

Jayaraman, N., K. Shastri, and K. Tandon. "The Impact of International Cross Listings on Risk and Return: The Evidence from American Depository Receipts." *Journal of Banking and Finance* 17 (1993), pp. 91–103.

Karolyi, G. Andrew. "What Happens to Stocks That List Shares Abroad? A Survey of the Evidence and its Managerial Implications." University of Western Ontario Working Paper, 1996.

Lee, Kwang Chul, and Chuck C. Y. Kwok. "Multinational Corporations vs. Domestic Corporations: International Environmental Factors and Determinants of Capital Structure." *Journal of International Business Studies* 19 (1988), pp. 195–217.

Lessard, D. and A. Shapiro. "Guidelines for Global Financing Choices." *Midland Corporate Finance Journal* 3 (1984), pp. 68–80.

Loderer, Claudio, and Andreas Jacobs. "The Nestlé Crash." *Journal of Financial Economics* 37 (1995), pp. 315–39.

McCauley, Robert, and Steven Zimmer. "Exchange Rates and International Differences in the Cost of Capital." In Y. Amihud and R. Levich (eds.), *Exchange Rates and Corporate Performance.* Burr Ridge, IL: Irwin, 1994, pp. 119–48.

Miller, Darius. "The Market Reaction to International Cross-listing: Evidence from Depository Receipts." *Journal of Financial Economics* 51 (1999), pp. 103–23.

Mittoo, Usha. "Additional Evidence on Integration in the Canadian Stock Market." *Journal of Finance* 47 (1992), pp. 2035–54.

Stapleton, Richard, and Marti Subrahmanyan. "Market Imperfections, Capital Market Equilibrium and Corporation Finance." *Journal of Finance* 32 (1977), pp. 307–21.

———. *Capital Market Equilibrium and Corporate Financial Decisions.* Greenwich, Conn.: JAI Press, 1980.

Stonehill, Arthur, and Kare Dullum. *Internationalizing the Cost of Capital.* New York: John Wiley and Sons, 1982.

Stulz, Rene. "On the Effect of Barriers to International Investment." *Journal of Finance* 36 (1981), pp. 923–34.

———. "Pricing Capital Assets in an International Setting: An Introduction." *Journal of International Business Studies* 16 (1985), pp. 55–74.

———. "The Cost of Capital in Internationally Integrated Markets: The Case of Nestlé." *European Financial Management* 1 (1995), pp. 11–22.

———. "Does the Cost of Capital Differ across Countries? An Agency Perspective." *European Financial Management* 2 (1996), pp. 11–22.

Stulz, Rene, and Walter Wasserfallen. "Foreign Equity Investment Restrictions, Capital Flight, and Shareholder Wealth Maximization: Theory and Evidence." *Review of Financial Studies* 8 (1995), pp. 1019–57.

Subrahmanyam, Marti. "On the Optimality of International Capital Market Integration." *Journal of Financial Economics* 2 (1975), pp. 3–28.

Pricing of Nontradable Assets: Numerical Simulations

To further explain the theoretical results presented in the preceding section, we provide a numerical illustration in which we assume a two-country and eight-firm world as described in Exhibit 16.13 to arrive at the equilibrium share prices and expected rates of return, or costs of equity capital, under the alternative structures of international capital markets.

Exhibit 16A.1 presents the equilibrium asset prices and the costs of equity capital for each of the eight firms as computed according to the asset pricing models presented earlier. Cross-listing domestic asset D1 on the foreign exchange in an otherwise segmented market decreases the equilibrium cost of equity capital from 22.59 percent (under segmentation) to 17.30 percent upon cross-listing. Clearly, international trading of the asset leads to a decrease in the cost of capital.

Once asset D1 is cross-listed, it will be priced (at $85.25) to yield the same expected rate of return that it would obtain under complete integration. Moreover, when the domestic asset is cross-listed, other domestic assets, which remain internationally nontradable, also experience a decrease in their costs of equity capital. Take asset D2 for example; the cost of capital falls from 27.34 percent under segmentation to 23.72 percent after cross-listing asset D1. This reflects the spillover effect generated by asset D1 when it becomes internationally tradable. Additionally, Exhibit 16A.1 shows that when foreign asset F1 is cross-listed in the domestic country, it will lower its own cost of equity capital as well as that of the other foreign firms. The exhibit shows that when F1 is cross-listed, its cost of equity capital falls from 26.28 percent to 19.03 percent, the same as if capital markets were completely integrated. Moreover, other foreign assets that remain internationally nontradable also experience a decrease in their costs of capital as a result of the spillover effect from the cross-listing of F1.

EXHIBIT 16A.1

International Capital Market Equilibria: The Effect of Cross-Listings

Asset	Complete Segmentation	Cross-Listing Asset D1	Cross-Listing Assets D1 and F1	Complete Integration
A. Equilibrium Asset Prices ($)				
D1	81.57	85.25	85.25	85.25
D2	78.53	80.83	80.37	83.34
D3	75.30	78.06	77.51	81.41
D4	71.88	75.10	74.45	79.34
F1	79.19	78.57	84.01	84.01
F2	75.87	75.11	78.36	81.99
F3	72.34	71.45	75.29	79.94
F4	68.62	67.59	72.02	77.76
B. Cost of Equity Capital (%)				
D1	22.59	17.30	17.30	17.30
D2	27.34	23.72	24.42	19.99
D3	32.80	28.11	29.02	22.84
D4	39.12	33.16	34.32	26.04
F1	26.28	27.28	19.03	19.03
F2	31.80	33.14	27.62	21.97
F3	38.24	39.96	30.97	25.09
F4	45.73	47.95	36.10	28.60

International Capital Budgeting

IN THIS BOOK, we take the view that the fundamental goal of the financial manager is shareholder wealth maximization. Shareholder wealth is created when the firm makes an investment that will return more in a present value sense than the investment costs. Perhaps the most important decisions that confront the financial manager are which capital projects to select. By their very nature, capital projects denote investment in capital assets that make up the productive capacity of the firm. These investments, which are typically expensive relative to the firm's overall value, determine how efficiently the firm produces the products it intends to sell and, thus, will also determine how profitable the firm will be. In total, these capital expenditure decisions determine the competitive position of the firm and the firm's long-run survival. Consequently, a valid framework for analysis of capital expenditure is important. The generally accepted methodology in modern finance is the **net present value (NPV)** discounted cash flow model.

In Chapter 15, we explored why a multinational corporation (MNC) would make foreign direct investment in another country. In Chapter 16, we discussed the cost of capital for a multinational firm. We saw that a firm that could source funds internationally, rather than just domestically, could feasibly have a lower cost of capital than a domestic firm because of its greater opportunities to raise funds. A lower cost of capital means that more capital projects will have a positive net present value to the multinational firm. Our objective in this chapter is to illustrate a proper method for a multinational firm to analyze an investment in a capital project in a foreign land.

Most readers will already be familiar with NPV analysis and its superiority over other capital expenditure evaluation techniques as a tool for maximizing shareholder wealth. Therefore, the chapter begins with only a brief review of the basic NPV capital budgeting framework. Next, the basic NPV framework is extended to an *adjusted present value (APV)* model. APV extends NPV in ways that are especially well suited to analysis of various cash flows that are unique to international expenditures. The chapter concludes with an illustrated mini case showing how to implement the APV decision framework.

17.1 Review of Capital Budgeting

The basic net present value (NPV) capital budgeting equation is:

$$NPV = \sum_{t=1}^{T} \frac{CF_t}{(1 + K)^t} + \frac{TV_T}{(1 + K)^T} - C_0 \tag{17.1}$$

403

where:

CF_t = expected after-tax cash flow for year t

TV_T = expected after-tax terminal value, including recapture of working capital

C_0 = initial investment at inception

K = weighted-average cost of capital

T = economic life of the capital project in years

The NPV of a capital project is the present value of all cash inflows, including those at the end of the project's life, minus the present value of all cash outflows. The *NPV rule* is to accept a project if NPV $\geq$ 0 and to reject it if NPV $<$ 0.[1]

For our purposes, it is necessary to expand the NPV equation. First, however, it is beneficial if we discuss annual cash flows. In capital budgeting, our concern is only with the change in the firm's total cash flows that are attributable to the capital expenditure. CF_t represents the **incremental** change in total firm cash flow for year t resulting from the capital project. Algebraically, CF_t is defined as:

$$CF_t = (R_t - OC_t - D_t - I_t)(1 - \tau) + D_t + I_t(1 - \tau) \qquad (17.2\text{a})$$
$$= NI_t + D_t + I_t(1 - \tau) \qquad (17.2\text{b})$$
$$= (R_t - OC_t - D_t)(1 - \tau) + D_t \qquad (17.2\text{c})$$
$$= NOI_t(1 - \tau) + D_t \qquad (17.2\text{d})$$
$$= (R_t - OC_t)(1 - \tau) + \tau D_t \qquad (17.2\text{e})$$
$$= OCF_t(1 - \tau) + \tau D_t \qquad (17.2\text{f})$$
$$= \text{nominal after-tax incremental cash flow for year } t$$

Equation 17.2a presents a detailed expression for incremental cash flow that is worth learning so that we can easily apply the model. The equation shows that CF_t is the sum of three flows, or that the cash flow from a capital project goes to three different groups. The first term, as Equation 17.2b shows, is expected income, NI_t, which belongs to the equity holders of the firm. Incremental NI_t is calculated as the after-tax, $(1 - \tau)$, change in the firm's sales revenue, R_t, generated from the project minus the corresponding operating costs, OC_t, minus project depreciation, D_t, minus interest expense, I_t. (As we discuss later in the chapter, we are only concerned with the interest expense that is consistent with the firm's optimal capital structure and the borrowing capacity created by the project.) The second term reflects the fact that depreciation is a *non*cash expense, that is, D_t is removed from the calculation of NI_t only for tax purposes. It is added back because this cash did not actually flow out of the firm in year t. D_t can be viewed as the recapture in year t of a portion of the original investment, C_0, in the project. The last term represents the firm's after-tax payment of interest to debtholders.

---

[1]The internal rate of return (IRR), payback method, and the profitability index are three additional methods for analyzing a capital expenditure. The IRR method solves for the discount rate, that is, the project's IRR, that causes the NPV to equal zero. In many situations, a project will have only a single IRR, and the IRR decision rule is to select the project if the IRR $\geq$ K. However, under certain circumstances a project will have multiple IRRs, thus causing difficulty in interpreting the simple decision rule if one or more IRRs are less than K. The payback method determines the period of time required for the cumulative cash inflows to "pay back" the initial cash outlay; the shorter the payback period, the more acceptable is the project. However, the payback method ignores the time value of money. The profitability index is computed by dividing the present value of cash inflows by the initial outlay; the larger the ratio, the more acceptable is the project. However, when dealing with mutually exclusive projects, a conflict may arise between the profitability index and the NPV criterion due to the scale of the investments. If the firm is not under a capital rationing constraint, it is generally agreed that conflicts should be settled in favour of the NPV criterion. Overall, the NPV decision rule is considered the superior framework for analyzing a capital budgeting expenditure. See Ross, Westerfield, Jaffee, and Roberts (2002, Chapter 6) for an overview of the NPV, IRR, payback, and profitability index methods.

Equation 17.2c provides a computationally simpler formula for calculating CF_t. Since $I_t(1 - \tau)$ is subtracted in determining NI_t in Equation 17.2a and then added back, the two cancel out. The first term in Equation 17.2c represents after-tax net operating income, $NOI_t(1 - \tau)$, as stated in Equation 17.2d.

Equation 17.2e provides an even simpler formula for calculating CF_t. It shows the result from Equation 17.2c of combining the after-tax value of the depreciation expense, $(1 - \tau)D_t$, with the before-tax value of D_t. The result of this combination is the amount τD_t in Equation 17.2e, which represents the tax saving due to D_t being a tax-deductible item. As summarized in Equation 17.2f, the first term in Equation 17.2e represents after-tax operating cash flow, $OCF_t(1 - \tau)$, and the second term denotes the tax savings from the depreciation expense.[2]

17.2 Adjusted Present Value

To continue our discussion, we need to expand the NPV model. To do this, we substitute Equation 17.2f for CF_t in Equation 17.1, allowing us to restate the NPV formula as:

$$NPV = \sum_{t=1}^{T} \frac{OCF_t(1 - \tau)}{(1 + K)^t} + \sum_{t=1}^{T} \frac{\tau D_t}{(1 + K)^t} + \frac{TV_T}{(1 + K)^T} - C_0 \qquad (17.3)$$

Following the well-known Modigliani-Miller approach to valuation, we know the value of a levered firm (V_l), that is a firm with debt in its capital structure, is greater than the value of an unlevered firm (V_u), a firm with no debt. The difference in value stems from the tax deductibility of interest payments on the debt. For perpetual debt at an interest rate (i), the annual tax savings via the tax deduction of interest is (τi Debt) where τ is the tax rate. Discounting the flow of annual tax saving at the rate i results in a present value of τDebt .

$$V_l = V_u + \tau\text{Debt} \qquad (17.4a)$$

Assuming the firms are ongoing concerns and the debt the levered firm issued to finance a portion of its productive capacity is perpetual, Equation 17.4a can be expanded as:

$$\frac{NOI(1 - \tau)}{K} = \frac{NOI(1 - \tau)}{K_u} + \frac{\tau I}{i} \qquad (17.4b)$$

where i is the levered firm's borrowing rate, $I = i$Debt, and K_u is the cost of equity for an **all-equity** financed firm.

Recall from Chapter 16 that the weighted average cost of capital can be stated as:

$$K = (1 - \lambda)K_l + \lambda i(1 - \tau) \qquad (17.5a)$$

where K_l is the cost of equity for a levered firm, and λ is the optimal debt ratio. K can be stated as:[3]

$$K = K_u(1 - \tau\lambda) \qquad (17.5b)$$

Equation 17.2a can be simplified to Equation 17.2d. This recognizes that NOI is independent of the firm's debt–equity ratio which is naturally the case, since NOI is computed *before* deduction of interest payments. From Equation 17.5b, if $\lambda = 0$ (that is, an all-equity financed firm), then $K = K_u$ and $I = 0$; thus, in Equation 17.4a $V_l = V_u$. However, if $\lambda > 0$ (that is, a levered firm), then $K_u > K$ and $I > 0$, thus, $V_l > V_u$. For Equation 17.4b to hold as an equality, it is necessary to add the present value of the

---

[2]Annual cash flows might also include incremental working capital funds. These are ignored here to simplify the presentation.

[3]To derive Equation 17.5b from Equation 17.5a, note that $K_l = K_u + (1 - \tau)(K_u - i)$ (Debt/Equity).

tax savings the levered firm receives. The value of a levered firm is greater than an equivalent unlevered firm earning the same NOI because the levered firm also has tax savings from the tax deductibility of interest payments to bondholders. The following example clarifies the tax savings to the firm from making interest payments on debt.

> **EXAMPLE 17.1** **Tax Savings from Interest Payments** Exhibit 17.1 provides an example of the tax savings arising from the tax deductibility of interest payments. The exhibit shows a levered firm and an unlevered firm, each with sales revenue and operating expenses of $100 and $50, respectively. The levered firm has interest expense of $10 and earnings, before taxes of $40, while the unlevered firm enjoys $50 of before-tax earnings, since it does not have any interest expense. The levered firm pays only $16 in taxes as opposed to $20 for the unlevered firm. This leaves $24 for the levered firm's shareholders and $30 for the unlevered firm's shareholders. Nevertheless, the levered firm has a total of $34 (= $24 + $10) of funds available for investors, while the unlevered firm has only $30. The extra $4 comes from the tax savings on the $10 before-tax interest payment. ∎

By direct analogy to the Modigliani-Miller equation for an unlevered firm, we can convert the NPV Equation 17.3 into the **adjusted present value (APV)** model:

$$APV = \sum_{t=1}^{T} \frac{OCF_t(1-\tau)}{(1+K_u)^t} + \sum_{t=1}^{T} \frac{\tau D_t}{(1+i)^t} + \sum_{t=1}^{T} \frac{\tau I_t}{(1+i)^t} + \frac{TV_T}{(1+K_u)^T} - C_0$$

(17.6)

The APV model is a **value-additive** approach to capital budgeting. That is, each cash flow is a source of value to be considered individually. In the APV model, each cash flow is discounted at a rate consistent with the risk inherent in that cash flow. The OCF_t and TV_T are discounted at K_u. The firm would receive these cash flows from a capital project, regardless of whether the firm was levered or unlevered. The tax savings due to interest, τI_t, are discounted at the before-tax borrowing rate, i, as in Equation 17.4b. The tax savings due to depreciation, τD_t, are also be discounted at i because they are relatively less risky than operating cash flows if tax laws are not likely to change radically over the economic life of the project.[4]

The APV model is useful for a domestic firm analyzing a domestic capital expenditure. If APV ≥ 0, the project should be accepted. If APV < 0, the project should be rejected. Thus, the model is useful for an MNC for analyzing one of its domestic cap-

EXHIBIT 17.1

Comparison of Cash Flows Available to Investors

	Levered	Unlevered
Revenue	$100	$100
Operating costs	−50	−50
Net operating income	50	50
Interest expense	−10	−0
Earnings before taxes	40	50
Taxes @ 0.40	−16	−20
Net income	24	30
Cash flow available to investors	$24 + 10 = $34	$ 30

---

[4]Booth (1982) shows under what circumstances the NPV and APV methods are precisely equivalent.

ital expenditures or for a foreign subsidiary of the MNC analyzing a proposed capital expenditure from the subsidiary's viewpoint.

17.3 Capital Budgeting from the Parent Firm's Perspective

The APV model as stated in Equation 17.6 is not useful for the MNC in analyzing a foreign capital expenditure of one of its subsidiaries from the MNC's, or parent's, perspective. In fact, it is possible that a project may have a positive APV from the subsidiary's perspective and a negative APV from the parent's perspective. This could happen, for example, if certain cash flows are blocked by the host country from being legally remitted to the parent or if extra taxes are imposed by the host country on foreign exchange remittances. A higher marginal tax rate in the home country may also cause a project to be unprofitable from the parent's perspective. If we assume that the MNC owns the foreign subsidiary but domestic shareholders own the MNC parent, it is the currency of the parent firm that is important because it is that currency into which the cash flows must be converted to benefit the shareholders whose wealth the MNC is attempting to maximize.

Lessard (1985) developed an APV model suitable for an MNC to use in analyzing a foreign capital expenditure. The model recognizes that foreign cash flows are eventually converted into the currency of the parent. APV is especially well suited to deal with special cash flows of the sort frequently encountered in foreign project analysis. Using the basic structure of the APV model developed in the previous section,

$$
\text{APV} = \sum_{t=1}^{T} \frac{\overline{S}_t OCF_t (1-\tau)}{(1+K_{ud})^t} + \sum_{t=1}^{T} \frac{\overline{S}_t \tau D_t}{(1+i_d)^t} + \sum_{t=1}^{T} \frac{\overline{S}_t \tau I_t}{(1+i_d)^t} + \frac{\overline{S}_T TV_T}{(1+K_{ud})^T}
$$

$$
- S_0 C_0 + S_0 RF_0 + S_0 CL_0 - \sum_{t=1}^{T} \frac{\overline{S}_t LP_t}{(1+i_d)^t} \tag{17.7}
$$

Several points are noteworthy about Equation 17.7. First, cash flows denominated in foreign currency are converted to the currency of the parent at the expected spot rate, S_t, applicable to year t. Second, the discount rates, K_{ud} and i_d, the cost of unlevered equity and the cost of debt, respectively, are identified (by subscript d) as the firm's *domestic* costs of capital. Once cash flows are converted to domestic currency, domestic costs of capital apply. Third, a distinguishing feature of *adjusted present value* is that specific cash flow streams or items are discounted at specific discount rates appropriate to the risk of the stream or item. For example, the net after-tax operating cash flow $S_t OCF_t (1-\tau)$ and the terminal value $S_T TV_T$ are risky cash flows for which it is appropriate to apply K_{ud}. On the other hand, a tax shield from the use of debt, $S_t \tau D_t$, or a concessionary loan, $S_t \tau I_t$, are cash flows for which the cost of borrowing, i_d, is appropriate. Finally, nowhere in the formula for adjusted present value do we see the Canadian tax rate. This reflects the fact that foreign-source income earned from active business by Canadian companies does not incur a Canadian tax liability.

In Equation 17.7, the OCF_t represents only the portion of net operating cash flow available for remittance that, indeed, can be effectively remitted to the parent firm. Cash flows earned in the foreign country that are blocked by the host government from being repatriated do not provide any benefit to the shareholders of the parent firm and, thus, are not relevant to the project valuation analysis. Likewise, cash flows that are repatriated in circuitous ways, such as through transfer price manipulation, are not included here.

As with domestic project analysis, it is important to include only incremental revenues and operating costs in calculating the OCF_t. An example will help illustrate the concept. An MNC may presently have a sales affiliate in a foreign country that is supplied by merchandise produced by the parent or a manufacturing facility in a third country. If a manufacturing facility is put into operation in the foreign country to satisfy local demand, sales may be larger overall than with just a sales affiliate if the foreign subsidiary is better able to assess market demand with its local presence. However, the former manufacturing unit will experience **lost sales** as a result of the new foreign manufacturing facility; that is, the new project has *cannibalized* part of an existing project. Thus, incremental revenue is not the total sales revenue of the new manufacturing facility but, rather, that amount minus the lost sales revenue. However, if the sales would be lost regardless, say, because a competitor who is better able to satisfy local demand is gearing up, then the entire sales revenue of the new foreign manufacturing facility is incremental sales revenue.

Equation 17.7 includes additional terms representing cash flows frequently encountered in foreign projects. The term S_0RF_0 represents the value of accumulated **restricted funds** (of amount RF_0) in the foreign land from existing operations that are freed up by the proposed project. These funds become available only *because* of the proposed project and are therefore available to offset a portion of the initial capital outlay. Examples are funds whose use is restricted by exchange controls or funds on which additional taxes would be due in the parent country if they are remitted. RF_0 equals the difference between the face value of these funds and their present value used in the best alternative. The extended illustration at the end of this chapter will help clarify the meaning of this term.

$$S_0CL_0 - \sum_{t=1}^{T} \frac{\overline{S_t}LP_t}{(1 + i_d)^t}$$

www.worldbank.org/
guarantees/

This website of the World Bank provides information on doing business in the developing world, including information on project financing.

The above term denotes the present value in the currency of the parent firm of the benefit of below-market-rate borrowing in foreign currency. In certain cases, a **concessionary loan** (of amount CL_0) at a below-market rate of interest may be available to the parent firm if the proposed capital expenditure is made in the foreign land. The host country offers this financing in its foreign currency as a means of attracting economic development and investment that will create employment for its citizens. The benefit to the MNC is the difference between the face value of the concessionary loan converted into the home currency and the present value of the similarly converted concessionary loan payments (LP_t) discounted at the MNC's normal domestic borrowing rate (i_d). The loan payments will yield a present value less than the face amount of the concessionary loan when they are discounted at the higher normal rate. This difference represents a subsidy the host country is willing to extend to the MNC if the investment is made. It should be clear that the present value of the loan payments discounted at the normal borrowing rate represents the size of the loan available from borrowing at the normal borrowing rate with a debt service schedule equivalent to that of the concessionary loan.

Recall that to calculate the firm's weighted-average cost of capital, it is necessary to know the firm's optimal debt ratio. When considering a capital budgeting project, it is never appropriate to think of the project as being financed separately from the way the firm is financed, for the project represents a portion of the firm. When the asset base increases because a capital project is undertaken, the firm can handle more debt in its capital structure. That is, the borrowing capacity of the firm has increased because of the project. Nevertheless, the investment and financing decisions are separate. There is an optimal capital structure for the firm; once this is determined, the cost of financing is known and can be used to determine if a project is acceptable. We do not mean to imply that *each* and every capital project is financed with the optimal portions of debt and equity. Rather, some projects may be financed with all debt or all equity or a suboptimal combination. What is important is that in the long run, the firm does not stray too far from its optimal capital structure so that overall the firm's assets are financed at the lowest cost. Thus, the interest tax shield term $S_t\tau I_t$ in the APV model recognizes the tax shields of the **borrowing capacity** created by the project, *regardless* of how the project is financed. Handling the tax shields in any other way would bias the APV favourably or unfavourably, respectively, if the project was financed by a larger or smaller portion of debt. This is an especially important point in international capital budgeting analysis because of the frequency of large concessionary loans. The benefit of concessionary loans, which are dependent on the parent firm making the investment, is recognized in a separate term.

Generality of the APV Model

APV includes many terms for cash flows frequently encountered in analyzing foreign capital expenditures. However, *all* possible terms are not included in the version presented as Equation 17.7. Nevertheless, the reader should now have the knowledge to incorporate into the basic APV model terms of a more unique nature for specific cash flows encountered in a particular analysis.

For example, there may be tax savings or deferrals that come about because of multinational operations. That is, the MNC may be able to shift revenues or expenses among its affiliates in a way that lowers taxes or be able to combine profits or affiliates from both low and high tax environments in a manner that results in lower overall taxes. Tax deferrals are possible by reinvesting profits in new capital projects in low-tax countries.

Through interaffiliate transfer pricing strategies, licensing arrangements, royalty agreements, or other means, the parent firm might be able to repatriate some funds that are meant to be blocked, or restricted, by the host country.[5] These cash flows are the counterpart to the unrestricted funds available for remittance as part of operating cash flows. As with the cash flows arising from tax savings or deferrals, it may be difficult for the firm to accurately estimate the size of these cash flows or their duration. Since these cash flows will exist regardless of how the firm is financed, they should be discounted at the all-equity rate.

One of the major benefits of the APV framework is the ease with which difficult cash flow terms, such as tax savings or deferrals and the repatriation of restricted funds, can be handled. The analyst can first analyze the capital expenditure as if they did not exist. Additional cash flow terms do not need to be explicitly considered unless the APV is negative. If the APV is negative, the analyst can calculate how large the cash flows from other sources need to be to make the APV positive and then estimate whether these other cash inflows will likely be that large.

Estimating the Future Expected Exchange Rate

The financial manager must estimate the future expected exchange rates, $\overline{S}_t$, in order to implement the APV framework. Chapter 5 provided a wide variety of methods for estimating exchange rates. One quick and simple way to do this is to rely on purchasing power parity (PPP) and estimate the future expected spot rate for year t as:

$$\overline{S}_t = S_0(1 + \overline{\pi}_d)^t/(1 + \overline{\pi}_f)^t \qquad (17.8)$$

where π_d is the expected long-run annual rate of inflation in the (home) domestic country of the MNC and $\overline{\pi}_f$ is the rate in the foreign land.

As noted in Chapter 5, PPP is not likely to hold precisely in reality. Nevertheless, unless the financial manager suspects that there is some systematic long-run bias in using PPP to estimate $\overline{S}_t$ that would result in a systematic over- or underestimate of the series of expected exchange rates, then PPP should prove to be an acceptable tool. Alternatively, the analyst may choose to use long-dated forward prices to estimate the future expected spot exchange rates.

---

[5]Chapter 18 covers interaffiliate transfer pricing strategies, licensing arrangements, and royalty agreements as methods the parent firm might use to repatriate funds restricted by the host country.

Illustrated MINI CASE | Research In Motion/Europe

Research In Motion (RIM) of Waterloo, Ontario, is a world leader in mobile communications. RIM developed and manufactures BlackBerry, the stunningly successful wireless handheld communicator with access to e-mail, Internet, and phone, along with organizer features.

Research in Motion has been exporting BlackBerries to Europe for several years. European sales are currently 9,600 units a year and have been increasing at a rate of 5 percent. The European marketing manager believes that a manufacturing facility in Europe offers real advantages in production efficiencies. A local presence in Europe is also strategically wise in view of the potential market expansion driven by European enlargement.

RIM is considering establishing a manufacturing and sales operation in Europe, to be based in the high-tech centre of Ulm, in the Province of Baden Wutenberg in Germany. Ulm is located about 100 kilometres west of Munich.

The European marketing manager, together with production managers in Canada, have drawn up plans for a wholly owned manufacturing facility in Ulm. A major attraction of locating in Ulm is that the Government of Baden Wutenberg has promised to arrange for a substantial portion of the construction cost to be financed at an attractive so-called *concessionary* interest rate if the plant is built there.

The Executive Committee of RIM has instructed the financial manager and her team to determine if the plan has financial merit. If the manufacturing facility is built, RIM will no longer export units from Canada to Europe.

On its current exports, RIM receives C$180 per unit of which C$40 represents the contribution margin. Twenty-five thousand units are forecast to be sold in Europe during the first year of operation. This volume will increase at the rate of 12 percent per year. European sales will be invoiced in euros. When the plant in Ulm begins operation, units will be priced at €110 each. Production cost is estimated to be €75 per unit, which results in a per-unit contribution of €35. Sales price and production costs in Europe are expected to keep pace with European inflation, which is forecast to be 3 percent per annum for the foreseeable future. By comparison, Canadian inflation is forecast to be 2 percent per annum. The current exchange rate is C$1.60/€1.

Construction of the manufacturing plant is estimated to cost €4,920,000. Since the capital expenditure on the plant and its equipment provide security in borrowing, we assume that the project expands RIM's borrowing capacity by C$1,770,000.

The basic corporate tax rate in Germany is 35 percent. The German tax authorities will allow the plant to be depreciated over an eight-year period. Little, if any, additional investment will be required over that time. The market value of the facility at the end of this period is difficult to estimate, but RIM believes that the plant should still be in good condition and have reasonable market value.

An attractive feature of the proposal is the special financing the German government is willing to arrange. If the plant is built in Ulm, RIM will be eligible to borrow €3,500,000 at a rate of 6 percent per annum. RIM's normal borrowing rate is 8 percent in dollars, and 9 percent in euros. The loan schedule calls for the principal to be repaid in eight equal installments. In dollar terms, RIM estimates its after-tax all-equity cost of capital to be 11 percent.

Here is a summary of the key points in the analysis:

The current exchange rate: $S_0 = \$1.60/€1$

Expected inflation, Europe: $\pi_f = 3$ percent per annum

Expected inflation, Canada: $\pi_d = 2$ percent per annum

The initial cost of the project in Canadian dollars is:

$$S_0 C_0 = C\$1.60 \times €4,920,000 = C\$7,872,000$$

For simplicity, we assume that PPP holds. Thus, the future path of the nominal exchange rate in Canadian dollars per Euro is:

$$S_t = S_0 (1 + \pi_d)^t/(1 + \pi_f)^t = 1.60 (1.02)^t / (1.03)^t$$

The before-tax incremental operating cash flow per unit in the first period of operations (t = 1) is €110 − 75 or €35. The nominal contribution margin on made-in-Europe Blackberries is €35 $(1 + \pi_f)^t$.

Export sales (unit volume) "lost" to the parent in Canada as manufacturing shifts to Europe are $9,600(1.05)^t$ units for year t .

Contribution margin per unit of "lost" sales in year t equals C$40(1 + π_d)t = C$40(1.02)^t.

The German tax rate, τ, is 35 percent.

Terminal value will initially be assumed to be zero.

Straight-line depreciation implies: D_t = €4,920,000 / 8 years = €615,000 per year.

RIM's cost of borrowing at the concessionary rate: i_c = 6 percent

RIM's Canadian dollar cost of borrowing: i_d = 8 percent

RIM's Canadian dollar cost of unlevered equity: K_{ud} = 11 percent

The last two items refer to the pretax cost of debt and the after-tax cost of (unlevered) equity capital that RIM faces in Canada. Thus, these are relevant "opportunity costs" that will be used as discount rates in appropriate places in the APV analysis.

The present value of the expected after-tax operating cash flows from RIM's proposed manufacturing facility in Europe is calculated in Exhibit 17.2. Column (a) presents the annual revenue in dollars from operating the new manufacturing facility. The figures in Column (a) are calculated for each year by multiplying the expected quantity of BlackBerries sold times the initial incremental operating cash flow of €35 per unit. This product is, in turn, multiplied by the European inflation factor of $(1 + \pi_f)^{t-1}$. For example, for year 2, the factor is $(1.03)^{2-1}$, which equals 1.03. Euro sales are then converted to dollars at the expected spot exchange rates. Column (b) reports annual lost sales revenue in dollars that will result from RIM (Canada) no longer selling to Europe.

EXHIBIT 17.2			Calculation of the Present Value of the After-Tax Operating Cash Flows				
			(a)		(b)	(a + b)	
Year (t)	$\bar{S}_t$	Quantity	$\bar{S}_t \times$ Quantity $\times$ €35 $\times (1.03)^{t-1}$ $	Quantity Lost Sales	Quantity Lost Sales $\times$ \$35.00 $\times (1.02)^{t-1}$ $	$\bar{S}_t OCF_t$ $	$\dfrac{\bar{S}_t OCF_t(1 - \tau)}{(1 + K_{ud})^t}$ $
1	1.5845	25,000	1,386,408	(10,080)	(411,264)	975,144	571,030
2	1.5691	28,000	1,583,832	(10,584)	(419,489)	1,164,343	614,254
3	1.5538	31,360	1,809,370	(11,113)	(427,879)	1,381,491	656,587
4	1.5388	35,123	2,067,024	(11,669)	(436,437)	1,630,588	698,177
5	1.5238	39,338	2,361,368	(12,252)	(445,165)	1,916,203	739,163
6	1.5090	44,059	2,697,627	(12,865)	(454,069)	2,243,559	779,674
7	1.4944	49,346	3,081,769	(13,508)	(463,150)	2,618,619	819,832
8	1.4799	55,267	3,520,613	(14,184)	(472,413)	3,048,200	859,752
							5,738,469

EXHIBIT 17.3

Calculation of the
Present Value of
the Depreciation
Tax Shields

Year (t)	$\bar{S}_t$	D_t €	$\dfrac{\bar{S}_t \tau D_t}{(1+i_d)^t}$ $
1	1.5845	615,000	315,793
2	1.5691	615,000	289,562
3	1.5538	615,000	265,510
4	1.5388	615,000	243,456
5	1.5238	615,000	223,233
6	1.5090	615,000	204,691
7	1.4944	615,000	187,688
8	1.4799	615,000	172,098
			1,902,031

Europe. These losses for the parent are calculated by multiplying the estimated quantity of lost sales in units by the contribution margin of C$40 per unit, which is, in turn, multiplied by the Canadian inflation factor $(1+\pi_c)^{t-1}$. The incremental dollar operating cashflow is the sum of columns (a) and (b). Taking into account the German tax and then discounting at RIM's unlevered discount rate, K_{ud} results in a present value of after-tax net operating income flows of C$5,738,469.

The present value of the depreciation tax shield ((Dt) is calculated in Exhibit 17.3. Tax savings on annual straight-line depreciation of €615,000 are converted to dollars at the expected future spot exchange rates and discounted to the present using the RIM's Canadian cost of borrowing, 8 percent. The present value of the depreciation tax shield is C$1,902,031.

The present value of the benefit of the concessionary loan is calculated in Exhibits 17.4 and 17.5. In Exhibit 17.4, the aim is to compute the present value of the concessionary loan payments in dollars. Since the annual principal payment on the €3,500,000 concessionary loan is the same each year, interest payments decline as the loan balance declines. For example, during the first year, interest of €210,000 (= 0.06 × €350,000) is paid on the full amount borrowed. During the second year, interest of €183,750 (= 0.06 × (€3,500,000 − 437,500)) is paid on the outstanding balance over year 2. The annual loan payment equals the sum of the annual principal payment and the annual interest charge. The sum of their present values in dollars, converted at the expected spot exchange rates and discounted at RIM's borrowing rate of 8 percent, is C$5,014,466. This sum represents the size of the equivalent loan available (in dollars) from borrowing at the normal borrowing rate with a debt service schedule equivalent to that of the concessionary loan.

EXHIBIT 17.4

Calculation of the
Present Value of the
Concessionary Loan
Payments

Year (t)	$\bar{S}_t$ (a)	Principal Payment (b) €	I_t (c) €	$\bar{S}_t LP_t$ (a) × (b + c) $	$\dfrac{\bar{S}_t LP_t}{(1+i_d)^t}$ $
1	1.5845	437,500	210,000	1,025,942	949,946
2	1.5691	437,500	183,750	974,793	835,728
3	1.5538	437,500	157,500	924,540	733,930
4	1.5388	437,500	131,250	875,172	643,277
5	1.5238	437,500	105,000	826,674	562,621
6	1.5090	437,500	78,750	779,036	490,925
7	1.4944	437,500	52,500	732,245	427,258
8	1.4799	437,500	26,250	686,290	370,781
		3,500,000			5,014,466

EXHIBIT 17.5	Calculation of the Present Value of the Benefit from the Concessionary Loan

$$S_0 CL_0 - \sum_{t=1}^{T} \frac{\overline{S}_t LP_t}{(1 + i_d)^t} = \$1.60 \times €3,500,000 - 5,014,466 = C\$585,534$$

EXHIBIT 17.6

Calculation of the
Present Value of the
Interest Tax Shields

Year (t)	(a) $\overline{S}_t$	(b) I_t €	(c) λ/Project Debt Ratio	(a × b × c × τ) $\overline{S}_t \cdot .5619τI_t$ $	$\dfrac{\overline{S}_t \cdot .5619τI_t}{(1 + i_d)^t}$ $
1	1.5845	210,000	0.56	65,438	60,591
2	1.5691	183,750	0.56	56,702	48,613
3	1.5538	157,500	0.56	48,130	38,207
4	1.5388	131,250	0.56	39,719	29,195
5	1.5238	105,000	0.56	31,467	21,416
6	1.5090	78,750	0.56	23,371	14,728
7	1.4944	52,500	0.56	15,429	9,003
8	1.4799	26,250	0.56	7.640	4,128
					225,879

Exhibit 17.5 concludes the analysis of the concessionary loan. It shows the difference between the dollar value of the concessionary loan and the equivalent dollar loan value calculated in Exhibit 17.4. The difference of C$585,534 represents the present value of the benefit of the below market rate financing of the concessionary loan.

The present value of the interest tax shield is calculated in Exhibit 17.6. The interest payments in column (b) of Exhibit 17.6 are drawn from column (c) of Exhibit 17.4. That is, we follow a conservative approach and base the interest tax shield on using the concessionary loan interest rate of 6 percent. The concessionary loan of €3,500,000 represents 71 percent of the project cost of €4,920,000. By comparison, the borrowing capacity created by the project is C$1,770,000, which implies an optimal debt ratio (for the parent firm of 40 percent = C$1,770,000/C$4,428,000) of the dollar cost of the project. Thus, only 56 percent (= 40%/71%) of the interest payments on the concessionary loan should be used to calculate the interest tax shield. Discounted at RIM's borrowing rate of 8 percent, the present value of the interest tax shield is C$225,879.

APV = PV of Net Operating Cash Flows (after German Tax)
+ PV of Depreciation Tax Shield
+ PV of the Benefit for the Concessionary Loan
+ PV of the Interest Rate Tax Shield
− Initial Cost of the Project in Canadian dollars

APV = C$5,738,469 + C$1,902,031 + C$585,534 + C$225,879
− C$7,872,000
= C$579,914

There appears little doubt that the proposed European manufacturing facility will be a profitable venture for RIM. Had the APV been negative or closer to zero, we would want to consider the present value of the after-tax terminal cash flow. We are quite uncertain as to what this amount might be, and fortunately in this case, we do not have to base a decision on this cash flow, which is difficult at best to forecast.

The European sales affiliate has accumulated €550,000 from past operations which can be used to partially finance the capital expenditure. These accumulated funds were earned under special tax concessions offered during the initial years of the sales operation and were taxed at a rate of 20 percent. If these funds are repatriated to Canada, additional tax at the 35 percent marginal rate would be owing.

To calculate the amount of the freed-up restricted remittances, it is first necessary to gross up the after-tax value of the €550,000 on which the European sales affiliate has previously paid taxes at the rate of 20 percent. This amount is €687,500 = €550,000/(1.20). The dollar value of this sum at the current spot exchange rate S_0 is C$1,100,000 = C$1.60(€687,500). If RIM decided not to establish a manufacturing facility in Germany, the €550,000 should be repatriated to the parent firm.

17.4 Risk Adjustment in Capital Budgeting

APV is suitable for analyzing a capital expenditure that has the average riskiness of the firm as a whole. Some projects may be more or less risky than average, however. The *risk-adjusted discount method* is the standard way to handle this situation. This approach requires adjusting the discount rate upward or downward for increases or decreases, respectively, in the systematic risk of the project relative to the firm as a whole. In the APV model presented in Equation 17.7, only the cash flows discounted at K_{ud} incorporate systematic risk; thus, only K_{ud} needs to be adjusted when project risk differs from that of the firm as a whole.[6]

A second way to adjust for risk in the APV framework is the *certainty equivalent method*. This approach extracts the risk premium from the expected cash flows to convert them into equivalent riskless cash flows, which are then discounted at the risk-free rate of interest. This is accomplished by multiplying the risky cash flows by a certainty-equivalent factor that is unity or less. The more risky the cash flow, the smaller is the certainty-equivalent factor. In general, cash flows tend to be more risky the further into the future they are expected to be received. We favour the risk-adjusted discount rate method over the certainty-equivalent approach because we find that it is easier to adjust the discount rate than it is to estimate the appropriate certainty-equivalent factors.[7]

17.5 Sensitivity Analysis

The way we have approached the analysis of RIM's expansion into Europe results in a point estimate of the APV through using expected values of the relevant cash flows. The expected values of these inputs are what the financial manager expects to obtain given the information at the time the analysis was performed. However, each cash flow has its own probability distribution. Hence, the realized value that may result for a particular cash flow may be different from expected. To examine these possibilities, the financial manager typically performs a sensitivity analysis. In a *sensitivity analysis,* different scenarios are examined by using different exchange rate estimates, inflation rate estimates, and cost and pricing estimates in the calculation of the APV. In essence, the sensitivity

[6]See Ross, Westerfield, Jaffee, and Roberts (2003) for a treatment of capital budgeting using discount rates adjusted for project systematic risk.
[7]See Brealey and Myers (2003, Chapter 9) for a more detailed discussion of the certainty equivalent method of risk adjustment.

analysis allows the financial manager a means to analyze the business risk, economic exposure, exchange rate uncertainty, and political risk inherent in the investment. Sensitivity analysis puts financial managers in a position to more fully understand the implications of planned capital expenditures. It also forces them to consider in advance actions that can be taken should an investment not develop as anticipated.

For example, if RIM's European unit sales in the base year are assumed to be 24,000 units, rather than 25,000, the APV of the project falls to C$291,970. Or, if the annual rate of growth of European unit sales is assumed to be 10 percent, rather than 12 percent, the APV of the project falls to C$127,338. Perhaps most telling of all is the sensitivity of APV to the "contribution" (selling price minus production costs) in Europe. If the contribution is €30, rather than €35, as a result of either a lower selling price or higher production costs than were assumed in the analysis, the APV falls to C$448,457 in which case the terminal value of the project becomes an important consideration in the accept/reject decision.

17.6 Real Options

Throughout this chapter, we have recommended the APV framework for evaluating capital expenditures in real assets, such as when a firm plans to set up production operations abroad. A decision based on APV relies on specific assumptions and forecasts involving revenues, operating costs, discount rates, exchange rates, and the like. When evaluated at appropriate APV discount rates, a project is accepted or rejected on the basis of whether APV is positive or negative. The evaluation exercise assumes that all relevant considerations involving future cash flows have been taken into account. It is often the case, however, that certain crucial, value-enhancing or value-destroying pieces of information are unavailable at the time of analysis or even at the time the project is scheduled to begin. Such information is typically *binary*, that is, one thing or the other will happen, one of which is favourable, and one of which is not. But we do not know which one will unfold.

In this situation, it is often wise to wait. Management has alternative paths—or *options*—that it can take until the new crucial information arrives. Option pricing theory can be useful for evaluating investment opportunities in such cases, for instance, as RIM's plans for Europe. In Chapter 9, we saw that option pricing is widely applied in the case of financial assets, such as foreign exchange. Now, with a little modification, we can apply option pricing theory to option-like situations that involve real projects. These are referred to as **real options**.

The firm is confronted with many possible real options over the life of a capital asset. For example, the firm may have a *timing option* about when to make the investment; it may have a *growth option* to increase the scale of the investment; it may have a *suspension option* to temporarily cease production; and it may have an *abandonment option* to quit the investment early. All of these situations can be evaluated as real options.

In international capital expenditures, the MNC is faced with the political uncertainties of doing business in a foreign host country. For example, a stable political environment for foreign investment may turn unfavourable if a different political party wins power by election—or worse, by political coup. Moreover, an unexpected change in a host country's monetary policy may cause a depreciation in its exchange rate versus the parent firm's home currency, thus adversely affecting the return to the shareholders of the parent firm. These and other political uncertainties make real options analysis ideal for use in evaluating international capital expenditures. Real options analysis, however, should be thought of as an extension of discounted cash flow analysis, not as a replacement of it, as the following example makes clear.

EXAMPLE | **17.2** | **Timing Option** Suppose the sales forecast for the first year of Research In Motion's operations in Europe had been only 23,000 BlackBerries, rather than 25,000. At the lower base year figure for unit sales, APV turns out to be C\$4,026 or, for all practical purposes, 0. It becomes questionable as to whether RIM ought to proceed with the construction of the manufacturing facility in Germany. Suppose further that there is substantial uncertainty as to whether the European Central Bank will tighten or loosen monetary policy. An expert advises RIM that a change in European monetary policy would cause the euro to either appreciate to C\$1.70/€ or depreciate to C\$1.50/€1. Under a restrictive monetary policy and euro appreciation, the APV of RIM's project rises to C\$95,536. With a more valuable euro, the present value of operating cash flows, the depreciation tax shield, the interest tax shield, and the value of the concessionary loan all become more valuable in Canadian dollar terms, more than offsetting the increased Canadian dollar cost of the initial investment. On the other hand, under a looser monetary policy and euro depreciation, the APV of RIM's project falls to a negative C\$87,483.

RIM's project analysts believe the effect of any change in monetary policy will be known in a year's time. Thus, RIM plans to put the project on hold until it learns what the European Central Bank decides to do. In the meantime, RIM can obtain a buy-option for a year on the parcel of land that would be its building site. The German landowner has offered to extend to RIM the option to purchase the land in one year's time for a fee of €10,000 or C\$16,000.

The situation is a classic example in which the real options framework is useful in evaluating a capital expenditure. The buy-option of €10,000 represents the option premium of the real option to buy the land and launch the project. The initial investment of €4,920,000 represents the exercise price of the option. RIM will only exercise its option if the European Central Bank decides to adopt a restrictive monetary policy that would result in euro appreciation that gives RIM's project a positive APV of C\$95,536. The €10,000 seems like a small amount to allow the flexibility to postpone a costly capital expenditure until crucial information is at hand. The following example explicitly values the timing option using the binomial option pricing approach.

EXAMPLE | **17.3** | **Valuing RIM's Timing Option** RIM's timing option can be valued with the use of the binomial option pricing model developed in Chapter 9. We use RIM's 8-percent borrowing cost in Canadian dollars and the 9-percent borrowing cost in euros as our estimates of the domestic and foreign risk-free rates of interest. Depending on the action of the ECB, the euro will either appreciate from C\$1.60/€ to C\$1.70/€, or 6.25 percent, or the euro will depreciate by an equal percentage to C\$1.50/€. Thus, $u = 1.0625$ and $d = 0.9375$. This implies that the risk-neutral probability of a depreciation of the euro is:

$$q = [((1 + i_d)/(1 + i_f)) - d]/(u - d)$$
$$= [(1.08/1.09) - 0.9375]/(1.0625 - 0.9375)$$
$$= 0.42$$

The probability of euro appreciation is $(1 - q)$ or 0.58.

The option will be exercised if the APV is positive, which occurs if the euro appreciates, and hence the value of the option is :

$$C = (0.58 \times C\$95,536)/1.08$$
$$= C\$51,306$$

Since C\$51,306 is substantially in excess of the C\$16,000 cost of the option to purchase the land, RIM is well advised to take advantage of the timing option in order to "buy time" and to wait and see what monetary policy the European Central Bank decides to pursue.

SUMMARY

This chapter presents a review of the NPV capital budgeting framework and expands the methodology into the APV model that is suitable for analyzing capital expenditures of an MNC in a foreign land.

1. The NPV capital budgeting framework in a domestic context is reviewed. The NPV is the difference between the present value of the cash inflows and outflows. If NPV ≥ 0 for a capital project, it should be accepted.

2. The annual after-tax cash flow formula was thoroughly defined and presented in a number of variations. This was necessary to expand the NPV model into the APV model.

3. The APV model of capital budgeting was developed by analogy to the Modigliani-Miller formula for the value of a levered firm. The APV model separates the operating cash flows from the cash flows due to financing. Each cash flow is discounted at a rate of discount commensurate with its inherent risk.

4. The APV model was further expanded to make it amenable for use by an MNC parent analyzing a foreign capital project. The cash flows were converted into the parent firm's home currency, and additional terms were added to the model to handle cash flows that are frequently encountered in international capital projects.

5. An illustrated mini case showing how to apply the APV model was presented and solved.

KEY WORDS

adjusted present value (APV), *406*
all-equity (cost of capital), *405*
borrowing capacity, *408*

concessionary loan, *408*
incremental cash flow, *404*
lost sales, *408*

net present value (NPV), *403*
real option, *415*
restricted funds, *408*
value-additivity, *406*

QUESTIONS

1. Why is capital budgeting analysis so important to the firm?
2. What is the intuition behind the NPV capital budgeting framework?
3. Discuss what is meant by the *incremental* cash flows of a capital project.
4. Discuss the nature of the equation sequence, Equations 17.2a to 17.2f.
5. What makes the APV capital budgeting framework useful for analyzing foreign capital expenditures?
6. Relate the concept of *lost sales* to the definition of incremental cash flows.
7. What problems can enter into the capital budgeting analysis if project debt is evaluated instead of the *borrowing capacity* created by the project?
8. What is the nature of a *concessionary loan,* and how is it handled in the APV model?
9. What is the intuition of discounting the various cash flows in the APV model at specific discount rates?
10. In the Modigliani-Miller equation, why is the market value of the levered firm greater than the market value of an equivalent unlevered firm?
11. Discuss the difference between performing the capital budgeting analysis from the parent firm's perspective as opposed to the project perspective.
12. Define the concept of a real option. Discuss some of the various real options a firm can be confronted with when investing in real projects.

PROBLEMS

1. The Alpha Company plans to establish a subsidiary in Hungary to manufacture and sell fashion wristwatches. Alpha has total assets of $70 million, of which $45 million is equity financed. The remainder is financed with debt. Alpha considered its current capital structure optimal. The construction cost of the Hungarian facility in forints is estimated at HUF2,400,000,000, of which HUF1,800,000,000 is to be financed at a below-market borrowing rate arranged by the Hungarian government. Alpha wonders what amount of debt it should use in calculating the tax shields on interest payments in its capital budgeting analysis. Can you offer assistance?

2. The current spot exchange rate between the Canadian dollar and the Hungarian forint is HUF150/$1. Long-run inflation in Hungary is estimated at 10 percent annually and 3 percent in Canada. If PPP is expected to hold between the two countries, what spot exchange rate should one forecast five years into the future?

3. The Beta Corporation has an optimal debt ratio of 40 percent. Its cost of equity capital is 12 percent and its before-tax borrowing rate is 8 percent. Given a marginal tax rate of 35 percent, calculate (a) the weighted-average cost of capital, and (b) the cost of equity for an equivalent all-equity financed firm.

4. Suppose that in the illustrated mini case in the chapter the APV for Research In Motion had been −C$60,000. How large would the after-tax terminal value of the project need to be before the APV would be positive and RIM would accept the project?

5. With regard to the RIM case, how would the APV change if:

   a. the forecast of $\bar{\pi}_d$ and/or $\bar{\pi}_f$ are incorrect?

   b. depreciation cash flows are discounted at K_{ud} instead of i_d?

   c. the host country did not provide the concessionary loan?

INTERNET EXERCISE

China is the focus of much new capital investment. Engineering and construction firms from around the world are competing to obtain some of this business. Concessionary financing often plays a part in whether a corporation can submit a winning bid. The website www.tradeport.org/ts/countries/china/mrr/mark0100.html discusses competition in the bidding on Light Rail Transport Projects in China. Read the discussion to learn how important concessionary financing is in structuring a deal.

MINI CASE 1

Dorchester

Dorchester is an old-line confectioner specializing in high-quality chocolates. Through its facilities in the United Kingdom, Dorchester manufactures candies that it sells throughout Western Europe and North America. With its current manufacturing facilities, Dorchester has been unable to supply the North American market with more than 290,000 kilograms of candy per year. This supply has allowed its sales affiliate, located in Halifax, to penetrate the North American market no farther west than Montreal and only as far south as Boston. Dorchester believes that a separate manufacturing facility located in Windsor, Ontario would allow it to supply the entire North American market. Dorchester currently estimates initial demand in the North American market at 390,000 kilograms, with growth at a 5-percent annual rate. A separate manufacturing facility would obviously free up the amount currently shipped to the United States and Canada. But Dorchester believes that this is only a short-run problem. They believe the economic development taking place in Eastern Europe will allow it to sell there the full amount presently shipped to North America within a period of five years.

Dorchester presently realizes £3 per kilogram on its North American exports. Once the Canadian manufacturing facility begins operating, Dorchester expects that it will be able to initially price its product at $7.70 per kilogram. This price would represent an operating profit of $4.40 per kilogram. Both sales price and operating costs are expected to keep track with the North American inflation which is running at 3 percent in both Canada and the United States and is expected to remain at that rate. In the United Kingdom, long-run inflation is expected to be in the 4- to 5-percent range, depending on which economic service one follows. The current spot exchange rate is $1.50/£1. Dorchester explicitly believes in PPP as the best means to forecast future exchange rates.

The manufacturing facility is expected to cost $7,000,000. Dorchester plans to finance this amount by a combination of equity capital and debt. The plant will increase Dorchester's borrowing capacity by £2,000,000, and it plans to borrow only that amount. The city of Windsor (Ontario) will provide $1,500,000 of debt financing for a period of seven years at 7.75 percent. The principal is to be repaid in equal installments over the life of the loan. At this point, Dorchester is uncertain whether to raise the remaining debt it desires through a domestic bond issue or a Eurodollar bond issue. It believes it can borrow pounds sterling at 10.75 percent per annum and dollars at 9.5 percent. Dorchester estimates its all-equity cost of capital to be 15 percent.

Revenue Canada Taxation will allow Dorchester to depreciate the new facility over a seven-year period. After that time, the confectionery equipment, which accounts for the bulk of the investment, is expected to have substantial market value.

Dorchester does not expect to receive any special tax concessions. Further, because the corporate tax rates in the two countries are the same—35 percent in the United Kingdom and in Canada—transfer pricing strategies are ruled out.

Should Dorchester build the new manufacturing plant in Canada?

MINI CASE 2

Timmins Gold Mining Company

The Timmins Gold Mining Company is contemplating expanding its operations. To do so it will need to purchase land that its geologists believe is rich in gold. Timmins' management believes that the expansion will allow it to mine and sell an additional 2,000 troy ounces of gold per year. The expansion, including the cost of the land, will cost C$500,000. The current price of gold bullion is C$275 per ounce and one-year gold futures are trading at C$291.50 = C$250(1.06). Extraction costs are C$225 per ounce. The firm's cost of capital is 10 percent. At the current price of gold, the expansion appears profitable: NPV = ($275 − 225) × 2,000/0.10 − C$500,000 = C$500,000. Timmins' management is, however, concerned with the possibility that large sales of gold reserves by Russia and the United Kingdom will drive the price of gold down to C$240 for the foreseeable future. On the other hand, management believes there is some possibility that the world will soon return to a gold reserve international monetary system. In the latter event, the price of gold would increase to at least C$310 per ounce. The course of the future price of gold bullion should become clear within a year. Timmins can postpone the expansion for a year by buying a purchase option on the land for C$25,000. What should Timmins' management do?

REFERENCES & SUGGESTED READINGS

Ang, James S., and Tsong-Yue Lai. "A Simple Rule for Multinational Capital Budgeting." *The Global Finance Journal* 1 (1989), pp. 71–75.

Booth, Lawrence D. "Capital Budgeting Frameworks for the Multinational Corporation." *Journal of International Business Studies* (Fall 1982), pp. 113–23.

Brealey, Richard A., and Stewart C. Myers. *Principles of Corporate Finance*, 7th ed. New York: McGraw-Hill/Irwin, 2003.

Coy, Peter. "Exploiting Uncertainty: The Real Options Revolution in Decision Making." *Business Week* (June 7, 1999), pp. 118–24.

Endleson, Michael E. "Real Options: Valuing Managerial Flexibility (A)." *Harvard Business School Note* (March 31, 1994).

Holland, John. "Capital Budgeting for International Business: A Framework for Analysis." *Managerial Finance* 16 (1990), pp. 1–6.

Lessard, Donald R. "Evaluating International Projects: An Adjusted Present Value Approach." In Donald R. Lessard (ed.), *International Financial Management: Theory and Application,* 2nd ed. New York: Wiley, 1985, pp. 570–84.

Luenberger, David G. "Evaluating Real Investment Opportunities." *Investment Science.* New York: Oxford University Press, 1998, pp. 337–43.

Luehrman, Timothy A. "Capital Projects as Real Options: An Introduction." *Harvard Business School Note* (March 22, 1995).

Luehrman, Timothy A. "Investment Opportunities as Real Options: Getting Started on the Numbers." *Harvard Business Review* (July–August 1998), pp. 51–67.

Modigliani, Franco, and Merton H. Miller. "Corporate Income Taxes and the Cost of Capital: A Correction." *American Economic Review* 53 (1963), pp. 433–43.

Ross, Stephen A., W. Westerfield, F. Jaffe, and G. Roberts. *Corporate Finance,* 3rd Canadian ed. New York: McGraw-Hill/Ryerson, 2003.

Shapiro, Alan C. "Capital Budgeting for the Multinational Corporation." *Financial Management* (Spring 1978), pp. 7–16.

CHAPTER | 18

Multinational Cash Management

CHAPTER OUTLINE

18.1 The Management of International Cash Balances

18.2 Reduction in Precautionary Cash Balances

18.3 Bilateral Netting of Internal and External Net Cash Flows

18.4 Transfer Pricing and Related Issues

18.5 Blocked Funds

Our primary concern in this chapter is with the efficient management of cash within a multinational corporation (MNC). We are concerned with the size of cash balances, their currency denominations, and where these cash balances are located among the MNC's affiliates. Efficient cash management techniques can reduce the investment in cash balances and foreign exchange transaction expenses, and it can provide for maximum return from the investment of excess cash. Efficient cash management techniques result in borrowing at the lowest rate when a temporary cash shortage exists.

We begin with an illustrated mini case that develops a centralized cash management system for an MNC. The system includes interaffiliate netting and a centralized cash depository. The benefits of a centralized system are clearly detailed. A second mini case illustrates transfer pricing and the unbundling of services as strategies to reposition cash among affiliates and, under certain circumstances, reduce the MNC's overall income tax liability. The chapter concludes with a discussion on moving blocked funds from a host country that has imposed foreign exchange restrictions.

18.1 Management of International Cash Balances

Cash management refers to the investment the firm has in **transaction balances** to cover scheduled outflows of funds during a cash budgeting period as well as funds tied up in precautionary cash balances. **Precautionary cash balances** are necessary in case the firm has underestimated the amount needed to cover transactions. Good cash management encompasses investing excess funds at the most favourable rate and borrowing at the lowest rate when there is a temporary cash shortage.

Many of the skills necessary for effective cash management are the same, regardless of whether the firm has only domestic operations or if it operates internationally. For example, the cash manager of a domestic firm should source funds internationally to obtain the lowest borrowing cost and to place excess funds wherever the greatest return can be earned. Firms with multinational operations, however, regularly deal in more than one currency, and hence the cost of foreign exchange transactions is an important factor in efficient cash management. Moreover, multinational operations require the firm to decide on whether the cash management function should be centralized at corporate headquarters (or elsewhere) or decentralized and handled locally by each affiliate. In this chapter, we make a strong case for centralized cash management.

Illustrated MINI CASE | Teltrex's Cash Management System

Teltrex International illustrates how centralized cash management works. Teltrex is an American multinational firm with headquarters in California's Silicon Valley. It manufactures quartz watches which it markets throughout North America and Europe. In addition to its manufacturing facilities in California, Teltrex has three sales affiliates in Canada, Germany, and the United Kingdom.

The foundation of any cash management system is its cash budget. The **cash budget** is a plan detailing the time and the size of expected cash receipts and disbursements. Teltrex prepares a cash budget in advance for the fiscal year (updating it periodically as the year progresses), using a weekly time interval as the planning frequency. Exhibit 18.1 presents a payments matrix for one week during the cash budget planning horizon; it summarizes all interaffiliate cash receipts and disbursements of Teltrex *and* the receipts from and disbursements to external parties with which Teltrex does business. Exhibit 18.1 is denominated in American dollars, the reporting currency of the parent firm. However, the functional currency of each foreign affiliate is the local currency.

Exhibit 18.1 shows, for example, that the American parent expects to receive the equivalent of $30,000* in Canadian dollar from its Canadian affiliate, the equivalent of $35,000 in euros from its German affiliate, and the equivalent of $60,000 in British pounds sterling from its affiliate in the United Kingdom. In total, it expects to receive $125,000 from interaffiliate transactions. The American parent also expects to receive $140,000 directly from external parties, say, from sales in the United States. In total, the parent expects to receive $265,000 in cash during the week. On the disbursements side, the American parent expects to make payments in dollars in the amounts of $20,000 to its Canadian affiliate, $10,000 to its German affiliate, and $40,000 to its British affiliate. It also expects to make direct disbursements of $120,000 to suppliers for component parts and to cover other operating costs. Analogous cash flows exist for the three affiliates.

Exhibit 18.1 shows that the equivalent of $350,000 in interaffiliate cash flows are expected to flow among the parent and its three affiliates. Note that no increase in cash in the MNC occurs as a result of interaffiliate transactions. Interaffiliate transactions effectively represent taking money out of one pocket of the MNC and putting it into another. However, Teltrex expects to receive the equivalent of $530,000 from external parties and make payments of $490,000 to other external parties. From these external transactions, a net increase of $40,000 in cash among the affiliates is expected during the week.

Netting Systems

Let us first consider the interaffiliate transactions that make up part of Exhibit 18.1. Later, we will examine the transactions Teltrex expects to have with external parties. Exhibit 18.2 presents only the portion of Teltrex's receipts and disbursements matrix from Exhibit 18.1 that concerns interaffiliate cash flows.

Exhibit 18.2 shows the amount that each affiliate is to pay and receive from the other. Without a netting policy, 12 foreign exchange transactions will take place among the four affiliates. In general, if there are N affiliates, there will be a maximum of $N(N - 1)$ transactions; in our case $4(4 - 1) = 12$. Exhibit 18.3 diagrams these 12 transactions.

Exhibit 18.3 indicates that the equivalent of $350,000 in funds flows among the four affiliates in 12 foreign exchange transactions. This represents a needless use of administrative time in arranging the transactions and a waste of corporate funds in

---

*$ denotes American Dollar.

| EXHIBIT 18.1 | | Cash Receipts and Disbursements Matrix for Teltrex ($000) | | | | | |

| | | Disbursements | | | | | |
Receipts	U.S.	Canada	Germany	U.K.	External	Total Internal	Total Receipts
U.S.	—	30	35	60	140	125	265
Canada	20	—	10	40	135	70	205
Germany	10	25	—	30	125	65	190
U.K.	40	30	20	—	130	90	220
External	120	165	50	155	—	—	490[a]
Total Internal	70	85	65	130	—	350	—
Total Disbursements	190	250	115	285	530[b]	—	1,370[c]

[a]Total cash disbursed by the American parent firm and its affiliates to external parties.
[b]Total cash received by the American parent firm and its affiliates from external parties.
[c]Balancing cheque figure.
Note: $350,000 is shifted among the various affiliates; $530,000 − $490,000 = $40,000 = increase in cash balances for Teltrex during the week.

| EXHIBIT 18.2 | | Teltrex's Interaffiliate Cash Receipts and Disbursements Matrix ($000) | | | | |

| | | Disbursements | | | | |
Receipts	U.S.	Canada	Germany	U.K.	Total Receipts	Net[a]
U.S.	—	30	35	60	125	55
Canada	20	—	10	40	70	(15)
Germany	10	25	—	30	65	0
U.K.	40	30	20	—	90	(40)
Total Disbursements	70	85	65	130	350	0

[a]Net denotes the difference between total receipts and total disbursements for each affiliate.

| EXHIBIT 18.3 |

Teltrex's Interaffiliate Foreign Exchange Transactions without Netting ($000)

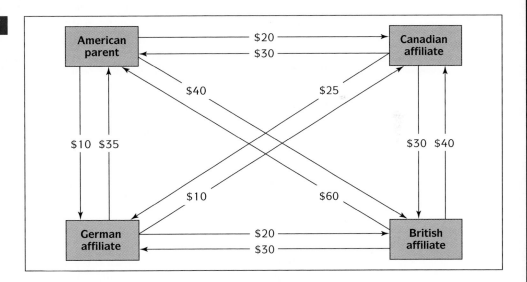

making the transactions. The cost of transferring funds is in the range of 0.25 percent to 1.5 percent of the transaction; this includes transaction expenses and the opportunity cost of funds tied up in interaffiliate float. If we assume a cost of 0.5 percent, the cost for transferring $350,000 is $1,750 for the week.

The 12 transactions can be reduced at least by half through bilateral netting. Under a **bilateral netting** system, each pair of affiliates determines the net amount due between them, and only the net amount is transferred. For example, the American parent and the Canadian affiliate would net the $30,000 and the $20,000 to be received from one another. The result is that only one payment is made; the Canadian

EXHIBIT 18.4

Bilateral Netting of
Teltrex's Interaffiliate
Foreign Exchange
Transactions ($000)

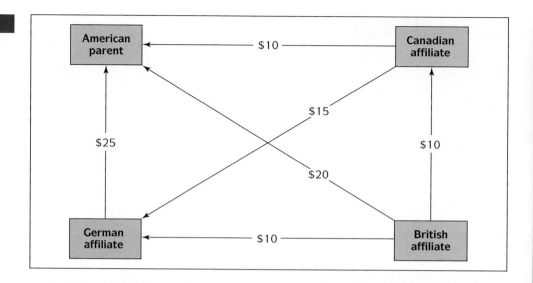

affiliate pays the American parent an amount equivalent to $10,000. Exhibit 18.4 shows the results of bilateral netting among Teltrex's four affiliates.

From Exhibit 18.4, it can be seen that a total of $90,000 flows among the four affiliates of Teltrex in six transactions. Bilateral netting can reduce the number of foreign exchange transactions among the affiliates to $N(N - 1)/2$, or less. The equivalent of $260,000 in foreign exchange transactions is eliminated through bilateral netting. At 0.5 percent, the cost of netting interaffiliate foreign exchange transactions is $450, a savings of $1,300 (= $1,750 − 450) over a non-netting system.

Exhibit 18.2 implies a way to limit interaffiliate transfers to no more than $(N - 1)$ separate foreign exchange transactions. Rather than stop at bilateral netting, the MNC can establish a multilateral netting system. Under a **multilateral netting** system, each affiliate nets all of its interaffiliate receipts against all of its disbursements. It then transfers or receives the balance, respectively, if it is a net payer or receiver. Recall from Exhibit 18.1 that total interaffiliate receipts will always equal total interaffiliate disbursements. Thus, under a multilateral netting system, the net funds to be received by the affiliates will equal the net disbursements to be made by the affiliates.

Exhibit 18.5 illustrates a multilateral netting system for Teltrex. Because the German affiliate's net receipts equal zero, only two foreign exchange transactions are necessary. The Canadian and British affiliates, respectively, pay the equivalent of $15,000 and $40,000 to the American parent firm. At 0.5 percent, the cost of transferring $55,000 is only $275 for the week, a savings of $1,475 (= $1,750 − 275) with a multilateral netting system.

Centralized Cash Depository

A multilateral netting system requires a certain degree of administrative structure. At a minimum, there must be a netting centre manager who has an overview of the interaffiliate cash flows from the cash budget. The **netting centre** manager determines the amount of the net payments and which affiliates are to make or receive them. A netting centre does not imply that the MNC has a central cash manager, however. Indeed, the multilateral netting system presented in Exhibit 18.5 suggests that each affiliate has a local cash manager who is responsible for investing excess cash and borrowing when there is a temporary cash shortage.

Exhibit 18.6 presents a modified diagram of multilateral netting for Teltrex with the addition of a centralized depository. Under a centralized cash management system,

EXHIBIT 18.5

Multilateral Netting of Teltrex's Interaffiliate Foreign Exchange Transactions ($000)

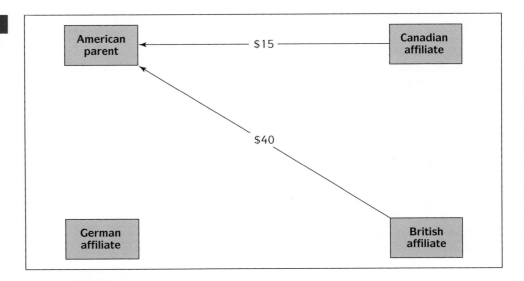

EXHIBIT 18.6

Multilateral Netting of Teltrex's Interaffiliate Foreign Exchange Transactions with a Centralized Depository ($000)

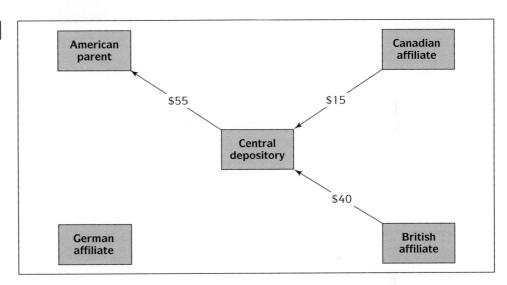

unless otherwise instructed, all interaffiliate payments will flow through the *central cash depository.*

As Exhibit 18.6 shows, the Canadian affiliate remits the equivalent of $15,000 to the central depository and the British affiliate remits the equivalent of $40,000. In turn, the central depository remits $55,000 to the American parent. One might question the wisdom of this system. It appears as if the foreign exchange transactions have doubled from $55,000 in Exhibit 18.5 to $110,000 in Exhibit 18.6. But that is not the case. The Canadian and British affiliates might be instructed to remit to the central depository in American dollars. Alternatively, the central depository could receive the remittances in Canadian dollars and British pounds sterling and exchange them for dollars before transferring the funds to the American parent. (There is the expense of an additional wire transfer, however.)

The benefits of a central cash depository derive mainly from the business transactions the affiliates have with external parties. Exhibit 18.7 presents a table showing the net amount of external receipts and disbursements each affiliate of Teltrex is expected to have during the week, as originally presented in Exhibit 18.1.

EXHIBIT 18.7

Expected Net Cash Receipts and Disbursements from Teltrex Transactions with External Parties ($000)

Affiliate	Receipts	Disbursements	Net
United States	$140,000	$120,000	$20,000
Canada	135,000	165,000	(30,000)
Germany	125,000	50,000	75,000
United Kingdom	130,000	155,000	(25,000)
			$40,000

EXHIBIT 18.8

Flow of Teltrex's Net Cash Receipts from Transactions with External Parties with a Centralized Depository ($000)

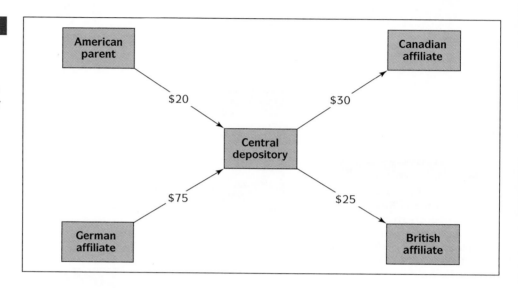

As Exhibit 18.7 shows, the American parent expects to have net receipts of $20,000 by the end of the week. Analogously, in dollars, the German affiliate expects net receipts of $75,000. The Canadian affiliate expects a cash shortage of $30,000, and the British affiliate expects a cash shortage of $25,000. In total, $40,000 of net receipts are expected for the MNC as a whole.

www.gcmltd.net/library.htm

This website provides links to various articles on international treasury management. See especially the article titled "Multicurrency Pooling."

With a **centralized cash depository,** excess cash is remitted to the central cash pool. Analogously, the central cash manager arranges to cover shortages of cash. The central cash manager has a global view of the MNC's overall cash position and needs. Consequently, there is less chance for *mislocated funds;* that is, there is less chance for funds being denominated in the wrong currency. Moreover, because of his global perspective, the central cash manager will know the best borrowing and investing rates. A centralized system facilitates *funds mobilization,* where systemwide cash excesses are invested at the most advantageous rates and cash shortages are covered by borrowing at the most favourable rates. Without a centralized cash depository, one affiliate might end up borrowing locally at an unfavourable rate, while another is investing temporary surplus funds locally at a disadvantageous rate. Exhibit 18.8 diagrams the cash payments for Teltrex depicted in Exhibit 18.7, showing the flows to and from the central cash pool.

Exhibit 18.8 shows that the American parent will remit $20,000 excess cash from transactions with external parties to the central cash pool, and similarly, the German affiliate will remit the $75,000 it has obtained. Both the Canadian and British affiliates will have their cash shortages of $30,000 and $25,000, respectively, covered by the central pool. In total, a net increase of $40,000 is expected at the central cash depository at the end of the week. The diagram shows that a total of $150,000 of cash is expected to flow to ($95,000) and from ($55,000) the cash depository.

Supplementary Material

18.2 Reduction in Precautionary Cash Balances

Up to this point, we have handled the multilateral netting of interaffiliate cash flows (Exhibit 18.6) *and* the net receipts of the affiliates from the transactions with external parties (Exhibit 18.8) as two separate sets of cash flows through the central cash depository. While it was easier to develop the concepts in that manner, it is not necessary, practical, or efficient to do it that way in practice. Instead, the two sets of net cash flows can be bilaterally netted, with the resulting net sums going through the central depository. This will further reduce the number, size, and expense of foreign exchange transactions for the MNC. Exhibit 18.9 calculates the net amount of funds from Teltrex affiliates to flow through the central depository.

Exhibit 18.9 shows the result of netting the cash receipts that would flow through the central cash depository via multilateral netting with the net cash flows that would flow through the central depository as a result of external transactions. The American parent will receive a single payment from the cash pool of $35,000 and the Canadian affiliate will receive $15,000. The German affiliate will remit to the central depository $75,000 and the British affiliate will remit $15,000. In total, the central depository receives $90,000 and disburses $50,000, for an expected net increase in cash of $40,000 for the week. Instead of two separate sets of cash flows totalling $55,000 from the multilateral netting and $150,000 from transactions with external parties, there is only one set of cash flows after the netting totalling $140,000. Thus, there is a saving on foreign exchange transactions of $65,000 for the week. Exhibit 18.10 diagrams the resulting $140,000 of cash flows for Teltrex that are calculated in Exhibit 18.9.

18.3 Bilateral Netting of Internal and External Net Cash Flows

An additional benefit of a centralized cash depository is that the MNC's investment in precautionary cash balances can be substantially reduced without a reduction in its ability to cover unforeseen expenses. To see how this is accomplished, consider the receipts and disbursements each affiliate of Teltrex expected to make with external parties during the week. Assume, for simplicity, that each affiliate will make *all* its planned payments to external parties before it receives any cash from other external sources. For example, from Exhibit 18.7, the Canadian affiliate expects to pay to external parties the equivalent of $165,000 before it receives any of the expected $135,000 in receipts. Thus, the Canadian affiliate will need a transactions balance of $165,000 to cover expected transactions.

		Net Excess Cash from	
EXHIBIT 18.9	**Net Receipts from**	**Transactions with**	
	Multilateral Netting[a]	External Parties[b]	**Net Flow[c]**
Affiliate			
United States	$55,000	$20,000	$35,000
Canada	($15,000)	($30,000)	$15,000
Germany	0	$75,000	($75,000)
United Kingdom	($40,000)	($25,000)	($15,000)
			($40,000)

EXHIBIT 18.9

Net Cash Flows of Teltrex Affiliates through the Central Cash Depository ($000)

[a]Net receipt from (payment to) the central depository resulting from multilateral netting, as shown in Exhibit 18.2.
[b]Net excess (shortage) of cash to be remitted to (covered by) the central depository, as shown in Exhibit 18.7.
[c]A positive amount in this column denotes a payment to an affiliate from the central cash depository; a negative amount denotes a payment from the affiliate.

EXHIBIT 18.10

Net Cash Flows of Teltrex Affiliates through the Central Cash Depository after Netting Multilateral Netting Payments and Net Payments from External Transactions ($000)

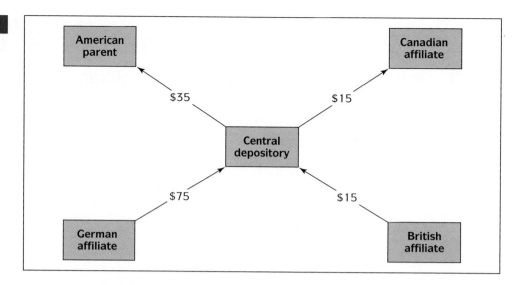

As previously mentioned, a firm keeps a precautionary cash balance to cover unexpected transactions during the budget period. The size of this balance depends on how safe the firm wants to be in its ability to meet unexpected transactions. The larger the precautionary cash balance, the greater is the firm's ability to meet unexpected expenses, and the lower is its risk of financial embarrassment and loss of credit standing. Assume that cash needs are normally distributed and that the cash needs of one affiliate are independent of the others. If Teltrex follows a conservative policy, it might keep three standard deviations of cash for precautionary purposes in addition to the cash needed to cover expected transactions for the planning period. Thus, the probability that Teltrex would experience a cash shortage is only 0.13 of 1 percent; it will have sufficient cash to cover transactions 99.87 percent of the time.

Under a decentralized cash management system, each affiliate would hold its own transaction balance and precautionary cash. Exhibit 18.11 shows the total cash held for transactions and precautionary purposes by each affiliate and by Teltrex as a whole.

As can be seen from Exhibit 18.11, Teltrex needs the equivalent of $490,000 in cash to cover expected transactions and an additional $615,000 in precautionary balances to cover unexpected expenses, for a total of $1,105,000. A centralized cash management system will greatly reduce the investment in precautionary cash balances. Under a centralized system, the amount of cash held by the MNC is viewed as a portfolio. Each affiliate will continue to hold cash sufficient to cover its expected cash transactions, but the precautionary cash balances are held by the central cash manager at the central cash depository. In the event one of the affiliates experiences a cash shortage, funds would be wired from precautionary cash held in the central cash pool.

EXHIBIT 18.11

Transaction and Precautionary Cash Balances Held by Each Teltrex Affiliate under a Decentralized Cash Management System

Affiliate	Expected Transactions (a)	Standard Deviation (b)	Expected Needs plus Precautionary (a + 3b)
United States	$120,000	$50,000	$ 270,000
Canada	165,000	70,000	375,000
Germany	50,000	20,000	110,000
United Kingdom	155,000	65,000	350,000
Total	$490,000		$1,105,000

From portfolio theory, the standard deviation of the portfolio of cash held by the centralized depository for N affiliates is calculated as:[1]

$$\text{Portfolio Std. Dev.} = \sqrt{(\text{Std. Dev. Affiliate 1})^2 + \ldots + (\text{Std. Dev. Affiliate } N)^2}$$

For our example,

$$\text{Portfolio Std. Dev.} = \sqrt{(\$50,000)^2 + (\$70,000)^2 + (\$20,000)^2 + (\$65,000)^2}$$

$$= \$109,659.$$

Thus, under a centralized system, only $328,977 (= 3 \times \$109,659) needs to be held for precautionary purposes by Teltrex's central cash manager. A total of $818,977 (= $490,000 + $328,977) is held by Teltrex. The reduction in precautionary cash balances under the centralized system is $286,023 (= $1,105,000 − $818,977), a sum that most likely can be used more profitably elsewhere, rather than standing by as a potential safety net.

The International Finance in Practice box on page 430 illustrates the use of many of the cash management techniques discussed in the first part of this chapter.

18.4 Transfer Pricing and Related Issues

Within a large business firm with multiple divisions, goods and services are frequently transferred from one division to another. The process brings into question the **transfer price** that should be assigned, for bookkeeping purposes, to the goods or services as they are transferred between divisions. Obviously, the higher the transfer price, the larger will be the gross profits of the transferring division relative to the receiving division. Even within a domestic firm, it is difficult to decide on the transfer price. Within an MNC, the decision is further compounded by exchange restrictions on the part of the host country where the receiving affiliate is located, a difference in income tax rates between the two countries, and import duties and quotas imposed by the host country.

Illustrated MINI CASE | Mintel Products Transfer Pricing Strategy

Low versus High Markup Policy

Mintel Products, Inc., manufactures goods for sale in the United States and overseas. Finished goods are transferred from the parent firm to its wholly owned sales affiliate for overseas retail sale. Mintel's financial manager, Hilary Van Kirk, has decided that the firm's transfer pricing strategy should be re-evaluated as part of a routine review of the operations of the sales affiliate. Van Kirk has decided to explore both low and high markup policies. The analysis is to be done in American dollars. She notes that both the parent firm and the sales affiliate have a 40-percent income tax rate, that the variable production cost of one unit is $1,500, and that the unit retail sales price charged by the sales affiliate to the final customer is $3,000. As a first step in her analysis, Van Kirk prepares Exhibit 18.12. The upper portion of the exhibit presents the analysis of a low markup policy, where the transfer price is set at $2,000. The lower portion of the exhibit analyzes the effect of a high markup policy, where the transfer price is $2,400 per unit.

Van Kirk notes from Exhibit 18.12 that the low markup policy results in larger pre-tax income, income taxes, and net income per unit in the selling country. On the other

---

[1]The standard deviation formula assumes that interaffiliate cash flows are uncorrelated with one another.

Disciplining European Cash: Currency Volatility Spurs Proactive Cash Management

Since 1992, international executives have focused mainly on adapting currency management techniques to the more volatile, riskier foreign-exchange market. But there's another, more subtle lesson to be learned from the new turbulence in currency markets: Sloppy cash management in Europe has become an unaffordable luxury.

This has not gone unnoticed. Many U.S. companies operating in Europe are seriously rethinking their cash management policies. Financial managers are more aware than ever of the need to monitor European cash positions closely. "The events of the last year have been a wake-up call," says Leonard Stolk, vice president at ABN AMRO Bank N.V. in Amsterdam. This is particularly true for U.S. and Asian firms.

Getting informed

The biggest reaction of rudely awakened senior executives has been to start managing cash proactively. For that to work, companies must have timely, comprehensive information on European cash positions. Many multinationals are therefore moving to centralize cash management, introducing more precision in handling and tracking cash positions, relying more on local-currency borrowing, and accelerating the remittance schedule of overseas cash balances.

John Perrotti, vice president and controller at Gleason Corp., readily acknowledges the "need to be more proactive in foreign exchange and cash management." Glea-

son, a $150 million Rochester, N.Y., multinational, derives more than two-thirds of its revenues from overseas. In 1992 only 32 percent of Gleason's revenues were generated in the Americas (South America included), with the remainder in Europe (25 percent of total) and the Asia-Pacific region. Gleason has machine-parts manufacturing, sales and service operations in the U.K., Germany, Italy and Belgium; it is setting up a direct affiliate in Spain (switching over from a local dealer).

"More and more of our European customers pay in their local currency," says Mr. Perrotti. This plus the currency markets' new volatility has increased Gleason's exposure and risk, making more disciplined cash management a must. "Our policy is to repatriate as much as we can," says Mr. Perrotti.

Last year cash from the U.K. operation was brought back to the U.S. as dividends at an exchange rate locked in at $1.90. (The rest of the European subs are either cash break-even or net debtors.) "That generated net savings to the company of $2 million," says Mr. Perrotti. Cash is not remitted blindly, however. Other factors, such as a sub's cash needs vs. cash needs in the U.S. and the tax impact, are also carefully considered.

Gleason has further shifted to using local borrowing facilities to help tighten cash management. With European interest rates more fluid, "we borrow more in the local currencies," says Mr. Perrotti. "We're also becoming more sensitive to local sourcing as a way of protecting local revenue flows."

hand, the high markup policy has the opposite effect, that is, higher taxable income, income taxes, and net profit per unit in the manufacturing country. She also notes that because the income tax rates are the same in both countries, the consolidated results are identical, regardless of whether the MNC follows a low or high transfer pricing scheme.

Exchange Restrictions

Van Kirk wonders if Mintel should be indifferent between the low and high markup policies, since the consolidated results are the same. She reasons, however, that if the distribution country imposes exchange restrictions limiting or blocking the amount of profits that can be repatriated to the manufacturing parent, Mintel would no longer be indifferent between the two markup policies. It obviously would prefer the high markup policy. According to Exhibit 18.12, the higher markup allows $240 per unit to be repatriated to the parent that otherwise may have been blocked. This amount represents the $400 higher markup minus the $160 additional taxes paid in the parent country.

Van Kirk notes that the low markup policy is disadvantageous from the host country's perspective. If the transferring affiliate attempts to reposition funds by changing from the low to the high markup policy, the exchange controls have been partially

Speedy repatriation

Advanced Logic Research, a $230 million Irvine, Calif., company, has also accelerated its remittance schedule. The company has two subsidiaries, in the U.K. and Germany, plus sales and marketing affiliates throughout Europe. Sales to the continent account for some 20 percent of the total, according to treasurer Vick Sial. Since all manufacturing is done in the U.S., Advanced Logic has no foreign cost structure to offset local-currency revenue naturally. So cash balances are remitted quickly to the U.S. in the form of intercompany payments to prevent a buildup of cash pools in volatile currencies.

But accelerated remittance is often easier said than done, since trade terms and collections practices can vary dramatically from one country to another. To speed up repatriation, companies must become familiar with each subsidiary's cash management environment, advises Dan Perkins, manager of Arthur Andersen's treasury consulting practice. For example, a company may have subsidiaries in the U.K., France and Italy. The U.S. parent sells product to the subs on 30-day terms. They then sell the product to local customers on 30-day terms in the U.K., 60-day in France, and 180-day in Italy. At the end of the 30-day period, the parent does not see the cash from the Italian and French subs and is effectively financing them and their customers.

"The U.S. parent can do one of two things," says Mr. Perkins. It can extend its own credit terms to match local market practice or require payment in 30 days and force the sub to borrow locally to finance its sales. The latter allows quick remittance of the funds back to the U.S.

Borrowing dollars may be cheaper in absolute terms, but there are benefits to setting up foreign credit facilities. (In any event, the interest expense should be factored into the subsidiary's margins and pricing to give the parent a true picture of profitability.) Local banking relations are a big step in developing the company's European business. Plus, the local-currency borrowing can act as a natural offset to local-currency revenues in case of devaluation.

The next generation

The sophistication of cash management is often a function of the size of the cash flow. Nordson Corp. of Westlake, Ohio, has taken proactive cash management a step further by instituting an intracompany netting system. The system, which senior treasury analyst Neechu Mei put in place two years ago, has helped the $600 million (60 percent international) machinery manufacturer to navigate the storm in the European currency markets.

How? It has developed a steady, centralized flow of information. The company has subsidiaries in almost every Western European country. That means its cash position is supersensitive to "rock and roll" currencies. "Subsidiaries file a monthly cash report," explains Ms. Mei. The report shows each sub's net cash position. Intracompany invoices are netted once a month. The U.S. parent buys and sells the local currencies, using forward contracts to hedge.

The netting system reduces the company's transaction cost, but more important, it allows Ms. Mei to monitor subsidiary exposure closely. It also enables the U.S. parent to use a system of intercompany loans to reduce the cost of borrowing. The monthly cash reports are studied carefully at the central treasury. If a large position is being accumulated, the parent can move it where it is most needed or remit it to the U.S.

Source: Excerpted from Nilly Landau, "Disciplining European Cash: Currency Volatility Spurs Protective Cash Management," *International Business*, December 1993, pp. 30 and 32. Used by permission.

bypassed and there is a loss of tax revenue in the host country. Thus, the host country may take measures to enforce a certain transfer price. She decides that she needs to brush up on how this might be accomplished and also to consider the effect of a difference in income tax rates between the two affiliates.

Differential Income Tax Rates

As a second step, Van Kirk prepares Exhibit 18.13, which examines the low versus the high markup policy when the tax rate in the transferring country is assumed to be 25 percent, or 15 percent less than the marginal tax rate of 40 percent in the receiving country.

Van Kirk notes from Exhibit 18.13 that the consolidated *taxable* income is $1,100 under both markup policies. However, Mintel would no longer be indifferent when there is a differential in the income tax rates. In the absence of governmental restrictions on the transfer price, the MNC would prefer a high markup policy when the tax rate in the parent country is lower than the tax rate in the receiving country. Consolidated net income for Mintel would be $60 [= ($2,000 − 2,400) × (0.25 − 0.40)] per unit greater under the high versus the low markup policy. The high markup policy results in $400 per unit of taxable income being shifted from the receiving country to the transferring country, where it is taxed at a 15 percent lower rate.

EXHIBIT 18.12

Low versus High
Transfer Pricing
Strategy between
Mintel Affiliates with
the Same Income
Tax Rate

	Manufacturing Affiliate	Sales Affiliate	Consolidated Company
Low Markup Policy			
Sales revenue	$2,000	$3,000	$3,000
Cost of goods sold	1,500	2,000	1,500
Gross profit	500	1,000	1,500
Operating expenses	200	200	400
Taxable income	300	800	1,100
Income taxes (40%)	120	320	440
Net income	180	480	660
High Markup Policy			
Sales revenue	$2,400	$3,000	$3,000
Cost of goods sold	1,500	2,400	1,500
Gross profit	900	600	1,500
Operating expenses	200	200	400
Taxable income	700	400	1,100
Income taxes (40%)	280	160	440
Net income	420	240	660

Consequently, the consolidated income taxes paid by Mintel drop from $395 to $335 per unit.

If the tax rate in the receiving country is lower than in the parent country, it is not clear that a low markup policy should be pursued. Van Kirk recalls that American MNCs are taxed on their worldwide income. Hence, income repatriated to the American parent from a receiving country with a low tax rate would be "grossed up" to its pretax amount so that American taxes could be figured. A credit for the taxes paid in the receiving country would be given against taxes owed in the United States. Thus,

EXHIBIT 18.13

Low versus High
Transfer Pricing
Strategy between
Mintel Affiliates with
Differential Income
Tax Rates

	Manufacturing Affiliate	Sales Affiliate	Consolidated Company
Low Markup Policy			
Sales revenue	$2,000	$3,000	$3,000
Cost of goods sold	1,500	2,000	1,500
Gross profit	500	1,000	1,500
Operating expenses	200	200	400
Taxable income	300	800	1,100
Income taxes (25%/40%)	75	320	395
Net income	225	480	705
High Markup Policy			
Sales revenue	$2,400	$3,000	$3,000
Cost of goods sold	1,500	2,400	1,500
Gross profit	900	600	1,500
Operating expenses	200	200	400
Taxable income	700	400	1,100
Income taxes (25%/40%)	175	160	335
Net income	525	240	765

pursuing a low markup policy would not result in a dollar tax savings if net income was to be repatriated. However, if the net income of the foreign subsidiary was to be reinvested in the host country, the low markup policy would result in a tax savings and allow more funds for reinvestment. Nevertheless, this would only be temporary, Van Kirk reasons. At some point, profitable investment opportunities would be exhausted, and the parent firm and its shareholders would desire some return on the investment made—and this means repatriation.

Regulations Affecting Transfer Prices

Van Kirk believes that governmental authorities within a host country would be quite aware of the motives of MNCs to use transfer pricing schemes to move blocked funds or evade tax liabilities. After doing some research, she learns that most countries have regulations controlling transfer prices. In the United States, the U.S. Internal Revenue Code Section 482: Allocation of Income and Deductions among Taxpayers stipulates that the transfer price must reflect an *arm's-length price,* that is, a price the selling affiliate would charge an unrelated customer for the good or service. The Internal Revenue Service (IRS) . . . "may distribute, apportion, or allocate gross income, deductions, credits, or allowances between or among such organizations . . . [if it is] necessary in order to prevent evasion of taxes or clearly to reflect the income of any such organizations . . ." Moreover, in the event of conflict, the burden of proof lies with the taxpayer to show that the IRS has unreasonably established the transfer price and determined taxable income.

She learns that there are three basic methods prescribed by the IRS, and recognized internationally, for establishing arm's-length prices of tangible goods. The method considered the best is to use a *comparable uncontrolled price* between unrelated firms. While this method seems reasonable and theoretically sound, it is difficult to use in practice because many factors enter into the pricing of goods and services between two business enterprises. The Code allows for some adjustments because differences in the terms of sale, the quantity sold, quality differences, and the date of sale are all factors that can realistically affect the sale price among various customers. Thus, what is a reasonable price for one customer may not be reasonable for another. The next best method is the *resale price* approach, which can be used if, among other things, there is no comparable uncontrolled sales price. Under this method, the price at which the good is resold by the distribution affiliate is reduced by an amount sufficient to cover overhead costs and a reasonable profit. However, it may be difficult to determine the value added by the distribution affiliate. The third method is the *cost-plus* approach, where an appropriate profit is added to the cost of the manufacturing affiliate. This method assumes that the manufacturing cost is readily accountable. Additionally, a group of methods collectively referred to as *fourth methods* can be applied to approximate arm's-length prices when the three basic methods are not applicable. The fourth methods include those based on financial and economic models and econometric techniques. The comparable uncontrolled price method and fourth methods are used for determining an arm's-length transfer price for intangible goods, whereas cost methods are used for pricing services.

The Organization for Economic Cooperation and Development (OECD) Model Tax Convention sets out the same methods as the IRS Code for use by member countries. Van Kirk concludes that all methods present operational difficulties of some type and are also difficult for the taxing authority to evaluate. Thus, transfer pricing manipulation cannot be completely controlled and the potential exists for manoeuvrability by the MNC to reposition funds or reduce its tax liability.

The International Finance in Practice box on pages 436–438 discusses the complexities the MNCs face in attempting to satisfy governmental authorities in transfer pricing disputes.

EXHIBIT 18.14

Low versus High Transfer Pricing Strategy between Mintel Affiliates with Differential Income Tax Rates and a 5-Percent Import Duty

	Manufacturing Affiliate	Sales Affiliate	Consolidated Company
Low Markup Policy			
Sales revenue	$2,000	$3,000	$3,000
Cost of goods sold	1,500	2,000	1,500
Import duty (5%)	—	100	100
Gross profit	500	900	1,400
Operating expenses	200	200	400
Taxable income	300	700	1,000
Income taxes (25%/40%)	75	280	355
Net income	225	420	645
High Markup Policy			
Sales revenue	$2,400	$3,000	$3,000
Cost of goods sold	1,500	2,400	1,500
Import duty (5%)	—	120	120
Gross profit	900	480	1,380
Operating expenses	200	200	400
Taxable income	700	280	980
Income taxes (25%/40%)	175	112	287
Net income	525	168	693

Import Duties

After some reflection, Van Kirk concludes that import duties are another factor that need to be considered. When a host country imposes an *ad valorem* import duty on goods shipped across its borders from another country, the import tax raises the cost of doing business within the country. An *ad valorem* duty is a percentage tax levied at customs on the assessed value of the imported goods. She reasons that an import tax will affect the transfer pricing strategy an MNC uses, but that, in general, the income tax will have the greatest after-tax effect on consolidated net income. To analyze the effect of an import duty on Mintel, she prepares Exhibit 18.14, which shows the low and high transfer price alternatives presented in Exhibit 18.13 with the imposition of a 5-percent import duty by the receiving country.

Comparison of Exhibits 18.13 and 18.14 shows Van Kirk that under the low markup policy, Mintel would receive $60 less (= $645 − 705) per unit if a 5-percent import duty was imposed by the host country. The $60 represents the after-tax cost of the $100 import duty on the $2,000 per-unit transfer price cost of the good. Mintel would still prefer the high markup policy as before, however, as it results in an increase in net income from $645 to $693 per unit. The difference in the net incomes between the two markup policies is only $48, in comparison with $60 without the 5-percent import tax. The loss of $12 represents the after-tax cost of an additional $20 of import duty per unit when the transfer price is $2,400 instead of $2,000 per unit.

Unbundling Fund Transfers

As Van Kirk knows, host countries are well aware of transfer pricing schemes used by MNCs to evade taxes within its borders or to avoid exchange restrictions. She wonders if there are ways to avoid suspicion from host country governmental authorities, and the administrative hassle likely to arise from such an inquiry, when the firm is merely trying to repatriate a sufficient amount of funds from a foreign affiliate to make the investment worthwhile. To learn more about transfer pricing strategies and related issues, she decides to attend a one-day seminar on the topic she saw advertised by a professional organization to which she belongs. She hopes it is beneficial, as the registration fee is $500 for the day!

As it turns out, the money was well spent. In addition to making the acquaintance of financial managers from other companies, one thing Van Kirk learned at the

Low versus High
Transfer Pricing
Strategy for Mintel with
Low Transfer Price and
Additional Royalty
Charge with Differential
Income Tax Rates

	Manufacturing Affiliate	Sales Affiliate	Consolidated Company
Low Markup Policy			
Sales revenue	$2,000	$3,000	$3,000
Cost of goods sold	1,500	2,000	1,500
Gross profit	500	1,000	1,500
Operating expenses	200	200	400
Taxable income	300	800	1,100
Income taxes (25%/40%)	75	320	395
Net income	225	480	705
High Markup Policy			
Sales revenue	$2,400	$3,000	$3,000
Cost of goods sold	1,500	2,400	1,500
Gross profit	900	600	1,500
Operating expenses	200	200	400
Taxable income	700	400	1,100
Income taxes (25%/40%)	175	160	335
Net income	525	240	765
Low Markup Policy and Royalty			
Sales revenue	$2,000	$3,000	$3,000
Royalty and fee income	400	—	—
Cost of goods sold	1,500	2,400	1,500
Gross profit	900	600	1,500
Operating expenses	200	200	400
Taxable income	700	400	1,100
Income taxes (25%/40%)	175	160	335
Net income	525	240	765

conference was that an MNC is likely to fare better if, instead of lumping all costs into a single transfer price, the parent firm unbundled the package to recognize the cost of the physical good and each service separately that it provides the affiliate. A detailing of the charges makes it easier, if ever necessary, to present and support to the taxing authority of a host country that each charge is legitimate and can be well substantiated. For instance, in addition to charging for the cost of the physical good, the parent firm could charge a fee for technical training of the affiliate's staff, a share of the cost of worldwide advertising or other corporate overhead, or a royalty or licensing fee as payment for use of well-recognized brand names, technology, or patents. The royalty or licensing fee represents remuneration for expense previously incurred by the parent for development or having made the product one that is desirable to own.

As a final step in her analysis, Van Kirk prepares Exhibit 18.15, which reproduces the low versus high markup policy analysis for Mintel with differential income tax rates presented in Exhibit 18.13. In addition, Exhibit 18.15 shows that a $2,000 transfer price and $400 per unit charge for royalties and fees results in the same consolidated net income of $765 as does the high markup policy with a $2,400 transfer price. By comparison, the low markup policy only provides $705 per unit consolidated net income. This is the case, regardless of whether a portion of the $480 net income of the sales affiliate is repatriated to the manufacturing affiliate as a dividend, because the tax rate in the distribution country is higher. As Van Kirk learned at the conference, the strategy of recognizing specific services may be acceptable to the host government, whereas the high markup policy may not, if $2,400 appears to be more than an arm's-length price for the transferred good.

Taking Shelter: As Congress Ponders New Tax Breaks, Firms Already Find Plenty

WASHINGTON—Congress is putting the final touches on a bill that would award corporate America billions of dollars in new tax breaks. But corporate America has already found plenty of breaks in current tax laws.

Thirteen years after Congress passed a tax-reform law intended to make every company pay its fair share, government and corporate records show that many profitable U.S. corporations are again paying little or no federal income tax.

The top federal income-tax rate for corporations is 35%. On paper. Yet even as they brag to shareholders about rising profits, companies are finding legal ways to reduce the amount of pretax income they report to the Internal Revenue Service. They establish financial subsidiaries in tax havens. They indulge in tax shelters so complex government auditors can't always understand them. They shift profits to low-tax countries by manipulating prices when doing business with their own overseas branches. And they take full advantage of the tax breaks that Congress has awarded over the years, while dispatching lobbyists to plead for still more.

Scot-free

Out of 2.3 million U.S. corporations, more than half paid no federal income tax at all between 1989 and 1995, according to a General Accounting Office study using the most recent IRS data available. Many of these were mom-and-pop operations. But four of every 10 companies with more than $250 million in assets or $50 million in gross receipts paid less than $100,000 to Uncle Sam in 1995. "You could probably make the case that a lot of small companies don't make much money," says Sen. Byron Dorgan, a North Dakota Democrat who has made a pet cause out of fighting corporate tax avoidance. "But it's pretty hard to make the case that a lot of large companies aren't making a lot of money."

Yet that's exactly the case many large companies are trying to make to the IRS, at a time when the U.S. is enjoying an extended economic boom and the stock market is constantly flirting with new records. Sure, after long years of deficits, the economy is producing big federal budget surpluses—$3 trillion projected over the next decade. But the bulk of that revenue is coming from individuals, not companies. "Revenues in general have really been skyrocketing, and the big action has been on the individual side," says Alan Auerbach, professor of law and economics at the University of California at Berkeley. "If you ask how much of this surplus has been on the corporate side, the answer is not much."

Tax bills

Annual federal revenue from personal income taxes is up 60% over the past six years, while revenue from corporate income taxes has increased just 30%. For the five years through calendar 1998, the government calculates that corporate profits increased 43%.

Companies aren't satisfied, though. In the $792 billion tax-cut bill the House just passed, corporate lobbyists have persuaded lawmakers to include $100 billion in tax cuts for business over 10 years. The Senate bill has about $50 billion in tax cuts for corporate America over 10 years.

One break, estimated to cut corporate tax bills by a total of $25 billion over a decade, would let global companies deduct from their U.S. returns more of the interest they pay abroad. Another, which would save companies $10 billion over the next 10 years and even more after being fully implemented in 2009, would repeal the corporate alternative-minimum tax. That tax was established in its current form in 1986 to make sure that profitable companies pay at least some taxes even if they have lots of deductions and credits.

Archer's view

Texas GOP Rep. Bill Archer, chairman of the House Ways and Means Committee, is skeptical that profitable corporations are really getting off easy. The alternative-minimum tax, he says, is a "job destroyer" because it punishes growing companies by making them pay taxes even if they deserve deductions for buying new equipment. And, he argues, reducing the tax burden on U.S.-based multinationals would make them less likely to merge with foreign companies and move their headquarters overseas, where they would pay even less to the IRS.

"If we don't do something to prevent our corporations from being gobbled up by foreign companies, we'll surely end up with less tax revenues," Mr. Archer says.

But the fact is that companies these days are already paying a smaller share of their profits to the federal government—31% in 1998, compared with 41% in 1989, the peak of the last business cycle, according to data in the newest Economic Report of the President.

That doesn't mean they are doing anything illegal. For the most part, executives are just using every bit of flexibility in the tax code to maximize their write-offs and minimize their taxable income, even as they play up their profits to investors.

Few companies release tax returns to the public. In annual reports, however, they tell shareholders how much they made before taxes and how much federal tax they must pay immediately, figures the GAO uses to calculate a company's effective tax rate. Although it's an imperfect method, the GAO considers it the most accurate because it excludes taxes that the companies report to shareholders, but can put off paying for years.

Take General Motors Corp., the largest corporation in the U.S. as measured by revenue. It reported $4.61 billion in worldwide pretax income in its 1998 annual report. "Your company is in better financial shape than it has been in many years," Chairman John F. Smith Jr. assured shareholders in June. But for 1998, the auto maker owed the IRS just $36 million—0.8% of its global pretax income. The same year, GM paid about two-thirds that much in compensation to Mr. Smith and his four top lieutenants—a total of $23.9 million for their salaries, bonuses, stock options and other remuneration.

Why was GM's tax bill so small? First, the company paid lots of taxes overseas, which can be credited against U.S. taxes. "When the day is done, we pay taxes that are equivalent to a statutory U.S. tax rate," says Mark Tanner, a GM spokesman. "We pay taxes to various governments overseas, and we're allowed to take credits for that. It's very difficult to compare a global company like GM to an individual company or individual person who has all of his or her operations or income in the U.S."

Indeed, GM reported to its shareholders that 27% of its pretax income—$1.23 billion—came from U.S. operations last year, although more than half of its car and truck production was here. (Mr. Tanner points out that vehicle-output figures ignore other GM businesses such as locomotives and financial services.) But only 13% of GM's current tax payments for 1998 went to federal, state or local tax collectors. The rest was paid to foreign governments. The company told shareholders it paid only 2.9% of U.S. profits to the federal government in current taxes.

Then there's the difference between the amount the company reported to its shareholders, whom it wants to impress with high profits, and the amount the company reported to the IRS, which it hopes to keep at bay. GM won't release its tax returns. But, among other things, such differences usually reflect the fact that tax laws allow companies to write off investments in equipment more rapidly than shareholder accounting methods do. In GM's case, there were also tax credits left over from the early 1990s, when the company ran huge losses and logged large employee-benefit payments on its books. GM won't say how much of a credit it claimed for those or other items in 1998.

GM points out that on top of the tax payments it made last year, it owed $145 million that it was allowed to defer. Assuming it eventually pays those taxes, it effective tax rate would rise to 14.7% for last year. But money paid tomorrow doesn't hurt as much as money paid today. To have $145 million for the IRS five years from now, for example, GM would need to set aside just $114 million now in an investment paying 5% interest.

Delay and accelerate

Congress has intentionally created ways for companies to put off tax payments and to collect tax credits that reduce future IRS bills. The tax code also lets companies take deductions for using up their equipment faster than it actually ages, a practice called accelerated depreciation.

Enron Corp. had $197 million of pretax income from its U.S. operations last year but, because of a variety of tax strategies, owed just 15% of that to the federal government. The company also had deferred tax credits, which reduced its effective federal tax rate to 8%. (Deferred credits, of course, are worth less than current credits, the same way deferred taxes hurt less than current taxes.) "Any taxpayer—a company or an individual—is going to make sure they pay what is legally required and not more," says Steve Kean, an Enron executive vice president.

"A company like ours that is making significant investments and is growing substantially is going to see lower effective tax rates," Mr. Kean continues. "But those investments and the growth they produce certainly add to the tax base and create additional tax revenues in the long run."

The corporate provisions of the 1986 Tax Reform Act passed partly because of popular outrage over reports that some big companies were paying less in taxes than their janitors were paying. Robert McIntyre, director of Citizens for Tax Justice, a group funded partly by organized labor, attracted a lot of media attention at the time with a report showing that 128 out of 250 large, profitable companies paid no federal income tax at all.

Tax reform lowered the top tax rates for companies and individuals, but eliminated many loopholes that the wealthy and corporations had used to avoid paying the statutory rates. The top corporate income-tax rate was lowered to 34% from 46%, then raised to 35% in 1993.

The reform has had some effect; corporate rate income taxes will provide 10% of total federal revenue this fiscal year, up from 8% in 1986.

But corporate tax payments aren't keeping pace with corporate profits, and critics of the system argue that a major reason is that companies are becoming more global, creating vast opportunities to shift to lower-tax countries, while moving their tax deductions to the U.S.

Transfer pricing

One way to do this is by playing with the price that one branch of the company charges another branch for goods and services. Say a U.S.-based company makes computers with parts from its subsidiary in a low-tax East Asian country. It can reduce its reported U.S. income—and increase its subsidiary's profit—by overpaying for those components. Or it can undercharge for exports to its overseas operations. Either way, the overall company can show a healthy profit while telling the IRS that not much of it is earned in the U.S.

Since overseas profits are taxed only when they come back to the U.S., the company can put off paying a chunk of its federal tax bill. And foreign companies with U.S. subsidiaries can minimize U.S. taxes because their non-U.S. profits aren't subject to U.S. tax.

continued

continued

The IRS estimates that transfer-pricing abuses cost the government $2.8 billion in lost revenue each year. Other estimates are much higher. Finance professors John S. Zdanowicz and Simon J. Pak of Florida International University in Miami believe that such methods led to $35.6 billion in lost federal revenue in 1998, with more companies joining the party each year. "Now that we've become a global economy, the idea is to shift income to countries where the net impact is to pay the lowest taxes," says Prof. Zdanowicz.

Tax watchers debate the accuracy of Florida International's lost-revenue estimates, but the study's anecdotal evidence is eye-catching. Combing through anonymous customers records, the researchers found $18,000 dot-matrix printers being imported from Japan and $2,600 radial tires coming from Indonesia. And somebody in the U.S. is exporting $12,000 helicopters to Italy and $135 howitzers to South Africa.

Corporations also take advantage of federal rules that let them shift profits to financial subsidiaries set up in low-tax locales such as Liechtenstein. The practice came about in 1996 after the Treasury allowed companies to choose whether a distant financial subsidiary would be considered part of the U.S. operation or part of a foreign branch. Treasury officials didn't foresee that this allowed U.S. companies to shift income to the financing unit, minimizing both U.S. and foreign taxes.

Here's how it typically works: The U.S. company sets up a financing arm, called a hybrid, in Liechtenstein, and tells the IRS that for U.S. tax purposes, it is part of the company's German manufacturing operation. The Liechtenstein company lends money to the German subsidiary at a very high interest rate, in essence moving some German profits to Liechtenstein. German authorities tax only the German subsidiary, as does the U.S. The profits in Liechtenstein escape high tax rates and still show up on the parent corporation's bottom line for shareholders. Treasury officials have tried to close the loophole, but the agency backed down last month under pressure from Congress and lobbyists.

Congressional staffers estimate that the practice will cost the government $10 billion over 10 years. "This thing is new and a lot of companies aren't doing it yet," says Mr. McIntyre of Citizens for Tax Justice. "But they're all going to do it if it works."

In the post-tax-reform world, companies are finding all sorts of complex new tax shelters, whose legality is tested only if IRS auditors can find them in corporate tax returns. "The proliferation of corporate tax shelters presents an unacceptable and growing level of tax-avoidance behavior," the Treasury said in a recent study.

Companies know that the safest tax savings come from Congress itself, and, with tax-reform enthusiasm fading, lawmakers are again bestowing valuable favors on business. The House bill, which President Clinton has vowed to veto, is bedecked with narrow tax breaks for companies that produce everything from plastic fishing-tackle boxes to steel. House and Senate negotiators will try to come up with a compromise this week.

But business lobbyists would have liked more than either the House or the Senate provides. Explains Dorothy Coleman, tax-policy director for the National Association of Manufacturers: "We thought that with the surpluses as large as projected, about one-third of the tax cuts should go to business."

Source: Michael M. Phillips, "Taking Shelter," *The Wall Street Journal,* August 4, 1999, pp. A1ff. Reprinted by permission of *The Wall Street Journal.* © 1999 Dow Jones & Company, Inc. All rights reserved worldwide.

Miscellaneous Factors

Transfer pricing strategies may be beneficial when the host country restricts the amount of foreign exchange that can be used for importing specific goods. In this event, a lower transfer price allows a greater quantity of the good to be imported under a quota restriction. This may be a more important consideration than income tax savings, if the imported item is a necessary component needed by an assembly or manufacturing affiliate to continue or expand production.

Transfer prices also have an effect on how divisions of an MNC are perceived locally. A high markup policy leaves little net income to show on the affiliate's books. If the parent firm expects the affiliate to be able to borrow short-term funds locally in the event of a cash shortage, the affiliate may have difficulty doing so with unimpressive financial statements. On the other hand, a low markup policy makes it appear, at least superficially, as if affiliates, rather than the parent firm, are contributing a larger portion to consolidated earnings. To the extent that financial markets are inefficient, or securities analysts do not understand the transfer pricing strategy being used, the market value of the MNC may be lower than is justified.

Obviously, transfer pricing strategies have an effect on international capital expenditure analysis. A very low (high) markup policy makes the APV of a subsidiary's capital expenditure appear more (less) attractive. Consequently, in order to obtain a meaningful analysis, arm's-length pricing should be used in the APV analysis to determine after-tax operating income, regardless of the actual transfer price employed. A separate term in the APV analysis can be used to recognize tax-savings from transfer pricing strategies. This was the recommended approach detailed in Chapter 17.

18.5 Blocked Funds

For a variety of reasons, a country may find itself short of foreign currency reserves and thus impose exchange restrictions on its own currency, limiting its conversion into other currencies so as not to further reduce scarce foreign currency reserves. When a country enforces exchange controls, the remittance of profits from a subsidiary firm to its foreign parent is blocked. The blockage may be only temporary, or it may be for a considerable period of time. A lengthy blockage is detrimental to an MNC. Without the ability to repatriate profits from a foreign subsidiary, the MNC might as well not even have the investment as returns are not being paid to the shareholders of the MNC.

Prior to making a capital investment in a foreign subsidiary, the parent firm should investigate the potential of future funds blockage. This is part of the capital expenditure analysis outlined in Chapter 17. The APV framework developed in that chapter only considers the expected operating cash flows that are available for repatriation.

Unexpected funds blockage after an investment has been made, however, is a political risk with which the MNC must contend. Thus, the MNC should be familiar with methods for moving blocked funds so as to benefit its shareholders. Several methods for moving blocked funds have already been discussed in this chapter and others. For example, transfer pricing strategies and unbundling services are methods the MNC might be able to use to move otherwise blocked funds. These methods were covered earlier in this chapter. Parallel and back-to-back loans discussed in Chapter 10 may also be used to reposition blocked funds. Moreover, in Chapter 13, leading and lagging of payments were discussed primarily as a means of controlling transaction exposure. However, leading and lagging payments may be used as a strategy for repositioning funds within an MNC. Additional strategies that may be useful for moving blocked funds are *export creation* and *direct negotiation*.

Export creation involves using the blocked funds of a subsidiary in the country in which they are blocked to pay for exports that can be used to benefit the parent firm or other affiliates. Thus, instead of using repatriated funds to pay for goods or services that will benefit the MNC, blocked funds are used. Examples include using consulting firms located in the host country where funds are blocked, instead of a firm in the parent country, to provide necessary consulting work that benefits the MNC; transferring personnel from corporate headquarters to the subsidiary offices, where they will be paid in the blocked local currency; using the national airlines of the host country, when possible, for the international travel of all MNC executives, where the reservations and fare payments are made by the subsidiary; and holding business conferences in the host country, instead of elsewhere, where the expenses are paid by the local subsidiary. All of these possibilities not only benefit the MNC, since these goods and services are needed, but they also benefit various industries within the host country.

Host countries desire to attract foreign industries that will most benefit their economic development and the technical skills of its citizens. Thus, foreign investment in the host country in industries that produce export goods, such as automobiles or electronic equipment, or in industries that will attract tourists, such as resort hotels, is desirable. This type of investment provides good employment and training for the country's citizens and is also a source, rather than a use, of foreign exchange. The host country should not expect an MNC to make beneficial investment within its borders if it is not likely to receive an appropriate return. Consequently, MNCs in desirable industries may be able to convince the host country government through direct negotiation that funds blockage is detrimental to all.

SUMMARY

This chapter discussed cash management in the multinational firm. Special attention was given to the topics of multilateral netting and transfer pricing policy. Illustrated case problems were used to show the benefits of centralized cash management and to examine transfer pricing strategies.

1. A multilateral netting system is beneficial in reducing the number of and the expense associated with interaffiliate foreign exchange transactions.

2. A centralized cash pool assists in reducing the problem of mislocated funds and in funds mobilization. A central cash manager has a global view of the most favourable borrowing rates and most advantageous investment rates.

3. A centralized cash management system with a cash pool can reduce the investment the MNC has in precautionary cash balances, saving the firm money.

4. Transfer pricing strategies are a means to reposition funds within an MNC and a possible technique for reducing tax liabilities and removing blocked funds from a host country that has imposed foreign exchange restrictions.

5. Unbundling fund transfers, export creation, and direct negotiation are other means for removing blocked funds from a host country that is enforcing foreign exchange restrictions.

KEY WORDS

bilateral netting, *423*
cash budget, *422*
cash management, *421*
centralized cash
  depository, *426*

multilateral
  netting, *424*
netting centre, *424*
precautionary cash
  balances, *421*

transaction
  balances, *421*
transfer price, *429*

QUESTIONS

1. Describe the key factors contributing to effective cash management within a firm. Why is the cash management process more difficult in an MNC?

2. Discuss the pros and cons of an MNC having a centralized cash manager handle all investment and borrowing for all affiliates of the MNC versus each affiliate having a local manager who performs the cash management activities of the affiliate.

3. How might an MNC use transfer pricing strategies? How do import duties affect transfer pricing policies?

4. What are the various means the taxing authority of a country might use to determine if a transfer price is *reasonable?*

5. Discuss how an MNC might attempt to repatriate blocked funds from a host country.

PROBLEMS

1. Affiliate A sells 5,000 units to Affiliate B per year. The marginal income tax rate for Affiliate A is 25 percent and the marginal income tax rate for Affiliate B is 40 percent. The transfer price per unit is currently $2,000, but it can be set at any level between $2,000 and $2,400. Derive a formula to determine how much annual after-tax profits can be increased by selecting the optimal transfer price.

2. Affiliate A sells 5,000 units to Affiliate B per year. The marginal income tax rate for Affiliate A is 25 percent and the marginal income tax rate for Affiliate B is 40 percent. Additionally, Affiliate B pays a tax-deductible tariff of 5 percent on imported merchandise. The transfer price per unit is currently $2,000, but it can be set at any level between $2,000 and $2,400. Derive (a) a formula to determine the effective marginal tax rate for Affiliate B, and (b) a formula to determine how much annual after-tax profits can be increased by selecting the optimal transfer price.

INTERNET EXERCISE

The Transfer Pricing Management Benchmarking Association conducts benchmarking studies to identify the best transfer pricing processes that will improve the overall operations of its members. Its website is www.tpmba.com. Go to this website to learn about the objectives of the association and the events it sponsors. You may be interested in receiving its free newsletter.

MINI CASE 1

Efficient Funds Flow at Eastern Trading Company

The Eastern Trading Company of Singapore purchases spices in bulk from around the world, packages them into consumer-size quantities, and sells them through sales affiliates in Hong Kong, the United Kingdom, and the United States. For a recent month, the following payments matrix of interaffiliate cash flows, stated in Singapore dollars, was forecast. Show how Eastern Trading can use multilateral netting to minimize the foreign exchange transactions necessary to settle interaffiliate payments. If foreign exchange transactions cost the company 0.5 percent, what savings result from netting?

Eastern Trading Company Payments Matrix (S$000)

	Disbursements				
Receipts	Singapore	Hong Kong	U.K.	U.S.	Total Receipts
Singapore	—	40	75	55	170
Hong Kong	8	—	—	22	30
U.K.	15	—	—	17	32
U.S.	11	25	9	—	45
Total disbursements	34	65	84	94	277

MINI CASE 2

Eastern Trading Company's Optimal Transfer Pricing Strategy

The Eastern Trading Company of Singapore ships prepackaged spices to Hong Kong, the United Kingdom, and the United States, where they are resold by sales affiliates. Eastern Trading is concerned with what might happen in Hong Kong now that control has been turned over to China. Eastern Trading has decided that it should re-examine its transfer pricing policy with its Hong Kong affiliate as a means of repositioning funds from Hong Kong to Singapore. The following table shows the present transfer pricing scheme, based on a carton of assorted, prepackaged spices, which is the typical shipment to the Hong Kong sales affiliate. What do you recommend that Eastern Trading should do?

Eastern Trading Company Current Transfer Pricing Policy with Hong Kong Sales Affiliate

	Singapore Parent	Hong Kong Affiliate	Consolidated Company
Sales revenue	S$300	S$500	S$500
Cost of goods sold	200	300	200
Gross profit	100	200	300
Operating expenses	50	50	100
Taxable income	50	150	200
Income taxes (31%/16.5%)	16	25	41
Net income	34	125	159

MINI CASE 3

Eastern Trading Company's New MBA

The Eastern Trading Company of Singapore presently follows a decentralized system of cash management where it and its affiliates each maintain their own transaction and precautionary cash balances. Eastern Trading believes that it and its affiliates' cash needs are normally distributed and independent from one another. It is corporate policy to maintain 2.5 standard deviations of cash as precautionary holdings. At this level of safety, there is a 99.37 percent chance that each affiliate will have enough cash holdings to cover transactions.

A new MBA hired by the company claims that the investment in precautionary cash balances is needlessly large and can be reduced substantially if the firm converts to a centralized cash management system. Use the projected information for the current month, which is presented below, to determine the amount of cash Eastern Trading needs to hold in precautionary balances under its current decentralized system and the level of precautionary cash it would need to hold under a centralized system. Was the new MBA a good hire?

Affiliate	Expected Transactions	One Standard Deviation
Singapore	S$125,000	S$40,000
Hong Kong	60,000	25,000
United Kingdom	95,000	40,000
United States	70,000	35,000

REFERENCES & SUGGESTED READINGS

Allman-Ward, Michele. "Globalization and the Cash/Treasury Manager." *Journal of Cash Management* 12 (1992), pp. 26–34.

Bogusz, Robert J. "The Renaissance of Netting." *Journal of Cash Management* 13 (1993), pp. 10–17.

Bokos, W. J., and Anne P. Clinkard. "Multilateral Netting." *Journal of Cash Management* 3 (1983), pp. 24–34.

Burns, Jane O. "Transfer Pricing Decisions in U.S. Multinational Corporations." *Journal of International Business Studies* 11 (1980), pp. 23–39.

Collins, J. Markham, and Alan W. Frankle. "International Cash Management Practices of Large U.S. Firms." *Journal of Cash Management* 5 (1985), pp. 42–48.

Diewert, W. Erwin. "Transfer Pricing and Economic Efficiency." In Alan M. Rugman and Lorraine Eden, eds., *Multinationals and Transfer Pricing*. New York: St. Martin's Press, 1985.

Griffiths, Susan. "International Pooling—Getting the Story Straight." *Journal of Cash Management* 12 (1992), pp. 5–7.

International Transfer Pricing. New York: Business International Corporation and Ernst and Young, 1991.

Pagar, Jill C., and J. Scott Wilkie. *Transfer Pricing Strategy in a Global Economy.* Amsterdam: IBFD Publications, 1993.

Prusa, Thomas J. "An Incentive Compatible Approach to Transfer Pricing." *Journal of International Economics* 28 (1990), pp. 155–72.

Shapiro, Alan C. "Payments Netting in International Cash Management." *Journal of International Business Studies* 9 (1978), pp. 51–58.

Srinivasin, Venkat, and Yong H. Kim. "Payments Netting in International Cash Management: A Network Optimization Approach." *Journal of International Business Studies* 17 (1986), pp. 1–20.

Tang, Roger Y. W. *Transfer Pricing in the 1990s: Tax and Management Perspectives.* Westport, Conn.: Quorum Books, 1993.

Tawfik, Mohamed Sherih. *An Optimal International Transfer Pricing System: A Nonlinear Multi-objective Approach.* Ph.D. dissertation, Pennsylvania State University, 1982.

Tax Aspects of Transfer Pricing within Multinational Enterprises: The United States Proposed Regulations. Paris: Organization for Economic Cooperation and Development, 1993.

U.S. Internal Revenue Code. Chicago: Commerce Clearing House, 1993.

Exports and Imports

TO HELP PROTECT elephants and rhinos from poachers, the Ugandan government needed 18 helicopters. Unfortunately, it did not have the $25 million needed to cover the cost. In stepped Gary Pacific, the head of countertrade for McDonnell Douglas Helicopters. He helped Uganda set up several local factories that are able to generate hard currency. One was a plant to catch and process Nile perch and another was a factory for making passion fruit and pineapple concentrate from fresh fruit. Additionally, Pacific found buyers for the output of these plants. After 14 months, Uganda had earned enough hard currency to start receiving the helicopters it needed.[1]

Foreign trade is obviously important for a country. In modern times, it is virtually impossible for a country to produce domestically everything its citizens need or demand. Even if it could, it is unlikely that it could produce all items more efficiently than producers in other countries. Without international trade, scarce resources are not put to their best uses. As the opening example illustrates, countries and firms will take even exotic steps to clinch a deal.

International trade is more difficult and risky, however, than domestic trade. In foreign trade, the exporter may not be familiar with the buyer and thus not know if the importer is a good credit risk. If merchandise is exported abroad and the buyer does not pay, it may prove difficult, if not impossible, for the exporter to have any legal recourse. Additionally, political instability makes it risky to ship merchandise abroad to certain parts of the world. From the importer's perspective, it is risky to make advance payment for goods that may never be shipped by the exporter.

The present chapter deals with these issues and others. The chapter begins with an example of a simple yet typical foreign trade transaction. The mechanics of the trade are discussed, delineating the institutional arrangements that have been developed over time to facilitate international trade in light of the risks we have identified. The three basic documents needed in a foreign trade transaction—a letter of credit, a time draft, and a bill of lading—are discussed in detail. It is shown how a time draft becomes a banker's acceptance, a negotiable money market instrument.

The second part of the chapter discusses the role of the Export-Import Bank, an independent government agency founded to offer competitive assistance to American exporters through loans, financial guarantees, and credit insurance. The chapter concludes with a discussion of various types of countertrade transactions, which include such trades as the Ugandan-McDonnell Douglas helicopter deal. Countertrade transactions can collectively be defined as foreign trade transactions in which the seller provides the buyer with goods or services in return for a reciprocal promise from the seller to purchase goods or services from the buyer.

---

[1]This example is from the 1992 article by Shelley Neumeier, entitled "Why Countertrade Is Getting Hot," in *Fortune* magazine.

19.1   A Typical Foreign Trade Transaction

www.Gopher://gopher.umsl.
edu:70/11/library/govdocs/
expguide

A comprehensive guide to
exporting that is designed to
help American firms learn the
costs and risks associated with
exporting and develop a
strategy for exporting. The
website also includes an export
glossary.

To understand the mechanics of a typical foreign trade transaction, it is best to use an illustration. Consider an American importer, who is an automobile dealer and who desires to purchase automobiles from a Japanese exporter, the manufacturer. The two do not know each other and are obviously separated by a great distance. If the Japanese manufacturer could have his way, he would have the American importer pay *cash in advance* for the shipment, since he is unfamiliar with the creditworthiness of the auto dealer.

If the auto dealer could have his way, he ideally would prefer to receive the cars on consignment from the auto manufacturer. In a *consignment* sale, the exporter retains title to the merchandise that is shipped. The importer only pays the exporter once he sells the merchandise. If the importer cannot sell the merchandise, he returns it to the exporter. Obviously, the exporter bears all the risk in a consignment sale. Second best for the auto dealer would be to receive the car shipment on credit and then to make payment, thus not paying in advance for an order that might not ever be received.

How can the situation be reconciled so that the foreign trade transaction is satisfactory to both the exporter and the importer? Fortunately for the auto dealer and the auto manufacturer, they are not the first two parties who have faced such a dilemma. Over the years, an elaborate process has evolved for handling just this type of foreign commerce transaction. Exhibit 19.1 presents a schematic of the process that is typically followed in foreign trade. Working our way through Exhibit 19.1 in a narrative fashion will allow us to understand the mechanics of a trade and also the three major documents involved.

Exhibit 19.1 begins with (1) the American importer placing an order with the Japanese exporter, asking if he will ship automobiles under a letter of credit. If the auto manufacturer agrees to this, he will inform the American importer of the price and the other terms of sale, including the credit terms. For discussion purposes, we will assume the length of the credit period is 60 days. The American importer will (2) apply to his bank for a letter of credit for the merchandise he desires to purchase, providing his bank with the terms of the sale.

A **letter of credit (L/C)** is a guarantee from the importer's bank that it will act on behalf of the importer and pay the exporter for the merchandise if all relevant documents specified in the L/C are presented according to the terms of the L/C. In essence, the importer's bank is substituting its creditworthiness for that of the unknown American importer.

The L/C is (3) sent via the importer's bank to the exporter's bank. Once the L/C is received, the exporter's bank will (4) notify the exporter. The Japanese exporter will (5) then ship the cars.

After shipping the automobiles, the Japanese exporter will (6) present to his bank a (60-day) time draft, drawn according to the instructions in the L/C, the bill of lading, and any other shipping documents that are required, such as the invoice and a packing list. A **time draft** is a written order instructing the importer or his agent, the importer's bank, to pay the amount specified on its face on a certain date (that is, the end of the credit period in a foreign trade transaction). A **bill of lading (B/L)** is a document issued by the common carrier specifying that it has received the goods for shipment; it can serve as title to the goods. The exporter's bank (7) presents the shipping documents and the time draft to the importer's bank. After taking title to the goods via the bill of lading, the importer's bank accepts the time draft, creating at this point a **banker's acceptance (B/A),** a negotiable money market instrument for which a secondary market exists. The importer's bank charges an acceptance commission, which is deducted at the time of final settlement. The acceptance commission is based on the term to maturity of the time draft and the creditworthiness of the importer.

One of several things can happen with the B/A. It can be returned to the Japanese exporter, who will hold it for 60 days and then present it for payment to the importer's

EXHIBIT 19.1   **Process of Typical Foreign Trade Transaction**

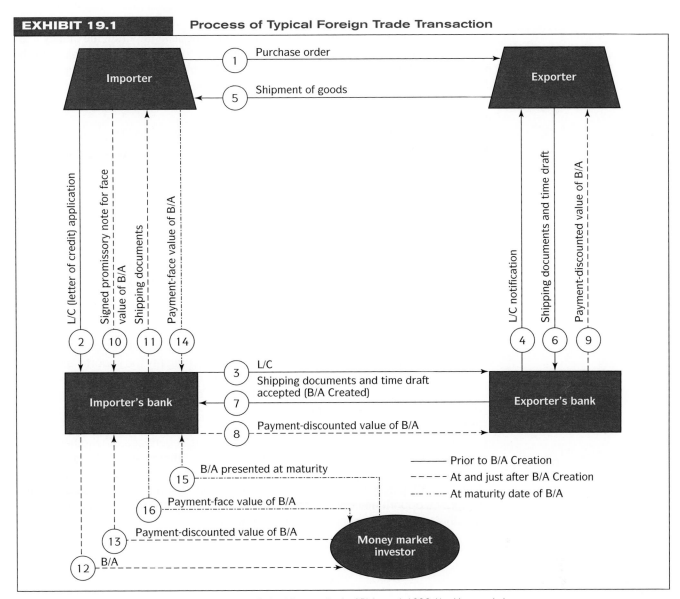

Source: Adapted from *Instruments of the Money Market,* Federal Reserve Bank of Richmond, 1986. Used by permission.

bank at maturity. Should the exporter suddenly find he needs funds prior to the maturity date, the B/A can be sold at a discount in the money market. Since their risks are similar, banker's acceptances trade at rates similar to rates for negotiable bank certificates of deposit. Alternatively, as in Exhibit 19.1, the Japanese exporter could instruct its bank to have the B/A (8) discounted by the importer's bank and (9) pay that amount to it. Analogously, the exporter's bank may decide to hold the B/A to maturity as an investment, and pay the Japanese exporter the discounted equivalent.

The American importer (10) signs a (60-day) promissory note with his bank for the face value of the banker's acceptance, due on the maturity date of the B/A. In return, the exporter's bank (11) provides the auto dealer with the shipping documents needed to take possession of the automobiles from the common carrier.

If the B/A is not held by the Japanese exporter or the exporter's bank, the importer's bank may hold it for 60 days until maturity when it will collect the face value from the American importer via the promissory note. Alternatively, as in Exhibit 19.1, the importer's bank may (12) sell the B/A in the money market to an investor at a (13) discount from face value. At maturity, the importer's bank will (14) collect the face value of the B/A via the promissory note from the American importer, the money market investor will (15) present the B/A for payment to the importer's bank, and the importer's bank will (16) pay the face value of the B/A to the investor. In the event of default by the American importer, the importer's bank will seek recourse against the importer. B/As usually have maturities ranging from 30 to 180 days; as such, they are only short-term sources of trade financing.

EXAMPLE 19.1 Cost Analysis of a Banker's Acceptance As mentioned in the previous discussion of the schematic describing a typical foreign trade transaction, the exporter may hold the B/A to maturity and collect payment at that time. Alternatively, the exporter may discount the B/A with the importer's bank or sell it at a discount in the money market.

Suppose the face amount of the promissory note is $1,000,000 and the importer's bank charges an acceptance commission of 1.5 percent. Since the note is for 60 days, the exporter will receive $997,500 = $1,000,000 × [1 − (0.015 × 60/360)] if he decides to hold the B/A until maturity. Thus, the acceptance commission is $2,500.

If 60-day B/A rates are 5.25 percent and the exporter discounts the B/A with the importer's bank, he will receive $988,750 = $1,000,000 × [1 − ([0.0525 + 0.0150] × 60/360)]. Thus, the importer's bank receives a discount rate of interest of 6.75 percent = 5.25 + 1.50 percent on its investment. At maturity the importer's bank will receive $1,000,000 from the importer. The bond equivalent yield it receives on its investment (which is figured on the actual number of days in a year instead of a 360-day banker's year) is 6.92 percent, or 0.0692 = ($1,000,000/$988,750 − 1) × 365/60.

The exporter pays the acceptance commission, regardless of whether he discounts the B/A or holds it to maturity, hence it is not marginal to a decision to discount the B/A. The bond equivalent rate the exporter receives from discounting the B/A is 5.38 percent, or 0.0538 = ($997,500/$988,750 − 1) × 365/60. If the exporter's opportunity cost of capital is greater than 5.38 percent compounded bimonthly (an effective annual rate of 5.5 percent), discounting makes sense; if not, the exporter should hold the B/A to maturity. ∎

19.2 Forfaiting

www.afia-forfaiting.g/
index.htm

The website of the Association of Forfaiters in the Americas, Inc. It provides information on forfaiting for exporters, importers, and financial institutions.

Forfaiting is a type of medium-term trade financing used to finance the sale of capital goods. Forfaiting involves the sale of promissory notes signed by the importer in favour of the exporter. The *forfait,* usually a bank, buys the notes at a discount from face value from the exporter. In this way, the exporter receives payment for the export and does not have to carry the financing. The forfait does not have recourse against the exporter in the event of default by the importer. The promissory notes are typically structured to extend out in a series over a period of from three to seven years, with a note in the series maturing every six months. Since forfaiting transactions are typically used to finance capital goods, they usually are for amounts of $500,000 or more. Forfaiting began in Switzerland and Germany, but it has now spread throughout most of Western Europe and into the United States. Forfait transactions are typically denominated in Swiss francs, euros, and American dollars.

19.3 Government Assistance in Exporting

Success in international trade is fundamentally important for a country. Success in exporting implies that there is demand for a country's products, that its labour force is benefiting from employment, and that some resources are used for technological

The Export-Import Bank and Affiliated Organizations

advancement. To be successful in international trade requires a country's export-oriented firms to be good marketers, that is, to be competitive in terms of product offerings, promotion, price, delivery capability, and service provided to importers. Equally important, however, is for firms to be competitive in terms of extending credit to importers.

Because of the benefits that accrue from exporting, the governments of most developed countries offer competitive assistance to domestic exporters in the form of subsidized credit that can be extended to importers. Also, credit insurance programs that guarantee financing extended by private financial institutions are common. In this section, we discuss the main features of programs available to American exporters.

In 1934, the **Export-Import Bank (Eximbank) of the United States** was founded, and subsequently chartered in 1945, as an independent government agency to facilitate and finance American export trade. Eximbank's purpose is to provide financing in situations where private financial institutions are unable or unwilling to because: (1) the loan maturity is too long; (2) the amount of the loan is too large; (3) the loan risk is too great; or (4) the importing firm has difficulty obtaining hard currency for payment.

To meet its objectives, Eximbank provides service through several types of programs. Some of the most important of these are working capital guarantees, direct loans to foreign borrowers, loan guarantees, and credit insurance.[2]

Through its *Working Capital Guarantee Program,* Eximbank facilitates the expansion of American exports by encouraging commercial lenders to make working capital loans to American exporters. The Eximbank loan guarantee covers 90 percent of the loan principal and accrued interest, and it is backed by the full faith and credit of the American government.

Through its *Medium and Long-Term Loan Program,* Eximbank will facilitate direct credit to foreign buyers of American exports. Disbursements go to the American exporter, and the export products go to the foreign importer. The *Long-Term Program* covers repayment terms in excess of seven years and a loan amount greater than $10 million. The *Medium-Term Program* covers repayment terms of seven years or less and loan amounts of $10 million or less. Both programs cover financing up to 85 percent of the export contract value. The *Private Export Funding Corporation (PEFCO),* established in 1970 by a group of commercial banks and industrial corporations, frequently cooperates in loans with the Eximbank under these programs by providing liquidity via the purchase of notes issued by Eximbank to finance the loans.

Through its *Medium and Long-Term Guarantee Program,* Eximbank guarantees the loans made by private financial institutions to foreign importers. Interest charged on these loans is usually at a floating rate. The guarantees, which commit the full faith and credit of the American government, cover financing up to 85 percent of the export contract value. The guarantees cover 100 percent of the loan principal and accrued interest against loss due to commercial and political risks. Guarantees covering only political risks are available.

Through its *Export Credit Insurance Program,* Eximbank helps American exporters develop and expand their overseas sales by protecting them against loss should a foreign buyer or other foreign debtor default for political or commercial reasons. Insurance policies may cover both comprehensive commercial and political credit risks, or only specific political risks.

In the United Kingdom, the *Exports Credits Guarantee Department (ECGD)* performs functions similar to those of the Eximbank and FCIA. Formed in 1919, the ECGD provides assistance to exporters through direct insurance coverage against nonpayment by the importer due to commercial and political risks and by guaranteeing bank loans to foreign borrowers. The exporter, who is considered to be the true beneficiary, pays to ECGD the guaranteed bank loan insurance premium.

---

[2]Much of the discussion in this section is drawn from the Export-Import Bank website, www.exim.gov/.

19.4 Countertrade

Countertrade is an umbrella term used to describe many different types of transactions, each "in which the seller provides a buyer with goods or services and promises in return to purchase goods or services from the buyer."[3] Countertrades may or may not involve the use of money. If money is not exchanged, the trade is a type of barter. Regardless, countertrade usually results in a two-way flow of commodities.

Countertrade arrangements can be traced back to prehistoric times, and they have been used throughout history whenever money was scarce. While it is difficult to determine the exact volume of countertrade, the practice is, nevertheless, widespread. According to Hammond (1990), some estimates put countertrade at only 5 percent of total world trade, whereas other estimates are as high as 40 percent. Moreover, countertrade transactions are not accounted for in official trade statistics. In the new millennium, the IMF, the World Bank, and the U.S. Department of Commerce estimate that as much as half of all international trade transactions will be conducted as countertrade.[4] Most recently, a surge of countertrade activity occurred in the 1980s, when the Third World debt crisis left the debtor countries without sufficient foreign exchange reserves or bank lines of credit to carry on normal commerce.[5]

Forms of Countertrade

Hennart (1989) identifies six forms of countertrade: barter, clearing arrangement, switch trading, buy-back, counterpurchase, and offset. The first three do not involve the use of money, whereas the latter three do.

Barter is the direct exchange of goods between two parties. While money does not exchange hands in a barter transaction, it is common to value the goods each party exchanges in an agreed-upon currency. It is often necessary to place a monetary value on the goods for accounting, taxation, and insurance purposes.

Hammond (1990) describes barter as "a rather primitive way to do business. It fosters bilateral trade which, in turn, under mercantilist economies and imperialistic policies, fostered a tight system of colonial dependency with protected markets and captive sources of raw materials." He notes that barter flourished until after World War II when the Bretton Woods fixed exchange rate system was established that provided for currency convertibility and fostered free trade.

Today, barter transactions are typically one-time exchanges of merchandise that take place when circumstances warrant. Schaffer (1989) describes a modern example of barter that took place between General Electric (GE) and Romania. GE had agreed to sell Romania a turbine generator for cash. The Romanian loan financing subsequently fell through, and in order to complete the deal, GE agreed to accept Romanian products, which it, in turn, sold for cash through its trading company.

A *clearing arrangement* (also called a bilateral clearing agreement) is a form of barter in which the counterparties (governments) contract to purchase a certain amount of goods and services from one another. Both parties set up accounts with each other that are debited whenever one country imports from the other. At the end of an agreed-upon period of time, any account imbalances are settled for hard currency, or by the transfer of goods. The clearing arrangement introduces the concept of credit to barter transactions and means that bilateral trade can take place that does not have to be immediately settled. Account balances are periodically determined, and any trade imbalances are settled in an agreed-upon currency. Anyane-Ntow and Harvey (1995) note that bilateral clearing agreements have usually taken place between Third World and Eastern European countries. They cite the 1994 agreement between China and Saudi Arabia with a $1 billion target as an example.

---

[3]Definition from Hennart (1990).
[4]See Anyane-Ntow and Harvey (1995, p. 47) for this estimate.
[5]See Chapter 6 for a discussion of the extent and severity of the Third World debt crisis.

A *switch trade* is the purchase by a third party of one country's clearing agreement imbalance for hard currency, which is, in turn, resold. The second buyer uses the account balance to purchase goods and services from the original clearing agreement counterparty who had the account imbalance. Anyane-Ntow and Harvey (1995) give the example of a switch trade when the United States exported fertilizers to Pakistan through a Romanian–Pakistani clearing agreement.

A *buy-back transaction* involves a technology transfer via the sale of a manufacturing plant. As part of the transaction, the seller agrees to purchase a certain portion of the plant output once it is constructed. As Hennart (1989) notes, money enters into the agreement in two ways. First, the plant buyer borrows hard currency in the capital market to pay the seller for the plant. Second, the plant seller agrees to purchase enough of the plant output over a period of time to enable the buyer to pay back the borrowed funds. A buy-back transaction can be viewed as a form of direct investment in the purchasing country. Examples of buy-back transactions include Japan's agreements with Taiwan, Singapore, and Korea to exchange computer chip production equipment for a certain percentage of the output.[6]

A *counterpurchase* is similar to a buy-back transaction, but with some notable differences. The two counterparties are usually an Eastern importer and a Western exporter of technology. The major difference between a buy-back and a counterpurchase transaction is that in the latter, the merchandise the Western seller agrees to purchase is unrelated and has not been produced on the exported equipment. The seller agrees to purchase goods from a list drawn up by the importer at prices set by the importer. Goods on the list are frequently items for which the buyer does not have a ready market. As an example of a counterpurchase, Anyane-Ntow and Harvey (1995) cite the agreement to exchange Italian industrial equipment for Indonesian rubber.

An *offset transaction* can be viewed as a counterpurchase trade agreement involving the aerospace/defence industry. Offset transactions are reciprocal trade agreements between an industrialized country and a country that has defence and/or aerospace industries. Hammond (1990) cites the example of the sale of F-16 jet fighters manufactured by General Dynamics to Turkey and Greece in exchange for olives, hydroelectric power projects, the promotion of tourism, and aircraft co-production.

Some Generalizations about Countertrade

Countertrade transactions became very prominent in international trade in the 1980s and 1990s. Arguments both for and against countertrade transactions can be made. Hammond (1990) notes that there are both negative and positive incentives for a country to be in favour of countertrade. Negative incentives are those that are forced upon a country or corporation whether or not it desires to engage in countertrade. They include the conservation of cash and hard currency, the improvement of trade imbalances, and the maintenance of export prices. Positive reasons from both the country and corporate perspectives include enhanced economic development, increased employment, technology transfer, market expansion, increased profitability, less costly sourcing of supply, reduction of surplus goods from inventory, and the development of marketing expertise.

Those against countertrade transactions claim that such transactions tamper with the fundamental operation of free markets, and, therefore, resources are used inefficiently. Opponents claim that transaction costs are increased, that multilateral trade is restricted through fostering bilateral trade agreements and that, in general, transactions that do not make use of money represent a step backward in economic development.

Hennart (1989) empirically studied all 1,277 countertrade contracts between June 1983 and December 31, 1986, that were reported in *Countertrade Outlook.* Of these transactions, 694 were clearing arrangements, 171 were classified as barters, 298 as counterpurchases, 71 as buy-backs, and 43 as offsets. The countries involved were

---

[6]See Anyane-Ntow and Harvey (1995, p. 48).

classified into the World Bank categories of: Developed, Organization of Petroleum Exporting Countries (OPEC) Members, Centrally Planned Economies (CPE), Middle-Income, and Low-Income.

Hennart found that each country grouping had a propensity to engage in certain types of countertrade transactions. OPEC, middle-income, and low-income countries used more counterpurchases, CPEs more buy-backs, and developed and middle-income countries engaged in more offsets. Barter was most common between two middle-income countries, between developed and middle-income countries, and between middle-income countries and CPEs.

Hennart claims the high frequency of buy-backs among CPEs is consistent with their use as a substitute for foreign direct investment. The reasons that CPEs and low-income countries do not actively engage in offset transactions are twofold: CPEs are not allowed to purchase Western weapons, and low-income developing countries cannot afford sophisticated weapons systems typically sold via offset transactions. Barter between two middle-income countries (the most frequent) is consistent with the two countries desiring to avoid the repayment of external debt. The absence of barter among the OPEC countries and among the developed countries is consistent with the use of barter to bypass cartels and commodity arrangements. The analysis of Marin and Schnitzer (1995) is consistent with Hennart's conclusions.

Whether countertrade transactions are good or bad for the global economy, it appears certain that they will increase in the near future as world trade increases.

SUMMARY

Export and import transactions and trade financing are the main topics discussed in this chapter.

1. Conducting international trade transactions is difficult in comparison with domestic trades. Commercial and political risks enter into the equation, which are not factors in domestic trade. Yet, it is important for a country to be competitively strong in international trade in order for its citizens to have the goods and services they need and demand.

2. A typical foreign trade transaction requires three basic documents: letter of credit, time draft, and bill of lading. A time draft can become a negotiable money market instrument called a banker's acceptance.

3. Forfaiting, in which a bank purchases at a discount from an importer a series of promissory notes in favour of an exporter, is a medium-term form of trade financing.

4. The Export-Import Bank provides competitive assistance to American exporters through direct loans to foreign importers, loan guarantees, and credit insurance to American exporters.

5. Countertrade transactions are gaining renewed prominence as a means of conducting international trade transactions. There are several types of countertrade transactions, only some of which involve the use of money. In each type, the seller provides the buyer with goods or services in return for a reciprocal promise from the seller to purchase goods or services from the buyer.

KEY WORDS

banker's acceptance (B/A), *444*
bill of lading (B/L), *444*
countertrade, *448*

Export-Import Bank (Eximbank) of the United States, *447*
forfaiting, *446*

letter of credit (L/C), *444*
time draft, *444*

QUESTIONS

1. Discuss some of the reasons why international trade is more difficult and risky from the exporter's perspective than is domestic trade.

2. What three basic documents are necessary to conduct a typical foreign commerce trade? Briefly discuss the purpose of each.

3. How does a time draft become a banker's acceptance?

4. Discuss the various ways the exporter can receive payment in a foreign trade transaction after the importer's bank accepts the exporter's time draft and it becomes a banker's acceptance.

5. What is a forfaiting transaction?

6. What is the purpose of the Export-Import Bank?

7. Do you think that a country's government should assist private business in the conduct of international trade through direct loans, loan guarantees, and/or credit insurance?

8. Briefly discuss the various types of countertrade.

9. Discuss some of the pros and cons of countertrade from the country's perspective and the firm's perspective.

10. What is the difference between a buy-back transaction and a counterpurchase?

PROBLEMS

1. Assume the time from acceptance to maturity on a $2,000,000 banker's acceptance is 90 days. Further assume that the importing bank's acceptance commission is 1.25 percent and that the market rate for 90-day B/As is 7 percent. Determine the amount the exporter will receive if he holds the B/A until maturity and also the amount the exporter will receive if he discounts the B/A with the importer's bank.

2. The time from acceptance to maturity on a $1,000,000 banker's acceptance is 120 days. The importer's bank's acceptance commission is 1.75 percent, and the market rate for 120-day B/As is 5.75 percent. What amount will the exporter receive if he holds the B/A until maturity? If he discounts the B/A with the importer's bank? Also determine the bond equivalent yield the importer's bank will earn from discounting the B/A with the exporter. If the exporter's opportunity cost of capital is 11 percent, should he discount the B/A or hold it to maturity?

INTERNET EXERCISE

The chapter indicated that banker's acceptances were negotiable money market instruments. You might be interested in including B/As in your portfolio. Fiscal Agents Financial Services Group is an investment advisory service specializing in helping investors structure portfolios to meet their needs. Go to www.fiscalagents. com/knowledge/inforeport/ba.shtml to learn what Fiscal Agents has to say about B/As as an investment.

MINI CASE

American Machine Tools, Inc.

American Machine Tools is a midwestern manufacturer of tool-and-die-making equipment. The company has had an inquiry from a representative of the Estonian government about the terms of sale for a $5,000,000 order of machinery. The sales manager spoke with the Estonian representative, but he is doubtful that the Estonian government will be able to obtain enough hard currency to make the purchase. While the American economy has been growing, American Machine Tools has not had a very good year. An additional $5,000,000 in sales would definitely help. If something cannot be arranged, the firm will likely be forced to lay off some of its skilled workforce.

Is there a way that you can think of that American Machine Tools might be able to make the machinery sale to Estonia?

REFERENCES & SUGGESTED READINGS

Anyane-Ntow, Kwabena, and Santhi C. Harvey. "A Countertrade Primer." *Management Accounting* (April 1995), pp. 47–50.

Celi, Louis J., and I. James Czechowicz. *Export Financing: A Handbook of Sources and Techniques.* Morristown, N.J.: Financial Executives Research Foundation, 1985.

Edwards, Burt. *Getting Paid for Exports.* Brookfield, Vt: Gower, 1990.

Francis, Dick. *The Countertrade Handbook.* New York: Quorum Books, 1987.

Guild, Ian, and Rhodri Harris. *Forfaiting.* New York: Universe Books, 1986.

Hammond, Grant T. *Countertrade, Offsets and Barter in International Political Economy.* New York: St. Martin's Press, 1990.

Hennart, Jean-Francois. "Some Empirical Dimensions of Countertrade." *Journal of International Business Studies* (Second Quarter, 1989), pp. 243–70.

Hill, Eric. "Bankers Acceptances." In *Instruments of the Money Market,* 6th ed., Timothy Q. Cook and Timothy D. Rowe, eds. Richmond, Va.: Federal Reserve Bank of Richmond, 1986.

Knight, Martin, James Ball, and Andrew Inglis-Taylor, eds. *Export Finance.* London: Euromoney Publications, 1988.

Machinery and Allied Products Institute. *A Handbook on Financing American Exports,* 4th ed. Washington, D.C.: Machinery and Allied Products Institute, 1984.

Marin, Dalia, and Monika Schnitzer. "Tying Trade Flows: A Theory of Countertrade with Evidence." *The American Economic Review* 85 (1995), pp. 1047–64.

Neumeir, Shelley. "Why Countertrade Is Getting Hot," *Fortune,* June 29, 1992, p. 25.

Rodriguez, Rita M. *The Export-Import Bank at Fifty.* Lexington, Mass.: Lexington Books, 1987.

Schaffer, Matt. *Winning the Countertrade War.* New York: John Wiley and Sons, 1989.

International Tax Environment

THIS CHAPTER provides a brief introduction to the international tax environment that will be useful to multinational firms in their tax planning. While taxation is a complex topic at the domestic level, it is even more so in the international sphere, where at least two and sometimes more tax systems interact to determine how much tax a corporation pays. This chapter is, at most, an introduction.

We begin with a discussion of two major objectives of taxation that have special relevance to international corporate taxation: *efficiency*, sometimes called "tax neutrality," and *national treatment*. We then turn to three categories of tax most pertinent to multinational enterprise: the corporate income tax, withholding taxes, and value-added tax. This is followed by an outline of how various nations adopt fundamentally different approaches to achieve similar policy objectives. The chapter goes on to examine the Canadian way of taxing multinational enterprise versus the American way. As we shall see, the Canadian system is remarkably simple, whereas the American way is remarkably complex. We develop an extensive illustration based on the American approach.

Some issues in taxation were introduced earlier in view of specific concerns at hand. For example, Chapter 17 on capital budgeting required basic knowledge of international taxation from the Canadian perspective. Chapter 18 on cash management investigated the role of intra-firm transfer pricing as a means to reduce the overall tax liability of a multinational corporation (MNC).

20.1 The Objectives of Taxation

Two fundamental policy objectives frame our thinking about the international tax environment: tax neutrality and national treatment.

Tax Neutrality

Tax neutrality is closely allied to economic efficiency. The issue is whether taxes impose costly distortions of investment decisions. Good tax policy tries to avoid penalizing investment. A neutral tax allows a nation to capture the full economic benefits of international investment, either inbound or outbound. In a world of highly mobile international capital, investment distortions caused by tax are the modern counterpart of trade distortions caused by tariffs.

Nations impose tax in a variety of ways. The most significant are personal income tax, sales taxes, corporate income tax, and value-added tax. International business is primarily concerned with corporate income tax, the tax that is most likely to distort investment decisions. For instance, if an MNC faces higher tax in one country than in another, then that MNC has an incentive to invest more in the low-tax country and less in the high-tax country. Likewise, as is often the case, when an MNC must choose between investing at home or abroad, it will invest more abroad if the burden of "home" taxation is greater than taxation abroad. Such tax-based bias in favour of foreign investment, we will see, is almost always the case for both Canadian and American firms-but for very different reasons.

The tax authorities of various countries recognize that MNC investment decisions are sensitive to taxation. No nation wants to discourage investment, domestic or otherwise. However, a nation can set only its own tax rules, rates, and regulations. Nations deal with joint tax concerns through bilateral tax treaties.

Tax treaties generally establish that MNCs must comply first with the taxation in the host country. A host country *always* has priority to tax those companies within its jurisdiction, an international understanding referred to as *national tax sovereignty*. The international question then is how does the home country of multinational enterprise tax the foreign-source income of the parent companies in that home country. We will turn to that issue in a moment.

National Treatment

The second pillar in the foundation of international taxation is **national treatment**. To abide by national treatment, a nation commits itself to taxing foreign-owned business in exactly that same way-with the same rules, rates and regulations-as it taxes domestic firms. National treatment is a commitment to no tax discrimination. National treatment combined with national tax sovereignty creates a situation where, in matters of corporate taxation, the host country of MNC sees no difference between foreign-owned and domestic corporations.

National treatment is enshrined in virtually every bilateral tax treaty as well as in most free trade agreements, such as the North American Free Trade Agreement (NAFTA).

Since the host country is both entitled and conveniently positioned to tax a foreign-owned firm first and since the host country levies corporate tax according to its own rules, rates and regulations, it is up to the *home country* to extend any special concession to foreign-source corporate income of the MNC that the home country considers to be appropriate. "Concession" usually involves relief of so-called "international double taxation." Relief of double taxation is exclusively the responsibility or prerogative of the home country of the MNC. For example, Canada is responsible for relief of double taxation on the foreign-source earnings of Barrick, CN, Domtar, Quebecor, or TD Bank. The United States is responsible for the relief of double-taxation of the foreign-source income of General Electric, General Motors, Disney, or IBM. Canada and the United States approach this responsibility in dramatically different ways.

The Canadian versus the American Way of Taxing Multinational Enterprise

Within Canada, all corporations, regardless of ownership, are liable for Canadian corporate tax on their in-Canada income. So, for example, income earned in Canada by Wal-Mart (Canada), which is foreign-owned, is taxed in exactly the same way as Canadian Tire which is wholly owned by Canadians. This reflects Canada's commitment to national treatment. Canada does not discriminate along the lines of nationality of corporate ownership. In our commitment to national treatment, Canada is in line with all modern industrial nations.

International taxation is substantially more complicated—and different among nations—in the case of home (or *residence*) taxation of foreign-source income. We are now referring to how Canada taxes, for instance, the American earnings of CN or how the United States taxes income that Wal-Mart earns in Canada. This is the perspective of the home country in regard to taxation of foreign-source corporate income.

When a Canadian-based multinational enterprise—such as Bombardier, McCain Foods, or Four Seasons Hotels—earns income in, say, the United States or Europe, such foreign-source corporate income is *not* subject to additional tax in Canada. This Canadian approach, known as *exemption*, differs significantly from the way that, say, the United States taxes the foreign-source income of American-based multinationals. We will turn to the United States in a moment, but a brief word on the logic of the Canadian approach is useful.

The rationale for Canada's exemption policy follows directly from Canada's recognition that virtually all countries are committed to national treatment together with the fact that it is not in Canada's interest to penalize outbound foreign direct investment. If Canada were to impose Canadian tax on foreign source earnings of Canadian MNCs after such firms had paid tax abroad, the foreign source earnings would be taxed twice—once by the foreign country and once again by Canada. No modern country wants to penalize outbound foreign direct investment in that way. However, a fundamental efficiency condition in international taxation, referred to as **capital export neutrality**, is not guaranteed by exempting earnings of Canadian FDI from Canadian taxation. Capital export neutrality calls for corporate income of Canadian corporations to be taxed at the same rate regardless of where in the world the income is earned. With exemption, Canadian MNCs can do themselves a favour by locating in low-tax jurisdictions. This is where Canada is being practical in its international tax affairs. Canada realizes that almost all countries in which Canadian MNCs have a serious interest, such as the United States, the EU, or other OECD nations, these countries have corporate tax rates that are quite similar to Canada. Canada accepts that for all practical purposes, other countries will tax the local income (called *source* income) of Canadian MNCs at approximately the same rate as Canada would tax such income. So, Canadian tax authorities leave foreign-source business income alone.

The United States, on the other hand, takes a fundamentally different approach to taxing the foreign-source income of its multinational enterprises. The United States taxes the worldwide income of American-based MNCs. For instance, the United States taxes the Canadian-source income of Wal-Mart. The U.S. Internal Revenue Service requires all American-based MNCs to compute an American tax liability on foreign-source income using American tax rules, rates, and regulations. At the same time, the United States also allows a *foreign tax credit* for taxes that American-owned MNCs pay to foreign governments. For instance, taxes that Wal-Mart pays to Ottawa are credited against Wal-Mart's American tax liability.

The American system of taxing foreign-source income of American-based MNCs has another significant feature known as *deferral*. While every American-based MNC must annually compute its American tax liability on foreign-source income using American rules, rates and regulations, they are not liable for the American tax until such income is repatriated to the United States in the form of dividends paid by the foreign subsidiary to the parent firm in the United States. The deferral provision creates a strong incentive for American-based MNCs to leave their earnings abroad, that is, they have an incentive to *not* repatriate. Since, as finance people recognize, a payment delayed is a payment reduced, the deferral provision in effect lowers the effective corporate tax rate on foreign-source earnings of American-based MNCs.

Taxes and Transfer Pricing

The way that a home country taxes the foreign-source income of its MNCs has implications for the effectiveness of transfer pricing as a means to lower taxes. In the Mintel example that we saw in Chapter 18, which takes the vantage point of an American-based MNC, Mintel realizes no tax advantage through transfer pricing. At most, transfer pricing allows Mintel to shift taxable income abroad and thereby delay—but not evade—the American tax liability.

On the other hand, an MNC with its home in Canada can always pursue a potential gain from shifting income out of Canada and into a lower tax jurisdiction. If a Canadian-based MNC maintains a high margin on transfers to Canada from a subsidiary in, say, low-tax Ireland (or a low margin on transfers from Canada to Ireland) income is shifted from Canada to Ireland. Less tax is paid in Canada, a bit more tax is paid in Ireland, and the MNC has, as a whole, saved tax.

A well-known example of such arrangements involves Irving Oil, the New Brunswick–based oil company. For many years, Irving imported crude oil from Venezuela destined for the Irving refinery in Saint John. The crude oil shipments from

Caracas to Saint John were channeled (in an accounting sense) through an Irving affiliate in Bermuda. By assigning a high transfer price to crude as it was "transferred" from Bermuda to Saint John, profits that would otherwise be reported in Canada were reported in low-tax Bermuda.[1]

Neither the U.S. Internal Revenue Service or the Canada Revenue Agency takes kindly to international accounting tricks that might cost them tax revenue to which they are otherwise entitled. . The tax auditors are vigilant. As a practical matter in how MNCs manage their internal transfer prices, strategies designed to save tax are less likely to involve actual *physically* transferred goods and more likely to involve intangibles such as management fees, royalties, and interest, on intrafirm loans. This was illustrated in "The Shell Case," in the International Finance in Practice box in Chapter 14.

20.2 | Types of Taxation

This section discusses the three basic types of taxation that national governments throughout the world use in generating revenue: income tax, withholding tax, and value-added tax.

Income Tax

Many countries in the world obtain a significant portion of their tax revenue from imposing an **income tax** on personal and corporate incomes. An income tax is a **direct tax,** that is, one that is paid directly by the taxpayer on whom it is levied. The tax is levied on **active income,** that is, income that results from production by the firm or individual or from services that have been provided.

One of the best guides detailing corporate income tax regulations in most countries is the PriceWaterhouseCoopers annual *Corporate Taxes: Worldwide Summaries.* Exhibit 20.1 is derived from the PriceWaterhouseCoopers summaries. It lists the normal, standard, or representative upper-end marginal income tax rates for domestic non-financial corporations for 125 countries. As the exhibit shows, national tax rates vary from a low of zero percent in such tax-haven countries as Bahrain, Bermuda, the British Virgin Islands, and the Cayman Islands to well over 40 percent in some countries. The current American marginal tax rate of 35 percent is positioned pretty well in the middle of the rates assessed by the majority of countries.

Withholding Tax

www.tax.kpmg.net

KPMG International, a global professional advisory firm, manages this website. A useful corporate tax survey that compares tax rates for 68 countries can be downloaded from this site.

www.taxup.com

This website provides tax and accounting information by country.

A **withholding tax** is a tax levied on passive income earned by an individual or corporation of one country within the tax jurisdiction of another country. **Passive income** includes dividends and interest income, and income from royalties, patents, or copyrights paid to the taxpayer. A withholding tax is an **indirect tax,** that is, a tax that is borne by a taxpayer who did not directly generate the income that serves as the source of the passive income. The tax is withheld from payments the corporation makes to the taxpayer and turned over to the local tax authority. The withholding tax assures the local tax authority that it will receive the tax due on the passive income earned within its tax jurisdiction.

Many countries have **tax treaties** with one another specifying the withholding tax rate applied to various types of passive income. Exhibit 20.2 lists the *basic* withholding tax rates Canada imposes on other countries through its tax treaties with them. For specific types of passive income, the tax rates may be different from those presented in the exhibit. Withholding tax rates imposed through tax treaties are bilateral; that is, through negotiation two countries agree to impose the same tax rate on one another on the same category of passive income.

---

[1]Irving Oil's transfer pricing arrangements prompted Revenue Canada Taxation (as the federal tax agency was then known) to reassess Irving's Canadian tax obligation, substantially raising Irving's Canadian tax bill. Irving challenged the reassessment. The case went all the way to the Supreme Court. The Supreme Court found in favour of Irving Oil.

EXHIBIT 20.1   Corporate Percentage Income Tax Rates from Certain Countries[a]

Country	Tax Rate	Country	Tax Rate	Country	Tax Rate	Country	Tax Rate
Antigua & Barbuda	40	Ecuador	25	Lithuania	15	Saudi Arabia	30
Argentina	35	Egypt	42	Luxembourg	22.88	Senegal	35
Australia	30	Estonia	35	Macau	15.75	Singapore	19.5
Austria	34	Faroe Islands	20	Malaysia	28	Slovak Republic	25
Azerbaijan	27	Fiji	32	Malta	35	Slovenia	25
Bahamas	0	Finland	29	Mauritius	25	Solomon Islands	30
Bahrain	0	France	35.43	Mexico	35	South Africa	30
Barbados	37.5	Gabon	35	Monaco	33.33	Spain	35
Belgium	40.17	Germany	26.38	Morocco	35	Sri Lanka	39.88
Bermuda	0	Ghana	32.5	Mozambique	35	Swaziland	30
Bolivia	25	Greece	37.5	Namibia	35	Sweden	28
Botswana	25	Guatemala	31	Netherlands	34.5	Switzerland	26∓
Brazil	15	Guyana	35	Netherlands Antilles	34.5	Tahiti	40
British Virgin Islands[b]	15/0	Hong Kong	16	New Caledonia	30	Taiwan	25
Brunei Darussalam	30	Hungary	18	New Zealand	33	Tanzania	30
Bulgaria	25	India	35.7	Nicaragua	25	Thailand	30
Cambodia	20	Indonesia	30	Nigeria	30	Trinidad & Tobago	35
Cameroon	38.5	Iran	25	Norway	28	Turkey	43.18
Canada	33.9	Ireland	16	Oman	30	Uganda	30
Cayman Islands	0	Isle of Man	18	Pakistan	45	Ukraine	30
Channel Islands, Guernsey	20	Israel	36	Panama	30	United Arab Emirates[c]	30
Channel Islands, Jersey	20	Italy	36	Papau New Guinea	25	United Kingdom	30
Chile	18	Ivory Coast	35	Paraguay	30	United States	35
China	30.9	Jamaica	33.33	Peru	27	Uruguay	30
Colombia	35	Japan	46.7	Philippines	32	Uzbekistan	24
Congo	40	Kazakstan	30	Poland	28	Venezuela	34
Costa Rica	30	Kenya	30	Portugal	33	Vietnam	32
Croatia	20	Korea	30.8	Puerto Rico	39	Zambia	35
Cyprus	25	Kuwait	55	Qatar	35	Zimbabwe	30.9
Czech Republic	31	Laos	45	Romania	25		
Denmark	30	Latvia	22	Russian Federation	35		
Dominican Republic	25	Liechtenstein	20	St. Lucia	33.33		

[a]The table lists normal, standard, or representative upper-end marginal tax rates for nonfinancial corporations.

[b]In the British Virgin Islands, a nonresident company incorporated as an international business company is tax exempt.

[c]Tax decrees have not been enforced, except for oil-producing companies where the tax rate is set by the ruler of each Emirate.

Source: Derived from PriceWaterhouseCoopers, *Corporate Taxes: Worldwide Summaries*, 2002.

The withholding tax rates presented in Exhibit 20.2 are for the most part *bilateral* in the sense that Canada and each of the nations represented in the exhibit have negotiated a bilateral tax treaty. All rates within a tax treaty are reciprocally equal. For example, within the Canada–United States tax treaty, the rate of withholding tax on interest payments from one country to the other is 10 percent. Canada withholds 10 percent on interest payments paid to the United States and the United States withholds 10 percent on interest payments paid to Canada. With respect to withholding tax rates on dividends, which tend to be important for corporations since intrafirm dividends are the mechanism for MNC subsidiaries to repatriate earnings to the parent firm, Exhibit 20.2 in most cases reports two withholding tax rates, for example "10 or 15" for China or "5 or 15" for the United States and most OECD nations. The higher rate applies to individual taxpayers and also to intracorporate dividends where the ownership share is small, say, less than 10 percent, whereas the lower rate applies to international intracorporate dividends (paid by a subsidiary to its parent). The rationale for the lower rate on corporate dividends is straightforward: the country from which the dividend is sent has already levied a corporate tax on the income that underlies the dividend.

Value-Added Tax

A **value-added tax (VAT)** is an indirect national tax levied on the value added in the production of a good (or service) as it moves through the various stages of production. There are several ways to implement a VAT. The "subtraction method" is frequently followed in practice.

EXAMPLE 20.1 | Value-Added Tax Calculation As an example of the subtraction method of calculating VAT, consider a VAT of 15 percent charged on a consumption good that goes through three stages of production. Suppose that Stage 1 is the sale of raw materials to the manufacturer at a cost of €100 per unit of production. Stage 2 results in a finished good shipped to retailers at a price of €300. Stage 3 is the retail sale to the final consumer at a price of €380. €100 of value has been added in Stage 1, resulting in a VAT of €15. In Stage 2 the VAT is 15 percent of €300, or €45, with a credit of €15 given against the value added in Stage 1. In Stage 3, an additional VAT of €12 is due on the €80 of value added by the retailer. Since the final consumer pays a price of €380, he effectively pays the total VAT of €57 (= €15 + €30 + €12), which is 15 percent of €380. Obviously, a VAT is the equivalent of imposing a national sales tax. Exhibit 20.3 summarizes the VAT calculation. ∎

In many European countries (especially the EU) and also Latin American countries, VAT has become a major source of taxation on private citizens. Many economists prefer a VAT in place of a personal income tax because the latter is a disincentive to work, whereas a VAT discourages unnecessary consumption. A VAT fosters national saving, whereas an income tax is a disincentive to save because the returns from savings are taxed. Moreover, national tax authorities find that a VAT is easier to collect than an income tax because tax evasion is more difficult. Under a VAT, each stage in the production process has an incentive to obtain documentation from the previous stage that the VAT was paid in order to get the greatest tax credit possible. Of course, some argue that the cost of record keeping under a VAT system imposes an economic hardship on small businesses.

A problem with VAT, especially in the EU, is that not all countries impose the same VAT tax rate. For example, in Denmark the VAT rate is 25 percent, but in Germany it is only 16 percent. Consequently, consumers who reside in a high-VAT country can purchase goods less expensively by simply shopping across the border in a lower-VAT

EXHIBIT 20.2 Treaty Withholding Tax Rates

Country	N/S	Dividends	Interest	Royalties
Algeria		15	15	0 or 15
Argentina	N	10 or 15	12.5	3,5,10 or 15
Armenia	N	25% imposed by Canada		
Australia		5 or 15	10	10
Austria		5 or 15	10	0 or 10
Azerbaijan	N	25% imposed by Canada		
Bangladesh		15	15	10
Barbados	N	15	15	0 or 10
Belgium		15 → [5 or 15]	15 → [10]	0 or 10 → [0 or 10]
Bolivia	S	25% imposed by Canada		
Brazil		15 or 25	15	15 or 25
Bulgaria		10 or 15*	10	0 or 10*
Cameroon**		15	15	15
Chile*		10 or 15	15	15
China PR. (not Hong Kong)	N	10 or 15	10	10
Columbia	N	25% imposed by Canada		
Costa Rica	S	25% imposed by Canada		
Croatia		5 or 15	10	10
Cuba	S	25% imposed by Canada		
Cyprus		15	15	0 or 10
Czech Rep.		5 or 15	10	10
Denmark		5 or 15	10	0 or 10
Dominican Rep.		18	18	0 to 18
Ecuador		5 or 15	15	10 or 15*
Egypt	N	15	15	15
Estonia		5 or 15	10	10*
Finland		10 or 15	10	0 or 10
France		5 or 15	10	0 to 10
Gabon		15 → [15]	25 → [10]	25 → [10]
Germany		5 or 15	10	0 or 10
Greece	N	25% imposed by Canada		
Guyana		15	15**	10
Hungary		5 or 15	10	0 or 10
Iceland		5 or 15	10	0 or 10
India		15 or 25	15	10, 15 or 20
Indonesia		10 or 15	10	10
Ireland	N	0 or 15	15	0 or 15
Israel		15	15	0 or 15
Italy		15 → [5 or 15]	15 → [10]	0 or 10 → [0, 5 or 10]
Ivory Coast		15**	15	10
Jamaica		15**	15	10
Japan		5 or 15	10	10
Jordan		10 or 15	10	10
Kazakhstan		5 or 15	10	10
Kenya		15 or 25	15	15
Korea, Rep. Of		15	15	15
Kuwait		25 → [5 or 15]	25 → [10]	25 → [10]
Kyrgyzstan		15*	15*	0 or 10
Latvia		5 or 15	10	10*
Lebanon		25 → [5 or 15]	25 → [10]	25 → [5 or 10]
Lithuania		5 or 15	10	10
Luxembourg		5 or 15**	10	0 or 10
Malaysia		15**	15	15
Malta		15**	15	0 or 10
Mauritius	N	25% imposed by Canada		
Mexico	N	10 or 15	15	0 or 15
Moldova		5 or 15	10	10
Mongolia		5 or 15	10	5 or 10
Morocco		15	15	5 or 10
Netherlands		5 or 15	10	0 or 10
New Zealand		15	15	15
Nigeria		12.5 or 15	12.5	12.5
Norway		5 or 15	10	0 or 10
Oman	N	25% imposed by Canada		
Pakistan**		15	15	0 or 15
Papua New Guinea		15**	10	10
Peru*†		10 or 15	15	15
Philippines		15**	15	10**
Poland		15	15	0 or 10
Portugal		10 or 15	10	10
Romania	N	15	15	10 or 15
Russia		10 or 15	10	0 or 10
Saint Lucia	N	25% imposed by Canada		
Senegal**		25 → [15]	25 → [15]	25 → [15]
Singapore		15	15	15
Slovak Republic		5 or 15	10	0 or 10
Slovenia		5 or 15	10	10
South Africa		5 or 15	10	6 or 10
Spain		15	15	0 or 10
Sri Lanka		15	15	0 or 10
Sweden		5 or 15	10	0 or 10
Switzerland		5 or 15	10	0 or 10
Tanzania		20 or 25	15	20
Thailand		15**	15**	5 or 15
Trinidad and Tobago		5 or 15	10	0 or 10
Tunisia		15	15	0, 15 or 20
Turkey	N	25% imposed by Canada		
Ukraine		5 or 15	10	0 or 10
United Arab Emirates		25 → [5 or 15]	25 → [10]	25 → [0 or 10]
United Kingdom		10 or 15 → [5 or 15]	10	0 or 10
United States	N	5 or 15	10	0 or 10
Uzbekistan		5 or 15	10	5 or 10
Venezuela		25 → [10 or 15]*	25 → [10]	25 → [5 or 10]
Vietnam		5, 10 or 15	10	7.5 or 10
Zambia		15	15	15
Zimbabwe		10 or 15**	15	10

This table summarizes withholding tax rates (%) under treaties that are in force, or are under negotiation. (Special rules may reduce the rates shown.) Rates in square brackets after an arrow are set out in a protocol, replacement treaty, or new treaty that is signed, but not in force. To the left of the bracket are the rates that are being replaced, i.e., the rate or rates in the existing treaty or protocol or, if no treaty is in force, the 25-percent rate imposed by Canada. Except for Ireland, if two or more dividend rates are provided, the lower (lowest) rate applies if the recipient is a company that owns/controls a specified interest of the payor.

A nil royalty rate generally applies to: copyright royalties and payments for a literary, dramatic, musical or other artistic work (but not royalties for motion picture films or works on film or videotape or other means of reproduction for use in television); and/or royalties for computer software, a patent or for information concerning industrial, commercial or scientific experience (but not royalties for a rental or franchise agreement).

N, S: Negotiations or renegotiation of tax treaty or protocol underway (N) or scheduled (S).

* If the other state concludes a treaty with another country providing for a lower rate, the lower rate will apply, with limits in some cases.

** The rate(s) apply to payments arising in Canada. Other rules may apply to payments arising in the other state.

† Rates apply after 2003. Until then, 25% imposed by Canada.

Source: Price Waterhouse Coopers Tax Facts and Figures, (Canada) 2003.

country. Indeed, *The Wall Street Journal* reports that Danish customers frequently *demand* the lower German VAT rate on their purchases in Denmark![2] This problem should eventually be resolved, or at least mitigated, in the EU countries as it is expected that a harmonization in VAT rates among member states will occur. The International Finance in Practice box on pages 464–465 presents an interesting discussion of VAT.

20.3 National Tax Environments

The international tax environment confronting an MNC or an international investor is a function of the tax jurisdictions established by the individual countries in which the MNC does business or in which the investor owns financial assets. There are two fundamental types of tax jurisdiction: the *worldwide* and the *territorial*. Unless some mechanism were established to prevent it, double taxation would result if all nations were to follow both methods simultaneously.

Worldwide Taxation

The **worldwide** or **residential** method of declaring a national tax jurisdiction is to tax national residents of the country on their worldwide income, no matter in which country it is earned. The national tax authority, according to this method, is declaring its tax jurisdiction over people and businesses. An MNC with many foreign affiliates would be taxed in its home country on its income earned at home and abroad. Obviously, if the host countries of the foreign affiliates of an MNC also tax the income earned within their territorial borders, the possibility of double taxation exists, unless a mechanism is established to prevent it.

Territorial Taxation

The **territorial** or **source** method of declaring a tax jurisdiction is to tax all income earned within the country by any taxpayer, domestic or foreign. Hence, regardless of the nationality of a taxpayer, if the income is earned within the territorial boundary of a country, it is taxed by that country. The national tax authority, according to this method, is declaring its tax jurisdiction over transactions conducted within its borders. Consequently, local firms and affiliates of foreign MNCs are taxed on the income earned in the *source* country. Obviously, if the parent country of the foreign affiliate also levies a tax on worldwide income, the possibility of double taxation exists, unless a mechanism is established to prevent it.

Foreign Tax Credits

The typical approach to avoiding double taxation is for a nation not to tax foreign-source income of its national residents. An alternative method, and the one the United States follows, is to grant to the parent firm **foreign tax credits** against American taxes for taxes paid to foreign tax authorities on foreign-source income.[3] In general, foreign tax credits are categorized as direct or indirect. A *direct* foreign tax credit is computed for direct taxes paid on active foreign-source income of a foreign branch of an American MNC or on the indirect withholding taxes withheld from passive income distributed by the foreign subsidiary to the American parent. For foreign subsidiaries of American MNCs, an *indirect* foreign tax credit is computed for income taxes *deemed paid* by the subsidiary. The deemed-paid tax credit corresponds to the portion of the distribution of earnings available for distribution that were actually distributed. For example, if a wholly owned foreign subsidiary pays out dividends equal to 50 percent of the earnings available for distribution, the deemed-paid tax credit is 50 percent of the foreign income taxes paid by the foreign subsidiary.

---

[2]See Horwitz (1993).

[3]In general, as Kuntz and Peroni (1994) note, the United States claims only a "limited taxing jurisdiction over nonresident alien individuals and foreign corporations. Foreign persons pay American taxes only on income that has a sufficient nexus with the American."

In a given tax year, an *overall limitation* applies to foreign tax credits; that is, the maximum total tax credit is limited to the amount of tax that would be due on the foreign-source income if it had been earned in the United States. The maximum tax credit is figured on worldwide foreign-source income; losses in one country can be used to offset profits in another. Excess tax credits for a tax year can be carried back two years and forward five years. Examples of calculating foreign tax credits for American foreign branch and subsidiary operations are provided in the next section. Value-added taxes paid may not be included in determining the amount of the foreign tax credit, but they are, nevertheless, indirectly expensed as part of the cost of a good or service.

Individual American investors may take a tax credit for the withholding taxes deducted from the dividend and interest income they received from the foreign financial assets in their portfolios.

20.4 Organizational Structures for Reducing Tax Liabilities

Countries differ in how they tax foreign-source income of their domestic MNCs. Additionally, regardless of the twin objectives of tax neutrality and tax equity, different forms of structuring a multinational organization within a country can result in different tax liabilities for the firm. Thus, it behooves management to be familiar with the different organizational structures that can be useful at various stages in the life cycle of the MNC for reducing tax liabilities. The following discussion on MNC organizational structure relates to American tax regulations.

Branch and Subsidiary Income

An overseas affiliate of an American MNC can be organized as a branch or a subsidiary. A **foreign branch** is not an independently incorporated firm separate from the parent; it is an extension of the parent. Consequently, active or passive foreign-source income earned by the branch is consolidated with the domestic-source income of the parent for determining the American tax liability, regardless of whether or not the foreign-source income has been repatriated to the parent. A **foreign subsidiary** is an affiliate organization of the MNC that is independently incorporated in the foreign country, and one in which the American MNC owns at least 10 percent of the voting equity shares. A foreign subsidiary in which the American MNC owns more than 10 but less than 50 percent of the voting equity is a *minority foreign subsidiary* or an *uncontrolled foreign corporation*. Active and passive foreign-source income derived from a minority foreign subsidiary is taxed in the United States only when remitted to the American parent firm via a dividend. A foreign subsidiary in which the American MNC owns more than 50 percent of the voting equity is a *controlled foreign corporation*. Active foreign-source income from a controlled foreign corporation is taxed in the United States only as remitted to the American parent, but passive income is taxed in the United States as earned, even if it has not been repatriated to the parent. A more detailed discussion on controlled foreign corporations is reserved for later in this section.

> **EXAMPLE 20.2** **Foreign Tax Credit Calculations** Exhibit 20.4 presents examples of calculating the foreign tax credits for both a foreign branch and a wholly owned foreign subsidiary of a American MNC in the host countries of Finland and Belgium. The examples use the actual domestic marginal income tax rates presented in Exhibit 20.1 and the withholding tax rates presented in Exhibit 20.2. Both Finland and Belgium tax foreign branch income at the same rate as domestic taxable income. The examples show the total tax liability for $100 of foreign taxable income when any excess foreign tax credits can be used and when they cannot. As a rule, excess tax credits can be carried back two years and forward

(continued)

EXHIBIT 20.4

Examples of
Calculating American
Foreign Tax Credits for
Branch and Subsidiary
Operations

	Finland		Belgium	
	Branch	**Subsidiary**	**Branch**	**Subsidiary**
Foreign income tax rate	29%	29%	40.17%	40.17%
Withholding tax rate	N/A	5%	N/A	5%
Taxable income	100	100	100	100
Foreign income tax	−29	−29	−40	−40
Net available for remittance	71	71	60	60
Withholding tax[a]	0	−4	0	−3
Net cash to American parent	71	67	60	57
Gross-up: Income tax	29	29	40	40
Gross-up: Withholding tax	0	4	0	3
American taxable income	100	100	100	100
American income tax at 35%	35	35	35	35
Less foreign tax credit:				
Income tax	−29	−29	−40	−40
Withholding tax	0	−4	0	−3
Net American tax (excess credit)	6	2	(5)	(8)
Total tax: Excess credit used	35	35	35	35
Total tax: Excess credit not used	35	35	40	43

[a]100 percent of the funds available for remittance are assumed to be declared as dividends.

EXAMPLE 20.2 Continued

five years. The examples assume that *all* after-tax foreign-source income available
for remittance is immediately remitted to the American parent.

   Exhibit 20.4 indicates that when the American MNC can use the full excess tax
credits, the total tax liability is $35 per $100 of foreign taxable income, or 35 percent, the same amount due on $100 of taxable income earned in the United States.
This is true: (1) regardless in which country the foreign affiliate is located; (2)
whether the foreign affiliate is established as a branch or a subsidiary; and (3)
regardless of the size of the income tax and withholding tax rates. An MNC that
consistently generates excess foreign tax credits will never be able to use them in
the allowable time. Thus, the more typical situation is that excess foreign tax credits go unused.

   When excess tax credits go unused, the foreign tax liability for a branch is
greater than the corresponding American tax liability when the foreign income tax
rate is greater than the American rate of 35 percent. For a foreign subsidiary, the
foreign tax liability is greater than the corresponding American tax liability when:
[foreign income tax rate + withholding tax rate − (foreign income tax rate × withholding tax rate)] is greater than the American income tax rate of 35 percent. To
illustrate, a foreign subsidiary in Belgium for which excess foreign tax credits cannot be used has a total tax liability of: $0.4017 + 0.05 − (0.4017 \times 0.05) = 0.4316$,
or 43.16 percent versus 35 percent in the United States.

   This example suggests that the management of an MNC should be aware of the current tax rates levied by various host countries when deciding where to locate foreign
affiliate operations. Moreover, the exhibit indicates that there can be a difference in the
tax liability due on foreign-source income, depending upon the organizational structure
selected for the foreign affiliate. Thus, the management of an MNC must be aware of
any differences in the taxation of income by a particular host country when deciding
whether to organize a foreign operation as a branch or subsidiary. For example, new

foreign affiliates frequently experience operating losses in the early years of operation. If this situation is expected, it may be beneficial for an American MNC to originally establish overseas operations as a foreign branch of the parent because branch operating losses are consolidated with the parent firm's earnings for tax purposes. Alternatively, when foreign-source income is to be reinvested abroad to expand foreign operations, it may be preferable to organize as a minority foreign subsidiary if the foreign income tax rate is less than the American income tax rate because the tax liability in the United States can be deferred until the subsidiary remits a dividend to the American parent.

Payments to and from Foreign Affiliates

In Chapter 18, we discussed transfer pricing strategies that may help an American MNC to minimize its global tax liability. Since the discussion there was sufficient, we will only recap the major points in this chapter. Recall that a *transfer price* was the accounting value assigned to a good or service as it was transferred from one affiliate to another. We learned that the higher the transfer price, the larger will be the gross profits of the transferring division relative to the receiving division. Consequently, it is beneficial to follow a high markup policy on transferred goods and services from the parent to a foreign affiliate when the income tax rate in the host country is greater than the tax rate in the parent country because there will be less taxable income remaining in the high-tax host country. However, when the parent country has the higher tax rate, it is not instantly clear that a low markup policy should be pursued. Since American MNCs are taxed on their worldwide income, earnings repatriated to the United States from a low-tax host country would be grossed up to figure the additional tax due in the United States. However, if foreign-source retained earnings were needed for reinvestment in the host country, a low markup policy would result in a tax savings (assuming, of course, that undistributed profits are not highly taxed by the host country).

We also learned from Chapter 18 that governmental authorities are quite aware of transfer pricing schemes used by MNCs to reduce their worldwide tax liability, and most countries have regulations controlling transfer prices. These regulations typically state that the transfer price must reflect an *arm's-length price,* that is, a price the selling affiliate would charge an unrelated customer for the good or service. However, an arm's-length price is frequently difficult to establish and evaluate; thus, there exists a window of opportunity for some manoeuvrability by an MNC to use transfer pricing strategies to reduce its worldwide tax liability.

Tax Havens

A **tax-haven** country is one that has a low corporate income tax rate and low withholding tax rates on passive income. Some major tax-haven countries, which are suggested by the income tax rates presented in Exhibit 20.1, are the Bahamas, Bahrain, Bermuda, British Virgin Islands, Cayman Islands, Channel Islands (Guernsey and Jersey), Hong Kong, and the Isle of Man. Additionally, in Hong Kong and Panama, foreign-source income is exempt from taxation.

In Ireland and the Netherlands Antilles, special tax incentives or tax holidays are granted for businesses that will earn hard currency or develop export markets. In Puerto Rico, certain businesses are granted a reduced flat income tax rate of 7 percent applicable to industrial development income, which, in some areas, may be further reduced to 0 percent. In Liechtenstein and in many instances in Switzerland, holding companies are exempt from certain income taxes.

Tax havens were once useful as locations for an MNC to establish a wholly owned "paper" foreign subsidiary that, in turn, would own the operating foreign subsidiaries of the MNC. Hence, when the tax rates in the host countries of the operating affiliates were lower than the tax rate in the parent country, dividends could be routed through the tax-haven affiliate for use by the MNC, but the taxes due on them in the parent country could continue to be deferred until a dividend was declared by the tax-haven subsidiary. These days the benefit of a tax-haven subsidiary for American MNCs has been greatly reduced

The Rise and Rise of VAT

Winston Churchill famously remarked that "there is no such thing as a good tax." Faced with a two percentage-point rise in the standard rate of value-added tax (VAT)—from 18.6% to 20.6%—earlier this month, many of the French will doubtless agree with him. France is, after all, already one of Europe's most heavily taxed countries. But leaving aside the question of whether more taxes (rather than bigger spending cuts) is the best way to cut France's budget deficit, the decision to get most of the new revenue from VAT makes sense.

VAT is paid throughout the production process—from the factory all the way through to the shop, with each intermediary (except the consumer) being able to claim back the tax paid. Its cousin, the retail-sales tax, which is used at the state level in America, is levied only at the time of sale to the consumer. Both are consumption taxes, levied when people spend money rather than when they earn it—as income taxes are.

Consumption taxes are usually hailed as an efficient means of taxation. A consumption tax is less likely to distort economic behavior than income taxes. With high marginal rates of income tax, individuals may have less incentive to work hard. With a consumption tax, their extra income is not taxed until it is spent. Consumption taxes can also be levied on a wide base. In theory, people should be taxed on everything they buy; in practice, things are a little more complicated. Many countries have numerous exemptions from VAT; others tax some goods at lower rates. The wider the tax base, the lower the tax rate needed to raise a given amount of revenue.

The main argument against consumption taxes is a political one. Personal allowances and higher rates for higher incomes mean that income taxes are progressive: the marginal rate of taxation (the rate people pay on the last dollar they earn) is always higher than the average rate. Consumption taxes, in contrast, are generally levied at a constant rate. This means that poor people, who consume a higher share of their current income than rich people, suffer—so consumption taxes are "unfair". This is true, though many economists argue that the most efficient response of a government should be to give poorer people benefits in cash rather than to distort the tax system.

Over the past 30 years, industrial countries have gradually shifted towards general consumption taxes. According to a new report by the Organisation for Economic Co-operation and Development (OECD) on consumption taxes, rich countries raised an average of only 3.5% of GDP from general consumption taxes in 1965. Three decades later the amount has doubled, to 7.0% (see chart).

Although countries still raise substantial amounts of money from some specific consumption taxes (especially on harmful goods such as alcohol or tobacco), part of this increase is due to a shift from specific taxes (such as excise taxes and import duties) to general ones such as VAT. The average amount of money raised from specific consumption taxes in OECD countries has fallen from 6% of GDP in 1965 to around 4% today. Half the increases in total tax revenue since 1965 has come from general consumption taxes, which now make up nearly a fifth of tax revenue in industrial countries.

VAT has become especially popular. In the 1960s only nine countries in the world levied VAT; now more than 90 do. Of the OECD countries, only America and Australia do not use value-added taxes. In the developing world, too, VAT has become the consumption tax of choice. All Latin American countries now have VAT, as do the ex-communist economies of Eastern Europe.

by two factors: One is that the present corporate income tax rate in the United States is not especially high in comparison with most non–tax-haven countries, thus eliminating the need for deferral; the second factor is that the rules governing controlled foreign corporations (the topic to be discussed next) have effectively eliminated the ability to defer passive income in a tax-haven foreign subsidiary. As the International Finance in Practice box on pages 466–467 suggests, however, certain tax advantages may obtain for dot.com companies domiciled in tax-haven countries that engage in e-commerce.

Controlled Foreign Corporation

The *Tax Reform Act* of 1986 created a new type of foreign subsidiary called a controlled foreign corporation. The purpose of the reform was to prevent the tax deferral of certain income in tax haven countries and to raise taxes by reducing the benefit gained by American MNCs from foreign tax credits. A **controlled foreign corporation (CFC)** is a foreign subsidiary that has more than 50 percent of its voting equity owned by American shareholders. An American shareholder is any American citizen, resident, partnership, corporation, trust, or estate that owns (or indirectly controls) 10 percent or more of the voting equity of the CFC. Thus, six nonaffiliated American shareholders each own-

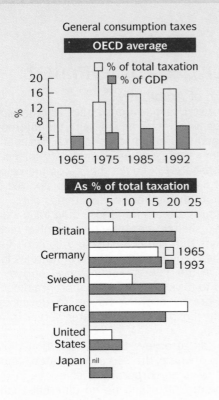

General consumption taxes

OECD average

☐ % of total taxation
■ % of GDP

As % of total taxation

☐ 1965
■ 1993

Britain
Germany
Sweden
France
United States
Japan — nil

In principle there is little economic difference between VAT and the American system of retail-sales taxes. Levied at the same rates, and covering the same number of goods and services (ideally all), both taxes should raise the same amount of money. However the different ways in which they are collected makes VAT more efficient. Under a retail-sales tax system, producers, wholesalers and retailers do not pay tax when they buy or sell from one another. VAT, in contrast, is paid throughout the production chain; registered intermediaries (but not the final consumer) reclaim VAT by presenting a set of invoices to the tax authorities.

This makes VAT much harder to avoid. While a good is being produced, sellers have an interest in proving they have paid the tax on their inputs in order to reduce the tax liability on their sales. With a retail-sales tax system, in contrast, the burden of collecting the tax lies entirely with the final seller of the good. If he fails to charge it, the tax on the whole value-added is lost. As the tax rises, the incentive to avoid it increases.

By limiting such incentives, governments can set VAT at higher rates than they could retail-sales taxes. It is no coincidence that sales taxes in America are, on average, below 8%, compared with a total OECD average for general consumption taxes of nearer 20%. Most economists reckon that 10% is the highest level at which a sales tax can be set without large-scale attempts at evasion. So, for countries which have high revenue requirements, VAT makes more sense.

Nonetheless, VAT rates are generally higher than they need be. Some services, such as financial services or insurance, are exempted by almost all countries, largely because it is difficult to work out exactly what the tax should be levied on. But usually the list of exemptions, or goods subject to lower rates, goes much further. In France many foods, medicine and books are taxed at the lower rate of 5.5%. Newspapers are taxed at only 2.1%.

Widening a VAT base is not popular—as Kenneth Clarke, Britain's chancellor found out when he tried to introduce VAT on fuel. On the other hand, any Frenchman who groans at the breakfast table at the thought of a 20.6% VAT rate should consider carefully the croissant on his plate and the newspaper in his hands.

Source: ©1995 The Economist Newspaper Group, Inc. Reprinted with permission.

ing exactly 10 percent of the voting equity would be required for a foreign corporation to be designated a CFC. Alternatively, a wholly owned subsidiary of an American MNC would be a CFC.

The undistributed income of a minority foreign subsidiary of an American MNC is tax deferred until it is remitted via a dividend. This rule is modified for Subpart F income of CFCs, which is subject to immediate taxation. **Subpart F income** includes income of a type that is relatively easy to transfer between countries and that is subject to a low foreign tax levy. Special rules apply for calculating foreign tax credits for CFCs. Much of the Subpart F income can be classified into four distinct categories or "baskets" of income: passive income, high withholding tax interest, financial services income, and shipping income. The allowable foreign tax credit limit is figured separately for each basket. Operating income of the CFC goes into the overall basket. The result is that high taxes paid in one country on income classified into one basket cannot be used to offset low taxes paid in another country on income classified into a different basket. This procedure results in more excess foreign tax credits, which are unlikely to be completely used.

INTERNATIONAL FINANCE
IN PRACTICE

As Dot-Coms Go Bust in America, Bermuda Hosts an Odd Little Boomlet

HAMILTON, Bermuda—Operating out of a hurricane-proof command center in a former U.S. military base, Paven Bratch is a tax examiner's nightmare.

Although his Internet company, music and video merchant Playcentric.com, has just 10 employees, didn't go live until September and has yet to turn a profit, it has the structure of a major multinational. Its computer servers are located here, its operating unit is in Barbados, and it has a distribution deal with a big record-store chain in Toronto. The 36-year-old Mr. Bratch figures this setup will save him so much on corporate income taxes and other expenses that he'll be able to undercut Amazon.com Inc.'s prices by more than 45% and still make a bundle.

"One thing that always amazes me is, why would anyone who's planning on generating a profit locate themselves in a full-tax jurisdiction?" he says.

'First Generation'
Plenty of dot-coms are asking themselves the same question these days. Undaunted by their industry's growing ranks of flameouts and hoping to emerge as one of the profitable few, dozens of them are popping up in tax havens around the world.

In Bermuda, they range from tiny publisher ISI Publications Ltd., which sells hard-to-find business books under the domain name Booksonbiz.com, to E*Trade Group Inc., the big online stockbroker, which is locating its international trading operations here. Further south, on the Caribbean island of Antigua, an American trader has set up Indextrade.com to allow small investors to bet on swings in market indexes, while in Cyprus, a former British jazz singer is doing a brisk business by listing vessels such as a Soviet-era submarine on Ships-for-sale.com.

"These merchants are the first generation who can really domicile anywhere," says Andrea Wilson, chief executive of Bermuda-based First Atlantic Commerce Ltd., which provides credit-card payment systems for e-businesses. "They can be a virtual corporation if they choose."

The trend started with Internet gambling companies, which fled to the Caribbean to avoid the long arm of U.S. law. But now, thanks to an explosion of new telecommunications links to places such as Bermuda and Britain's Channel Islands—and an ambitious push by promoters in such countries as Panama to set up facilities capable of hosting hundreds or thousands of Web sites each—more-legitimate Internet companies are starting to make the leap offshore.

A Wealth of Ambiguity
There are serious questions about whether some of the structures would pass muster with the Internal Revenue Service and its foreign counterparts. But many accountants figure there's enough ambiguity in the industrial world's offshore tax codes that e-commerce companies could, at least theoretically, rack up tax-free profits for years before the authorities sort things out.

The issues are often murkier than for a standard offshore tax shelter, because they involve technological innovations that the U.S. Treasury couldn't have anticipated when it began laying the ground rules for offshore taxation in the 1960s. For instance, nobody's entirely sure how to tax the earnings of a programmer who sells his software by allowing buyers to download it from a Web site hosted on a computer server in a zero-tax jurisdiction.

Some tax attorneys take the position that the sale takes place where the server is located, and that the business owes no corporate or sales tax in the buyer's home country. "It would be no different than you or I getting on a plane, flying to the Bahamas, and buying a T-shirt in the hotel," says Lazaro Mur, a Miami tax attorney.

New telecommunications options have brought Bermuda and much of the Caribbean even closer than a plane ride away. Cable & Wireless PLC's phone monopoly among former British colonies in the region is breaking up, and C&W's new competitors are starting to lace the seabed with modern fiber-optic lines, breaking down old technological barriers to working offshore.

At the same time, so-called server farms—warehouses built to accommodate row upon row of computer servers—are sprouting up to accommodate high-tech newcomers. At Fort Clayton, a former U.S. military base in Panama, local entrepreneurs plan to open a 50,000-square-foot "high-tech hotel" later this month they say will be capable of hosting as many as 1.2 million Web sites.

HavenCo, a self-proclaimed "data haven," announced plans last year to host Web sites from an antiaircraft platform abandoned by the British after World War II. The North Sea platform has a colorful history: In 1966, a retired British army major seized control of it and has operated it for years as the sovereign "Principality of Sealand."

Ryan Lackey, HavenCo's chief technical officer, says the company, which spent the summer upgrading electrical power and air conditioning on Sealand, has more than

30 servers up and running, connected to the mainland by satellite and wireless service, and hopes to expand to as many as 5,000.

He says the company has fielded "several thousand" sales inquiries. "The big thing people really want is e-mail servers, because in the past people have been getting their e-mail servers subpoenaed," he says. He adds that HavenCo would only comply with subpoenas issued by the Court of Sealand. "But there's no Court of Sealand, so it's very unlikely."

Tax savings are the big selling point for many of the installations. "Offshore + Ecommerce = Tax Free Heaven," screams a banner ad for Bahamas.net, which offers server facilities in the Bahamas for as low as $2,200 a month.

Bermuda, which has a rich history of helping foreigners shave taxes, also is doing its best to encourage the migration offshore. Its two biggest banks, Bank of Bermuda Ltd. and Bank of N.T. Butterfield & Son Ltd., have launched major e-commerce initiatives, establishing systems to allow online merchants to bill customers in several major currencies. A common refrain among business leaders on this tiny fishhook-shaped island is that Bill Gates would be a much-richer man today if he had originally established Microsoft here.

The pitch helped reel in Robert Edwards, an editorial cartoonist who lives in Canterbury, England. Not long ago he went looking for help in setting up a Web site to sell works by him and about 30 other artists from around the world. Tipped off to Bermuda by a visiting delegation of businesspeople, he registered his company online through Appleby, Spurling & Kempe, a local law firm here, and was quickly directed to Web designers, a hosting site and a credit-card intermediary, First Atlantic.

Late last year, at a total cost of less than $200,000, his Drawnandquartered.com went live, offering 4,000 artworks, which can be downloaded online with a credit card, for $200 and up. His company doesn't pay any income or sales taxes, and he only has to pay personal-income tax on the salary he draws. "I'm a perfect example of how it can be done," he says.

Playcentric's Mr. Bratch, a former Procter & Gamble Co. manager, says he relied on advice from an international tax attorney in structuring the online retailer, which will market its compact disks, videos and DVDs partly through packaged-goods makers who want to reward loyal customers. Mr. Bratch, a Canadian citizen, put his operating unit in Barbados, which, unlike Bermuda, has a tax treaty with Canada, in order to take advantage of the Caribbean nation's corporate income-tax rate of just 2%.

He says he located his computer operations in Bermuda because of its extensive banking and telecommunications infrastructure. Its attractions include a state-of-the-art server facility built in an old U.S. naval base by 360networks Inc.'s TeleBermuda International unit, which laid an undersea fiber-optic cable to the U.S. in 1997.

Tax considerations also helped lure Todd Middagh, chief executive of Originals Online Ltd., to Bermuda. His brainchild: a site that will allow importers, exporters and shipping companies to swap legally binding trade documents online, instead of wasting days with couriers. "It's a digital product, global in nature, 24-hours-a-day worldwide," says Mr. Middagh, who has already attracted the interest of several major grain companies, including Archer Daniels Midland Co.

"We're going to be in almost every jurisdiction over time," he says. Meanwhile, Mr. Middagh, a native of Canada, will be presiding over the company from his house here, which overlooks the Atlantic Ocean.

Scott Rubman, a Long Island, N.M., real-estate attorney whose family has long been in the fur trade, is putting together Furs.com, a Bermuda-based site that plans to match mink farmers in, say, Norway, with fur-coat manufacturers in North America and China. As an American, Mr. Rubman may face a bigger hurdle in shielding any offshore profits from taxation. Unlike many other countries, the U.S. taxes its citizens on their income world-wide.

"If you move offshore strictly to evade taxes, that's something the U.S. will always look at," says Mr. Rubman, who is getting plenty of advice from U.S. tax experts. "When you have a legitimate business purpose to transact business offshore, I'd think the U.S. would be supportive of that."

And if the U.S. isn't supportive? Cryptographer Vince Cate thinks he has that covered. In 1998, the onetime Carnegie-Mellon University Ph.D. candidate walked into the U.S. Embassy in Barbados and renounced his American citizenship, declaring that he was henceforth a citizen of Mozambique, thanks to a document he purchased for $5,000 over the Internet.

Then, he went back to the Caribbean island of Anguilla, where he had developed a reputation as a computer-encryption visionary. Among his many ventures, he has taken over the operations of an online marketer of driver's-license information that had run afoul of a new privacy law in Texas. Mr. Cate plans to build the business without paying a cent of taxes.

"Because I'm not a U.S. citizen, I'm not in the United States, and Anguilla has no taxes, I don't believe I have any problem," he says.

Source: Michael Allen, *The Wall Street Journal*, January 8, 2001, pp. A1, A8. Reprinted by permission of *The Wall Street Journal*, ©2001 Dow Jones & Company, Inc. All Rights Reserved Worldwide.

SUMMARY

This chapter provided a brief introduction to the international tax environment that confronts MNCs and investors in international financial assets.

1. The twin objectives of taxation are tax neutrality and tax equity. Tax neutrality has its foundations in the principles of economic efficiency and equity. Tax equity is the principle that all similarly situated taxpayers should participate in the cost of operating the government according to the same rules.

2. The three basic types of taxation are income tax, withholding tax, and value-added tax. Corporate income tax rates from many countries were listed and compared. Similarly, the withholding tax rates for certain countries for various types of foreign-source income for which Canada has bilateral tax treaties were listed and compared.

3. Nations often tax the worldwide income of resident taxpayers and also the income of foreign taxpayers doing business within their territorial boundaries. If countries simultaneously apply both methods, double taxation will result unless a mechanism is established to prevent it. The concept of the foreign tax credit as a means to eliminate double taxation was developed. Examples were presented from the perspective of an American MNC showing the calculation of the foreign tax credits for branch and subsidiary operations in three countries with different corporate income tax rates.

4. Different forms of organizational structure can affect the tax liability of an MNC. Specifically, there are differences in taxation between branch and subsidiary operations. Transfer pricing strategies, subsidiary operations in tax-haven countries, foreign-controlled corporations, and foreign sales corporations were also defined and discussed.

KEY WORDS

active income, *456*
capital-export
    neutrality, *455*
controlled foreign
    corporation (CFC), *464*
direct tax, *456*
foreign branch, *461*
foreign subsidiary, *461*
foreign tax credits, *460*

income tax, *456*
indirect tax, *456*
national treatment, *454*
passive income, *456*
residential taxation, *460*
source taxation, *460*
Subpart F income, *465*
tax haven, *463*
tax neutrality, *453*

tax treaty, *456*
territorial taxation, *460*
value-added tax
    (VAT), *458*
withholding tax, *456*
worldwide taxation, *460*

QUESTIONS

1. Discuss the twin objectives of taxation. Be sure to define the key words.

2. Compare and contrast the three basic types of taxation that governments levy within their tax jurisdiction.

3. Show how double taxation on a taxpayer may result if all countries were to tax the worldwide income of their residents and the income earned within their territorial boundaries.

4. What methods do taxing authorities use to eliminate or mitigate the evil of double taxation?

5. There is a difference in the tax liability levied on foreign-source income depending upon whether a foreign branch or subsidiary form of organizational structure is selected for a foreign affiliate. Please elaborate on this statement.

PROBLEMS

1. There are three production stages required before a pair of skis produced by Fjord Fabrication can be sold at retail for NOK2,300. Fill in the following table to show the value added at each stage in the production process and the incremental and total VAT. The Norwegian VAT rate is 24 percent.

Production Stage	Selling Price	Value Added	Incremental VAT
1	NOK 450		
2	NOK1,900		
3	NOK2,300		
			Total VAT

INTERNET EXERCISE

The website www.taxsites.com is a comprehensive site that provides links to many other websites categorized into the following topics: country-specific sites, IRS Resources, European Union and VAT, Students and Scholars, Tax Associations, Other Resources, Tax Treaties, and Governments. For example, go to the Worldwide-Tax section under Other Resources and learn about the history of taxation.

MINI CASE

Sigma Corp.'s Location Decision

Sigma Corporation of Boston is contemplating establishing an affiliate operation in the Mediterranean. Two countries under consideration are Spain and Cyprus. Sigma intends to repatriate all after-tax foreign-source income to the United States. At this point, Sigma is not certain whether it would be best to establish the affiliate operation as a branch operation or a wholly owned subsidiary of the parent firm.

In Cyprus, the marginal corporate tax rate is 25 percent. Foreign branch profits are taxed at the same rate. In Spain, corporate income is taxed at 35 percent, the same rate as in the United States. Additionally, foreign branch income in Spain is also taxed at 35 percent. The American withholding tax treaty rates on dividend income are 5 percent with Cyprus and 10 percent with Spain.

The financial manager of Sigma has asked you to help him determine where to locate the new affiliate and which organizational structure to establish. The location decision will be largely based on whether the total tax liability would be smallest for a foreign branch or a wholly owned subsidiary in Cyprus or Spain.

REFERENCES & SUGGESTED READINGS

Bischel, Jon E., and Robert Feinscheiber. *Fundamentals of International Taxation,* 2nd ed. New York: Practicing Law Institute, 1985.

Gamme, Malcolm, and Bill Robinson. *Beyond 1992: A European Tax System, Proceedings of the Fourth Institute for Fiscal Studies Residential Conference.* London: Chameleon Press, July 1989.

Horst, Thomas. "American Taxation of Multinational Firms." *American Economic Review* (July 1977), pp. 376–89.

Horwitz, Tony. "Continental Shift: Europe's Borders Fade and People and Goods Can Move Freely." *The Wall Street Journal, (*May 18, 1993).

Isenberg, Joseph. *International Taxation: American Taxation of Foreign Taxpayers and Foreign Income,* Vols. I and II. Boston: Little, Brown, 1990.

Jones, Sally M., and Ray M. Sommerfeld. *Federal Taxes and Management Decisions.* Burr Ridge, Ill.: Irwin, 1995–96.

Kaplan, Richard L. *Federal Taxation of International Transactions: Principles, Planning and Policy.* St. Paul, Minn.: West, 1988.

Kopits, George, ed. *Tax Harmonization in the European Community: Policy Issues and Analysis.* International Monetary Fund Occasional Paper, No. 94, Washington, D.C., June 1992.

Kuntz, Joel D., and Robert J. Peroni. *American International Taxation,* Vols. I and II. Boston: Warren, Gorham and Lamont, 1994.

Metcalf, Gilbert E. "Value-Added Taxation: A Tax Whose Time Has Come?" *Journal of Economic Perspectives* 9 (1995), pp. 121–40.

Pratt, James W., and William N. Kulsrud. *Corporate, Partnership, Estate, and Gift Taxation.* Burr Ridge, Ill.: Irwin Taxation Series, 1996.

PriceWaterhouseCoopers. *Corporate Taxes: Worldwide Summaries.* New York: John Wiley and Sons, Inc., 2002.

American Internal Revenue Code, Part III. Income From Sources Without the United States. Chicago: Commerce Clearing House, 1993.

Corporate Governance around the World

THE RECENT SPATE of corporate scandals and failures, including Enron, World-Com, and Global Crossing in the United States, along with Nortel Networks and Hollinger in Canada, has raised serious questions about the way public corporations are governed around the world. Other well-publicized examples of serious corporate misconduct include Credit Lyonnais of France, Parmalat of Italy, the Daewoo Group of South Korea, and HIH, a major insurance group, of Australia. When "self-interested" managers take control of the company, they sometimes engage in actions that are profoundly detrimental to the interests of shareholders and other stakeholders. For example, such managers may give themselves excessive salaries and indulgent perquisites, squander resources for corporate empire building, divert the company's cash and assets for private benefits, engage in cronyism, and steal business opportunities from the company. A recent report in the *Harvard Business Review* (January 2003) describes how American executives "treat their companies like ATMs, awarding themselves millions of dollars in corporate perks." In many less developed and transitional countries, corporate governance mechanisms are either very weak or virtually nonexistent. In Russia, for example, a weak corporate governance system allows managers to divert assets from newly privatized companies on a large scale.

When managerial self-dealings are excessive and left unchecked, they can have serious negative effects on corporate values and the proper functions of capital markets. In fact, there is a growing consensus around the world that it is vitally important to strengthen **corporate governance** to protect the rights of shareholders, curb managerial excesses, and restore confidence in capital markets. *Corporate governance* can be defined as *the economic, legal, and institutional framework in which corporate control and cash flow rights are distributed among shareholders, managers, and other stakeholders of the company*. Other stakeholders may include workers, creditors, banks, institutional investors, and even the government. As we will see later, corporate governance structure varies a great deal across countries, reflecting divergent cultural, economic, political, and legal environments.

21.1 Governance of the Public Corporation: Key Issues

The *public corporation*, which is jointly owned by a multitude of shareholders protected with limited liability, is a major organizational innovation of vast economic consequences. The majority of global corporations that drive economic growth and innovations worldwide, including Microsoft, General Electric (GE), IBM, Toyota, Sony, British Petroleum (BP), Nokia, and DaimlerChrysler, are chartered as public corporations, rather than as private companies. The genius of public corporations stems from their capacity to allow efficient sharing or spreading of risk among many investors, who can buy and sell their ownership shares on liquid stock exchanges and let professional managers run the company on behalf of shareholders. This efficient risk-sharing mechanism enables public corporations to raise large amounts of capital at relatively low costs and undertake many investment projects that individual entre-preneurs or private investors might eschew because of the costs and/or risks. Public corporations have played a pivotal role in spreading economic growth and capitalism worldwide for the last few centuries.

However, the public corporation has a key weakness—namely, the conflicts of inter-est between managers and shareholders. The separation of the company's ownership and control, which is especially prevalent in such countries as the United States and the United Kingdom, where corporate ownership is highly diffused, gives rise to possible conflicts between shareholders and managers. In principle, shareholders elect the board of directors of the company, which, in turn, hires managers to run the company for the interests of shareholders. In the United States, managers are legally bound by the "duty of loyalty" to shareholders. Managers are, thus, supposed to be agents working for their principals, that is, shareholders, who are the real owners of the company. In a public company with diffused ownership, the board of directors is entrusted with the vital tasks of monitoring the management and safeguarding the interests of shareholders.

In reality, however, management-friendly insiders often dominate the board of directors, with relatively few outside directors who can independently monitor the management. In the case of Enron and similarly dysfunctional companies, the boards of directors grossly failed to safeguard shareholder interests. Furthermore, with dif-fused ownership, few shareholders have strong enough incentive to incur the costs of monitoring management themselves when the benefits from such monitoring accrue to all shareholders alike. The benefits are shared, but not the costs. When company own-ership is highly diffused, this "free-rider" problem discourages shareholder activism. As a result, the interests of managers and shareholders are often allowed to diverge. With an ineffective and unmotivated board of directors, shareholders are basically left without effective recourse to control managerial self-dealings. Recognition of this key weakness of the public corporation can be traced at least as far back as to Adam Smith's *Wealth of Nations* (1776), which stated:

> The directors of such joint-stocks companies, however, being the managers rather of other people's money than of their own, it cannot well be expected that they should watch over it with the same anxious vigilance with which the partners of a private copartnery fre-quently watch over their own. . . . Negligence and profusion, therefore, must always pre-vail, more or less, in the management of the affairs of such a company.

Two hundred years later, Jensen and Meckling (1976) provided a formal analysis of the "agency problem" of the public corporation in their celebrated paper "Theory of the Firm: Managerial Behavior, Agency Costs, and Ownership Structure." The Jensen-Meck-ling agency theory drew attention to this vitally important corporate finance problem.

It is suggested, however, that outside the United States and the United Kingdom, diffused ownership of the company is more the exception than the rule. In Italy, for instance, the three largest shareholders control, on average, about 60 percent of the shares of a public company. The average comparable ownership by the three largest shareholders is 54 percent in Hong Kong, 64 percent in Mexico, 48 percent in Ger-many, 40 percent in India, and 51 percent in Israel.[1] These large shareholders (often including founding families of the company) effectively control managers and may run the company for their own interests, expropriating outside shareholders in one way or another. In many countries with concentrated corporate ownership, conflicts of interest are greater between large controlling shareholders and small outside share-holders than between managers and shareholders.

---

[1] Source: La Porta, R., F. Lopez-de-Silanes, A. Shleifer, and R. Vishny, "Law and Finance," *Journal of Political Economy* 106 (1998), pp. 1113–55.

In a series of influential studies, La Porta, Lopez-de-Silanes, Shleifer, and Vishny (LLSV, hereafter) document sharp differences among countries with regard to (1) corporate ownership structure, (2) depth and breadth of capital markets, (3) access of firms to external financing, and (4) dividend policies. LLSV argue that these differences among countries can be explained largely by how well investors are protected by law from expropriation by the managers and controlling shareholders of firms. LLSV also argue that the degree of legal protection of investors significantly depends on the "legal origin" of countries. Specifically, English common law countries, such as Canada, the United States, and the United Kingdom, provide the strongest protection for investors, whereas French civil law countries, such as Belgium, Italy, and Mexico, provide the weakest. We will revisit the issue of law and corporate governance later in the chapter.

Shareholders in different countries may, indeed, face divergent corporate governance systems. However, the central problem in corporate governance remains the same everywhere: *how to best protect outside investors from expropriation by the controlling insiders so that the former can receive fair returns on their investments.* How to deal with this problem has enormous practical implications for shareholder welfare, corporate allocation of resources, corporate financing and valuation, development of capital markets, and economic growth. In the rest of this chapter, we will discuss the following issues in detail:[2]

- Agency problem
- Remedies for the agency problem
- Law and corporate governance
- Consequences of law
- Corporate governance reform

21.2 The Agency Problem

Suppose that the manager (or entrepreneur) and the investors sign a contract that specifies how the manager will use the funds and also how the investment returns will be divided between the manager and the investors. If the two sides can write a **complete contract** that specifies exactly what the manager will do under each of all possible future contingencies, there will be no room for any conflicts of interest or managerial discretion. Thus, under a complete contract, there will be no **agency problem**. However, it is practically impossible to foresee all future contingencies and write a complete contract. This means that the manager and the investors will have to allocate the rights (control) to make decisions under those contingencies that are not specifically covered by the contract. Because the outside investors may be neither qualified nor interested in making business decisions, the manager often ends up acquiring most of this **residual control right**. The investors supply funds to the company but are not involved in the company's daily decision making. As a result, many public companies come to have "strong managers and weak shareholders."

Having captured residual control rights, the manager can exercise substantial discretion over the disposition and allocation of investors' capital. Under this situation, the investors are no longer assured of receiving fair returns on their funds. In the contractual view of the firm described above, the agency problem arises from the difficulty that outside investors face in assuring that they actually receive fair returns on their capital.[3]

---

[2] Our discussion here draws on the contributions of Jensen and Meckling (1976), Jensen (1989), La Porta, Lopez-de-Silanes, Shleifer, and Vishny (1997–2002), and Denis and McConnell (2002).

[3] The contractual view of the firm was developed by Coarse (1937) and Jensen and Meckling (1976).

With the control rights, the manager may allow himself or herself to consume exorbitant perquisites. For example, Steve Jobs, the CEO of Apple Computer, reportedly has a $90 million company jet at his disposal.[4] Sometimes, the manager simply steals investors' funds. Alternatively, the manager may use a more sophisticated scheme, setting up an independent company that he owns and diverting to it the main company's cash and assets through *transfer pricing*. For example, the manager can sell the main company's output to the company he owns at below market prices or buy the output of the company he owns at above market prices. Some Russian oil companies are known to sell oil to manager-owned trading companies at below market prices and not always bother to collect the bills.[5]

Self-interested managers may also waste funds by undertaking unprofitable projects that benefit themselves but not investors. For example, managers may misallocate funds to take over other companies and overpay for the targets if it serves their private interests. Needless to say, this type of investment will destroy shareholder value. What is more, the same managers may adopt anti-takeover measures for their own company in order to ensure their personal job security and perpetuate private benefits. In the same vein, managers may resist any attempts to be replaced even if shareholders' interests will be better served by their dismissal. These **managerial entrenchment** efforts are clear signs of the agency problem.

As pointed out by Jensen (1989), the agency problem tends to be more serious in companies with "free cash flows." **Free cash flows** represent a firm's internally generated funds in excess of the amount needed to undertake all profitable investment projects, that is, those with positive net present values (NPVs). Free cash flows tend to be high in mature industries with low future growth prospects, such as the steel, chemical, tobacco, paper, and textile industries. It is the *fiduciary duty* of managers to return free cash flows to shareholders as dividends. However, managers in these cash-rich and mature industries will be most tempted to waste cash flows to undertake unprofitable projects, destroying shareholders' wealth but possibly benefiting themselves.

There are a few important incentives for managers to retain cash flows. First, cash reserves provide corporate managers with a measure of independence from the capital markets, insulating them from external scrutiny and discipline. This will make life easier for managers. Second, growing the size of the company via retention of cash tends to have the effect of raising managerial compensation. As is well known, executive compensation depends as much on the size of the company as on its profitability, if not more. Third, senior executives can boost their social and political power and prestige by increasing the size of their company. Executives presiding over large companies are likely to enjoy greater social prominence and visibility than those running small companies. Also, the company's size itself can be a way of satisfying the executive ego.

In the face of strong managerial incentives for retaining cash, few effective mechanisms exist that can compel the managers to disgorge cash flows to shareholders. Jensen cites a revealing example of this widespread problem (1989, p. 66):

> A vivid example is the senior management of Ford Motor Company, which sits on nearly $15 billion in cash and marketable securities in an industry with excess capacity. Ford's management has been deliberating about acquiring financial service companies, aerospace companies, or making some other multibillion-dollar diversification move—rather than deliberating about effectively distributing Ford's excess cash to its owners so they can decide how to reinvest it.

He also points out that in the 1980s, many Japanese public companies retained enormous amounts of free cash flow, far exceeding what they needed to finance profitable internal projects. For example, Toyota Motor Company, with a cash hoard of more than

---

[4] Source: *Financial Times* (November 27, 2002), p. 15.

[5] Source: A. Shleifer and R. Vishny, "A Survey of Corporate Governance," *Journal of Finance* (1997).

$10 billion, was known as the "Toyota Bank." Lacking effective internal control and external monitoring mechanisms, these companies went on an overinvestment binge in the 1980s, engaging in unprofitable acquisitions and diversification moves. This wasteful corporate spending is, at least in part, responsible for the economic slump that Japan has experienced since the early 1990s.

The preceding examples show that the heart of the agency problem is the conflicts of interest between managers and the outside investors over the disposition of free cash flows. However, in high-growth industries, such as biotechnology, financial services, and pharmaceuticals, where companies' internally generated funds fall short of profitable investment opportunities, managers are less likely to waste funds in unprofitable projects. After all, managers in these industries need to have a "good reputation," as they must repeatedly come back to capital markets for funding. Once the managers of a company are known for wasting funds for private benefits, external funding for the company may dry up quickly. The managers in these industries, thus, have an incentive to serve the interests of outside investors and build a reputation so that they can raise the funds needed for undertaking their "good" investment projects.

21.3 Remedies for the Agency Problem

Obviously, it is a matter of vital importance for shareholders to control the agency problem; otherwise, they may not be able to get their money back. It is also important for society as a whole to solve the agency problem, since the agency problem leads to waste of scarce resources, hampers capital market functions, and retards economic growth. Several governance mechanisms exist to alleviate or remedy the agency problem:

1. Board of directors
2. Incentive contracts
3. Concentrated ownership
4. Debt
5. Overseas share listings
6. Market for corporate control

In the following sections, we discuss the corporate governance role of each of these mechanisms.

Board of Directors

In most countries in the so-called Anglo–corporate tradition, including Canada and the United States as well as the United Kingdom, shareholders have the right to elect the board of directors, which is legally charged with representing the interests of shareholders. If the board of directors remains independent of management, it can serve as an effective mechanism for curbing the agency problem. For example, studies show that the appointment of outside directors is associated with a higher turnover rate of CEOs following poor firm performances, thus curbing managerial entrenchment. In the same vein, in a study of corporate governance in the United Kingdom, Dahya, McConnell, and Travlos (2002) report that the board of directors is more likely to appoint an outside CEO after an increase in outsiders' representation on the board. But due to the diffused ownership structure of the public company, management often gets to choose board members who are likely to be friendly to management. As can be seen from the International Finance in Practice box "When Boards Are All in the Family," the insider-dominated board becomes a poor governance mechanism.

The structure and legal charge of corporate boards vary greatly across countries. In Germany, for instance, the corporate board is not legally charged with representing the interests of shareholders. Rather, it is charged with looking after the interests of stakeholders (e.g., workers, creditors, and so on) in general, not just shareholders. In Germany, there are two-tier boards consisting of supervisory and management boards.

When Boards Are All in the Family

There is much talk these days about the need to increase the independence of directors on company boards. That has been obvious for a long time. Indeed, it is fairly easy to spot those boards for which chief executives have handpicked friends or business associates who are not truly independent.

This characteristic is a reliable indicator of whether a chief executive acts as a baronial owner of the company, or as one chosen by—and responsible to—the stakeholders. In fact, one can argue that making boards more independent is the single most important thing we can do in the current reform climate to restore public confidence.

By now it is well documented that boards dominated by their chief executives are prone to trouble. W.R. Grace is a good example. Peter Grace, the company's chief executive, was too powerful. He controlled his board as if the enterprise were his personal fief.

Even though the business was foundering in the late 1990s, the board allowed Mr Grace to negotiate a retirement package that included generous perks—including use of a corporate jet and a company-owned apartment. The directors also sold a subsidiary to Mr Grace's son and bestowed other benefits that they neglected to disclose to shareholders. This non-disclosure was against the law and resulted in an SEC-type enforcement action.

Another example is Apple, whose board I was once asked, briefly, to consider joining. Apart from Steve Jobs, the CEO, the board currently has only four members while Mr Jobs searches for a replacement for his friend Larry Ellison of Oracle, who resigned from Apple's board in September.

That is all to the good, as Mr Ellison attended fewer than half of Apple's board meetings anyway. Bill Campbell, another director, is nominally independent but may not be truly so. Mr Campbell, who chairs the company's audit committee, qualifies as an independent director, because he is not currently connected with Apple. But he formerly worked at Apple and sold his software company, Claris, to Apple.

Another member of Apple's audit committee, Jerome York, is the chief executive of MicroWarehouse, whose Mac Warehouse catalogue was responsible for nearly $150m of Apple's $5.4bn sales in 2001. As a former chief financial officer for International Business Machines and Chrysler Mr York is well qualified but his presence on the all-important audit committee had to be treated as an exceptional circumstance by the Nasdaq market.

Such choices, to my mind, can yield bad judgment. In January 2000, for example, Apple's board awarded Mr Jobs 20m shares, worth $550m if the share price increased 5 per cent over 10 years. They also authorised the company to buy a $90m Gulfstream jet for him. The share price sank, putting Mr Jobs's options under water. So the board granted him 7.5m more shares. At the time of the grant, Apple shares were underperforming other stocks in their industry sub-class by 28 per cent.

There is plenty of evidence that public scrutiny and a spotlight can help improve corporate governance. The California Public Employees' Retirement System began pressing underperforming companies to change the composition of their boards in 1993. Calpers drew up a list of corporate governance standards: make independent directors a majority on boards; let these directors meet the chief executive separately three times a year; make boards perform an annual assessment of their own performance, and so on.

A study by Wilshire Associates looked at the performance of 62 companies named by Calpers as poor performers. These companies' stocks underperformed the Standard & Poor's 500 index by an average of 89 per cent in the five years before they were singled out. After the spotlight was shone on them, they outperformed the index by an average of 23 per cent over five years.

This does not, of course, mean all companies will fail without a model board of directors. At Warren Buffett's Berkshire Hathaway, the seven directors include Mr Buffet's wife, his son, his business partner Charlie Munger, a partner at his company's law firm and a co-investor with Berkshire Hathaway in other companies.

Mr Buffett makes a persuasive argument that the best directors may well be those who have the greatest personal economic stake in the company. But the correlation of seduced boards with underperforming or ethically flawed enterprises suggests that independent overseers are much less likely to give into temptation or corruption.

Source: Arthur Levitt, *Financial Times*, November 27, 2002. p. 15. Reprinted with permission.

Based on the German *codetermination* system, the law requires that workers be represented on the supervisory board. Likewise, some American companies have labour union representatives on their boards, although it is not legally mandated. In the United Kingdom, the majority of public companies voluntarily abide by the *Code of Best Practice* on corporate governance recommended by the *Cadbury Committee*. The code recommends that there should be at least three outside directors and that the board chairman and the CEO should be different individuals. Apart from outside directors, separation of the chairman and CEO positions can further enhance the independence of the board of directors. In Japan, most corporate boards are insider dominated and are primarily concerned with the welfare of the *keiretsu* to which the company belongs.

Incentive Contracts

As previously discussed, managers capture residual control rights and thus have enormous discretion over how to run the company. But they own relatively little of the equity of the company they manage. To the extent that managers do not own equity shares, they do not have cash flow rights. Although managers run the company at their own discretion, they may not significantly benefit from the profit generated from their efforts and expertise. Jensen and Murphy (1990) show that the pay of American executives changes only by about $3 per every $1,000 change of shareholder wealth; executive pay is nearly insensitive to changes in shareholder wealth. This situation implies that managers may not be very interested in the maximization of shareholder wealth. This "wedge" between managerial control rights and cash flow rights may exacerbate the agency problem. *When professional managers have small equity positions of their own in a company with diffused ownership, they have both power and a motive to engage in self-dealings.*

Aware of this situation, many companies provide managers with **incentive contracts**, such as shares and share options, in order to reduce this wedge and better align the interests of managers with those of investors. With the grant of shares or share options, managers can be given an incentive to run the company in such a way that enhances shareholder wealth as well as their own. Against this backdrop, incentive contracts for senior executives have become common among public companies in both Canada and the United States. As we have seen lately, however, senior executives can abuse incentive contracts by artificially manipulating accounting numbers, sometimes with the connivance of auditors (for example, Arthur Andersen's involvement's with the Enron debacle), or by altering investment policies so that they can reap enormous personal benefits. It is, thus, important for the board of directors to set up an independent compensation committee that can carefully design incentive contracts for executives and diligently monitor their actions.

Concentrated Ownership

An effective way to alleviate the agency problem is to concentrate shareholdings. If one or a few large investors own significant portions of the company, they will have a strong incentive to monitor management. For example, if an investor owns 51 percent of the company, he or she can definitely control the management (he can easily hire or fire managers) and will make sure that shareholders' rights are respected in the conduct of the company's affairs. With **concentrated ownership** and high stakes, the free-rider problem afflicting small, atomistic shareholders dissipates.

In the United States and the United Kingdom, concentrated ownership of a public company is relatively rare. For publicly traded firms on the major American and British exchanges, the largest single owner of shares of any one company seldom holds more than 2 to 3 percent of the shares. While corporate ownership is characterized by widely dispersed share holdings, financial institutions have emerged as the major share holders.

Canada's corporate structure is characterized by a substantial degree of family ownership, such as the Westons, Thomsons, Irvings, Aspers, or McCains. Firms with strong family ownership either do not publicly trade shares at all or they retain family control through substantial family ownership of traded shares. On the other hand, many large Canadian firms are subsidiaries of multinationals and, as such, are not subject to demanding disclosure requirements.

Elsewhere in the world, however, concentrated ownership is the norm. In Germany, for example, commercial banks, insurance companies, other companies, and families often own significant blocks of company shares. Similarly, extensive cross-holdings of equities among *keiretsu* member companies and main banks are commonplace in Japan. Also in France, cross-holdings and "core" investors are common. In Asia and

Latin America, many companies are controlled by founders or their family members. In China, the government is often the controlling shareholder for public companies. Previous studies indicate that concentrated ownership has a positive effect on a company's performance and value. For example, Kang and Shivdasani (1995) report such positive effects for Japan, and Gorton and Schmid (2000) for Germany. This suggests that large shareholders indeed play a significant governance role.

Of particular interest here is the effect of managerial equity holdings. Previous studies suggest that there can be a nonlinear relationship between managerial ownership share and firm value and performance. Specifically, as the managerial ownership share increases, firm value may initially increase, since the interests of managers and outside investors become better aligned (thus reducing agency costs). But if the managerial ownership share exceeds a certain point, firm value may actually start to decline as managers become more entrenched. With larger shareholdings, for example, managers may be able to more effectively resist takeover bids and extract larger private benefits at the expense of outside investors. If the managerial ownership share continues to rise, however, the alignment effect may become dominant again. When managers are large shareholders, they do not want to rob themselves. To summarize, there can be an "interim range" of managerial ownership share over which the entrenchment effect is dominant.

This situation is illustrated in Exhibit 21.1, depicting a possible relationship between managerial ownership share and firm value. According to Morck, Shleifer, and Vishny (1988), who studied the relationship for *Fortune* 500 American companies, the first turning point (x) is reached at about 5 percent and the second (y) at about 25 percent. This means that the "entrenchment effect" is roughly dominant over the range of managerial ownership between 5 percent and 25 percent, whereas the "alignment effect" is dominant for the ownership shares less than 5 percent and exceeding 25 percent.[6] The relationship between managerial ownership and firm value is likely to vary across countries. For instance, Short and Keasey (1999) indicate that the inflection point (x) is reached at 12 percent in the United Kingdom, a much higher level of man-

EXHIBIT 21.1

The Alignment versus Entrenchment Effects of Managerial Ownership

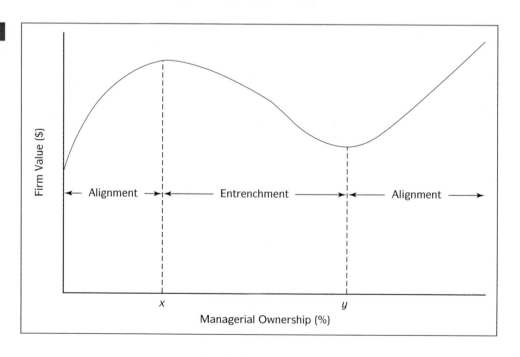

[6] It is noted that the authors actually used "Tobin's q" to measure firm value. Tobin's q is the ratio of the market value of company assets to the replacement costs of the assets.

agerial ownership than in the United States. They attribute this difference to more effective monitoring by British institutional investors and the lesser ability of British managers to resist takeover.

Debt

Although managers have discretion over how much of a dividend to pay to shareholders, debt does not allow such managerial discretion. If managers fail to pay interest and principal to creditors, the company can be forced into bankruptcy and its managers may lose their jobs. Borrowing and the subsequent obligation to make interest payments on time can have a major disciplinary effect on managers, motivating them to curb private perks and wasteful investments and trim bloated organizations. In fact, debt can serve as a substitute for dividends by forcing managers to disgorge free cash flow to outside investors, rather than wasting it. For firms with free cash flows, debt can be a stronger mechanism than stocks for credibly bonding managers to release cash flows to investors.[7]

Excessive debt, however, can create its own problem. In turbulent economic conditions, equities can buffer the company against adversity. Managers can pare down or skip dividend payments until the situation improves. With debt, however, managers do not have such flexibility and the company's survival can be threatened. Excessive debt may also induce the risk-averse managers to forgo profitable but risky investment projects, causing an underinvestment problem. For this reason, debt may not be such a desirable governance mechanism for young companies with few cash reserves or tangible assets. In addition, companies can misuse debt to finance corporate empire building. Daewoo, a Korean *chaebol*, borrowed excessively to finance global expansion until it went into bankruptcy; its debt-to-equity ratio reached 600 percent before bankruptcy.

Overseas Share Listings

Companies domiciled in countries with weak investor protection, such as Italy, Korea, and Russia, can bond themselves credibly to better investor protection by listing their shares in countries with strong investor protection, such as the United States and the United Kingdom. In other words, foreign firms with weak governance mechanisms can opt to outsource a superior corporate governance regime available in the United States via cross-listings. Suppose that Benetton, an Italian clothier, announces its decision to list its shares on the New York Stock Exchange (NYSE).[8] Since the level of shareholder protection afforded by the American Securities Exchange Commission (SEC) and the NYSE is much higher than that provided in Italy, the action will be interpreted as signalling the company's commitment to shareholder rights. Then, investors both in Italy and abroad will be more willing to provide capital to the company and value the company shares more. Generally speaking, the beneficial effects from American listings will be greater for firms from countries with weaker governance mechanisms.

Studies confirm the effects of cross-border listings. Specifically, Doidge, Karolyi, and Stulz (2002) report that foreign firms listed in the United States are valued more than those from the same countries that are not listed in the United States. They argue that firms listed in the United States can take better advantage of growth opportunities and that controlling shareholders cannot extract as many private benefits. It is pointed out, however, that foreign firms in mature industries with limited growth opportunities are not very likely to seek American listings, even though these firms face more serious agency problems than firms with growth opportunities that are more likely to seek American listings. In other words, firms with more serious problems are less likely to seek the remedies.

---

[7] Leveraged buy-outs (LBOs) can also be viewed as a remedy for the agency problem. LBOs involve managers or buyout partners acquiring controlling interests in public companies, usually financed by heavy borrowing. Concentrated ownership and high level of debt associated with LBOs can be effective in solving the agency problem.

[8] Benetton is actually listed on the New York Stock Exchange.

Market for Corporate Control

Suppose a company continually performs poorly and all of its internal governance mechanisms fail to correct the problem. This situation may prompt an outsider (another company or investor) to mount a takeover bid. In a hostile takeover attempt, the bidder typically makes a tender offer to the target shareholders at a price substantially exceeding the prevailing share price. The target shareholders thus have an opportunity to sell their shares at a substantial premium. If the bid is successful, the bidder will acquire the control rights of the target and restructure the company. Following a successful takeover, the bidder often replaces the management team, divests some assets or divisions, and trims employment in effort to enhance efficiency. If these efforts are successful, the combined market value of the acquirer and target companies will become higher than the sum of stand-alone values of the two companies, reflecting the synergies created. The market for corporate control, if it exists, can have a disciplinary effect on managers and enhance company efficiency.

In the United States and the United Kingdom, hostile takeovers can serve as a drastic governance mechanism of the last resort. Under the potential threat of takeover, managers cannot take their control of the company for granted. In many other countries, however, hostile takeovers are quite rare. This is so partly because of concentrated ownership in these countries and partly because of cultural values and political environments disapproving hostile corporate takeovers. But even in these countries, the incidence of corporate takeovers has been gradually increasing. This can be due, in part, to the spreading of equity culture and the opening and deregulation of capital markets. In Germany, for instance, takeovers are carried out through transfer of block holdings. In Japan, as in Germany, interfirm cross-holdings of equities are loosening, creating capital market conditions that are more conducive to takeover activities. To the extent that companies with poor investment opportunities and excess cash initiate takeovers, it is a symptom, rather than a cure, of the agency problem.

21.4 | Law and Corporate Governance

When outside investors entrust funds to the company, they receive certain rights that are legally protected. Among these are the rights to elect the board of directors, receive dividends on a pro-rata basis, participate in shareholders' meetings, and sue the company for expropriation. These rights empower investors to extract from management fair returns on their funds. However, the content of law protecting investors' rights and the quality of law enforcement vary a great deal across countries. According to the studies of La Porta, Lopez-de-Silanes, Shleifer, and Vishny (LLSV), many of the observed differences in international corporate governance systems arise from the differences in how well outside investors are protected by law from expropriation by managers and other corporate insiders. LLSV argue that the legal protection of investor rights systematically varies, depending on the historical origins of national legal systems.

Legal scholars show that the commercial legal systems (for example, company, security, bankruptcy, and contract laws) of most countries derive from relatively few **legal origins**:

- English common law
- French civil law
- German civil law
- Scandinavian civil law

The French and German civil laws derived from the Roman law, whereas the Scandinavian countries developed their own civil law tradition that is less derivative of Roman law. The civil law tradition, which is the most influential and widely spread, is based on the comprehensive *codification of legal rules*. In contrast, English common law is formed by the *discrete rulings* of independent judges on specific disputes and *judicial precedent*.

These distinct legal systems, especially **English common law** and **French civil law**, spread around the world through conquest, colonization, voluntary adoption, and subtle imitation. The United Kingdom and its former colonies, including Australia, Canada, India, Malaysia, Singapore, South Africa, New Zealand, and the United States, have the English common law system. France and the parts of Europe conquered by Napoleon, such as Belgium, the Netherlands, Italy, Portugal, and Spain, ended up with the French civil law tradition. Further, many former overseas colonies of France, the Netherlands, Portugal, and Spain—such as Algeria, Argentina, Brazil, Chile, Indonesia, Mexico, and the Philippines—also ended up with the French civil law system. The German civil law family comprises Germany and the Germanic countries of Europe, such as Austria and Switzerland, and a few East Asian countries, such as Japan, Korea, and Taiwan. The Scandinavian civil law family includes the four Nordic countries: Denmark, Finland, Norway, and Sweden. Thus, in most countries, the national legal system did not indigenously develop but, rather, was transplanted from one of several legal origins. Although national legal systems have evolved and adapted to local conditions, it is still possible to classify them into a few distinct families. Such a classification is provided in Exhibit 21.2. The exhibit also provides the indexes for shareholder rights and rule of law for each country as computed by LLSV (1998).

Exhibit 21.2 shows that the average shareholder rights index is 4.00 for English common law countries, 2.33 for both French and German civil law countries, and 3.00 for Scandinavian civil law countries. Thus, English common law countries tend to offer the strongest protection for investors, French and German civil law countries offer the weakest, and Scandinavian civil law countries fall in the middle. The quality of law enforcement, as measured by the rule of law index, is the highest in Scandinavian and German civil law countries, followed by English common law countries; it is lowest in French civil law countries.

Clearly, there is a marked difference in the legal protection of investors between the two most influential legal systems, namely, English common law and French civil law. A logical question is: Why is the English common law system more protective of investors than the French civil law system? According to the prevailing view, the state historically has played a more active role in regulating economic activities and has been less protective of property rights in civil law countries than in common law countries. In England, control of the court passed from the crown to Parliament and property owners in the 17th century. English common law thus became more protective of property owners, and this protection was extended to investors over time. This legal tradition in England allows the court to exercise its discretionary judgment or "smell test" over which managerial self-dealings are *unfair* to investors. In France as well as in Germany, parliamentary power was weak, and commercial laws were codified by the state, with the role of the court confined to simply determining whether the codified rules were violated or not. Since managers can be creative enough to expropriate investors without obviously violating the codified rules, investors receive low protection in civil law countries.

In a recent study, Glaesser and Shleifer (2002) offer an intriguing explanation of the English and French legal origins based on the divergent political situations prevailing in the Middle Ages. In France, local feudal lords were powerful and there were incessant wars. Under this turbulent situation, there was a need for the protection of adjudicators from local powers, which can only be provided by the king. France came to adopt a royal judge-inquisitor model based on the *Justinian code* of the Roman Empire in the 13th century. According to this model, judges appointed by the king collect evidence, prepare written records, and determine the outcome of the case. Understandably, royal judges were mindful of the preferences of the king. The French legal tradition was formalized by the *Code Napoleon*. Napoleon extensively codified legal rules, *bright line rules* in legal terms, and required state-appointed judges to merely apply these rules. In England, in contrast, local lords were less powerful, and war was

EXHIBIT 21.2

Classification of Countries by Legal Origins

Legal Origin	Country	Shareholder Rights Index	Rule of Law Index
1. English common law	Australia	4	10.00
	Canada	5	10.00
	Hong Kong	5	8.22
	India	5	4.17
	Ireland	4	7.80
	Israel	3	4.82
	Kenya	3	5.42
	Malaysia	4	6.78
	New Zealand	4	10.00
	Nigeria	3	2.73
	Pakistan	5	3.03
	Singapore	4	8.57
	South Africa	5	4.42
	Sri Lanka	3	1.90
	Thailand	2	6.25
	United Kingdom	5	8.57
	United States	5	10.00
	Zimbabwe	3	3.68
	English-origin average	**4.00**	**6.46**
2. French civil law	Argentina	4	5.35
	Belgium	0	10.00
	Brazil	3	6.32
	Chile	5	7.02
	Colombia	3	2.08
	Ecuador	2	6.67
	Egypt	2	4.17
	France	3	8.98
	Greece	2	6.18
	Indonesia	2	3.98
	Italy	1	8.33
	Jordan	1	4.35
	Mexico	1	5.35
	Netherlands	2	10.00
	Peru	3	2.50
	Philippines	3	2.73
	Portugal	3	8.68
	Spain	4	7.80
	Turkey	2	5.18
	Uruguay	2	5.00
	Venezuela	1	6.37
	French-origin average	**2.33**	**6.05**
3. German civil law	Austria	2	10.00
	Germany	1	9.23
	Japan	4	8.98
	South Korea	2	5.35
	Switzerland	2	10.00
	Taiwan	3	8.52
	German-origin average	**2.33**	**8.68**
4. Scandinavian civil law	Denmark	2	10.00
	Finland	3	10.00
	Norway	4	10.00
	Sweden	3	10.00
	Scandinavian-origin average	**3.00**	**10.00**

Note: Shareholder rights index scales from 0 (lowest) to 6 (highest). Rule of law index scales from 0 (lowest) to 10 (highest).
Source: Rafael La Porta, Florencio Lopez-de-Silanes, Andrei Shleifer, Robert W. Vishny, "Law and Finance," *Journal of Political Economy* 106 (1998), pp. 1113–55.

EXHIBIT 21.3

**Does Law Matter? :
Italy versus the United
Kingdom**

	Italy	U.K.
Legal origin	French civil law	English common law
Shareholder rights	1 (low)	5 (high)
Ownership by three largest shareholders	58%	19%
Market cap/GDP	71%	248%
Listed shares	247	2,292

Note: Shareholder rights refer to the antidirector rights index as computed by La Porta, Lopez-de-Silanes, Shleifer, and Vishny (1998). Both the ratio of stock market capitalization to GDP and the number of listed shares are as of 1999.
Source: Various studies of LLSV and the CIA's *World Factbook*.

less frequent. In a more peaceful England, which partly reflects the country's geographical isolation, local magnates were mainly afraid of royal power and preferred adjudication by a local jury that was not beholden to the preferences of the crown and was more knowledgeable about local facts and preferences. Initially, the jury consisted of 12 armed knights who were less likely to be intimidated by local bullies or special pressure groups. After the *Magna Carta* of 1215, local magnates basically paid the crown for the privilege of local, independent adjudication and other rights. The divergent legal developments in England and France came to have lasting effects on the legal systems of many countries.

21.5 Consequences of Law

Protection of investors' rights not only has interesting legal origins, but the concept is shown to have major economic consequences on the pattern of corporate ownership and valuation, the development of capital markets, economic growth, and others. To illustrate, let us consider two European countries, Italy and the United Kingdom. As shown in Exhibit 21.3, Italy has a French civil law tradition with weak shareholder protection, whereas the United Kingdom, with its common law tradition, provides strong investor protection. In Italy (UK), the three largest shareholders own 58 percent (19 percent) of the company, on average. Company ownership is thus highly concentrated in Italy and more diffuse in the United Kingdom. In addition, as of 1999, only 247 companies are listed on the stock exchange in Italy, whereas 2,292 companies are listed in the United Kingdom. In the same year, the stock market capitalization as a proportion of the annual GDP was 71 percent in Italy but 248 percent in the United Kingdom. The stark contrast between the two countries suggests that protection of investors has significant economic consequences. Concentrated ownership can be viewed as a rational response to weak investor protection, but it may create a different agency conflict between large controlling shareholders and small outside shareholders. We now discuss some of the issues in detail.

**Ownership and
Control Pattern**

Companies domiciled in countries with weak investor protection may need to have concentrated ownership as a substitute for legal protection. With concentrated ownership, large shareholders can control and monitor managers effectively and solve the agency problem. LLSV (1998), indeed, found that corporate ownership tends to be more concentrated in countries with weaker investor protection. As can be seen from Exhibit 21.4, the three largest shareholders own 43 percent of companies on average in English common law countries, and 54 percent of companies on average in French civil law countries.

If large shareholders benefit only from pro-rata cash flows, there will be no conflicts between large shareholders and small shareholders. What is good for large shareholders should be good for small shareholders as well. Since investors may be able to derive private benefits from control, however, they may seek to acquire control rights

EXHIBIT 21.4	Consequences of Law: Ownership and Capital Markets		

Legal Origin	Country	Ownership Concentration	External Cap/GNP	Domestic Firms/Population
1. English common law	Australia	0.28	0.49	63.55
	Canada	0.40	0.39	40.86
	Hong Kong	0.54	1.18	88.16
	India	0.40	0.31	7.79
	Ireland	0.39	0.27	20.00
	Israel	0.51	0.25	127.60
	Kenya	na	na	2.24
	Malaysia	0.54	1.48	25.15
	New Zealand	0.48	0.28	69.00
	Nigeria	0.40	0.27	1.68
	Pakistan	0.37	0.18	5.88
	Singapore	0.49	1.18	80.00
	South Africa	0.52	1.45	16.00
	Sri Lanka	0.60	0.11	11.94
	Thailand	0.47	0.56	6.70
	United Kingdom	0.19	1.00	35.68
	United States	0.20	0.58	30.11
	Zimbabwe	0.55	0.18	5.81
	English-origin average	**0.43**	**0.60**	**35.45**
2. French civil law	Argentina	0.53	0.07	4.58
	Belgium	0.54	0.17	15.50
	Brazil	0.57	0.18	3.48
	Chile	0.45	0.80	19.92
	Colombia	0.63	0.14	3.13
	Ecuador	na	na	13.18
	Egypt	0.62	0.08	3.48
	France	0.34	0.23	8.05
	Greece	0.67	0.07	21.60
	Indonesia	0.58	0.15	1.15
	Italy	0.58	0.08	3.91
	Jordan	Na	na	23.75
	Mexico	0.64	0.22	2.28
	Netherlands	0.39	0.52	21.13
	Peru	0.56	0.40	9.47
	Philippines	0.57	0.10	2.90
	Portugal	0.52	0.08	19.50
	Spain	0.51	0.17	9.71
	Turkey	0.59	0.18	2.93
	Uruguay	na	na	7.00
	Venezuela	0.51	0.08	4.28
	French-origin average	**0.54**	**0.21**	**10.00**
3. German civil law	Austria	0.58	0.06	13.87
	Germany	0.48	0.13	5.14
	Japan	0.18	0.62	17.78
	South Korea	0.23	0.44	15.88
	Switzerland	0.41	0.62	33.85
	Taiwan	0.18	0.86	14.22
	German-origin average	**0.34**	**0.46**	**16.79**
4. Scandinavian civil law	Denmark	0.45	0.21	50.40
	Finland	0.37	0.25	13.00
	Norway	0.36	0.22	33.00
	Sweden	0.28	0.51	12.66
	Scandinavian-origin average	**0.37**	**0.30**	**27.26**

Note: Ownership concentration measures the average share ownership by three largest shareholders. External Cap/GNP is the ratio of the stock market capitalization held by minority shareholders (other than three shareholders) to the gross national product for 1994. Domestic Firms/Population is the ratio of the number of domestic firms listed in a given country to its population (million) in 1994.
Source: Various studies of LLSV.

exceeding cash flow rights. Dominant investors may acquire control through various schemes, such as:

1. Shares with superior voting rights
2. Pyramidal ownership structure
3. Interfirm cross-holdings.

Many companies issue shares with differential voting rights, deviating from the one-share one-vote principle. By accumulating superior voting shares, investors can acquire control rights exceeding cash flow rights. In addition, large shareholders, who are often founders and their families, can use a **pyramidal** structure in which they control a holding company that owns a controlling block of another company, which, in turn, owns controlling interests in yet another company, and so on. Also, cross-holdings of equities among a group of companies, such as *keiretsu* and *chaebols*, can be used to concentrate and leverage voting rights to acquire control. Obviously, a combination of these schemes may also be used to acquire control.

Hutchson Whampoa, the third most valuable public company in Hong Kong, provides an interesting example of pyramidal control structure. The company is 43.9 percent controlled by another public company, Cheung Kong Holdings, which is the fifth-largest publicly traded company in Hong Kong. Cheung Kong Holdings, in turn, is 35 percent controlled by the Li Ka-Shing family. The cash flow rights of the Li family in Hutchson Whampoa are, thus, 15.4 percent ($0.35 \times 0.439 = 0.154$), but the family's control rights in Hutchson Whampoa is 43.9 percent. The chain of control of Hutchson Whampoa is illustrated in Exhibit 21.5. In Korea, the ownership structure can be more complicated. Take Samsung Electronics, Korea's most valuable company. Lee Keun-Hee, the chairman of the Samsung *chaebol* and the son of Samsung's founder, controls 8.3 percent of Samsung Electronics directly. In addition, Lee controls 15 percent of Samsung Life, which controls 8.7 percent of Samsung Electronics and 14.1 percent of Cheil Chedang, which controls 3.2 percent of Samsung Electronics and

EXHIBIT 21.5

Hutchson Whampoa:
The Chain of Control

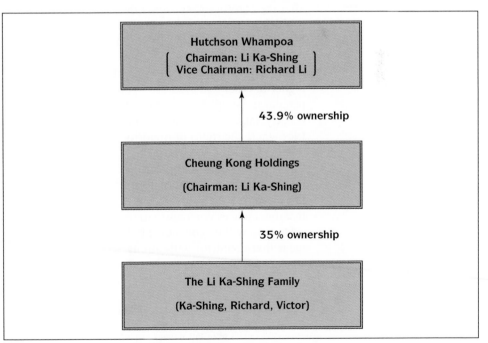

Source: R. La Porta, F. Lopez-de-Silanes, and A. Shleifer and R. Vishny, "Corporate Ownership around the World," *Journal of Finance* 54 (1999), p. 483.

11.5 percent of Samsung Life. This byzantine web of cross-holdings enables Lee to exercise an effective control of Samsung Electronics.[9]

As in Asia, concentrated ownership and a significant wedge between control and cash flow rights are widespread in continental Europe. Exhibit 21.6 illustrates the pyramidal ownership structure for Daimler-Benz, a German company, at the beginning of the 1990s.[10] The company has three major block holders: Deutsche Bank (28.3 percent), Mercedes-Automobil Holding AG (25.23 percent), and the Kuwait government (14 percent). The remaining 32.37 percent of shares are widely held. The pyramidal ownership structure illustrated in Exhibit 21.6 makes it possible for large investors to acquire significant control rights with relatively small investments. For example, Robert Bosch GmbH controls 25 percent of Stella Automobil, which, in turn, owns 25 percent of Mercedes-Automobil Holding, which controls 25 percent of Daimler-Benz AG. Robert Bosch can possibly control up to 25 percent of the voting rights of Daimler-Benz AG with only 1.56 percent cash flow rights in the company.

Private Benefits of Control

Once large shareholders acquire control rights exceeding cash flow rights, they may extract **private benefits of control** that are not shared by other shareholders on pro-rata basis. A few studies document the existence and magnitude of private benefits. Nenova (2001) computed the premium for voting shares relative to nonvoting shares in different countries. The voting premium, defined as the total vote value (value of a vote times the number of votes) as a proportion of the firm's equity market value is only about 2 percent in the United States and 2.8 percent in Canada. This implies that private benefits of control are not very significant in both countries. In contrast, the voting premium is 23 percent in Brazil, 9.5 percent in Germany, 29 percent in both in Italy and Korea, and 36 percent in Mexico, suggesting that in these countries, dominant shareholders extract substantial private benefits of control. Unless investors can derive significant private benefits of control, they will not pay substantial premiums for voting shares over nonvoting shares.

Dyck and Zingales (2003), on the other hand, computed "block premium," that is, the difference between the price per share paid for the control block and the exchange price after the announcement of the control transaction, divided by the exchange price after the control transaction. Obviously, control blocks will command premiums only if block holders can extract private benefits of control. Similar to Nenova's findings, Dyck and Zingales report that during the period 1990–2000, the average block premium was only 1 percent in Canada, the United Kingdom, and the United States, and 2 percent in Australia and Finland. The average block premium, however, was much higher in other countries—65 percent in Brazil, 58 percent in the Czech Republic, 27 percent in Israel, 37 percent in Italy, 16 percent in Korea, and 34 percent in Mexico. Clearly, large shareholders extract significant private benefits of control in those countries where the rights of minority shareholders are not well protected.

Capital Markets and Valuation

The legal analysis of corporate governance predicts that investor protection promotes the development of external capital markets. When investors are assured of receiving fair returns on their funds, they will be willing to pay more for securities. To the extent that this induces companies to seek more funds from outside investors, strong investor protection will be conducive to large capital markets. LLSV (1997) empirically document that countries with strong shareholder protection tend to have more valuable stock markets and more companies listed on stock exchanges per capita than countries

---

[9] Examples here are from R. La Porta, F. Lopez-de-Silanes, A. Shleifer and R. Vishny, "Corporate Ownership around the World," *Journal of Finance* 54 (1999), pp. 471–517.

[10] This example is from Julian Franks and Colin Mayer, "Ownership and Control of German Corporations," *Review of Financial Studies* 14 (2001), pp. 943–77. Note that the ownership structure of Daimler-Benz has been significantly altered since 1990.

EXHIBIT 21.6 Ownership Structure of Daimler-Benz AG, 1990

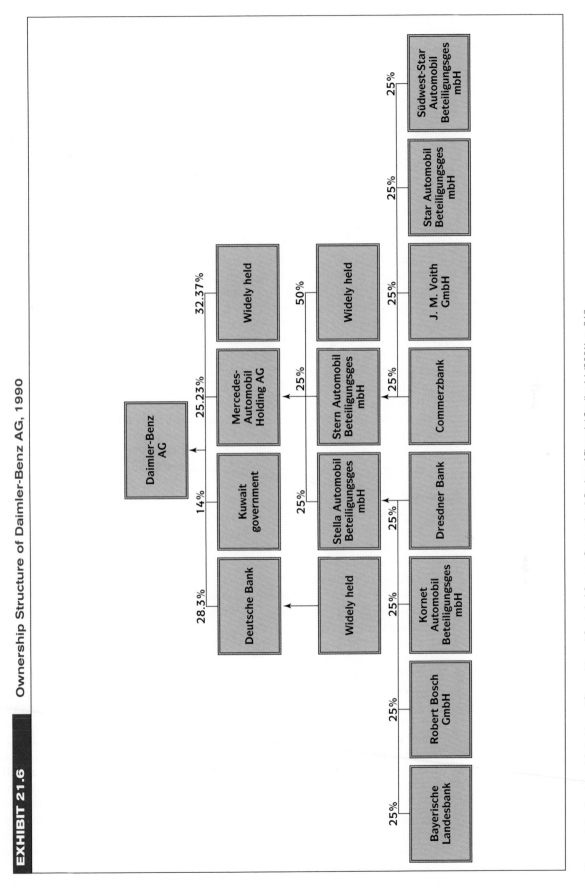

Source: Julian Franks and Colin Mayer, "Ownership and Control of German Corporation," *Review of Financial Studies* 14 (2001), p. 949.

with weak protection. Also, a few studies report that higher insider cash flow rights are associated with higher valuation of corporate assets, whereas greater insider control rights are associated with lower valuation of corporate assets. Exhibit 21.4 shows that the stock market capitalization held by minority shareholders (excluding the three largest shareholders) as a proportion to the GNP for the year 1994 is 0.60 in English common law countries and 0.21 in French civil law countries. The exhibit also shows that the number of domestic firms listed on stock exchanges per population (million) is about 35 in English common law countries, compared with only 10 in French civil law countries.

Weak investor protection can also be a contributing factor to sharp market declines during a financial crisis. In countries with weak investor protection, insiders may treat outside investors reasonably well as long as business prospects warrants continued external financing. However, once future prospects dim, insiders may start to expropriate the outside investors as the need for external funding dissipates. The accelerated expropriation can induce sharp declines in security prices. Johnson, Boon, Breach, and Friedman (2000) provide evidence that during the Asian financial crisis of 1997–1998, stock markets actually declined more in countries with weaker investor protection.

The existence of well-developed financial markets, promoted by strong investor protection, may stimulate economic growth by making funds readily available for investment at low cost. Earlier, Schumpeter (1934) argued that financial development promotes economic growth. Several studies now document the empirical link between financial development and economic growth, supporting the Schumpeter hypothesis.[11] According to Beck et al. (2000), financial development can contribute to economic growth in three major ways: (1) It enhances savings; (2) it channels savings toward real investments in productive capacities, thereby fostering capital accumulation; and (3) it enhances the efficiency of investment allocation through the monitoring and signalling functions of capital markets.

www.worldbank.org/
privatesector/cg/

This site discusses corporate governance reform.

21.6 Corporate Governance Reform

In the wake of the Asian financial crisis of 1997–1998 and the spectacular failure of several major companies, such as Daewoo, Enron, and WorldCom, scandal-weary investors around the world are demanding corporate governance reform. The failure of these companies hurts shareholders as well as other stakeholders, including workers, customers, and suppliers. Many employees who invested heavily in company shares for their retirement were dealt severe financial blows. It is not just the companies' internal governance mechanisms that failed; auditors, regulators, banks, and institutional investors also failed in their respective roles. Failure to reform corporate governance will damage investor confidence, stunt the development of capital markets, raise the cost of capital, distort capital allocation, and even shake confidence in capitalism itself.

Objectives of Reform

During the 1980s, when the economies of Germany and Japan were strong performers, the governance systems of the two countries received much attention and admiration. In both Germany and Japan, banks and a few permanent large shareholders play the central role in corporate governance. This "bank-centred" governance system was seen as guiding corporate managers to pursue long-term performance goals and also as effectively supporting companies when they were in financial distress. In contrast, the "market-centred" governance system of the United States was viewed as inducing short-term-oriented corporate decisions and being ineffectual in many ways. However, as the American economy and its stock market surged ahead in the 1990s, with Germany and Japan lagging behind, the American-style market-centred governance system replaced the German-Japanese system as a subject of admiration. The American market-oriented system seemed the wave of the future. But then, the subsequent slowdown

---

[11] Examples include King and Levine (1993), Rajan and Zingales (1998), and Beck, Levine, and Loayza (2000).

of the American economy and stock market and the shocking corporate scandals again dethroned the American system. It seems fair to say that no country has a perfect system for other countries to emulate.

There is a growing consensus that corporate governance reform should be a matter of global concern. Although some countries face more serious problems than others, existing governance mechanisms have failed to effectively protect outside investors in many countries. What should be the objective of reform? Our discussion in this chapter suggests a simple answer: *Strengthen the protection of outside investors from expropriation by managers and controlling insiders.* Among other things, reform requires (1) strengthening the independence of boards of directors with more outsiders, (2) enhancing the transparency and disclosure standard of financial statements, and (3) energizing the regulatory and monitoring functions of securities commissions, such as the Ontario Securities Commission (OSC), the flagship securities commission in Canada, or the Securities and Exchange Commission (SEC) in the United States, and stock exchanges. In many developing and transition countries, it may be necessary to first modernize the legal framework.

Political Dynamics

www.brt.org/

This site discusses the principles of corporate governance.

However, as we have seen from the experiences of many countries, governance reform is easier said than done. First of all, the existing governance system is a product of the historical evolution of the country's economic, legal, and political infrastructure. It is not easy to change historical legacies. Second, many parties have vested interests in the current system, and they will resist any attempt to change the status quo. For example, Arthur Levitt, chairman of the SEC during much of the 1990s, attempted to reform the accounting industry, but it successfully resisted the attempt through the use of lobbyists and advertising. In Levitt's words (*The Wall Street Journal*, June 17, 2002, p. C7): "The ferocity of the accounting profession's opposition to our attempt to reform the industry a few years ago is no secret. . . . They will do everything possible to protect their franchise, and will do so with little regard for the public interest." This earlier failure to reform the accounting industry contributed to the breakout of corporate scandals in the United States. It is noted that the former executives of WorldCom were indicted for allegedly orchestrating the largest accounting fraud in history, with the help of conniving auditors.[12] In another example, following the Asian financial crisis, the Korean government led efforts to reform the country's *chaebol* system but met with stiff resistance from the founding families, which were basically afraid of losing their private benefits of control. Nevertheless, reform efforts in Korea were partially successful, partly because the weight and prestige of the government were behind them and partly because public opinion was generally in favour of reform.

To be successful, reformers should understand the political dynamics surrounding governance issues and seek help from the media, public opinion, and nongovernmental organizations (NGOs). The role of NGOs and the media can be illustrated by the success of the People's Solidarity for Participatory Democracy (PSPD) in Korea, organized by Hasung Jang of Korea University. The PSPD and Professor Jang have utilized legal pressure and media exposure to create public opinion and shame corporate executives into changing their practices. For example, PSPD successfully challenged the transfer pricing of SK Telecom. Specifically, SK Telecom transferred huge profits to two subsidiaries, Sunkyung Distribution, which is 94.6 percent owned by SK Group Chairman Choi Jong-Hyun, and Daehan Telecom, fully owned by Choi's son and his son-in-law, thereby expropriating outside shareholders of SK Telecom. The PSPD exposed this practice to the media, and the episode was reported in the *Financial Times* as well as local newspapers and television. Facing unfavourable public opinion, SK Telecom finally agreed to stop the practice.[13]

---

[12] *New York Times*, (September 2, 2002), p. A16.
[13] Alexander Dyck and Luigi Zingales, "The Corporate Governance Role of the Media," Working paper (2002).

Facing public uproar following the American corporate scandals, politicians took actions to remedy the problem. The American Congress passed the **Sarbanes-Oxley Act** in 2002. The major components of the *Sarbanes-Oxley Act* are:

- Accounting regulation—The creation of a public accounting oversight board charged with overseeing the auditing of public companies and restricting the consulting services that auditors can provide to clients.

- Audit committee—The company should appoint independent "financial experts" to its audit committee.

- Executive responsibility—Chief executive and finance officers (CEO and CFO) must sign off on the company's quarterly and annual financial statements. If fraud causes an overstatement of earnings, these officers must return any bonuses.

The New York Stock Exchange (NYSE) is also currently considering various measures to protect investors. These measures call for, among other things: (1) listed companies to have boards of directors with a majority of independents; (2) the compensation, nominating, and audit committees to be entirely composed of independent directors; and (3) the publication of corporate governance guidelines and reporting of annual evaluation of the board and CEO. These measures, if properly implemented, should improve the corporate governance regime in the United States.

The Cadbury Code of Best Practice

Like the United States, the United Kingdom was hit by a spate of corporate scandals in the 1980s and early 1990s, resulting in the bankruptcy of such high-profile companies as Ferranti, Colorol Group, BCCI, and Maxwell Group. The "scandalous" collapse of these prominent British companies was popularly attributed to their complete corporate control by a single top executive, weak governance mechanisms, and the failure of their boards of directors. Against this backdrop, the British government appointed the *Cadbury Committee* in 1991 with the broad mandate to address corporate governance problems in the United Kingdom. Sir Adrian Cadbury, CEO of Cadbury Company, chaired the committee.[14] The work of the committee led to successful governance reform in the United Kingdom.

In December 1992, the Cadbury Committee issued its report, including the *Code of Best Practice* in corporate governance. The code recommends that (1) boards of directors of public companies include at least three outside (nonexecutive) directors, and that (2) the positions of chief executive officer (CEO) and chairman of the board (COB) of these companies be held by two different individuals; boards of directors of most British companies were dominated by insiders, with the positions of CEO and COB often held by the same individuals. Specifically, the code prescribed that:

> The board should meet regularly, retain full and effective control over the company and monitor the executive management. There should be a clearly accepted division of responsibilities at the head of a company, which will ensure a balance of power and authority, such that no one individual has unfettered power of decisions. Where the chairman is also the chief executive, it is essential that there should be a strong and independent element on the board, with a recognized senior member. The board should include non-executive directors of significant calibre and number for their views to carry significant weight in the board's decisions.

The **Cadbury Code** has not been legislated into law, and compliance with the code is voluntary. However, the London Stock Exchange (LSE) currently requires that each listed company show whether the company is in compliance with the code and explain why if it is not. This "comply or explain" approach has apparently persuaded many

---

[14] For a detailed discussion of the Cadbury Committee and its effect on corporate governance in the United Kingdom., refer to Dahya, McConnell, and Travlos (2002).

companies to comply, rather than explain; currently, 90 percent of all LSE-listed companies have adopted the Cadbury Code. According to a study by Dahya, McConnell, and Travlos (2002), the proportion of outside directors rose from 26 percent before the adoption to 47 percent afterward among those companies newly complying with the code. On the other hand, joint CEO/COB positions declined from 37 percent of the companies before the adoption to 15 percent afterward. This means that even though the compliance is voluntary, the Cadbury Code has made a significant impact on the internal governance mechanisms of British companies. The Dahya et al. study further shows that the "negative" relationship between CEO turnover and the company performance became stronger after the introduction of the Cadbury Code. This means that the job security of chief executives has become more sensitive to the company performance, strengthening managerial accountability and weakening its entrenchment.

SUMMARY

In the wake of recurrent financial crises and high-profile corporate scandals and failures in the United States and abroad, corporate governance has attracted a lot of attention worldwide. This chapter provides an overview of corporate governance issues, with the emphasis on intercountry differences in the governance mechanisms.

1. The public corporation, which is jointly owned by many shareholders with limited liability, is a major organizational innovation with significant economic consequences. The efficient risk-sharing mechanism allows the public corporation to raise large amounts of capital at low cost and profitably undertake many investment projects.

2. The public corporation has a major weakness, the agency problem associated with the conflicts of interest between shareholders and managers. Self-interested managers can take actions to promote their own interests at the expense of shareholders. The agency problem tends to be more serious for firms with excessive free cash flows but without growth opportunities.

3. To protect shareholder rights, curb managerial excesses, and restore confidence in capital markets, it is important to strengthen corporate governance, defined as the economic, legal, and institutional framework in which corporate control and cash flow rights are distributed among shareholders, managers, and other stakeholders of the company.

4. The central issue in corporate governance is: how to best protect outside investors from expropriation by managers and controlling insiders so that investors can receive fair returns on their funds.

5. The agency problem can be alleviated by various methods, including (a) strengthening the independence of boards of directors, (b) providing managers with incentive contracts, such as shares and share options, to better align the interests of managers with those of shareholders, (c) concentrated ownership so that large shareholders can control managers, (d) using debt to induce managers to disgorge free cash flows to investors, (e) listing shares in the London or New York stock exchanges where shareholders are better protected, and (f) inviting hostile takeover bids if the managers waste funds and expropriate shareholders.

6. Legal protection of investor rights systematically varies across countries, depending on the historical origins of the national legal system. English common law countries tend to provide the strongest protection, French civil law countries the weakest. The civil law tradition is based on the comprehensive codification of legal rules, whereas the common law tradition is based on the discrete rulings by independent judges on specific disputes and judicial precedent. The English common law tradition, based on independent judges and local juries, evolved to be more protective of property rights, which were extended to the rights of investors.

7. Protecting the rights of investors has major economic consequences in terms of corporate ownership patterns, the development of capital markets, economic growth, and more. Poor investor protection results in concentrated ownership, excessive private benefits of control, underdeveloped capital markets, and slower economic growth.

8. Outside the United States and the United Kingdom, large shareholders, often founding families, tend to control managers and expropriate small outside shareholders. In other words, large, dominant shareholders tend to extract substantial private benefits of control.

9. Corporate governance reform efforts should be focused on how to better protect outside investors from expropriation by controlling insiders. Often, controlling insiders resist reform efforts, as they do not like to lose their private benefits of control. Reformers should understand political dynamics and mobilize public opinion to their cause.

KEY WORDS

agency problem, *473*
Cadbury Code, *490*
complete contract, *473*
concentrated
    ownership, *477*
corporate governance, *471*
English common law, *481*

free cash flow, *474*
French civil law, *481*
incentive
    contracts, *477*
legal origin, *480*
managerial entrenchment,
    474

private benefits of control,
    486
pyramidal, *485*
residual control right, *473*
Sarbanes-Oxley Act, 490

QUESTIONS

1. The majority of major corporations are franchised as public corporations. Discuss the key strength and weakness of the "public corporation." When do you think the public corporation as an organizational form is unsuitable?

2. The public corporation is owned by a multitude of shareholders but run by professional managers. Managers can take self-interested actions at the expense of shareholders. Discuss the conditions under which the so-called agency problem arises.

3. Following corporate scandals and failures in the United States and abroad, there is a growing demand for corporate governance reform. What should be the key objectives of corporate governance reform? What kind of obstacles can thwart reform efforts?

4. Studies show that the legal protection of shareholder rights varies a great deal across countries. Discuss the possible reasons why the English common law tradition provides the strongest protection of investors and the French civil law tradition the weakest.

5. Explain "the wedge" between control and cash flow rights and discuss its implications for corporate governance.

6. Discuss different ways that dominant investors may establish and maintain control of a company with relatively small investments.

7. The *Cadbury Code of the Best Practice,* adopted in the United Kingdom, led to a successful reform of corporate governance in the country. Explain the key requirements of the code, and discuss how it contributed to the success of reform.

8. Many companies grant shares or share options to managers. Discuss the benefits and possible costs of using this kind of incentive compensation scheme.

9. It has been shown that foreign companies listed on American stock exchanges are valued more than those from the same countries that are not listed in the United

States. Explain why American-listed foreign firms are valued more than those that are not. Also explain why not every foreign firm wants to list shares in the United States.

10. Explain "free cash flows." Why do managers like to retain free cash flows instead of distributing it to shareholders? Discuss what mechanisms may be used to solve this problem.

INTERNET EXERCISE

It is often mentioned that the United States has a "market-centred" corporate governance system, whereas Germany has a "bank-centred" system. Review the website of OECD, www.oecd.org/daf/corporate-affairs/governance/ or any other relevant websites and answer the following questions:

(a) Compare and contrast the corporate governance systems of the two countries.

(b) How did the two countries come to have the particular governance systems?

(c) What are the consequences of the different governance systems in the two countries?

REFERENCES & SUGGESTED READINGS

Beck, T., R. Levine, and N. Loayza. "Finance and the Sources of Growth." *Journal of Financial Economics* 58 (2000), pp. 261–300.

Claessens, S., S. Djankov, and L. H. P. Lang. "The Separation of Ownership and Control in East Asian Corporations." *Journal of Financial Economics* 58 (2000), pp. 81–112.

Coase, Ronald. "The Nature of the Firm." *Economica* 4 (1937), pp. 386–405.

Dahya, Jay, John McConnell, and Nickolaos Travlos. "The Cadbury Committee, Corporate Performance, and Top Management Turnover." *Journal of Finance* 57 (2002), pp. 461–83.

Denis, D., and J. McConnell. "International Corporate Governance." Working Paper (2002).

Demsetz, H., and K. Lehn. "The Structure of Corporate Ownership: Causes and Consequences." *Journal of Political Economy* 93 (1985), pp. 1155–77.

Doidge, C., A. Karolyi, and R. Stulz. "Why Are Foreign Firms Listed in the American Worth More?" Working Paper, NBER (2002).

Dyck, A., and L. Zingales. "The Corporate Governance Role of the Media." Working Paper (2002).

Dyck, A., and L. Zingales. "Private Benefits of Control: An International Comparison." *Journal of Finance* 58 (2003).

Franks, J. R., and C. Mayer. "Ownership and Control of German Corporations." *Review of Financial Studies* 14 (2001), pp. 943–77.

Glaesser, E., and A. Shleifer. "Legal Origin." *Quarterly Journal of Economics* 117 (2002), pp. 1193–229.

Gorton, G., and F. A. Schmid. "Universal Banking and the Performance of German Firms." *Journal of Financial Economics* 58 (2000), pp. 28–80.

Holstrom, B., and S. N. Kaplan. "Corporate Governance and Merger Activity in the U.S.: Making Sense of the 1980s and 1990s." Working Paper, NBER (2001).

Jensen, M. "Eclipse of the Public Corporation." *Harvard Business Review* (1989), pp. 61–74.

Jensen, M., and W. Meckling. "Theory of the Firm: Managerial Behavior, Agency Cost, and Ownership Structure." *Journal of Financial Economics* 3 (1976), pp. 305–60.

Jensen, M., and K. Murphy. "Performance Pay and Top Management Incentives." *Journal of Political Economy* 98 (1990), pp. 225–63.

Johnson, S., P. Boon, A. Breach, and E. Friedman. "Corporate Governance in the Asian Financial Crisis." *Journal of Financial Economics* 58 (2000), pp. 141–86.

Johnson, S., R. La Porta, F. Lopez-de-Silanes, and A. Shleifer. "Tunneling." *American Economic Review* 90 (2000), pp. 22–27.

Kang, J., and A. Shivdasani. "Firm Performance, Corporate Governance, and Top Executive Turnover in Japan." *Journal of Financial Economics* 38 (1995), 29–58.

King, R. and R. Levine. "Finance and Growth: Schumpeter Might Be Right." *Quarterly Journal of Economics* 108 (1993), pp. 717–38.

La Porta, R., F. Lopez-de-Silanes, and A. Shleifer. "Legal Determinants of External Finance." *Journal of Finance* 52 (1997), pp. 1131–50.

———. "Law and Finance." *Journal of Political Economy* 106 (1998), 1113–55.

———. "Corporate Ownership around the World." *Journal of Finance* 54 (1999), pp. 471–517.

———. "Investor Protection and Corporate Governance." *Journal of Financial Economics* 58 (2000), pp. 3–27.

———. "Investor Protection and Corporate Valuation." *Journal of Finance* 57 (2002), pp. 1147–69.

Lemmon, M. L., and K. V. Lins. "Ownership Structure, Corporate Governance, and Firm Value: Evidence from the East Asian Financial Crisis." Working Paper (2001).

Morck, R., A. Shleifer, and R. Vishny. "Management Ownership and Market Valuation: An Empirical Analysis." *Journal of Financial Economics* 20 (1988), pp. 293–315.

Nenova, T., "The Value of Corporate Votes and Control Benefits: A Cross-Country Analysis." Working Paper (2001).

Rajan, R., and L. Zingales. "Financial Dependence and Growth." *American Economic Review* 88 (1998), pp.559–86.

Reese, W. A., Jr., and M. S. Weisbach. "Protection of Minority Shareholder Interests, Cross-listings in the United States, and Subsequent Equity Offerings." Working Paper, NBER (2001).

Shleifer, A., and R. Vishny. "A Survey of Corporate Governance." *Journal of Finance* 52 (1997), pp. 737–83.

Short, H., and K. Keasey. "Managerial Ownership and the Performance of Firms: Evidence from the UK." *Journal of Corporate Finance* 5 (1999), pp. 79–101.

Smith, Adam. *An Inquiry Into the Nature and Causes of the Wealth of Nations.* (1776).

Schumpeter, J. *The Theory of Economic Development.* Translated by R. Opie. Cambridge, MA: Harvard University Press, 1934.

Stulz, R., and R. Williamson. "Culture, Openness, and Finance." *Journal of Financial Economics* (2003).

Zingales, L. "The Value of the Voting Right: A Study of the Milan Stock Exchange Experience." *Review of Financial Studies* 7 (1994), pp. 125–48.

Glossary

A

Active Income   Income which results from production or services provided by an individual or corporation.

Adjusted Present Value (APV)   A present value technique which discounts a firm's cash flows at different rates depending on the risk of the cash flows.

Agency Market   A market in which the broker takes the client's order through the agent, who matches it with another public order.

Agency Problem   Managers who are hired as the agents working for shareholders may actually pursue their own interests at the expense of shareholders, causing conflicts of interest. Agency problems are especially acute for firms with diffused share ownership.

All-Equity Cost of Capital   The required return on a company's shares in the absence of debts.

All-in-Cost   All costs of a swap, which are interest expense, transaction cost, and service charges.

American Depository Receipt (ADR)   A certificate of ownership issued by an American bank representing a multiple of foreign shares that are deposited in an American bank. ADRs can be traded on the organized exchanges in the United States or in the over-the-counter (OTC) market.

American Option   An option which can be exercised at any time during the option contract.

American Terms   A foreign exchange quote in which the US dollar is on the top of the ratio, for example S = $ / £ or S($/£) = $1.5000/£. From the American dollar perspective, this is commonly called a "direct quote" (in dollars) or, less frequently, "US $ equivalent".

Arbitrage   The capture of zero-risk profits as a result of momentarily mispricing of similar assets.

Ask Price   *See* Offer Price.

B

Back-to-Back Loan   A loan involving two parties—two companies located in different countries. Each company borrows funds in its capital market and relends to the other company.

Balance of Payments   A country's record of international transactions presented in a double-entry bookkeeping form.

Balance of Payments Identity   The Balance of Payments *must* balance. A surplus (deficit) on Current Account equals a corresponding deficit (surplus) on Capital Account.

Balance Sheet Hedge   Intended to reduce translation exposure of a multinational corporation (MNC) by eliminating the mismatch of exposed net assets and exposed net liabilities denominated in the same currency.

Bank Capital Adequacy   The amount of equity capital and other securities a bank holds as reserves against risky assets to reduce the probability of a bank failure.

Banker's Acceptance (B/A)   A negotiable money market instrument for which a secondary market exists and is issued by the Importer's Bank once the bill of lading and time draft are accepted. It is essentially a promise that the bank will pay the draft when it matures.

Basle Accord   Established in 1988 by the Bank for International Settlements, this act established a framework to measure bank capital adequacy for banks in the Group of Ten and Luxembourg.

Bearer Bond   A bond in which ownership is demonstrated through possession of the bond.

Beta   A statistical measure of the systematic risk of a company's shares. Beta is the coefficient on the independent variable "market return" in a regression of the returns of a company's shares against the return on the market.

Bid Price   The price at which dealers will buy a financial asset.

Bilateral Netting   A system in which a pair of affiliates determines the net amount due between them and only this amount is transferred.

Bill of Lading (B/L)   In exporting, a document issued by a common carrier specifying that it has received goods for shipment and which can also serve as title to the goods.

Bimetallism   A double standard maintaining free coinage for both gold and silver.

Borrowing Capacity   The maximum amount of debt that a firm is willing to take on.

Brady Bonds   Loans converted into collateralized bonds with a reduced interest rate devised to resolve the international debt crisis in the late 1980s. Named after the U.S. Treasury Secretary Nicholas Brady.

Bretton Woods System   An international monetary system created in 1944 to promote postwar exchange rate stability and coordinate international monetary policies. Otherwise known as the gold-exchange system.

C

Cadbury Code   The Cadbury Committee appointed by the British government issued the *Code of Best Practice* in corporate governance for British companies, recommending, among other things, appointing at least three outside board directors and having the positions of CEO and board chairman held by two different individuals.

Call   A call gives the holder the right but not the obligation to purchase an asset at a specified price within a specified period.

Call Market   A market in which market and limit orders are accumulated and executed at specific intervals during the day.

Call Option   The right but not the obligation to purchase an asset (e.g., a share) for a specified price at a specified price on or before a specified date.

Capital Account   Balance-of-payment entry capturing all sales and purchases of financial assets, real estate, and businesses.

Capital Asset Pricing Model (CAPM)   A formal model that relates the expected (or required) rate of return on risky assets to systematic risk.

Capital-Export Neutrality   The idea that an ideal tax is one which is effective in raising revenue for the government and, at the same time, does not prevent economic resources from being deployed most efficiently no matter where in the world the highest return can be earned.

Capital-Import Neutrality   An international tax arrangement where the structure of tax does not favour domestic capital over foreign capital or *vice versa*.

Capital Structure   Refers the relative amounts of debt and equity used to finance a company.

Cash Budget   In cash management, a plan which details the time and size of expected receipts and disbursements.

Cash Management   The handling of cash within a firm, such as the investment a firm has in transaction balances, funds tied up in precautionary cash balances, investment of excess funds at the most favourable rate, and borrowing at the lowest rate when there is a temporary cash shortage.

Central Cash Depository   In an MNC, it is a central cash pool in which excess cash from affiliates is collected and invested or used to cover systemwide shortages of cash.

Civil Law   A system of law made explicit in Acts (in contrast to common law which is based on precedents of past judgments).

Clearinghouse   An integral part of the institutional structure of financial markets. The Canadian Derivatives Clearing Corporation (CDCC), for example, associated with the Montreal Stock Exchange, is the issuer, clearinghouse, and guarantor of interest rate, equity, and index derivative contracts traded on the MSE. LIFFE (International Financial Futures and Options Exchange) in London is an major clearinghouse for foreign exchange derivative contracts.

Client Market   In foreign exchange dealings, for example, the market in which individual or industrial clients arrange transactions (in contrast to the interbank market, which exclusively involves banks trading in large volumes.)

Closed-End Country Fund (CECF)   A country fund (fund invested exclusively in the securities of one country) which issues a given number of shares that are traded on the host country exchange as if it were an individual share. These shares are not redeemable at the underlying net asset value set in the home market.

Commission   A fee paid to a broker to carry out a transaction in a financial market.

Comparative Advantage   David Ricardo used the notion of comparative advantage to justify international trade. Specifically, if countries specialize production in those industries where they can produce goods and services more efficiently (in relative terms) than other countries, and engage in trade, all countries will be better off.

Competitive Effect   Refers to the effect of exchange rate changes on the firm's competitive position, which, in turn, affects the firm's operating cash flows.

Complete Contract   Refers to the contract that specifies exactly what each party will do under all possible future contingencies.

Composite Currency Bond   A bond denominated in a currency basket, such as European Currency Unit (ECU), instead of a single currency. Also called *Currency Cocktail Bonds*.

Concessionary Loan   A loan below the market interest rate offered by the host country to a parent MNC to encourage capital expenditures in the host country.

Concentrated Ownership   Ownership of a company's shares is concentrated when they are held by a relatively few shareholders.

Conservative Principle   The accounting principle whereby assets are valued at the lower of cost or market value.

Contingent Claim Security   *See* Derivative Security.

Contingent Exposure   The risk due to uncertain situations in which a firm does not know if it will face exchange risk exposure in the future.

Continuous Market   A market in which market and limit orders can be executed any time during business hours.

Contract Size   In a futures contract, the number of units of the underlying asset that are involved in one contract are specified as the contract size.

Controlled Foreign Corporation (CFC)   A foreign subsidiary in which American shareholders own more than 50 percent of the voting equity shares.

Conversion Effect   Refers to the fact that the dollar amount converted from a given cash flow from foreign operation will be affected by exchange rate changes.

Convertible Bond   A corporate bond that can be converted to a specific number of the issuing company's shares.

Corporate Governance   The economic, legal, and institutional framework in which corporate control and cash flow rights are distributed among shareholders, managers, and other stakeholders of the company.

Correspondent Banking Relationship   A formal cooperative operating relationship between two banks in two different countries to serve the international banking needs of commercial and corporate customers.

Cost of Capital   The required rate of return on a risky investment.

Counterparty   One of the two parties involved in financial contracts who agrees to exchange cash flows on particular terms.

Countertrade   Transactions in which parties exchange goods or services. If these transactions do not involve an exchange of money, they are a type of barter.

Country Risk   In banking and investment, it is the probability that unexpected events in a country will influence its ability to repay loans and repatriate dividends. It includes political and credit risks.

Covered Interest Arbitrage   A situation which occurs when interest rate parity (IRP) does not hold, thereby allowing certain arbitrage profits to be made without the arbitrageur investing any money out of pocket or bearing any risk.

Cross-Border Acquisition   A takeover or outright purchase of a company based in one country by a company based in another country, such as when in 1998 Nortel Networks (Canada) acquired Bay Networks (United States).

Cross-Border Merger   A merger of a companies from two different countries, such as in 2003 when Manulife Financial (Canada) merged with John Hancock (United States).

Cross Exchange Rate   An exchange rate between a currency pair where neither currency is the American dollar.

Cross-Currency Interest Rate Swap   Typically called a "currency swap." One counterparty exchanges the debt service obligations of a bond denominated in one currency for the debt service obligations of the other counterparty that are denominated in another currency.

Cross-hedging Involves hedging a position in one asset by taking a position in another asset.

Cross-Listing The act of directly listing securities on foreign financial exchanges. Cross-listing will require meeting the listing and disclosure standards of foreign exchanges.

Crowd Trading An equity trading arrangement in which traders and specialists congregate around a trading post at the stock exchange to execute orders.

Cumulative Translation Adjustment (CTA) Used in the current rate method of translating foreign currency financial statements, this equity account allows balancing of the balance sheet by accounting for translation gains and losses.

Currency Against Currency In dealers' language, a foreign exchange transaction in which the American dollar is not involved. Virtually all interbank foreign exchange transactions involve the American dollar on one side of the transaction. "Currency against currency" is an exception in which one non-dollar currency is exchanged for another non-dollar currency, for example, the Euro for Yen.

Currency Board An extreme form of the fixed exchange rate regime under which local currency is fully backed by the American dollar or another chosen standard currency.

Currency Futures A standardized foreign exchange contract with a future delivery date that is traded on organized exchanges.

Currency Swap One counter party exchanges the debt service obligations of a bond denominated in one currency for the debt service obligations of the other counter party denominated in another currency.

Current Account Balance-of-payment entry representing the exports and imports of goods and services, and unilateral transfer.

Current/Noncurrent Method In dealing with foreign currency translation, the idea that current assets and liabilities are converted at the current exchange rate while noncurrent assets and liabilities are translated at the historical exchange rates.

Current Rate Method In dealing with foreign currency translation, the idea that all balance sheet accounts are translated at the current exchange rate except shareholder's equity, which is translated at the exchange rate on the date of issuance.

D

Daily Price Limit The maximum allowable movement in the price of a security—such as a bond or a share—as specified by the exchange.

Dealer Market A market in which the broker takes the trade through the dealer, who participates in trades as a principal.

Debt-for-Equity Swap The sale of sovereign debt for American dollars to investors desiring to make equity investment in the indebted nation.

Delivery Month The month in which settlement of a futures contract must be completed.

Derivatives Hedge A hedge in which derivatives (calls, puts, futures, or forwards) are purchased or sold so as to create a distribution of payoffs that offset foreign exchange exposure.

Derivative Security A security whose value is contingent upon the value of the underlying security. Examples are futures, forward, and options contracts.

Direct Quotation A foreign exchange quote expressed in terms of units of domestic currency per one unit of a foreign currency—1.25 Canadian dollars per one American dollar is a direct quote from the Canadian perspective (C$1.25/US$1)

Direct Tax A tax paid directly by the taxpayer on whom the tax is levied.

Diversification of the Market A strategy for managing operating exposure in which a firm diversifies the market for its product. Thus, exchange rate changes in one country may be offset by opposite exchange rate changes in another.

Domestic (Foreign) Country Market Portfolio A broad index, such as the S&P TSX in Toronto, the S&P 500 in New York, the FTSE in London, or the Nikkei in Tokyo, that is representative of a diversified portfolio of the equities in the nation.

Draft A written order instructing the importer or his agent to pay the amount specified on its face at a certain date.

Dual Currency Bond A straight fixed-rate bond which pays coupon interest in the issue currency but at maturity pays the principal in a currency other than the issue currency.

E

Economic Exposure The possibility that cash flows and the value of the firm may be affected by unanticipated changes in the exchange rates.

Edge Act Bank Federally chartered subsidiaries of American banks which may engage in the full range of international banking operations. These banks are located in the United States.

Efficient Market Hypothesis Hypothesis stating that financial markets are informationally efficient in that the current asset prices reflect all the relevant and available information.

Elasticity of Demand A measure of the sensitivity of demand for a product with respect to its price.

English Common Law Law which is not contained within a specific Act is known as common law. It is built up by the courts and their judgments. English Common Law acknowledges the origins of this form of law (in contrast with the French or German Civil Law) and its use in most English-speaking countries.

EURIBOR The rate at which interbank deposits of the euro are offered by one prime bank to another in countries that make up the European Monetary Union (EMU) as well as prime banks in non-EMU EU countries and major prime banks in non-EU countries.

Euro Introduced in 1999, the common European currency of the 11 countries of the European Union (EU) that make up the EMU.

Eurobank A financial institution that accepts deposits in foreign currencies and makes foreign currency loans.

Eurobond A bond issue denominated in a particular currency but sold to investors in national capital markets other than the issuing country.

Eurocommercial Paper Notes with maturities up to 360 days issued by companies in international money markets.

Eurocredit A medium-term loan for large corporate and governmental bodies denominated in European currencies from a syndicate of banks.

Eurocurrency   A time deposit of money in an international bank located in a country other than the country which issues the currency.

Euronote   The paper associated with short-term (usually less than seven months) commercial borrowings in the Euro-markets.

European Central Bank (ECB)   The central bank of the 11 countries that make up the EMU, responsible for maintaining price stability via monetary policy.

European Currency Unit (ECU)   A basket currency made up of a weighted average of the currencies of the 12 members of the European Union. The precursor of the euro.

European Monetary System (EMS)   Replaced the Snake in 1979. A system to establish monetary stability in Europe and promote European economic and political unification.

European Monetary Union (EMU)   The monetary union of 11 countries of the EU that irrevocably fixed their exchange rates and use the common euro currency.

European Option   An option which can be exercised only at the maturity date of the contract.

European System of Central Banks (ESCB)   The new monetary arrangement in Europe, in which the European Central Bank (ECB) in Frankfurt takes overall responsibility for monetary policy in the European Union, while the central banks of the member-states assume the responsibilities of regional banks.

European Terms   A foreign exchange quote in which the dollar is on the bottom of the ratio S = £ / $ or S(£/$) = £0.6548/$. From the dollar perspective, this is commonly called an "indirect quote" (in foreign currency) or, less frequently, "currency per $."

European Union (EU)   A regional economic integration in Western Europe, currently with 15 member states, in which all barriers to the free flow of goods, capital, and people have been removed. EU plans to complete economic unification including a single currency.

Exchange Rate Mechanism (ERM)   The procedure, prior to the introduction of the euro, by which EMS member countries collectively manage their exchange rates based on a parity grid system, a system of par values between ERM countries.

Exchange Rate Pass-Through   The relationship between exchange rate changes and the price adjustments of internationally traded goods.

Exchange-Traded   A security, such as a futures contract, that is traded on an exchange.

Exchange-Traded Funds   Portfolios of shares and/or bonds that are traded on formal exchanges.

Exercise Price   The prespecified price paid or received when an option is exercised.

Expanded Opportunity Set   In international portfolio construction, the increase in opportunities to invest in foreign assets.

Export Development Corporation (EDC)   The agency of the Canadian federal government that provides finance on commercial terms to purchasers of Canadian exports.

Export-Import Bank (Eximbank) of the United States   Chartered in 1945, it is an independent government agency which facilitates and finances American export trade by financing exports in situations where private financial institutions are unable or unwilling to provide financing.

Exposure Coefficient   The coefficient obtained from regressing the home currency value of assets on the foreign exchange rate under consideration. This provides a measure of the firm's economic exposure to currency risk.

Exposure Netting   Hedging only the net exposure by firms which have both payables and receivables in foreign currencies.

F

FDI Flow   An aggregate measure of the amount of foreign direct investment that flows into a country (or out of a country) in a given year.

FDI Stock   An aggregate measure of the accumulated total amount of foreign direct investment in a country.

Financial Hedges   Refers to hedging exchange risk exposure using financial contracts, such as currency forward and options contracts.

Fisher Effect   Theory stating that the nominal interest rate is the sum of the real interest rate and the expected inflation rate.

Flexible Sourcing Policy   A strategy for managing operating exposure that involves sourcing from areas where input costs are low.

Floating Rate Note   Medium-term bonds which have their coupon payments indexed to a reference rate, such as the three-month American dollar LIBOR.

Foreign Bond   Refers to a bond offered by a foreign borrower to the investors in a national capital market and denominated in that nation's currency. Example: An American company selling yen-denominated bonds in Japan to local investors.

Foreign Branch   An overseas affiliate of an MNC which is not an independently incorporated firm but is, rather, an extension of the parent.

Foreign Branch Bank   A branch of a bank of which the owner is foreign. Branches have no corporate independence from the parent bank. If the Royal Bank, based in Toronto, sets up a branch in Bermuda, the parent bank in Canada owns all the assets and is fully responsible for all the liabilities of the Bermuda branch.

Foreign Currency Transaction   Any transaction involving an exchange of foreign currencies.

Foreign Direct Investment (FDI)   Investment by a multinational corporation in one country that sets up operations in another country; gives the MNC a measure of control.

Foreign Exchange Markets   Encompass the conversion of purchasing power from one currency into another, bank deposits of foreign currencies, and trading in foreign currency spot, forward, futures, swap, and options contracts.

Foreign Exchange Risk   The risk of facing uncertain future exchange rates.

Foreign Subsidiary   An affiliate organization of an MNC which is independently incorporated in a foreign country.

Foreign Tax Credit   Used to avoid double taxation on a parent firm with foreign subsidiaries. It is the credit given to the parent firm against taxes due in the host country based on the taxes paid to foreign tax authorities on foreign-source income.

Forfaiting A form of medium-term trade financing used to finance exports in which the exporter sells promissory notes to a bank at a discount, thereby freeing the exporter from carrying the financing.

Forward Expectations Parity Theory stating that the forward premium or discount is equal to the expected change in the exchange rate between two currencies.

Forward Market A market for trading foreign exchange contracts initiated today but to be settled at a future date.

Forward Market Hedge A method of hedging exchange risk exposure in which a foreign currency contract is sold or bought forward.

Forward Premium/Discount The amount over (under) the spot exchange rate for a forward rate that is often expressed as an annualized percent deviation from the spot rate.

Forward Rate A market-determined rate of exchange of one currency for another that is agreed today for fulfillment at a specific time in the future.

Forward Rate Agreement An interbank contract that is used to hedge the interest rate risk in mismatched deposits and credits.

Free Cash Flow It represents a firm's internally generated fund in excess of the amount needed to finance all investment projects with positive net present values.

French Civil Law *See* "Civil Law."

Full Service In reference to a bank, a bank that is involved in both commercial (retail) and investment banking.

Fully Integrated World Capital Markets Global markets without barriers caused by institutional deficiencies, transaction costs, or regulations.

Functional Currency For a foreign subsidiary of an MNC, it is the currency of the primary economic environment in which the entity operates. This is typically the local currency of the country in which the entity conducts most of its business.

Futures Contract A standardized contract to buy or sell an asset, foreign exchange, or commodity at a specific time in the future at a specific price.

G

General Agreement on Tariffs and Trade (GATT) A multilateral agreement between member countries to promote international trade. The GATT played a key role in reducing international trade barriers.

Gold Exchange Standard A monetary system in which countries hold most of their reserves in the form of a currency of a particular country. That country is on the gold standard.

Gold Standard A monetary system in which currencies are defined in terms of their gold content. The exchange rate between a pair of currencies is determined by their relative gold contents.

Greenfield Investment A foreign direct investment that takes the form of new plant and equipment and associated operations as opposed to a takeover.

Gresham's Law Under the bimetallic standard, the abundant metal was used as money while the scarce metal was driven out of circulation, based on the fact that the ratio of the two metals was officially fixed.

H

Hedger One who creates offsetting positions in an asset and a derivative security on that asset.

Hedging via the Invoice Currency A method of hedging exchange risk exposure by invoicing in terms of the home currency of the firm.

Home Bias In portfolio holdings, the tendency of an investor to hold a larger portion of the home country securities than is optimum for diversification of risk.

I

Incentive Contracts A contract, typically an employment contract or a contract for managerial services, in which the employee (or manager) is rewarded on the basis of measurable performance that is positively related to the value of the firm.

Income Tax A direct tax levied on the active income of an individual or corporation.

Incremental Cash Flow The change in corporate cash flow that results from undertaking a project. Incremental "project" cash flow is generally built up from component changes in cash flows in the project—in revenues, costs, changes in working capital, and so on.

Indirect Quotation A foreign exchange quote expressed in terms of units of foreign currency per one unit of the domestic currency—US$0.80/C$1 is an indirect quote from the Canadian perspective.

Indirect Tax A tax levied on a taxpayer's income which was not directly generated by the taxpayer and serves as passive income for the taxpayer.

Initial Margin An initial collateral deposit needed to establish an asset position.

In-the-Money A call option, for example, is in-the-money when the price of the option is greater than the exercise price.

Intangible Assets The proprietary assets, such as trademarks, good-will (reputation, and patented technology, that are crucial to the commercial uniqueness of a company.

Integrated World Capital Markets A situation in which capital is unrestricted from flowing across international borders and, as a result, interest rates and rates of return on risky assets are determined by global financial markets factors and conditions.

Interbank Market The market for loans and for currencies in which only banks are involved. Transactions are in large amounts among highly informed traders.

Interest Rate Parity (IRP) An arbitrage equilibrium condition holding that the interest rate differential between two countries should be equal to the forward exchange premium or discount. Violation of IRP gives rise to profitable arbitrage opportunities.

Internalization Theory A set of propositions that deal with the way in which multinational companies establish "internal markets" for trade among divisions of the company.

International Asset Pricing Model (IAPM) A model of asset valuation that takes account of the investors' opportunity to hold a globally diversified portfolio of assets. In this case, which assumes a high degree of international financial integration, individual assets (company shares) are "priced" in terms of global risks and financial conditions.

International Banking Facility (IBF)   Banking operation within domestic American banks that act as foreign banks in the United States and, as such, are not bound by domestic reserve requirements or FDIC insurance requirements. They seek deposits from non-American citizens and can make loans only to foreigners.

International Debt Crisis   Extreme disruption of currency and loans markets in a country generally associated with monetary instability, exchange rate volatility, and rapid outflows of short-term capital.

International Fisher Effect   A theory stating that the expected change in the spot exchange rate between two countries is the difference in the interest rates between the two countries.

International Monetary System   The institutional framework within which international payments are made, movements of capital are accommodated, and exchange rates among currencies are determined.

Internationally Non-Tradable Asset   A financial asset that trades only in its home capital market.

Internationally Tradable Asset   A financial asset that trades on several exchanges in the world—for example, New York, Toronto, London, and Tokyo—and can be readily bought or sold by anyone, anywhere.

Intrinsic Value   The immediate exercise value of an American option.

J

Jamaica Agreement   International monetary agreement in January 1976 by which flexible exchange rates were accepted and gold was abandoned as an international reserve asset.

J-curve Effect   Refers to the initial deterioration and eventual improvement of the trade balance following a depreciation of a country's currency.

L

Law of One Price   The requirement that similar commodities or securities should be trading at the same or similar prices.

Lead/Lag Strategy   Reducing transaction exposure by paying or collecting foreign financial obligations early (lead) or late (lag) depending on whether the currency is hard or soft.

Legal Origin   Refers to alternative national or cultural sources from which legal systems are derived; for example, English common law or French civil law.

Less Developed Countries   Poorer, industrially under-developed nations, typically with immature financial markets.

Letter of Credit (L/C)   A guarantee from the Importer's Bank that it will act on behalf of the importer and pay the exporter for merchandise if all documentation is in order.

Limit Order   An order away from the market price which is held until it can be executed at the desired price.

Liquidity   The ability of securities to be bought and sold quickly at close to the current quoted price.

London Interbank Offered Rate (LIBOR)   The interbank interest rate at which a bank will offer Eurocurrency deposits to another bank in London. LIBOR is often used as the basis for setting Eurocurrency loan rates. The loan rate is determined by adding a risk premium to LIBOR.

Long   Holding an asset. In a long position, a rise or fall in the value of an asset is captured or borne by the asset holder.

Lost Sales   In capital budgeting, the prospect that a new project—say, to manufacture widgets—will reduce the sale of another of the firm's products—say, gizmos—since widgets and gizmos are substitutes.

Louvre Accord   An agreement in 1987, prompted by the dollar's decline, in which the G-7 countries (i) cooperate to achieve greater exchange rate stability, and (ii) consult and coordinate their macroeconomic policies.

M

Maastricht Treaty   Treaty signed in December 1991 states that the European Union will irrevocably fix exchange rates among member countries by January 1999 and introduce a common European currency which will replace individual national currencies.

Maintenance Margin   Collateral needed to maintain an asset position.

Managed Float System   Established by the Louvre Accord in 1987, it allows the G-7 countries to jointly intervene in the exchange market to correct over- or undervaluation of currencies.

Managerial Entrenchment   The ability of managers of corporations to resist market discipline in respect to their own self-serving behaviour or managerial ineptitude. Managerial entrenchment reflects relatively weak corporate governance on the part of the shareholders and the Board.

Market Completeness   A market is complete if each state of the economy is matched by security payoff.

Market Imperfections   Various frictions, such as transaction costs and legal restrictions, that prevent the markets from functioning perfectly.

Market Order   An order executed at the best price available (market price) when the order is received in the market.

Market Portfolio   A broad index, such as the S&P TSX 300, of the corporate share prices in a country.

Marking-to-Market   The process of establishing daily price gains and losses in the futures market by the change in the settlement price of the futures contract.

Maturity Date   The date on which a contract—such as a call, a put, or a futures contract—expires.

Measure of Aggregate Risk Aversion   A statistical index of the degree to which the capital market exhibits a preference to avoid risk in the form of volatility.

Merchant Bank   Banks which perform traditional commercial banking as well as investment banking activities.

Monetary/Nonmonetary Method   In dealing with foreign currency translation, the idea that monetary balance sheet accounts, such as accounts receivable, are translated at the current exchange rate, while nonmonetary balance sheet accounts, such as shareholder's equity, are converted at the historical exchange rate.

Money Market Hedge   A method of hedging transaction exposure by borrowing and lending in the domestic and foreign money markets.

Multilateral Netting   A system in which all affiliates each net their individual interaffiliate receipts against all their disbursements and transfer or receive the balance, respectively, if it is a net payer or receiver.

Multinational Corporation (MNC)   Refers to a firm that has business activities and interests in multiple countries.

N

National Neutrality   The idea that an ideal tax on taxable income would tax all income in the same manner by the taxpayer's national tax authority, regardless of where in the world it is earned.

National Treatment   In matters of taxation, national treatment requires that foreign-owned corporations are taxed exactly as domestic corporations.

Negotiable Certificate of Deposit (NCD)   A negotiable bank time deposit.

Net Present Value (NPV)   A capital budgeting method in which the present value of cash outflows is subtracted from the present value of expected future cash inflows to determine the net present value of an investment project.

Netting Centre   In multilateral netting, it determines the amount of net payments and which affiliates are to make or pay them.

North American Free Trade Agreement (NAFTA)   Created in 1994, it includes the United States, Canada, and Mexico as members in a free trade area. NAFTA aims to eliminate tariffs and import quotas over a 15-year period.

Notional Principal   A reference amount of principal used for determining payments under various derivative contracts.

O

Offer Price   The price at which a dealer will sell a financial asset.

Offshore Banking Centre   A country in which the banking system is organized to allow external accounts beyond the normal economic activity of the country. Their primary function is to seek deposits and grant loans in currencies other than the host country currency.

Open Interest   The total number of short or long contracts outstanding for a particular delivery month in the derivative markets.

Operating Exposure   The extent to which the firm's operating cash flows will be affected by random changes in the exchange rates.

Operational Hedges   Long-term, operational approaches to hedging exchange exposure that include diversification of the market and flexible sourcing.

Optimal International Portfolio   A portfolio of shares and bonds from around the world that offers the highest ratio of expected return to risk as measured in one (reference) currency, such as the Canadian dollar.

Optimum Currency Area   A geographical area that is suitable for sharing a common currency by virtue of a high degree of factor mobility within the area.

Option   A contract giving the owner the right, but not the obligation, to buy or sell a given quantity of an asset at a specified price at some date in the future.

Options Market Hedge   Use of put and call options to limit the downside risk of transaction exposure while preserving the upside potential. The price of such flexibility is the option premium.

Out-of-the-Money   A call option, for example, is out-of-the-money when the price of the option is less than the exercise price.

Over-the-Counter (OTC) Market   Trading market in which there is no central marketplace; instead, buyers and sellers are linked via a network of telephones, telex machines, computers, and automated dealing systems.

P

Par Value   The nominal or face value of shares or bonds.

Parallel Loan   A loan involving four parties—two parent firms located in different countries and two foreign subsidiaries. The parent firms borrow in their capital markets and relend to the other's subsidiary.

Partially Integrated World Financial Markets   The global asset pricing relationship where some financial assets are not traded internationally due to regulatory restrictions, transaction costs, or institutional barriers.

Passive Income   Income not directly generated by an individual or corporation, such as interest income, royalty income, and copyright income.

Plaza Accord   G-5 agreement in 1985 that depreciation of the dollar is desirable to correct the American trade deficits.

Political Risk   Potential losses to the parent firm resulting from adverse political developments in the host country.

Portfolio Investment   Cross-border investment in the form of bonds or noncontrolling equity. The latter refers, for example, to shares in a foreign company in which case the shareholder holds an insufficient number of shares to control the company, usually defined to be 10 percent or less of the total number of shares outstanding.

Portfolio Risk Diversification   Portfolio risk is minimized by investing in multiple securities which do not have strong correlations between one another.

Precautionary Cash Balance   Emergency funds a firm maintains in case it has underestimated its transaction cash balance.

Premium   To compensate for risk in equities, a rate of return in excess of the risk-free rate. In option pricing, the amount per share that an option buyer pays to the seller.

Price Discovery   The process of determination of market prices for financial assets and exchange rates through the interactions of many buyers and sellers in a free market place.

Price-Specie-Flow Mechanism   Under the gold standard, it is the automatic correction of payment imbalances between countries. This is based on the fact that under the gold standard, the domestic money stock rises or falls as the country experiences inflows or outflows of gold.

Pricing to Market   When an exporter sets price for an exported product in light of local market conditions in the importing country. When pricing to market, an exporter tends not to change the price of the product denominated in the foreign currency following a change in the exchange rate.

Primary Market   The market in which new security issues are sold to investors. In selling the new securities, investment bankers can play a role either as a broker or a dealer.

Private Benefits of Control   Corporate control structured such that the benefits of ownership (influence on corporate decisions or perquisites) are unevenly shared, typically to the advantage of shareholders who hold large share positions and to the detriment of minority shareholders.

Privatization   Act of a country divesting itself of ownership and operation of business ventures by turning them over to the free market system.

Product Differentiation   Creating a perception among consumers that a firm's product(s) are different from those offered by competitors, thereby reducing price sensitivity of demand.

Product Life Cycle   The view that a manufactured product goes through a cycle that begins with invention and product-development in a high-income market for domestic consumption. Foreign demand is met through exports. As export demand increases, production shifts to low-cost foreign sites. As the foreign site of production becomes the low-cost site, the product is exported to the country in which it was first developed.

Purchasing Power Parity (PPP)   A theory stating that the exchange rate between currencies of two countries should be equal to the ratio of the countries' price levels of a commodity basket.

Put   An option to sell an underlying asset at a prespecified price.

Pyramidal   A structure of corporate ownership, often associated with European companies, in which the owners of companies that own other companies wield significant corporate control with relatively small capital commitment.

Q

Quality Spread Differential (QSD)   The difference between the fixed interest rate spread differential and the floating interest rate spread differential of the debt of two counterparties of different creditworthiness. A positive QSD is a necessary condition for an interest swap to occur that ensures that the swap will be beneficial to both parties.

Quantity Theory of Money   An identity stating that for each country, the general price level times the aggregate output should be equal to the money supply times the velocity of money.

R

Random Walk Hypothesis   A hypothesis stating that in an efficient market, asset prices change randomly (i.e., independently of historical trends), or follow a "random walk." Thus, the expected future exchange rate is equivalent to the current exchange rate.

Real Exchange Rate   Measures the degree of deviation from PPP over a period of time, assuming PPP held at the beginning of the period.

Real Option   The application of options pricing theory to the evaluation of investment options in real projects.

Registered Bond   A bond whose ownership is demonstrated by associating the buyer's name with the bond in the issuer's records.

Reinvoice Centre   A central financial subsidiary of a multinational corporation where intrafirm transaction exposure is netted and the residual exposure is managed.

Reporting Currency   The currency in which an MNC prepares its consolidated financial statements. Typically, this is the currency in which the parent firm keeps its books.

Representative Office   An office of a bank established in a foreign country for liaison between the head office of the bank and the financial institutions (including banks), companies, commissions, and private and public institutions in the foreign country.

Residential Taxation   *See* Worldwide Taxation.

Residual Control Rights   Refers to the right to make discretionary decisions under those contingencies that are not specifically covered by the contract.

Restricted Funds   A situation in which a multinational enterprise is restricted from moving money (dividends or capital repatriations) out of a foreign country in which it has an investment.

Retail Market   In the market for foreign exchange, the market that serves the needs of individuals and industry (approximately 10 percent of transaction volume, with the rest involving banks and non-bank dealers.)

Reversing Trade   A trade in either the futures or forward market that will neutralize a position.

S

Sarbanes-Oxley Act   The U.S. Congress passed this law in 2002 to strengthen corporate governance. The act requires the creation of a public accounting oversight board. It also requires that the CEO and the CFO sign off the company's financial statements.

Secondary Market   A market in which investors buy and sell securities to other investors; the original issuer is not involved in these trades. This market provides marketability and valuation of the securities.

Segmented Capital Market   When capital is unable to flow easily and costlessly across borders because of legal, institutional, or technical restrictions, thus preventing cross-border equalization of interest rates and/or an international equilibrium in rates of return on risky assets.

Shareholder Rights   The individual and/or collective legal rights of shareholders in respect of the company whose shares they own. Shareholders generally exercise their rights through the corporate Board of Directors.

Shareholder Wealth Maximization   This represents the most important objective of corporate management that managers of companies should keep in mind when they make important corporate decisions. Managers can maximize shareholder wealth by maximizing the market value of the firm.

Sharpe Performance Measure (SHP)   A risk-adjusted performance measure for a portfolio which gives the excess return (above the risk-free interest rate) per standard deviation risk.

Shelf Registration   Allows bond issuer to pre-register a securities issue which will occur at a later date.

Short Selling   Selling an asset that you do not own with the intention of buying it back ("covering") at a later date at a lower price. The short seller captures the difference in price.

Single-Currency Interest Rate Swap   Typically called an "interest rate swap." There are many variants; however, all involve swapping interest payments on debt obligations that are denominated in the same currency.

Smithsonian Agreement   In December 1971, the G-10 countries agreed to devalue the American dollar against gold and most major currencies in an attempt to save the Bretton Woods system.

Snake   European version of fixed exchange rate system which appeared as the Bretton Woods system declined.

Source Taxation   *See* Territorial Taxation.

Special Drawing Rights (SDR)   An artificial international reserve created by the International Monetary Fund (IMF) which is a currency basket currently comprising five major currencies.

Specialist   On exchange markets in the United States, each share is represented by a specialist who makes a market by holding an inventory of the security.

Speculator   A participant in a financial market whose sole interest is to make money from changes in the price of financial assets. "Buy low, sell high."

Spot (Exchange) Rate   Price at which foreign exchange can be sold or purchased for immediate (within two business days) delivery.

Spot Market   The market in which assets are bought or sold for "on-the-spot" delivery.

Standardized Contract   A contract, such as a foreign exchange futures contract, that specifies a specific amount of foreign exchange in the contract as well as the time of expiry and various other conditions.

Sterilization of Gold   At the time, for example, in the early part of the 20th century, that monetary systems were on the gold standard, an influx of gold into a country would increase the money supply and thus create inflationary pressures. Sterilization was a process of placing gold in an "inactive" account in the nation's treasury so as to prevent the money-expanding effect.

Straight Fixed-Rate Bond   Bonds with a specified maturity date that have fixed coupon payments.

Striking Price   *See* Exercise Price.

Stripped Bond   A synthetic zero coupon bond created by an investment bank via selling the rights to a specific coupon payment or the bond principal of a coupon bond, typically a U.S. Treasury bond.

Subpart F Income   Income of controlled foreign corporations which is subject to immediate American taxation and includes income that is relatively easy to transfer between countries and is subject to a low foreign tax levy.

Subsidiary Bank   A foreign subsidiary of a bank that has legal independence from the parent bank. Harris Bank of Chicago is a subsidiary of the Bank of Montreal. The Bank of Montreal's liability to Harris Bank is limited to BMO's capital in Harris Bank (in contrast to the unlimited liability that a parent bank has with respect to a foreign branch bank).

Swap Bank   A generic term to describe a financial institution which facilitates currency and interest rate swaps between counterparties.

Swap Broker   Function of a swap bank in which it matches counterparties but does not assume any risk of the swap; however, it does receive a commission for this service.

Swap Dealer   Function of a swap bank in which it makes a market in one or the other side of a currency or interest rate swap.

Swap Transaction   The simultaneous spot sale (purchase) of an asset against a forward purchase (sale) of an approximately equal amount of the asset.

Syndicate   A group of Eurobanks banding together to share the risk of lending Eurocredits.

Synergistic Gains   In a corporate merger or acquisition, the gains that result from enhanced efficiency that arise from the merger or acquisition over and above the simple combining of assets.

Systematic Risk   Represented by "beta" in the Capital Asset Pricing Model, systematic risk is a measure (in fact, a regression coefficient) of the relationship between the returns of an asset (a company's shares, for example) and the return on a broad index of shares.

T

Tax Equity   The idea that all similarly situated taxpayers should participate in the cost of operating the government according to the same rules.

Tax Haven   A country that has a low corporate income tax rate and low withholding tax rates on passive income.

Tax Neutrality   A principle in taxation, holding that taxation should not have a negative effect on the decision-making process of taxpayers.

Tax Treaty   A bilateral agreement between nations that governs matters of taxation of mutual concern.

Technical Analysis   A method of predicting the future behaviour of asset prices based on their historical patterns.

Temporal Method   In dealing with foreign currency translation, the idea that current and noncurrent monetary accounts as well as accounts which are carried on the books at current value are converted at the current exchange rate. Accounts carried on the books at historical cost are translated at the historical exchange rate.

Territorial Taxation   A method of declaring tax jurisdiction in which all income earned within a country by any taxpayer, domestic or foreign, is taxed.

Theory of Comparative Advantage   An argument which supports the existence of international trade. This theory states that it is mutually beneficial for countries to specialize in production of goods for which they can produce most efficiently and then engage in trade.

Time Draft   A written order instructing the importer or the importer's bank to pay a specific sum of money on a certain date. Used in import-export trade financing.

Time Value   In the price of a derivative security, such as a call option on a foreign currency, "time value" refers to the market value of an in-the-money option that is in excess of the spot rate of exchange minus the exercise price.

Tobin Tax   A tax on the international flow of hot money proposed by Professor Tobin for the purpose of discouraging cross-border financial speculation.

Trade Balance   The difference between a nation's credits on traded goods (exports) and its debits (imports).

Transaction Cash Balance   Funds a firm has marked to cover scheduled outflows during a cash budgeting period.

Transaction Exposure   The potential change in the value of financial positions due to changes in the exchange rate between the inception of a contract and the settlement of the contract.

Transfer Price   The price assigned, for bookkeeping purposes, to the receiving division within a business for the cost of transferring goods and services from another division.

Translation Exposure   The effect of an unanticipated change in the exchange rates on the consolidated financial reports of a MNC.

Translation Exposure Report   A corporate report that indicates the foreign exchange exposure that exists for each foreign currency in which the MNC has exposure.

Triangular Arbitrage   The process of trading American dollars for a second currency and subsequently trading this for a third currency. This third currency is then traded for American dollars. The purpose of such trading is to earn arbitrage profit via trading from the second currency to the third.

Triffin Paradox   Under the gold exchange standard, the reserve-currency country should run a balance of payments deficit, but this can decrease confidence in the reserve currency and lead to the downfall of the system.

U

Uncovered Interest Rate Parity   This parity condition holds that the difference in interest rates between two countries is equal to the expected change in exchange rate between the countries' currencies.

Universal Bank   International banks that provide such services as consulting in foreign exchange hedging strategies, interest rate and currency swap financing, and international cash management.

V

Value Additivity   The decomposition of the adjusted present value of a project into additive components.

Value-at-Risk   An analysis which provides a confidence interval on the probability of maximum loss that can occur during a given period of time.

Value-Added Tax (VAT)   An indirect national tax which is levied on the value added in the production of a good or service as it moves through the various stages of production.

Variation Margin   Variation margin is paid on a daily basis on margin accounts in foreign exchange futures contracts in order to reduce the exposure to risky positions.By demanding variation margin, clearing organizations address their exposure to participants' accumulation of significant adverse price movements.

W

Weighted Average Cost of Capital (WACC)   A corporate discount rate on an investment project that takes account of the mix of finance (debt and equity) used to finance the project. WACC equals the cost of debt times its proportional share in the mix of finance plus the cost of equity times its proportional share in the mix of finance.

Wholesale Market   In the market for foreign exchange, the core of the market (close to 90 percent of transaction volume) involving banks and non-bank dealers.

Withholding Tax   An indirect tax levied on passive income earned by an individual or corporation of one country within the tax jurisdiction of another country.

World Beta   A measure of the sensitivity of an asset or portfolio to the world market movements. This is a measure of the world systematic risk.

World Equity Benchmark Shares (WEBS)   WEBS are exchange-traded, open-end country funds designed to closely track national stock market indexes. WEBS are traded on the American Stock Exchange (AMEX).

World Market Portfolio   A concept of a global portfolio represented by an index that comprises all shares in the world. A working approximation is an overall index consisting of all major national stock market indexes weighted by their respective shares of total global market capitalization.

World Systematic Risk   Represented by "beta" in the International Capital Asset Pricing Model, world systematic risk is a measure (in fact, a regression coefficient) of the relationship between the returns of an asset (a company's shares, for example) and the return on a global stock index.

World Trade Organization (WTO)   Permanent international organization created by the Uruguay Round to replace GATT. The WTO will have power to enforce international trade rules.

Worldwide Taxation   A method of declaring national tax jurisdiction in which national residents of the country are taxed on their worldwide income, regardless of which country it is earned in.

Writer   A term for the one who "sells" an option.

Y

Yankee Bond (Stock)   Bond (stock) directly sold to American investors by foreign companies.

Z

Zero Coupon Bond   A bond that pays no coupon interest and simply returns the face value at maturity.

Zero-Sum Game   A game in which one side gains at the of the other. An option, such as a call or a put, is a zero-sum game.

Index